Enhancing Virtual Reality Experiences with Unity 2022

Use Unity's latest features to level up your skills for VR games, apps, and other projects

Steven Antonio Christian

BIRMINGHAM—MUMBAI

Enhancing Virtual Reality Experiences with Unity 2022

Group Product Manager: Rohit Rajkumar

Publishing Product Manager: Nitin Nainani

Senior Editor: Divya Anne Selvaraj and Mark D'Souza

Technical Editor: Joseph Aloocaran and Simran Ali

Book Project Manager: Aishwarya Mohan

Copy Editor: Safis Editing

Proofreader: Safis Editing

Indexer: Sejal Dsilva

Production Designer: Nilesh Mohite

DevRel Marketing Coordinator: Nivedita Pandey

First published: November 2023

Production reference: 1131023

Published by Packt Publishing Ltd.

Grosvenor House

11 St Paul's Square

Birmingham

B3 1RB, UK.

ISBN 978-1-80461-953-7

`www.packtpub.com`

Two years have passed since I began this book, a time when every page written was a stepping stone in my personal and professional journey. I discovered, I faltered, and I stood tall, striking a fine balance between my medical pursuits and my passion for XR development. It was a journey that whispered the secrets of resilience, that painted a canvas of innovation, bright and bold, before my very eyes. Yet, this journey was not a solitary venture; it was nurtured by a community that stood by me, unwavering.

To my mother, Shalanda, and my partner, Tyne, your love was my beacon of hope; your trust, my stronghold. To my father, Steven Christian, your legacy is the wellspring from which I draw inspiration; your unyielding faith has laid the groundwork for my enduring aspirations.

This narrative of my life is enriched by those who've supported my dreams. From my humble beginnings (tinkering with phone modifications in high school, taking on the field as a college football player, and sharing my journey of app development and animated experiences on YouTube) to venturing into entrepreneurship and blossoming as a medical school technologist, your cheer, your applause, and your reassurances have kept me grounded.

To the loved ones who are no longer with us in person but continue to shine in my heart and spirit – my beloved grandmother, my cousin Marschell, and my dear friends Greg, Quint, and Alain – your memory is a guiding light, each one a luminous star on my life's constellation. You push me to reach beyond the known, to innovate, and to evolve. This journey and the work encapsulated within these pages are a testament to your lasting influence on my life.

And so, to each of you, I dedicate this book. Your essence is woven into its narrative, echoing in the silence between the lines, making it more than just a chronicle of knowledge, but a monument to our shared history and an homage to our enduring bond.

– Steven Christian, MAIS

M.D., Ph.D. Candidate in Integrative Neuroscience at the University of Nevada, Reno '27

Foreword

In a world where the boundaries of reality are being redefined and reimagined, Steven Christian emerges on the world's stage as a visionary author who joins the forefront of the technological revolution using virtual reality (VR). Prepare to embark on an extraordinary voyage where the power of imagination, creativity, and technology intertwine to illuminate Steven's blueprint using the Unity game engine to further galvanize the development of extended reality (XR) experiences.

Enhancing Virtual Reality Experiences with Unity finds at center stage an author who courageously blends his life experiences as a college athlete, visual artist, animator, founder of Iltopia Studios, former surgical patient, and now M.D./Ph.D. student who is determined to make a global impact leveraging emerging technology and culture. His contributions to advancing medicine will undoubtedly be invaluable and mirror his voice that resonates on the numerous stages onto which he's been invited to share his knowledge and passion.

The creation of immersive experiences using VR continues to impact every field of human endeavor. Beyond sharing knowledge of using Unity to create immersive experiences, Steven provides a window into the creative fuel that powers his imagination and curiosity.

Enhancing Virtual Reality Experiences with Unity is not just a book but a cornerstone that will empower, accelerate curiosity, and guide creators toward a future where they can craft more meaningful and impactful experiences within the realm of VR and beyond.

Patrick B. Thomas MD, MMCi, FACS

Director of Digital Innovation in Pediatric Surgery at The University of Nebraska Medical Center College of Medicine

Contributors

About the author

Steven Antonio Christian is a former football player turned creator, writer, animator, and the founder of Iltopia Studios. Holding a master's degree from Oregon State University, he's known for projects such as the *Eyelnd Feevr* AR immersive storytelling experience and the Analog-AR headset. An instructor at Portland Community College and a Unity Certified Instructor, he is currently pursuing an M.D./Ph.D. in Integrative Neuroscience at the University of Nevada as the first Black American M.D./Ph.D. student in Nevada's state history. His work is celebrated on platforms such as The Wall Street Journal and Unity for Humanity. Passionate about community uplifting, Steven's primary goal is to entertain, educate, and empower through his art and provide hope for African American youth to pursue careers in technology and medicine.

Dedicated to the pillars of my life, the memories that guide me, and the dreams we've built together.

About the reviewer

Vishal Pandey is a co-founder and CTO at MythyaVerse, an innovative start-up focusing on VR and AI solutions for wellness and productivity. He possesses a strong academic background, with a B.Tech. in computer science and an M.Tech. in data science, and is currently pursuing a Ph.D. at IIT Roorkee. Previously, as a research fellow at the Defence Research and Development Organization, Vishal played a key role in building XR products for cognitive training in defense research in India. He has multiple published papers in the field of human-computer interaction, solidifying his status as an XR thought leader and innovator. Vishal's commitment to pushing the boundaries of technology continues to make a lasting impact in the industry.

Table of Contents

Part 2: Technical Skills for Building VR Experiences in Unity (Assets, GameObjects, Scripts, and Components)

2

3

4

Using Game Objects, Materials, and Prefabs 97

5

Implementing Animation – Physics and Colliders 131

6

Lighting Your Worlds and Experiences 155

7

Creating Immersion with Sound 193

8

Working with C#, Unity Events, and Input Actions 203

9

Unlocking the Power of Render Pipelines 243

Part 3: Projects: Putting Skills Together

10

Design Thinking for Virtual Reality Experiences 261

11

Adding Audio to a Virtual Reality World 287

12

Building an Art Gallery 309

13

Animating a Virtual Reality Experience 339

14

Recording Virtual Reality Videos 379

15

Enhancing Virtual Reality Rigs 387

16

Triggering Actions in Virtual Reality 411

17

Destroying Objects in Virtual Reality 429

Part 4: Final Touches

18

Preface

Virtual reality *(***VR***) has unequivocally established itself as one of the most revolutionary mediums of the 21st century. It has unleashed a new paradigm in games, entertainment, education, and many other industries, radically transforming the way we interact with digital environments.*

Unity, the world's leading platform for creating interactive, real-time 3D content, plays a vital role in enhancing VR development. The engine's flexibility, extensive capabilities, and broad compatibility with VR hardware make it the tool of choice for creating VR experiences. Its ease of use for building on Android/Mobile devices and for projects centered around both utility and entertainment opens up an expansive canvas for VR developers.

The importance of learning about Unity for VR development cannot be overstated. This is where Enhancing Virtual Reality Experiences with Unity 2022 comes into play. It encapsulates a three-pillar approach to mastering VR development:

Explore*: Understand the principles of VR and Unity's interface and delve into its features, tools, and utilities that can be harnessed to create compelling VR experiences.*

Create*: Apply the knowledge gained to create VR projects. From basic to complex, you will build a variety of VR experiences for headsets, computers, and mobile devices.*

Innovate*: Break the boundaries of conventional VR experiences. Learn how to integrate traditional gaming and animation tools and create immersive worlds that push the frontiers of what's possible with VR.*

Enhancing Virtual Reality Experiences with Unity 2022 is a project-based exploration of VR that bridges the gap between creativity and technology. It leverages my years of experience in VR development to deliver a comprehensive guide that combines both creative and technical skills to develop and improve your VR workflow.

The book presents a development framework to kickstart and scale your VR projects, introducing you to the basics of creating VR projects, and deepening your understanding of **Extended Reality** *(***XR***) development. You will learn to utilize many features and tools of the Unity game engine, helping you build truly immersive experiences.*

In essence, this book provides you with a solid foundation in VR and the Unity game engine, empowering you to create innovative projects that push the boundaries of what is currently possible in VR. It's time to embark on your VR development journey and shape the future of this exciting medium.

Who this book is for

This book invites individuals of all experience levels to explore the compelling universe of virtual reality. From novices with a budding interest in VR to accomplished developers eager to refine their abilities, this book delivers a profound journey into the heart of VR development.

This guide acts as a comprehensive introduction for newcomers, demystifying VR terminology and techniques, enabling you to confidently traverse the virtual landscape. For those with a grounding in Unity and C#, the book offers an opportunity for skill enhancement and creativity expansion within this intricate tech realm. In essence, it offers a lifeline for creators aspiring to integrate VR into their creative workflows and push their boundaries with this emerging technology.

This book also addresses the specific needs of our audience. Our readers grapple with translating skills from various industries into VR, generating innovative ideas based on their existing skill sets, and creating impactful VR projects. We will focus on these challenges and provide comprehensive guidance on pivotal features such as the XR Interaction Toolkit, animation system and timeline, and world-building and kitbashing techniques.

The journey, from beginning to end, is planned to equip you with practical skills and a deepened appreciation of VR development's transformative power. Regardless of your current proficiency, this book aims to ignite your creativity and inspire you to explore the limitless possibilities of virtual reality.

What this book covers

Chapter 1, Philosophy of Building Immersive Experiences, opens your journey into the world of VR by setting the foundations, revealing the art behind crafting impactful, immersive experiences, and highlighting the exciting potential VR can offer to developers and users alike.

Chapter 2, Building Virtual Reality Scenes in Unity, empowers you with the ability to navigate the world-renowned Unity game engine, laying the groundwork for your very own VR projects and paving the path for a deep understanding of Unity's tools and possibilities.

Chapter 3, Working with Inputs and Interactions, uncovers the secrets of creating intuitive and engaging interactions, enhancing your understanding of VR input systems and equipping you with the skills to create immersive and natural user experiences.

Chapter 4, Using GameObjects, Materials, and Prefabs, dives into the essential building blocks of Unity. From game objects to prefabs and materials, you'll master the art of asset manipulation, opening doors to more efficient and creative development processes.

Chapter 5, Implementing Animation – Physics and Colliders, brings your VR world to life by adding movement, physics, and interaction triggers. This exploration of Unity's animation system unlocks the potential to create dynamic, responsive environments that elevate the immersion of your VR experiences.

Chapter 6, Lighting Your Worlds and Experiences, enlightens you on the power of lighting in creating visually stunning, mood-enhancing virtual landscapes, thereby driving the overall immersive quality of your VR projects.

Chapter 7, Creating Immersion with Sound, explores the sonic aspect of VR, delving into Unity's robust audio toolkit. With this knowledge, you will enrich your VR experiences with captivating, immersive, and spatial audio, adding another layer of immersion to your VR world.

Chapter 8, Working with C#, Unity Events, and Input Assets, strengthens your understanding of C# programming, XR namespaces, and Unity's Event System, allowing you to harness the true power of scripting in VR and creating highly interactive experiences.

Chapter 9, Unlocking the Power of Render Pipelines, navigates through Unity's render pipelines, empowering you to select the ideal one for your project, optimize visuals and performance, and understand the nuances of VR rendering.

Chapter 10, Design Thinking for Virtual Reality Experiences, applies the principles of design thinking to the 3D realm, giving you a fresh perspective on VR development and enabling you to build purposeful, user-centered experiences that engage and inspire.

Chapter 11, Adding Audio to a Virtual Reality World, turns up the volume on your VR skills, revealing how to infuse your VR worlds with sound, and enhancing the sensory depth of your creations, making them feel more real and immersive than ever.

Chapter 12, Building an Art Gallery, combines your gained knowledge into a practical project, guiding you step by step to construct a virtual art gallery filled with interactive and aesthetically pleasing elements.

Chapter 13, Animating a Virtual Reality Experience, immerses you in the realm of VR storytelling, demonstrating how to craft animated sequences and narratives in VR, thereby enhancing user engagement and delivering memorable experiences.

Chapter 14, Recording Virtual Reality Videos, pushes the boundaries of your VR journey, guiding you to produce 360-degree videos within Unity that can be shared and experienced worldwide, widening the reach of your creative efforts.

Chapter 15, Enhancing Virtual Reality Rigs, elevates your understanding of VR rigs, revealing how to implement advanced features such as hand animations, locomotion functions, and interactor controls, thereby expanding the functionality and usability of your VR experiences.

Chapter 16, Triggering Actions in Virtual Reality, shows you how to create interactive events in VR, introducing concepts such as VR menus, action triggers, scene portals, and physics-based elements, thereby adding more depth and engagement to your virtual world.

Chapter 17, Destroying Objects in Virtual Reality, adds an exhilarating twist to your VR creations by teaching you how to incorporate destructible elements and effects, introducing a sense of chaos and excitement that keeps users engaged and entertained.

Chapter 18, Optimizing Your Virtual Reality Experiences, rounds off your journey by emphasizing the importance of optimization, exploring the tools and techniques to improve performance without compromising on quality and ensuring your VR experiences run smoothly across different platforms and devices.

To get the most out of this book

To truly harness the knowledge encapsulated within this book, it is recommended to have the latest version of Unity installed. This guide has been crafted with Unity 2021 in mind and is expected to be compatible with all subsequent versions. A prerequisite for an optimal learning experience would be to have XR Interaction Toolkit 2.0 installed, as certain features may be inaccessible in previous versions of the toolkit.

For the most seamless journey, all code and projects have been created using a Windows computer and an Oculus Quest 2 headset. However, the content should remain applicable for Mac users and compatible with other VR headsets that may emerge in the future.

This guide assumes that you are equipped with basic computer literacy. While prior knowledge of Unity and XR development could be beneficial, it is by no means necessary. The book is structured to guide you step by step, from the rudimentary to the complex, ensuring a comprehensive understanding of VR development.

Software/hardware covered in the book	Operating system requirements
Unity 2021.x.x or later	Windows, macOS, or Linux
A VR headset such as Oculus Quest 2	

Venturing into the world of VR development with Unity involves a straightforward setup process. Here are the key steps to get started:

1. **Download Unity Hub**: Begin by downloading Unity Hub from the Unity website. Unity Hub is available for Windows, Mac, and Linux computers. It's important to note that Unity cannot be installed on mobile platforms, iPads, or tablets.
2. **Set up your Unity license**: Next, set up a free personal license or an educational license for development with Unity. Instructions for this can be found on the Unity website.
3. **Ensure adequate storage space**: Make sure you have at least 50 gigabytes of free space on your computer. This will accommodate all the necessary Unity files, as well as any plugins and developer kits required for the projects in this book.
4. **Acquire a VR headset**: Lastly, to fully experience and test your VR projects, you'll need a VR headset. For Windows users, you can test some aspects of your VR projects directly in the Unity Editor. However, for Linux or Mac users, a headset will be essential to test and experience the VR projects you create.

By following these steps, you'll be well prepared to dive into the fascinating world of VR development with Unity. Happy creating!

If you are using the digital version of this book, we advise you to type the code yourself or access the code from the book's GitHub repository (a link is available in the next section). Doing so will help you avoid any potential errors related to the copying and pasting of code.

Upon completion of this book, we encourage readers to apply the skills and knowledge gained to create their own VR projects. This could mean designing an immersive VR game, an educational simulation, or a stunning VR art exhibit – the possibilities are endless!

Consider sharing your projects with the wider VR community, such as on Unity's community forums or on other platforms such as GitHub. Not only will this provide you with valuable feedback but it can also contribute to the collective learning of the community.

Continue to explore and stay updated with advancements in VR technologies. The field of VR is ever-evolving, and there's always more to learn!

Download the example code files

You can download the example code files for this book from GitHub at `https://github.com/PacktPublishing/Enhancing-Virtual-Reality-Experiences-with-Unity-2022`. If there's an update to the code, it will be updated in the GitHub repository.

We also have other code bundles from our rich catalog of books and videos available at `https://github.com/PacktPublishing/`. Check them out!

Conventions used

There are a number of text conventions used throughout this book.

`Code in text`: Indicates code words in text, database table names, folder names, filenames, file extensions, pathnames, dummy URLs, user input, and Twitter handles. Here is an example: "If I had an animation project, I would name it Animation_FightScenes_002. If I created a world-building scene, I would name it WorldBuilding_TropicalIsland_023."

A block of code is set as follows:

```
foreach (AudioSource source in audioSources)
        {
            source.clip = audioClip;
            source.spatialBlend = 1f;
        }
Play();
```

When we wish to draw your attention to a particular part of a code block, the relevant lines or items are set in bold:

```
[default]
exten => s,1,Dial(Zap/1|30)
exten => s,2,Voicemail(u100)
exten => s,102,Voicemail(b100)
exten => i,1,Voicemail(s0)
```

Any command-line input or output is written as follows:

```
$ mkdir css
$ cd css
```

Bold: Indicates a new term, an important word, or words that you see onscreen. For instance, words in menus or dialog boxes appear in **bold**. Here is an example: "Click Add Layer, and create a new layer called Floor in User Layer 8."

> **Tips or important notes**
> Appear like this.

Get in touch

Feedback from our readers is always welcome.

General feedback: If you have questions about any aspect of this book, email us at `customercare@packtpub.com` and mention the book title in the subject of your message.

Errata: Although we have taken every care to ensure the accuracy of our content, mistakes do happen. If you have found a mistake in this book, we would be grateful if you would report this to us. Please visit `www.packtpub.com/support/errata` and fill in the form.

Piracy: If you come across any illegal copies of our works in any form on the internet, we would be grateful if you would provide us with the location address or website name. Please contact us at `copyright@packt.com` with a link to the material.

If you are interested in becoming an author: If there is a topic that you have expertise in and you are interested in either writing or contributing to a book, please visit `authors.packtpub.com`.

Share Your Thoughts

Once you've read *Enhancing Virtual Reality Experiences with Unity 2022*, we'd love to hear your thoughts! Scan the QR code below to go straight to the Amazon review page for this book and share your feedback.

`https://packt.link/r/1-804-61953-1`

Your review is important to us and the tech community and will help us make sure we're delivering excellent quality content.

Download a free PDF copy of this book

Thanks for purchasing this book!

Do you like to read on the go but are unable to carry your print books everywhere?

Is your eBook purchase not compatible with the device of your choice?

Don't worry, now with every Packt book you get a DRM-free PDF version of that book at no cost.

Read anywhere, any place, on any device. Search, copy, and paste code from your favorite technical books directly into your application.

The perks don't stop there, you can get exclusive access to discounts, newsletters, and great free content in your inbox daily

Follow these simple steps to get the benefits:

1. Scan the QR code or visit the link below

`https://packt.link/free-ebook/9781804619537`

2. Submit your proof of purchase
3. That's it! We'll send your free PDF and other benefits to your email directly

Part 1: Philosophy and Basics of Understanding Virtual Reality

In this thought-provoking part of the book, we delve into the core philosophical underpinnings of **virtual reality** (**VR**), shedding light on the *why* before the *how* of VR creation. This part will not just prepare you technically but also mentally, equipping you with the right mindset and conceptual understanding necessary to create truly immersive experiences. This journey is about more than just understanding VR—it's about truly living it.

This part includes the following chapter:

- *Chapter 1, Philosophy of Building Immersive Experiences*

1
Philosophy of Building Immersive Experiences

Welcome to *Enhancing Virtual Reality Experience with Unity*! In this book, we will explore not only what it takes to build **virtual reality** (**VR**) experiences, but also how to expand on that knowledge to create innovative experiences with VR. You will be able to create amazing projects in VR on your own in no time as we progress through this book. We will follow a series of step-by-step tutorials to complete projects aimed at giving you the skills you need to be proficient at VR development.

VR can encompass many content and concept areas, but we will cover the major areas so that you have a good foundation and understanding as you continue your journey as a developer. Ultimately, the goal is to create VR experiences that are fun and engaging.

This chapter will explore some of the foundational concepts of **immersive experiences**, VR, and using the **Unity** game engine. The goal is to first understand some of the philosophy around what immersive experiences are and why we build experiences with this technology. Before we dive deep into VR, we will expand your concept of VR by first defining immersive experiences and introducing VR within that context. VR goes beyond making games for headsets. It is a medium that can be applied to a variety of industries and applications, such as healthcare, education, therapy, design, entertainment, and so on. We will break down the various components that comprise the experiences and introduce some of the hardware that is necessary to develop and participate in those experiences. In this way, before we begin developing, you will have a better idea of what to expect when you open Unity to start building your experiences.

In this chapter, we will cover the following topics:

- What is an immersive experience?
- What are the essential components of an immersive experience?
- Understanding XR, AR, VR, and MR
- How does VR work?
- Approaching VR development

What is an immersive experience?

Immersion is a core concept of how we experience the world around us. It can be minimal (sitting in a park and reading a book) or maximal (going scuba diving in the ocean as you feel the weightlessness from the water pressure pushing against your body), but the fact remains that immersion is a constant in our lives. Quite frankly, we don't have any concept of what a lack of immersion is because the experiences we have involve some level of immersion.

Medical students are trained to test the functions of the human body so that patients can have a fully immersive experience. As the body declines due to age and disease, we see that things become less immersive, and ultimately, quality of life diminishes. Immersion affects our perceptions and informs our reality to an extent. Nevertheless, there is no box that we can put the concept of immersion into because it is all-encompassing.

The *Merriam-Webster Dictionary* defines *immersion* as "*a state of being deeply engaged or involved, deep mental involvement.*" We can also use the more literal definition: "*to plunge into something that surrounds or covers especially: to plunge or dip into a fluid.*" Both definitions overlap in many ways because they allude to an ever-present stimulus. When we talk about immersive experiences, we are referring to the concept of how the surrounding environment provides stimuli that inform our perceptions. In those conversations, we often describe what we see, smell, feel, hear, and believe to be true based on what engaged our senses at that moment.

An immersive experience is an illusion that makes you feel like you are inside or part of an environment. We perceive the environment as tangible (real), but it is intangible. This environment engages your senses through the use of technology and feedback to mimic real-world phenomena: when you walk, you hear footsteps; running blurs your surroundings; and looking at lights disrupts your vision.

We are familiar with this notion as **extended reality** (**XR**) or **mixed reality** (**MR**) – that is, placing digital objects in the real world and directly interacting with them as if they were actually there. We can use hardware such as **head-mounted displays** (**HMDs**) and **infrared sensors** to augment physical spaces with digital objects and enhance the experience within the space.

However, before we learn more about MR, we must talk about the role of the senses in immersion. Senses are the focal point of our experiences. Without them, we are unable to interpret information or engage with the world around us. If we hear a loud noise, we will cover our ears and try to leave the source of the noise. When we are confronted with the source in the future, our negative experience will inform us how we should respond to that source. Let's say we were immersed in an environment with a loud noise. That noise provided an unpleasant experience for our ears, and we responded by removing the stimulus. We care about what appeals to our experiences because, in this example, the noise shaped the experience. If the noise wasn't as loud, it would likely have improved the experience.

Understanding immersion through the senses

We should all be familiar with the major senses: touch, sight, hearing, smell, and taste. We often associate those senses with experience and actions. If you want to taste, you will eat food; if you want to see, you will watch TV; if you want to smell, you will breathe in an aroma; if you want to touch, you will hold something; and if you want to hear, you will listen to music. Those actions toward a stimulus engage the senses and provide us with an experience. Each sense alone provides us with a different way to experience the world around us.

If our senses are tied to our experiences, they become the anchors of an immersive experience. We can say that an immersive experience is something that incorporates multiple senses into one experience. Think of immersion as being on a spectrum, rather than it being all or nothing. You can't remove immersion completely because it is tied to our senses. Unless you lose all of your ability to sense, you can't completely remove immersion. Rather, it is on a scale of less immersive to more immersive.

For example, imagine you are walking down a busy street in the middle of rush hour in a major city. You are rushing from a lunch date back to work, so you are holding part of your lunch on your way back. While doing so, someone dumps spoiled milk on you from their balcony. It reeks! In this scenario, you can imagine the type of experience you would have in that situation. Based on the description, you can also isolate each part of that experience into their respective senses:

- **Touch**: You can feel the food in your hand as you hold your lunch. When the milk lands on you, you feel the liquid on your skin and clothes (fun fact – we can't feel wetness, but we can feel the difference in pressure and temperature of the liquid compared to the air on our skin).
- **Sight**: You see tons of cars and people out in the city. Maybe you can even see some buildings and have the sun shining in your eyes.
- **Smell**: You could be smelling the food you are eating, the smog and sewage of the city, or even the stench of the spoiled milk that was spilled onto you.
- **Taste**: You could taste the food you had for lunch, or maybe some of the spoiled milk got into your mouth; you probably have a bad taste in your mouth now.
- **Hearing**: In a busy city, you might hear car horns, engines revving, people talking, and even the sound of the spoiled milk hitting the ground as it also covers you.

When it comes to immersion, you can't get more immersed than this! The experience I have described incorporates all the senses (*Figure 1.1*) and would leave you with a vivid and lasting memory:

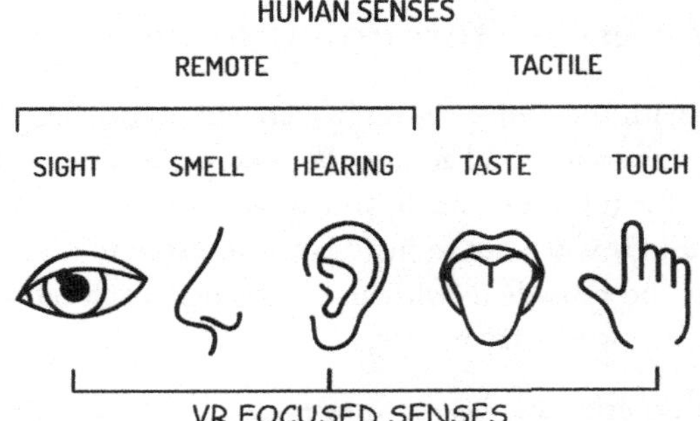

Figure 1.1 – Human senses that focus on VR include sight, hearing, and touch

When we talk about applications of immersive technology, especially VR, we are in some ways trying to use technology to mimic what we would experience in real life. Research suggests that experiences are more memorable when more senses are tied to those experiences. If you can find ways to build experiences that incorporate the senses in believable ways, the user will feel more engaged, and they will walk away from the experience more informed. We will explore some techniques in future chapters to achieve these goals.

What makes something immersive?

When we talk about being less immersive, we simply mean that we start to remove our senses from the experience. When you remove touch, you can't feel anything; remove sight, you can't see the world around you; remove smell, you can't enjoy aromas; remove hearing and everything is quiet; and remove taste and you cannot enjoy food. The more senses you remove, the less immersive the experience is. Going back to the idea of removing immersion completely, can you do that and still be alive?

Think about the experiences we enjoy and see if you can define what senses are used to make it immersive:

- Reading a book involves seeing and touching
- Listening to music involves listening
- Watching TV involves seeing and listening
- Talking on the phone involves talking and listening
- Swimming involves moving and seeing
- Playing video games involves touching, seeing, and hearing
- Driving a car involves touching, seeing, and hearing

When we talk about these experiences, one crucial component is interaction. We aren't in stasis: we are acting and reacting to the world around us. Even if the experience is passive, there is a level of interactivity that keeps us engaged. When the experience requires us to perform an action, that makes it interactive. Let's not confuse interaction with immersion. They are two separate concepts involved in the same experience. You may listen to music, watch a movie, or read a book. Those are passive experiences, but the act of turning the page, changing the channel with a remote, or rewinding a song gives you a level of interaction that keeps you engaged.

To make VR experiences immersive, use the elements of immersion as a guide. We know that immersive experiences are more engaging for users, and the focal point of immersive experiences is our senses. By developing experiences focused on what we see, feel, and do, we can create applications that have a true impact on the VR industry and community. Note that this is independent of the content or industry. These approaches and philosophies can be applied to a variety of industry applications because they speak to the core component of what makes VR different than other mediums such as animation, cinema, or console games. It is the ability to immerse the user in an experience.

How to make experiences immersive

So, how do you make something more immersive? Simple – involve more senses in the experience. Compared to text, video is more immersive because it involves two senses rather than one. Reading incorporates sight and listening incorporates hearing, but watching a movie involves both seeing and listening. To make reading more immersive, add sound. To make listening to music more immersive, add haptic feedback to feel the sound vibrations. When you are thinking about immersion, think about building off the native experience rather than exchanging one element for another. I would not consider video to be the same as immersive reading because you are replacing text with images. Although you are adding sound, you are taking away the text-based visual.

Adding sound to a quiet reading experience such as background music or sound effects can make the reading experience more immersive without taking away the core element of the experience.

With VR, you can take the concept of immersive experiences and build on that framework using technology and digital assets. VR uses interactions in a completely virtual world to let you walk, run, jump, and navigate with motion. Even though you can't touch the object in the world, haptics can provide limited vibrational feedback. Ultimately, you can see the objects, hear the objects, and orient yourself in spaces among the objects. Compared to being behind a computer screen or gamepad, VR is more immersive because you are in the very location you want to explore, not a proxy of it. You don't control the character; you are the character.

Now that we have introduced what an immersive experience is and its various components, we can explore what components are essential to achieving such experiences within VR. This will help simplify how to approach building immersive experiences and make the process seem less daunting.

What are the essential components of an immersive experience?

The point of explaining and defining immersion and immersive experiences in the preceding section was intentional. When we talk about VR or any other variation of XR, we are talking about different types of experiences that engage the user in distinct ways. It is important to understand that as fact rather than opinion because some technical aspects and elements make the experiences what they are. They can be clearly defined and formulaic. With most VR experiences, the user will have an experience with an HMD such as an Oculus Quest. With **augmented reality** (**AR**), the user will most likely have an experience through their smartphone. The list can go on.

The true impact as a creator and developer is taking the core elements of a formulaic experience and infusing abstract and creative elements into it so that people have a memorable experience they want to share with friends and colleagues or even promote to the world. At face value, all VR experiences are a variation of putting on a plastic headset and responding to stimuli that are not real, but the experiences people reflect on afterward with VR are a lot more formative and expressive. They will describe what they did, what they saw, and how the VR experience made them feel. The following are some examples of general (non-specific) experiences that can be enhanced using VR:

- **Entertainment through 360-degree videos**: You can immerse yourself in the video as if you are there. 360 videos provide a passive VR experience that allows you to see in all directions rather than at just a monitor screen in front of you. Think about someone base jumping with a 360-camera attached to them. In VR, you can tag along with them as they go on an epic adventure.
- **Games**: Instead of sitting on the couch with a controller, you can be the player in the game dodging all the obstacles and scoring all the points. Such games include the following:
    - **Story/role-playing games**: You take on the persona of a character in a story and evolve as the story progresses.
    - **FPS games**: First-person shooters allow you to go to battle with others in a game of survival. You can navigate environments to evade gunfire and take out opposing players.
    - **Foraging/exploration games**: Games where you can traverse vast worlds, climb high peaks, and scavenge for resources. These games normally focus on puzzles and creating lighthearted experiences.
    - **Sports games**: Instead of going to the field or the court in real life, you can play your favorite sport in VR.
    - **Artistic games**: These games are abstract because they are all about using interactions to elicit a certain effect. This can mean shooting paintballs at a 100-foot canvas to make a painting or fishing in a field on another planet.
    - **Survival games**: Much like first-person shooters, you are immersed in an environment where the goal is to think outside the box to increase your chance of survival.

- **Social/virtual meetings**: You can meet up with friends, watch movies, and go to meetings in virtual environments with friends across the globe. Geographic locations won't hinder you from connecting with others.
- **Medicine**: You can improve patient outcomes in a variety of areas, from therapy to training. With VR, you can create simulation modules for healthcare professionals to improve their training and provide immersive learning experiences for patients to better understand their health.
- **Education**: In the classroom, VR can give students the ability to explore learning in a more exploratory way. This allows them to retain information better. Students can go on museum and gallery tours to places across the globe and interact with content beyond a textbook.
- **Military training**: You can make training more accessible and cheaper with simulations of the tasks at hand. The military uses VR to simulate combat environments.
- **Utility/productivity**: VR can be used to extend your office beyond its physical location. Instead of using a computer monitor, your headset can create countless virtual monitors so that you can multitask and work in a variety of locations. Want to work on a project on the beach with a 200-foot monitor screen? You can do that in VR.
- **Real estate**: You can tour homes from your living room using digital replicas of the places you intend to learn more about. Digital twins allow for deep exploration of real-world locations without you having to physically be there.
- **Engineering**: You can design and prototype before you move to manufacturing. This saves countless work hours and allows for rapid revisions and iterations, thus saving money.
- **Exercise**: Instead of going to a workout class, you can bring the workout class to you. In VR, you can gamify your workouts with others and/or in fantastical ways using digital enhancements.
- **Content creation**: You can ditch the keyboard and mouse to sculpt and paint content for projects in VR. If you like the kinetic experience of sculpting but still want to work digitally, you can put on a headset and do what you do best in the way that feels the most natural.

Skills required to build immersive experiences

Some technical and nontechnical skills are valuable in the XR industry and for developing VR experiences that will have an impact. In many cases, if you have developed skills and worked on projects in other industries, you can integrate those skills into making engaging immersive experiences. Understand that you do not exist within a vacuum. You have skills and ideas that can push the culture of XR forward in new and exciting ways. I can speak from personal experience. I was a Division 1 college football player who did software development for Windows Mobile in the early 2000s. When Windows Mobile went defunct, I shifted to comic illustration and visual storytelling. My creative endeavors evolved from newspaper comics to webcomics, to animation on YouTube, to live-action visual effects, and ultimately to XR creation. I did all that while playing football, retiring, and getting into medical school. Over this 10+ years' creative and professional journey, I developed skills in a variety of areas that further informed my workflow and ideas to create and pursue.

The reason your skills are so valuable is because XR is just a medium. It is a manifestation of the ideas you think of and write on paper. Those ideas can become books, animated shows, live-action movies, training modules, mobile apps, and so on. You just so happen to want to create VR experiences. In many ways, there are projects and ideas only you can produce to a specific end because you ultimately infuse your skills and experiences into the work you do. Whether it is naming conventions or artistic style, the things you create will have a touch of you in them. If 10 developers and creators get the same prompt, which is a brief description of a project idea that a client or developer hopes to create, you will get 10 different projects. Some will be better than others based on the utilization of tools and execution of the prompt. Here are the skills that will prove most useful to you when you are trying to build immersive experiences:

- **Project management**: Immersive experiences can be large in scale and require experience managing multiple elements. If you don't know how to navigate both people and a variety of content sources, you can easily become overwhelmed. Although this is often lost on developers and creators, project management skills are crucial to completing projects. To build a portfolio and further your career, you must be able to complete projects.
- **Creative direction**: XR has yet to reach its peak market value. As a result, grand ideas exist that are yet to be manifested and translated into experiences. The value of a creator and developer is not only measured by the technical skills you offer but also by the vision you present to explore the technology and push it to new heights with your ideas. Having experience in a variety of content creation workflows and pipelines can help you explore the possibilities of XR. Creative directors develop and manage projects from ideas to finished products. They typically have experience in a variety of areas, such as marketing, illustration, business, product development, and more. These skills serve as valuable assets on the creative journey.
- **Software development**: Having technical skills is very valuable in developing XR experiences. Although Unity makes building experiences easier, to get the most out of the medium and the platform, you need to know how to open the hood and unlock certain features. Even if you aren't a seasoned coder, being familiar with code structures and functions can lead to major growth and innovations in the space.

Technological components of building immersive experiences

Every immersive experience has the same core elements. The difference among all experiences is the degree to which each of the core elements is incorporated. Whether you are doing a simulation or playing a game, you will need animation, a user interface, lighting, and audio. Creating experiences is more about navigating the required elements to fit the scope of the project rather than redefining what it means to build an experience. Innovation is taking what already exists and improving upon it with ideas that show the true potential of the tools and the medium. The following comprise some of the core components of building immersive experiences:

- **Game engine**: Most VR experiences are built on game engines because of their ability to render objects in real time instead of pre-rendering the objects, such as animation and compositing software. In this book, we will be using the Unity game engine, the most versatile engine used to build XR applications and games. Another popular engine is Unreal Engine.
- **Rendering**: I mentioned that game engines use real-time rendering to provide a platform for building interactive experiences. Within Unity, there are render pipelines that determine the way objects are rendered within the experience. The difference in rendering pipelines is usually device-dependent. There are render pipelines for lower-end devices such as smartphones and high-definition pipelines for higher-end devices. Since VR headsets have hardware specifications, knowing which one to use for your project early in the development process is crucial to providing the best experience for your users.
- **3D content**: You can't have a virtual experience without 3D content (2D content on some occasions). In a virtual experience, you interact with the 3D objects in the world you are experiencing. This content can comprise characters, buildings, environments, and even digital twins. Content can make or break the experiences you build because the user chooses the VR experiences they want based on the content in the experience.
- **Shaders**, **materials**, and **textures**: Often associated with 3D content, shaders, materials, and textures provide an element of variation to the 3D world that can elicit various emotions and responses. They provide the color and character to the polygons and pixels of the digital world. If 3D models are the architecture and foundation for the world, then materials and shaders are the paint and decorations. When the materials, shaders, and textures are used correctly, they become recognizable and familiar to the user.
- **Levels design** and **architecture**: Design is crucial to experiences because you need to give users environments to anchor their experiences to. Without a map to navigate or cities to traverse, they have no direction.
- **Audio**: Sound is crucial to having an immersive experience. Hearing the sound of your feet on the pavement as you walk or increasing the volume of music as you walk closer to the source creates something subtle yet impactful. If you can create and integrate sounds, you can harness an important component of an immersive experience.
- **UX/UI**: User interfaces are the blueprints of interactions within the experiences. If you design a world but people don't know how to explore the world, then you need to find ways to design elements that feel natural and intuitive.
- **Animation**: Animation brings life to a static world. In a real-time game engine, VR makes animation an integral part of the interactive experiences. It is often the element people respond to the most because animation alters the world as time progresses. If we were playing a sports game, the location of the animated character or object can determine how the player would respond. In a still world, a player has no incentive to engage in the experience.

- **Lighting**: Nothing is fun if you can't see. Lighting 3D environments is a necessary skill because it gives you full control of every element that can improve visibility and influence mood.
- **Performance**: Not every experience will work on every device. Being able to develop something vast but also performant can maximize your reach and leave a lasting impression on users.
- **Software development**: Even though we interact with the content we see in a virtual world, those interactions are dependent on elements that you code and integrate using *C#*. Knowing how to utilize code so that it works for your project can unlock unlimited possibilities.

Now that we understand what immersive experiences are and the components that make up such experiences, let's dive deeper into XR.

Understanding XR, AR, VR, and MR

Extended reality (**XR**) is the umbrella term that's used to explain technology that engages our senses. This includes providing information, recreating worlds, or enhancing the world in real time. It was developed to enable more immersive experiences using digital objects. When we look at how digital objects are used, it is often through a 2D experience. This experience can include animation, word processing, video games, and even training simulations. Incorporated digital content can include images, and 3D designs that are rendered on a screen. But why should we spend hours building 3D content only to experience it in 2D? XR provides a way out of this limitation by creating a pathway for viewing 3D content in a 3D space. If we think in 3D and build in 3D, then we must have a way to experience our content in 3D.

XR is an umbrella term for **augmented reality** (**AR**), **virtual reality** (**VR**), and **mixed reality** (**MR**) (*Figure 1.2*). On the surface, people often confuse the three, but it would be valid to say that even if they are different from each other, they all comprise XR.

Within XR, we can think of AR, VR, and MR on a spectrum just like immersion. On one side, you have a completely digital world with digital objects, and on the other side, you have a physical world with digital objects. The consistent component across each experience is the digital objects, but the difference is how connected to the physical world the experience is. There are specific hardware and sensors that contribute to attaining these experiences, but we will get to that a bit later.

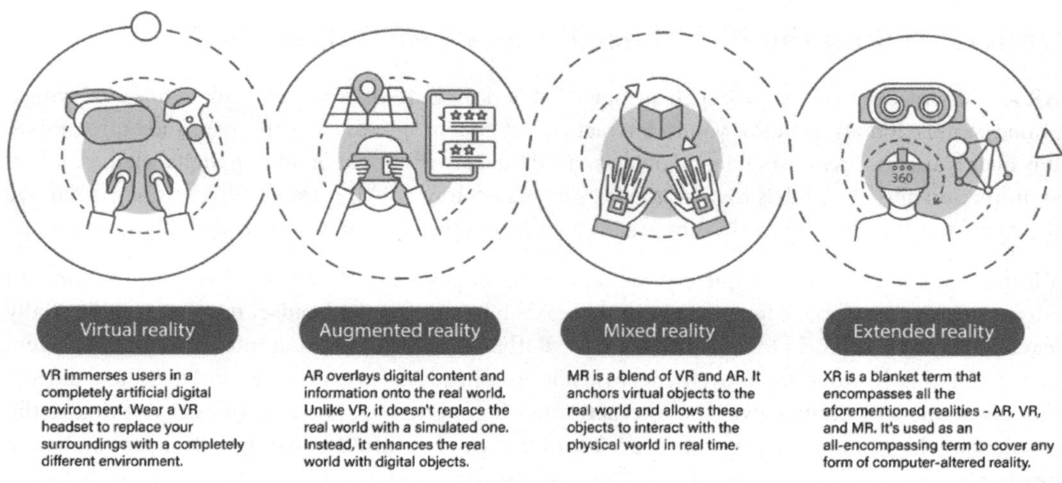

Figure 1.2 – Overview of VR, AR, MR, and XR

AR is when you have an experience that places digital objects in a completely physical world. This experience is dependent on sensors from a device that can scan the surrounding area to create a believable experience for the user. You are usually adding digital elements to the screen of a live camera feed. The camera feed is most likely from a smartphone or webcam. There are AR headsets such as HoloLens that create more immersive experiences, but they place those experiences into another category (MR). AR can also incorporate audio such as Bose glasses, which infuse audio into your environment without the need for headphones. Some popular AR experiences are found on smartphones: Pokémon Go, Snapchat face filters, and IKEA Place.

VR is when you have an experience in a completely digital world. In VR, you are not tied to the physical world. You can think of it as being inside a computer, like in Tron, or inside your favorite game. You can walk, run, and jump as an avatar in the digital world. Compared to AR, VR is not sensor-heavy, but it does require specific hardware to get the most out of the experience. At most, you would require a headset such as the Oculus Quest, but you can also use Google Cardboard, where you can use your phone with a low-cost headset case to have bite-sized experiences.

MR lies somewhere in the middle of that spectrum. It combines both AR and VR elements, allowing real words and digital objects to interact seamlessly. Instead of removing yourself from the physical world to have more interactions with digital objects in the digital world, you are integrating more sensors to track your body so that you can interact with digital objects in the physical world. In this experience, you are combining camera sensors with HMDs to scan the world around you, scan your body, and build an immersive environment that combines the best of AR and VR. Devices such as HoloLens and Magic Leap allow you to do that.

Understanding the difference between AR, VR, and MR

AR uses interactions on a screen such as toggles, sliders, or buttons. You can think of this as playing a phone game. AR does not allow you to interact with digital objects outside of screen and button input. It is mainly used for rendering digital objects in a digital environment or adding digital elements such as animation and 3D models to print media. The major draw to AR is the fact that it doesn't remove the user from the physical world they are in. It enhances the real environment with digital content.

VR uses interactions in a completely virtual way. Compared to AR, VR requires a headset and an adequate amount of space for most experiences. When you put the headset on, you are essentially leaving the physical world for the digital world. Rather than having button interactions on a screen, you are making gestures and movements instead. Most headsets have joysticks and handheld devices that give you more control over the interactions. VR experiences, because they are not tied to the physical world, will have larger-scale experiences that can last minutes to hours. Because you have a headset on, you are inside the game as if you were the real character. You don't control the character. You are the character.

MR is often confused with AR because the core element of AR (placing digital objects in the real world) is wrapped within MR. The key differentiator is that in MR, your hands are usually free because you have an HMD rather than a smartphone, so sensors can track and occlude your hands, and you can interact with digital objects naturally with simple hand gestures. You can think of it as AR with hand tracking and object interactions, or VR in the real world. If we revisit the spectrum analogy, again, MR lies somewhere in the middle of AR and VR.

As a comic book artist and visual storyteller, I delve into the distinct attributes of each XR branch. My webcomic, *Eyelnd Feevr*, weaves immersive tales on paper and elevates them with the fusion of technology on digital platforms. These technologies breathe life into comics in unparalleled ways: AR animates characters off the pages, VR submerges readers into the comic's universe, and MR intertwines the narrative with tangible reality. The depth and richness of Afro-centric narratives present vast possibilities to harness these innovations, enriching the storytelling journey.

With that, we have covered what XR is and the difference between AR, VR, and MR. You should now have a better understanding of which medium would be used for which experiences you want to pursue. If you want people to be in an experience for an extended period, go with VR. If you want people to have an experience that is accessible and affordable, go with AR. If you want people to experience the best of the real and digital world combined, go with MR. Since this is a book focused on VR experiences, let's get a little more background on how VR came to be.

Brief history of VR

The exact moment when VR was developed is currently disputed. There were references to the idea of an artificial world noted back in the early 1900s. Thomas G. Zimmerman and Jaron Lanier developed the first commercial applications of virtual technology at the company VPL Research. The main purpose of VR was for flight simulations, automotive design, and military training. This usage lasted from the 1970s to the 1990s. By the early 90s, VR started to become more mainstream. Nintendo, SEGA, and Apple were developing products as line extensions of their already popular products. By the 21st century, we started to see different mobile form factors and more portable solutions. Since then, there has been an ever-growing industry and landscape of applications using VR to where it is now seen as a medium rather than an application. The shift from an application to a medium allows VR to be industry-agnostic. Whether it is print publishing, healthcare, or higher education, VR can be used to engage customers, clients, and students.

With our increased background on VR and how it can be used to build experiences, we will now explore how it works, and what is required to create the experiences we want.

How does VR work?

VR may seem difficult to comprehend but by the end of this book, this mountain will seem more like a manageable hill. Two areas of understanding are required to fully comprehend how VR works: development and engagement. The latter requires less explanation, so we will start with that first.

VR experiences require devices specifically for VR applications. They can be smartphones or HMDs. To engage in a VR experience, you can either open the application on your phone or open the application on your headset. With the application active, you can enjoy the experience until you are ready to exit.

Developing for VR is a bit more time-consuming and intricate. Before you begin developing a VR experience, it is always good to write out a roadmap. This can include features you want to integrate, assets you want to utilize, and even interactions you want to have. This can be a checklist or a narrative description.

When you are building experiences, recall the list of elements I mentioned in the *Technological components of building an immersive experience* section. Developing a good workflow is easier when you can formulate a plan with the elements you have access to. You will need audio, animation, and 3D models. What will those look like and sound like?

Using that as a guide, you can gather all of your assets from other sources, such as Blender, Photoshop, or even asset marketplaces.

When you have all your assets, you can open Unity and begin to build out each scene of the experience. You may combine C# code with music, 3D models, character animation, and object interactions all into one experience.

After you have a prototype, you can integrate testing into the development process. Since we experience on devices, it is best to test on those devices early and often. When you finish, you build and export the VR experience to your intended device (headset or smartphone) and enjoy the experience. We will expand on how to develop VR experiences later, but this should help establish a standard process as you gain more experience.

How do we experience VR?

The most popular way to experience VR is with a headset or HMD. The headset will render a visual in each eye separately. This is called **stereoscopic rendering**. This is different from seeing through an open viewport, which is a full-screen view, similar to what we see with most smartphone experiences.

Once you have the headset on, you can load an experience onto your headset, and you can enjoy the experience.

Some experiences will require you to clear out a space to move around, and others will work perfectly in a seated position. All this depends on what you intend to do in VR. The only thing hindering you is your desires.

Hardware, software, and platforms that support VR development and engagement

Even though we will be focusing on developing VR experiences in Unity using an Oculus Quest as the test device, it is important to be aware and familiar with other tools since all the stuff we will be learning can easily be applied to other tools that are mentioned. More importantly, as time goes on, higher-end devices will become more accessible, and creators will always explore various tools to meet the scope of what the client needs:

- **Headsets**: VR headsets allow the user to enter an immersive digital world by simply putting on a headset. There are a variety of headsets available on the market at a range of price points. Let's discuss some of the popular headsets and what features make them unique for VR:

    - *Desktop-based headsets* require a computer to use. Some VR experiences require high-end graphics rendering and computer processing to play, and these headsets will allow you to plug into a USB port and engage. The limiting factor is that you must have a hardline connection to enjoy VR:

        - *PlayStation VR* is a console-based VR system developed by Sony to work with the Sony **PlayStation** (**PS**). It allows you to experience high-end console games through VR. To do so, you also need a PS4 or PS5, a PS camera, and a VR system (headset and handheld controllers). This is great for users who don't have an expensive computer but have a PS4 or PS5 game console. More importantly, by utilizing PS Network, you can play games with friends fairly easily in VR.

        - *HTC Vive* is a VR headset developed by HTC. It uses two sensors in the corners of the room to map your surroundings and track your movements while the headset is also connected to a computer. It uses two hand controllers to track finger and hand movements. It provides a fully immersive experience but may require a computer with good processing power to run smoothly. Unlike PSVR, which uses the PS's library of games, HTC Vive uses the SteamVR library, an online-based VR gaming software.

   - *Oculus Rift S* is a connected VR headset by Oculus (Meta). It provides a fully immersive experience with high-end graphics comparable to a console gaming experience. It has two touch controllers that provide hand and finger tracking. You do not need additional sensors to use the headset. The price point and the minimal setup hardware make this a solid headset for the price.
   - *HP Reverb G2* is a connected VR headset by Hewlett Packard. Much like the Oculus Rift S, it provides a fully immersive experience with a headset and hand controllers that support touch input and hand tracking. This headset is capable of playing on lower-end computers, but to get the best experience, a computer with a good graphics card and processor is recommended. It has one of the best displays of any headset with a 2K (2,160 pixel x 2,160 pixel) per eye resolution. It also comes with off-ear speakers that improve the quality of the audio out of the box. For the price, this is one of the more premium VR options on the market.
   - *Valve Index* is a PC-powered VR headset by Valve. It is a fully immersive VR headset that requires an external base station for full tracking capabilities. It comes with two sensors you must mount to a wall for body tracking, and two controllers for touch input and hand tracking. It is one of the most expensive headsets on the market, but that comes with some perks. First, it is one of the most comfortable headsets to wear for long periods. Visually, it also provides a good pixel density at a high frame rate, allowing you to get the crispest picture possible without the lag.
- *Mobile VR* is another category of VR experiences that often trade accessibility for quality. It follows the basic concept of VR as you use your phone to play the experiences with or without a case you can wear on your head. It does not provide hand or body tracking, but you can use a Bluetooth controller to interact with elements in the experience. Typically, with mobile VR, the headset case is device agnostic as it serves solely as a phone holder. In this case, you usually choose one based on the comfort and the price rather than the software features. The quality of the VR experience is usually determined based on your mobile device:
   - Android phones are the most popular phones for mobile VR. They have a lot of support behind them from Google, Samsung, and the open developer community on the internet. Because Android is open source, there are very few barriers hindering developers from developing VR experiences. This provides some of the most innovative games and applications on the market. Interestingly enough, almost all VR headsets are Android-based, so the difference in experiences is normally due to the lack of sensors and processing power of the Android smartphone.
   - iPhone's VR is simple, but it can be limited. If you want to have a VR experience on iPhones, you simply choose the VR app you downloaded from the App Store, place the iPhone into a VR head-mounted case, and enjoy. Again, much like Android phone VR experiences, you don't have hand or body tracking, and the processing power is not as high. You can use a Bluetooth remote to interact with objects, but you can expect these experiences to

be more passive, such as watching 360 videos. Unlike Android, iPhone does not have as much developer support, and the experiences available are restricted to ones you can find on the App Store. iOS is a good introduction to VR for early adopters, but it only skims the surface of possibilities for intermediate to advanced users.

- *Standalone headsets* do not require a computer connection to run, although some games may require a connected device. Standalone headsets are unique because they provide the portability of a mobile device and the quality of a desktop headset. They are the most popular category of headsets because they have the best features for the price. They require an internet connection and most of the experiences that are played are stored on the device. It is likely that if you meet someone who has a VR device, it will be a standalone headset:
  - *Oculus Quest 2* is a standalone headset by Oculus (Meta). It is the most popular headset on the market at the time of writing. It does not require a PC but is capable of supporting connected experiences as a hybrid device. It has a high refresh rate for a standalone headset and supports hand tracking and gestures with two hand controllers. It is the most versatile headset because it can play a variety of experiences from a variety of platforms.
  - *Lenovo Mirage VR S3* is a standalone headset developed by Lenovo. Like other standalone headsets, it does not require a PC to use. It only comes with one remote control, so you will have limited hand gestures and interactions with this headset experience. A unique feature of this device is that its memory can be expanded with a microSD card.

- **Platforms**: These are integral to the VR experience because they serve as hubs for navigating the virtual world and accessing games and applications. Without a VR platform, your headset is just a paperweight with futuristic sensors. Platforms provide you with access to different games and marketplaces, depending on the supported headset, although there is overlap in the content that each platform offers:
  - *SteamVR* is a customizable VR platform by Valve that allows you to launch apps and games and interact with objects in VR. It supports most VR headsets on the market. SteamVR is a one-stop shop for everything you would want to do with your headset.
  - *Oculus VR* is the default platform for Oculus headsets. Although this is specific to Oculus headsets, it is good to mention because most people who have a VR headset have an Oculus. Oculus is similar to SteamVR in terms of its customizability and access to popular marketplace applications. Oculus VR supports a hybrid mode that allows you to choose if you want to render things with your computer by plugging it in or with your headset as a standalone device.
  - *Windows Mixed Reality* is a VR platform for Windows operating systems. It provides VR experiences for compatible devices such as the HP Reverb. In Windows Mixed Reality, you can choose from a variety of apps and games available on your computer.

    - **Open Source Virtual Reality** (**OSVR**) is an open source VR platform that supports a variety of devices on Windows, Android, OSX, and Linux. It is more of a developer kit, but the focus of OSVR is to improve the standard for smooth VR experiences.

- **Accessories**: They can improve your day-to-day experience in VR. These options are normally hardware-focused and not software-focused, but since this book is about enhancing VR experiences, I figured the physical comfort should at least be covered. This will not be a comprehensive list or endorsement of particular products. My goal is to make you aware of what is available so that you can make more informed decisions about the experiences you want to have:

    - *Haptic feedback gloves and suits* provide extended sensory input through direct feedback. With gloves and suits, you can feel the difference between a hard, soft, and smooth virtual surface. It fills the gap of touch sensation that is left void with virtual objects. When we talk about making experiences more immersive, improving touch sensation with additional hardware can do that.
    - *Sensory masks* allow users in VR to smell in VR. These masks simulate natural, relaxing, and realistic smells and add them to your VR experiences. They work as attachments to your headset that you can use in your development process to provide sensations such as water mist, heat, wind, and vibration for your different VR scenarios.
    - *Omnidirectional treadmills* provide a unique opportunity to improve mobility within VR. One of the limiting factors of VR is the physical space available for you to navigate in VR. Even in the most robust VR experiences, because of space limitations, we are stuck with using joysticks to explore virtual worlds. You may be able to duck under objects or jump over fences, but locomotion is often hindered for logistical and safety reasons. Omnidirectional treadmills do that by giving you the means to walk in any direction for an unlimited time virtually while also having a small physical footprint. If you want to have a more realistic simulation of movement in VR, look into one of these.
    - *Headphones* that connect directly to the headset provide a better audio experience. It makes you feel more immersed because the audio quality is not obstructed by sounds from your environment. If you want to improve the audio quality, you can get some headphones.
    - *Extended batteries*. If you have a standalone headset such as an Oculus Quest, one of the biggest selling points is also its limiting factor. Yes, I am talking about battery life. Standalone headsets are great because you are not tethered to a computer. Although that can be liberating, it does mean your experiences have a time limit. With an extended battery, you can extend that time limit without compromising comfort.

- **Game and rendering engines**: These are the premier software for developing experiences for VR. Their ability to render elements in real time allows for interaction-based experiences that react and respond to user engagement:
  - *Unity* is one of the most popular engines for AR, VR, and mobile gaming. It is very versatile and can be used to create applications for a variety of industries. We will be focusing on VR development in Unity for this book primarily.
  - *Unreal Engine* is another popular game engine known for rendering high-fidelity experiences in real time. It supports a wide range of VR platforms and provides avenues for developers to use Python and C++ in their development processes.
  - *Godot* is an open source game engine that uses modules to expand the features of the platform. It has a huge library of tools to build games and other experiences for a range of platforms. The Godot gaming community is growing, and more support is available as a result.
  - *CryEngine* is a reliable second-tier engine that's used for games and provides a great toolset to build VR experiences. It offers great visuals and a sandbox of options that are relevant to VR development. It does not have as much support as Unity or Unreal, but it's open source and can fulfill all the needs you may have to get started.
  - *AppGameKit* is a great game engine for beginners and hobbyists that provides developers with the tools needed to learn game development. You can expand its features by installing the VR extension. Here, you can develop VR games with a library of common interactions you will find in most games. Compared to other engines where you can make VR applications, AppGameKit focuses primarily on game development.
  - *Blender* can support VR development. Blender is great for content creation, and the latest version allows you to connect to an Oculus Quest. With Blender, you can view your model creation in a virtual space and traverse the elements. You can also model objects in VR, but there are not as many tools to build interactive games and applications as there are for most engines.
  - *Amazon Sumerian* is a lesser-known software developed by Amazon that allows you to render VR experiences with **Amazon Web Services** (**AWS**). It is a popular platform for early developers because it does not require programming or 3D skills to build experiences. More importantly, these experiences can work with a variety of devices, from smartphones to high-end headsets.
  - *Sketchup Studio* is a 3D modeling tool that allows you to create models specific to construction and architecture. It has a VR feature where you can create those models in VR. If you are familiar with CAD and construction-specific tools, Sketchup may be a good avenue for exploring VR.

- **Software development kits (SDKs)**: These are a set of tools, sample scenes, and code examples that allow developers to create games and applications for specific platforms and hardware. In most cases, you download the SDK from a reputable website and utilize it within a compatible software, such as Unity:
    - *Steam VR Plugin* allows you to develop VR experiences in a game engine such as Unity and Unreal and distribute those experiences on the Steam VR marketplace – one of the largest marketplaces in the world. This SDK also allows you to add Steam-specific features to your experiences, such as achievements and matchmaking.
    - *Open VR SDK* is a developer kit by Valve that is used to make VR experiences for a variety of hardware. It builds off of the foundation that SteamVR provides to give developers more features for their hardware-specific interactions.
    - *Oculus Integration SDK* allows you to develop VR experiences for Oculus in the Unity game engine. It has all the tools needed to go from concept to finished project and make it available for Oculus users.
    - *Virtual Reality Toolkit* is a collection of scripts and interactions that work for a variety of VR experiences. At the time of writing, it is only compatible with the Unity game engine.
    - *Dev Kit* allows you to develop experiences for PSVR. Compared to other SDKs, where you can download them and start developing very quickly, with PSVR, you must become a registered developer first.
    - *Cardboard SDK* (formerly Google VR) is a developer kit that allows you to make VR experiences for Android and iOS. It supports motion tracking, stereoscopic rendering, and user interaction for mobile devices out of the box to let you create engaging VR experiences on a smartphone.
    - *PICO Unity XR SDK* is used to develop experiences for the Lenovo Mirage. It supports games and applications built on the Android platform.
- **Content creation**: These tools allow creators to create 3D objects and animated assets for their VR experiences. Game engines are perfect for rendering elements in real time, but those objects need to be created and optimized for rendering. That includes having a low poly count, textures, materials, and even the right real-world scale. You can do all of that in content creation software:
    - *Maya* is an industry standard for game development and animation. Most 3D characters and animated assets for games made in Unity and Unreal are made with Maya. If you need a tool that does everything you want for VR, Maya is a safe choice that has applications in other industries.
    - *Cinema 4D* is a 3D animation powerhouse. It is used by a variety of entertainment industries due to its ability to provide high-quality renders and simulations. Although the simulations and renders do not translate to Unity, Cinema 4D has superb modeling, animation, and polygon reduction tools to make your VR scene more performant.

- *Blender* is one of the most versatile tools a content creator can have. It can support 3D modeling, 3D animation, 2D animation, texturing, 3D mesh optimization, and 3D world-building. Pretty much anything you can think of, Blender can do. You can create your content here and export it to an engine to render it.
- *ZBrush* is a 3D sculpting program that gives you the ability to create 3D models and objects as if you are sculpting with clay. It has a variety of tools to streamline your process and give you the highest quality creations.
- *Photoshop* is a dependable 2D content creation tool. It is great for prototyping user interfaces, designing interactive UI elements, creating decals, and 2D animation. Game engines are not the best at creating professional-looking UI themes, but Photoshop can be used to address that.
- *Oculus Medium* is a tool that allows you to create content in VR using the Oculus VR headset. You can create 3D models using sculpting and traditional modeling techniques. Medium has a robust array of painting tools to texture your models to your liking.

We know what VR is, we are familiar with all the hardware and software (*Figure 1.3*), and we know what applications can be made. With this foundation, we can begin to explore VR development. The next section will cover ways to approach VR development. Instead of diving deep into Unity and building prototypes, it is wise to expand on the workflow I mentioned earlier in this chapter so that you can approach development with confidence and efficiency:

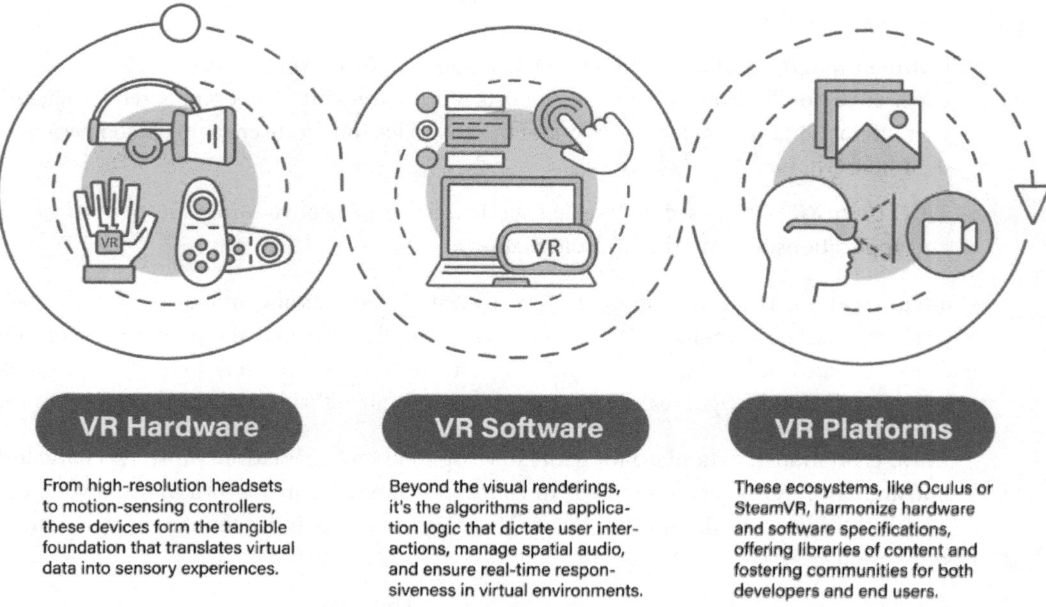

VR
VR
VR Hardware
From high-resolution headsets to motion-sensing controllers, these devices form the tangible foundation that translates virtual data into sensory experiences.
VR Software
Beyond the visual renderings, it's the algorithms and application logic that dictate user interactions, manage spatial audio, and ensure real-time responsiveness in virtual environments.
VR Platforms
These ecosystems, like Oculus or SteamVR, harmonize hardware and software specifications, offering libraries of content and fostering communities for both developers and end users.

Figure 1.3 – Core elements of VR development

Approaching VR development

I mentioned earlier in this chapter that VR development involves many components: 3D assets, animation, sounds, code, and more. The key to building VR experiences successfully and efficiently is all about navigating the required components and utilizing them effectively within your project.

How do you do that? Well, the short answer is trial and error. You have to spend time exploring the tools and making things. You may be rusty when you work on your first project, but by the 100th project, you will feel pretty comfortable with your ability to create. Regardless of whether you are a beginner, intermediate, or advanced developer, we will cover some techniques to put you on the right track. Acknowledging the importance of repetition to master these concepts, this section delves into the development of VR experiences using the principle of **design thinking**. As we explore these fundamental ideas, *Chapter 10, Design Thinking for Virtual Reality Experiences*, will revisit them, enhancing our grasp and underscoring their significance in our workflow.

Setting expectations for projects

VR development can be a lengthy process. It can take months, if not years, to complete a project. Sometimes, those experiences meet our expectations, and other times, they don't. Throughout this process, you want to set yourself up for success at every turn, no matter how big or small the project is. With that being said, you want to develop a growth mindset. This means that with every experiment and project, your goal is not to be perfect – it is to constantly improve. You want to test your limits and capabilities and push the ideas you want to pursue as far as possible. The tools you are learning to use and the skills you apply to your projects are just a means to that end goal. Going back to the 100-project analogy, compared to your first project, your 100th project will not be perfect, but it will be better than your first. Your 200th project will be even better than your 100th. Quite often, you will look back at old projects that you were proud of and think, "I'm much better now." That is the point!

Let's say you have an idea for a project, such as a fully immersive massive multiplayer open-world role-playing game with dragons, unlockable achievements, and a robust character creation system, and you want it to work on both low-end headsets and high-end headsets smoothly. You must ask yourself, "What am I capable of developing now, and what will I be able to do later?" Pulling references from our favorite games and applications, we must understand that they were created by teams of people who devoted years, thousands of dollars, and countless resources to them. More importantly, they earned years of foundational education to know how to implement core elements and features. Can one person develop this? Yes, but it will not happen overnight. A developer's most unspoken qualities are patience and persistence.

Developing VR experiences is all about improving – that's why we call it *developing*. There is always something to improve. Ultimately, your goal, as a developer, is to develop experiences that can be usable. In VR, that means that you can interact with objects, traverse digital worlds, and not get motion sickness in the process. More importantly, your goal is to take an experience that works on your high-powered computer, export it as an application, and have it run smoothly on an HMD. If you can do that, you are on the right track.

Navigating available resources

One thing you will ask in your development process is: "Do I have to make everything in my VR experience?" The short answer is no. You don't have to make every single model or character in your VR experience. There are games and applications on the market from developers that have little to no experience with 3D modeling, texturing, scripting, producing audio, and even animation. What they are successful at is coming up with interesting ideas and using the resources available to bring them to life. How do they do that? We will discuss this briefly here.

Major game engines such as Unity and Unreal have huge communities that come together all in the name of making games. With that large community comes a market for sharing and selling assets. You can find these in the respective marketplaces of the mentioned game engines. They are amazing places to find a wide range of assets for an affordable price. You may even find some stuff for free or in a blowout sale. In the marketplace, you will find 3D models and animation, 2D sprites and animation, music and sound effects, VFX, particle systems, templates for games, premade level designs, scripts to optimize your game, and more – literally anything you can think of you can find.

If you want to explore resources outside of the marketplace for content, you have pretty decent options:

- *Sketchfab* is one of the leading platforms for 3D content on the web, or you can download 3D models from users who post their content. So long as it is a `.fbx` or `.obj` file, you can implement it into your project fairly easily.
- *TurboSquid* is an alternative market that allows you to buy 3D content. It is not specifically for games or XR experiences, but the content can be modified to work with any project you may have.
- *ArtStation* is one part portfolio and another part marketplace. Here, you can find inspiration from other users who post content, and you can download and purchase that content if the users make it available. ArtStation is a wonderful place to go if you need to get out of your creative block because it has such a talented creative community.
- *Mixamo* is a huge library of animations that can be utilized in any project. Whether you are looking for a walk cycle or some stock interactions for non-playable characters, this is a great place to go to get your characters moving. More importantly, they offer rigging for any humanoid character to apply those animations perfectly. This is a free resource with a great community of support.

If you need help with development and coding, there are some places you can explore as well:

- *Unity Forums* are great places to start when you are looking for a solution. There are experienced Unity developers who know the Unity game engine inside and out. Even if they don't know how to fix problems for XR experiences specifically, they can walk you through possible solutions because of their experience with the Unity game engine.

- *Unity Discord* is an alternative to forums. Unlike forums where you could be waiting for days if not weeks for an answer to your inquiry, Unity Discord gives you access to the same support team in real time. They have specific groups for XR development and VR that you can post questions in. You may get responses from developers or one of the thousands of other members who may be able to help you.
- *Stack Overflow* is a perfect place to find help when you are stuck in the development process. The community is large and spans a variety of industries and coding languages. More than likely, if you post your problem, someone may have a solution. Often, you can simply copy and paste those solutions into your projects so that you can move on to the next task.
- *YouTube* is a great place to find help with problems others may be facing. A simple search in the search bar can lead you down a path of learning how to create a certain element or how to code a certain feature. When I got started, I made a point to follow certain Youtubers who created work I eventually wanted to create.

We are in a day and age where a simple internet search can help you tremendously. As a solo developer, being able to create experiences with high-quality assets, even if I don't know how to create those myself, is liberating because I can focus on the core of my ideas and innovate in ways that speak to my interests.

Developing an efficient workflow

The final thing to discuss is the workflow. How do we take all the knowledge, skills, and assets we've acquired and apply them to a project? There is a methodology I follow that has helped me with projects from a variety of industries, such as healthcare, animation, and even bookmaking that I can share with you. The purpose of a workflow is to streamline your creative process so that you can focus your energy on the creative process rather than figuring out the steps to create the project. Although that does not seem like much of a problem, it can be taxing when you are working on large projects or exploring things you never did before. With a workflow, you will know what steps you need to take to create something before you even start working on the project. That in part gives you a level of confidence that is increasingly valuable as you embark on your experimental journeys. You may not know what it will look like when it is finished, but you know how to get to the finish line. That is half the battle right there!

Let's say you have an idea you want to work on. You are excited about the possibilities, and you are eager to get to work. Before you begin a project, remember that everything starts on paper. It can be a napkin, a notebook, or even a document on your phone. The goal is to take that idea and transfer it from your brain to something tangible. Doing this does two things for you:

- It converts a project that is floating in the ether of your brain into something tangible that you can see and touch. You can share it with your peers, and you can deconstruct it and reconstruct it.
- The act of writing something down forces you to articulate it in a way that makes sense. When we have an idea in our head, it is normally a collection of elements that make up a project.

We can think about it, but when someone asks us about our idea, we often find it difficult to provide a concise description of it. You have an idea, but the idea is only as good as how well you can communicate it to yourself and others. Writing it down will help you articulate it and fill in gaps with details you probably did not think of initially.

Let's try out an example.

Brainstorming ideas for developing projects

Brainstorming for a project could go through the following seven stages, starting with idea creation:

1. **Idea**: A cool VR experience that is fun to play.

   How much should you write down for our idea? Well, the short answer is however much you want/need to get the point across. You will eventually be expanding on the idea, but if you need a starting point that is not too daunting, start with one to two sentences. Briefly describe what it is you want to create.

2. **Writing down a brief description**: I want to make a cool VR experience that is fun to play where you can be a superhero for a day.

   When you write down your brief description, you may have the urge to elaborate on what the experience is and some of the features involved in it. That is what we want. The purpose is to demystify and uncover elements of the experience so that you can turn those elements into actionable items you can apply your skills. Once you know what type of project you have, then you will know what elements you need, and how to acquire those elements. With your brief done, you can expand on it by adding a list of features. This can be elements of the user experiences, particular content, certain themes, and more. Think of this as a brain dump for your project. Get it all out and on paper. If you get stuck, don't worry. We will revisit this later.

3. **Creating a feature list**:

   - An open VR world where people can run, walk, and fly
   - You can save people and fight bad guys
   - You can go to the highest mountain and watch the sunset
   - There is a level-up system where you can earn more interactions and features
   - You can customize your character

   With this feature list, the project is starting to become clearer and clearer. You should be able to visualize the experience more than when it was in your head because articulating it on paper makes the idea more concrete.

4. **Research**: Now, you can start doing some research. Research is valuable because you want to know what is out there already. If you are making a commercial game, you want to see if there is an idea similar to yours. You may need to tweak it or pivot to differentiate it from others. You

can also look for inspiration on functionality, themes, artistic style, and more. We don't live in a vacuum, and your creative process should not exist in a vacuum either. As you create stuff and put it out into the world, others are doing the same. This can be a valuable resource early on when you are exploring new ideas. It allows you to see what is possible. To do this, you can start with a Google search based on some keywords from your feature list. Formulate a list of terms you can search on the internet. Start with five keywords and add more if you need to. You may get enough from a few searches, but that is not always the case. Regardless, the goal is to give you enough inspiration to expand on your current ideas. Some good places to start are Google, YouTube, Twitter, Instagram, ArtStation, and Pinterest.

5. **Shortlisting keywords**: Based on your research, you may notice that some words or phrases seem to appear more frequently and feel more relevant. Write some of them down. You could have a list that looks like this:

    - Superhero VR experiences
    - Flying in VR
    - Games with superpowers
    - Action-adventure VR experiences
    - Cool VR interactions
    - VR fighting games

    You can use these keywords to fine-tune your research.

6. **Creating a mood board**: You did a bunch of searches and found a bunch of cool ideas people are working on. Some of those ideas you want to explore in your experiences and others you don't. By this time, you should have a better idea of what your experience is and what it is not. What do you do with all this? Make a mood board.

    A mood board is a document that helps you organize the elements, features, and inspirations of your project. Create different sections on your mood board to place elements you like or don't like. If you see a feature in a game you like, add it to your mood board. If you see a color palette, add it to your mood board. If you like a character style, add it to your mood board. If you played a game you hated, add it to your mood board. Some great tools to help with creating one are *PureRefs*, *Google Docs*, *Microsoft Word*, *Milanote*, and *Pinterest*. They work great for giving you a digital canvas to organize ideas and references. The following figure shows you how you could organize a mood board you create:

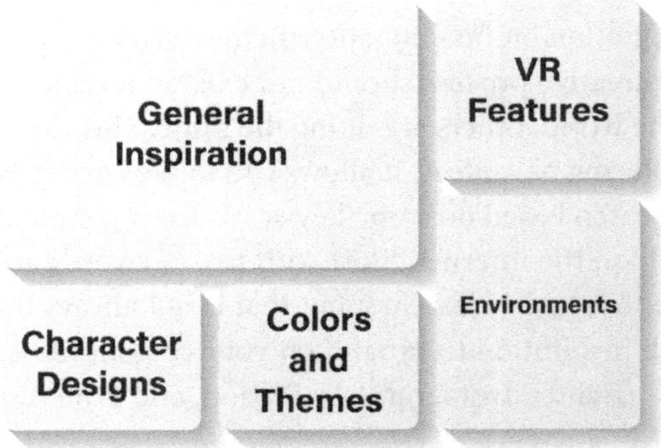

Figure 1.4 – Mood board example

With our mood board, we can elaborate on the list and expand it with more details. There may be some features that are nice to have now and some nice to have later. Maybe you want to have everything be in a particular style. Maybe there are some vague ideas in your feature list that need to be fleshed out more. Think about what it is the user will be doing and how it will make them feel. What is the experience you are trying to provide for them? What elements of your experience will the users be excited the most about? Take this time to address those questions.

7. **Creating a detailed feature list**: Once you have answered the questions, you can create a more detailed feature list compared to what we did in *step 3*. Your list could now look like this:

   - An open world where people can explore in VR:
     - They can navigate three settings: a city, forest, and space environment
     - They can run up buildings
     - They can fly to the tops of mountains
     - They can walk on the moon
   - Users can interact with people and objects using common VR interactions:
     - They can punch bad guys
     - They can open doors and enter buildings
     - They can shoot projectiles and use weapons
   - Users can enjoy dynamic levels and environments:
     - They can watch the sunset on top of a mountain
     - They can do yoga in the park
     - They can enjoy a concert with other non-playable characters

  - As the user plays the game, they can customize their character:
    - They can unlock and buy gear to equip themselves
    - They can level up their skills
    - They can improve their abilities through training
    - They can add and remove various superpowers

The feature list we have now is more focused on something we want to build rather than an idea we have. Everyone has ideas, but what differentiates this from others is that we are focusing more on the user experience. Remember, people care about VR because it provides us with a unique and immersive user experience. If we don't consider that early in the development process, then we will lose sight of what our goal is: making innovative VR experiences. We are not done, though. We need to convert this list into actionable items. This is a crucial step because this will be our guide for creating every element of the experience. That is why we call it a roadmap.

Planning development details using a roadmap

Based on the features we mentioned, we can split the elements into categories that make sense for us to develop. I like to label my categories based on the type of assets so that I can understand what it would require to include that element in my experience. Afterward, we will have a comprehensive list of what our VR experience will be made of, a list of *to-dos* to direct us, and all we would need to do is create those elements and implement them into the experience. We can use the following roadmap:

- **Characters**:
  - Enemies:
    - Grunt enemy model
    - Boss enemy model
    - Attack animations
    - Character grunts
  - Main character:
    - Various customizable elements, such as hair and clothing
    - Level up system
  - Non-playable characters:
    - Low poly mesh characters
    - Idle and walk animations

        - Stock conversation audio
    - To-do: Record audio, character animation, character design, 3D model and texture, and create character controllers for each type of character
- **Environments**:
    - City scene:
        - Buildings, roads, streetlights, sidewalks, cars, city blocks
        - Park, school, intersections, city hall, and more
        - City ambiance sounds
        - Objects that emit audio
    - Forest scene:
        - Terrain with grass, rocks, birds, and trees
        - Walking paths and natural landmarks
        - Nature sounds
        - Objects that emit audio
    - Space scene:
        - Moon terrain, Sun, stars, and space environment
    - To-do: Design 3D environments, populate environments with objects and characters, add sounds to various audio sources, and set boundaries for character navigation
- **User interface**:
    - Menu screens:
        - Buttons, text, scene navigation
    - Pause screen:
        - Buttons, text, scene navigation, game settings
    - Heads-up displays:
        - UI design, health bar, map indicator
    - To-do: Design the interface screens and create each element according to the color palette and theme

- **User interactions**:
    - Character controller
    - Flying system
    - Shooting projectiles
    - Grabbing objects
    - Fighting system
    - To-do: Code each system
- **Rewards**:
    - Superpowered abilities:
        - To-do: different VFX for the abilities
    - Level-up system:
        - To-do: Code the system and use particle and sound effects for user feedback

We can elaborate on the roadmap even more, but you get the gist. You list all of the elements needed for a particular experience and try to think about what the technical requirements are. Some things may only need to be recorded; others may need to be rendered. Figure out what you need to do for that element and add it to the roadmap. The bulk of the prep work is done. You should have a familiarity with the project that will inform you what your first objective would be. Regardless of where you start, you aren't going to have that element finished before you move on to the next element. Your development process should still be at a high level. Focus on the core elements of the experience and not the itty-bitty details. There will be time for that later. Right now, we just need to lay the foundation that we can build on. If we shortcut this process, then we will be sure to regret it in the future because our project's foundation will not be able to fully support our aspirations for the project. In the *Roadmapping* section of *Chapter 10, Design Thinking for Virtual Reality Experiences*, we will cover a full concept of the roadmapping process that we will be able to flesh out with more details and eventually put into practice in *Chapters 11* to *17*.

Developing a prototype based on your mood board and roadmap

Using the *to-dos* as a guide, we can perform some steps to prepare us for making our prototype. We can divide what we need to do into three stages:

1. **Sketching/drafting**:
    - **Coding**: Before we spend countless hours coding in Visual Studio, we can create some of the necessary scripts and place comments describing what we intend to do instead of coding. We may not need all the code to get up and running but having a plan can provide us with directions we can do ourselves or collaborate with others on.

- **Character design**: It can take time to develop one character let alone a whole cast. Start with sketching the character design in a side and front pose. This will help you when you begin modeling because it is easier to replicate a premade character than modeling on the fly.
- **Environment design**: Just like character design, building an environment that can take on a life of its own can be time-consuming. A way to mitigate some of the problems is to create a map of your environments. Include everything from city blocks, key landmarks, points of interest, and more. Think of all the elements that make up an area and include them. When you plan out all the areas of a location, you can simply move elements to those areas of the map and cut out most of the guesswork. Another opportunity is to do concept art for how the environment should look and feel. You can design buildings and objects and visualize settings you want to replicate in the experience. Again, the goal is to take the guesswork out of the creative process.
- **Sound recording**: Audio is a crucial component of an immersive experience. Even if you are not a sound design expert, there are things you can do to create the best auditory experience for the user. Think about all the sounds in your experience and try to create a comprehensive list you can use to build a library of sounds. You may have started doing that in your roadmap, but if not, here is your opportunity. You will need sounds for cars, sword slashes, people talking, footsteps, grunts, and more. You can record them yourself, or you can get them from a third party. Regardless, building a library based on your needs is a great way to prepare for your prototype.
- **User interface design**: User interfaces benefit the most from planning because you can do most of the designing of the buttons, text, and visual elements, and then import them into your experience for coding, regardless of whether it is a menu screen, pause screen, character HUD, or something else. Sketch out the locations of each element and prepare them for prototyping.
- **Animation**: Develop a list of all the animated elements that need to be made for the different situations. Animating can be time-consuming, so knowing what to animate can minimize the time needed to spend on the process. Some of these assets can be purchased or downloaded from third parties.

You will get to a point where you want to start putting things together. When that point comes, it means you are ready to prototype.

2. **Prototyping**: I normally encourage developers to get to the prototype phase as quickly as possible, but only if they have the other stuff done. Again, we are in the business of building experiences, not making pitch decks. We want to make things we can show users instead of creating documents that describe the experiences we want to make. If we are talking about building full experiences, the preparation work will take longer, but if we are trying to develop an element of the experience, we can jump into the prototyping phase with minimal prep work. The purpose of this phase is to make something that we can quickly use with a headset. It will

be rough and buggy but getting to a prototype sooner allows us to address the problems early before the project becomes too big to manage:

- **Code**: We can follow our comments from our previous steps to implement any interactions we want. This can include downloading SDKs and toolkits to lighten the developmental load of our projects. This will not be production-ready code, but just enough to test out the features.
- **Characters**: We don't need fully rendered, high-quality characters right now. We just need simple meshes with a character rig and character controller. They can be place markers for our final character designs. We focus on their interactions with the environment and players right now.
- **Environments**: We will be introduced to the term grayboxing later in this book, but the concept is all about using primitive shapes to build environments. We can color code them based on whether they are buildings, cars, or trees, but don't focus on the details right now. So long as the environment is to scale and has all the core elements, you can be satisfied with a world of cubes, spheres, and prisms.
- **Sounds**: You should have a decent number of sounds in a library at this point. You can swap them out later if you want. The goal is to start playing around with different sound combinations in your prototype early so that you can capture the different effects you want a user to experience.
- **User interfaces**: User interfaces also do not need to be pretty. They just need to be functional. For a prototype, it will be good enough to have simple buttons, sliders, and scenes that you can navigate. Focus on being able to load scenes within your experience, point buttons to specific results, and load whatever information you want to load on the screen. The beautiful themes can come later.
- **Animation**: You can get pretty far without having animation right now. Much like building a sound library, you can build an animation library to use for your projects. If you have little to no experience with animation, Mixamo and Marketplaces are great places to build your library. Since most of the VR interactions will be code-based for your player, the animation assets will typically be used for enemies, non-playable characters, and objects in your environment.

Having a prototype is a feat in and of itself. Test it out and see how far you have come. If you have friends and colleagues, have them try it too. Feedback early in the process is very valuable. Make note of all the things that work and don't in the experience so that you can quickly address them before you add more elements to the experience. When you are satisfied with where the experience is, you can begin polishing the experience. This can come in a variety of forms. If you are creating all the assets yourself, that would mean that you would be spending the majority of your time building 3D models and characters, animating, designing environments, and more. If you are using primarily third-party assets, you would be kitbashing and implementing those assets into your project in place of the cubes and low poly meshes. More than likely, you are doing a combination of both. With that being said, the goal here is to make the game look as polished as possible. Add all the code you need, replace all the characters, integrate all the sounds and animation you want from your library, and spruce up your UI screens.

By this time, your experience has taken on a life of its own. What started as an idea is now an interactive experience that occupies gigabytes on your hard drive. It looks good and sounds good when you are in the experience, but now, we need to make sure it runs well on a device. We will discuss some good optimization techniques later in this book. At this point, you want to try to optimize all your assets and content: compress audio and image files, clean up your code, bake all your lights, reduce keyframes in your animation, and more. This will help improve your frame rate and minimize the number of crashes your experience may have as people try to run them in a variety of settings and contexts.

Beyond this, you will continue to improve on different features of your experience, and on some occasions, rebuild it to correct some of the mistakes you made early in the development process. Like I said before, you are not making a final product – you are developing experiences. That developmental process is never-ending. The experiences will never be fully completed because there is always room for improvement. What you are doing is creating experiences that are good enough to share with others.

With that, we have gone through a full project workflow that you can follow to make your development process more efficient. You know the steps required to build the experience. Now, you can spend more time applying those steps and focusing on the creative process.

3. **Creating a workflow checklist**: To make prototype development even simpler, you can turn it into a checklist you can reuse over and over to keep you on track. This is something you can expand on and make your own, but we will be using this later in this book as we dive deeper into developing VR experiences:

   I. Get your idea on paper.

   II. Write a brief one to two-sentence description.

   III. Create a feature list.

   IV. Create a keyword list to do research.

   V. Create a mood board of inspiration and ideas.

   VI. Expand on your list of features.

   VII. Create a roadmap for your project.

   VIII. Sketch out elements, including menus, designs, code, assets, concepts, and more.

   IX. Prototype features such as scenes, UIs, interactions, and animation.

   X. Test our experience, in the editor and on the device.

   XI. Polish our experience by creating final assets, kitbashing, and populating worlds.

   XII. Optimize our experience for function and performance.

With this refined roadmap, you will be better equipped to build, test, and deploy your VR experience in Unity.

Summary

In this chapter, we covered a variety of topics that are essential for orienting ourselves in a VR developer's mindset. We covered the basics of what an immersive experience is, what the different types of immersive experiences are, and what elements distinguish each of them. We then explored the various components and technical skills required to build VR experiences.

VR is a medium that incorporates various hardware such as HMDs and motion controllers with software to create experiences that go beyond games. VR has applications in the healthcare, entertainment, and education industries too.

At the end of this chapter, we explored how to set up expectations for ourselves and our projects. We went through all the necessary steps required to complete a full project and developed a checklist we can use in future chapters to improve our creative process and VR development workflow.

In the next chapter, we will dive deep into the Unity game engine. We will learn the basics of what it is and how to use it to build VR experiences.

Part 2: Technical Skills for Building VR Experiences in Unity (Assets, GameObjects, Scripts, and Components)

This part is the technical bedrock of the book. Here, you will navigate the vibrant landscape of Unity, the world's leading platform for creating interactive, real-time content. By engaging with a plethora of tools and techniques available in Unity, you'll gain the technical prowess necessary to bring your creative visions to life. This part will serve as your comprehensive guide to mastering the tangible, hands-on skills that bring VR experiences into existence.

This part includes the following chapters:

- *Chapter 2, Building Virtual Reality Scenes in Unity*
- *Chapter 3, Working with Inputs and Interactions*
- *Chapter 4, Using GameObjects, Materials, and Prefabs*
- *Chapter 5, Implementing Animation – Physics and Colliders*
- *Chapter 6, Lighting Your Worlds and Experiences*
- *Chapter 7, Creating Immersion with Sound*
- *Chapter 8, Working with C#, Unity Events, and Input Assets*
- *Chapter 9, Unlocking the Power of Render Pipelines*

2
Building VR Scenes in Unity

In this chapter, we will learn how to navigate the Unity game engine and build a template scene of key components that we will use for future projects. We will create a new project, set up all the necessary packages and settings for building VR experiences, navigate the **Package Manager**, **Inspector**, and **Editor**, and lastly test our first Unity VR scene on a device. After the test is complete, we will build a template of this scene we can use for future projects.

By the end of this chapter, you will have an understanding of how to convert a blank Unity scene or premade template into a functional VR development environment. This will include importing the required developer kit packages, creating an empty scene, placing a VR rig and plane in the scene, and testing out the experience. After this chapter, you will feel confident in the basics of VR scene components to where you can continue to add to the scenes and incorporate whatever preexisting Unity knowledge you may have.

In this chapter, we will cover the following topics:

- Setting up a Unity project
- Navigating the Unity game engine
- VR setup
- Headset setup
- VR scene setup
- Testing in the Editor
- Testing on a device

Technical requirements

The complete source code for this chapter can be found at https://github.com/PacktPublishing/Enhancing-Virtual-Reality-Experiences-with-Unity-2022/tree/main/EnhancingVRExperiencesFullProject/Assets/_VRProjectAssets/Scenes/Chapter_2.

Setting up a Unity project

To begin creating VR projects, we first need to install the **Unity Editor**. This is the most crucial part of the development process because, without the Editor, we would be stuck trying to figure out how to connect hardware and sensors with the experiences we hope to build manually. Using the foundation Unity has built for developing games, we can harness its power to build experiences tailored to our needs.

Installation

The first thing we need to do is visit the Unity website. Open a web browser and navigate to https://unity.com/. On the web page, you will want to select **Plans and Pricing** in the top-right corner. Clicking this link will take you to the license selection page (*Figure 2.1*):

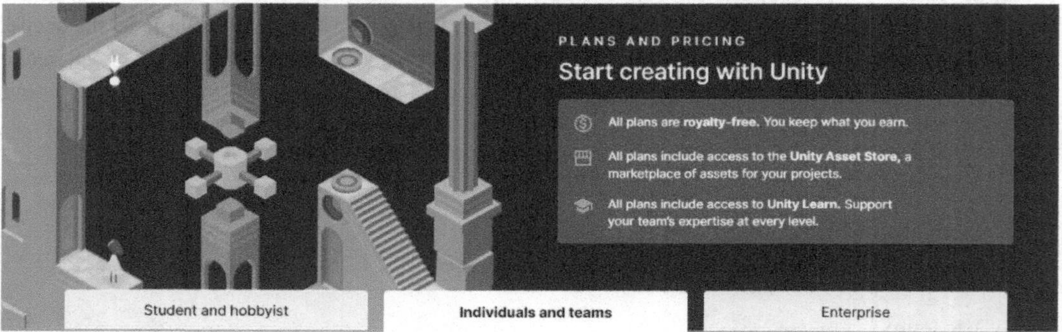

Figure 2.1 – The Plans and Pricing section

If you represent a business or corporation that meets the minimum earning threshold, you will need to choose a license option from the **Enterprise** tab. If you represent a small to medium-sized business that has employees and collaborators working on the same projects together, select the **Individuals and teams** tab and select a license option. Finally, if you are an indie developer, hobbyist, or student, select the **Student and hobbyist** tab. Most people will select the **Individuals and teams** tab, after which they can select a personal license to begin (*Figure 2.2*):

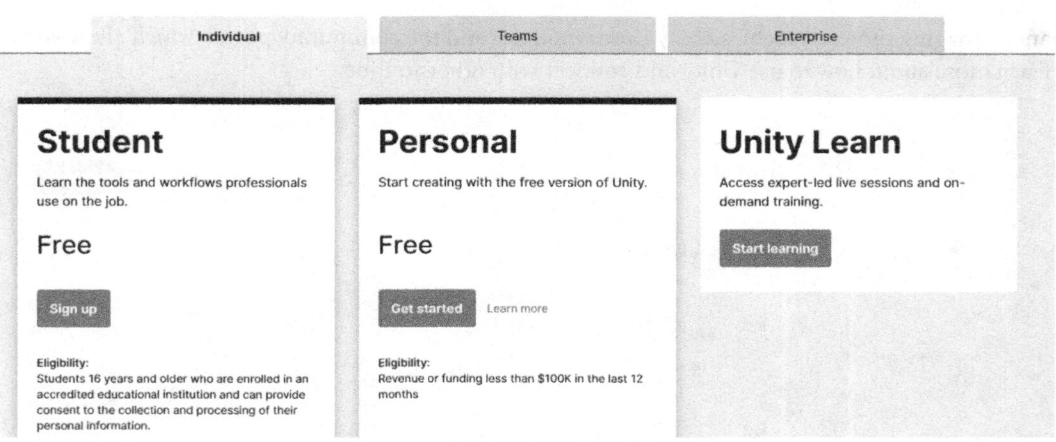

Figure 2.2 – The Individual tab's license options

If you are a student or hobbyist, you will need to select **Sign up** under the **Student** subcategory or **Get started** under the more commonly opted-for **Personal** subcategory.

If you choose to select a **Student** license, you have to fill out a form for Unity to verify that you are a student at an accredited university. This does not give you immediate approval and it can take some time for your license to be activated – usually days to weeks. So, you may need to select a personal license to get started in the meantime. If you are considering a **Student** license, you will have access to premium Unity features that are not available for **Personal** licenses.

Once you've selected your license option, you will be taken to a new window that allows you to download the right version of **Unity Hub** for your operating system. Unity only supports three operating systems: *Windows*, *Linux*, and *Mac*. As of the most recent release of Unity 2021, Macs with the Silicon M1 or M2 processor are now natively supported. Download the right operating system version you want to use the Unity Editor on and install it in the proper location.

You will notice that there is no option to download Unity for iPad, Android, or Chromebooks. Those devices are not supported, even if they have the right hardware specs. There are a variety of reasons for this, but in short, understand that Unity is only available for Mac, Windows, and Linux.

Unity Hub

Once you've finished downloading and installing Unity, you can't just hop right into making projects. Unity operates slightly differently from most software you may be used to. There are some things you need to set up first. This is a one-time process that will allow you to jump right into creating projects in the future. When you open Unity for the first time, you will be opening **Unity Hub** (*Figure 2.3*), not the Unity Editor. Unity Hub is a portal where you can manage multiple installations of the Unity Editor, create new projects, access remote projects, and manage supported device platforms. This is your one-stop shop for all your Unity needs. Some additional features in Unity Hub go beyond creating and managing projects, such as Unity Learn modules and the community portal, which allow you to learn more about how to use Unity and connect with others online:

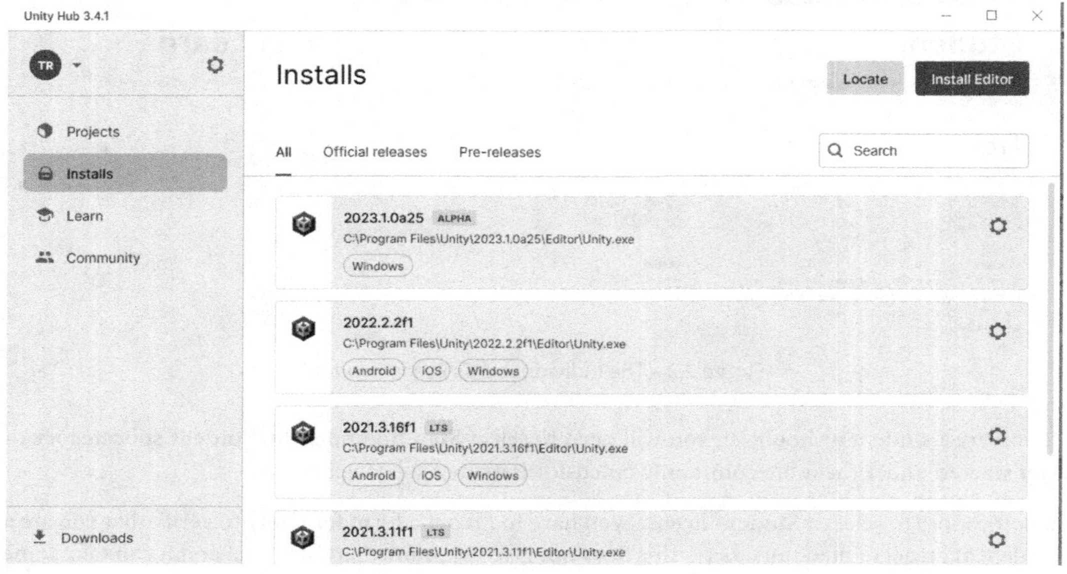

Figure 2.3 – The Unity Hub interface

The main tabs in Unity Hub are as follows (*Figure 2.3*):

- **Projects**: This is where you access your projects in the Unity Editor. You can organize them based on name and date, you can open projects from remote and local locations, and you can create new projects using a variety of available templates.

Note

Unity projects can be quite large and can take up a significant amount of disk space. It is recommended to have a dedicated storage drive for your VR projects.

- **Installs**: Here, you can install any version of the Unity Editor, from official releases to pre-releases. If you have a particular device you want to build on, you can select your desired platform module for the Editor version of your choosing.
- **Learn**: This area gives you access to Unity's very own Unity Learn platform. Here, you can watch hours of online tutorials, follow hundreds of step-by-step blog-style tutorials, or download and explore beginner projects. If you want to dive deep into everything Unity, this is the place to go.
- **Community**: This is where you can find the community resources. You can also access **Unity Blog** to read the latest articles from the Unity team, get questions answered in **Unity Forum**, or get live help from the Unity tech team.

You may be wondering, "How do I open a project?" You must do that using a particular set of steps. We will discuss those now. Typically, with software, to open a project, you open the software and then start a new project. When you are finished working on the project, you save it to your computer. When you want to work on it again, you can open the software and load the project file.

However, Unity does not work that way, partly because there are a lot of files that go into a Unity project. Instead of a standalone app, Unity uses Unity Hub to manage projects and the Unity Editor to edit projects. Unity does that because there are tons of different versions of the Unity Editor and depending on the version, you will have access to different features. Some projects require the latest Unity features, and others require stable features that have been around for years. This means that you can have multiple Editor versions installed and, depending on the project, you can open the right Editor for the right project from Unity Hub.

In short, you can have multiple Unity Editors with one Unity Hub. To open a project in Unity Hub, you must open Unity Hub, download a version of the Unity Editor in the **Installs** tab, create a new project in the **Projects** tab, and select the Unity version you downloaded to edit the new project (*Figure 2.4*):

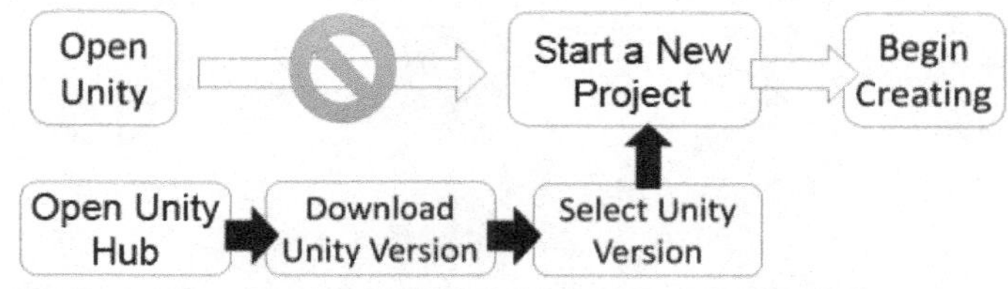

Figure 2.4 – How Unity Hub works

It may not be as intuitive as other software, but it does make it easier to navigate different projects as you get more comfortable working in Unity.

Licenses

At this point, you may have your license set up in the Unity Editor, but if you don't, click the gear icon in the top-left corner. This will take you to the license settings of Unity Hub. Here, you can change and manage the licenses you have for using Unity. Some people have a license for their student account, personal account, and work account. You can switch between them all or activate a new one here.

There are different Unity Editor features available with different license options. Pro and Enterprise licenses offer more features than personal licenses, while Student licenses offer Pro features, but cannot be used for commercial projects.

If you would like to know more about installing Unity, you can visit `https://docs.unity3d.com/Manual/GettingStartedInstallingUnity.html`.

Unity Editor version

Now that we know what Unity Hub is and how the installation process works, let's install the Unity Editor. Go to the **Installs** tab of Unity Hub. You will notice that there are tabs for official releases and pre-releases. We will discuss those momentarily. Click **Install Editor** in the top right. A pop-up screen will appear for you to select the Editor version you want to download and use (*Figure 2.5*):

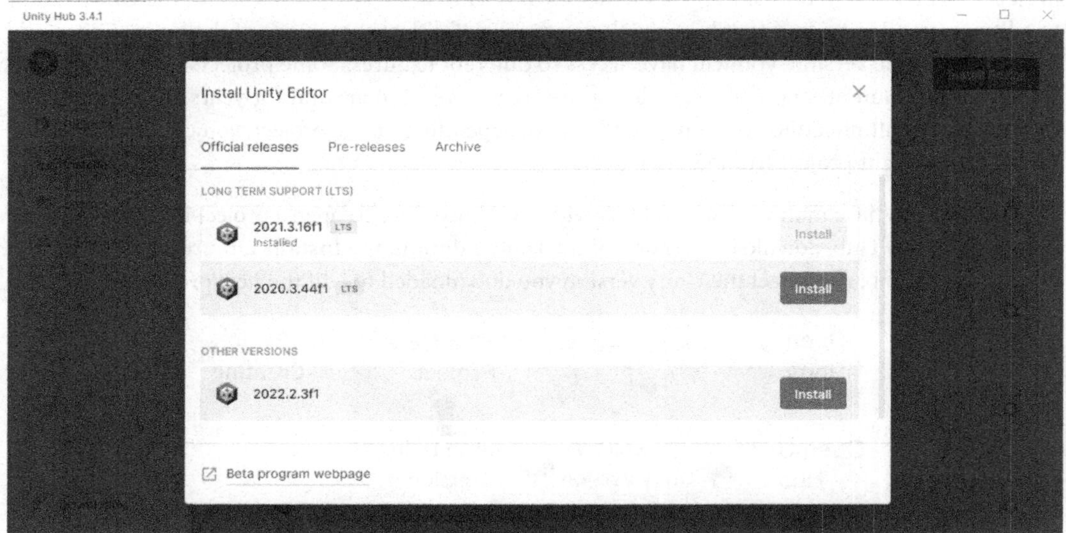

Figure 2.5 – The Install Unity Editor menu

It can be jarring seeing all the options and numbers for the different versions at first. The version number represents the year, version, and iteration of the particular Unity release. Each number gives you a glimpse of how recent the Editor version is. *2019.4.40f* is the version that was made in 2019 and is the 4th version and the 40th update, whereas *2021.3.5* is the 5th update to the 3 version of the 2021 Editor release. Unity is notorious for constantly releasing new versions and updating features of the Editor. Let's take a look at the different areas of the **Install Unity Editor** menu:

- **Official releases** comprises the official supported release that Unity offers:
    - **LONG-TERM SUPPORT (LTS)** is the most stable version of Unity for each release year. If you have a project you are working on for clients, use this one.
    - **OTHER VERSIONS** are other supported releases that are not yet stable, but close to it. These are not great for client projects but are good for testing out new features that will be coming to future stable releases.
- **Pre-releases** are experimental versions of Unity that will have new features coming to Unity in the next few years:

    - **ALPHA** is the earliest of early releases and is the most buggy. This is not recommended for current projects.
    - **BETA** is not as buggy but it does have some great features to explore. Again, this is not recommended for projects.

- **Archive** is the repository for older releases. If you want to use a particular version number of the Editor and you don't see it in the menu, you can download it from their archive.

Ideally, you will want to install the latest stable release of Unity. You don't need to update it every time they release a new update, though. When you find the right Editor, click **Install**. This will take you to another pop-up menu where you can select all the modules you want to use in the Unity Editor.

> **Note**
> When choosing your Unity Editor version, be sure to check the compatibility of the VR hardware you will be developing for as there might be different restrictions and limitations with certain Editor versions.

Modules

Once you have chosen a version of the Unity Editor you wish to use, you will be taken to the **Add Modules** menu. Here, you can select all the modules you need to build experiences for the various devices Unity supports. There are four categories of modules to download:

- **DEV TOOLS**: This category allows you to write code and process information in a development environment. If you want to use any scripting or render pipeline features in Unity, you need to install a dev tool such as **Visual Studio**. In *Chapter 8*, we will cover C# scripting, so be sure to download this.
- **PLATFORMS**: This category allows you to download modules for any device Unity supports. The modules here are crucial for exporting experiences you build in Unity. Current devices include game consoles, Android, iOS, Windows, Linux, MacOS, WebGL, and dedicated servers. For VR development, we will select Android and Windows build support.
- **LANGUAGE PACKS**: If you want to use the Unity Editor in a language other than English, you can download a language pack from this category to translate the Editor into the proper language. Supported languages include Japanese, Korean, and Chinese.
- **DOCUMENTATION**: This category gives you access to the Unity documentation package. Instead of searching online for information on the Unity Editor, you can access everything you need to know within Unity.

For our VR project, we will be selecting **Android Build Support**. Once you've selected your Unity modules, select **Continue** in the bottom-right corner. You may then be asked to agree to Microsoft

Visual Studio Community 2019's terms and conditions, as well as the Android SDK and NDK License Terms from Google before you can click **Install**. Unity will begin to install all the files needed to create Unity projects.

> **Note**
>
> This process can take time, especially if you are also installing multiple modules. Be aware of the disk space required, disk space available, and internet speed during this process as those are factors that can impact the total installation time for the Unity Editor of your choice.

Project templates

With the Editor and modules installed, you can now create a new Unity project. When you go back to the **Projects** tab in Unity Hub, select **New project**. The next page will be where you can choose your project template (*Figure 2.6*). Unity provides a variety of templates you can use to learn more about game development for consoles and mobile devices. They also have templates for cinematography and animation. We will only focus on 3D core templates for our projects, but you can learn more about the other project templates at `https://docs.unity.cn/ru/2021.1/Manual/ProjectTemplates.html`:

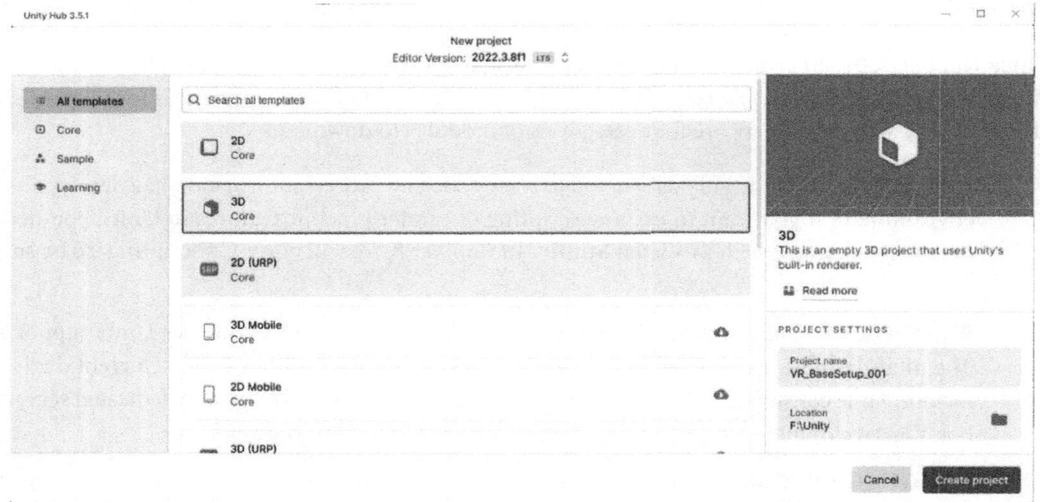

Figure 2.6 – The All templates menu for creating a new Unity project

Creating a new project

Once you've selected your template, you will be prompted to name your project and select a folder to save it to. I use a simple naming convention for most of my projects to help me keep track of them. Since names are arbitrary and can lose meaning when out of context, I try to stick to a system that helps me recall what the project is and the purpose of creating it. My naming system is `Category_ProjectName_ BuildNumber`. This naming convention is a personal preference, and it is by no means a requirement. I follow this naming convention to keep my projects organized. Different developers may use different naming conventions based on their preferences, and I encourage you to explore alternatives that work better for you. An example of mine would be `VR_BaseSetup_001`. If I had an animation project, I would name it `Animation_FightScenes_002`. If I were creating a world-building scene, I would name it `WorldBuilding_TropicalIsland_023`. You will notice that I separated the words with an underline instead of a space. I do that because you can run into issues with building projects to devices and debugging experiences if you have too many spaces in file directory names. It is best to avoid using spaces in the naming of your folders, files, and projects in Unity to avoid any unwanted errors during the building process. For our first project, let's select the **3D core** template, name it `VR_Basics_001`, and click **Create project**.

Once you have named your project and created it, you will be able to see a sample scene surrounded by several windows. In the following section, we will understand what each window's components can be used for.

Navigating the Unity interface

The Unity Editor interface is comprised of windows that enable developers to create with a variety of features and tools. Some windows allow you to tweak settings, some enable optimizations, and others allow for world-building and 3D modeling.

The Scene view

The center window is the **Scene** view. This is the main view you will be working in to design your experiences. It includes all the game objects, cameras, and elements that players will be navigating in the experiences we create. In the **Scene** view, you will see everything that will make up your experience. You can manipulate objects in 3D space and add and remove 3D objects in the 3D environment. To learn how to navigate the **Scene** view, visit `https://docs.unity3d.com/Manual/SceneViewNavigation.html`.

The Game view

The window next to the **Scene** window is the **Game** window. In this window, you can see what the main camera in your scene sees. Whatever happens in front of the camera, you will see in this view. This is the "player's perspective." You cannot move freely in this view compared to the **Scene** view. Think of this as the screen where you would render out games and animation. It shows the scene with all the lighting settings.

Within the **Game** view, you have options to modify various elements:

- **Screen resolution**: By selecting the **Free Aspect** dropdown, you can select various screen resolutions to fit your desired device resolution or aspect ratio
- **Scale**: You can zoom in and out of the current resolution of your **Game** window
- **Maximize on play**: The **Game** view will automatically be in full-screen mode when you enter play mode
- **Mute audio**: Your scene's audio will be muted when you enter play mode
- **Stats**: This shows the frame rate and other stats related to your rendering performance

The Hierarchy window

Hierarchy is the area that shows you everything that is included in the scene. It is shown as a list of items in a tree-like structure with parent objects and child objects. If you have it in your **Scene** view, then it will appear here. There are very good development techniques that use **Hierarchy** that we can use in the future.

Hierarchy object order

If you select an object in the **Scene** view, it will be selected in the **Hierarchy** window and vice versa. You can arrange objects in the hierarchy to navigate large element collections and stay organized.

As mentioned in the previous section, you can make objects children of other objects, where they are contained within them, and parents of other objects, where they can contain objects. You can also make empty objects that are used solely for separating the categories of objects in the list.

The Project window

The **Project** window is where all of your files are. I mentioned earlier that a Unity project contains many files. This is where you can access those files. From 3D models to scripts, to music and video, this is where you access them. You can create a variety of folders to organize all your folders, and you can create new assets within the **Project** window to expand your projects' content and features. The **Project** window is the inventory window for your project. In that inventory, you have the flexibility to import any supported assets into your project, including 3D models, textures, audio files, scripts, and more.

The Inspector window

The next major window is the **Inspector** window. You will be using this window a lot to integrate many of the features you have in your Unity experiences. The **Inspector** window shows all the settings and components of an object you inspect in the **Hierarchy**, **Scene**, or **Project** windows. In the **Inspector** window, you can change values for an object's location in the **Scene** view, add/remove scripts, and modify the elements for different functionality within your project, such as the position, scale, and rotation of any object in your Unity scene.

Package Manager

The Unity Package Manager is a window in the Unity Editor that serves as the library or repository for all the plugins and assets within the Unity Editor. Here, you can add and remove native features to the Editor to tailor the development environment to your project's needs. Some packages include render pipelines, AI tools, version control, animation tools, and much more. Think of it as your plugin hub. To access the Package Manager, go to **Window** in the toolbar and select **Package Manager**. To learn more about the Unity Package Manager, visit `https://docs.unity3d.com/Manual/upm-ui.html`.

Adding custom extensions is a great way to customize your Unity Editor. You can import extensions and packages from a variety of sources that will automatically update, similarly to how default Unity extensions do:

- **From fdisk** allows you to import extensions from your local disk drive
- **From git** allows you to import extensions from a GitHub repository
- **From tarball** allows you to import extensions from a `.tarz` file
- **By name** allows you to search for an extension based on a name

Later in this chapter, we will be adding a custom package called XR Interaction Toolkit.

Build Settings

Build Settings is a section that allows you to create builds for specific devices. Builds are exported files and packages of your application that are used for particular devices. Those include `.apk` for Android, `.exe` for Windows, and `.dmg` for macOS. Since Unity is capable of exporting builds to multiple platforms through its module extensions, you can control the settings of those exports in **Build Settings**.

To access **Build Settings**, go to **File**, and then select **Build Settings**. In **Build Settings**, you will see a section at the top called **Scenes in Build**. This section tells you which Unity scenes in your project will be included in your build. To add a scene, you simply select the scene in your **Project** window and drag it into the **Scenes in Build** window, or if you have an open scene you want to include, you can select the **Add Current** button at the bottom right of **Scenes in Build** window. If you do not add a scene to the scenes list, it will not be included in the build. This is useful for developers because it allows you to create demo and test scenes to prototype different features, but also exclude them from the build of the game without you having to delete them. If you build without adding any scenes, Unity will build an application with the existing open scene only. We will discuss how to use this window when we cover scene management in the *Switching between scenes with portals* section of *Chapter 8*.

If you look at the left-hand side of the **Scenes** list, you will notice numbers. Those numbers indicate the order of the scenes in your build. This order allows you to control different scene management properties within an application, as well as build a navigation system. When you build an application, **Scene 0** will be the first scene that's loaded by default.

Below is the **Platforms** section. This allows you to choose what platform you want to build to. Below that section is a button for **Project Settings**, where you can modify the settings for your whole project, such as adding a name, app icon, and much more. This allows you to tweak how the project will appear on the different platforms you export to. Lastly, if you want to build to a platform, select **Build** to build an application file that you can load to a device and share with others, or **Build And Run** to build to an attached device and run the experience.

Platforms

In the **Platforms** section, you can find a list of platforms that Unity supports. The current platform in the list is indicated by a Unity logo next to its icon. These platforms allow you to develop experiences for particular devices. You can enable certain platforms by downloading the module for that platform in the **Installs** section of Unity Hub. You cannot build to a specific platform if you do not have that module installed.

If you want to switch from one platform to another, select the platform that you want to switch to from the menu, and then select the **Switch Platform** button below the window. When the platform switches successfully, there will be a Unity icon on the icon for that platform. Before working on a project, it is best to choose the platform you are developing for and switch to that platform before starting development.

Project Settings

Project Settings allows you to configure the project as well as the export you intend on building. Whether you want to unlock preview Unity packages or tweak the default audio settings, you can do that here. Visit `https://docs.unity3d.com/Manual/comp-ManagerGroup.html` to learn more about all the different **Project Settings** features.

Play mode

In the center top of the Unity Editor, you will find a play button, a pause button, and a forward button.

The play button allows you to run your scene and utilize the real-time rendering engine to test and play your experience. When you press play, you will be automatically sent to the **Game** view. You have the option to go back to the **Scene** view during play mode.

The pause button allows you to pause the rendering engine while in play mode so that you can examine your scene and modify elements. Note that anything you change and modify in play mode will not be saved and will revert to what it was before you entered play mode.

Now that we have a good idea of how the Unity engine works, we can focus on building our first experience.

VR setup

Before we begin setting up our project, we want to make sure we have specific modules installed to run our experiences:

- Android build support for standalone headsets
- Windows build support for PC-based headsets

With those modules installed, you can create a new project (**Unity Hub | Projects | Create New**). Name it `VR_Basics_001`, Select the folder where you wish to save it, and select the right Editor. For the template, select **3D Core** (shown in *Figure 2.6*). Then, select **Create project**:

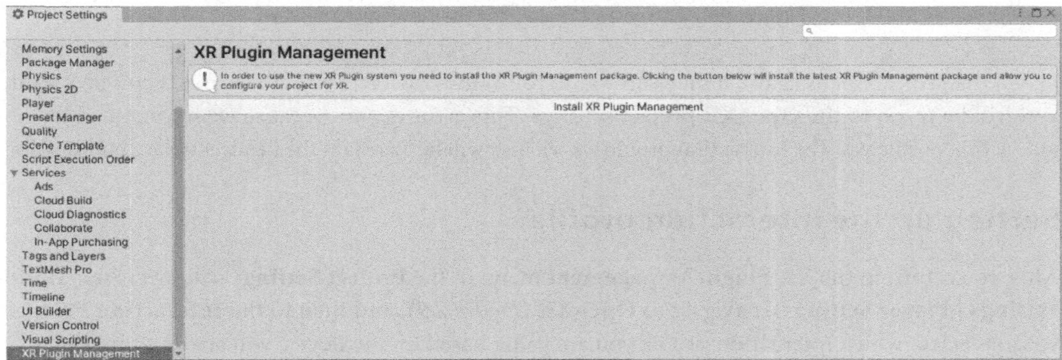

Figure 2.7 – The XR Plugin Management pre-installation window

Once the project has been created and the Unity Editor is open, we will want to open **Project Settings** (**File | Build Settings | Project Settings**). Go to the **XR Plugin Management** tab and select **Install XR Plugin Management** (*Figure 2.7*). This will do all the heavy lifting for you when you are trying to build VR experiences and interacting with those experiences in the Unity Editor with a headset.

You will now see plugin providers you can enable for various VR workflows. Those include **Oculus**, **OpenXR**, and **Unity Mock HMD**. OpenXR is the plugin that supports the most headsets. They are moving to this one because it provides a universal input system that can be translated across devices. This is important for developers because you only need to build once for all devices and not build specifically for each device you want to run the experience on. Each headset has different hardware and buttons, and that can be time-consuming for developers to navigate if the project's scope increases. Instead of needing a plugin for Oculus, Steam VR, and other platforms, this provides a standard.

Select **OpenXR** and wait for it to compile. This will automatically switch your project to the new input system and restart. A dialog window will appear (*Figure 2.8*). Select **Yes** and wait for the project to reload:

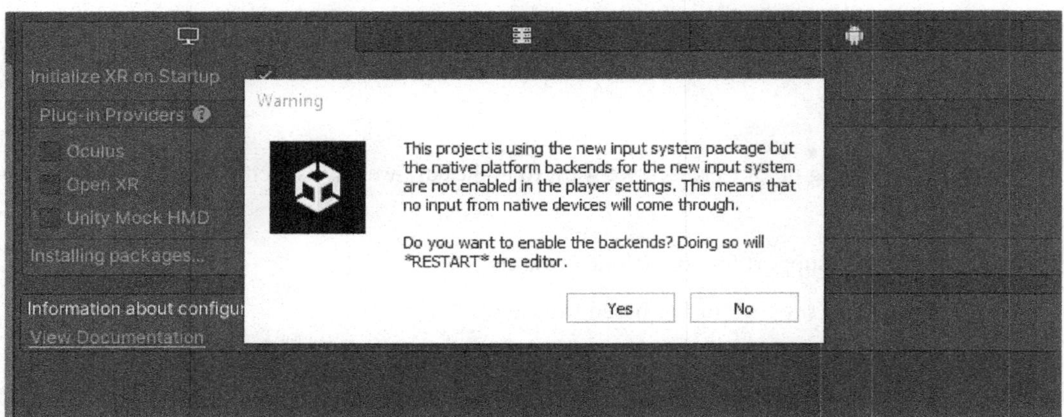

Figure 2.8 – The restart dialog for the new input system

When the project opens again, it may show an error in the console. Select the error, then select **Edit**; you will be taken to the **OpenXR** project settings. This error occurs because we have not added an interaction profile yet. The interaction profile we will use will be based on the headset we are building for.

Setting up the interaction profile

After you return to the **XR Plugin Management** menu in the **Project Settings** window (**File** | **Build Settings** | **Player Settings**), navigate to **OpenXR** (*Figure 2.9*), and then to the **Interaction Profiles** section. Select which interaction profile you are using based on the device you are building for:

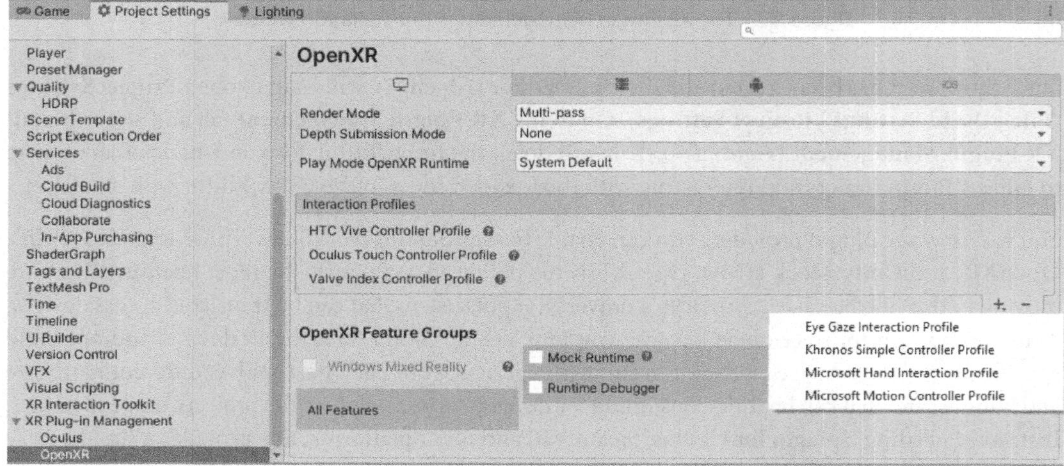

Figure 2.9 – The OpenXR menu

You can choose from Oculus, Valve, Eye Gaze, HTC Vive, Khronos, and Microsoft (*Figure 2.9*). You can add as many as you would like to your project.

For **Render Mode**, you can choose between **Single pass** and **Multi-pass. Single pass** takes one rendered image and uses that image for both eyes. This is the reason your view in the headset will only display on one eye, or have a duplicate on both eyes. **Multi-pass** does two render calls. This will render a separate picture for each eye individually. This provides a better visual experience but requires more performance because it renders twice as much.

Android VR

Most standalone VR headsets are Android-based devices. To set them up, go to **XR Plugin Management** in **Project Settings** and select the **Android** tab. Select **Oculus** for Oculus headsets and standalone builds (*Figure 2.10*). Select **OpenXR** for other Android-based headsets that are not Oculus headsets and are standalone devices (they don't require a PC):

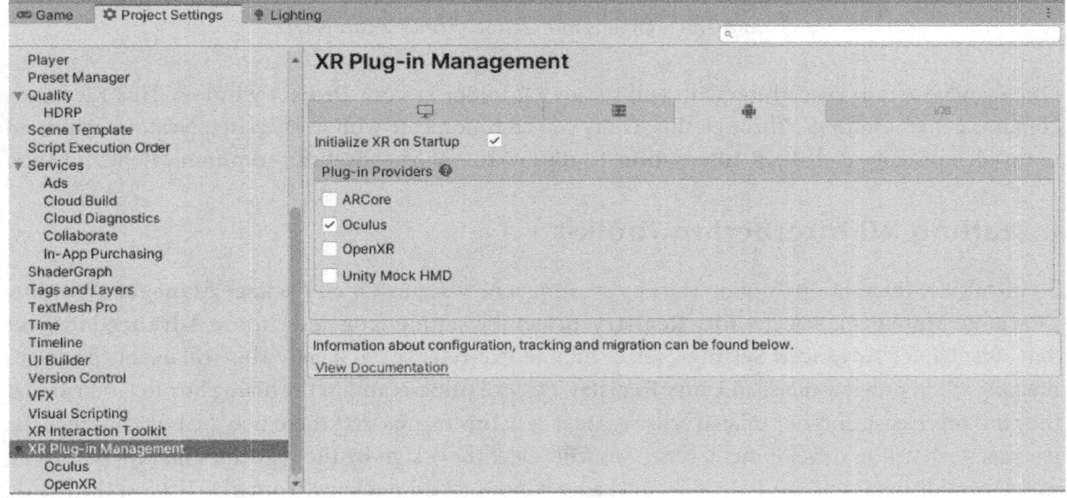

Figure 2.10 – XR Plugin Management settings for Oculus

When you select **Oculus**, a new package will be installed that will add an Oculus interaction profile settings tab under **XR Plugin Management** on the left (*Figure 2.11*).

For the **Oculus** interaction profile (*Figure 2.11*), set the rendering mode to **Multi-pass**. For the target device, you can choose **Quest** if you want the build to run on the Quest 1. This will have to be more performant; otherwise, it will not run well. You can choose **Quest 2** if you want the build to run on the Quest 2:

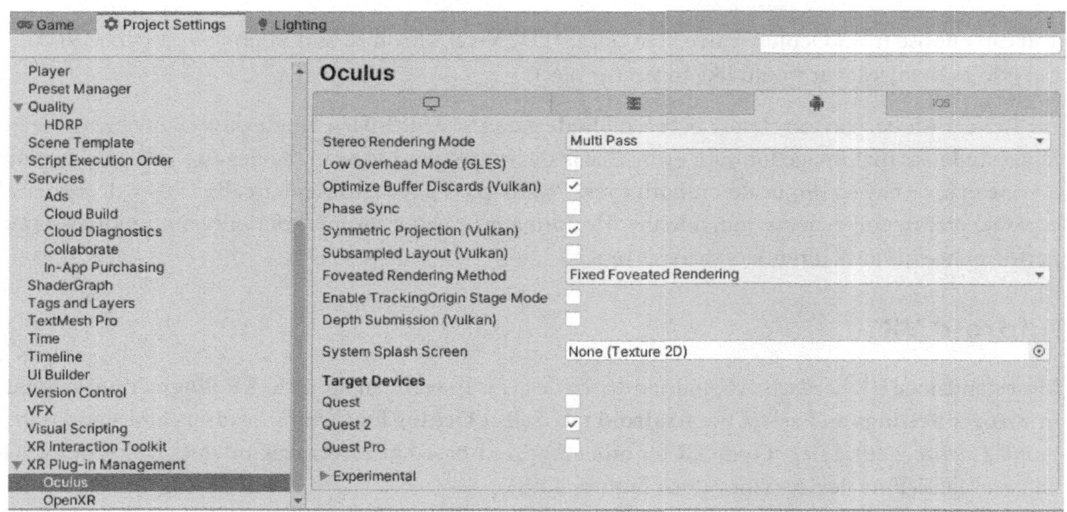

Figure 2.11 – Oculus interaction profile settings tab

Once you've set up everything, you will see an `XR` folder in your **Project** window. This `XR` folder contains general settings. Through this, Unity can communicate with the headset. Next, we will need to install a package called **XR Interaction Toolkit** so that the headset can communicate with Unity.

Installing XR Interaction Toolkit

To install XR Interaction Toolkit, start by creating a new scene. Open **Package Manager** (**Window | Package Manager**). Select **Unity Registry**. Select the settings cog and choose **Advanced Project Settings**. Under **Advanced Settings**, select **Enable Pre-release Packages**. This will enable packages that are still in preview mode in **Unity Registry**. Select **I understand** in the dialog box to confirm that they are prerelease and not official release packages. This means that there may be bugs because the packages are still in development. Next, we will select the + sign by the registry. This will allow you to select additional options to import packages. Choose **Add package from git URL**. In the dialog box, input `com.unity.xr.interaction.toolkit` and then select **Add** (*Figure 12*). This will download XR Interaction Toolkit:

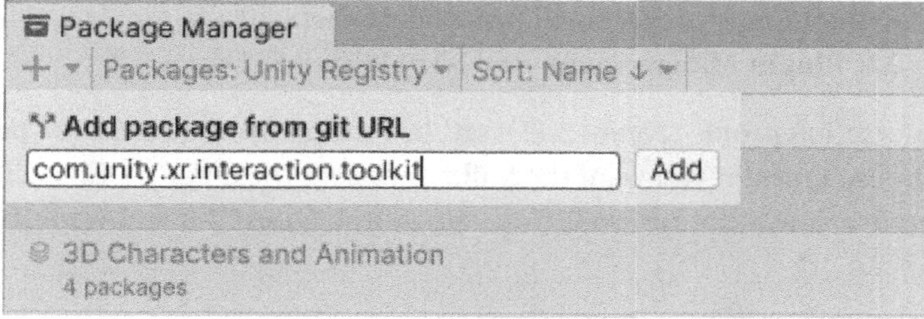

Figure 2.12 – Installing the XR Interaction Toolkit package from a URL

Once this has happened, click **Add**. Afterward, select **I Made a Backup** to proceed.

This package will give us a lot of preinstalled interactions to use out of the box. Select **Samples** from the XR Interaction Toolkit package and import the starter assets. This will preconfigure many of the input actions we want to use. You will see new folders in your `Assets` folder in the **Project** window. The `XRI` folder is the toolkit we just installed. The `Samples` folder we installed with XR Interaction Toolkit contains sample inputs we will be using for our base VR rig. There are five default input assets: **XRI Default Continuous Move**, **XRI Default Continuous Turn**, **XRI Default Left Controller**, **XRI Default Right Controller**, and **XRI Default Snap Turn** (*Figure 2.13*). In each setting asset, you can add the input assets to the presets for each device by clicking the button at the top of each one in the **Inspector** window. Select the default input actions to see all the actions:

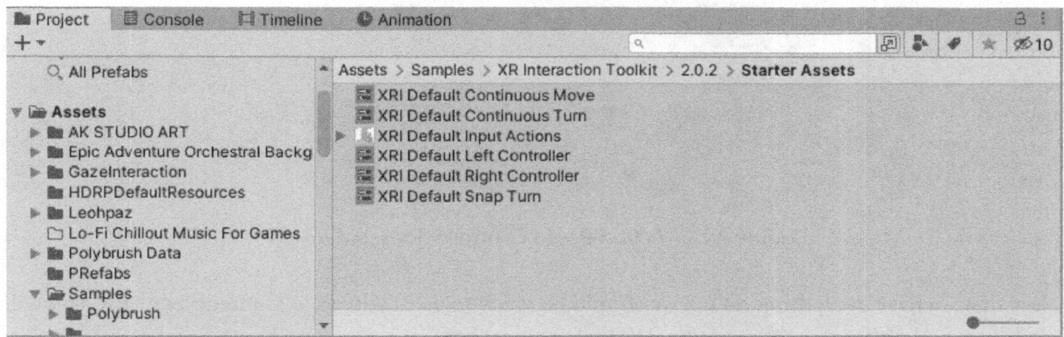

Figure 2.13 – The default sample XRI input action assets

To edit the presets, go to **Edit** | **Project Settings** | **Preset Manager**. You should see five total presets from the ones that we just installed (*Figure 2.14*). Under **Action-Based Controller**, add a filter for the left and right-hand sides of each of the actions. The toolkit does not do that automatically, so it will not be able to differentiate between the left and right controller interactions unless you specifically designate the left and right-hand sides. The labels for left and right are not case-sensitive, so you can label it however you want:

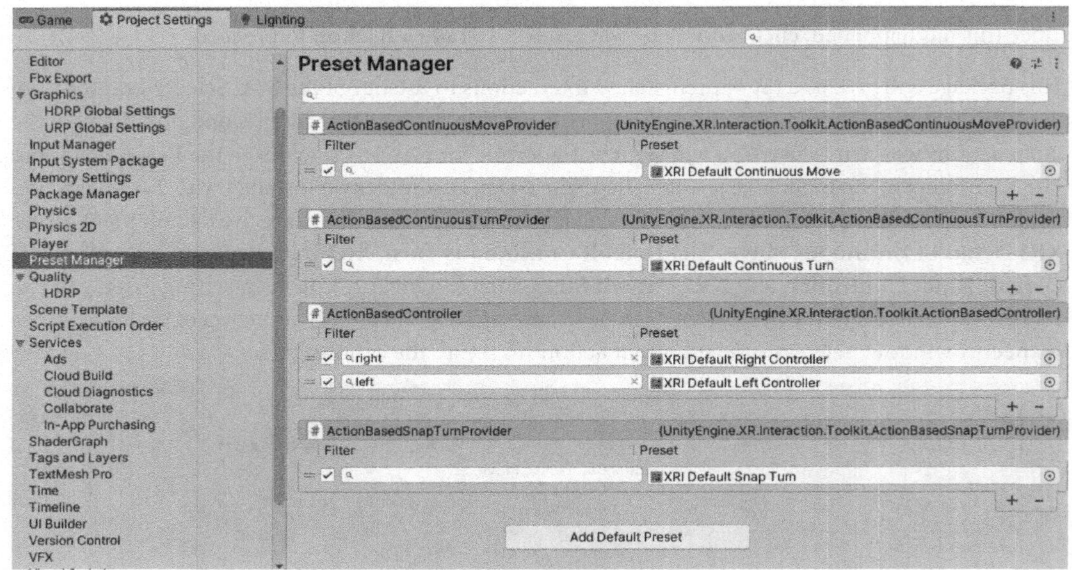

Figure 2.14 – Action-Based Controller Preset Manager

Now that we have everything set up, we should be ready to go. If you go to **Gameobject** | **XR**, you will see a bunch of options to choose from. We will explore them later when we begin building our scenes.

Headset setup

In our demos, we will be using the Oculus Quest to test our experiences. To set up your Oculus Quest, we must enable unknown sources for the device. Open the Oculus app and select **Settings**. Go to the **General** tab, select **Unknown sources**, and check **Allow**. This will let you use your Oculus Quest outside of the Oculus Store and directly within the Unity Editor. This will allow you to bypass the build process if you have a PC. If you are using a Mac for development, your only option for testing on the Oculus is building to the device.

Setting up developer mode

If you have an Oculus Quest 2, it is best to set up developer mode. Developer mode allows you to run, debug, and test applications directly on your headset. To put your headset in developer mode, follow these steps:

1. Put on the headset and sign in with an account.
2. Go to **Settings** | **System** | **Developer** and turn on **USB connection**.
3. Connect the headset to a computer using the provided USB-C cable.
4. Click **Allow** when the prompt appears.

5. Accept the **Allow USB Debugging** prompt and make sure the **Always allow from this computer** box is checked.

Once you've done this, you are ready to go!

VR scene setup

Now, it is time to build a VR scene. This scene will allow us to test our VR interactions using our headset directly in the Editor. To set up our scene, we will create a new scene in the **Project** window (*right-click* | **Create** | **Scene**) and name it `VR_Basics_000`. Within the scene we created, add a plane (*right-click* | **3D Object** | **Plane**) and label it `Ground`. Add an action-based XR rig (*right-click* | **XR** | **XR Origin (VR) [formerly Action-Based]**). With the rig GameObject selected, you will see three arrows (*Figure 2.15*). The blue arrow is pointing forward, the green arrow is pointing upward, and the red arrow is pointing right. These coordinates are important because when you set up your rig, you need to make sure you know which way you will be facing and whether the left and right-hand sides are configured correctly:

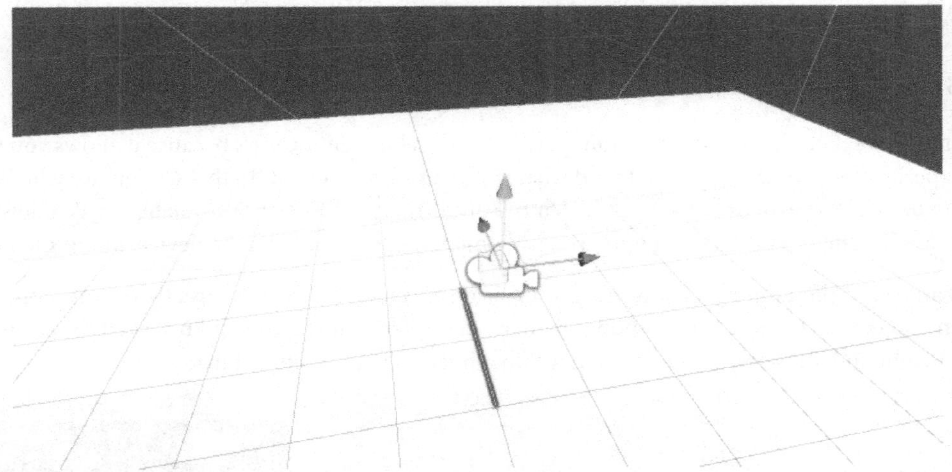

Figure 2.15 – XR Origin (VR) GameObject displaying three directional arrows

Under the rig, you will see the camera offset GameObject, and within that, you will see the main camera and left and right controllers. Each controller should have action settings for their respective sides. If you see that things are off, delete `XR Origin` and follow the previous steps to fix the setup. Then, add another `XR Origin` to your scene.

Next, we will add an **Input Action Manager** setting. In the `XR Interaction Manager` GameObject, select **Add Component** and type `input action manager`. Now, you can add an interaction asset from the samples. Select the + sign in the `Input Action Manager` component, select **Object Picker** icon to the right of the **Element 0** reference slot, and select **XRI Default Input Actions** (*Figure 2.16*). This should be the only one that appears. If you added the `XR Origin (VR)` component, the `Input Action Manager` component may be on the `XR Origin` GameObject already. Different versions of XR Interaction Toolkit may have different default setups:

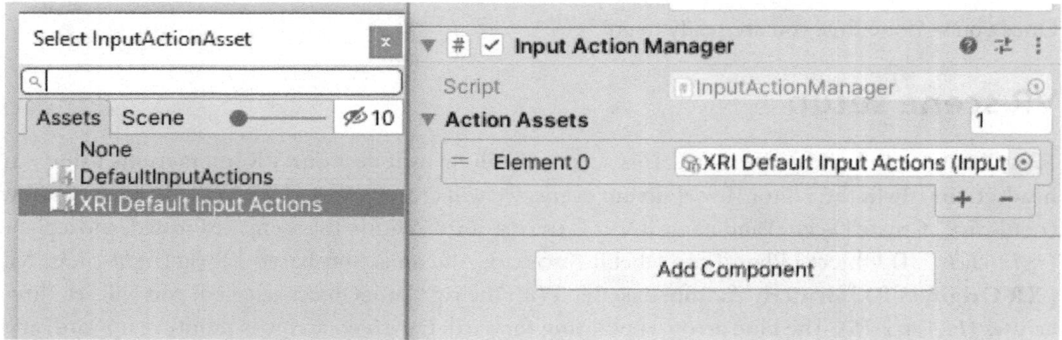

Figure 2.16 – The Input Action Manager component

With that, we have completed the setup process for our first VR scene. Now, we can test it out.

Testing in the Editor

Testing your experiences is an important part of the development process because it allows you to try the experience as a user and see firsthand what works and what doesn't. In this section, we will discuss how to test our VR experience within the Unity Editor. This process is only available for Windows OS. If you are developing on Mac or Linux, you can only test experiences on the device, not in the Editor.

You can test in the Editor by connecting your headset (Oculus Quest 2) directly to your computer. When you connect your device, a popup will appear. Select **Allow**. You will be asked to set up your floor height and VR boundaries. If you have not already, enable Oculus Link:

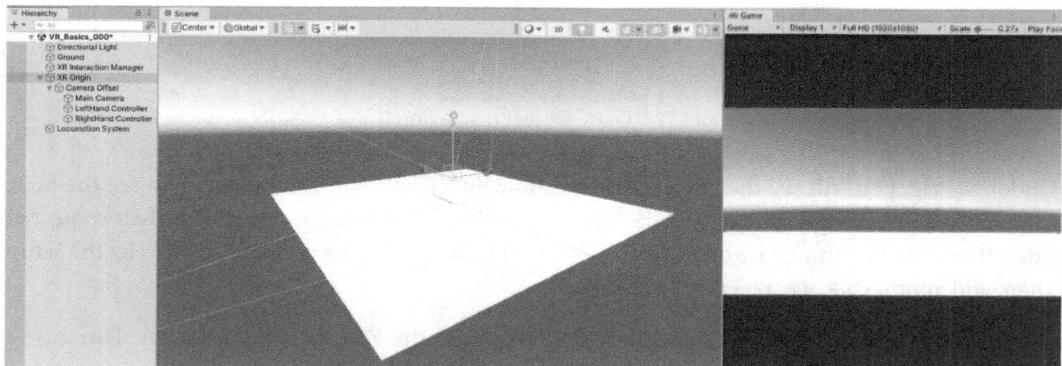

Figure 2.17 – Final VR_Basics_000 scene running in play mode

Press play to run the scene in VR (*Figure 2.17*), and put on your headset. You should be in the scene you built in Unity at this point. Both hands should appear as rods when you move the joystick controllers. You will be located in the center of the scene where the `XR origin` is placed. You can't do much because we have not added any locomotion functions, but you are in VR! Congratulations!

With this, we can explore how to add locomotion and interactions in the next chapter.

Testing on a device

As mentioned in the previous section, Linux and Mac do not support testing VR experiences in the Unity Editor. As an alternative, you can test them on your device. Similar to building applications for mobile phones, you can build directly to the headset. First, go to **Build Settings** in the **File** menu (*Figure 2.18*) and add the VR scene you want to test to the **Scenes In Build** list by selecting **Add Open Scenes**. Switch the platform to Android. The Unity icon will appear next to the selected platform. Select **Build And Run** to test the scene on your device. Before you select **Build And Run**, you will want to make sure that the headset is connected to the computer. After you build it to the device, you will be able to see the experience in action:

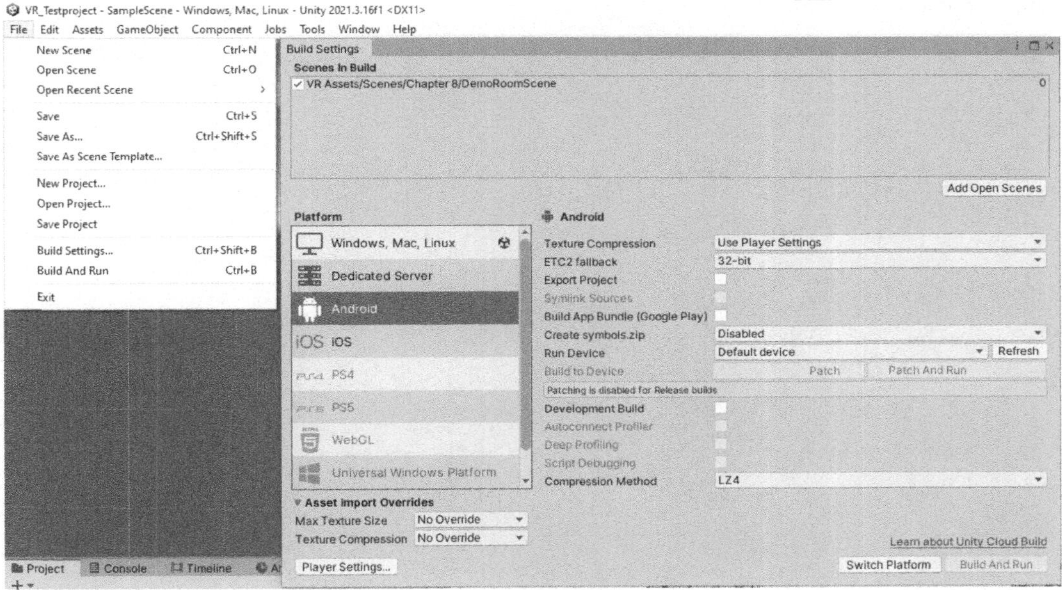

Figure 2.18 – The Build Settings screen

Summary

VR experiences are very powerful and lend to great experiences. Using the Unity Editor to build these experiences unlocks heaps of creative potential for developers and consumers alike.

So far, we've covered the basics of Unity Hub and how to create a new project with a default template. If you want to explore all the other templates, you can. With our new project created, we installed the XR Interaction Toolkit and Interaction profiles for our desired device. We then created a VR scene with a ground plane and VR rig that can communicate with our headset.

With our simple scene, we can look around with our headsets on. We can't move around in VR yet, but we took a big step in our VR development journey, and that is creating a VR scene that will run on a device. We can officially say we are a VR developer now because we achieved such a crucial milestone. Moving forward, we will be building off what we learned in this chapter to further enhance the VR scenes we can build now.

In the next chapter, we will look at the different interaction profiles that we downloaded from the XR Interaction Toolkit samples, and how they can be used to navigate a virtual scene and interact with different objects.

3

Working with Inputs and Interactions

Making realistic interactions in VR is key to making memorable immersive experiences.

In VR, we don't just rely on joysticks and buttons; we also apply natural gestures to interact with the world. We kneel to pick things up, we clench our fists to hold objects, we wave our arms to swing swords, and so on. The act of punching in real life is similar to performing a punching action in VR. We must acknowledge how we interact in VR and incorporate that into our development process.

It is in our best interest to explore this area of development because users are attracted to VR to explore digital worlds and free themselves of the limitations of the real world. Incorporating interactions that make users feel free creates a framework for memorable experiences in VR.

Part of the development process is testing the limits of the medium and pushing it beyond what is expected.

Since we set up our basic VR scene in the *VR setup* section in *Chapter 2*, and we know how to build rigs for VR experiences, It's time to talk about inputs and interactions. **Inputs** and **interactions** are crucial to VR experiences because they are the summation of actions that allow us to have effects within our VR scene. By definition, inputs and interactions are things that are done to influence other actions or objects. In the context of VR, those are your physical movements, and they have a direct effect on virtual objects and controller keystrokes that initiate commands. Default inputs include trigger press, grip press, and joystick movement. Other input controls will be discussed in *Chapter 8* when we integrate **C# code** into our experiences.

The interactions we will discuss in this chapter are **ray interactions**, **direct interactions**, **gaze interactions**, **snap locomotion**, **continuous locomotion**, and **teleportation**. Once we've explored the main interactions and locomotion features, we will expand on them at the end of this chapter by briefly integrating **haptic feedback** into our controllers, adding **attach points** to our virtual objects (to specify how objects will be held), and creating **socket interactions** (to anchor interactable objects to static positions in the world) for those virtual objects in our demo scene. Each form of interaction has its strengths and weaknesses. By the end of this chapter, you will have a better understanding of how interactions can be used within your experiences.

In this chapter, we will cover the following topics:

- Why do interactions matter?
- Setting up a demo scene with primitive shapes
- Setting up the locomotion system for our VR rig
- Adding interactor components to our VR controllers and virtual objects
- Adding haptic feedback to our VR controllers
- Adding attach points to virtual objects
- Adding socket interactors to our demo scene

Technical requirements

The complete source code for this chapter can be found at `https://github.com/PacktPublishing/Enhancing-Virtual-Reality-Experiences-with-Unity-2022/tree/main/EnhancingVRExperiencesFullProject/Assets/_VRProjectAssets/Scenes/Chapter_3`.

Why do interactions matter?

Interactions are important because we're trying to mimic real-world experiences and phenomena in VR. The reason people are attracted to VR is because they're able to have that physical experience in a virtual world and do things that go beyond what is physically possible in the real world. The vital part of the interactions that we have in VR is that they mimic actions of our daily lives. If the interactions we have in VR don't resonate with users, then we inadvertently reduce the incentive to return to those experiences because they feel "off." Therefore, our goal as developers is to create the most believable and relevant interactions possible so that when a user engages in the experiences we build, they can have something that resonates with them.

The possibilities that interactions allow are limitless. Think about being able to build a virtual scene in any part of the universe, whether it's fictional or possible, and navigating that space through VR. Looking at it from a game development perspective, anything that you would script for buttons can be done with motion. If you're not interested in making games, you could build worlds that you can traverse with your friends. You could go exploring and find hidden gems in these out-of-the-world experiences.

You can go swimming with sharks and whales deep in the ocean. You can battle hordes of zombies and protect the president in the White House. You can battle wizards and warlocks in space or on the moon. You can meditate in a black hole or travel across deep space in search of hidden treasure. You can even design 3D structures and make out-of-this-world murals that can last forever in the digital world. The possibilities are endless.

Essentially, anything that you can think of is possible, and you have the tools that are required to make those things a reality. It's all about setting your mind to a specific goal of what you want to see and then applying the skills that we will learn in this book to bring those things to life.

But before all that, let's set up a demo scene for our interactions to live and work in.

Setting up a demo scene using primitive shapes

The first thing we're going to do before we get everything set up for interactions is turn our *base scene* into a working **demo scene**. A demo scene is an environment that is used to showcase the features and functionality of an experience. This is important because, with demo scenes, you're able to rapidly prototype the ideas that you have without having to waste time on all the other details of the environment you are testing in. We're not at the point where we need to build worlds and explore specific interaction use cases – we're just testing what is possible with our basic knowledge of VR. That includes walking around and engaging with different objects. Our demo scene is going to focus on making simple interactions possible.

First, we are going to create an environment we can use to test all of the interactions. We will create it using **primitive shapes**, which we will then learn how to replace with other 3D models in *Chapter 4*. **Primitives** are basic 3D shapes that can be created and used as the building blocks for more complex objects. These shapes are considered *primitive* because they are simple and basic, and can be used to construct more complex models. Some examples of primitives include spheres, cubes, cylinders, and planes. The scene we are going to create now will include a simple table with some objects placed on top of it. To create the scene, go through the following steps:

1. We will start by creating a new scene (I will name my newly created scene `00_Base_Demo`), adding a plane to it from the **3D Object** menu, and naming the plane `Floor`.
2. Create a folder in the `Assets` folder called `Materials`, and create a new material for the floor.
3. Use a gray color for the floor material, as shown in *Figure 3.1*. We will dive deeper into materials in *Chapter 4*. Right now, we will just use Unity's standard materials:

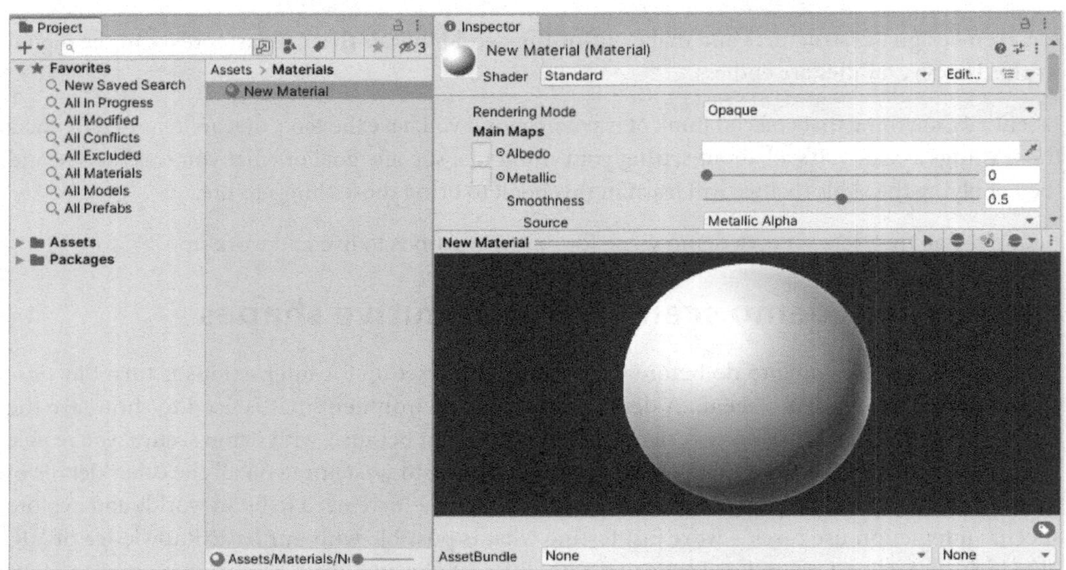

Figure 3.1 – The Materials folder and the floor material

4. With our floor created, let's create our table to put objects on. Start by creating an empty **GameObject** (**GO**) and name it `Table`.
5. Under the `Table` GO, add a cube.
6. Raise the cube transform to `.5` on the Y axis.
7. Name the cube `TableBase` and give it a new material.
8. Create another cube under the `Table` GO, name it `TableTop`, and raise the transform to `1` on the Y axis. Using the **Rect** tool, reduce the **Y** scale value to `.2`. Set the **Z** scale value to `1.6` and the **X** scale value to `1.8` (*Figure 3.2*).
9. Create another material for the `TableTop` GO:

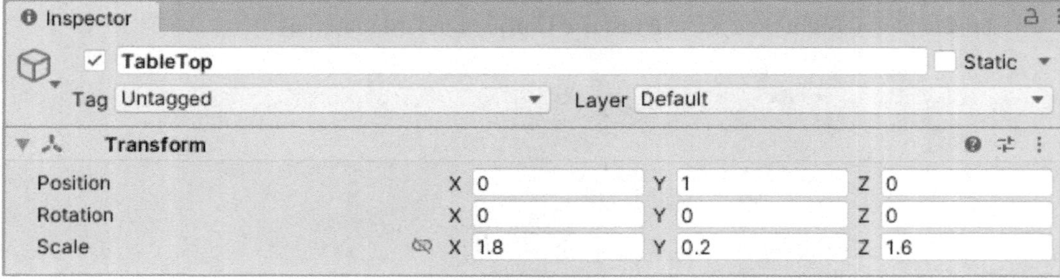

Figure 3.2 – Transform values for the TableTop GO

We now have a table to place objects on in the center of the scene (*Figure 3.3*):

Figure 3.3 – Table made from primitive shapes

With our table complete, let's create objects to place on the table:

1. First, let's create a new empty GO and name it `VRObjects`. We will use this as a container for the objects we will be interacting with in the scene. This will serve as an anchor so that all the objects will be on the same plane when we lay them out on the table.
2. Place `VRObjects` at the level of the tabletop.
3. For this demo scene, we will add one of each primitive shape for object interactions. As children of the `VRObject` GO, add a cube, sphere, capsule, and cylinder.
4. Resize them so that they can fit on the table with room between them. I chose a scale of `.25` for the **XYZ** scale for each.
5. Orient the shapes so that they are resting at the level of the tabletop, and give each shape a new material and color (*Figure 3.4*):

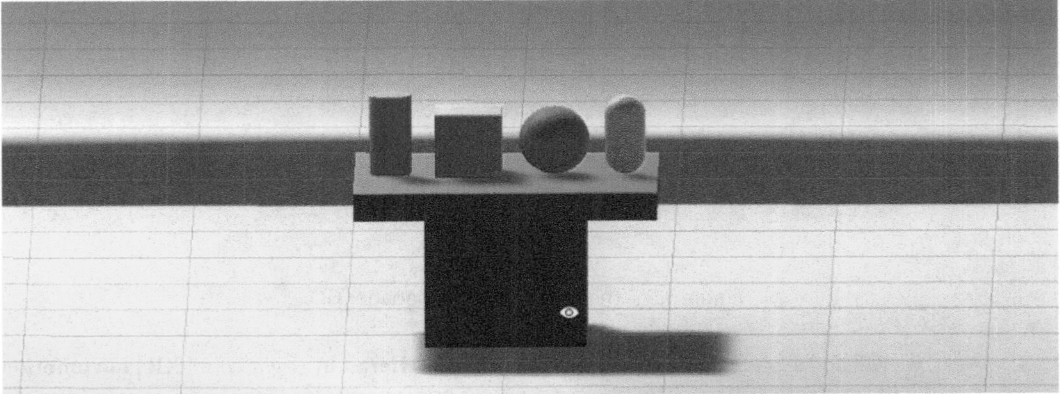

Figure 3.4 – Basic shapes on our table in the demo scene

With the table and shapes done, we can now work on adding interactions to our VR rig using a locomotion system.

Setting up the locomotion system

With our base demo complete, let's set up our **locomotion**. By locomotion, I am referring to adding the ability for the user to move the VR rig around the VR scene using the joystick inputs on the hand controllers. The locomotion system enables the user to move around the virtual environment, allowing for a more immersive experience and the ability to interact with the environment more naturally. It is important for the player to feel comfortable and not experience motion sickness when experiencing VR.

I like to work non-destructively, meaning I always save and back up my projects so that I can recover anything if I make mistakes. Instead of creating a new scene, let's duplicate the demo scene and name it `01_Locomotion_Setup`. Duplicating will retain all the data in the scene for us to change and modify while retaining a backup. Now, to establish our locomotion system, we must follow these steps:

1. In the locomotion setup scene, add our `Action based XR rig` GO, as we did in the *VR scene setup* section in *Chapter 2*. Add the `XR Origin` GO (*right-click* | **XR** | **XR Origin**).
2. If the `Input Action Manager` component is on the `XR Origin` GO, then add the `XRI Default Input Actions` asset to the dedicated slot. If not, add `Input Action Manager` to the `XR Interaction Manager` GO (*Figure 3.5*), and add the `XRI Default Input Actions` asset at the top of the slot:

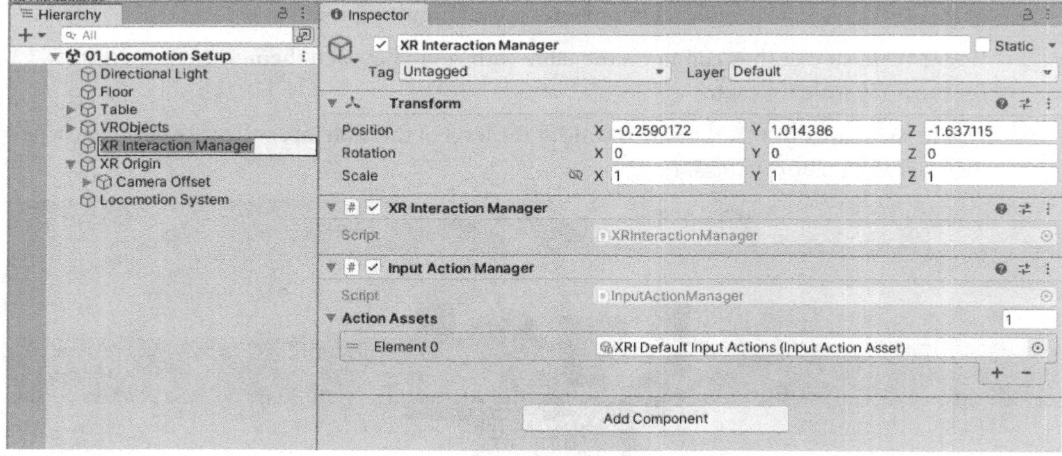

Figure 3.5 – The XR Interaction Manager GO

3. Next, we will add a `Locomotion System` GO to our **Hierarchy** (*right-click* | **XR** | **Locomotion System[Action-Based]**). In the `Locomotion System` GO (*Figure 3.6*), you will see a `Locomotion System` component and a `Teleportation Provider` component:

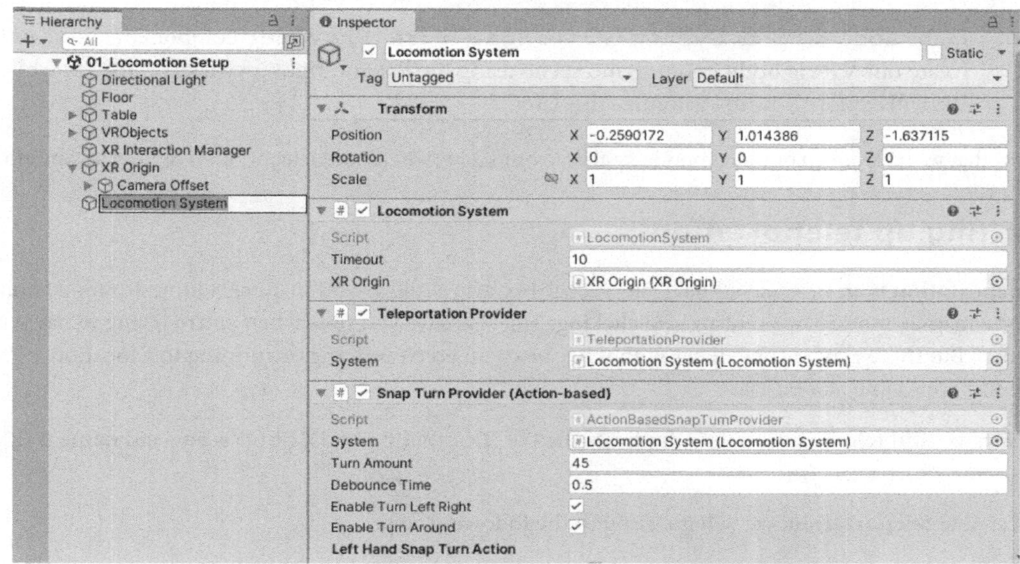

Figure 3.6 – The XR Locomotion System GO

4. Place the `XR Origin` GO in the reference slot for `Locomotion System`. `Teleportation Provider` allows us to quickly add teleportation features to our VR rig.
5. In the `Locomotion System` GO, you'll see a component for `Locomotion System`, a component for `Teleportation Provider`, and a component for `Snap Turn Provider (Action-based)` (*Figure 3.6*). Under the `Snap Turn Provider` component, under `Left Hand Snap Turn Action` and `Right Hand Snap Turn Action`, make sure that the `XRI LeftHand Locomotion` and `XRI RightHand Locomotion` inputs have been added to the reference slots correctly (*Figure 3.7*). If they haven't been added, be sure to add the correct ones to the corresponding hands:

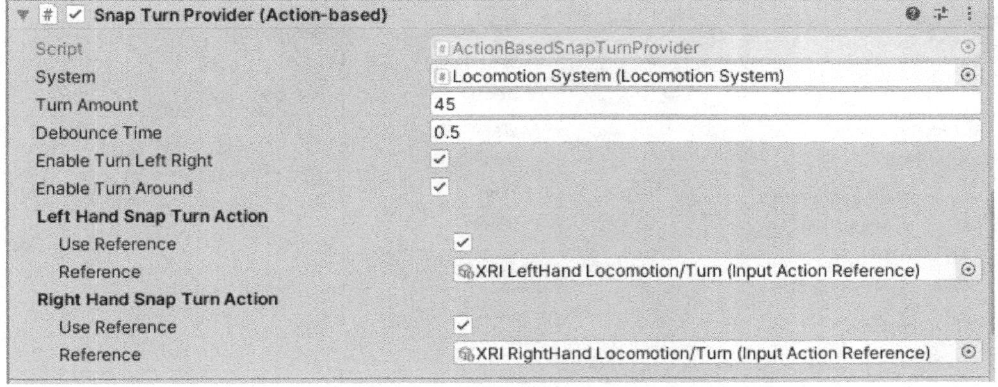

Figure 3.7 – The Snap Turn Provider (Action-based) component

6. In the `Locomotion System` GO, the `Snap Turn Provider` component allows us to rotate our VR rig body in our demo scene using the left and right joysticks on the controller. We will explore how to customize this later.

Now that we have added our locomotion system to our scene, we can add teleportation or fluid locomotion.

Setting up teleportation

Teleportation is an easy way to navigate a scene because it allows you to quickly jump from one point of the map to another by pointing and clicking. This will save you time when you're trying to navigate a map. But there can be some flaws with it because you aren't walking or running to a location – you are just appearing at a location.

Before we add **teleportation**, let's duplicate the `01_Locomotion_Setup` scene and name it `02_Teleportation_Setup`.

To enable **teleportation**, we will go through the following steps:

1. Find the `Teleportation Provider` component that we have on our `Locomotion System` GO (*Figure 3.6*). This will enable the teleportation features for our VR rig.
2. Enable teleportation on our `Floor` GO by selecting it and adding a `Teleportation Area` component. This component enables the VR rig to teleport to any part of the enabled area using a **raycast** and **trigger press**.

   A **raycast** is a line that's used for detecting collisions in a virtual environment. The line starts at the hand controller and points onward. A **trigger press** is an event that occurs when the button on the front of the VR controller is pressed. This is typically pressed with the index finger:

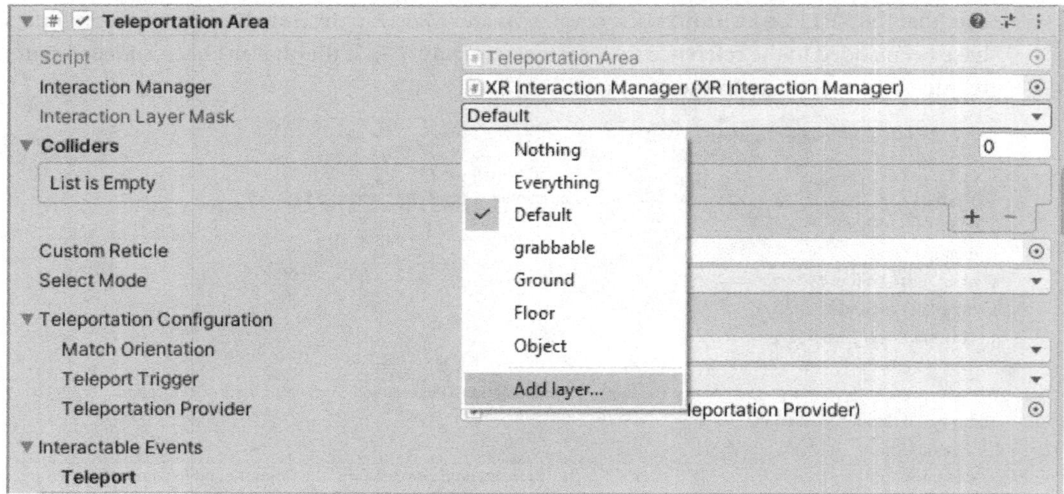

Figure 3.8 – The Teleportation Area component

3. In the `Teleportation Area` component, we want to designate a specific layer called `Floor` in the **Interaction Layer Mask** dropdown menu so that we only teleport to areas on the `Floor` layer. Click **Add layer...** and create a new layer called `Floor` in **User Layer 8**.
4. Set the `Floor` GO to the `Floor` layer in **Inspector**.
5. Add the `Floor` layer to **Interaction Layer Mask** and uncheck the `Default` layer as well.
6. In the `Teleportation provider` slot of the `Teleportation Area` component, add the `Locomotion System` GO.

With that, we have set up teleportation and snap turning. Now, we can test it on our device. In play mode, we can look around and move our hands. Our hands are still represented with red rods. If we move the joysticks, we will be able to snap turn to rotate our VR rig. When we point our hands down to the ground, the red rods will turn white, indicating that we have enabled an interaction (*Figure 3.9*). When we press the grip button on one of the joysticks, we will teleport to the location that we were pointing to. Anywhere you point to in the teleportation area we designated will allow support teleportation. With that, we have achieved our first locomotion in VR!

Figure 3.9 – Testing teleportation in the VR scene

With that, we've set up teleportation and snap turning. We can now test it in play mode by moving and turning the VR rig using joysticks. We can also teleport by pressing the grip button on a joystick while pointing to an area on the floor plane. By doing this, we have achieved our first locomotion in VR.

With our first locomotion test complete, let's learn how to enable teleportation on specific areas of the floor instead of the whole floor.

Teleportation areas

Teleportation areas are specific areas on the map that you can teleport to. This can be used in combination with fluid locomotion to provide variation for the user.

First, we will duplicate our `02_Teleportation_Setup` scene and name it `03_Teleportation_Areas`.

To create a teleportation area, go through the following steps:

1. Create an `empty` GO and call it `TeleportationAreas`. **Zero out** the transforms by setting each of the transform values to `0` and place the `TeleportationAreas` GO slightly above the floor plane.
2. Add a plane to the `TeleportationAreas` GO, name it `Area1`, and reduce the scale to `.15`.
3. Give `Area1` a new material with a different color. I chose a pink/violet material color.
4. Add a `Teleportation Area` component to `Area1` and change **Interaction Layer Mask** to `Floor`.
5. Add the `Locomotion System` GO to the **Teleportation Provider** reference slot.

Next, we'll need to deactivate the `Floor` GO's `Teleportation Area` component so that we can utilize the teleportation area sections that we just created without impacting the functionality. We can then spread our `Teleportation Area` across our map.

To deactivate the `Teleportation Area` component on the `Floor` GO and distribute our teleportation area GOs, go through the following steps:

1. On the `Floor` GO, deactivate the `TeleportationArea` component.
2. Set **Interaction Layer Mask** to **Nothing** so that we don't enable teleportation when we point our hands to the floor, just when we point toward the designated teleportation areas planes.
3. Duplicate the `Area1` GOs three times and rename them `Area2`, `Area3`, and `Area4`, respectively.
4. Place them at the four corners of the floor map (*Figure 3.10*):

Figure 3.10 – Demo scene with teleportation areas at the four corners of the floor map

When we test it out, nothing will happen when we point our hands to the ground. The red rods won't turn white. When we point our rods to the teleportation areas, the red rod will turn white, and we can teleport to that location. Now, teleportation only works when you point the rods coming from the hand controllers to specific areas on the floor.

In the next section, we will explore the different turning actions we can add to our VR rig.

Snap and continuous turning

Before we continue with locomotion, let's explore turning, specifically **snap turn** and **continuous turn**. You may have noticed from the previous section that during the test, you could move the joysticks to rotate the VR rig left or right. The rig uses **snap turning** to rotate at a specific angle rather than a smooth rate. Snap turning is connected to the joystick controllers and can be modified by accessing the `Snap Turn Provider` component of the `Locomotion system` GO. If you want to make the turning smoother, you can change `Snap Turn Provider` to `Continuous Turn Provider`.

Before we begin, duplicate the `03_Teleportation_Area` scene and rename it `04_SnapAndSmoothTurning`.

To have snap turning on the right joystick and smoother turning on the left joystick, go through the following steps:

1. Go to the `Locomotion System` GO and find the `Snap Turn Provider (Action-Based)` component (*Figure 3.11*). You will notice that snap turning is enabled for both joysticks. This means that the joystick on both controllers will enable snap turning:

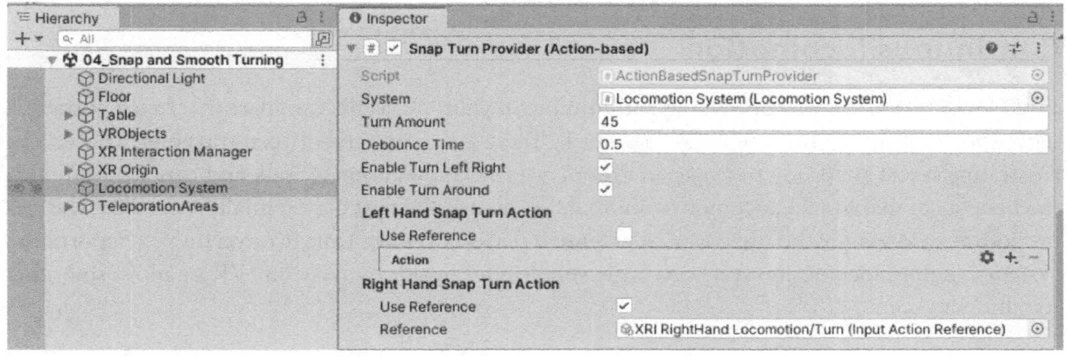

Figure 3.11 – The Snap Turn Provider (Action-based) component

2. If you only want to enable it on one controller, check **Use Reference** for the controller you want to use. Uncheck **Use Reference** to disable turning for the left controller.
3. Add a `Continuous Turn Provider (Action-based)` component to the `Locomotion System` GO (*Figure 3.12*):

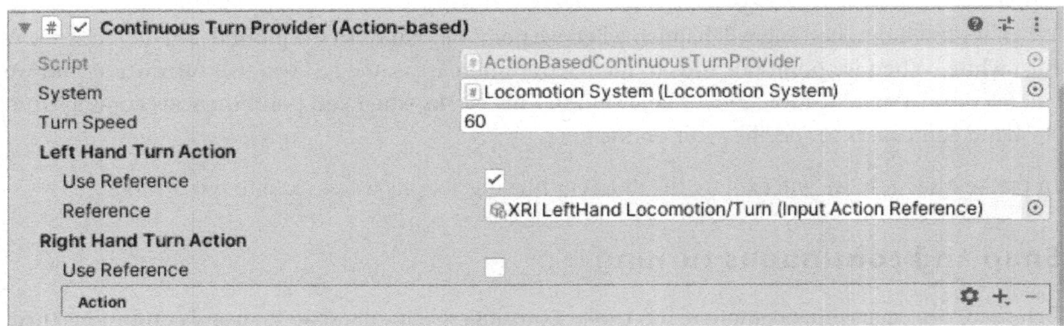

Figure 3.12 – The Continuous Turn Provider (Action-based) component

4. Under the component, add the `Locomotion System` GO to the **System** reference slot, and disable the **Use Reference** box under `Right Hand Turn Action` so that the `Continuous Turn Provider` component only references the left joystick.
5. You can increase or decrease the turning speed by modifying the **Turn Speed** value. This will determine how fast you will turn when you move the left joystick left or right.

Our turning controls have been configured with snap turning on the right joystick and continuous turning on the left joystick. We can now test out the experience with our new turning actions.

Most controllers move the left joystick and look around with the right joystick, so we can only enable snap turning on the right joystick. In the next section, we will introduce fluid motion so that we can navigate a map as if we are walking and map that to the left joystick.

Continuous locomotion

Fluid locomotion is a way of walking and running in your VR scene. Compare that to teleportation, where you're jumping from point A to point B. There is no time in between traveling. This can be frustrating if you are trying to create an experience that allows users to walk and run. Be aware that the benefits of making the locomotion more fluid come at the cost of potentially increasing the risk of motion sickness for the user over an extended period of usage time. Converting a teleportation system to a fluid locomotion system is fairly simple. Our goal is to make our VR rig move smoother in our demo scene.

Before we begin, let's duplicate the `04_SnapAndSmoothTurning` scene and rename it `05_Continous_Locomotion`.

To convert `Locomotion System` from teleportation to fluid locomotion, go through the following steps:

1. Find the `Locomotion System` GO in **Hierarchy** and add a `Continuous Move Provider (Action-based)` component.

2. In the `Continuous Move Provider` component (*Figure 3.13*), add `Locomotion System` to the **System** reference slot, and deselect **Use Reference** under `Right Hand Move Action`:

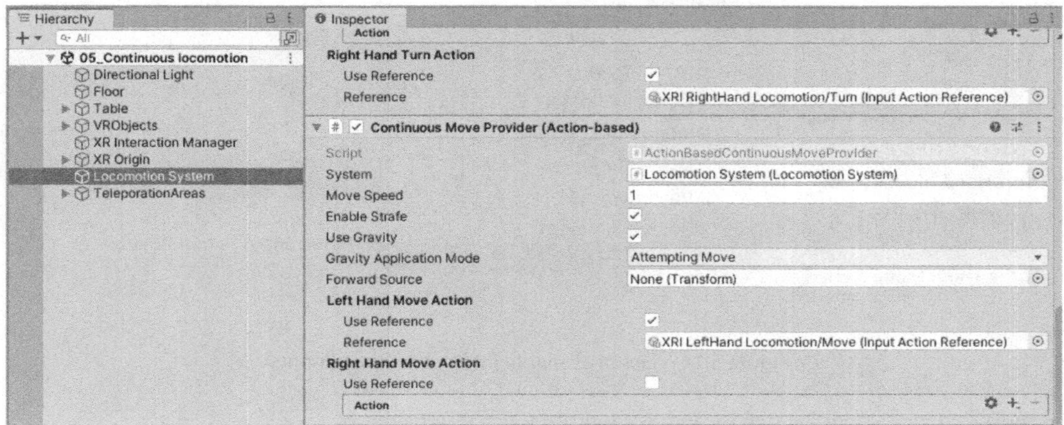

Figure 3.13 – The Continuous Move Provider (Action-based) component

3. In the `Continuous Turn Provider` component, uncheck **Use Reference** for `Left Hand Turn Action` and check **Use Reference** for `Right Hand Turn Action`.
4. Deactivate `Snap Turn Provider` for both hand turn actions.

Remember, we want to *move* with our *left joystick* and *rotate* with our *right joystick* to mimic traditional console controls. Test smooth locomotion in play mode, then move on to adding object interactions.

> **Note**
>
> This is a common approach to locomotion based on the traditional gamepad standard for video games. The beauty of being a developer in VR is that you can develop your layout with physical gestures in mind to replace the standard conventions.

Congratulations – we can now move and look around freely in VR using both teleportation and traditional locomotion! Now, we can focus on creating some interactions, such as grabbing objects. In the next section, we will incorporate **interactor components** into our VR rig.

Adding interactor components

In this section, we will delve into the topic of **object interactions** in VR. *Object interactions* refer to the ability of users to grab and manipulate virtual objects as if they were real-life objects. To enable object interactions in VR, developers must use interactor components.

Several types of interactor components can be used to create engaging VR experiences, as shown in *Figure 3.14*:

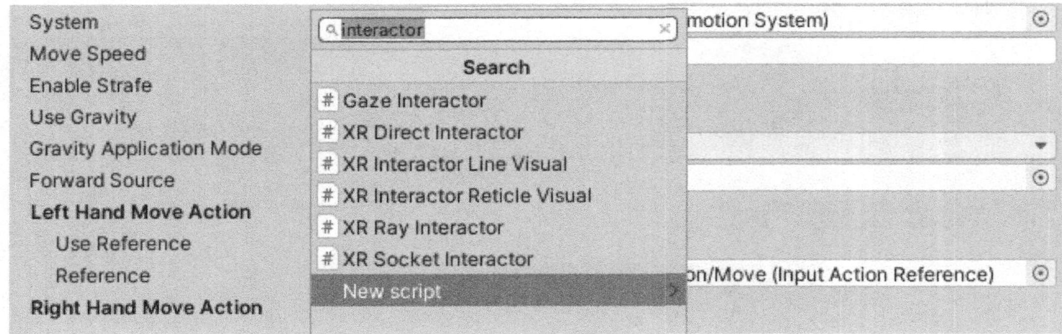

Figure 3.14 – List of available interactor components

In this section, we will cover four types of interactor components: **ray interactors**, **direct interactors**, **gaze interactors**, and **socket interactors**.

Ray interactors allow users to interact with objects by pointing at them with a virtual *ray* emitted from a controller. **Direct interactors** enable users to directly grab and manipulate objects using hand controllers. **Gaze interactors** allow users to interact with objects simply by looking at them, without the need for any physical input device. Finally, **socket interactors** enable objects to be placed in specific *sockets* or locations in the VR environment.

Each of these interactor components has its own unique set of capabilities and potential uses. By the end of this chapter, you will have a better understanding of what interactors are, how they can be used, and the possibilities they offer for creating immersive and interactive VR experiences for your users.

In the next section, we will set up the `Ray Interactor` component on our VR controller

Ray interactors

The **ray interactor** is one of three default interactor components in XR Interaction Toolkit; it allows you to interact with objects using a pointing ray emitted from the hand controllers. It is similar to the ray that's used for teleportation but it's used to grab and manipulate objects in VR. It is great for interacting with objects from a distance.

Let's set up our scene by first duplicating the `05_ContinousLocomotion` scene and renaming it `06_RayInteractions`.

In **Hierarchy**, we will find the `Hand Controller` GO with attached `XR Ray Interactor` and `Line Visual` components (*Figure 3.15*); these are set up by default:

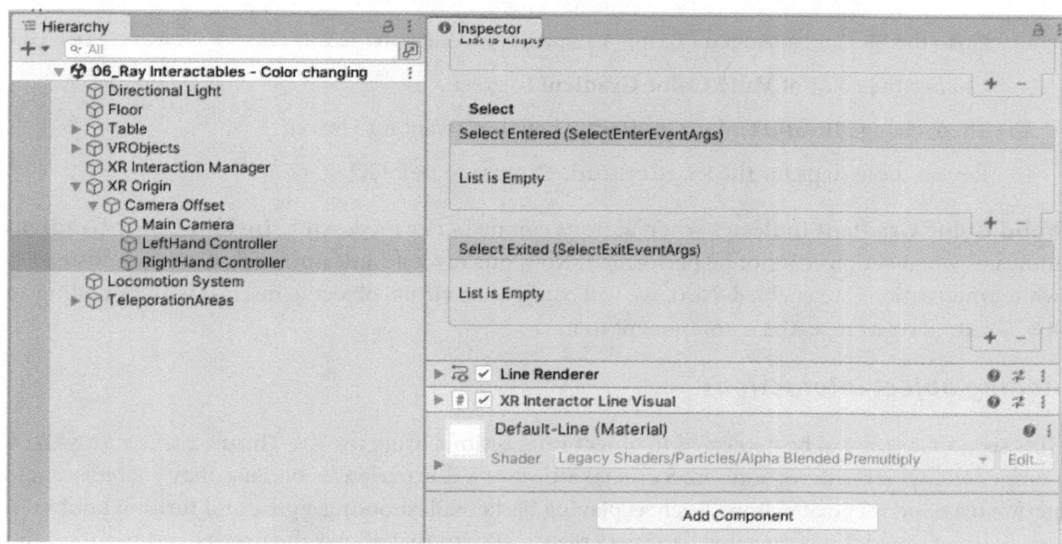

Figure 3.15 – The default components on the Hand Controller GO

During testing, the hand controller's **raycast** will be white when it's not interacting with anything. This can be difficult to see on light-colored surfaces. To change the color of the raycast and improve its visibility, we will modify the `XR Interactor Line Visual` component in the next subsection.

Changing the color of the XR Interactor Line Renderer Visual component

As a reminder, the hand rods turn from red to white when they're pointing to an active *teleportation area* and can perform an action when clicked while white. We can customize the hand rod properties to fit our VR experience theme using the `XR Interactor Line Visual` component:

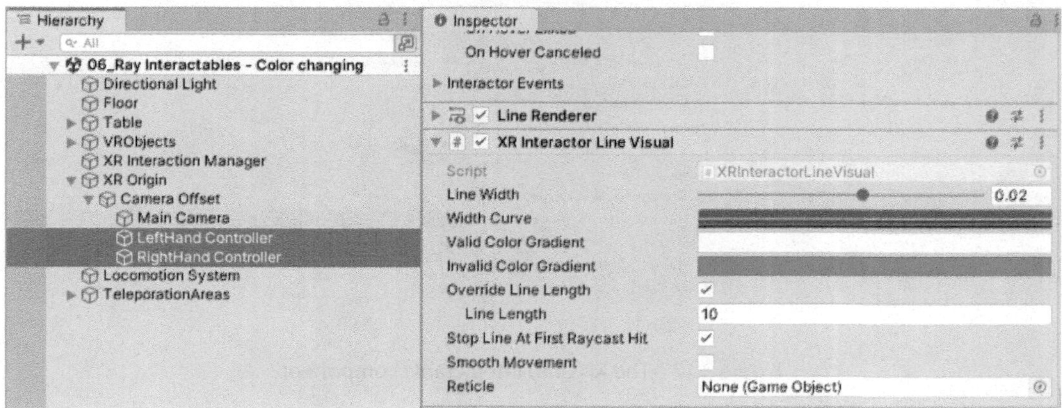

Figure 3.16 – The XR Interaction Line Visual component

1. Go to the `XR Interactor Line Visual` component in the `LeftHand Controller` GO.
2. Change the color of **Valid Color Gradient** to green.
3. Then, change **Invalid Color Gradient** if you don't want it to be red.
4. Repeat these steps for the `RightHand Controller` GO.

Valid Color Gradient indicates when actions can be performed, while **Invalid Color Gradient** indicates when actions cannot be performed. Now, our raycast indicators will turn green instead of white when actions are enabled. Next, we will configure a virtual object to interact with by adding an `XR Grab Interactable` component to it.

Adding object interactions

This section is going to be dedicated to **object interactions** using the `XR Grab Interactable` component. Object interactions are a crucial aspect of VR experiences because they enable users to perform a wide range of actions, such as playing basketball, shooting a gun, and turning knobs. To create these interactions, developers must create a system that allows the user's hand motions and trigger presses to interact with virtual objects in specific conditions. The `XR Grab Interactable` component allows developers to create and modify these conditions so that they work for different objects and situations. This system is essential for creating immersive and interactive VR experiences that respond to the user's actions realistically and believably:

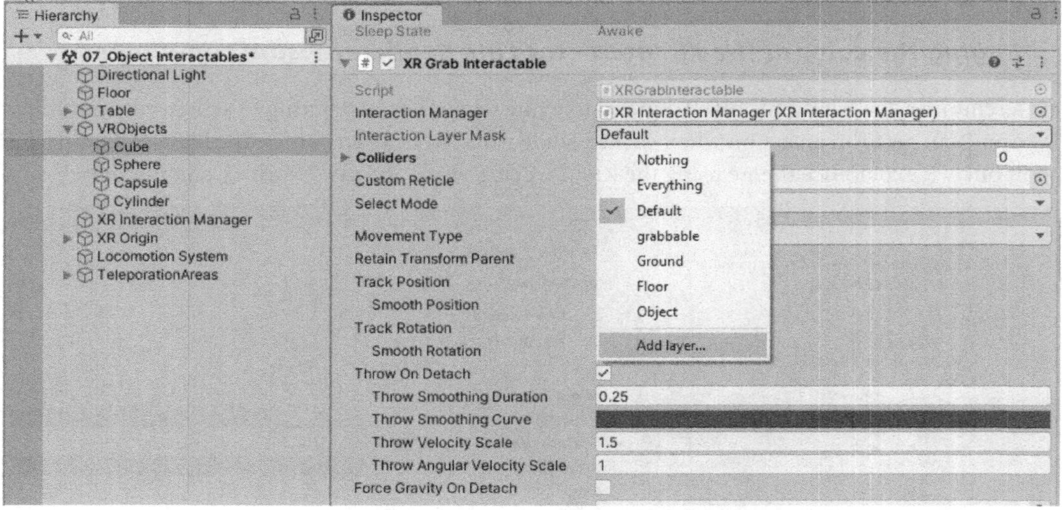

Figure 3.17 – The XR Grab Interactable component

We will duplicate the `06_RayInteractables` scene and rename it `07_ObjectInteractables`.

To create our first interactable VR object, go through the following steps:

1. In **Hierarchy**, we will revisit our four basic shapes in the `VRObjects` GO.
2. Select the `Cube` GO from the list of available objects.
3. Add an `XR Grab Interactable` component to it. When you add it, it will also add a `Rigidbody` component.
4. Select the **Interaction Layer Mask** dropdown menu and select **Add layer...**.
5. Add a new interaction layer called `Object` in the `User Layer 9` slot.
6. Go back to the `Cube` GO and set **Interaction Layer Mask** to `Object`.

When we enter play mode and test out our object interactions using the `Cube` GO and the ray interactor, we will notice that the color of the hand rod changes only when it is pointed at the cube. When the trigger button is pressed while the rod's color has changed, the cube will be grabbed by the hand and when the trigger button is released, the cube will fall to the ground. This is a basic example of how object interactions work in VR:

Figure 3.18 – Holding the Cube GO while in play mode

In *Chapter 5*, we will delve deeper into the topic of physics in Unity and how it can be applied to VR experiences. **Physics** plays an important role in creating realistic and believable interactions between virtual objects and the user.

Next, will discuss **anchor controls**, which are used to improve the object interactions with the ray interactor. These controls allow developers to fine-tune the position and orientation of virtual objects, making the interactions more precise and realistic.

Anchor control

As mentioned in the previous section, anchor controls allow you to extend the reach of the object you are holding, similar to stretching your arm. You can use the joystick of the hand you are using to extend or retract the object and also rotate it. This feature can be used in puzzle games and problem-solving experiences to improve object interactions and make them more engaging:

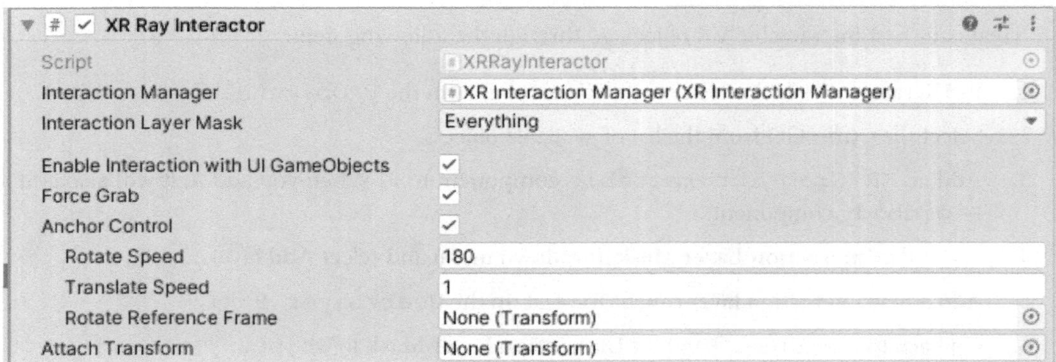

Figure 3.19 – The anchor control settings of the XR Grab Interactable component

When testing the anchor controls, it may feel awkward when using the same joystick for movement and extending the object as it can cause unintentional movement. The feature works best when it's used with the joystick that's used for rotation and turning as the VR headset is already used for looking around, so the rotation is not noticed. Therefore, it's recommended to deactivate **Anchor Control** on the left joystick and keep it enabled on the right joystick:

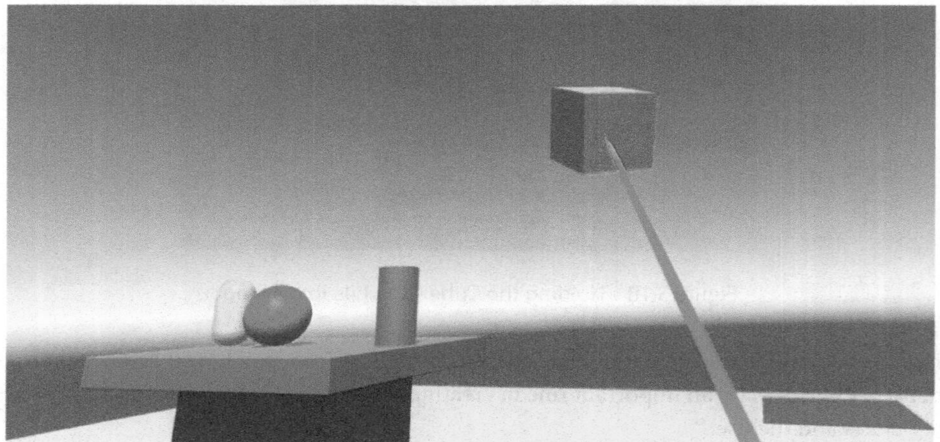

Figure 3.20 – Using Anchor Control with the right joystick

In the next section, we will explore direct object interactions using the `XR Direct Interactor` component as an alternative to the `XR Ray Interactor` component.

Direct interactors

The `Direct Interactor` component is the second **interactor component** that we will cover. Unlike the `Ray Interactor` component, it requires physical contact with `Object Interactable` to interact with it. This means that you cannot use this component to interact with objects from a distance. This component is used to simulate the sense of physically holding and manipulating objects in the virtual space. It can be used to create realistic and immersive experiences such as grasping a virtual object, turning a virtual knob, or pulling a virtual lever. It allows users to interact with objects more naturally and intuitively, making the VR experience more engaging and believable.

We will use `LeftHand Controller` for our direct interactions because `RightHand Controller` is already set up for ray interactions, and it works best when using anchor controls, as we saw in the previous section.

Duplicate the `07_ObjectInteractables` scene and rename it `08_DirectInteractables`.

To add the **direct object interactions** to our `LeftHand Controller`, go through the following steps:

1. Select the `LeftHand Controller` GO in **Hierarchy**.
2. Remove `XR Ray Interactor` from the `LeftHand Controller` GO. If you don't, you will receive an error message stating **you can only contain one XRBaseInteractor component.**
3. Add the `XR Direct Interactor` component (*Figure 3.21*):

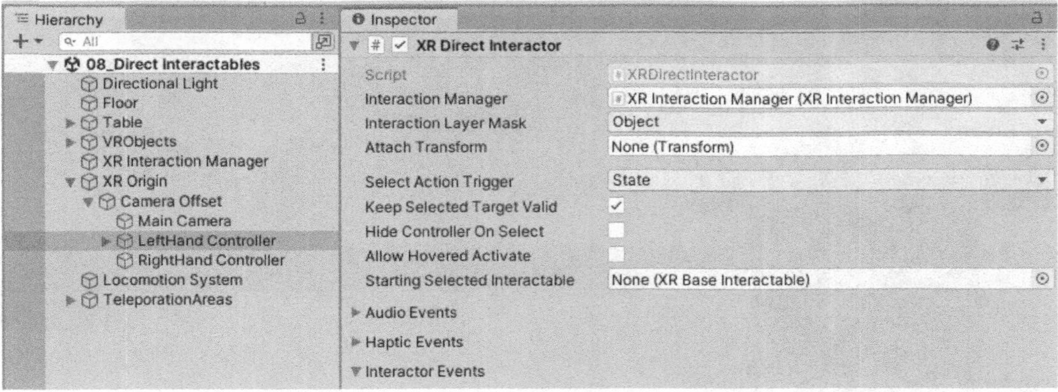

Figure 3.21 – The XR Direct Interactor component

4. Set **Interaction Layer Mask** to `Object`.

The next thing we need to do is add a proxy for our hand. This allows Unity to know when our hand is supposed to be touching an object in VR. To do that, follow these steps:

1. Add a `Sphere` object (*right-click* | **Create** | **3D Object** | **Sphere**) as a child of the `LeftHand Controller` GO and name it `HandSphere`.
2. In the `HandSphere` GO, click the **Is Trigger** checkbox on the `Sphere Collider` component to enable it.
3. Set **Scale** to `.45` and move it to `.15` in the **Z** position (*Figure 3.22*):

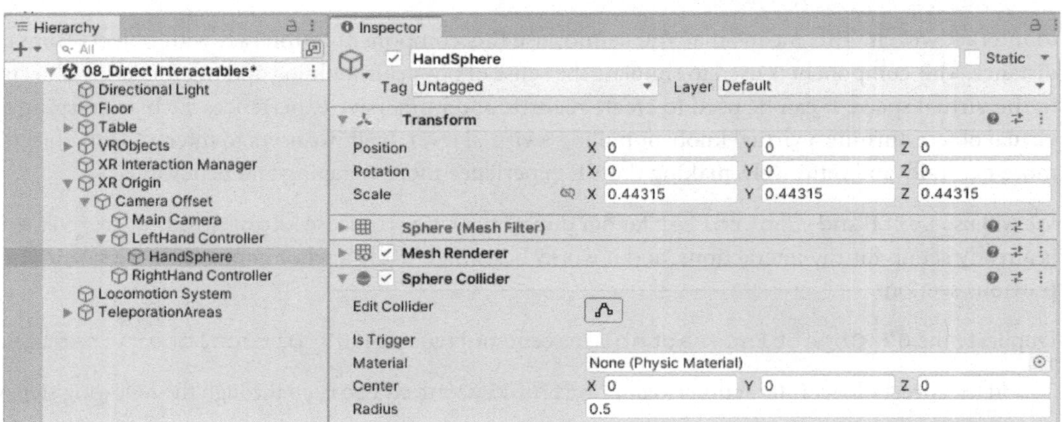

Figure 3.22 – The HandSphere GO in Hierarchy

4. Create a new material called `Hand` and add it to the `HandSphere` GO.
5. Make the material a transparent blue or teal color:

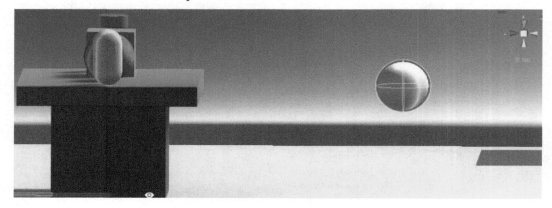

Figure 3.23 – The HandSphere GO in the VR rig

6. Copy the `Sphere Collider` component from the `HandSphere` GO and add it to the `LeftHand Controller` GO.
7. Resize the `Sphere Collider` bounding box on the `LeftHand Controller` GO to fit the `HandSphere` GO and delete the `Sphere Collider` component from the `HandSphere` GO.

Now, we can test our direct interactions. When we walk up to the `Cube` GO, we can press the left-hand control trigger when `HandSphere`, which is a virtual representation of the user's hand, comes into contact with `Cube`. This will cause `Cube` to be anchored to the anchor point of `HandSphere`. When we release the trigger, `Cube` will fall to the ground. This simulates the feeling of physically holding and releasing an object.

With this, we have both direct and ray interactions working in our VR rig, allowing users to interact with objects in different ways. The direct interaction allows for a more realistic and immersive experience as it simulates the feeling of physically holding and manipulating objects, while the ray interaction allows for interaction with objects from a distance. Having both types of interactions in our VR rig enables us to create a more versatile and engaging experience for the users.

In the next section, we will explore gaze interactions using a custom package from a GitHub repository.

Gaze interactions

The next interactor component we will discuss is `Gaze Interactor`. Unlike the ray and direct interactors, gaze interactors are not included by default in XR Interaction Toolkit. These comprise a third-party component developed by *Tomaz Saraiva* that was made available to the community for free via his GitHub repository.

Gaze interactions were more popular in the early days of VR development, particularly when VR was mainly smartphone-based. With the advent of hand controllers, gaze interactions have been used less frequently. Gaze interactions require the user to look at an object for a certain amount of time to activate or interact with it. There is a buffer in the gaze interaction to prevent unintentional triggers as looking around is a natural part of interacting in VR, and just because you look at something does not mean you want to interact with it.

If we compare the gaze interactor with the direct and ray interactors, it works similarly to the ray interactor, but the interaction is based on time rather than a trigger press.

Gaze setup

To install the `Gaze Interactor` component, go through the following steps:

1. Go to *Tomaz Saraiva's GitHub* at `https://github.com/tomazsaraiva/unity-gaze-interaction`).
2. Click on **Releases** at the bottom right of the screen to go to the download screen.
3. Download the latest version as a Unity package.
4. Install the Unity package by using the **Package Manager** area or dragging the downloaded package into the `Assets` folder in the **Project** tab.
5. Once the package has been installed, we can configure gaze interactions on our VR rig. First, we will duplicate the `08_DirectInteractables` scene and rename it `09_GazeInteractables`.
6. We can then navigate to the `GazeInteraction` folder and look for the `Gaze_Interactable` and `Gaze_Interactor` prefabs in the `Prefabs` folder.

These follow the same concept as the other interactor and interactable components. We will focus on setting up our **gaze reticle** first.

Gaze reticle

For the gaze interactions to work, we must set up our reticle. A reticle is a small cross-shaped or circular visual element that is placed in the center of the user's field of view and is often used as a cursor or aiming point. In the case of gaze interactions, the reticle is used to indicate the object that the user is currently looking at and can interact with. It can be a simple dot, crosshair, or a more complex 3D object that follows the user's gaze. The reticle can be customized to suit the needs of the application and make the interactions more intuitive and user-friendly. The reticle is also used to indicate the state of the interaction, such as when the object is ready to be interacted with, or if the interaction is currently in progress.

In addition, the reticle can be used to provide feedback to the user, such as when the user is looking at an object that cannot be interacted with or if the interaction is not possible at that moment. Reticles can also be used to provide additional information to the user, such as the distance between the user and the object.

The reticle also serves as a way to communicate to the user that the gaze interaction is active and that the user can interact with the objects in the virtual environment by simply looking at them.

To set up our gaze reticle, go through the following steps:

1. Go to the `Main Camera` GO in the VR rig in **Hierarchy** (*Figure 3.24*).
2. Add a `Gaze_Interactor` prefab from the `Prefabs` folder as a child of the `Main Camera` GO.
3. Create a new layer in the top right of **Inspector** called `GazeInteraction`
4. Set **Layer Mask** in the `Gaze_Interactor` GO to `GazeInteraction`.
5. Set **Min Detection Distance** to `0`.
6. Set **Max Detection Distance** to `6`.
7. Set **Time to Activate** to `6`.

   Min Detection Distance and **Max Detection Distance** are measured in meters to indicate the range for how close and how far `Gaze Interactor` will work on objects (*Figure 3.24*). **Time to Activate** indicates the number of seconds it takes for `Gaze Interactor` to trigger an action when you stare at something:

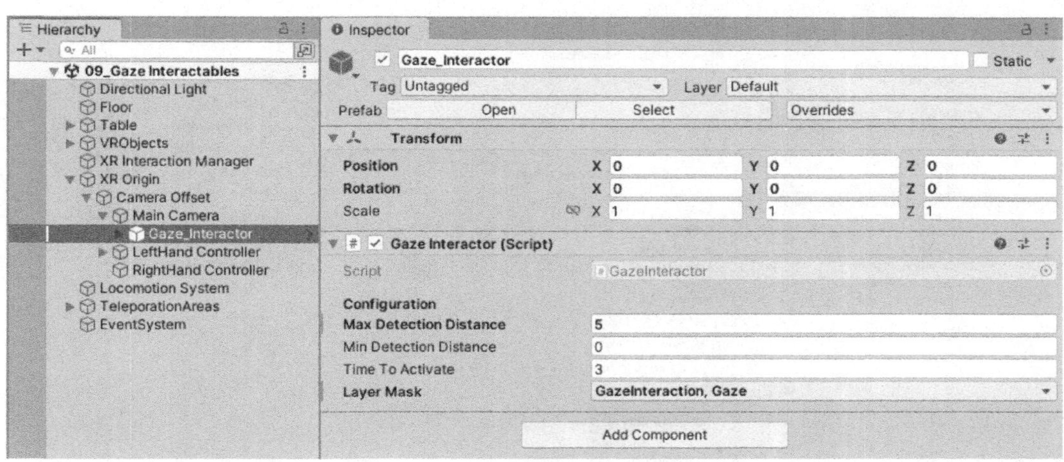

Figure 3.24 – The Gaze Interactor GO

8. Add the `gaze_reticle` prefab to the `Gazeinteraction` prefab folder (`Gazeinteraction | Resources | Prefabs`) as a child of the `Gaze_Interactable` GO (*Figure 3.25*):

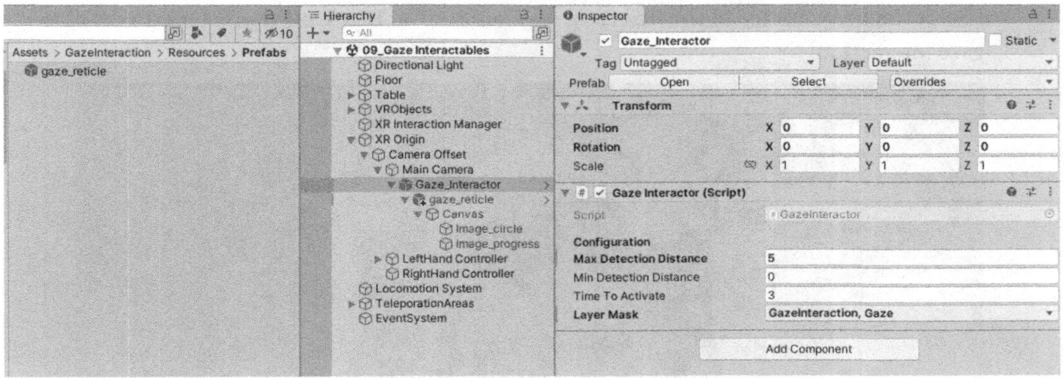

Figure 3.25 – The gaze reticle set up in Hierarchy

In the next section, we will set up our virtual object for **gaze interactions**.

Gaze events

Previously, we used the `Cube` GO for ray and direct object interactions. We will now use the `Capsule` GO for gaze interactions by performing the following steps:

1. Take the `Gaze_Interactable` prefab and make it a child of the `Capsule` GO:

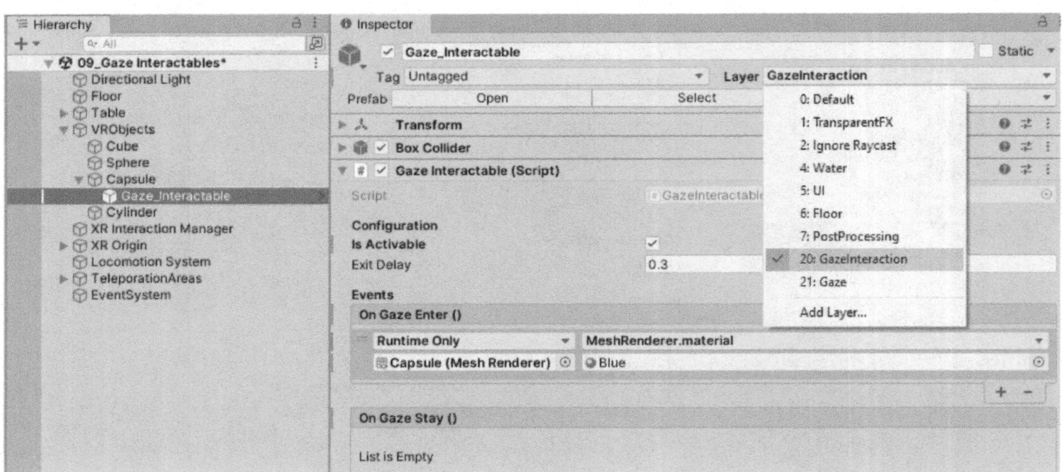

Figure 3.26 – The Gaze_Interactable GO as a child of the Capsule GO

2. Enable the **isActivable** box in the `Gaze Interactable` component.
3. The box collider on the prefab should be placed around the `Capsule` GO. You can edit the size of the box collider in the **Scene** view (*Figure 3.27*). **Box Collider** is used to register the gaze interaction:

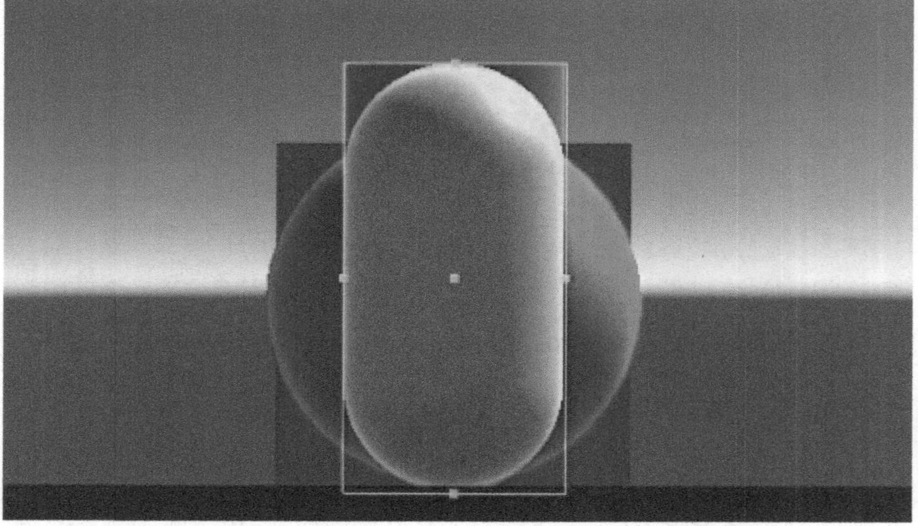

Figure 3.27 – Box collider bounding box around the Capsule GO

4. Set the prefab's **Layer** to `GazeInteraction`.

We can now test the gaze interactions with the `Capsule` GO. By putting on your headset and looking at the `Capsule` GO, you will be able to see the reticle, which we set up on the `Gaze Interactor` component, appear as a blue dot on the `Capsule` GO, indicating that we are currently looking at it.

As you look away from the `Capsule` GO, the reticle will disappear and when you look back at it, the reticle will reappear. To trigger actions when we look at the `Capsule` GO, we need to enable events on the `Gaze Interactor` component. This way, we can detect when the user is looking at the `Capsule` GO and perform certain actions, such as picking it up or interacting with it in some other way. Let's go to the **Events** section of the `Gaze Interactor` component, where we will see various event parameters:

- `On Gaze Enter`: When you first look at the object; you usually see this event trigger during the first frame you look at while viewing the object.
- `On Gaze Stay`: When you continue to look at the object after the first frame; this event parameter will override `On Gaze Enter` if both the `Enter` and `Stay` parameters are used.
- `On Gaze Exit`: When you look away from the object.
- `On Gaze Activated`: When you trigger an action after the `Time to Activate` time has triggered an action. As you may recall, the `Time to Activate` time will count down to 0 when you gaze upon an object. When the countdown hits 0, it will trigger the `On Gaze Activated` event parameter.

Let's set up a series of materials that can be used to indicate which gaze event we are triggering. To set up these events, perform the following steps:

1. Click + on each event slot.
2. Drag the `Capsule` GO from **Hierarchy** to the event slots.
3. Select the function | **MeshRenderer** | **Material material** for each slot.
4. Create a material for the orange, green, purple, red, and blue colors (*Figure 3.28*). We will drag the material color we chose into the event reference slot:

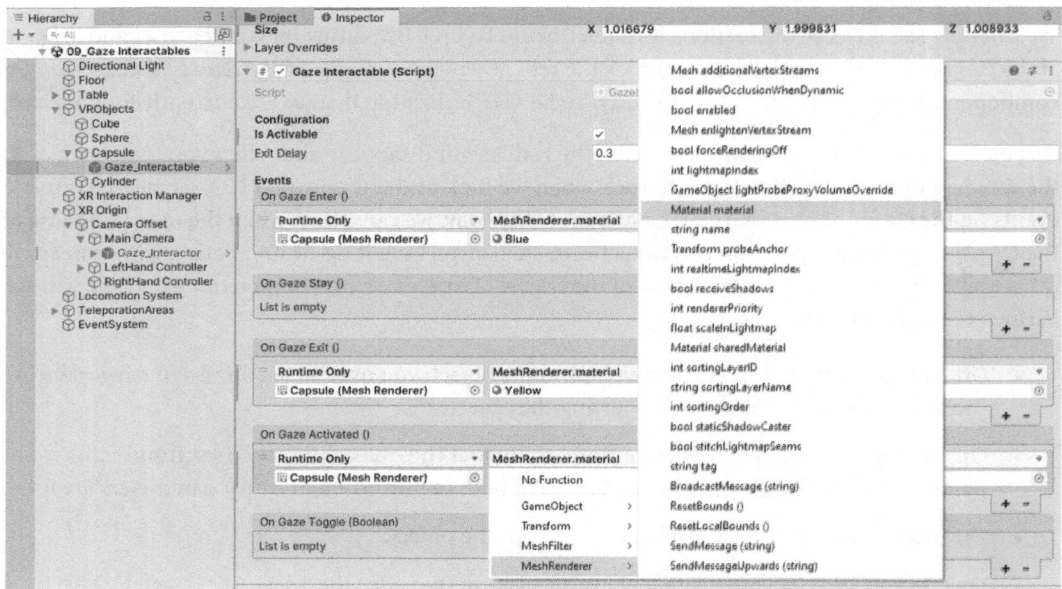

Figure 3.28 – Material and Gaze Interactor component setup

5. Set `On Gaze Enter` to a `Blue` material.
6. Set `On Gaze Stay` to a `Green` material.
7. Set `On Gaze Exit` to a `Yellow` material since that is the original color of the `Capsule` GO.
8. Set `On Gaze Activated` to a `Red` material.

To create a dynamic and interactive VR experience, it's important to set up events that trigger actions when the user interacts with virtual objects. In this case, we will set up events for our gaze interactions with the `Capsule` GO. We used the `On Gaze Enter`, `On Gaze Stay`, and `On Gaze Exit` events to change the color of the `Capsule` GO when the user looks at it:

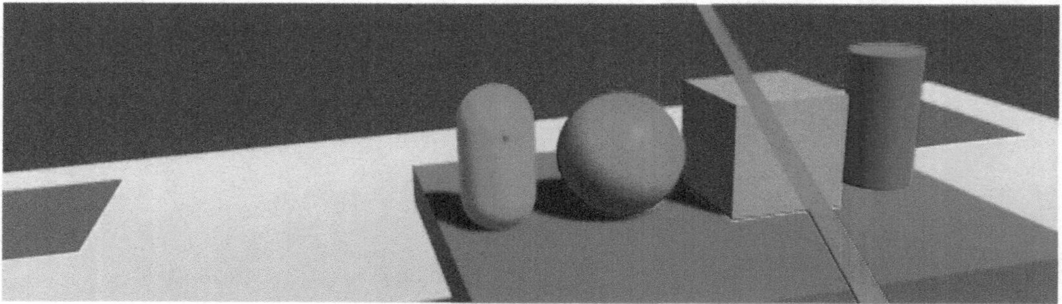

Figure 3.29 – Testing the gaze reticle and indicator

When we test this out in play mode, we will see the reticle appear when we look at the `Capsule` GO. The reticle is a visual indicator that helps the user know what they are looking at. The reticle will also have a pinwheel that will fill up when the `On Gaze Activate` event is triggered. Additionally, we will see the color of the `Capsule` GO change as we interact with it.

It's also worth noting that since gaze interactions are typically used to interact with distant objects, they can be combined with other interactions such as direct and ray interactions. This allows us to create a more versatile and dynamic VR experience.

In the next section, we will work on incorporating multiple object interactions on a single virtual object.

Multiple object interactions

To enable multiple object interactions on a single VR object, you can add multiple interactor components to the object. For example, you can add a `Ray Interactor` component, a `Direct Interactor` component, and a `Gaze Interactor` component to the same VR object. This will allow the object to be interacted with using different methods, such as pointing and clicking with a hand controller, walking up to the object, and looking at the object for a certain period.

You can also set up different events for each interactor component, such as changing the color of the object when it is interacted with using the `Ray Interactor` component and playing a sound when it is interacted with using the `Direct Interactor` component. It's also important to keep in mind that the order in which the interactors are added to the object and the order of the events on each interactor component will determine which interaction takes precedence when multiple interactions are possible.

Let's duplicate the `09_GazeInteractables` scene and rename it `10_MultipleObjectInteractables`.

To add multiple interactions to a virtual object, go through the following steps:

1. In **Hierarchy**, rename `Cube` to `Cube - Grab`, `Sphere` to `Sphere - Multi`, `Capsule` to `Capsule - Gaze`, and `Cylinder` to `Cylinder - Multi` to indicate in **Hierarchy**, which objects correspond to which enabled object interactions.
2. With `Cylinder` and `Sphere` selected, we will add two components: `Gaze Interactable` and `XR Grab Interactable`.
3. For the `Gaze Interactable` events, we will enable `On Gaze Enter`, `On Gaze Exit`, and `On Gaze Activated`.
4. In the `XR Grab Interactable` component, set **Interaction Layer Mask** to `Object`.
5. In the **Layer** menu of both GOs, set **Layer** to `GazeInteraction`.
6. For the `Gaze interactions` events, we will repeat the steps we performed in the previous section for the `Capsule` material colors for `Cylinder` and `Sphere`.

7. Place the `Cylinder` GO in the `Gaze Event` reference slot.
8. Set the functions to `MeshRenderer.material` (*Figure 3.30*):

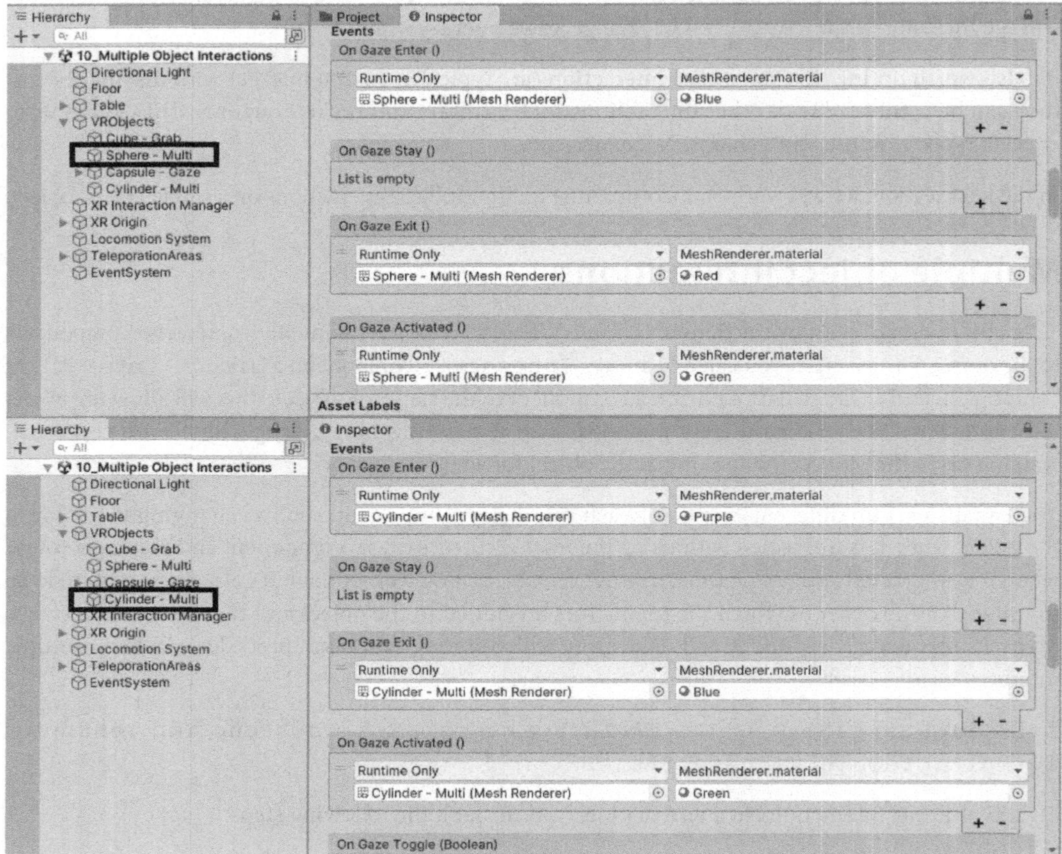

Figure 3.30 – Sphere (top) and Cylinder (bottom) gaze event material setup

9. Set **Exit delay** to `0.3`.
10. Repeat *steps 8* and *9* for the `Sphere` GO.

When we test out the scene, all the objects that have the `Gaze Interactor` component will work as the `Capsule` GO does, and all the ones that have the `XR Grab Interactable` component can be used with direct and ray interactions. At this point, we know how to set up objects that can respond to gaze, ray, and direct interactions.

In the next section, we will learn how to incorporate haptic feedback to enhance the immersion of our VR experience.

Adding haptic feedback to our VR controllers

Haptic feedback, also known as **haptics**, is the use of vibrations or other tactile sensations to communicate information or provide a sense of touch in a virtual or remote environment. In VR, haptic feedback can be used to simulate the feeling of holding or touching objects and add an extra layer of realism to the experience. For example, when you pick up an object in VR, the controller you are holding may vibrate to give you the sensation of grasping something.

In our demo scene, we will use XR Interaction Toolkit's built-in haptic feedback system to add haptic feedback to our objects that can be interacted with. This system allows us to add haptic vibrations to specific events, such as when an object is picked up or when a button is pressed. We can also adjust the strength and duration of the haptic feedback to suit the specific interaction.

For example, when you pick up an object in VR, the controller you are holding may vibrate to give you the sensation of grasping something. The strength of the vibration could be made stronger when you pick up a heavier object, or weaker when you pick up a lighter object. Similarly, when you press a button in VR, the controller could vibrate to give you the sensation of pressing a physical button.

By incorporating haptic feedback into our VR experience, we can create a more immersive and realistic experience for the user. It can make the virtual world feel more tangible and responsive, making it easier for the user to suspend their disbelief and fully immerse themselves in the experience.

Please note that this only works for ray and direct interactions and not gaze interactions.

Let's duplicate the `10_MultiObjectInteractables` scene and rename it `11_HapticFeedback`.

To enable **haptic feedback** on our VR hand controllers, complete the following steps:

1. Go to the `LeftHand Controller` and `RightHand Controller` GOs in **Hierarchy** and select them to view their components in **Inspector**.
2. Enable **Haptic Events** in the `XR Direct Interactor` and `XR Ray Interactor` components (*Figure 3.31*):

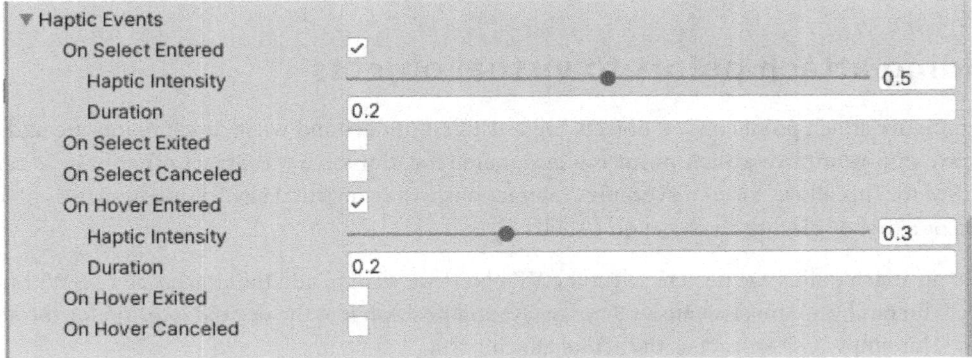

Figure 3.31 – The Haptic Events settings

3. For **Haptic Intensity**, input `.5` for heavy intensity and `.3` for light intensity.
4. For **Duration**, input `.5` for heavy intensity and `.2` for light intensity.

Haptic events work similarly to gaze events and follow the same naming conventions (*Figure 3.32*). The difference is that with haptic events, you can set the intensity and the duration of the rumble of the controller. Light interactions can have minimal feedback, and heavy interactions can have more intense feedback:

Event Name	Fired When
OnFirstHoverEnter	The first interactor begins hovering over the interactable.
OnHoverEnter*	Any interactor begins hovering over the interacable.
OnHoverExit*	Any interactable stops hovering over the interactable.
OnLastHoverExit	The last interactor has stopped hovering over the interactable.
OnSelectEnter*	An interactor has begun selecting the interactable.
OnSelectExit*	An interactor has deselected the interactable.
OnActivate	An interactor has activated this interactable.
OnDeactivate	An Interactor has deactivated this interactable.

* These events can also trigger audio and haptic feedback on interactors.

Figure 3.32 – Chart of haptic and audio event functions

Haptics is a subtle way to simulate physical resistance in an experience. Controllers have haptic capabilities, so you might as well utilize them to your advantage.

In the next section, we will explore attach points, which we can use to control how VR objects are held and positioned on our controllers during an interaction.

Adding attach points to virtual objects

To configure attach points on VR objects, we must first understand what attach points are and why they are important. An **attach point** is a designated location on a VR object other objects can be *attached* to. This allows for more complex interactions within a virtual environment, such as holding a gun or a tool or placing an object on a shelf.

To set up attach points, we need to select the VR object we want to add the attach point to. Within the object's hierarchy, we must create an `Empty` GO and position it at the desired location for the attach point. This empty GO will act as the actual attach point.

Once the `Empty` GO is in place, we will need to add it to the **Attach Transform** reference slot on the `XR Interactor` component. We will test this feature out with our `Cylinder` GO.

Let's duplicate the `11_HapticFeedback` scene and rename it `12_AttachPoints`.

To configure an attach point on the `Cylinder` GO, go through the following steps:

1. Go to **Hierarchy** and select our `Cylinder - Multi` GO.
2. Create an `Empty` GO as a child of `Cylinder` and name it `CylinderAttachPoint`.
3. In the **Scene** view, move the `CylinderAttachPoint` transform to the bottom right-hand corner of the object (*Figure 3.33*):

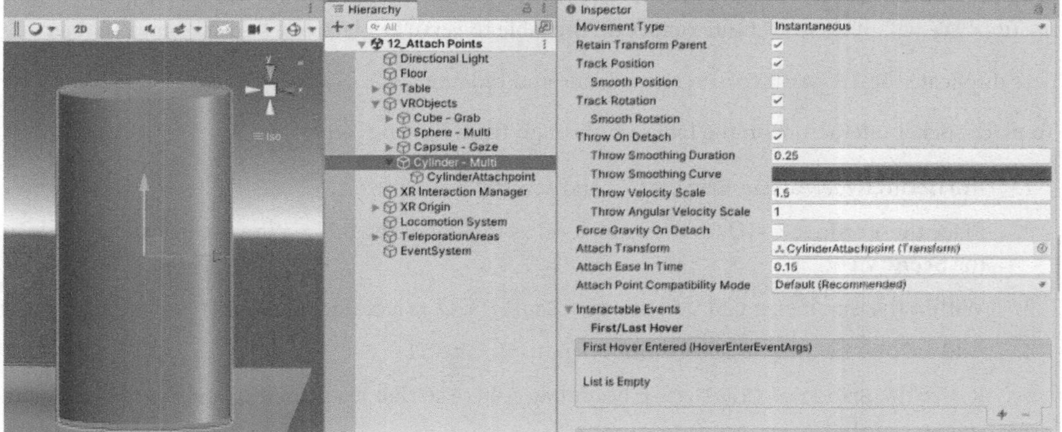

Figure 3.33 – The attach point on the Cylinder GO

4. Add the `CylinderAttachPoint` empty to the **Attach Transform** reference slot in the `XR Grab Interactable` component.

When configuring attach points on VR objects, we can control the location at which the object is anchored to the user's hand in our VR experience. This can be accomplished by using an empty GO as an attach point and positioning it at the desired location on the object. By doing this, we can create more realistic and immersive object interactions as the object will be anchored to the hand in a specific location instead of the center of the object. This allows for more complex interactions and a more realistic experience for the user.

In the next section, we will delve into the concept of socket interactors, which are another powerful tool for creating realistic and immersive object interactions in VR.

Adding socket interactors to our demo scene

Socket interactors are a type of interactor that allows you to place objects in specific locations with precision and feedback. This can be achieved by providing a socket or a designated location where the object can be placed. This socket can be visualized as a preview and can provide feedback when the object is placed correctly or incorrectly.

The object being placed can also snap to the socket to ensure it is in the correct location. This can greatly enhance the interactivity and realism of the VR experience, especially in scenarios where objects need to be placed in specific locations, such as puzzles or problem-solving experiences. Additionally, since the objects are not affected by physics when being placed in the socket, attaching them can prevent unwanted movement or collision of objects, providing a more seamless and polished experience for the user. We will place socket interactors on the table to serve as place markers for our VR objects.

Let's duplicate the `12_AttachPoints` scene and rename it `13_SocketInteractors`.

To place socket interactors on the table, go through the following steps:

1. In **Hierarchy**, create an `Empty` GO and rename it `Sockets`.
2. Place the `Sockets` GO on the same level as the top of the table using the transform tools in the **Scene** view.
3. Within the `Sockets` GO, add another `Empty` GO as a child and name it `Socket1`.
4. Add a `Sphere Collider` component to `Socket1`.
5. Resize the `Sphere Collider` bounding sphere so that it sits on the same level as the table (*Figure 3.35*).
6. Add the `XR Socket Interactor` component to `Socket1`.
7. Set **Layer Mask** to `Object`.
8. Add a new `Empty` GO as a child to `Socket1` and name it `AttachPoint`.
9. Place the `AttachPoint` GO in the **Attach Transform** reference slot.
10. Add a `Plane` GO as a child of `Socket1` and rename it `SocketIndicator`.
11. Resize the XYZ scale of `SocketIndicator` to `.02`. This will serve as an indicator for where the socket is located on the table:

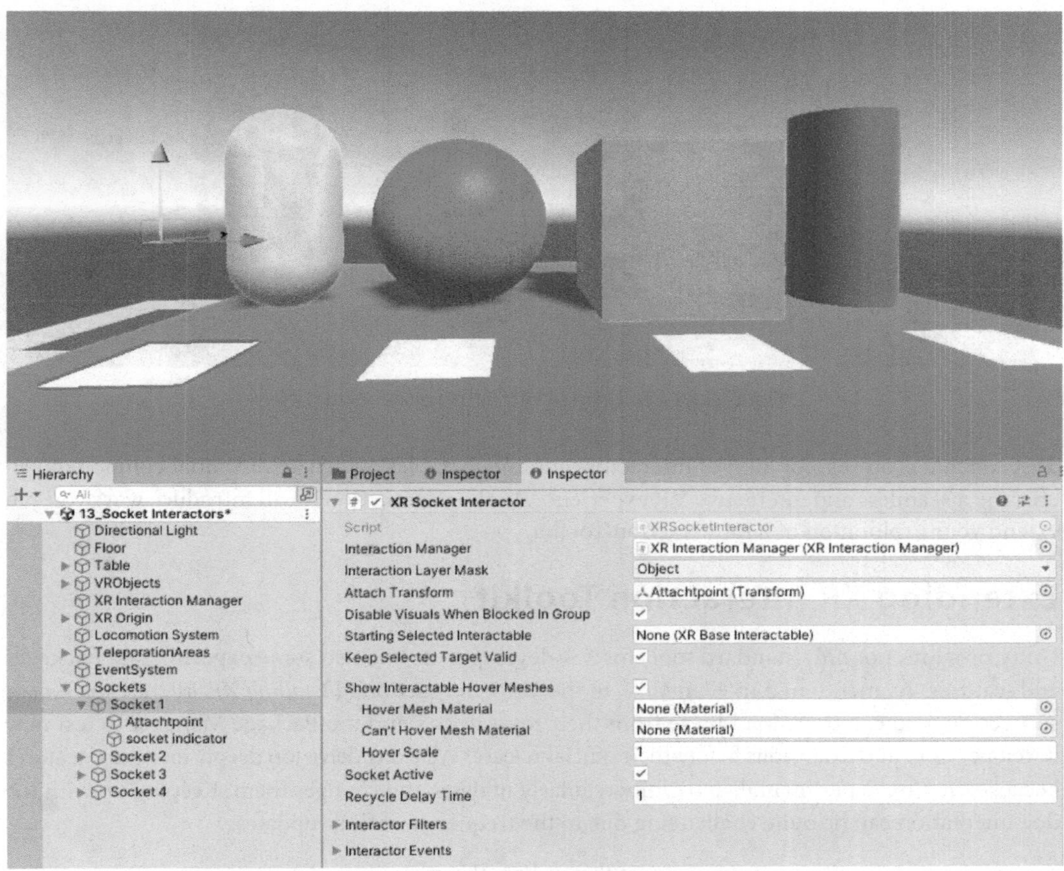

Figure 3.34 – The Socket1 GO collider (top) and its settings (bottom)

Before we test it out, it is important to note that the objects we will be using with the socket should have their **Collision Detection** set to **Continuous Dynamic** in the `Rigidbody` component.

We can also duplicate the `Socket1` GO and place the duplicates around the table to have multiple socket locations for different objects. When we test out the socket, any object held near the collider area of the socket will show a blue silhouette preview of the object's placement. The placement is based on the attach point's location, as we covered in the previous section. Once an object has been placed, it will remain in that spot unless it's moved. If we try to add another object to an occupied socket, it will display a red object preview (*Figure 3.35*):

Figure 3.35 – Testing sockets with primitive objects

This concludes our exploration of interactors and interactables, which are essential components in creating a seamless and interactive VR experience. In the next section, I will introduce ways you can extend your exploration of XR Interaction Toolkit.

Extending XR Interaction Toolkit

Unity provides not only standard tools for VR development but also some experimental packages and features. As mentioned in *Chapter 2*, in the *VR setup* section's *Installing XR Interaction Toolkit* subsection, you can download these from their repositories and the Package Manager to test new developer tools and extensions before their official release. We won't delve too deeply into these features because they are experimental, and Unity regularly updates and changes them. Keeping up with the documentation can be quite challenging due to the frequency of their updates.

Nevertheless, Unity offers a sample project that utilizes the most up-to-date features of XR Interaction Toolkit. These will be included in the latest build of the toolkit. Among these are a scene with starter assets for VR development right out of the box, a VR device simulator that allows you to simulate different head-mounted displays and controllers, and presets for input interactions using the Unity input system. There are also predefined XR Interaction Toolkit behaviors for standard VR interactions, camera effects for altering the VR experience while moving to reduce motion sickness, improved gaze interaction support for XR Interaction Toolkit, and poke interactions with controllerless hand interactions.

These are all highly experimental and can often be very buggy, depending on the release. We don't recommend using any of these sample or experimental features in projects intended for immediate release.

To download the samples and import them into your current project, follow these steps:

1. Open **Package Manager** (**Windows** | **Package Manager**).
2. Press the + icon in the top left to open the **Import Package** dialog box.
3. Select **Add package by name** and input `com.unity.xr.interaction.toolkit.`
4. Select **Add** to import the sample package.

You can find two main scenes in the `samples` folder, and the features will likely differ depending on when you import this package. The `Starter Assets Demo` scene can be found in the `Assets\Samples\XR Interaction Toolkit[version]\Starter Assets` folder, and the `Hands Interaction Demo` scene can be found in the `Assets\Samples\XR Interaction Toolkit[version]\Hands Interaction Demo` folder. We encourage you to explore these two scenes and keep an eye on the progress of various features coming to XR Interaction Toolkit. To learn more about upcoming features, visit `https://docs.unity3d.com/Packages/com.unity.xr.interaction.toolkit@2.4/manual/whats-new-2.4.0.html`.

Mastering XR Interaction Toolkit and understanding its operation can empower you to create innovative experiences using cutting-edge tools. When new tools are released, the documentation may not be comprehensive initially, which can be frustrating. However, by going through this chapter, we hope you have gained comfort and familiarity with some of the core features of XR Interaction Toolkit, thus forming a foundation for when new features are added.

Summary

This chapter provided a comprehensive understanding of the various interactions and locomotion features that can be used in VR experiences. By setting up a demo scene, we were able to explore different forms of interactions, such as ray, direct, gaze, snap, continuous, and teleportation. We also looked at how to incorporate haptic feedback, attach points, and socket interactors to enhance the realism and immersion of our VR experience. We now have a foundation we can build on that includes interacting with objects from a distance, interacting with them directly, changing the way we navigate virtual spaces, and much more. These are the core interactions that every VR experience should have and at this point, you should have a better understanding of how to use these interactions within your experiences. Remember that the key to VR development is a mix of planning features, adding components to GOs within the scene, and testing in the editor. With the basic foundations in place, we can now move on to the next chapter, where we will explore the use of GOs, prefabs, and assets to enhance the VR experience further.

4

Using Game Objects, Materials, and Prefabs

In this chapter, we will delve deeper into the world of GOs in Unity and explore how they can be utilized to enhance the visual quality of VR experiences. We will cover a variety of essential topics, including creating a custom grid with primitive GOs, assigning custom materials to GOs, and replacing VR hands and objects with custom game objects. Additionally, we will delve into the use of **ProBuilder** and **Polybrush** to create custom 3D shapes and environments, as well as the use of Unity packages and **FBX Exporter** for project organization and asset management.

Throughout the chapter, we will work on several projects that will help solidify your understanding of these concepts. These projects will include creating a custom grid of primitive GOs with custom materials, replacing VR hands with custom game objects from the Unity Asset Store, and creating a custom VR demo room to test advanced VR features. By the end of this chapter, you will have a solid understanding of game objects and how they can be used to enhance the visual quality of your VR experiences.

As we continue on in the book, we will build on this foundation by focusing on developing a more robust demo scene for testing VR experiences in future chapters. This will include adding animation and physics in *Chapter 5*, lighting and post-processing effects in *Chapter 6*, sound in *Chapter 7*, code with C# in *Chapter 8*, and expanding the render pipeline assets in *Chapter 9*. By the end of *Chapter 10*, we will have produced a fully functional demo scene that allows us to build on our knowledge of Unity and increase the usability of our VR features.

In this chapter, we will cover the following topics:

- Creating a grid with primitive GOs
- Creating a materials library
- Assigning custom materials to GOs

- Creating a custom VR demo room with ProBuilder
- Designing a demo room floor plan with Google Drawings
- Converting the floor plan into a 3D room with ProBuilder
- Decorating the VR demo room with Polybrush and vertex painting
- Creating prefabs with our GOs
- Organizing project assets with folders in the **Project** tab
- Exporting project assets with Unity packages and FBX Exporter

Before we begin, let's take a step back and go over the basics of GOs, which will provide a foundation for the rest of the chapter.

Technical requirements

The complete source code for this chapter can be found at `https://github.com/PacktPublishing/Enhancing-Virtual-Reality-Experiences-with-Unity-2022/tree/main/EnhancingVRExperiencesFullProject/Assets/_VRProjectAssets/Scenes/Chapter_4`.

Creating a grid with Primitive GOs

GOs are the building blocks of Unity scenes. They can be anything from simple shapes to complex characters and vehicles. Each GO has a `Transform` component that defines its position, rotation, and scale in the scene. It also has one or more other components that determine its behavior and appearance. GOs can be organized into hierarchies for the easy management of complex scenes. They are important because they form the foundation of Unity scenes and are the primary way to represent and manipulate objects within the engine. They provide organization, reusability, modularity, and improved performance.

To learn more about GOs, visit the Unity documentation here: `https://docs.unity3d.com/Manual/GameObjects.html`.

In this section, we will create a scene consisting of four different primitive shapes arranged in a 3 x 4 object grid. Each shape will be placed 2 meters (m) apart from one another. The shapes will include small (0.5 m), medium (1 m), and large (2 m) sizes. By the end of this section, we will have a grid of different-sized primitive shapes.

Let's create a new scene and name it `04_04_01_Primitives`.

To create a scene in Unity with different-sized primitive shapes in a grid, go through the following steps:

1. Create a plane and position it at (`0,0,0`) on the **X**, **Y**, and **Z** axes in the `Transform` component.
2. Create an empty GO and name it `Primitives_Holder`. This will be used to hold all of our primitive shapes on the same level.
3. Create a `Cube` GO and position it at (`0,0,0`) on the **X** and **Z** axes.
4. Name this GO `Cube_0.5`.
5. Scale it down to `0.5` on all axes.
6. Raise the Y position by `0.25` so that the cube is sitting on top of the plane. Remember that the anchor point of the primitive cube is located in the center of the GO, so placing the `Cube` GO on the top of the plane requires the value of the Y position to be half the value of the Y scale (*Figure 4.1*).
7. Repeat *step 3* to create two more `Cube` GOs, naming them `Cube_1` and `Cube_2`, respectively.
8. Set the **Y** position for `Cube_1` to `.5`.
9. Set the **X**, **Y**, and **Z** scale for `Cube_2` to `2`, and set the **Y** position to `1`.
10. Position `Cube_1` at `(0,0,2)` on the **Z** axis.
11. Position `Cube_2` at `(0,0,4)` on the **Z** axis.
12. Create a new empty GO and name it `Cubes`, then place the `Cube` GOs inside it as children.

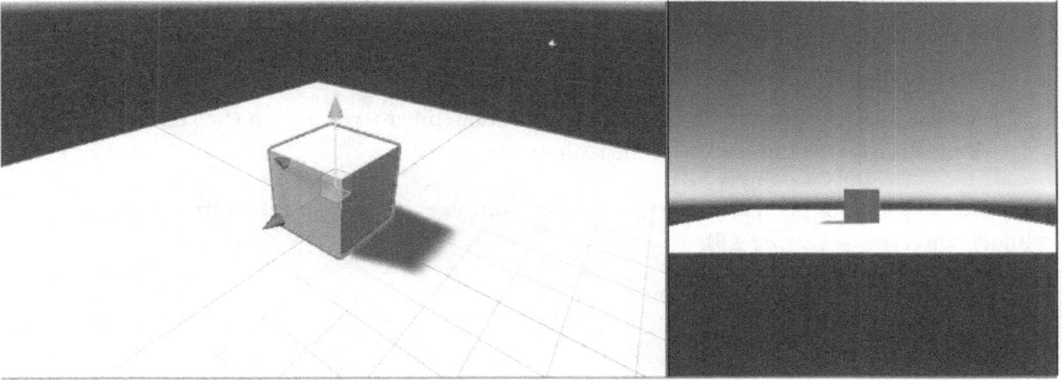

Figure 4.1 – Cube GO on the 3D plane

We will focus on the sphere, capsule, and cylinder primitive shapes. We will create a parent object for each shape and arrange them in a similar grid pattern as we did for the cubes (*Figure 4.2*).

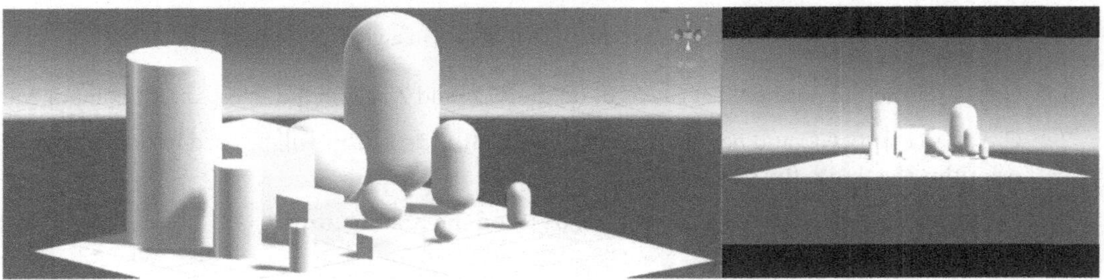

Figure 4.2 – Cylinders, spheres, and cubes in a grid on the 3D plane

To finish the grid with the sphere, capsule, and cylinder, go through the following steps:

1. Create a `Sphere` GO and duplicate it twice to get three `Sphere` GOs.
2. Name the first one `Sphere_0.5`, the second one `Sphere_1`, and the third one `Sphere_2`.
3. For `Sphere_0.5`, reduce its scale to `0.5` and set the **Y** position to `0.25`.
4. For `Sphere_1`, leave the scale as is, set the **Y** position to `0.5`, and move it back in the **Z** position to `2`.
5. For `Sphere_2`, increase its scale to `2`, set the **Y** position to `1`, and move it back in the **Z** position to `4`.
6. Create an empty parent object for the spheres and move it to the right by setting the **X** position to `2`.
7. Repeat the same process for the capsules.
8. Repeat the same process for the cylinders but remember to raise each `Cylinder` GO in the **Y** position by the same value as the scale.

Now you have a set of primitive shapes (small, medium, and large) in the form of a cube, sphere, cylinder, and capsule (*Figure 4.3*).

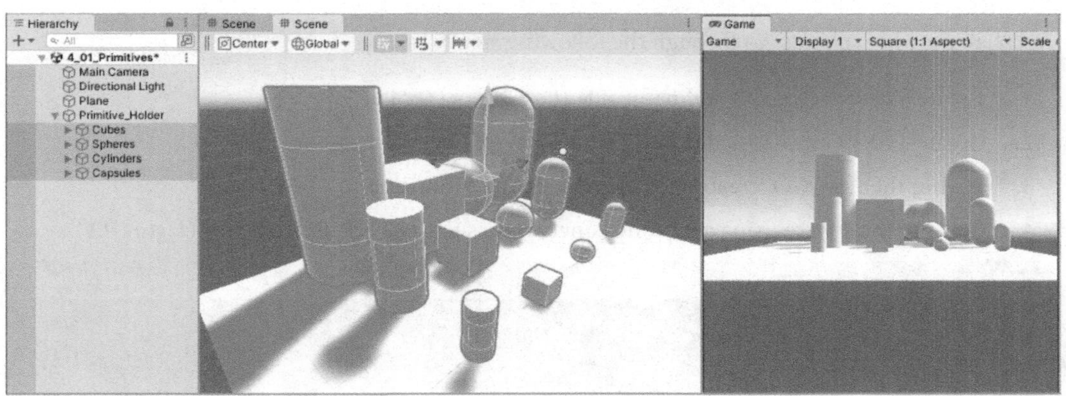

Figure 4.3 – Capsules, cylinders, spheres, and cubes in a grid on the 3D plane

This section taught you how to create a scene in Unity with different-sized primitive shapes arranged in a grid pattern, and how to procedurally create a similar pattern for different primitive shapes.

In the next section, we will create a grid of spheres that we can use to assign custom materials to. This will serve as our materials library for future projects.

Creating a materials library

We will be creating a grid of spheres that we can use to assign custom materials to. We call this a *materials library*. This grid of spheres will serve as our materials library for future projects. By creating a materials library, we will be able to easily access and apply different materials to our 3D models without having to create new materials each time. Additionally, having a materials library will make it easier to maintain consistency in our projects.

We will begin by creating a grid of spheres in a 3D modeling software of your choice. Then, we will assign different materials to each sphere. These materials can be textures, colors, or even patterns. Once we have assigned materials to each sphere, we will be able to easily select and apply them to other 3D models in our project.

Creating a grid of spheres

We will be building a materials grid in Unity. This grid will serve as a library of different materials that we can use in future projects. We will be using spheres to assign custom materials to, and we will create a naming convention for these materials to make them easily identifiable. By the end of this section, you will have a grid of spheres with different materials that can be used as a reference for future projects.

Before we get started, let's duplicate the `4_01_Primitives` scene and name it `4_02_Materials Grid`.

To create a grid of spheres, go through the following steps:

1. Create a new empty GO and name it `Materials Grid`.
2. Create a new empty GO and name it `Red`.
3. Within the `Red` GO, create a sphere and set the **Y** position to `0.5`.
4. Rename the sphere using a naming convention, such as `Red_Standard` (*Figure 4.4*).

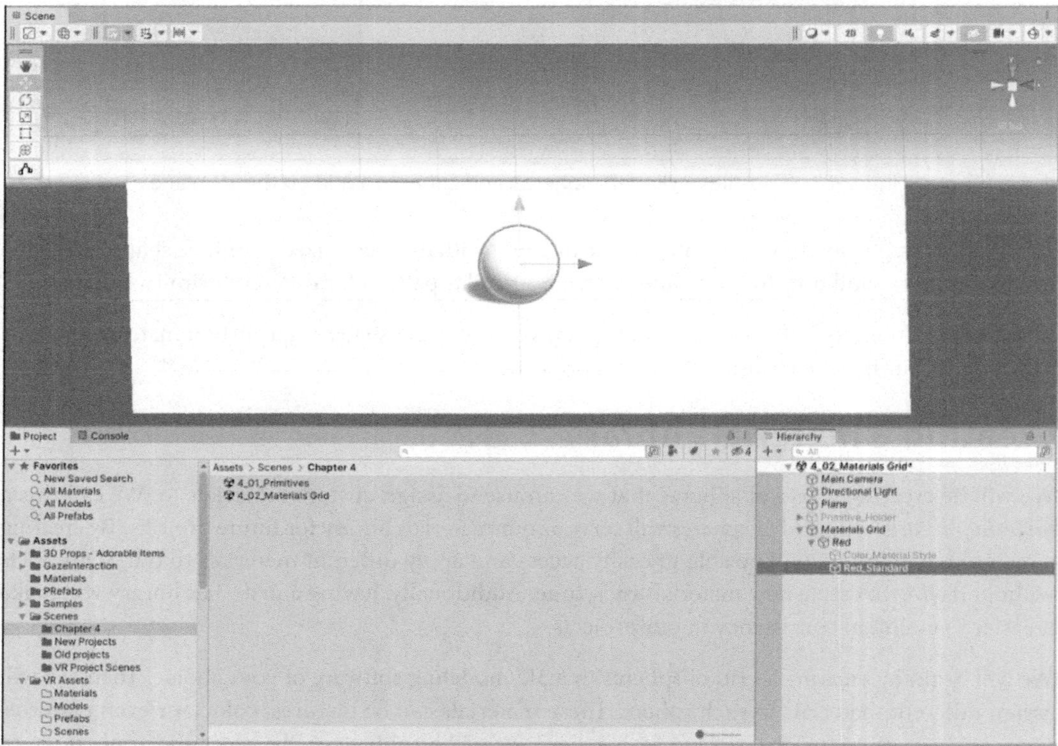

Figure 4.4 – First sphere in the materials grid

5. Duplicate the `Red_Standard` sphere five times. You should have six spheres in total.
6. Change the `Standard` part in each name to `Metallic`, `Unlit`, `Emission`, and `Specular`, respectively, to represent the different material styles we will create (*Figure 4.5*). There should be five total spheres in the `Red` parent GO.

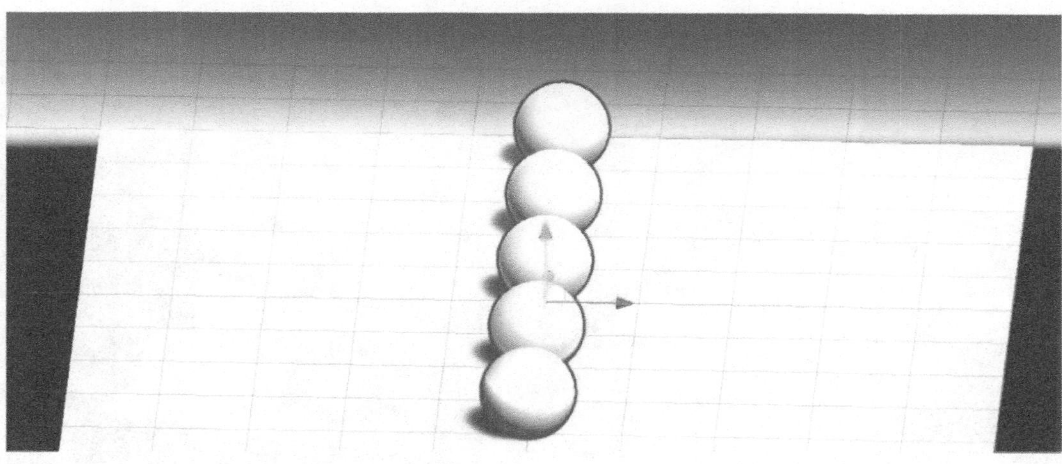

Figure 4.5 – Row of spheres aligned

7. Align each sphere in a row by adding `2` to the **Z** position value of each subsequent sphere until they are aligned (*Figure 4.5*).
8. Duplicate the `Red` GO that has the five spheres in a row.
9. Change the color in each of the duplicate rows' names to `Orange`, `Yellow`, `Green`, `Blue`, and `Violet`, respectively. There should now be parent folders representing the six colors (*Figure 4.6*).

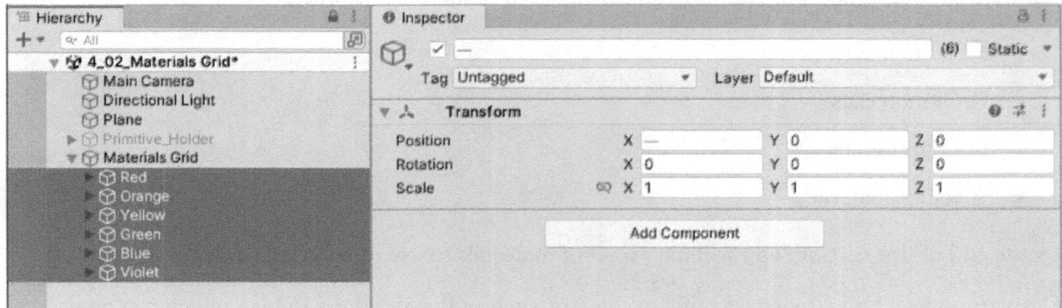

Figure 4.6 – Color-coded folders

10. Arrange the spheres in a grid layout to create a visual representation of the materials library (*Figure 4.7*) by changing the **X** position on the parent GO for each color. You should not directly change the position of the individual spheres in the row. Each row should be separated on the **X** position by `2` units.

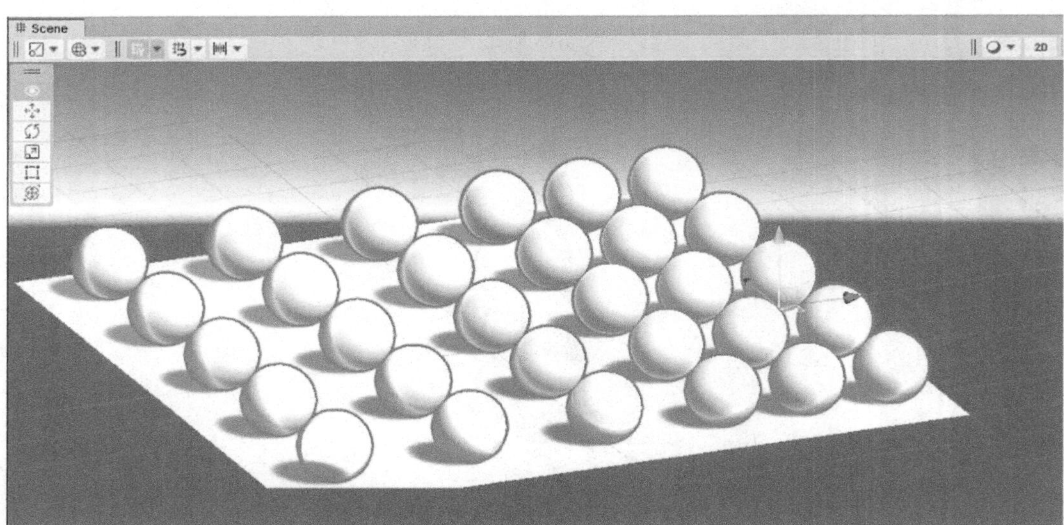

Figure 4.7 – Row of spheres aligned in a grid

In the next section, we will create a library of custom materials.

Creating custom materials

We will be creating various materials in Unity for a VR development project. We will start with a red standard material and then duplicate it four times to create the following:

- Metallic materials
- Unlit materials
- Emission materials
- Specular materials

By the end of this section, you will have a set of materials to use in your VR project.

Unity provides a wide variety of built-in shaders, such as the *Standard Shader*, which can be used to create realistic materials with the following features and properties:

- Reflections
- Ambient occlusion
- Advanced effects

Additionally, developers can create custom shaders using Unity's **ShaderLab** language, Unity's **Shader Graph** package using the Universal Render Pipeline and High Definition Render Pipeline, or by using third-party tools such as Shader Forge or Amplify Shader Editor.

Materials are applied to objects using the `Mesh Renderer` component, and once a material is applied to an object, you can use the material's properties to control the appearance of the object, such as the following:

- Color
- Texture

You can create materials in Unity by doing the following:

- Right-clicking in the project window and selecting **Create | Material**
- Clicking on the **Create** button in the **Assets** menu

Once you have created a material, you can assign it to a GO by doing the following:

- Dragging and dropping it onto the `Mesh Renderer` component in the **Inspector** window
- Using scripts to create, assign, and modify materials

The Standard Shader, Standard Specular Shader, and Unlit Shader are all built-in shaders that are provided by Unity. Each of them is suited for different purposes and has its own set of features and properties:

- **Standard Shader**: The Standard Shader is a versatile and widely used shader that is suitable for most types of materials. It provides a wide range of features, such as support for multiple lights, reflections, and advanced lighting models, making it well suited for creating realistic materials such as metal, glass, and plastic.
- **Standard Specular Shader**: The Standard Specular Shader is a variant of the Standard Shader that uses a specular lighting model rather than a standard lighting model. This means that it calculates highlights and reflections based on the angle of the surface to the camera, making it well suited for creating materials that have a high specular component, such as metal.
- **Unlit Shader**: The Unlit Shader is a simple shader that does not take into account any lighting information. This means that it does not calculate any reflections, shadows, or other lighting-related effects. This makes it well suited for creating simple, flat, or 2D-like materials, such as text, or simple UI elements.

Keep in mind that these properties are just a subset of the properties that are available for Unity's built-in shaders, and custom shaders can have their own set of properties. Additionally, some properties may not be available for all shaders, so it's important to check the documentation for the specific shader you are using to see which properties are available and how to use them. If you would like to learn more about materials, visit the Unity documentation here: `https://docs.unity3d.com/Manual/Materials.html`.

Now that we have briefly covered what materials are, let's proceed to creating our library.

To create a library of custom materials, go through the following steps:

1. In the **Project** tab, find the `Assets` folder and create a new folder called `Materials`.
2. In the `Materials` folder, create a new material.
3. Name the material based on the naming convention we used for the sphere, such as `Red_Standard`.
4. Create a material corresponding to each sphere that is located in the grid scene.
5. Select the `Red_Standard` material, and then go to the **Shader** dropdown in **Inspector**.
6. Set **Rendering Mode** to **Opaque**.
7. Change the color value to red, with **RGB** values of `255` on the red (**R**) channel and `0` on the green and blue channels (**G** and **B**). Also, set the alpha (**A**) value to `255` to make it opaque (*Figure 4.8*).

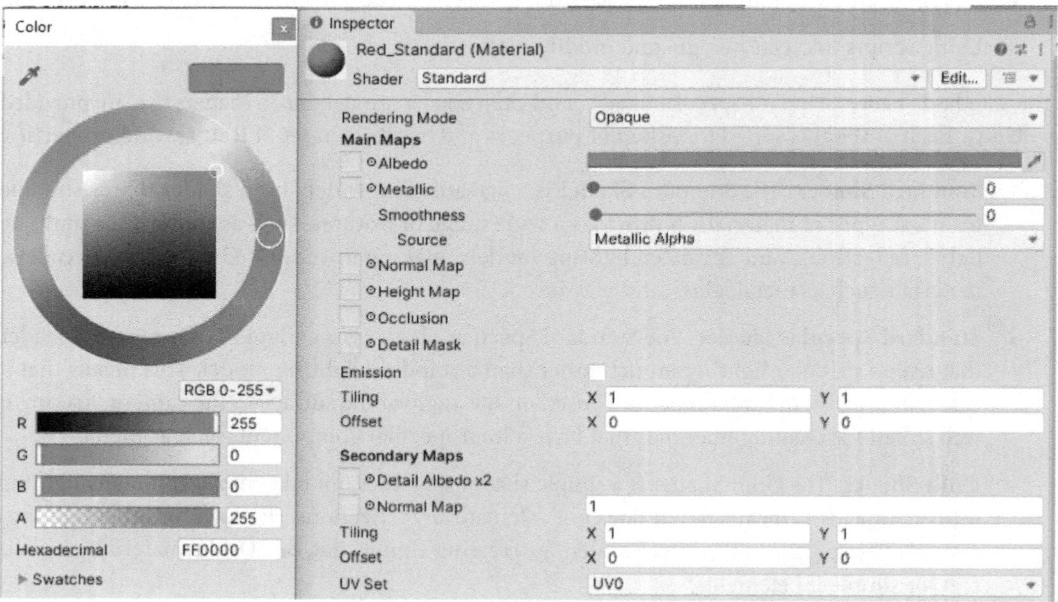

Figure 4.8 – Red_Standard material setup and swatches (lower left).

8. Drag the `Red_Standard` material onto the corresponding `sphere` GO in the scene.
9. Reduce the **Metallic** and **Smoothness** values on the red standard material to `0`.
10. Select all the red materials in the `Materials` folder and change their color to red.
11. Go to the `Red_Metallic` material, set the **Metallic** value to `0.75`, and set **Smoothness** to `0.75`.
12. Set **Rendering Mode** to **Transparent**.

13. Replace the default material on the `Red_Metallic` sphere GO with the `Red_Metallic` material.
14. Go to the `Red_Unlit` material, change the **Standard** material to an `Unlit` material, and use the color red.
15. Replace the default material on the `Red_Unlit` sphere GO with the `Red_Unlit` material.
16. Go to the `Red_Emission` material and check the **Emission** box on the material. Set the **Emission** RGB values to `25`, `100`, and `100`. Increase the intensity to `2`.
17. Replace the default material on the `Red_Emission` sphere GO with the `Red_Emission` material.
18. Go to the `Red_Specular` material, change the **Standard** material to a **Standard (Specular Setup)** material, and use the color red.
19. Change **Rendering Mode** to **Transparent** (*Figure 4.9*).

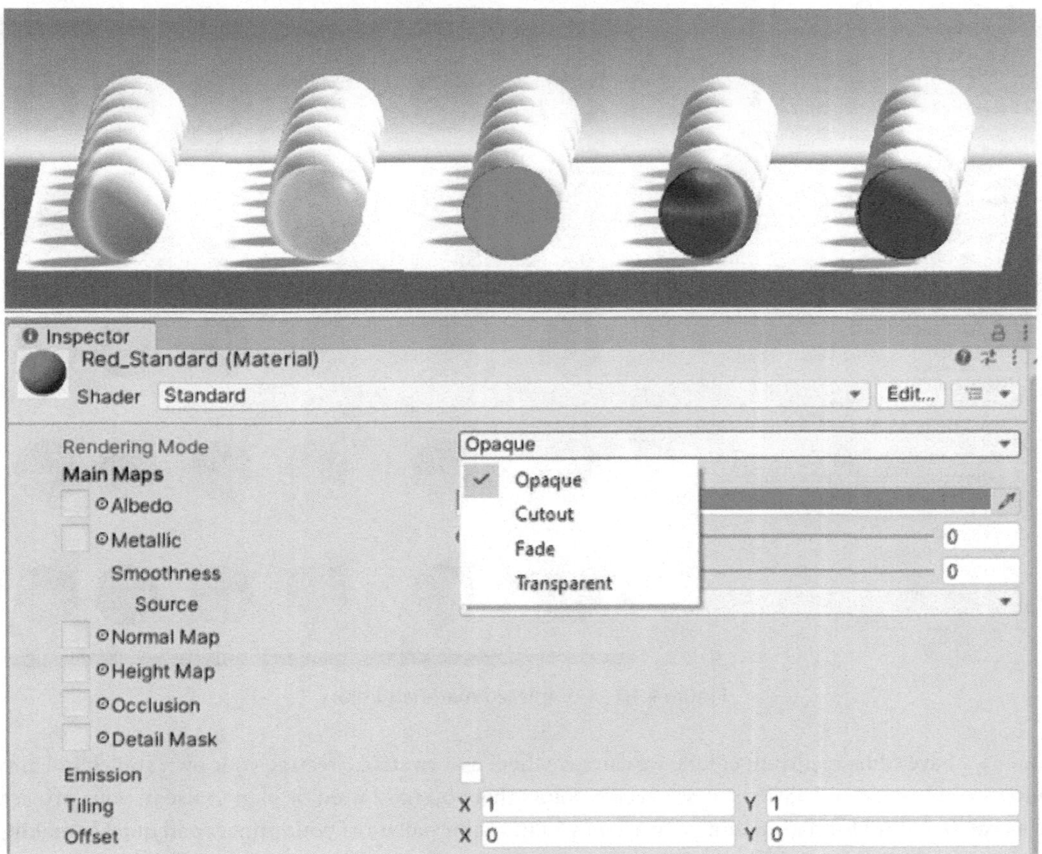

Figure 4.9 – Specular setup

20. Set **Smoothness** to `0.6`, and decrease the color value to `25`.
21. Replace the default material on the `Red_Specular` sphere GO with the `Red_Specular` material.
22. To create an orange material set, duplicate all the red materials and rename them to `Orange`.
23. For each of the orange materials, use the RGB values `255`, `130`, `0` to change the color to orange.
24. Place the corresponding materials on the corresponding sphere GOs.
25. Repeat *steps 23 and 24* to create yellow materials, using the RGB values `255`, `250`, `0`.
26. Repeat *steps 23 and 24* to create green materials, using the RGB values `0`, `255`, `0`.
27. Repeat *steps 23 and 24* to create blue materials, using the RGB values `0`, `0`, `255`.
28. Repeat *steps 23 and 24* to create violet materials, using the RGB values `100`, `0`, `255`.

We now have a grid containing our library of materials (*Figure 4.10*).

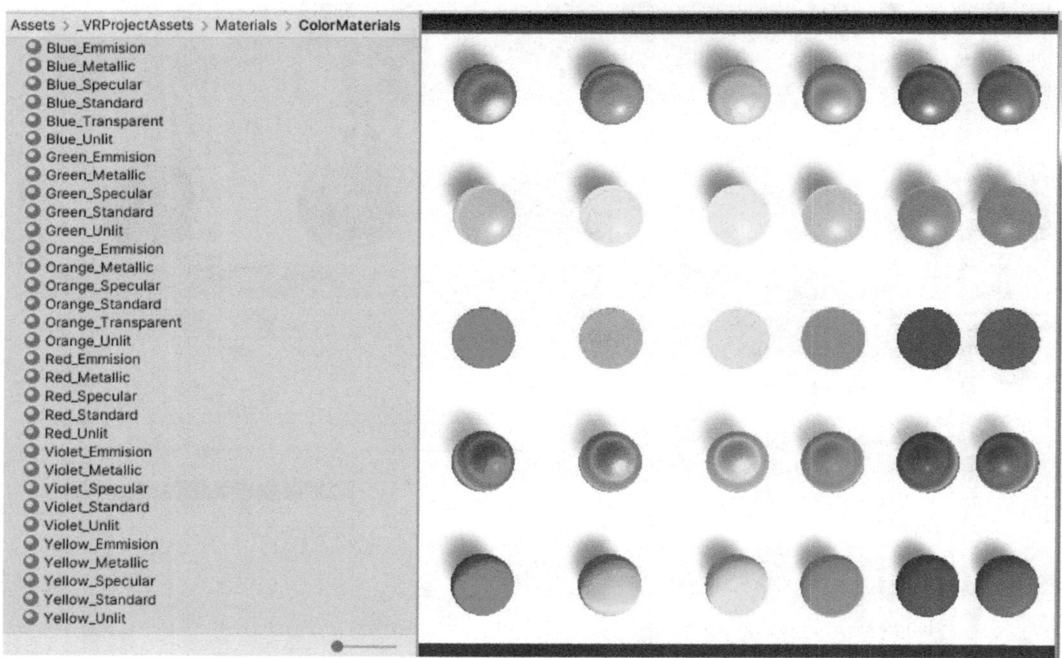

Figure 4.10 – Completed materials library

Since we have some recurrent colors, we can save them as a **swatch**. Creating your own swatch in Unity allows you to save and easily access specific colors that you have used or plan to use in your project. This can be useful for maintaining consistency in the color palette of your project and quickly making changes to the colors of different materials or objects. Additionally, creating a swatch library allows you to easily organize and manage different colors, making it easier to find and apply the colors you need. To save a color in Unity using the **Swatches** feature, complete the following steps:

1. Locate the color picker in the materials **Inspector**.
2. Select the color you want to save.
3. In the **Swatches** dropdown, click **Create New Library**.
4. Give the new library a name, for example, `Basic Colors`.
5. A new swatch library will appear. Click **Add New** to create a new preset for the color you just selected.
6. The new preset will be added to the **Basic Colors** library.
7. To access this library later, go to the color picker and select the **Basic Colors** library from the **Swatches** dropdown.
8. You can also add more colors to the **Basic Colors** library by repeating *steps 1–6* with different colors.

   This way, you can keep a consistent color palette and easily apply these colors to your materials and meshes. You can also see different color swatches at the bottom of the editor that are already created, such as red, orange, yellow, green, blue, and violet (*Figure 4.8*).

In this section, we created a materials grid in Unity. We used spheres to assign custom materials to and created a naming convention for these materials to make them easily identifiable. We also created a visual representation of the materials library by arranging the spheres in a grid layout. By now, you now have a reference library of different materials that can be used in future projects.

In the next section, we will download and apply custom assets and materials from the Asset Store to our VR rig to visualize our VR controllers as hands.

Assigning custom materials and assets to GOs

One important aspect of a VR rig is the visual representation of the hands, as this allows the user to see and interact with virtual objects in a realistic way.

To enhance the visual experience, we can add custom visuals for the hands on our VR rig. This can be done by exploring options available on the **Unity Asset Store**, which is a marketplace that offers a wide range of assets and tools for Unity developers. For our example, we will be downloading custom VR hand assets and a custom transparent ghost shader.

Custom VR hand assets are pre-made 3D models of hands that can be imported and used in Unity to replace the default primitive cubes or spheres that are often used to represent hands in VR. These assets can be more detailed and realistic, providing a more immersive experience for the user.

A custom transparent ghost shader is a type of shader that controls how light interacts with a 3D object. It is responsible for adding transparency, and we will use it to make the hands appear more see-through, giving the user a more realistic experience.

Once we have downloaded these assets, we will apply them to our VR controller Game objects to give us a visual for our VR hands. This will replace the default primitive spheres and cubes, providing a more visually appealing and realistic experience for the user. This is important for VR development in Unity as it enhances the overall user experience and immersion.

Let's proceed to the Asset Store!

Downloading assets from the Asset Store

The Unity Asset Store is a marketplace where creators can share and sell assets for Unity projects. These assets include 3D models, textures, audio, animations, and code. The Asset Store can be accessed through the Unity Editor or on the web. It allows users to quickly search and import assets to speed up development. There are free and paid options available and you can filter your search by category, price, and publisher.

Once an asset is selected, it can be added to your project and downloaded through the Unity Package Manager. This is important for VR development in Unity as it allows developers to easily add custom visuals for VR hands instead of using primitive shapes. If you want to learn more about the Unity Asset Store, visit the Unity documentation here: `https://docs.unity3d.com/Manual/AssetStore.html`.

We will download two assets from the Asset store: **Stylized - Simple Hands** (from `https://assetstore.unity.com/packages/3d/characters/stylized-simple-hands-221297`) and **Ghostly Hand Shader** (from `https://assetstore.unity.com/packages/vfx/shaders/ghostly-hand-shader-free-vr-212412`).

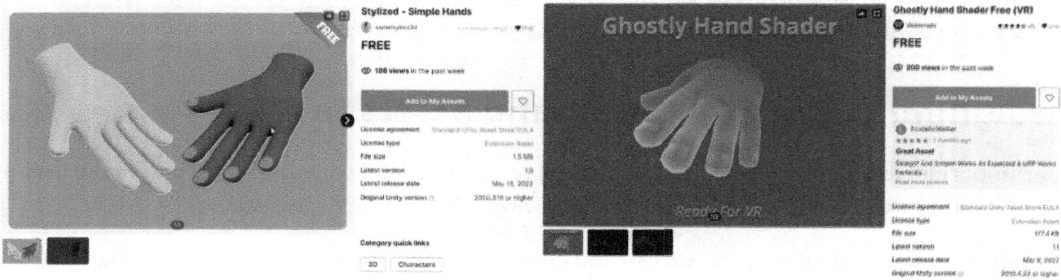

Figure 4.11 – Stylized - Simple Hands (left) and Ghostly Hand Shader (right) assets on Unity Asset Store

After downloading the hand assets and shaders from the asset store, go through the following steps:

1. Click **Add to My Assets** and then **Accept** in the Unity Asset Store.
2. Click **Open in Unity** to open the Package Manager with the new asset highlighted in the **My Assets** tab.
3. Click **Download** and then **Import** to import the asset into your project.

In the next section, we will apply the assets we downloaded to our VR rig.

Replacing VR hands with custom GOs

For most VR experiences, seeing your hands is an essential part of the experience. So, what we're going to do is replace the `HandSphere` GOs that we had with a new `3D Mesh Hand` GOs.

Before we get started with adding our Asset Store assets, let's duplicate the `4_02_MaterialsGrid` scene from the last chapter and name it `4_03_VRHands`.

To replace the VR hand GOs on the VR controllers, go through the following steps:

1. In the `VR hands` scene, locate the `Controller` GO and replace the standard sphere with a mesh.
2. In the scene, select the `Stylized - Simple Hands` prefab and place it where the `RightHand Controller` GO is located.
3. Rotate the prefab 80 degrees on the **X** axis and 90 degrees on the **Y** axis.
4. Decrease the scale of the prefab by 50 percent (`0.45` on each axis).
5. Rotate the prefab 80 degrees on the **X** axis and 90 degrees on the **Y** axis.
6. Decrease the scale of the prefab by 50 percent (`0.45` on each axis).

   Your VR hands are now replaced with the stylized hand model (*Figure 4.12*).

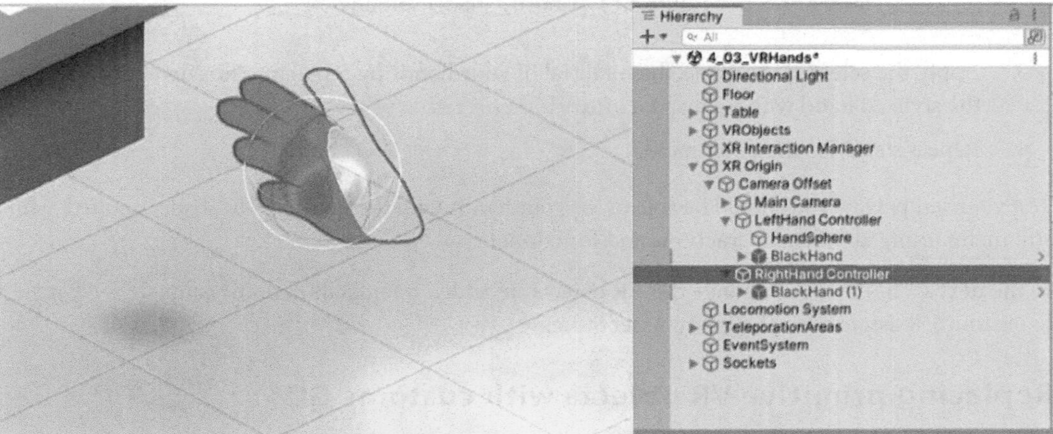

Figure 4.12 – VR hands setup

In the next section, we will replace the shader on our VR hands with the ghostly shader we downloaded from the Unity Asset Store.

Replacing the shader and materials on VR hands

To add the ghostly shader to our VR hands, go through the following steps:

1. Navigate to the `GhostlyHand` | `Materials` folder in the **Project** tab.
2. Select the `Example Hand Gradient` material and modify the settings to your liking (*Figure 4.13*).

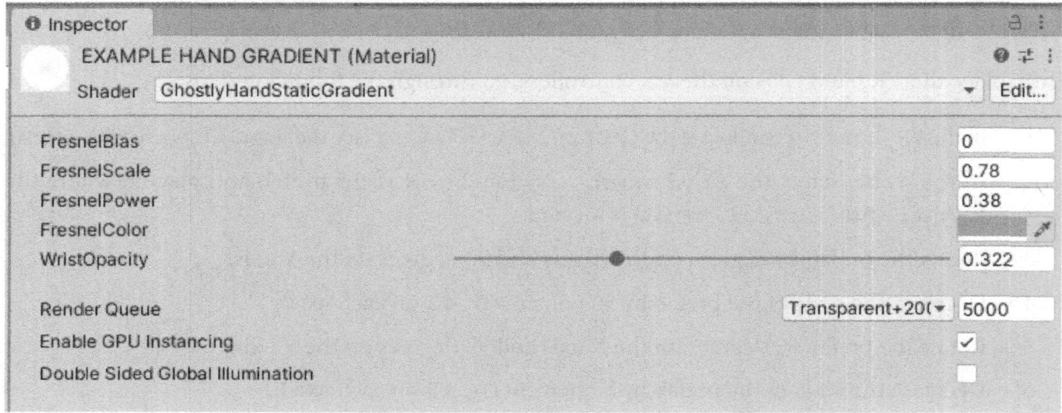

Figure 4.13 – Ghostly Shader settings

3. Apply the selected shader to the material of your hands by replacing the current material on the stylized hand with `Example Hand Gradient.`
4. Repeat *step 3* for the other hand.

Test your setup. Now you should be able to see your hands with the new ghostly Shader applied, while still maintaining all other interactions and functionality.

In the next section, we will change the VR objects we added interactable components to in *Chapter 3* to custom VR assets from the Unity Asset Store.

Replacing primitive VR objects with customs GOs

Replacing primitive 3D objects with custom 3D objects with more details from the asset store in VR scenes can greatly enhance the realism and immersion of the experience. Custom 3D objects with more details can add a sense of depth and realism to the environment, making it feel more like a real-world location. Additionally, custom 3D objects can be designed to have a more accurate and realistic look and feel, which can make it easier for the user to interact with and understand the objects in the scene. Overall, using custom 3D objects with more details can greatly improve the overall quality and realism of the VR experience.

Before we get started with adding our Asset Store assets, let's duplicate the `4_03_VRHands` scene from the last chapter and name it `4_04_CustomeVRObjects`.

To replace the primitive VR objects in our demo scene with more detailed objects, go through the following steps:

1. Go to the Unity Asset Store: `https://assetstore.unity.com/packages/3d/props/food/food-pack-free-demo-225294`.
2. Download the food object pack by going to **Food Pack | Free Demo**.
3. Import the downloaded assets into your project.
4. In the `Food Pack - Demo | Prefabs` folder, select the food objects you want to use in your scene.

   I chose **Coffee Cup**, **Ketchup Bottle**, **Peach**, and **Sake Cup**.
5. Change the material of the selected food objects to **Standard** to correct any issues with the materials.

Now, to replace the virtual objects on your table, go through the following steps:

1. Select the object you want to replace. The objects that are being replaced are a cylinder, capsule, sphere, and cube with a coffee cup, ketchup bottle, peach, and sake cup, respectively.
2. Place the new food object prefabs as children of the existing objects in **Hierarchy**.
3. Resize the custom prefab so that it fits within the bounds of the primitive object.
4. Hide the `Mesh Renderer` of the original parent GO so that only the new food objects are visible (*Figure 4.14*).

Figure 4.14 – Replacing the primitive prefab with a cup asset

5. Repeat *steps 6 and 7* for each object you wish to replace.
6. To add a gaze interaction, change the material of the food object when the player looks at it as we did in *Chapter 3* (*Figure 4.15*).
7. Change the material back to the original when the player's gaze leaves the object.
8. Test the scene to ensure everything works correctly.

Figure 4.15 – Primitive VR objects replaced with custom VR objects

These can be replaced with any other objects as per your requirements.

In the next section, we will design a demo room floor plan using Google Drawings, convert the plan into a 3D model using ProBuilder, and decorate it using Polybrush and custom assets from the Asset Store.

Creating a custom VR demo room with ProBuilder

In this section, we will be creating a VR demo room, starting from the ground up. We will begin by using Google Drawings to design the floor plan for our demo room, visualizing the layout and dimensions of the space. This floor plan will serve as the blueprint for our 3D model, which will be created using ProBuilder. ProBuilder is a powerful tool in Unity that allows us to create and modify 3D models quickly and easily. With ProBuilder, we will convert the floor plan into a fully realized 3D space, complete with walls, flooring, and ceilings.

Once the basic structure of the demo room is in place, we will then turn our attention to decorating the space. Using Polybrush and custom assets from the Unity Asset Store, we will add furniture, artwork, and other decorative elements to the room, giving it a unique and personalized feel. Polybrush allows us to paint and sculpt on 3D models, giving us complete control over the look and feel of our assets. With the combination of Polybrush and custom assets, we will have the ability to create a truly unique and immersive demo room, ready to showcase our VR projects.

In the next section, we will start our design process by creating a floor plan for our demo room using Google Drawings.

Designing a demo room floor plan with Google Drawings

We will now take a break from Unity and work in Google Drawings to create a floor plan for our 3D demo room. Designing a floor plan for a 3D room in Google Drawings is a good idea because it allows you to plan out the layout and dimensions of the room before creating it in 3D software. This allows you to make changes and adjustments to the layout more easily and quickly, as well as visualize the space in a clear and easy-to-understand manner. Additionally, using Google Drawings allows you to easily share and collaborate on the design with others, making it a great option for team projects. Using a floor plan can also help you ensure that the room is functional and efficient and that all necessary elements are included in the design. It also helps you to save time and avoid errors while modeling a 3D room. Overall, creating a floor plan in Google Drawings can help you to create a well-designed and functional 3D room.

To create a floor plan in Google Drawings, go through the following steps:

1. Go to Google Drawings: `https://docs.google.com/drawings`.
2. Next, open the demo room and focus on creating a floor plan.
3. Use the **Square** tool to draw the main room we have in our demo scene already.
4. Draw a large room that is connected to the main scene by a couple of hallways.
5. Draw two more small rooms on the side of the large room.
6. Group the different shapes together to create the hallways, large room, and small rooms (*Figure 4.16*).

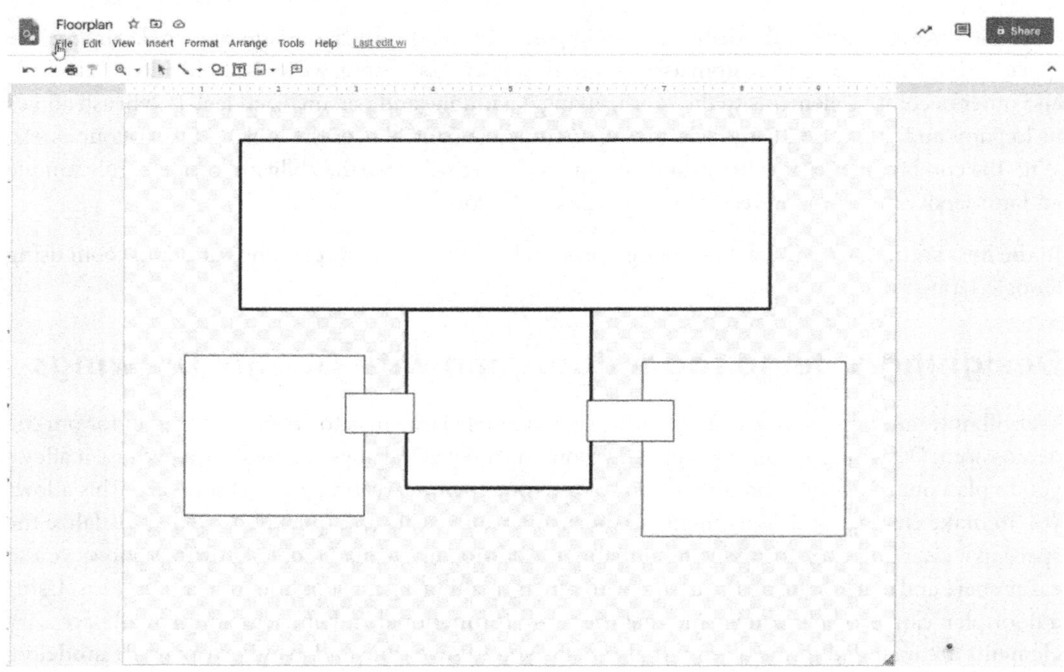

Figure 4.16 – Google Drawings floor plan

7. Download the floor plan as a JPEG and save it to a folder called `floor plan`.
8. Import the floor plan into Unity by going to the `Textures` folder, creating a new folder called `floor plan`, and dragging the `.jpg` texture into it.
9. In Unity, select the texture and change the import settings in **Inspector** to **Sprite 2D UI**.
10. Click **Apply** to apply the changes.

We can now use the imported floor plan texture as a guide to build out the scene, creating different rooms and hallways as shown in the floor plan.

In the next section, we will convert the 2D image into a 3D model using ProBuilder.

Converting the floor plan into a 3D room with ProBuilder

Now that we have our custom shapes and are able to replace different things with 3D objects from the asset store, it's time to beef up our demo scene by creating a custom container environment for us to navigate. We will do that using ProBuilder.

ProBuilder is a Unity extension that allows you to create and edit 3D geometry directly within the Unity Editor. It provides a set of tools to easily create and manipulate 3D shapes, such as spheres, cubes, and cylinders, as well as more complex meshes. ProBuilder also includes tools for editing and optimizing meshes, such as welding vertices and extruding faces. It allows you to create and edit 3D geometry in Unity without the need for external 3D modeling software, making it an efficient and powerful tool for prototyping and production. It also allows you to export your meshes to other 3D modeling software if needed.

To use ProBuilder in Unity, you will first need to download and install the ProBuilder extension from the Unity Asset Store. Once installed, you will be able to access ProBuilder's tools and features directly from the Unity Editor. Here are some basic steps to get started with ProBuilder:

1. Create a new ProBuilder object by going to the **GameObject** menu and selecting **3D Object** | **ProBuilder** |**[Shape]**, where **[Shape]** can be a cube, sphere, cylinder, and so on. A new GO will be created in the scene with the chosen shape.
2. Edit the object by selecting it in the scene and using ProBuilder's editing tools. These tools are located in the **ProBuilder** panel, which can be accessed by selecting **Window** | **ProBuilder**.
3. Optimize the object by using ProBuilder's tools for optimizing meshes, such as welding vertices and reducing the number of faces. These tools can be found in the **ProBuilder** panel under **Edit** | **Optimize**.
4. Apply materials to the object just like any other GO in Unity. You can drag and drop materials from the **Project** window onto the object in the scene, or you can assign them programmatically through scripting.
5. Export the object by using the **ProBuilder** | **Export** option in the **ProBuilder** panel. This will allow you to export the object to a variety of file formats, such as FBX or OBJ.

ProBuilder has many more features, such as UV mapping and texturing. Additionally, ProBuilder is integrated with Unity's workflow, so you can use it with other Unity tools and features, such as physics, lighting, and scripting. It's recommended to go through the ProBuilder documentation, tutorials, and examples to get familiar with all its features and how it can be used in different scenarios. To learn more about ProBuilder, visit `https://docs.unity3d.com/Packages/com.unity.probuilder@5.0/manual/index.html`.

Before we begin, let's duplicate the `4_04_CustomeVRObjects` scene from the last chapter and name it `4_05_DemoRoom`.

To convert the floor plan image into a 3D model using ProBuilder, go through the following steps:

1. Add your floor plan image to the `DemoRoom` scene and rotate it 90 degrees on the **X** axis so that when viewed from above, it is oriented correctly.
2. Position the image at the center of the scene and scale it so that it fits within a box (*Figure 4.17*).

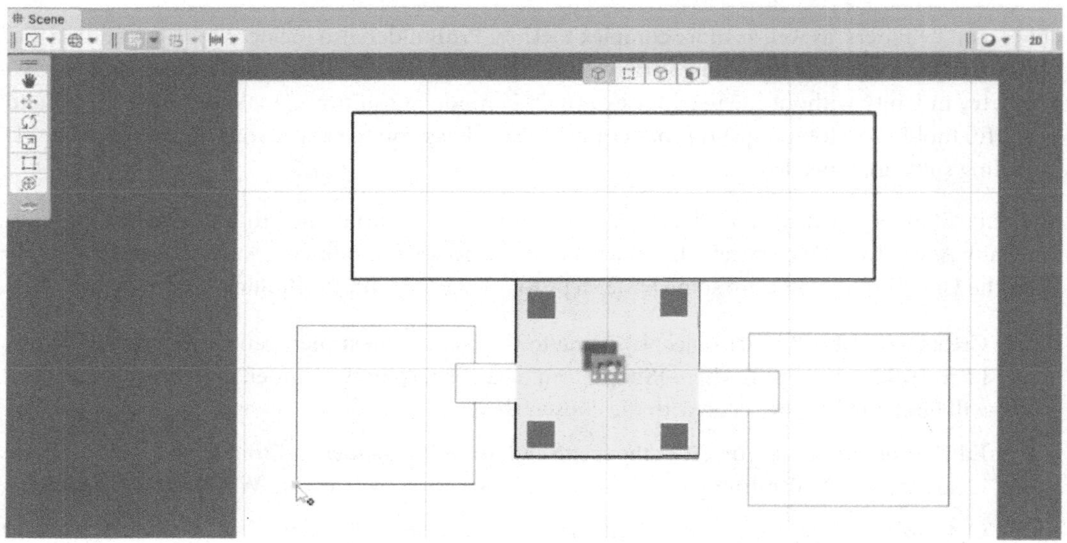

Figure 4.17 – Floor plan image aligned with demo room

3. Create a new parent object and name it `DemoRoom`.
4. Install the ProBuilder package from the Unity Registry.
5. In the **ProBuilder** window, select **New Poly Shape** and set the position to `(0,0,0)`.
6. Use the **New Poly Shape** tool to trace over the outline of your floor plan image, creating a new shape. Wherever you click, there will be a vertex point that will comprise a shape.
7. Place a vertex on the outside of every corner that you want for the overall demo room. Do not include points within the overall structure you want, just the outer-most points.
8. To close and complete the shape, click on the first vertex you made.
9. Use the **Poly Shape Tool | Extrusion** feature to create walls for your room by specifying the desired height as `4` and selecting the box for **Flipped Normals**.
10. Click **Quit Editing** to complete the demo room 3D model (*Figure 4.18*).

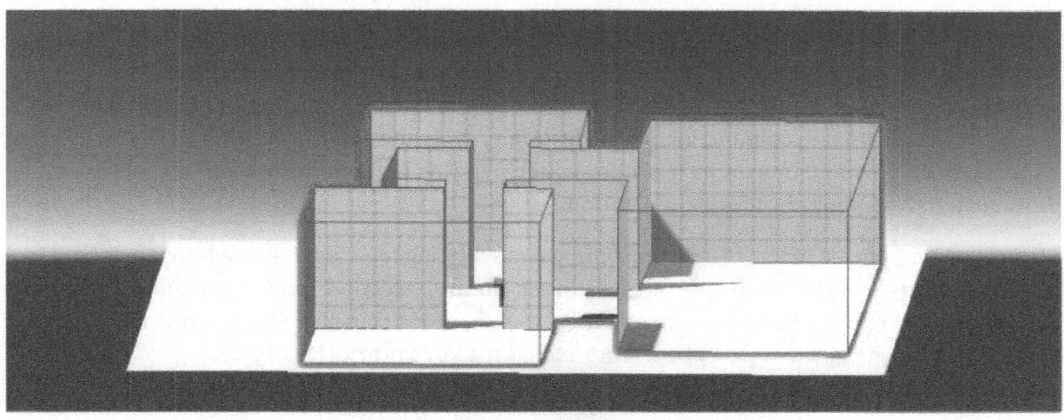

Figure 4.18 – Completing the extruded 3D room

11. Exit the ProBuilder editing mode and name the new shape `rendered room`.

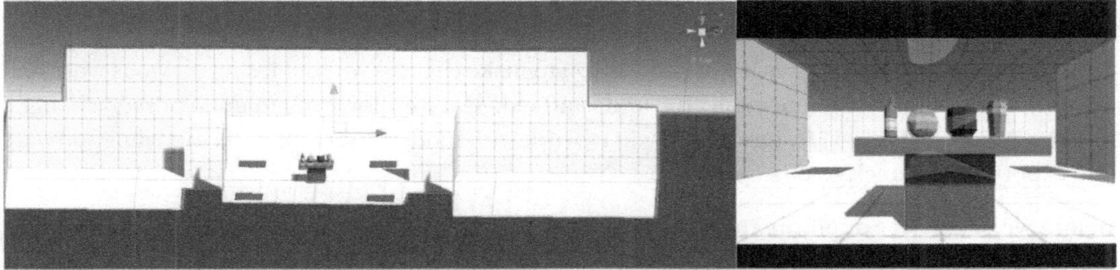

Figure 4.19 – Final Demo Room ProBuilder mesh

12. Add the `rendered room` object to the `DemoRoom` parent object and center the pivot point for extra room to move around in the scene.
13. Save your scene and test navigating through the different rooms.

In the next section, we will decorate the room with Polybrush.

Decorating the VR demo room with Polybrush and vertex painting

Our demo room is complete and it's time to decorate it. We will change the colors of the floor and walls to different materials we have already created and add some furniture by downloading it from the asset store.

Polybrush is a Unity extension that allows you to paint and sculpt 3D models directly within the Unity Editor. It provides a set of tools that make it easy to paint and sculpt textures, materials, and colors onto 3D models. It also allows you to edit the geometry of models, creating new shapes and forms. Polybrush can be used in conjunction with other Unity tools and extensions, such as ProBuilder and Unity's terrain system. Some of its features include painting and sculpting tools, geometry editing tools, material blending, and Unity integration.

The major components of Polybrush are painting and sculpting tools, geometry editing tools, material blending, Unity integration, brush settings, brush library, selection tools, layers, undo and redo, and import and export. To learn more about Polybrush, visit `https://docs.unity3d.com/Packages/com.unity.polybrush@1.1/manual/index.html`.

To use Polybrush, you need to download and install the Polybrush extension from the Unity Asset Store. Once installed, you can access Polybrush's tools and features through Unity's menu. You can use the painting and sculpting tools to add textures, materials, and colors to your models. The geometry editing tools can be used to sculpt, extrude, and smooth the shape of the mesh. The material blending feature allows you to blend multiple materials on the same mesh. You can also use the brush settings to fine-tune the brush to suit your needs and your project, and the brush library to use predefined brushes or create and save your own. The selection tools allow you to make precise changes to specific parts of the mesh, and the layers feature allows you to make changes without losing previous work and to work on specific areas of the mesh. The undo and redo feature allows you to undo or redo changes, and the import and export feature allows you to work with models from other 3D modeling software and export your models to other software.

Before we begin, let's duplicate the `4_05_DemoRoom` scene from *Chapter 3* and name it `4_06_DecoratedRoom`.

To decorate the room with Polybrush, go through the following steps:

1. Open the Package Manager and install the ProBuilder and Polybrush packages (*Figure 4.20*).

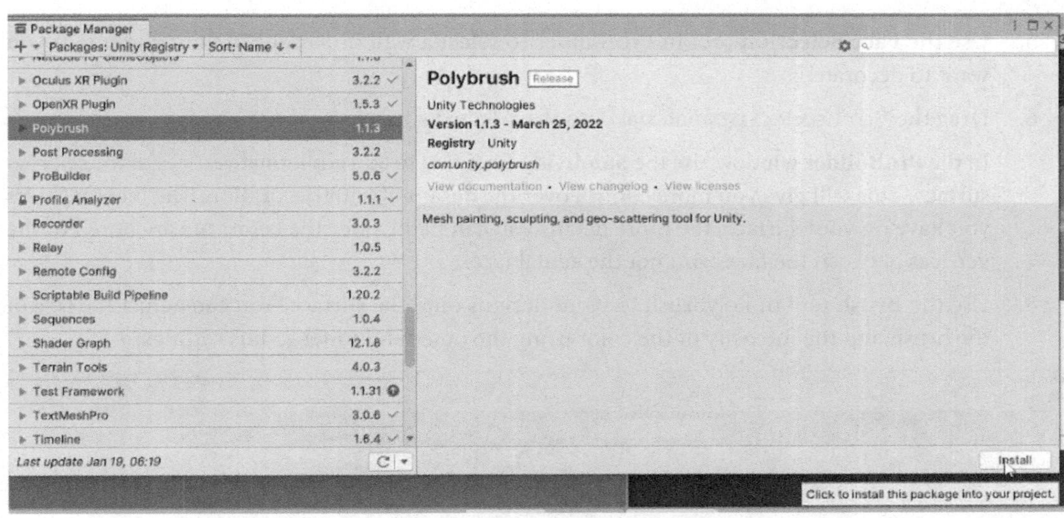

Figure 4.20 – Installing Polybrush

2. Once installed, open the ProBuilder window and create a basic room layout.
3. Next, open the Polybrush window and select the **Vertex Paint** tab.
4. Create a new material called `VertexPaint` and change the **Shader** to **Polybrush | Standard Vertex Color** (*Figure 4.21*).

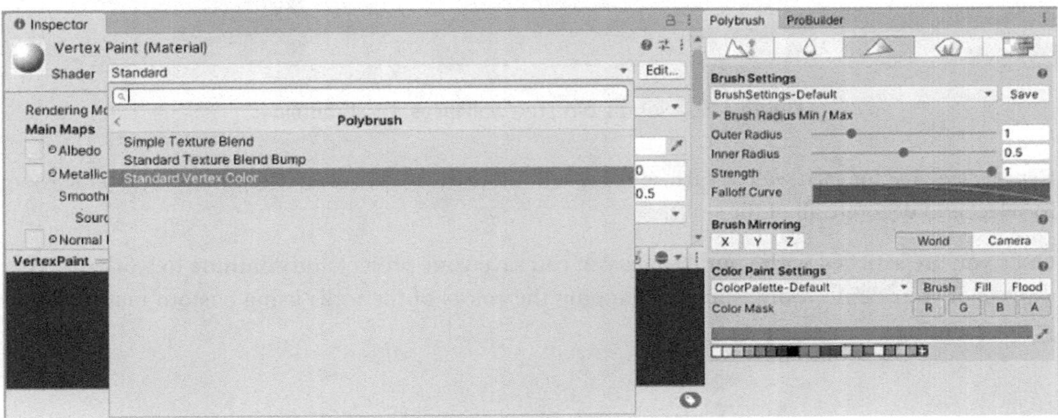

Figure 4.21 – Vertex Paint Material and Brush settings in Polybrush

5. Use the **Face Selection** tool in ProBuilder to select a wall or surface in your room that you want to decorate.
6. Drag the `VertexPaint` material onto the selected surface.
7. In the **ProBuilder** window, use the **Subdivide Face** tool to add additional vertices to the selected surface. This will give you more control over the design of your decoration. The more vertices you have on your surface, the more details you can paint since the colors are anchored to the vertices between the faces and not the actual faces.
8. Use the **Brush** tool in Polybrush to paint designs onto the surface. You can adjust the size of the brush and the intensity of the color using the outer and inner radius settings.

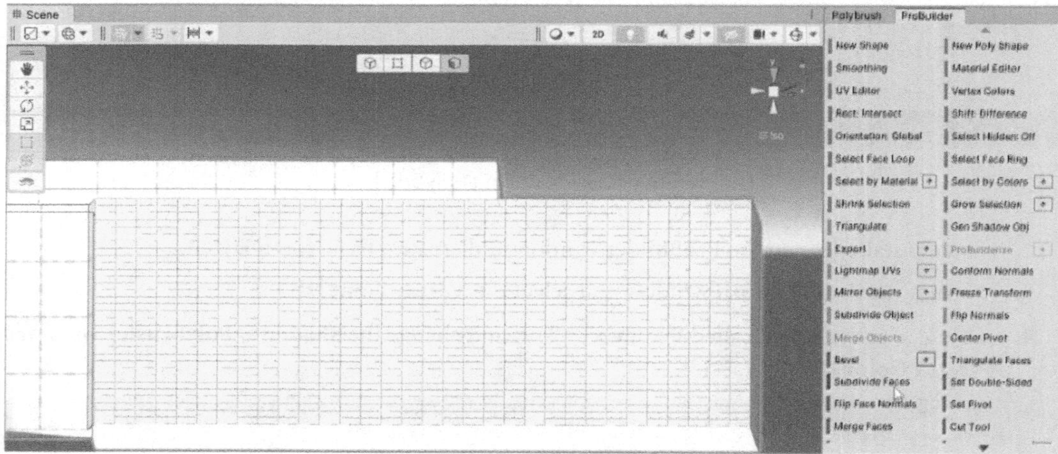

Figure 4.22 – Subdividing the wall faces with ProBuilder

Repeat *steps 5–8* for each wall or surface that you want to decorate. Feel free to rotate around the room to select and decorate all of the walls.

Once you are satisfied with your design, you can save your project and continue to work on other aspects of your demo room, such as changing the colors of the walls using custom materials and vertex painting.

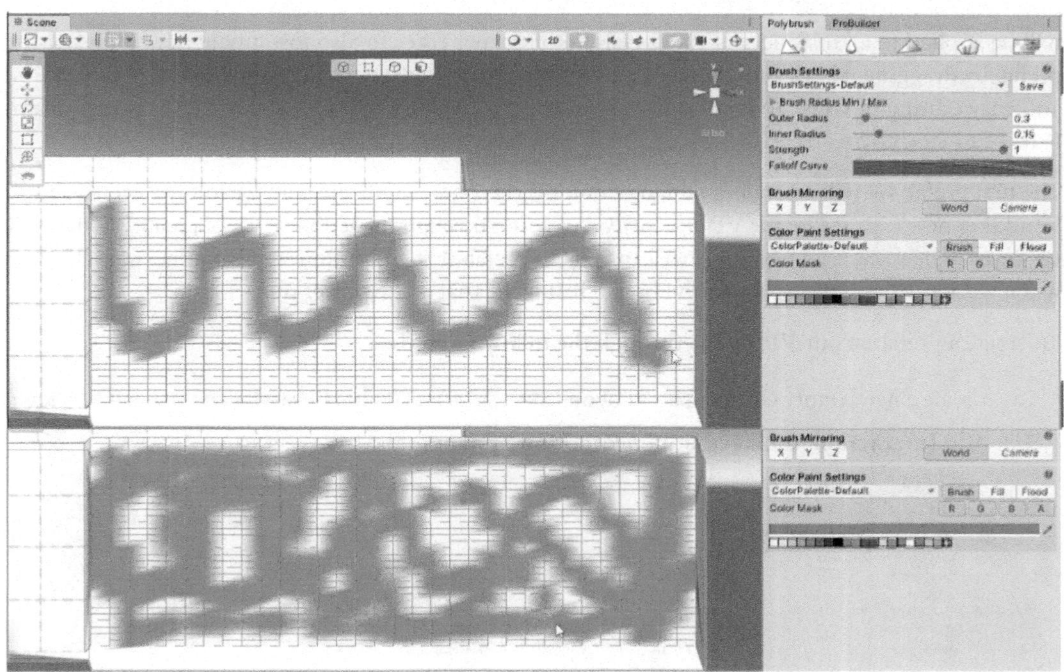

Figure 4.23 – Vertex painting wall faces using Polybrush

If you want to decorate `DemoRoom` with custom assets, such as furniture, you can do that by following the steps we used for replacing the VR objects in the previous sections of this chapter. A good asset pack to use is **VOXEL Furniture FREE**: `https://assetstore.unity.com/packages/3d/props/furniture/voxel-furniture-free-170365`.

In the next section, we will create prefabs of our demo room and assets so that we can reuse them in our scene while also being able to modify them procedurally across our project.

Creating prefabs with our GOs

We have our different GOs and scenes, and all these things work great within the scene. But what if we wanted to have a scene that has objects that we can modify, and then it could update on all the other scenes You'll notice that every time we make a new project, we duplicate our scene, and then anything that happens in the scene that we worked on now won't work on the other scenes. So, a way to create instances of objects that update across scenes is through the use of prefabs.

Prefabs in Unity are preconfigured GOs that can be reused multiple times in a scene or across multiple scenes. They are like templates or blueprints of GO and can contain any combination of components, such as scripts, meshes, and materials. To create a prefab, you can select a GO in a scene, drag it into the **Project** window, give it a name, and make changes to it in the **Inspector** window. These changes will be applied to all instances of the prefab in the scene. You can also instantiate new copies of the prefab by dragging it back into the scene. Using prefabs allows reusability, consistency, organization, and easy editing of GOs. To learn more about prefabs, visit `https://docs.unity3d.com/Manual/Prefabs.html`.

The first prefab we will create is a prefab of our VR rig. As we continue with various projects, we will be adding new features to our VR rig. Instead of going through the tedious task of creating a new VR rig for each new scene and exercise, we can create a prefab that will automatically update in each scene when we apply the settings across the prefab instance. That is the power of prefabs!

To create a prefab of our VR rig, go through the following steps:

1. Create a new, empty GO as a parent of our `XR Origin` GO in **Hierarchy** and name it `VR Rig`.
2. Add **Interaction Manager** and **Locomotion System** to the `VR Rig` GO.

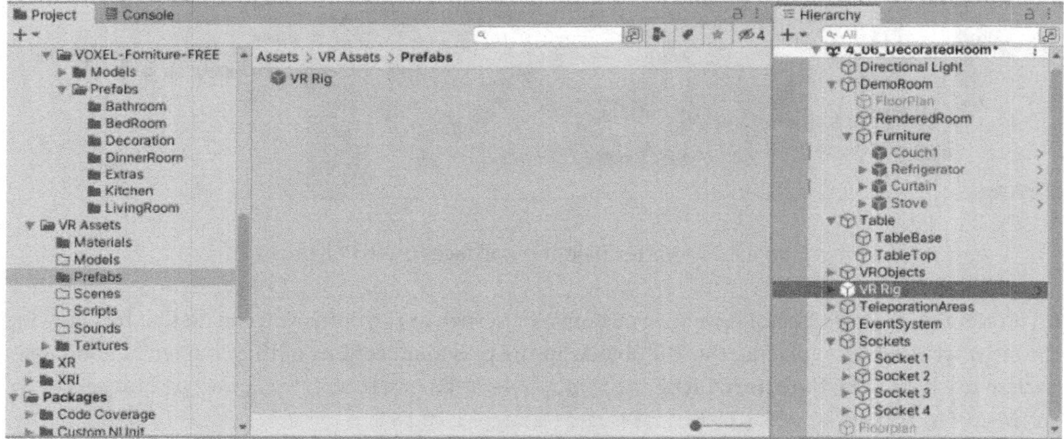

Figure 4.24 – Prefab of our VR Rig

3. Drag and drop the `VR Rig` GO into the `Prefabs` folder in the **Project** tab.
4. Repeat *steps 1–3* for other objects in your project that you want to use as prefabs, such as `Teleportation Area` and `XR Socket Interactor`.
5. Turn your entire demo room into a prefab by dragging and dropping all objects into the `Prefabs` folder.

In the next part of this exercise, we will learn about how we can use prefab variants to have a variation of the same object that updates automatically in our project.

Prefab variants are variations of a prefab that can be used to create different versions of a prefab while still maintaining a link to the original prefab. This means changes can be made to all variations at once. To create a prefab variant, you can create a prefab first and then right-click on it in the **Project** window and select **Create Prefab Variant**. This will create a new prefab with a link to the original prefab, and changes made to it will not affect the original prefab. We will utilize prefab variants in future chapters as we progress through projects. To learn more about prefab variants, visit `https://docs.unity3d.com/Manual/PrefabVariants.html`.

We can create prefab variants of our teleportation areas because we have a lot of them in our scene and sometimes want to give them different features, such as colors, without changing all the teleportation area prefabs across the project.

Before we begin, instead of duplicating a scene like we normally do, let's create an empty scene and name it `4_07_PrefabDemoRoom`.

To create a prefab variant of our teleportation area, go through the following steps:

1. In the new scene, drag and drop the prefab `VR Rig demo room` from our `Prefabs` folder.
2. Add an **Event System** to the scene and enable the new input system in **Inspector** to remove the error dialog box that appears in the **Event System** component in **Inspector**.
3. Add a `Teleportation` prefab to our demo scene and place it in a location.
4. Change the color of the teleportation area plane to the `Red_Emissive` material or another material from our materials library.
5. Drag that prefab from **Hierarchy** to the `Prefab` folder.
6. A dialog box will appear. Select **Prefab Variant**.
7. Repeat *step 5 and 6* for any additional prefab variants.

We can now create prefabs with different visual features that function exactly the same to give our scene some variation. Prefab variants are a great way to build on our understanding of GOs, materials, and shaders to enhance our VR experiences easily.

In the next section, we will learn how we can use folders in the **Project** tab to organize all the assets in our project.

Organizing project assets with folders in the Project tab

In Unity, the **Project** tab is where you can organize and access all of the assets in your project. One way to keep your project organized is to use folders to group related assets together. To create a new folder, right-click in the **Project** tab and select **Create | Folder**. You can then name the folder and drag and drop assets into it. You can also create subfolders within a folder by right-clicking on the parent folder and selecting **Create | Folder**. This allows you to create a hierarchical structure for organizing your assets. Additionally, you can also search for assets within a specific folder by clicking on the folder and using the search bar at the top of the **Project** tab. Keep in mind that changes made to the folders in the **Project** tab will only affect the organization of the assets in the editor and will not affect the file structure on your computer.

To organize the assets in your project with folders, go through the following steps:

1. Start by creating a new folder for your assets. You can name it `VR Assets` or something similar.

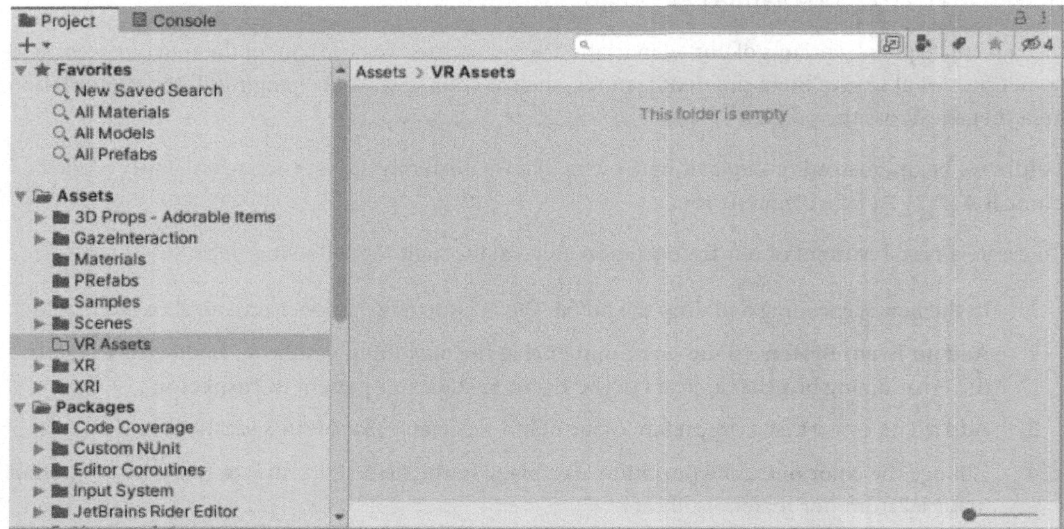

Figure 4.25 – Empty VR Assets parent folder

2. Inside the `VR Assets` folder, create subfolders for different types of assets you plan to use, such as materials, prefabs, scripts, models, textures, sounds, and scenes.
3. As you acquire new assets, put them in the appropriate subfolder. For example, if you download a new 3D model, put it in the `models` subfolder.
4. If you have existing assets that are not organized, go through them and move them to the appropriate subfolders.
5. As you work on your project, you may need to create additional subfolders to keep things organized. For example, if you have a lot of different scenes, you may want to create a subfolder within the `Scenes` folder to store them all.
6. To find specific assets quickly, you can use the search bar to narrow down your options.

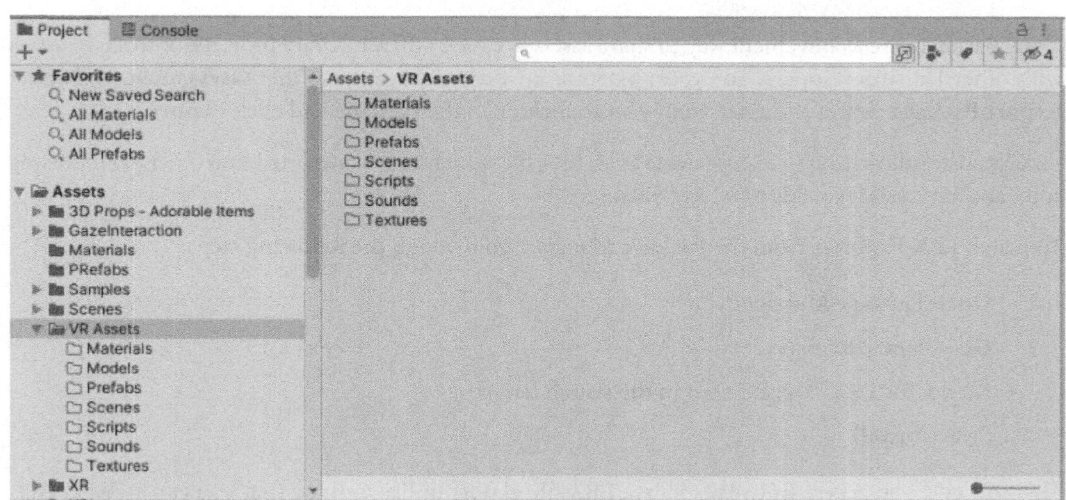

Figure 4.26 – Final folder structure for file organization

Remember, organization is key to staying efficient and being able to find the assets you need quickly.

7. Lastly, consider adding other useful folders, such as an `Animation` folder.

Now that we have a way to organize our folders, try to use it to optimize your workflow and limit the amount of bloat in your project. This will be useful if you want to conserve space on your computer hard drive.

In the next section, we will export project assets as Unity packages and FBX files.

Exporting project assets with Unity packages and FBX Export

Exporting assets from Unity can be done in multiple ways, such as exporting as a file type (`FBX`, `OBJ`, or `COLLADA`) that can be imported into other 3D modeling software, creating and exporting Unity packages that can be used in other Unity projects, creating and exporting asset bundles for downloadable content, exporting the project as a standalone executable or web player through **Build Settings**, using plugins for specific platforms, and using cloud services such as Google Cloud Platform, AWS, and Microsoft Azure. The available options may vary depending on the Unity version and platform being used. Always test exported assets to ensure their proper functioning on the destination software or platform.

In Unity, there are several ways to export project assets, including Unity packages and FBX export.

Unity packages are a convenient way to share assets between different Unity projects, or to share assets with other Unity developers. To export assets as a Unity package, go to the **Assets** menu and select **Export Package**. Select the assets you want to include in the package and click **Export**.

FBX Exporter allows you to export assets as an FBX file, which can be imported into other 3D modeling software, such as Maya, 3ds Max, and Blender.

To install FBX Exporter from the Package Manager, go through the following steps:

1. Go to **Package Manager**.
2. Go to **Unity Registry**.
3. Search for `FBX Exporter` in the search bar.
4. Select **Install**.

This will give you access to Unity's native FBX file export utility tools so that you can convert GOs into files that can be used in other programs.

To export assets as an FBX file, select the assets in the **Assets** tab, go to the **Assets** menu, and select **Export Selected**. Choose the FBX file format and select the destination for the exported file.

It's important to note that the export options available may depend on the version of Unity you are using and the platform you are targeting. Additionally, you should always test the exported assets to ensure that they work correctly in the destination software or platform.

To export a custom Unity package, go through the following steps:

1. Right-click on the asset or scene you want to export.
2. Select **Export Package**.
3. Select the dependencies of the asset or scene you want to export.
4. Click **Export** and save the package with a name (e.g., `DemoRoom`).

The exported package will be in the form of a Unity package that can be dragged and dropped into another project or uploaded to an app store. Next, we will use the FBX Exporter utility from the Unity Registry to export our `DemoRoom` GO as an FBX so we can edit it in another program, such as Blender or Cinema 4D.

To export a `.fbx` file using the FBX Exporter utility, go through the following steps:

1. Download and install the FBX Exporter utility package from the Unity Package Manager.

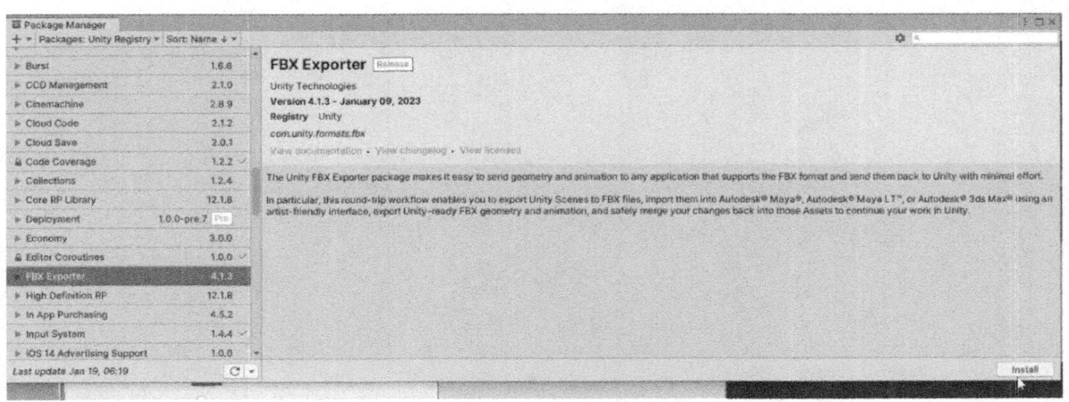

Figure 4.27 – Installing FBX Exporter

2. Right-click on the asset or scene you want to export.
3. Select **Convert to FBX**.
4. Select the desired settings (the default settings should suffice) and click **Convert**.

The exported asset will be in the form of an FBX file and can be imported into other programs, such as Autodesk Maya, 3ds Max, or Blender, for further modifications.

Both of these methods work well together and can be used to export assets in Unity. With these methods, you can easily move assets from one project to another or export them for use in other programs.

That concludes this chapter.

Summary

This chapter has provided a comprehensive overview of GOs and their crucial role in enhancing the visual quality of VR experiences in Unity. Our understanding of custom materials, creating custom 3D shapes and environments using ProBuilder and Polybrush, and proper asset management should by now have been reinforced through hands-on projects and practical applications. You should now be able to use these techniques to create a customized grid, replace VR hands with custom game objects, and design a demo room using Google Drawings, ProBuilder, and Polybrush.

We are well equipped to move forward and develop a more robust demo scene by incorporating animation and physics in *Chapter 5*.

5
Implementing Animation – Physics and Colliders

VR is an immersive experience that requires realistic and interactive elements to truly captivate its audience. To create these interactive experiences in Unity, it's essential to have a strong understanding of animation, physics, and colliders. This is the focus of this chapter.

In this chapter, we will dive into the basics of animation in Unity, including animation clips and creating animation clips from keyframes in Unity Timeline. We will learn how to utilize the physics system to complement our animation and create believable interactions in VR. We will also explore the use of **colliders** and **Rigidbodies** to give our animations a more realistic look and feel. Ultimately, we will explore ways to make our VR rig and demo scene more representative of the real world. One thing to note is that Unity is a powerful tool that can utilize animations created in other programs, such as Blender and Maya, to provide more detailed and complex animations for your VR projects. In the *Downloading animations from Mixamo* section in *Chapter 13*, we will explore how to import external animation files to be used in a VR animation project.

By the end of this chapter, readers will have learned how to create an animation clip, use the physics system to simulate and animate objects, create triggers for enhanced interactions, and record animations and interactions using the Unity Recorder.

Some of the projects we will cover include adding physics using Rigidbody, adding colliders for object and environment interactions, creating a physically based VR rig, creating an animation clip for an object, adding animations to objects with the timeline, and triggering animations with **gaze** and **Raycast**.

Overall, this chapter will provide readers with the essential skills to create immersive VR experiences with animation, physics, and colliders in Unity. With a solid foundation in these areas, the possibilities for creating unique and engaging VR experiences are endless.

In this chapter, we will cover the following projects:

- Adding physics using Rigidbody components
- Adding colliders for physics interactions
- Adding accurate human body physics to the VR rig
- Creating an animation clip for GOs
- Adding animations to objects with the timeline
- Creating animation clips from timeline keyframes
- Triggering animations with Gaze and Raycast components

Technical requirements

The complete source code for this chapter can be found at `https://github.com/PacktPublishing/Enhancing-Virtual-Reality-Experiences-with-Unity-2022/tree/main/EnhancingVRExperiencesFullProject/Assets/_VRProjectAssets/Scenes/Chapter_5`.

Introducing Unity's physics system

In this chapter, we're going to look at using Unity's physics system and implementing that into the animation and the components that we can add to our VR objects and our VR rig to give it more of a realistic experience and feeling. The first two things we're going to look at are two components. One is a Rigidbody and another is a collider. These are crucial for allowing us to add physics to different game objects. We've seen a little bit of that in the previous chapters that we added colliders to with our 3D objects, but now we will be adding them to the VR rig and objects.

Using the physics and animation systems in Unity can help you add realism and immersion to your VR projects. Here are some ways to use these systems in your VR projects:

- **Rigidbodies and colliders**: Unity's physics engine allows you to add physics-based interactions to your VR objects by using Rigidbodies and colliders. You can attach Rigidbodies to objects to make them affected by gravity and other forces, and you can attach colliders to objects to define their physical shape and create collisions. Having too many Rigidbodies in your scene comes at the price of impacting performance. This can impact low-end devices the most.
- **Physics materials**: You can use physics materials to define the properties of an object's surface, such as friction and bounciness. This can be used to create realistic interactions between objects in your VR scene. Unlike regular materials where you can apply it to `Mesh Renderer` components on GOs, physical materials can only be applied to `collider` components on GOs.

- **Raycasting**: Unity's physics engine also allows you to use Raycasting to detect whether there is an intersection point between a line (or "ray") from the user's controllers and the collider containing objects in the scene. This is useful for creating interactions such as grabbing and throwing objects in your VR scene.
- **Animation system**: Unity's animation system allows you to create animations for your VR objects and characters. You can use the **Animation** window to create and edit animations and use scripting to control animation playback and blending. Unity's animation system also supports animation blending, which allows for smooth transitions between different animations.

Unity's built-in physics and animation systems are also compatible with VR development. You can use Unity's physics engine to create realistic interactions between objects in your VR scene, and you can use Unity's animation system to create animations for your VR objects and characters.

What is a Rigidbody component?

In Unity, a Rigidbody, as shown in *Figure 5.1*, is a component that allows a GO to be affected by physics simulations such as gravity, forces, and collisions. They can also affect other GOs with colliders and Rigidbodies during physics simulations, such as pushing and knocking over objects.

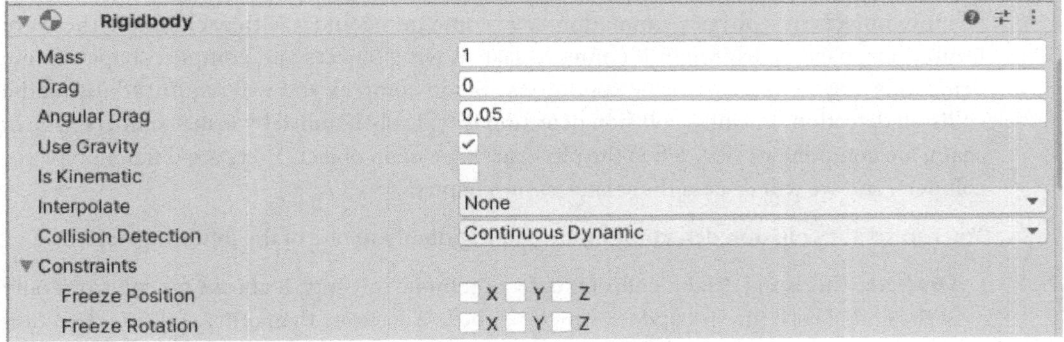

Figure 5.1 – Rigidbody component

A Rigidbody has the following main features:

- **Mass**: You can set the mass of a Rigidbody, which determines how it behaves in response to forces and collisions. A heavier object will have more inertia and be harder to move. We will want to set this to values in kilograms that simulate the real world.
- **Dynamics** (`isKinematic`): A Rigidbody can be set to be dynamic or kinematic, and this determines how it interacts with other Rigidbodies and forces. Dynamic Rigidbodies are affected by physics simulations, while kinematic Rigidbodies are not. When `isKinematic` is enabled, the GO with the Rigidbody will not be affected by forces or collisions from other GOs.

- **Interpolation**: You can use interpolation to smooth the motion of a Rigidbody over time, which can reduce jitter and improve the overall look of the physics simulation.

  In Unity, you can set the interpolation mode of a Rigidbody to one of the following options:

  - **Interpolate**: This option interpolates the motion of the Rigidbody between physics updates, which can help to smooth out jittery motion
  - **Extrapolate**: This option extrapolates the motion of the Rigidbody between physics updates, which can be useful when the physics engine is running at a lower frame rate than the rendering engine
  - **None**: This option disables interpolation, which can be useful when you want to have complete control over the motion of the Rigidbody using scripting

  Interpolation is the process of smoothing the motion of a Rigidbody over time. This can help to reduce jitter and improve the overall look of the physics simulation. When choosing which interpolation mode to use, you should consider the requirements of your project and the performance of your game.

- **Collision Detection**: You can use colliders to define the physical shape of a Rigidbody and create collisions between objects. Collision detection is the process of determining when two or more objects in a physics simulation have come into contact with each other. There are limitations, particularly when it comes to fast-moving objects and complex shapes. Some detections may not register if the conditions are too complex and will require adjusting the collision detection. In Unity, collision detection is typically handled by using colliders, which, again, are components that define the physical shape of an object. There are different types of colliders, and we will discuss these later in the chapter.

  You can set the **collision detection mode** of a Rigidbody to one of the following options:

  - **Discrete**: This is the default collision detection mode in Unity. It checks for collisions only at the end of each physics update, which can be less accurate than other collision detection modes but can be more efficient in terms of performance.
  - **Continuous**: This collision detection mode checks for collisions continuously during the physics update, which can be more accurate than discrete collision detection but can also be more computationally expensive. This mode is recommended when using fast-moving objects or objects with high-frequency motion.
  - **Continuous Dynamic**: This collision detection mode is a combination of the Discrete and Continuous modes. It's more accurate than Discrete mode and more efficient than Continuous mode. It's specially designed for objects that are both fast-moving and have a high-frequency motion.

  Collision detection is used in a variety of situations in a physics simulation, such as detecting when a player's character has come into contact with a solid object in the game world, detecting when a projectile has hit a target, or detecting when two objects have come into contact with each other.

- **Constraints**: You can use constraints to limit the movement of a Rigidbody in certain directions. For example, you can use a constraint to prevent an object from rotating around a specific axis as well as the position of the GO:
  - **Freeze Position**: You can restrict the GO from altering the position based on physics interactions.
  - **Freeze Rotation**: You can restrict the GO from rotating on the *X*, *Y*, or *Z* axis. This is great for stopping unnecessary rotational movement in response to physics interactions with slopes and gravity.

This setting can really help create physically based experiences in VR. Often, they are crucial in making believable interactions that follow the laws of physics in a way that is assumed and expected by the user. When you throw an object, you expect it to fall down as it goes in the direction you throw it. The foundational principles of force and gravity will stop the object from floating in the air or floating away and ultimately meet our expectations. Our job as developers is to use tools such as Unity that can handle all those complex calculations so that we can utilize them in the experiences we aim to create.

Now that we have a deeper understanding of Rigidbodies, let's create a physically based VR rig by adding a Rigidbody to it.

Adding physics using Rigidbodies

In this subsection, we will be discussing the steps to add physics to our VR rig in Unity. With the help of Unity's physics system, we will be creating opportunities for different interactions and making the VR experience more immersive. Adding physics to the VR rig by way of a Rigidbody can significantly impact the user's experience, and it is important to be aware of that moving forward. Physics simulations can cause unexpected movements that may make the user feel uncomfortable. It's important to test the rig regularly to minimize undesirable effects and plan for modifications and alternatives if issues were to arise.

We first need to set up a fresh demo scene using the prefabs we created in *Chapter 4*. To recap, we created prefabs for our VR rig, demo room, teleportation areas, and socket interactors. In this section, we will utilize the `DemoRoom` prefab to test our physics simulations on our VR rig.

To set up our new demo scene with the prefabs we created earlier, take the following steps:

1. Start with a new scene and name it `5_01_RigidbodyAndCollider`.
2. From the `Prefabs` folder we made in *Chapter 4*, add a `DemoRoom` prefab.
3. Add a `VR Rig` prefab to a location in the `DemoRoom`.
4. Delete the main camera, as we only need one camera located on the `VR Rig`.
5. Add an `Event System` GO (*right-click* | **UI** | **Event System**).
6. In the `Event System` GO, click **Replace with InputSystemUIModule**.

Now that we have our demo scene created, we can now add the Rigidbody component to our VR rig to apply gravity, mass, drag, and velocity to our virtual body.

To add a Rigidbody component to our VR rig, take the following steps:

1. In the VR Rig prefab in our scene, select the XR Origin GO.
2. Add a Rigidbody component to the XR Origin.
3. In the **Freeze Rotation** section of the Rigidbody component, select **X**, **Y**, and **Z** to freeze all rotation. We handle the rotations using our VR controllers and headset, so enabling these will lead us to being knocked over by objects that are falling to the side when the ground is not level. We will modify the values of the Rigidbody later.
4. Move the camera up to 0.06 units on the **Y** axis.
5. Save the scene.

With these steps, you have added a Rigidbody and collider component to your VR rig in Unity. This will help you create realistic interactions and enhance the VR experience for your users.

Next, we will add a collider to our VR rig to simulate interactions that restrict us from going through objects and affecting them when we touch them.

Introducing collider components

In Unity, a collider is a component that defines the physical shape of an object and is used to detect collisions between objects in a physics simulation. This does not affect the appearance of the GO because that is determined by the MeshRenderer component. Colliders are usually attached to GOs that have a Rigidbody component, which allows them to be affected by physics simulations such as gravity, forces, and collisions.

When two colliders with Rigidbodies come into contact with each other, the Unity physics engine will calculate the collision and apply the appropriate forces to the involved Rigidbodies. This process is called **collision resolution**. The physics engine uses the properties of the colliders, such as mass and collision material, to determine how the objects should react to the collision.

There are different types of colliders in Unity, each suited for different shapes of objects:

- **Box collider**: A box-shaped collider is defined by its center and size. This type of collider is useful for creating collisions with objects that have a rectangular shape.
- **Sphere collider**: A sphere-shaped collider is defined by its center and radius. This type of collider is useful for creating collisions with objects that have a round shape.
- **Capsule collider**: A capsule-shaped collider is defined by its center, radius, and height. This type of collider is useful for creating collisions with objects that have a cylindrical shape.

- **Mesh collider**: This collider takes the shape of a 3D model. This type of collider is useful for creating collisions with objects that have a complex shape. Compared to the other collider types, this has the most impact on performance because of how complex the object's shape can be.
- **Terrain Collider**: This collider is used to represent terrains and landscapes; it can be used to create collisions with the terrain GOs and objects that interact with it using the Unity terrain system. This is common for large environments.

We should now be familiar with the importance of colliders in Unity. We can now add one to our VR rig. I will show you an easy way to add a collider that gives you the exact dimensions for simulating a human body in VR.

Adding colliders for interactions

In this section, we will add a capsule collider to our VR rig to complete our physically based VR rig.

To add a capsule collider to our VR Rig, take the following steps:

1. Add a new `Capsule` 3D object as a child of our `XR Origin` GO.
2. Zero out the position of the capsule so that it is in the center of the VR rig.
3. Copy the `Capsule Collider` component from the `Capsule` GO (*Figure 5.2*) to the `XR Origin` GO.

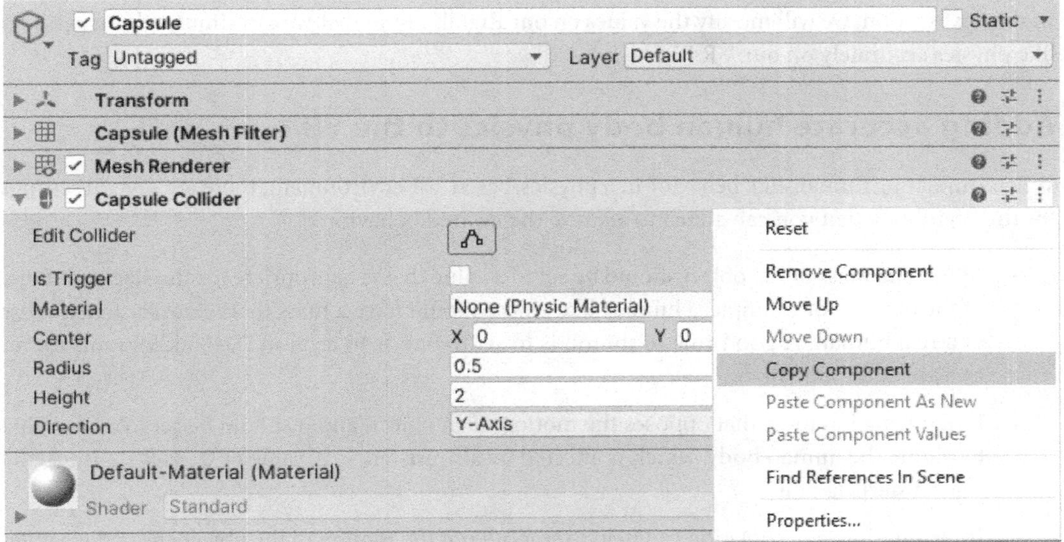

Figure 5.2 – Capsule Collider component

4. Delete the capsule.

You now have a capsule collider on your VR rig. Since the Unity standard units for the 3D capsule are two meters tall by one meter wide, we can modify the collider dimensions (**Edit Collider**) to fit our desired body height and width that our VR rig represents.

The testing of the VR rig in Unity's play mode will confirm that the added physics components are working as expected. They will prevent the VR rig from going through walls or objects. This shows that the implementation of physics in the VR rig has been successful.

We can now create a prefab of our physics-based VR rig for future use as we did with the original VR rig and the demo room. This version of the VR rig will be a prefab variant of the original and not a completely new prefab.

To create a prefab variant of our physics-based VR rig, take the following steps:

1. Go to the `VR Rig` prefab in **Inspector** and rename it `VR Rig Physics Variant`.
2. Navigate to the `prefab` folder in the **Project** tab where the other prefabs we made reside.
3. Drag the `VR Rig Physics Variant` prefab into the `Prefabs` folder.
4. Click **Prefab Variant** to create a variant of the original prefab. Do not click **Original Prefab** because it will lose its previous connections to the original prefab that this is a variant of.

With these steps, you have added physics to your VR rig in Unity and created a prefab variant of it. This will allow you to keep the original VR rig intact and have a separate version for physics-based interactions.

In the next section, we will modify the values on our Rigidbody so that we can simulate human body-like physics accurately on our VR Rig.

Adding accurate human body physics to the VR rig

When simulating human-like behavior in a physics-based VR environment, there are several settings for the Rigidbody that you can adjust to achieve the desired behavior:

- **Mass**: The mass of the object should be set to a value that is appropriate for the size and shape of the object. For example, a human-like object should have a mass that is similar to the mass of a real human. A good rule of thumb is to set the mass to around 70–85 kilograms for an average adult human.
- **Drag**: Drag is a force that opposes the motion of an object, and it should be set to a low value to mimic the human body, which is affected by air resistance. A value of `0.1-0.2` is usually a good starting point.
- **Interpolation**: Interpolation can help to smooth out the motion of the object and reduce jitter. Interpolation should be set to **Interpolate** or **Extrapolate**.

- **Collision Detection**: Collision detection should be set to **Continuous** or **Continuous Dynamic**. These modes check for collisions more frequently, which can help to ensure that collisions are detected accurately.
- **Angular Drag**: This is a force that opposes the rotation of an object and it should be set to a low value. A value of `0.05-0.1` is usually a good starting point.

It's important to note that the best settings for simulating human-like behavior in a physics-based VR environment will depend on the specific requirements of your project. The settings mentioned previously are a good starting point, but you may need to adjust them based on the specific behavior you are trying to achieve. You may also need to tweak other settings such as the size, shape, and properties of the collider component to achieve the desired behavior.

To simulate real-world physics on our VR rig, take the following steps:

1. Find the `Rigidbody` component on our `XR Origin` GO.
2. Set **Mass** to `75` kilograms.
3. Set **Drag** to `0.15`.
4. Set **Angular Drag** to `0.05`.
5. Set **Interpolation** to **Interpolate**.
6. Set **Collision Detection** to **Continuous Dynamic**.
7. For the `Capsule Collider`, you can change the height of the collider to match your desired height in meters.
8. If you change the height of your `Capsule Collider`, change the height of the main camera in your VR rig so that it is at an accurate eye level for your VR rig.

We want to simulate real-world physics accurately by using relevant values that accurately reflect the world we live in. This allows us to create believable interactions and experiences that we can push to the edge of reality.

Using colliders as barriers

In Unity, colliders can be used to create barriers that prevent objects from passing through them. This can be useful for creating walls, floors, and other types of obstacles in your VR projects.

> **Note**
>
> While colliders can establish barriers, users can still move through them in a VR setting unless their VR rig or controllers incorporate colliders and Rigidbodies. This is due to the VR hardware's direct movement tracking, which Unity's physics engine doesn't influence.

Here's an example of how to add colliders as barriers in Unity:

1. **Create a GO**: Create a new GO in your scene that will serve as the barrier. This could be a simple cube or any other shape that you like.
2. **Add a collider component**: Add a collider component to the GO. There are different types of colliders in Unity, such as the box collider, sphere collider, and capsule collider. Each type of collider is suited for different shapes of objects.
3. **Configure the collider**: Configure the collider component by adjusting its size and position to match the shape of the barrier. You can also set the collider's material to define the collision behavior.
4. **Test the barrier**: Test the barrier by moving other objects in the scene and observing whether they collide with the barrier as expected.
5. **Tweak the settings**: If necessary, tweak the collider's settings, such as the size, position, and material, to ensure that the barrier behaves as expected.

It's important to note that in order for the collision to work, the object that is colliding with the barrier should have a `Rigidbody` component. Otherwise, the collider will be seen as a trigger and won't stop the object from passing through.

If you look at the `DemoRoom` prefab, you will notice that the `RenderedRoom` GO we created already has a mesh collider on it. Most GOs you create and add to your scene will have the accurate colliders on them by default. If you want to have the ability to go through them (which is what we will explore more in *Chapter 8*), you can select `isTrigger`. For now, we will work with the fact that we have a demo scene that we can use with the physics system. We can now move on to applying animations to the `DemoRoom` to create more engaging and dynamic interactions.

Introducing Unity's animation system

The animation system in Unity is a set of tools and components that allow you to create and control animated characters and objects in your game or application. The system is based on the concept of animation clips, which are collections of keyframe data that define the positions, rotations, and other properties of objects over time.

There are several key components of the animation system in Unity:

- **The Animation window**: This is the main interface for creating, editing, and previewing animation clips. It allows you to create keyframes, adjust the timing of animations, and preview the animations in real time.
- **The Animator component**: This component is used to control the playback of animations and blend multiple animations together. It also allows you to create complex animation behaviors using state machines and transition conditions.

- **The Animation component**: This component is used to play back animation clips on GOs. It allows you to control the playback speed, looping, and other properties of the animation.
- **The Animation event**: This is a feature that allows you to trigger events in your game or application at specific points in an animation using C# scripting.
- **The Humanoid and Generic Animation Rig**: These are two types of animation rigs that you can use to create and control animations of human-like characters and other types of objects.

Now that we know what Unity's animation system is, we can explore one of my favorite animation tools in Unity: Unity Timeline. We will use this to create our animation clips and control our animation interactions.

Working with Unity Timeline

Unity Timeline is a visual tool for creating cinematic sequences, cutscenes, and gameplay events in Unity. It allows you to create a timeline of events, and assign animations, audio, camera movements, and other actions to specific points in the timeline.

With Unity Timeline, you can create complex and dynamic sequences by controlling multiple GOs, animations, and audio tracks in a single timeline. It also allows you to create interactive sequences by using Timeline control tracks.

Here are some of the main features of Unity Timeline:

- **Visual Editing**: Unity Timeline provides a visual interface for creating and editing timelines, which makes it easy to create and manage complex sequences
- **Multi-track support**: Unity Timeline supports multiple tracks for different types of assets, such as animation, audio, and camera movement
- **Playback control**: Unity Timeline allows you to control the playback of the timeline, including adjusting the speed, looping, and playing in reverse
- **Timeline control tracks**: Unity Timeline allows you to create interactive sequences by using Timeline control tracks, which allow you to pause, resume, or jump to different parts of the timeline based on user input
- **Customizable**: Unity Timeline allows you to create custom tracks and clips and allows you to use a script to control the timeline
- **Timeline asset**: Unity Timeline is a type of asset that allows you to save and reuse timelines across different scenes and projects

Using Unity Timeline to create cinematic sequences, cutscenes, and gameplay events in Unity involves several steps:

- **Create a new Timeline asset**: To create a new timeline, go to the **Assets** menu and select **Create | Timeline**. This will create a new empty timeline asset in your project.
- **Add tracks to the timeline**: To add tracks to the timeline, right-click on the timeline and select **Add Track**. You can add tracks for different types of assets, such as animation, audio, and camera movement.
- **Add clips to the tracks**: To add clips to the tracks, drag and drop the desired assets from the **Project** window to the appropriate track in the timeline. You can also create new clips by right-clicking on the track and selecting **Create | Clip**.
- **Adjust the timing and properties of the clips**: To adjust the timing and properties of the clips, select the clip and use the controls in the **Inspector** window. You can adjust the start and end time, the looping behavior, and other properties of the clip.
- **Add control tracks**: To add control tracks, right-click on the timeline and select **Add Control Track**. You can use control tracks to pause, resume, or jump to different parts of the timeline based on user input.
- **Preview and test the timeline**: To preview and test the timeline, press the play button in the Unity Editor or build and run the game. You can also use the scrubber in the timeline window to preview the timeline at different points.
- **Customizable and scripting**: Unity Timeline allows you to create custom tracks and clips, and it allows you to use a script to control the timeline. You can write code to control the timeline, and you can also use the provided events to be notified when the timeline reaches certain points.

Using Unity Timeline involves creating a new `Timeline` asset, adding tracks to the timeline, adding clips to the tracks, adjusting the timing and properties of the clips, adding control tracks, and previewing and testing the timeline.

Now that we have a brief overview of the animation system and Unity Timeline, let's add a timeline to our scene.

Creating an animation clip for GOs

In this lesson, we will learn about the animation system in Unity and how to use it to create animations for our VR rig. We will create two door animations using Unity Timeline, one for the left door and one for the right door.

Before we get started, duplicate the `5_01_RigidbodyAndCollider` scene and rename it `5_02_AnimationTimeline`.

To create two doors we can animate, take the following steps:

1. Create two empty objects in the scene.
2. Name one `LeftDoor` and duplicate it to create another one and name it `RightDoor`.
3. Place each door in their respective positions. Since my `DemoRoom` is at the transform position `0, 0, 0`, I can set the left door at `-6.2, 0, -.084`.
4. Set the `RightDoor` at `6.54, 0, -1.31`.
5. Create a cube as a child for each door.
6. Raise the cube to `2.084` units in the **Y** transform position.
7. Make the scale `3` units by `3` units by `4` units.
8. Duplicate the cube and place it under the other door's parent object.
9. Zero out the position of both cubes.

Now you have two different doors: a left door and a right door. We can now add custom animations.

To set up our Unity Timeline to create our door animation, take the following steps:

1. Go to the Unity Editor and select the **Window** menu.
2. Select **Timeline** from the menu options (**Window** | **Sequencing** | **Timeline**). A new timeline window will appear.
3. Right-click in the **Hierarchy** and select `Create Empty`.
4. Name the empty GO `DemoAnimationsTimeline`.
5. Create a new folder in your VR assets organization folder called `Animations`.

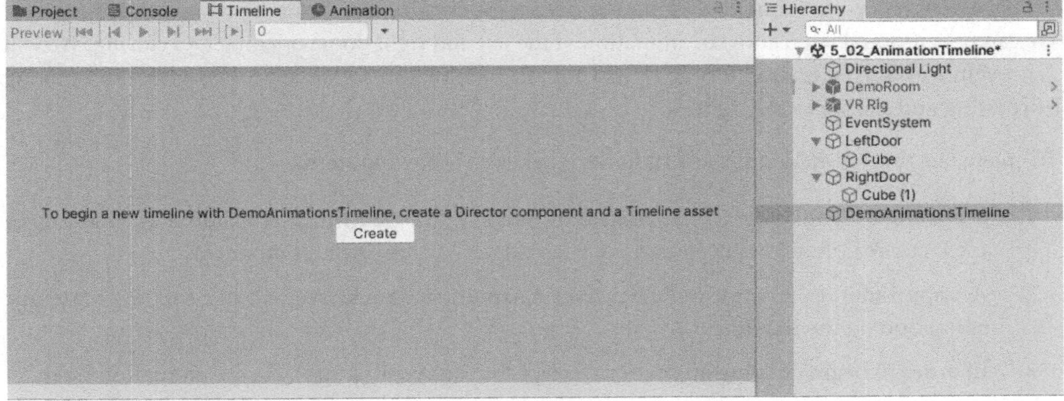

Figure 5.3 – Timeline window without a timeline asset

6. While selecting the `DemoAnimationsTimeline` GO in **Hierarchy**, select **Create** in the **Timeline** window to create a new `Timeline` asset.
7. Save the timeline as `timeline playable` in the `Animations` folder.
8. In the **Inspector** for the `DemoAnimationsTimeline`, change the wrap mode to **Loop**.
9. Set the **Play on Awake** option to on.
10. In the **Timeline** window settings menu (gear icon in the top-left of the **Timeline** window), change the frame rate to **Film: 24 fps**.

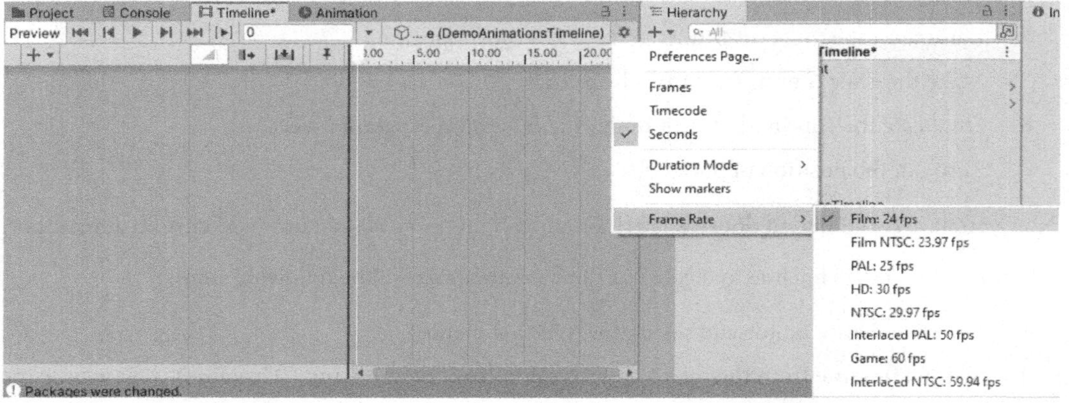

Figure 5.4 – Frame rate settings for the timeline asset

11. Click on the lock icon to keep the timeline active when you select another GO in **Hierarchy**.

We have now set up our **Timeline** window and asset for creating new animations in our demo scene. We can now proceed to creating an animation of the left and right doors opening and closing. We will first begin with the animation for the right door. This animation will involve the right door opening by rotating and sliding to the right.

To create our first animation for our right door, take the following steps:

1. Select the `RightDoor` GO in **Hierarchy** and drag it to the timeline to add it as a binding to the `DemoAnimationsTimeline Playable Director` component.
2. A popup menu will appear. Select **Add Animation Track**. We will use this to create our animation on the timeline.
3. In order to begin creating animations, select the red record button on the animation track.
4. Go to frame `0` in the timeline and add a key for the position of the `Transform` component for the door in **Inspector** (right-click **Position**).

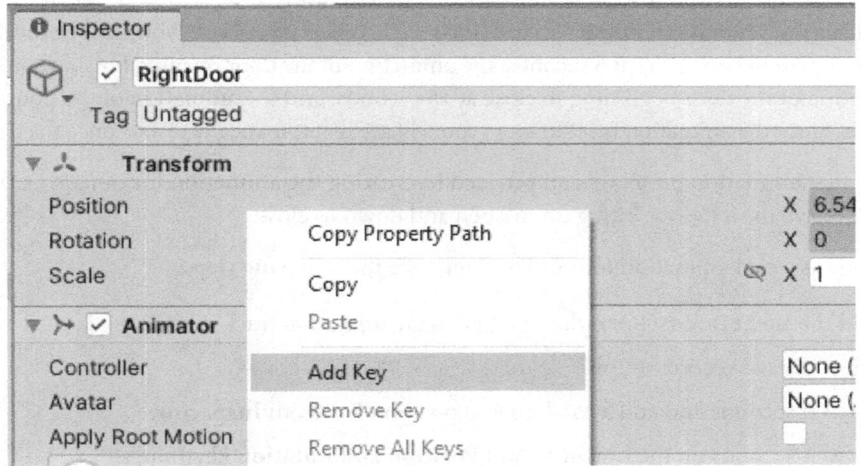

Figure 5.5 – Adding a new keyframe from the Inspector window

5. Repeat *step 4* but add a key for the rotation. You should see a diamond on the timeline indicating that you successfully added an animation keyframe.
6. Go to `5` seconds on the timeframe and create **Rotation** and **Position** keys in **Inspector**. This is the moment before the animation begins.
7. Go to `7` seconds on the timeline. We will create the animation keys that open the door.
8. Rotate the `RightDoor` GO to `90` degrees in the **Y** axis and move it `-3` units in the **Z** axis. This part of the animation is where the door is open.
9. Go to `15` seconds on the timeline. This will be the time that the door will remain open. We will add position and rotation keys from **Inspector**.
10. Go to `17` seconds on the timeline. We will create the animation keys to close the door.
11. Set the **Y** rotation to `0`.
12. Set the **Z** position to `-1.3`.
13. Deselect the red record button to save the animation.

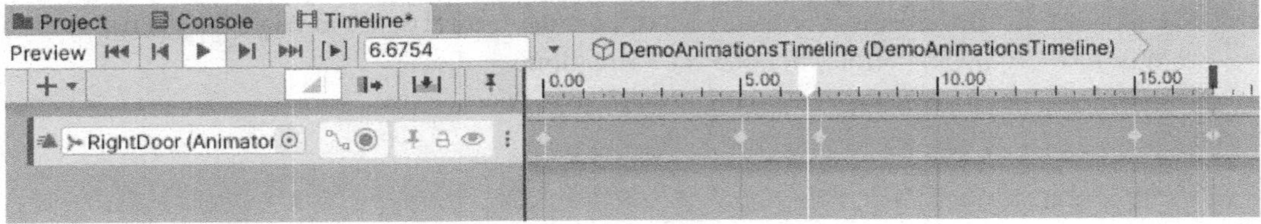

Figure 5.6 – RightDoor GO animation keys

We now have our animation for our `RightDoor` GO. When you play it, you will see the animation of the door opening beginning at 5 seconds, the animation of the door opening finishing at 7 seconds, the animation of the door beginning to close at 15 seconds, and the animation of the door closing at 17 seconds. Since the animation is set to loop, you will see it automatically restart once the door closes.

With our first animation done, we can proceed to creating the animation for our `LeftDoor` GO. This will involve the left door lifting up to open and down to close.

To create our second animation for our left door, take the following steps:

1. Add the `LeftDoor` GO to the timeline as an animation track.
2. Select the red record button.
3. Go to `0` seconds and add a rotation and position key from **Inspector**.
4. Go to `5` seconds on the timeline. Add **Position** and **Rotation** keyframes.
5. Go to `7` seconds on the timeline. We will not begin the animation for lifting the door up.
6. Set the **Y** position to `3.5`.
7. Go to `15` seconds and add keyframes for **Position** and **Rotation**.
8. Go to `17` seconds to complete the animation.
9. Set the **Y** position to `0`.
10. Deselect the red record button to save the animation.

We now have our second animation for our `LeftDoor` GO. When you press play, the animation will begin lifting up at 5 seconds, complete the lift at 7 seconds, begin closing at 15 seconds, and complete the close at 17 seconds.

You may often want to tweak the animation clips after they are completed. You can do that very easily by opening the **Animation** window to edit the timing and sequence of keyframes individually. This gives you more control over the characteristics of each animation keyframe that goes beyond the **Timeline** window.

To modify the animation keyframes on the Timeline animation track, take the following steps:

1. On the `RightDoor` animation track, select the three vertical dots and select **Edit in Animation Window** (*Figure 5.7*). This will open the animation window.

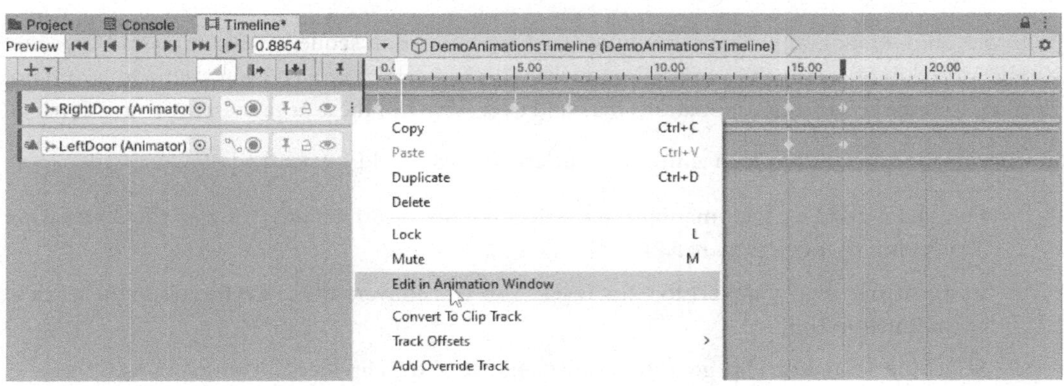

Figure 5.7 – Accessing the Animation Window

2. Select individual keyframes or groups of keyframes by clicking on **Timeline** near the keyframes and dragging a selection box around the desired keyframes to change when they initiate movement on the timeline. This will make your animation more dynamic and less rigid.
3. Modify the keyframes as desired to stagger the animation or make it longer or shorter.

> **Note**
>
> Any modifications you make in the **Animation** window will automatically be saved in the **Timeline** window.

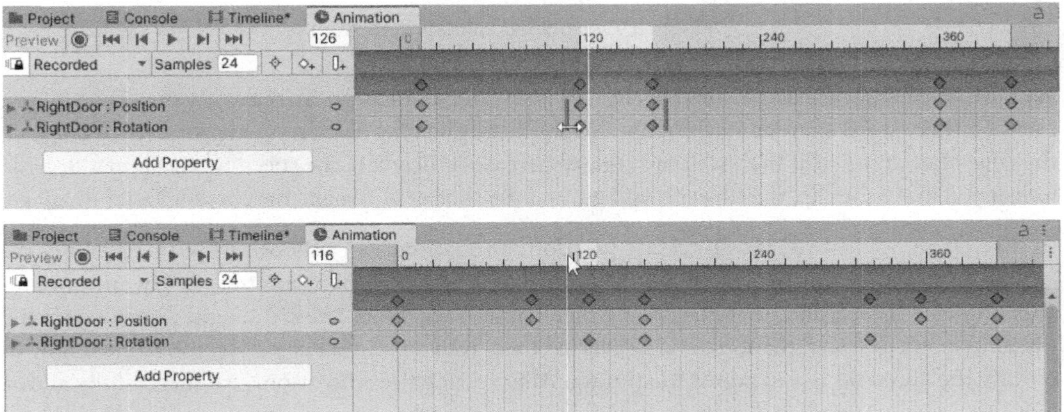

Figure 5.8 – Animation window before edits (top) and after edits (bottom)

With our animations complete, we can now save both animation sequences as animation clips that can be reused in other timeline animation tracks. This is great for repurposing animations and not needing to recreate the same animations over and over. Think of these as prefabs for animations.

To convert the animations on an animation track to animation clips, take the following steps:

1. On the `RightDoor` animation track, select the three vertical dots to open the **Animation Track** options menu (*Figure 5.7*).
2. In the menu, select **Convert to Clip Track**. This will convert all the keyframes in the track to one animation clip.
3. Select the animation clip, go to **Inspector**, and name the clip `RightDoorAnimation`.
4. Repeat *step 1* and *step 2* for the `LeftDoor` animation track.
5. Name the `LeftDoor` animation clip `LeftDoorAnimation`.

Figure 5.9 – Modified animation clips

We have successfully created animation clips for both door animations. To make it more dynamic, you can modify the speed of the animation clips even further by holding *Shift* on your keyboard and dragging the edge of each side clip to the left or right to increase or decrease the speed of the animation. The longer you make the clip, the slower it will go, and the shorter you make the clip, the faster it will go.

In this lesson, we learned how to create two door animations in Unity using Unity Timeline. We created an animation for the right door that moves to the left and then back to the right and another animation for the left door that lifts up and then comes back down. We created the doors, set up the timeline, created two animations, and converted them into animation clips. We also learned how to modify the animations and adjust the timing. After testing the animations, we successfully added loops to the doors. Now that we have completed this lesson, we have a better understanding of how to create animations in Unity.

In the next section, we will learn how to trigger animations to play using ray and gaze interactors.

Adding animations to objects with Timeline

In this subsection, you will learn how to trigger animations using a Raycast in Unity. You will be using a Raycast to detect a gaze interaction and play an animation timeline. This lesson will guide you through the process step-by-step so that you can complete it successfully.

Before we begin, duplicate the `5_02_AnimationTimeline` scene and rename it `5_03_AnimationTriggers`.

We will first create a cube on the wall right next to the doors that we can use to trigger the animations for each door. We will then configure the cube for ray interactions and gaze interactions.

To set up the Raycast target with a cube as a trigger indicator, go through the following steps:

1. Create an empty GO in **Hierarchy** and name it `RayAnimationTrigger`.
2. Add a cube to the `RayAnimationyTrigger` GO.
3. Place the cube on the wall by the `RightDoor`.

Figure 5.10 – Placement of the RayAnimationTrigger GO on the wall next to the RightDoor GO

4. Set the **X** scale of the `RayAnimationTrigger` GO to `0.2`.
5. Set the **XYZ** position to `5.15, 2, .75`.
6. Add an `XR Interactable` component to the `RayAnimationTrigger`.
7. Go to the **Interactable Events** section and press the + to set the event that you want to trigger.

We will want to trigger the animation timeline for the right door individually without triggering the left door. We can do that by creating a timeline specifically for the right door animation clip we made in the last section.

To create the animation timeline for the right door, take the following steps:

1. Select the `RightAnimationTrigger` GO and right-click.
2. Select **Create Empty Game Object** and name it `RightDoorOpenTimeline`.
3. Create a new animation timeline asset in the **Timeline** window for the `RightDoorOpenTimeline`.
4. Go to the `Animations` folder, save it, and set the frame rate to `24`.
5. Add the `RightDoor` GO to the timeline as an animation track.
6. Go to `DemoAnimationsTimeline`.
7. In the **Timeline** window, copy the `RightDoorAnimation` animation clip.
8. Go to the `RightDoorOpenTimeline` and paste the `RightDoorAnimation` animation clip in the animation track.
9. Cut the animation clip at `3.3` seconds by moving the time indicator on the timeline and pressing *S* to split the clip. We can now make the animation clip start sooner when the animation is triggered.
10. In the `Playable Director` component for the `RightDoorOpenTimeline`, set the wrap mode to `none` and turn off **PlayOnAwake**.

We have our animation timeline set to play only when we trigger it. With this complete, we can go back to our interactable event on the `RayAnimatorTrigger` and trigger the `RightDoorOpenTimeline` asset to play.

To trigger **Timeline Asset** to play the `RightDoorOpenTimeline` animation, take the following steps:

1. Select the `RayAnimationTrigger` GO and navigate to the **Interactable Events** section.
2. Under the `Select Entered` event, press the + to add an event reference slot.
3. Drag the `RightDoorOpenTimeline` GO to the `Event` reference slot.
4. Select the play function for the `Playable Director` (**No Function** | **Playable Director** | **Play()**).

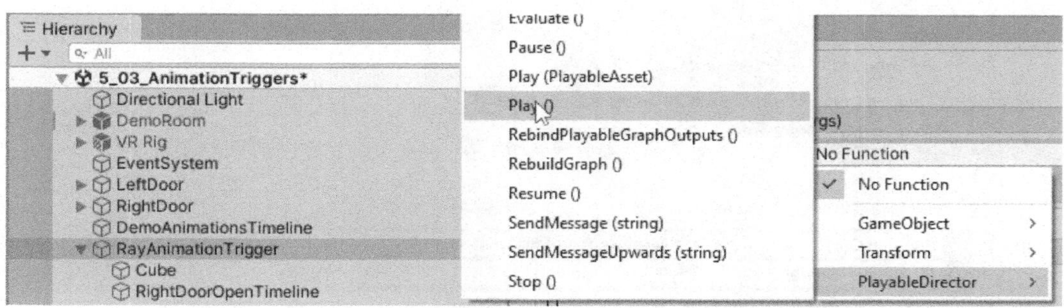

Figure 5. 11 – Selecting the play function in Select Entered event

With the play function connected to the selected event, we can provide indicators for when we are interacting with the `RayAnimationTrigger` GO. We can do that by changing the color of the cube depending on the interaction conditions. If you recall, we did this in *Chapter 3* and *Chapter 4* by swapping out different materials.

5. Go to the **Hover** section on `RayAnimationTrigger`.
6. Press the + under the `Hover Entered` event to create a new event reference slot.
7. Select the cube and add it to the `Hover Entered` event reference slot.
8. Access the cube mesh material function (**No Function | MeshRenderer | Material material**). This is for when the ray interacts with the cube trigger.
9. Repeat *steps 6–8* for the `Hover Exited` event. This will be for when the Raycast is removed from the cube trigger.
10. Set the material on `Hover Entered` to a `Green_Emission` material.
11. Set the material on `Hover Exited` to a `Red_Standard` material.
12. Repeat *steps 6–8* for the `Select Entered` event. This will be for when the Raycast triggers an event on the cube.
13. Set the material on `Select Entered` to a `Violet_Metallic` material.

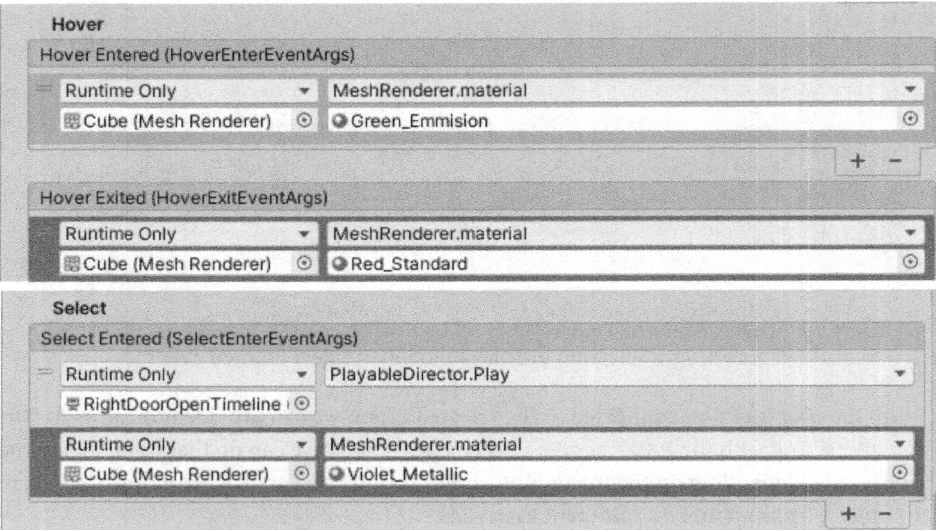

Figure 5.12 – Interactable Events Hover (top) and Select Setup (bottom)

Everything for our `RayAnimationTrigger` is complete. Test the animation to make sure it works. When you place the ray over the cube, it will turn green, when it exits it will turn red, and when you press the trigger button on the controller, it will turn purple and the door animation will turn on.

We have the ray trigger animation complete. Now we can proceed to adding the gaze interaction to trigger the same animation.

Trigger animation with gaze and Raycast

Triggering gaze interactions is just as simple as the ray interactions if you recall from *Chapter 3*, yet the benefits can be enormous in immersive experiences.

To trigger an animation function from a gaze interaction, go through the following steps:

1. Go to the `cube` GO that is a child of `RayAnimatorTrigger`.
2. Add a `Gaze Interactable` component to it.
3. Navigate to the **Events** section on the `Gaze Interactable` component.
4. For `On Gaze Enter ()`, set the material for the cube to `Blue_Metallic`.
5. For `On Gaze Exited ()`, set the material for the cube to `Red_Standard`.
6. For `On Gaze Activated ()`, set the material for the cube to `Yellow_Specular`.
7. Also set the `Gaze Activated ()` to trigger play on the `Playable Director` component on the `RightDoorOpenTimeline`.

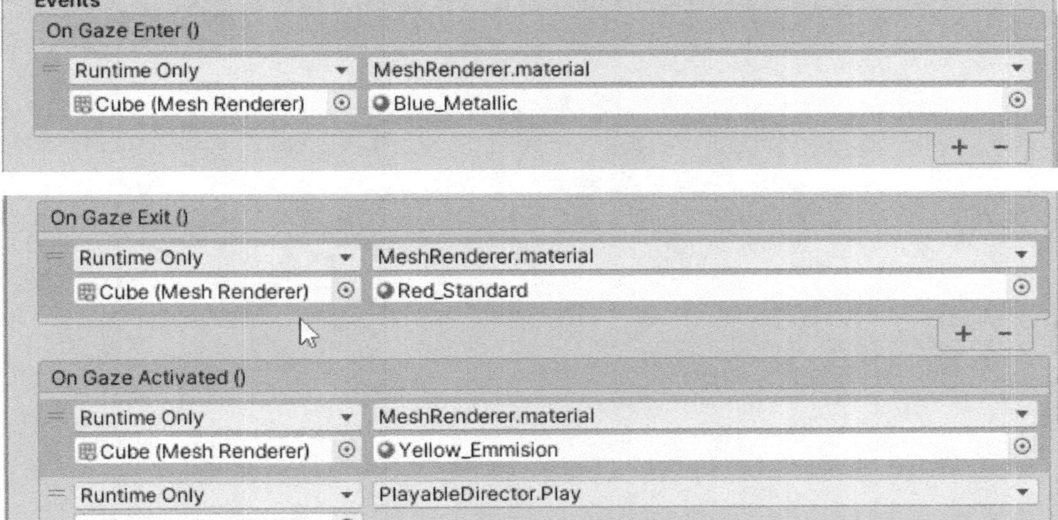

Figure 5.13 – Gaze Interactable Events setup

8. Create a new layer by going to the **Layer** dropdown menu in the **Inspector** of a GO and select **Add Layer**. Navigate to a free layer and add the term `Gaze` to an empty slot. I chose layer slot 21.
9. Set the **Cube Layer** in the **Inspector** to **Gaze** so that the `Gaze Interactor` component on the main camera can recognize it.
10. Set the **Exit Delay** to `.3`.
11. Enable **Is Activable**.

We can now test out our gaze interactions in our demo scene. When you look at `RayAnimationTrigger` on the wall, it will turn blue and the reticle will countdown. When the reticle completes, it will activate the playable director animation and turn yellow. When you look away from the cube, it will turn red. We have successfully triggered custom animation with a Raycast interaction and gaze interaction.

Summary

In this chapter, you learned how to trigger animations using a Raycast and a gaze interaction in Unity. You set up a Raycast target, created an animation timeline, triggered a function to play the timeline, and triggered an animation function from a gaze interaction. By following the steps, you should now have a working animation trigger interaction framework that you can use in your VR projects.

In the next chapter, we will explore Unity's lighting system and how lights can be used to alter and enhance our VR scenes.

6
Lighting Your Worlds and Experiences

Lighting plays a critical role in VR development and has the power to make or break the overall experience of an application. The right lighting system can help to create an immersive and believable environment that is engaging and enjoyable for users.

In this chapter of our book, we will be diving into the intricacies of the lighting system in Unity. As you progress through the chapter, you will learn about all the essential components of the lighting system, including directional lights, spot lights, point lights, and area lights. These components play a crucial role in creating dynamic and realistic lighting in your VR environment.

Additionally, we will also be discussing the use of skybox materials and emissive materials, which are essential in creating a believable and immersive environment. Another important aspect of lighting in Unity is light baking, which is the process of pre-computing lighting information to improve performance in real-time scenarios.

One of the most exciting parts of this chapter is the discussion on post-processing effects and local and global volumes. Post-processing effects add a layer of realism to your virtual environment by simulating real-world camera effects such as bloom, chromatic aberration, and vignetting. With the use of local and global volumes, you can control the overall mood, look, and feel of your VR environment by adjusting various post-processing effects.

By the end of this chapter, you will have a comprehensive understanding of the lighting system in Unity and how to use it to create dynamic and realistic VR environments. Whether you are a beginner or an experienced Unity developer, this chapter is sure to enhance your knowledge and skills in lighting and post-processing.

In this chapter, we will cover the following topics:

- Getting to know the Unity lighting system
- Simulating indoor lighting
- Modifying quality settings for lighting
- Introducing post-processing

Technical requirements

The complete source code for this chapter can be found at `https://github.com/PacktPublishing/Enhancing-Virtual-Reality-Experiences-with-Unity-2022/tree/main/EnhancingVRExperiencesFullProject/Assets/_VRProjectAssets/Scenes/Chapter_6`.

Getting to know the Unity lighting system

Unity's lighting system is a powerful tool for creating realistic and immersive environments in games and other interactive experiences. The lighting system is based on **physically based rendering** (**PBR**), allowing Unity to simulate the physical properties of light and how it interacts with objects in the real world. It allows developers to control the way light interacts with objects in their scenes and create complex lighting effects such as shadows, reflections, and ambient occlusion to provide more realistic and believable lighting effects in their VR experiences. Let's have a look at this in a bit more detail, as follows:

- **Shadows**: The effect in Unity's lighting system that simulates the way light is blocked by objects in a scene, creating areas of darkness. This can greatly enhance the realism of lighting in a VR environment.
- **Reflections**: The ability of Unity's lighting system to simulate the way light reflects off surfaces in a scene. This can add depth and detail to VR environments and create more convincing reflections in mirrors and other reflective surfaces.
- **Ambient occlusion**: A technique used in Unity's lighting system to simulate the way ambient light is scattered or blocked by nearby objects, creating more natural-looking shadows and adding depth to the scene.

The system includes both real-time and baked lighting options, depending on the needs of the project, as outlined here:

- **Real-time lighting**: The dynamic lighting system in Unity updates in real time based on changes in the environment. This is particularly important in VR as it helps to create a more immersive and responsive experience for the user.

- **Lightmap**: A pre-computed lighting solution in Unity that uses baked lighting information to create a more efficient and optimized lighting experience. This can be useful in VR as it helps to reduce computational load on the system, ensuring smooth and stable performance, but does not allow for real-time lighting adjustments.

Unity's lighting system also supports a range of light types, including point lights, spotlights, directional lights, and area lights, each of which can be customized to achieve different lighting effects. Additionally, the system includes features for handling reflections and global illumination, which can further enhance the realism of the lighting in a scene. Global Illumination is the ability of Unity's lighting system to simulate the way light is scattered and bounced around a scene, creating more natural-looking lighting and shadows. This can greatly enhance the realism of lighting in VR environments. To learn more about the lighting system and global illumination, visit `https://docs.unity3d.com/Manual/LightingInUnity.html`.

With this brief introduction to the lighting system, we will proceed to explore each of the different elements, starting with directional lights.

Directional lights

Lighting is an essential aspect of VR as it helps to create a scene that can be navigated and illuminates details in the virtual world. In this section, we will look at how to use directional lighting to control the lighting in a scene.

A directional light in Unity's lighting system is a light source that illuminates all objects in a scene from a single direction, simulating the effect of a distant light source such as the sun. The direction is determined by the rotation of the directional light GO.

The components of a directional light in Unity include the following:

- **Direction**: The direction in which the light is shining, specified using a vector that is determined by the rotation of the transform component on the GO.
- **Intensity**: The brightness of the light, specified as a numerical value.
- **Color**: The color of the light, specified as an RGB value.
- **Shadows**: A toggle to turn on or off the shadow-casting capabilities of the light.
- **Shadow resolution**: The resolution of the shadows generated by the light, specified as a numerical value.
- **Shadow type**: The type of shadows generated by the light, such as hard shadows or soft shadows.
- **Shadow distance**: The distance at which shadows will be cast by the light, specified as a numerical value.
- **Shadow strength**: The opacity of the shadows generated by the light, specified as a numerical value.

- **Bias**: A value that helps to adjust the position of shadows generated by the light, reducing shadow artifacts such as shadow acne. *Note*: Setting this value too high can cause shadows to detach from the casting object.

To learn more about directional lights, visit the Unity documentation:

`https://docs.unity3d.com/Manual/Lighting.html`

To modify how directional lights affect lighting in the scene, go through the following steps:

1. Create an empty scene. There will be a `Directional Light` GO in the center by default. The directional light represents the sun and controls the scene.
2. Use the **Rotation** tool to rotate the `Directional Light` GO and observe how it affects the scene. As you rotate the light, you will notice that the horizon changes and the light in the environment gets darker or lighter depending on the angle.

To better understand how a directional light works, place a plane and a cube in the scene:

1. Create a plane and set its position to `0, 0, 0`.
2. Add a `Cube` GO and set the **Y** position to `.5` to place it on top of the plane (*Figure 6.1*).
3. As you rotate the directional light, you will see how it affects the shadows on the cube.

   You can control the intensity and color of the light and the strength of the shadows.

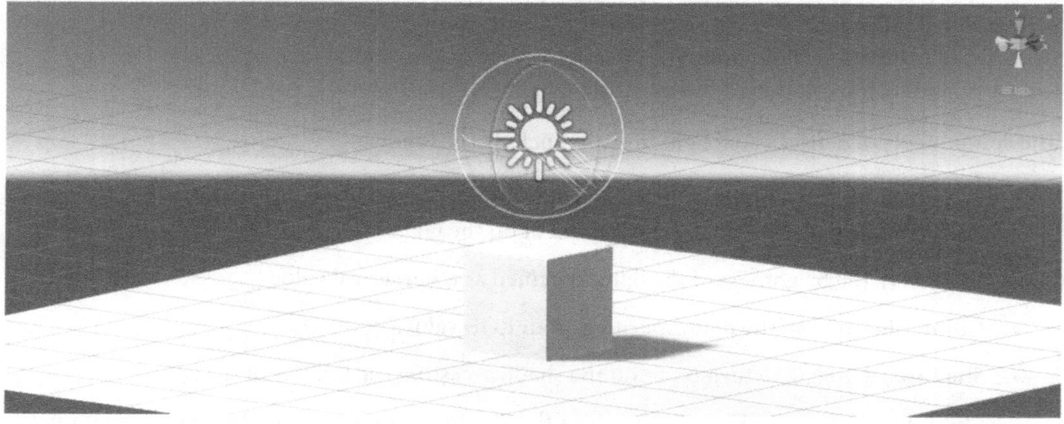

Figure 6.1 – Directional Light GO casting a shadow on the cube

> **Note**
>
> The location (transform position) of the `Directional Light` GO does not affect the way the sun moves or hits the objects in the scene. Only the rotation of the light affects shadows. The reason is that a directional light is considered to be infinitely far away, so its position doesn't matter.

`Directional Light` GOs can be used to create a wide range of lighting effects, from simulating the sun in an outdoor scene to creating a backlight in an indoor environment. They are an important tool in the toolkit of any Unity developer looking to create high-quality lighting in their projects. We have seen how to use a `Directional Light` GO to control the lighting in a scene and how to adjust the light's intensity, color, and shadows. We have also learned that only the rotation of a `Directional Light` GO affects shadows and not the location of the GO.

Lighting window

The **Lighting** window allows us to create lighting assets and effects for our scenes. It allows developers to adjust various settings related to the lighting system in their projects. We will learn how to use this window to generate lighting and create lightmaps for our scene.

To access the **Lighting** window, go through the following steps:

1. Go to **Windows | Rendering | Lighting**.
2. Selecting **Lighting** will open the **Lighting** settings window.

The **Lighting** window has different tabs that you can use to adjust the way light interacts with objects in your scene, as outlined here:

- **Scene**: This tab provides an overview of the lighting in the scene and allows you to adjust global lighting settings such as the ambient light and skybox
- **Environment**: This tab provides options for controlling the environmental lighting in a scene, including settings for sky, fog, and other atmospheric effects
- **Realtime Lightmaps**: This tab shows all the real-time lightmaps that are created
- **Baked Lightmaps**: This tab shows all the baked lightmap files created

The **Lighting** window also includes a number of other tools and options for controlling the lighting in a scene, such as the ability to preview lighting and shadows in real time, and the ability to bake and save lighting information to disk. Overall, the **Lighting** window is an essential tool for any Unity developer looking to create high-quality lighting in their projects.

In the next section, we will talk about baking lightmaps and how it impacts performance.

Baking lightmaps

Lightmaps are pre-computed lighting information in Unity that is used to create a more efficient and optimized lighting experience in a scene. Essentially, lightmaps are 2D textures that contain information about the lighting in a scene, including information about shadows, reflections, and ambient occlusion that is only associated with static objects that do not change during runtime.

In VR development, lightmaps can have a significant impact on performance. This is because they allow Unity to perform many of the lighting calculations in advance, rather than in real time. This reduces the computational load on the system, helping to ensure smooth and stable performance even in complex and demanding VR environments. Developers should use lightmaps judiciously and should optimize their size and resolution to balance visual quality and performance.

Using lightmaps can also help to reduce the number of dynamic lights in a scene, which can be a major source of performance overhead. By using pre-computed lighting information, developers can achieve high-quality lighting effects (*Figure 6.2*) with a much lower impact on performance, making lightmaps an important tool for creating optimized and performant VR experiences.

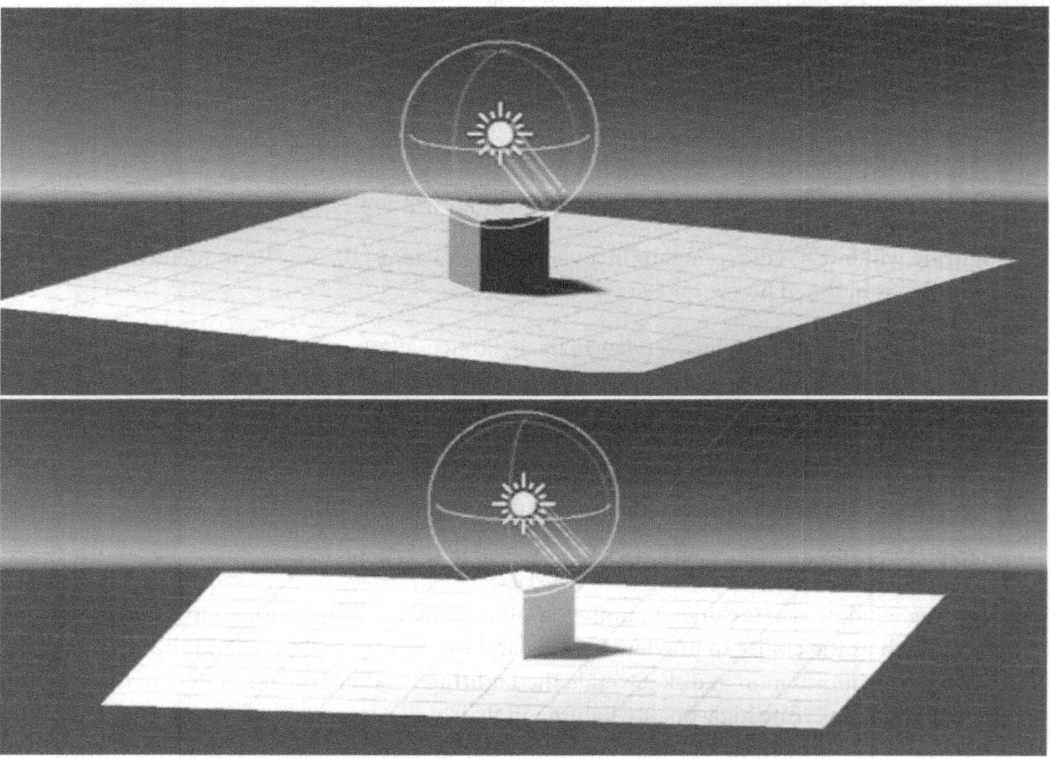

Figure 6.2 – Real-time lighting (top) versus baked lighting (bottom)

It's worth noting that lightmaps are not always the best solution for every VR project, as they are only appropriate for scenes with relatively static lighting. In scenes with dynamic lighting or rapidly changing lighting conditions, real-time lighting may be a better option. However, for many VR projects, lightmaps can provide an effective and efficient way to create high-quality lighting with minimal performance overhead.

To learn more about lightmapping, visit `https://docs.unity3d.com/Manual/Lightmappers.html`.

To bake our lightmaps in our scene, go through the following steps:

1. Open the **Lighting** window (**Window | Rendering | Lighting**).
2. In the **Scene** tab, select **New Lighting Settings** to create a new `Lighting Settings` asset for this specific scene.
3. Enable **Runtime Global Illumination** and **Realtime Environment Lighting**.
4. In the **Environment** tab, add the `Directional Light` GO to the `Sun Source` reference slot.
5. To incorporate our objects in our scene in the lightmaps, select the objects you want to include in **Hierarchy**.
6. In **Inspector**, enable **Contribute Global Illumination** in the **Lighting** section of the `Mesh Renderer` component. This will enable the GO with a mesh and any children under the GO.
7. Select **Generate Lighting** in the **Lighting** window to create lightmaps for our scene based on the current lighting settings. This process may take some time, but after it's done, you will have a new folder with lighting data and reflection probe data.

We have learned about the **Lighting** settings window. We have seen how to use this window to generate lighting and create lightmaps for our scene. We have also learned how to create new lighting settings and use them to create different lighting effects.

In the next section, we will cover environment lights and how custom skyboxes alter our scene lighting.

Skybox and environment lights

We will now learn how to create a skybox material. A skybox is an environment that surrounds a scene and provides an illusion of an infinite and vast space. It is typically used to simulate sky, clouds, and other atmospheric elements, and can greatly enhance the visual quality of a scene. Whether you're creating a realistic outdoor environment or a fantastical sky-based world, a skybox is an essential tool for creating immersive and believable environments in Unity.

Skybox material is the material applied to a skybox to control its appearance. This material typically uses a skybox shader, which is a specialized shader designed to display a skybox texture in a way that simulates the appearance of a 3D environment.

Key features of a skybox in Unity include the following:

- **Cubemap**: The skybox material uses a special type of texture called a cubemap to provide the background for the skybox. A cubemap is a cube-shaped texture that can be used to create a 3D environment, with each face of the cube representing a different direction in 3D space.
- **Skybox shader**: A skybox shader is a specialized shader designed to display the cubemap texture in a way that simulates the appearance of a 3D environment. This shader can be customized to control the appearance of the skybox, including its color, brightness, and other visual effects.

Unity's skybox system supports dynamic skies, allowing you to create animated skies that change over time. This can be useful for simulating day/night cycles or other dynamic atmospheric effects (*Figure 6.3*). We saw this when we were rotating the `Directional Light` GO. Depending on the angle of the `Directional Light` GO, you will see different locations of the sun and different time-of-day simulations:

Figure 6.3 – Custom skybox and environment lighting applied to the Plane and Cube GOs

A skybox can also impact the overall lighting in a scene, particularly the ambient light. This can be useful for creating more realistic and immersive environments, as it allows you to control the overall brightness and color of the scene based on the skybox.

To learn more about skyboxes, visit `https://docs.unity3d.com/Manual/sky.html`.

Now that we have a deeper understanding of skyboxes, we can create a custom skybox and add it to our **Lighting** window to create custom environment lighting.

To create a custom skybox material, go through the following steps:

1. Go to the `Materials` folder in the **Project** tab.
2. Create a new material and name it `Skybox_Simple`.
3. Select the `Skybox_Simple` material.
4. Change the material shader to a procedural skybox (**Skybox/Procedural**; see *Figure 6.4*).

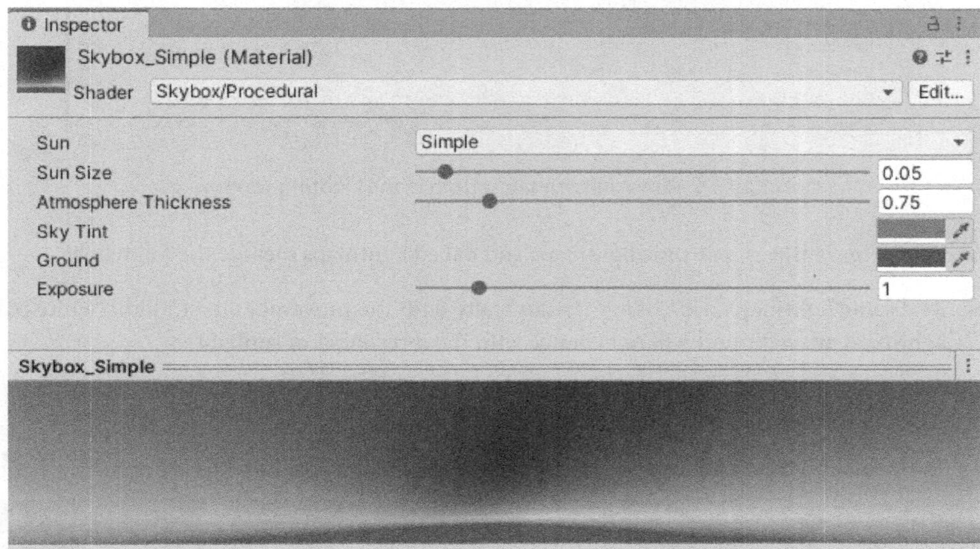

Figure 6.4 – Custom procedural skybox material settings

5. For **Sun**, set to **Simple**.
6. Set **Sun Size** to `.05`.
7. Set **Atmospheric Thickness** to `.75`.
8. Set **Exposure** to `1`.
9. Add the `Skybox_Simple` material to the `Skybox Material` reference slot in the **Lighting** window's **Environment** tab.
10. Select **Generate Lighting** to update the environment lighting with the new skybox material (*Figure 6.5*).

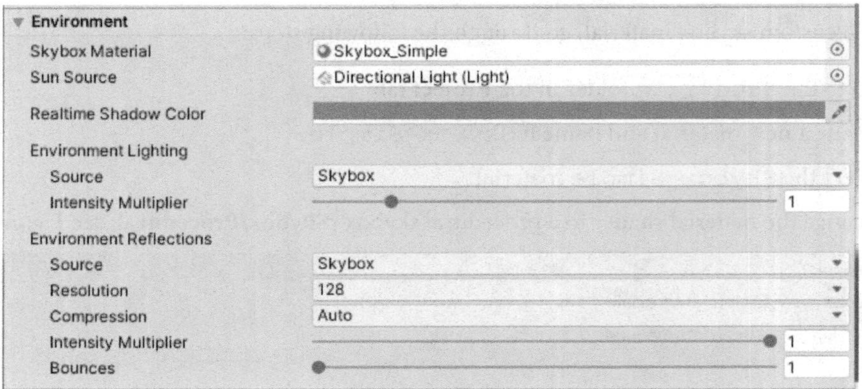

Figure 6.5 – Environment tab setting in the Lighting window

Some differences between real-time lightmaps and baked lightmaps include the following:

- Real-time lightmaps will change dynamically with the movement of sunlight, while baked lightmaps are static and will not change with the movement of sunlight
- Baked lightmaps can improve performance but will also show artifacts when objects in the scene move (*Figure 6.6*)
- To update the baked lightmaps, simply generate lighting again after adjusting the sunlight:

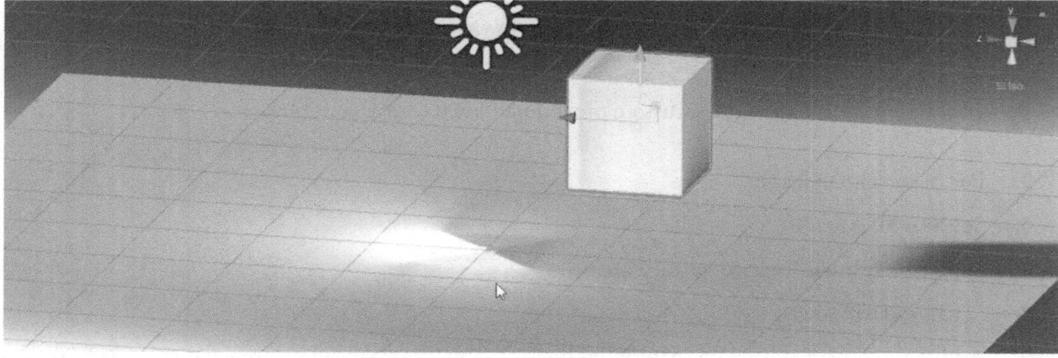

Figure 6.6 – Baked lighting artifacts when objects are moved after lightmaps are created

In this section, we learned how to create a skybox material and modify its settings in Unity for VR development. We also learned about the differences between real-time and baked lightmaps and how to generate lighting data for the scene.

In the next section, we will simulate indoor lighting using a `Directional Light` GO and light baking.

Simulating indoor lighting

In this section, we will be focusing on simulating indoor lighting using the lighting system. We will start by removing the main plane and keeping the simple skybox. Next, we will add the demo room and VR rig back into the scene. We will then replace the emissive materials with regular standard materials and set up the lighting for the indoor demo room. Finally, we will create a high-quality skybox material to enhance the overall look and feel of the indoor lighting.

Before we begin, create a new scene called `06_03_IndoorLighting`.

To set up our indoor lighting scene, go through the following steps:

1. Go to our `Prefabs` folder in the **Project** tab.
2. Add a `DemoRoom` prefab.
3. Add a `VR Rig` prefab.
4. Remove the **Main Camera**.
5. Add an `Event System` GO.
6. In the `Event System` GO, select **Replace with InputSystemUIInputModule**.
7. Create a `DarkGrey_Standard` material for the walls.
8. Create a `LightGrey_Standard` material for the ground.
9. Apply them to the ground and walls of the `DemoRoom` prefab.
10. In the prefab **Overrides** menu, apply overrides to the original prefab.

In `DemoRoom`, we have emissive materials that we want to swap out for regular materials. If you have any emissive materials in your scene, replace those emissive materials with standard materials that are not emissive. We will revisit emissive materials later in this chapter in the subsection entitled *Emissive materials*.

Next, we will apply lighting settings to our `DemoRoom` prefab to simulate an indoor lighting environment.

To simulate indoor lighting in our `DemoRoom` prefab, go through the following steps:

1. Create a `Cube` GO and name it `RenderedRoom`.
2. Increase the **XYZ** scale so that it surrounds the perimeter of the `DemoRoom` prefab. We do this so that unwanted sunlight does not affect the inside of the `DemoRoom` prefab.
3. Make all the GOs in the `DemoRoom` prefab a child of the `RenderedRoom` prefab.
4. In the `RenderedRoom` **Inspector** under the `Mesh Renderer` component, select **Contribute to Global Illumination** (*Figure 6.7*).
5. Select to **Apply to all children** in the pop-up menu.
6. For **Receive Global Illumination**, select **Lightmaps**.

7. In the **Lighting** window **Scene** tab, select **New Lighting Settings**.
8. Enable **Ambient Occlusion**.
9. Select **Generate Lighting** to bake our lightmaps. Afterward, you will notice that everything within the walls of the `DemoRoom` prefab is now dark. This is exactly what we want.

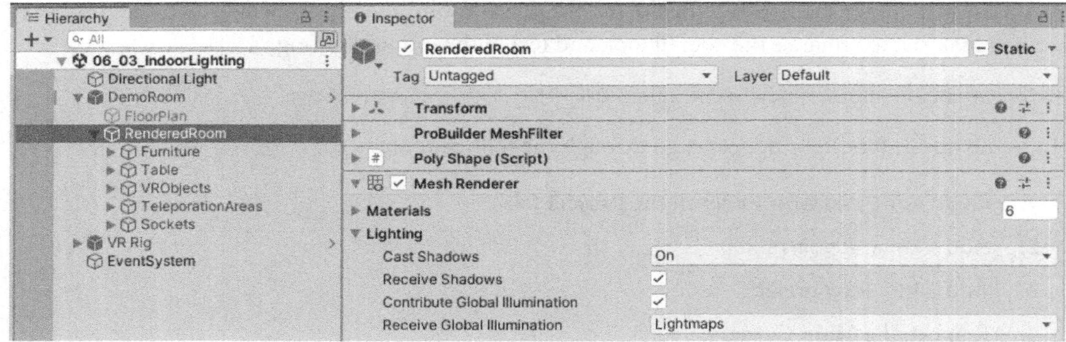

Figure 6.7 – RenderedRoom GO lighting settings

Now that we have a dark room that is blocked by the sunlight from our `Directional Light` GO, we can proceed to use light components to illuminate our `DemoRoom` prefab.

In the next section, we will use spot lights to illuminate our dark `DemoRoom` prefab.

Spot lights

A spot light is a light source that emits light in a cone shape, which is defined by the angle of the light source and the size of the cone. It can be used to simulate focused light sources such as flashlights and car headlights.

Spot lights are an important tool for illuminating dark VR rooms in Unity. They emit light in a cone shape, which is defined by the angle of the light source and the size of the cone. This makes them particularly useful for creating focused light sources, such as flashlights, car headlights, and spotlights.

Key features of spot lights in Unity include the following:

- **Color**: You can adjust the color of the light to match the mood or atmosphere of your scene
- **Intensity**: You can adjust the intensity of the light to control how bright or dim it is
- **Spot angle**: You can adjust the angle of the light to control the size of the cone and the area that is illuminated by the light
- **Range**: You can adjust the range of the light to control how far it can illuminate objects

In this subsection, we will start by adding a spot light to the scene, converting it to a ceiling light, and adjusting settings to create a reusable prefab to add ceiling lights throughout the `DemoRoom` prefab.

To add a spot light to the dark `DemoRoom` prefab, go through the following steps:

1. In **Hierarchy**, create a spot light (*right-click* | **Light** | **Spotlight**).
2. Set the **X** rotation setting to `90`. This will make the spot light face downward (*Figure 6.8*). You will notice that there are no light rays visible. That is called volumetric lighting. Unity does not support that out of the box, but we can simulate it with a mesh later in the chapter.
3. Set **Spot Angle** to `100`.
4. Set **Range** to `6`.
5. Set **Intensity** to `7`.
6. Set **Shadows** to **Soft Shadows**.
7. Set **Mode** to **Mixed**.

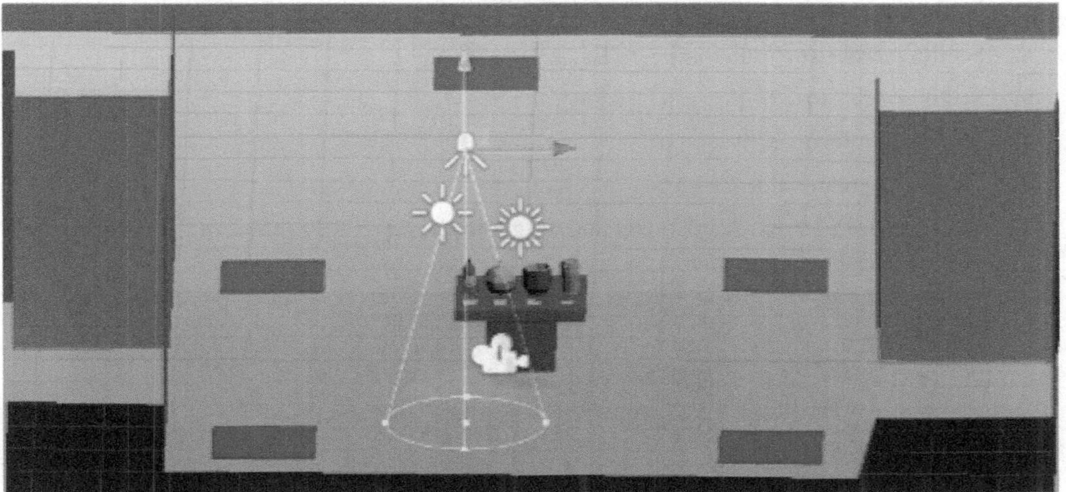

Figure 6.8 – Spot light GO pointing toward the ground

We have a pretty solid spot light we can use to illuminate our `DemoRoom` prefab from the ceiling. We can now convert this to a ceiling light and then a prefab to be reused.

To create our ceiling lights, go through the following steps:

1. Create an empty GO.
2. Name it `Ceiling`.
3. Raise the **Y** position value to `3.8`.

4. Create another empty GO.
5. Name it `CeilingLight`.
6. Place the spot light GO as a child of the `CeilingLight` empty GO.
7. Set the **X**, **Y**, and **Z** positions to `0`.

To create a 3D visual for our ceiling light (*Figure 6.9*), go through the following steps:

1. Add a 3D `Cylinder` GO as a child of the `CeilingLight` GO.
2. Name it `LightBase`.
3. Set the **Y** position to `.15`.
4. Set the **Y** scale to `.15`.
5. Change the material to `Blue_Standard`.
6. Create a `Sphere` GO as a child of the `CeilingLight` GO.
7. Name it `LightBulb`.
8. Set the **X** scale to `.7`.
9. Set the **Z** scale to `.7`.
10. Set the **Y** scale to `.3`.
11. Change the material to `Yellow_Unlit`.
12. Select the `Ceiling Light` GO and drag it to the `Prefabs` folder in the **Project** tab to create a prefab we can reuse.

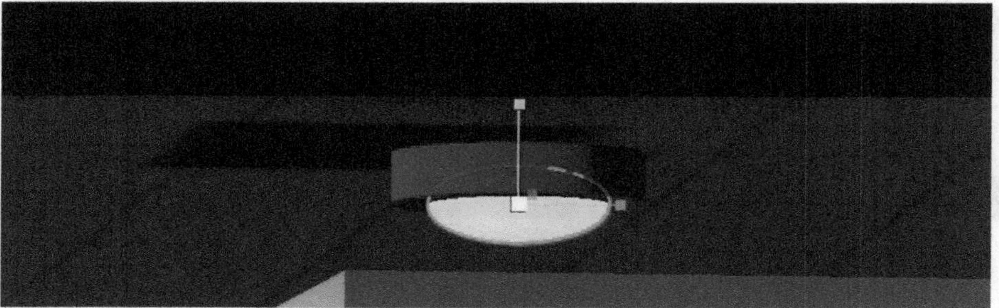

Figure 6.9 – Ceiling light 3D visual made with primitives

To distribute ceiling lights around the `DemoRoom` prefab, go through the following steps:

1. Go to the `Prefabs` folder in the **Project** tab.
2. Select the `CeilingLights` prefab and drag it to the scene.
3. Make it a child of the `Ceiling` GO.

4. Set the **Y** position to `0`. This will place the height at the ceiling level of `3.8` that we set earlier in the chapter.

I chose three lights to illuminate the main room and the two rooms on the side (*Figure 6.10*). You can add as many lights as you would like:

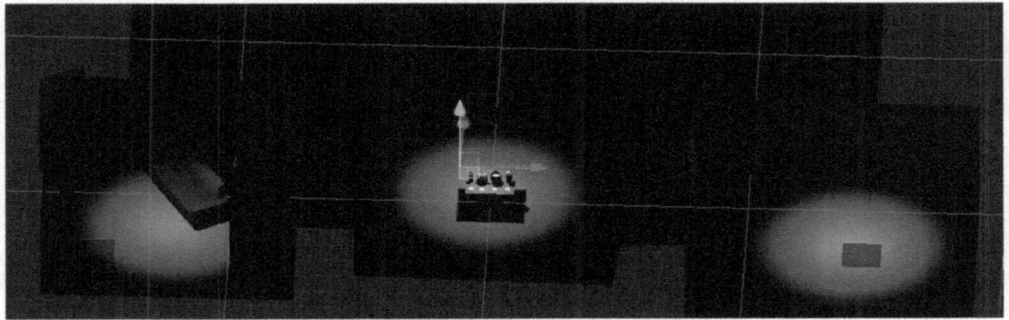

Figure 6.10 – Spot lights applied to three dark areas of our demo room

Spot lights are important for illuminating dark VR rooms because they allow you to create focused light sources that can be used to highlight specific objects or areas in a scene. This can help to create a more dynamic and engaging experience for the user, as well as to increase visibility and reduce confusion in the virtual environment. Additionally, spot lights can be used to create interesting shadows and highlights that can add depth and dimensionality to your scene.

In this section, we learned how to create and distribute spot lights and ceiling lights in Unity to illuminate our VR environment. We used the Unity engine to create and modify our lights to create the desired lighting effects. Now that we have our ceiling lights in place, we can easily light up our demo room and add more lights as needed.

In the next section, we will create point lights as an alternative to spot lights to illuminate our scene in all directions.

Point lights

Point lights are a type of light source in Unity that emits light in all directions from a single point. This makes them ideal for creating light sources that simulate lightbulbs, candles, and other similar sources of light.

Key features of point lights in Unity include the following:

- **Color**: You can adjust the color of the light to match the mood or atmosphere of your scene
- **Intensity**: You can adjust the intensity of the light to control how bright or dim it is
- **Range**: You can adjust the range of the light to control how far it can illuminate objects

In this section, we will be creating a 3D lamp model and adding a point light to it. We will also be distributing the lamps around the demo room to illuminate it.

Before we begin, duplicate the `06_04_SpotLights` scene and rename it `06_05_PointLights`.

To create a 3D lamp model for our point light (*Figure 6.11*), go through the following steps:

1. Create an empty GO and name it `Ground`.
2. Create an empty GO as a child and name it `Lamp`.
3. Add a `Cylinder` GO as a child of `Lamp` and name it `LampStem`.
4. Set the **X** and **Z** scale to `.15`.
5. Set the **Y** scale to `.75`.
6. Set the **Y** position to `.75`.
7. Create a `Cylinder` GO as a child of the `Lamp` GO and name it `LampBase`.
8. Set the **Y** scale to `.05`.
9. Set the **X** and **Z** scale to `.4`.
10. Set the **Y** position to `.05`.
11. Create a `Sphere` GO as a child of the `Lamp` GO.
12. Name it `Bulb`.
13. Set the **X** and **Z** scale to `.2`.
14. Set the **Y** position to `1.65`.
15. Set the **Y** scale to `.4`

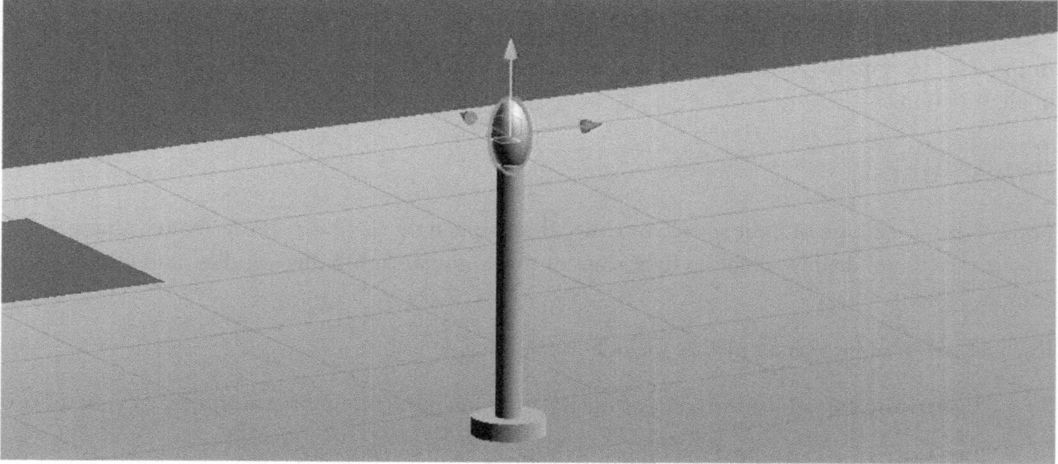

Figure 6.11 – Lamp 3D visual created from primitives

We now have a 3D model of the lamp, and we can add our point light to illuminate the surrounding area in all directions.

To add a point light to our `Lamp` GO, go through the following steps:

1. Add a `Point Light` GO as a child of the `Bulb` GO.
2. Set **Range** to `5`.
3. Set **Intensity** to `3`.
4. Set **Mode** to **Mixed**.
5. Change the material of the `Bulb` GO to `Yellow_Standard`.

With the lamp now complete with the point light for illumination, we can make this a prefab by dragging the `Lamp` GO into the `Prefabs` folder in the **Project** tab and reuse it throughout our `DemoRoom` prefab to provide light in all directions (*Figure 6.12*):

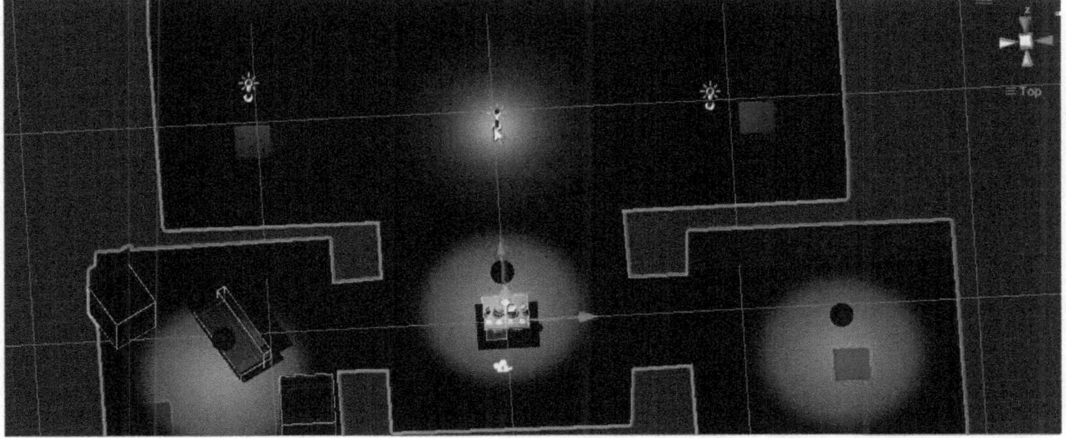

Figure 6.12 – Three lamps with point lights placed in the demo room

Point lights are important for illuminating dark VR rooms because they provide a general source of light that can be used to illuminate a large area. This can help to increase visibility and reduce confusion in the virtual environment, as well as to create a more dynamic and engaging experience for the user. Additionally, point lights can be used to create interesting shadows and highlights that can add depth and dimensionality to your scene. In this section, we learned how to create a 3D lamp model in Unity and add a point light to it. We also learned how to distribute lamps around the demo room to illuminate it. We modified the light's intensity and range to make it more effective.

Now you have a good understanding of how to create lamps and light up a room in Unity, we can revisit emissive materials to simulate the glow of lightbulbs on our ceiling lights and lamps.

Modifying quality settings for lighting

Before we move to emissive materials, you may have noticed that there is a limit to how many active lights there are.

To change the quality settings to improve the light count, go through the following steps:

1. Navigate to the **Project Settings** tab.
2. Select **Quality Settings**.
3. Change **Quality** to `Medium`.
4. Set **Pixel Light Count** to `10` (*Figure 6.13*). Be aware that increasing the pixel light count can negatively impact the performance of low-end devices, so monitor their performance and adjust the pixel light count as necessary to achieve a balance between visual quality and performance.

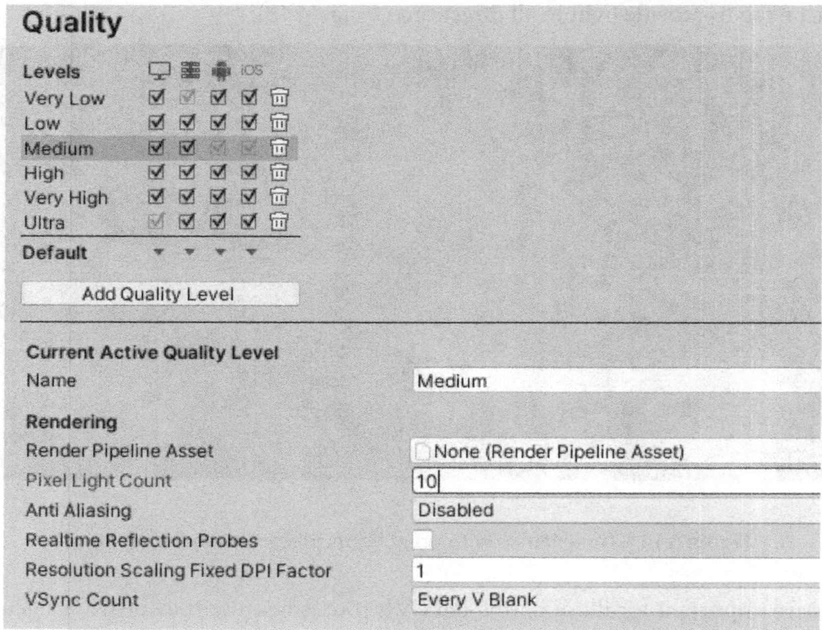

Figure 6.13 – Quality settings for optimizing the amount of available lights rendered in our demo scene

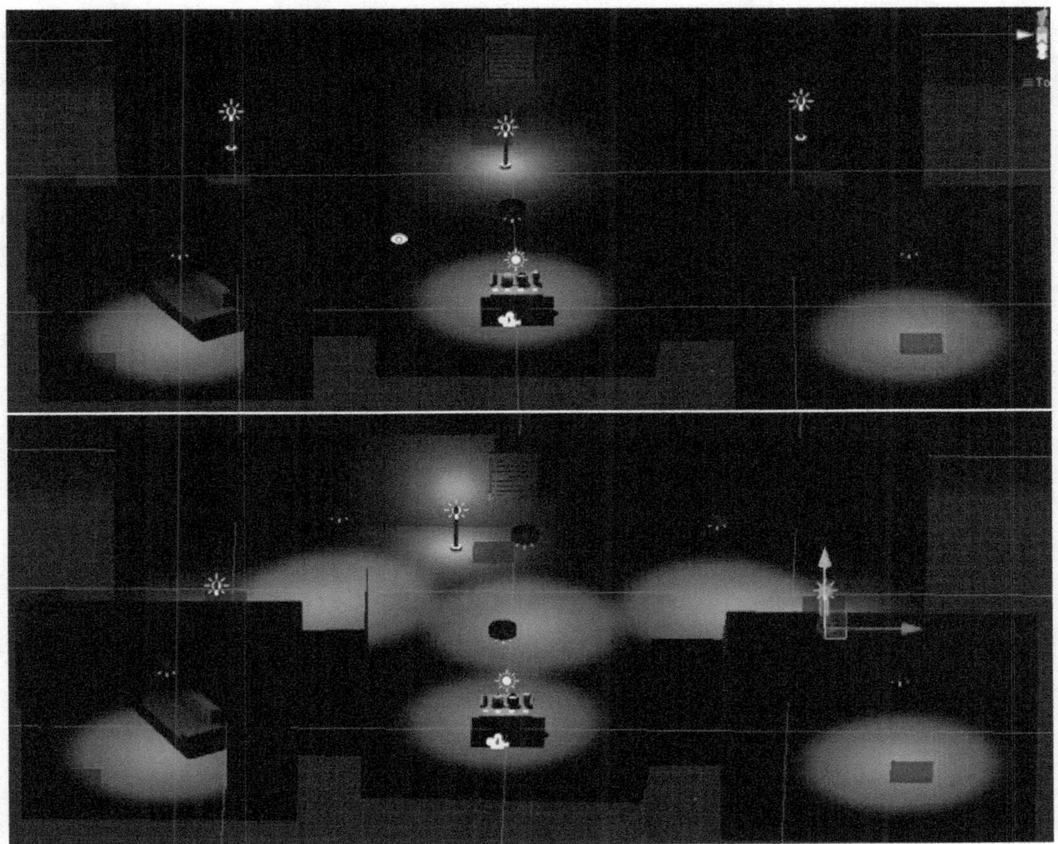

Figure 6.14 – Optimizing rendered lights in our demo scene: before (top) and after (bottom)

We can now give our lightbulbs a glow with emissive materials.

Emissive materials

Emissive materials are materials in Unity that emit light, simulating glow or self-illumination. They are a powerful tool for adding visual interest and realism to your VR scenes, particularly in dark environments.

Emissive materials are important for illuminating dark VR rooms and providing a simulation of glow to GOs because they can help to create an immersive and believable environment. They can also be used to add visual interest and highlight certain elements in the scene, drawing the user's attention to important objects or areas. Additionally, emissive materials can help to create a sense of depth and dimensionality in your VR environment, as the glowing elements will cast shadows and interact with other objects in the scene.

Key features of emissive materials in Unity include the following:

- **Color**: You can adjust the color of the emissive light to match the mood or atmosphere of your scene
- **Intensity**: You can adjust the intensity of the emissive light to control how bright or dim it is
- **Compatibility with other lighting systems**: Emissive materials can be used in conjunction with other lighting systems, such as point lights and directional lights, to create a more dynamic and visually interesting scene

In this subsection, we'll create an emissive material for our lightbulb to make it glow white with a tint of yellow. Finally, we'll save the prefab override to apply the changes to all lights in the scene.

Before we begin, duplicate the `06_05_PointLights` scene and rename it `06_06_EmissiveMaterials`.

To create an emissive material for the lights (*Figure 6.15*), go through the following steps:

1. In the `Materials` folder in the **Project** tab, create a new material.
2. Name it `White_EmissiveLight`.
3. Add this material to the `Bulb` GO of the `Lamp` GO.
4. In the **Material** settings in **Inspector**, set **Metallic** to `0`.
5. Set **Smoothness** to `0`.
6. Enable **Emission**.
7. Set **Emission Color** to `RGB = 191,191,15`.
8. Set **Intensity** to `3.8`.

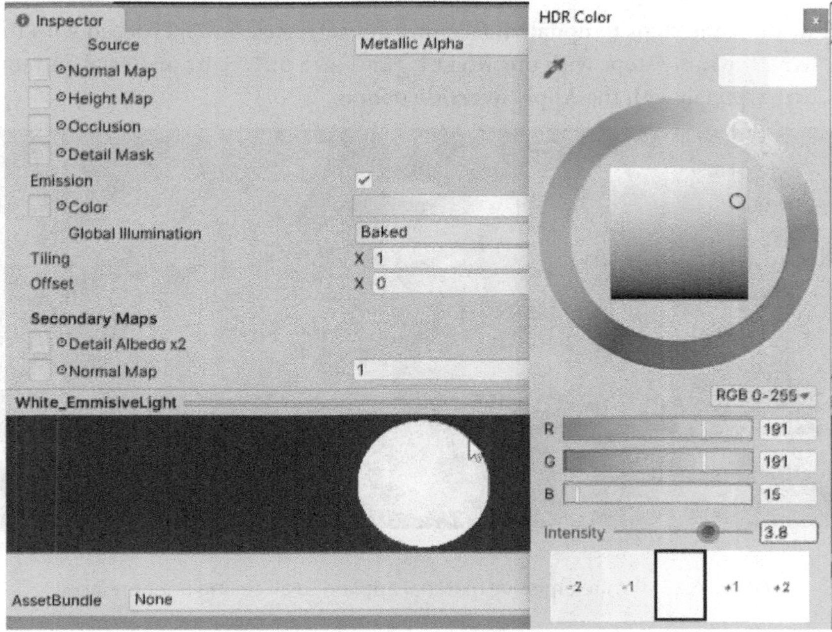

Figure 6.15 – Lightbulb emissive material settings

We have the lightbulb of our lamp glowing to simulate the light it is emitting from the point light attached to it (*Figure 6.16*). This makes a more believable lighting experience. We can now apply an override to all the edits we did to the prefab so that they update across all the other lap prefabs in our scene and project. This, again, is the power of prefabs! Edit once and update them all.

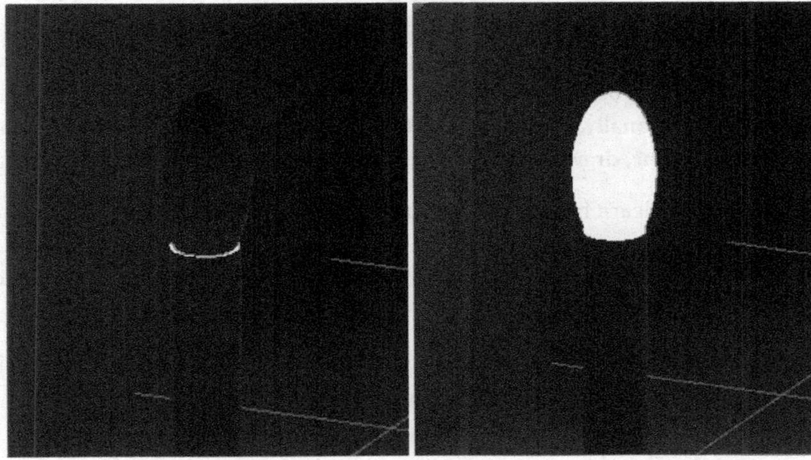

Figure 6.16 – Applying the white emissive material to the lightbulb before (left) and after (right)

We can follow the same steps to update the ceiling lights (*Figure 6.17*). Proceed with that on your own by applying the same steps with our `White_EmissionLight` material and updating the `CeilingLight` prefab with the **Apply override** option.

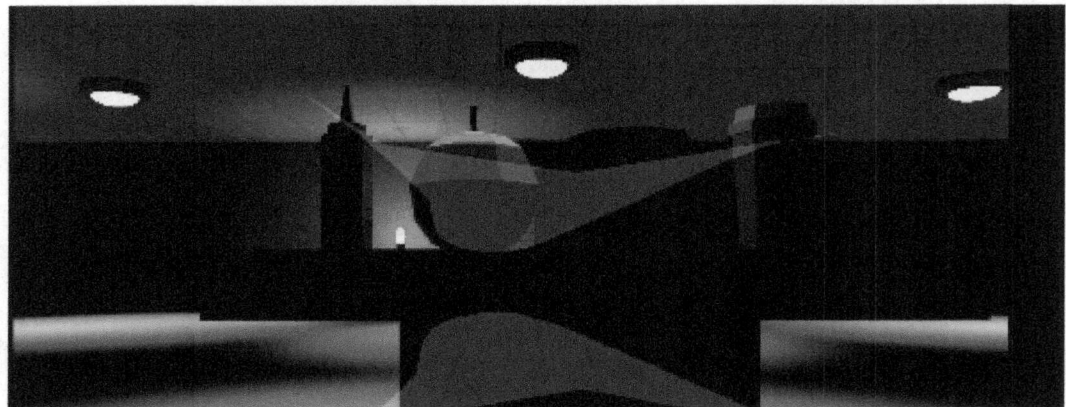

Figure 6.17 – White emissive material applied to all ceiling light prefabs

Our lights now glow and give the scene a more realistic and immersive look.

In the next section, we will use emissive materials and `Mesh Renderer` components to simulate light rays coming from the ceiling lights.

Visualizing light rays

Visualizing light rays in Unity using emissive materials and `Mesh Renderer` components is important for illuminating dark VR rooms and providing a simulation of glow to GOs because it allows you to create believable and immersive light effects. Light rays can help to create a sense of depth and dimensionality in your VR environment, as they will cast shadows and interact with other objects in the scene. Additionally, visualizing light rays can help to add visual interest and highlight certain elements in the scene, drawing the user's attention to important objects or areas.

In this subsection, you will learn how to add light rays to ceiling lights in Unity to enhance the visual effects of your VR environment. By the end of this section, you will have a clear understanding of how to create a light ray mesh and apply a light ray material to it, which will be applied to all ceiling lights in the VR environment.

Before we begin, duplicate the `06_06_EmissiveMaterials` scene and rename it `06_07_CeilingLightRays`.

To visualize light rays with a `Mesh Renderer`, go through the following steps:

1. Select the `CeilingLight` prefab.
2. Create a `Cylinder` GO as a child of the `CeilingLight` prefab.
3. Name it `LightRay`.
4. Remove the `Capsule Collider` component on the cylinder.
5. Set the **X** and **Z** scale to `7`.
6. Set the **Y** scale to `2`.
7. Set the **Y** position to `-2`.
8. Open the **Probuilder** window.
9. Select **Probuilderize**.
10. In the **Probuilderize** options, set the **Smoothing Threshold** to `4`.
11. Select **Probulderize** to complete the process.
12. Select the **Face Selection** tool from the **Probuilder** tool menu in the **Scene** view.
13. Select all faces on top of the cylinder.
14. With all the top faces selected, use the **Scale** tool to shrink them smaller. Make the faces small enough to fit under the `CeilingBase` GO (*Figure 6.18*).
15. Use the **Move** tool to align the top cylinder faces with the `CeilingBase` GO (*Figure 6.18*).

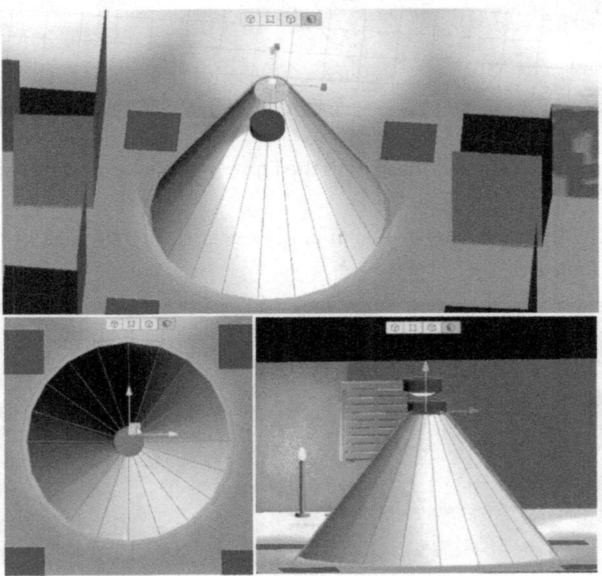

Figure 6.18 – Modifying the cylinder to simulate a light ray

Next, we will create a light ray material and apply it to the mesh we just created (*Figure 6.19*). To do that, go through the following steps:

1. Create a new material and name it `LightRay`.
2. Apply the `LightRay` material to the `LightRay` mesh.
3. Set the material shader to **Standard**.
4. Set the **Rendering Mode** option to `Fade`.
5. Set **Albedo Color** (**R**,**G**,**B** values) to `250, 250, 75`.
6. Set **Albedo Alpha** to `75`.
7. Enable **Emission**.
8. Set **Emission Color** (**R**,**G**,**B** values) to `40, 40, 40`.
9. Set **Intensity** to `1`.

Figure 6.19 – Light ray mesh with the light ray emissive material applied

We have completed the light ray. Now, we can apply overrides to the rest of the `CeilingLight` prefabs in the scene (*Figure 6.20*):

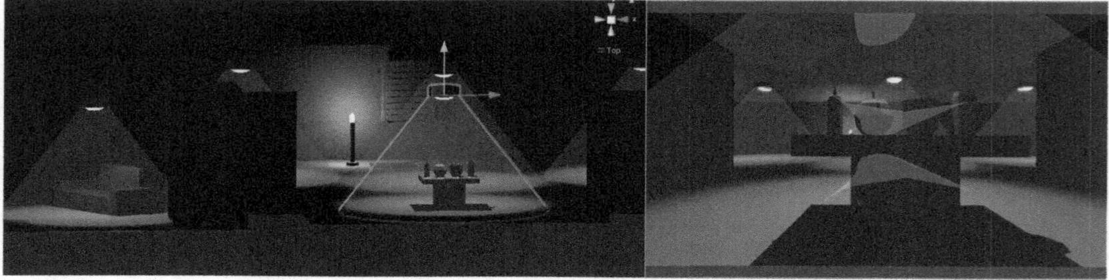

Figure 6.20 – Light rays applied to all CeilingLight prefabs

Now, your lights will stand out and show the light rays expanding in an interesting way, making your VR environment look even better.

In the next section, we will set up some area lights to give our `DemoRoom` prefab a unique character.

Area lights

An area light is a light source that emits light from a rectangular or circular shape. It can be used to simulate large light sources such as windows, skylights, and fluorescent lights.

Area lights in Unity are a type of light source that emits light from a defined rectangular area, rather than a single point light or a spot light. They are used to simulate more complex lighting scenarios, such as illuminating a room or a large outdoor space. Key features of area lights in Unity include the following:

- **Shape**: Area lights have a rectangular shape and emit light in all directions, making them ideal for simulating large light sources such as windows or overhead lights
- **Intensity**: The intensity of an area light can be adjusted to control how bright the light is, just as with other light sources in Unity
- **Shadows**: Area lights can cast soft, volumetric shadows, which are useful for creating realistic lighting in a VR environment
- **Bounce light**: Area lights can also be used to bounce light off of objects in a scene, which can help to create more natural lighting scenarios

Area lights are different from other light sources in Unity because they emit light from a defined area rather than a single point or a spot light. Area light allows for more complex and realistic lighting scenarios, which can help to create a more immersive VR experience.

In this section, we will start by creating a new empty object, which we will call `AreaLight`. Then, we will create a light panel, which will be our first area light. After that, we will rotate a quad to make it face in the same direction as the light panel, and place the light panel on the wall. After that, we will add an emission to the light panel and choose a color for it. Then, we will bake the area light and create prefab variants of the light panel.

Before we begin, duplicate the `06_07_CeilingLightRays` scene and rename it `06_08_AreaLights`.

To create our first area light (*Figure 6.21*), go through the following steps:

1. Create an empty GO and name it `AreaLights`.
2. Create another empty GO as a child of `AreaLights`.
3. Name it `LightPanel`.
4. Create an `AreaLight` GO (*right-click* | **Lights** | **Area Light**) as a child of the `LightPanel` GO.

5. Set **Shape** to `Rectangle`.
6. Set **Range** to `31`.
7. Set **Width** to `2`.
8. Set **Height** to `2`.
9. Set **Color** to `Yellow`. This color does not need to be exact.
10. Add a `Quad` GO as a child of the `LightPanel` GO. This allows you to visualize the direction of the `AreaLight` GO better when setting it up. This will not actually contribute to the lighting of the scene.
11. Set the **Y** rotation to `-90` to have the `Quad` GO face the same direction as the `AreaLight` GO.
12. Place a `LightPanel` GO on the wall by setting the **Y** position to `2.3`.
13. Set the **Z** position to `-5`.
14. Change the quad material to `Yellow_Emission` from our `Materials` folder in the **Project** tab.

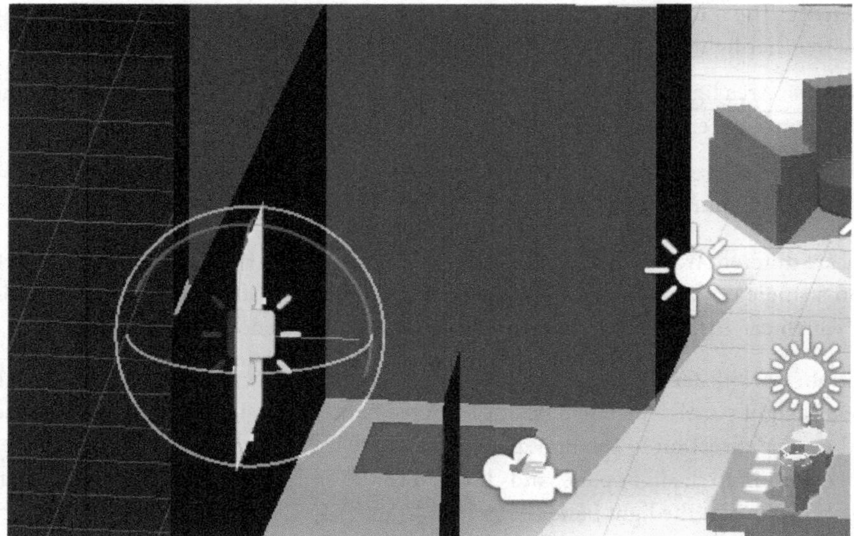

Figure 6.21 – Area light panel placed on the wall

We have our first `AreaLight` panel GO complete. Now, we can set up the lighting for our scene so that we can bake the area light and visualize it in our scene. The way this works is that we will have the `AreaLight` GO emit a color that bounces off of surrounding surfaces, and the `Quad` GO will have an emissive material of the same color that simulates the glow from the `AreaLight` GO. As with the other lights we created, it is all about creating an illusion of emission that contributes to a believable environment.

To bake our area light (*Figure 6.22*), go through the following steps:

1. Go to the **Lighting** window.
2. Remove the **Lighting Settings** asset in the **Scene** tab.
3. In the **Baked Lightmaps** tab, remove any **Lighting Data** assets.
4. Select **Generate Lighting**.

After the lighting is generated (*Figure 6.22*), you may see that the `AreaLight` GO does not appear on surrounding surfaces as much as you would like it to. You can turn off the other lights and *rebake* the lighting to see the area light. This will make the `AreaLight` emission more apparent:

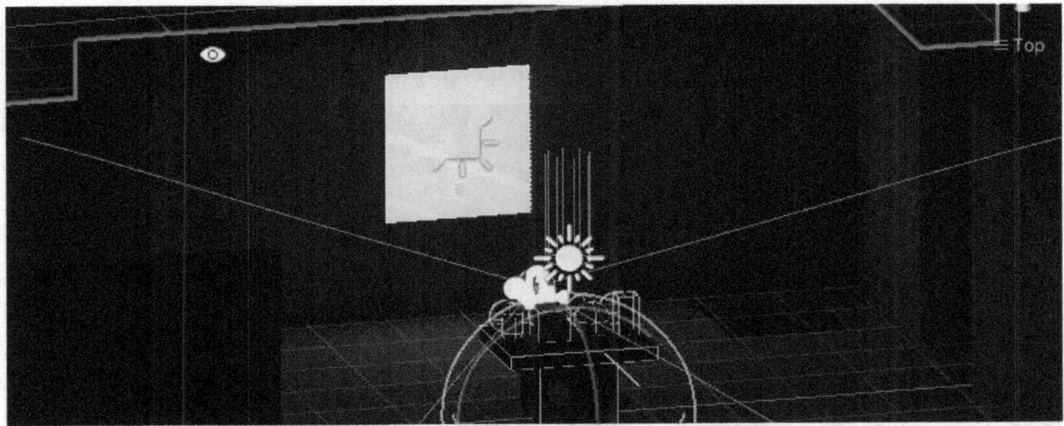

Figure 6.22 – Area light panel showing bounced light after baking lights

If you want to increase the strength of the `AreaLight` GO, do the following:

1. Increase the value of **Range** to `55`.
2. Select **Generate Lighting**.
3. If it is bright enough, turn the `LightPanel` GO into a prefab.

Now that we have a working `LightPanel` GO with an `AreaLight` GO, to make a prefab variant of our `LightPanel` GO, go through the following steps:

1. Change the material on the `Quad` GO to `Green_Emission`.
2. Change the `AreaLight` color to `Green_Emission`.
3. Make it a prefab variant called `LightPanel_Green`.

The next variant we will create is a `LightPanel` variant for the ceiling. We can change the size and position of the variant to lie along the ceiling.

To create a ceiling light panel (*Figure 6.23*), go through the following steps:

1. Add a new `LightPanel` prefab to the scene.
2. Set the **Y** position to `3.8`.
3. Set the **Z** position to `10`.
4. Set the **X** rotation to `90`.
5. Set the **X** scale to `15`.
6. Set the **Y** scale to `.3`.
7. Keep the color set at **Yellow**.
8. Make it a prefab variant called `LightPanel_Yellow`.
9. Duplicate the `LightPanel` GO and spread it evenly along the ceiling:

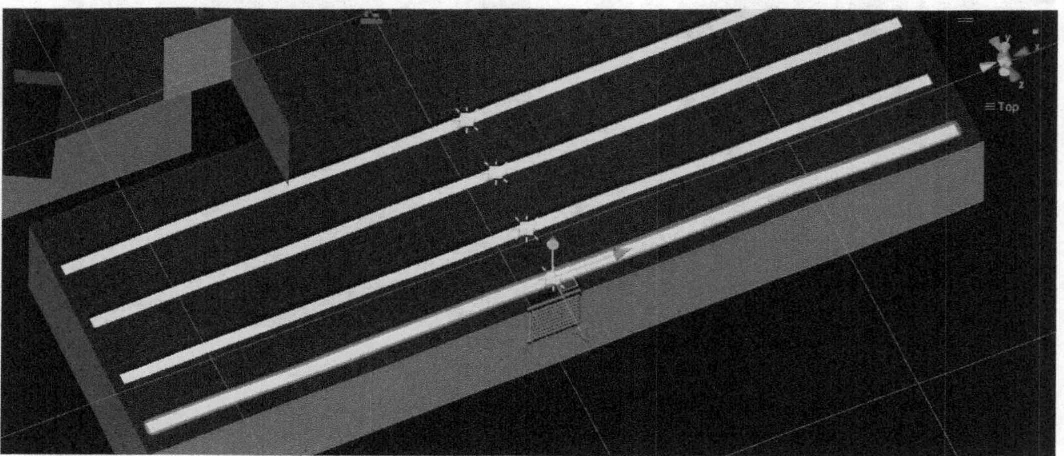

Figure 6.23 – Area lights applied to the ceiling

To create a horizontal wall `LightPanel` variant (*Figure 6.24*), go through the following steps:

1. Add a `LightPanel` prefab to the scene.
2. Set the **X** rotation to `180`.
3. Set the **X** position to `-9`.
4. Set the **Y** position to `2`.
5. Set the **Z** position to `14`.
6. Set the **X** scale to `3`.
7. Set the **Y** scale to `.5`.

8. Change the material on the `Quad` GO to `Red_Emission`.
9. Change the `AreaLight` color to `Red`.
10. Make it a prefab variant called `LightPanel_Red`.
11. Duplicate it and spread it across the wall evenly.

Figure 6.24 – Light panels applied to the wall

To create a vertical wall `LightPanel` GO (*Figure 6.25*), go through the following steps:

1. Add a `LightPanel` prefab to the scene.
2. Set the **X** rotation to `180`.
3. Set the **Z** rotation to `90`.
4. Set the **Y** rotation to `-90`.
5. Set the **X** position to `14`.
6. Set the **Y** position to `2`.
7. Set the **Z** position to `7`.
8. Set the **X** scale to `1.5`.
9. Set the **Y** scale to `.5`.
10. Change the material on the `Quad` GO to `Violet_Emission`.
11. Change the `AreaLight` color to violet or pink.
12. Make it a prefab variant called `LightPanel_Violet`.
13. Duplicate it and spread it evenly along the wall.

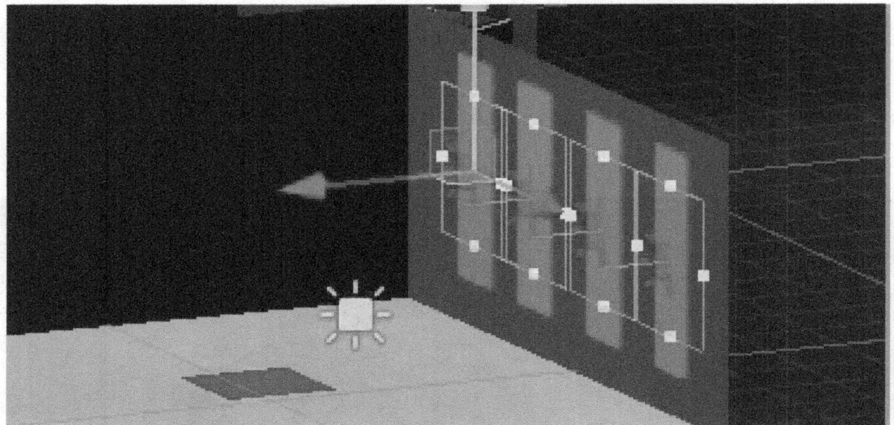

Figure 6.25 – Four LightPanel_Violet prefabs applied to the wall

With all the `LightPanel` GO created, you can now generate lighting (before you start baking, clear all the bake data) and watch the scene illuminate with various colors (*Figure 6.26*). Afterward, you can reactivate the ceiling lights and lamps on the ground to combine both real-time and baked lighting:

Figure 6.26 – Area lights in the demo room without ceiling light (top) and with ceiling lights (bottom)

In this subsection, we learned how to create an area light in Unity. We started by creating a new empty object, which we named `AreaLight`, and then created a light panel, which was our first area light. We added an emission to the light panel and chose a color for it. Then, we baked the area light and created prefab variants of the light panel. Finally, we added a spot light to the main camera to make it easier to navigate dark rooms. By following these steps, you will be able to create an area light and make your VR development projects even better.

By using area lights to simulate windows, overhead lights, or other large light sources, you can create a more realistic and immersive environment for the user. Additionally, the ability to cast soft, volumetric shadows and bounce light off of objects can help to create a more natural lighting scenario and provide a more convincing illusion of a real, 3D space.

This completes the overview of Unity's lighting system and the various lighting components we can use to illuminate our scene. Before we conclude this chapter, we will look at applying post-processing effects to our camera to enhance the visual style of our renders.

Introducing post-processing

Post-processing in Unity refers to a set of techniques and effects that can be applied to a scene after the main rendering has been completed. This can include effects such as color correction, bloom, depth of field, and many others. Key features of post-processing in Unity include the following:

- **A wide range of effects**: Unity provides a large number of post-processing effects that can be applied to a scene, ranging from simple color correction to more complex effects such as bloom, depth of field, and motion blur
- **Customizability**: Each post-processing effect in Unity can be customized and adjusted to suit the specific needs of a project, allowing developers to fine-tune the look of their VR environments
- **Easy to use**: Post-processing effects in Unity can be easily applied to a scene using the Unity post-processing stack, which is a set of tools and scripts that simplify the process of adding post-processing effects to a scene

Post-processing is important for VR development because it allows developers to create more immersive and visually stunning VR environments. By applying post-processing effects developers can create a more convincing illusion of a real, 3D space, and make the VR experience more visually engaging and appealing to users (*Figure 6.27*):

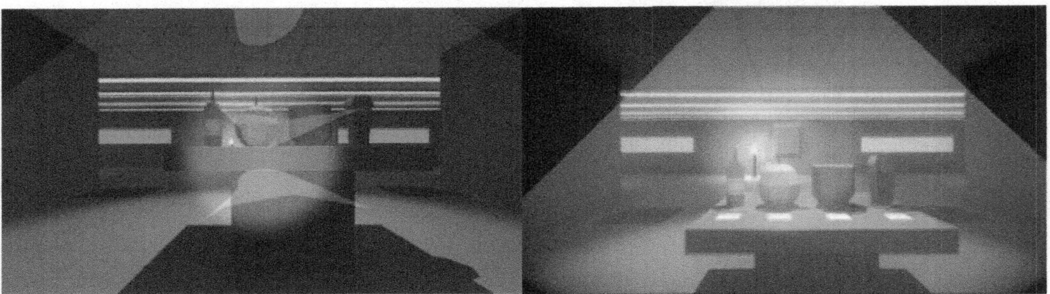

Figure 6.27 – Post-processing effects not applied (left) and applied (right)

There are a variety of post-processing effects that can be applied in Unity to enhance the look of a scene. Some of the most commonly used post-processing effects include the following:

- **Bloom**: Bloom is an effect that simulates the way light scatters in a scene, creating a bright glow around light sources
- **Depth of field**: Depth of field is an effect that simulates the way a camera lens focuses light, making objects in the foreground appear sharp and in focus, while objects in the background appear blurred
- **Motion blur**: Motion blur is an effect that simulates the way objects appear to blur as they move quickly through a scene
- **Color correction**: Color correction is an effect that allows developers to adjust the color balance, saturation, and hue of a scene, to create a specific mood or look
- **Ambient occlusion**: Ambient occlusion is an effect that simulates the way light is absorbed in a scene, creating more realistic shadows and shading
- **Screen space reflection**: Screen space reflection is an effect that simulates reflections on reflective surfaces in a scene, such as mirrors or water
- **Vignette**: Vignette is an effect that darkens the edges of a scene, creating a more focused, cinematic look
- **Film grain**: Film grain is an effect that simulates the look of film grain, adding a textured, organic quality to a scene

These are just a few of the available post-processing effects. If you want to learn more about them in detail, visit `https://docs.unity3d.com/Packages/com.unity.postprocessing@3.2/manual/index.html`.

In this section, we will be learning how to install and set up the post-processing stack in Unity to enhance the look and feel of our VR scene. The post-processing effects will allow us to change the appearance of the camera and make it more visually appealing.

To install the post-processing stack package, go through the following steps:

1. Go to **Package Manager**.
2. Under **Unity Registry**, find **Post Processing**.
3. Install the latest version.

Now that you have it installed, you need to set up your camera and layers to activate the `Postprocessing` component in your scene. To do that, go through the following steps:

1. Create a new `Layer` GO and name it `PostProcessing`.
2. Enable post-processing on the `MainCamera` GO in our `VR Rig` prefab.
3. Add a `Post-processing layer` component to the `MainCamera` GO.
4. Set the `Layer` object in the `Post-processing layer` component to `Postprocessing`.
5. Set **Anti-Aliasing** mode to `FXAA`.
6. Enable **Fast Mode**.

We now have our post-processing package enabled on our main camera and in our scene. We can now set up our Post-Processing Volumes to control the effects we place in our scene. There are two different volumes we can use: Global and Local.

In the next section, we will create a Global Post-Processing Volume.

Global Post-Processing Volume

A **Global Post-Processing Volume** is a feature in Unity that allows developers to control post-processing effects in a scene at a global level. With Global Post-Processing Volumes, developers can define a specific set of post-processing effects that will be applied to all cameras in a scene, providing a consistent look and feel across the entire experience.

Global Post-Processing Volumes are particularly useful for VR development, where it is important to ensure a consistent look and feel across the entire experience, regardless of the position of the user's head or the orientation of their device. With Global Post-Processing Volumes, developers can create a consistent look and feel for their VR experience, helping to reduce visual distractions and improve the overall sense of immersion.

In this subsection, we will be learning how to create a Global Post-Processing Volume and add various post-processing effects to enhance the visuals in our VR scene.

To create a Global Post-Processing Volume, go through the following steps:

1. In our scene, create an empty GO.
2. Name it `Postprocessing`.

3. Create a `Cube` GO as a child and name it `PostProcessingVolume`.
4. Delete the `MeshRenderer` component from the `Cube` GO.
5. Add a `Post-Process Volume` component to the `Cube` GO.
6. Enable `isGlobal`.
7. Under **Profiles**, select **New** to create a new profile asset.

We have created a Global Post-Processing Volume to affect our whole scene; now, we need to add post-processing effects to apply to our scene. To do that, follow these steps:

1. In the **Overrides** section, select **Add Effect**.
2. A dropdown menu will appear with all the available post-processing effects.
3. Add an **Ambient Occlusion** effect to boost the shadows in the corners and adjacent meshes.
4. Add a **Bloom** effect to enhance the glow from all the lights we placed in our scene. This effect really makes the emissive materials pop!
5. Add a **Chromatic Aberration** effect to distort the RGB layers.
6. Add a **Vignette** effect to narrow the field of view along the edges of the screen.

The post-processing stack is very robust, and I urge you to explore all the different settings and effects to create interesting styles and visual effects.

In this section, we learned how to create a Global Post-Processing Volume in Unity to enhance the visual effects of our VR scene. By adding various post-processing effects such as ambient occlusion, bloom, chromatic abrasion, and vignette, we were able to create a more stylized and visually appealing VR experience.

In the next section, we will convert our global volume into a local volume that applies post-processing effects in specific areas of the scene.

Local Post-Processing Volume

Local Post-Processing Volume is a feature in Unity that allows developers to control post-processing effects in a specific area of a scene. With Local Post-Processing Volumes, developers can define a set of post-processing effects that will only be applied to cameras within a certain range or volume.

Local Post-Processing Volumes are useful for adding special effects to specific areas of a scene, such as creating a unique look and feel for a specific room or location. For example, a Local Post-Processing Volume could be used to add a specific color grading effect to a dark room, creating a unique mood or atmosphere. Local Post-Processing Volumes are also useful for VR development, where they can be used to create unique visual experiences in different parts of a VR environment, helping to reinforce a sense of place and increase immersion.

In this section, we'll be covering the process of setting up a Local Post-Processing Volume in Unity. This will allow you to create a non-global volume and apply post-processing effects within a specific area or room in your VR environment.

To create a Local Post-Processing Volume (*Figure 6.28*), go through the following steps:

1. Duplicate our `PostprocessingVolume` GO and rename it `PostProcessingVolume_Local`.
2. Create a new post-processing profile.
3. Uncheck **Is Global**.
4. In the `Box Collider` component, select **Edit Collider** to make the collider large enough to surround the large room.
5. Enable **Is Trigger**.
6. In the `Postprocessing` component, add any post-processing effects you would like to apply to the volume.

We have created a local volume that triggers effects when you enter the large part of our demo room (*Figure 6.28*). Pick and choose which effects you would like to apply to it when you enter the area covered by the volume collider.

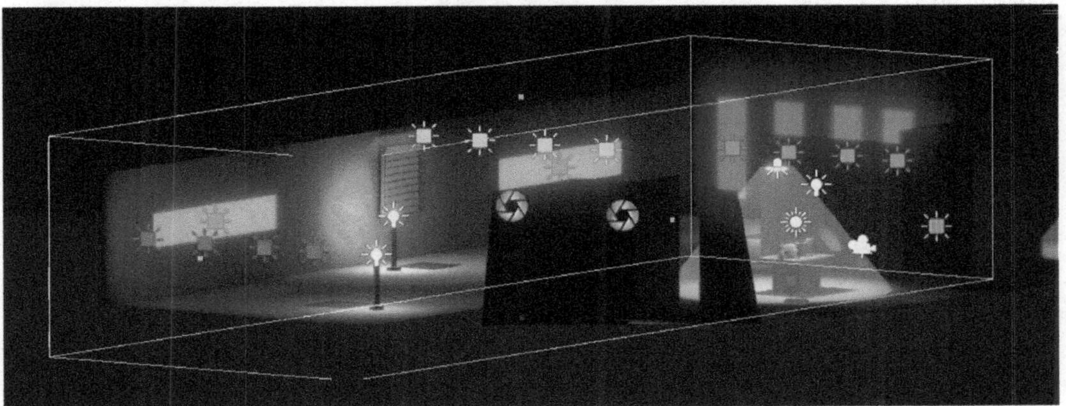

Figure 6.28 – Local Post-Processing Volume around the main demo room

When you walk into the volume, it will change abruptly. If you want to gradually apply the effects as you enter the local volume, you can use the **Blend Distance** setting. The blending distance determines the area over which the effects of one Post-Processing Volume will blend into the effects of another Post-Processing Volume.

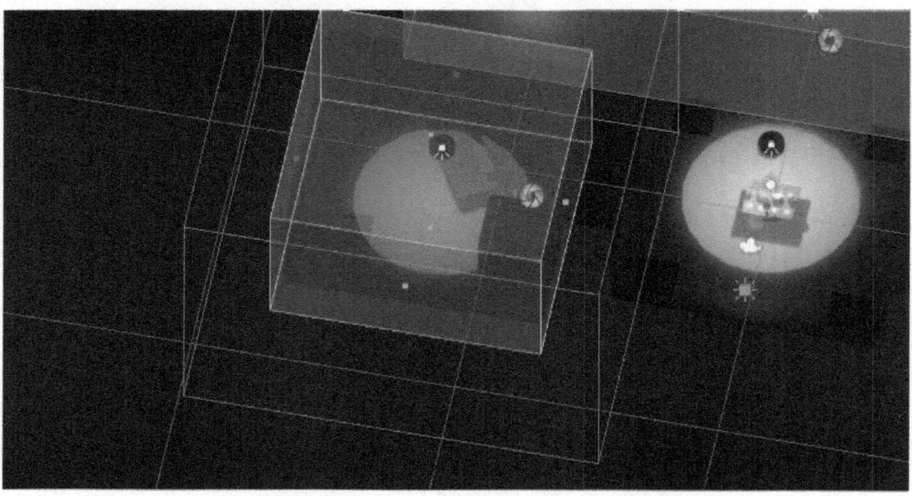

Figure 6.29 – Local Post Processing Volume applied to the left room

Blend Distance is an important feature for creating a smooth and seamless experience in VR development, as it can be used to control the transition between different post-processing effects in different areas of a scene.

Now that we have a better understanding of global and local volumes, you can create multiple volumes in different areas of the `DemoRoom` prefab to apply different effects to them (*Figure 6.30*).

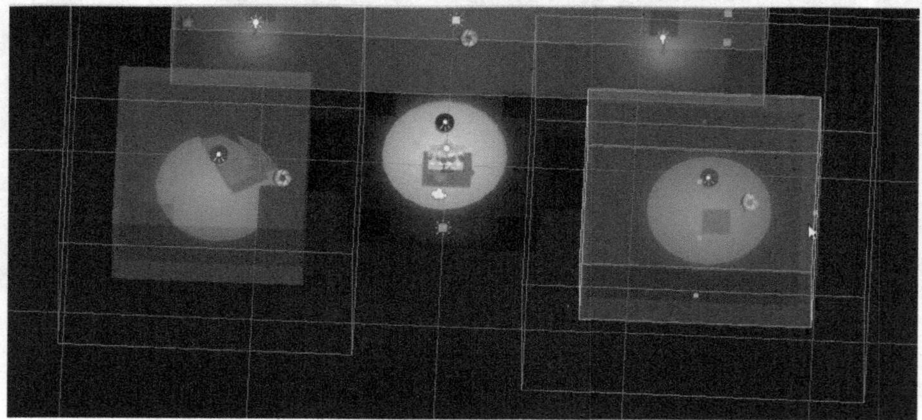

Figure 6.30 – Local Post-Processing Volumes applied to both small rooms

In this subsection, we covered how to set up a Local Post-Processing Volume in Unity. By following these steps, you can apply post-processing effects within specific areas or rooms in your VR environment, creating a more immersive experience for your players.

Summary

This chapter has provided an in-depth exploration of the lighting system in Unity and its various components. From directional lights, spot lights, point lights, and area lights, to skybox materials, emissive materials, light baking, post-processing effects, and local and global volumes, this chapter covers all the essential elements of lighting in Unity. Now that you are at the end of this chapter, you will have a solid understanding of how to use lighting and post-processing to create dynamic and realistic VR environments. Whether you are just starting out or are an experienced Unity developer, this chapter will give you the knowledge and skills you need to take your VR development to the next level. In the next chapter, we will explore audio and sound effects.

7

Creating Immersion with Sound

When thinking about VR, the visual aspect of VR is often the focus for many VR developers. The majority of our attention is given to the graphics, animations, and user interface design. However, sound is equally important in VR development, as it plays a crucial role in creating an immersive and believable experience.

Sound is an essential aspect of our daily lives, providing us with information about our environment, including the location, movement, and nature of objects around us. In VR, sound can be used to provide cues that can help users to better understand the virtual world they are in. For example, footsteps can indicate the presence of an NPC, while wind sounds can suggest the user is on a high mountain.

Sound can also enhance the sense of immersion in a VR environment. When the sound is well-designed and implemented, it can make the virtual world feel more real and believable. The use of spatial audio effects, for instance, can give users a sense of the distance and location of objects in the virtual world, just as they would in the physical world. This can help to create a more engaging and convincing experience, making users feel like they are truly inside the virtual environment.

Unity's audio system provides developers with a wide range of tools and features to create a rich and immersive audio experience in VR. This includes the ability to create background audio across a scene, add sound effects to VR controllers using audio events, and use 3D audio sources to create spatial audio effects. In addition, developers can use the Unity Asset Store to access a wealth of sound assets that can be used to further enhance the audio experience in VR.

In this chapter, we will cover the following topics:

- Downloading audio assets from the Unity Asset Store
- Adding background music with a 2D audio source
- Adding audio events to the VR rig
- Adding spatial audio with 3D audio sources

Sound is a critical component of VR development, and by leveraging the powerful tools and features provided by Unity's audio system, developers can create truly immersive and engaging virtual experiences for their users.

Technical requirements

The complete source code for this chapter can be found at `https://github.com/PacktPublishing/Enhancing-Virtual-Reality-Experiences-with-Unity-2022/tree/main/EnhancingVRExperiencesFullProject/Assets/_VRProjectAssets/Scenes/Chapter_7`.

Getting to know Unity's audio and sound system

Unity's audio and sound system is a feature of the Unity game engine that allows developers to add and manipulate audio in their games. It includes features such as spatial audio, real-time mixing, and support for various audio file formats. Developers can use Unity's audio and sound system to create immersive audio experiences in their games, including sound effects, music, and dialogue.

There are several core features and key topics related to Unity's audio and sound system, including the following:

- **Audio sources and listeners**: These components are used to play audio and control how it's heard by the player
- **Spatial audio**: This feature simulates the way sound travels in real life, creating an immersive audio experience that matches the game's environment
- **Audio effects**: Unity's audio system includes a range of built-in effects, such as reverb and distortion, that can be applied to audio sources to modify their sound
- **Audio mixers**: These allow developers to create complex audio mixes by combining multiple audio sources and applying effects to them
- **Audio file formats**: Unity supports a range of audio file formats, including WAV, MP3, and Ogg Vorbis
- **Scripting and programming**: Developers can use C# scripting to program audio behaviors, such as triggering sound effects or controlling the audio volume
- **Optimization**: Unity provides tools for optimizing audio performance, such as audio compression and batching, to ensure that the game runs smoothly on a variety of devices

In this chapter, we will add a global audio source to play background music. Then, we will apply sound effects to our object interactions and VR controllers. Lastly, we will create a local audio source to create spatial audio effects. Before we begin, we will download audio files from the Unity Asset Store.

To download the required audio files for this chapter, take the following steps:

1. Go to the Unity Asset Store at `https://assetstore.unity.com/`.
2. Download **RPG Essentials Sound Effects - FREE!** at `https://assetstore.unity.com/packages/audio/sound-fx/rpg-essentials-sound-effects-free-227708`.
3. Download **Epic Adventure Orchestral Background Music (Free Sample)** at `https://assetstore.unity.com/packages/audio/music/orchestral/epic-adventure-orchestral-background-music-free-sample-23837`.
4. Download **Lo-Fi Chillout Music For Games** at `https://assetstore.unity.com/packages/audio/music/lo-fi-chillout-music-for-games-213270`.
5. Download **3D Radio** at `https://assetstore.unity.com/packages/3d/props/radio-230712`.
6. After you download all the preceding files, go to the Package Manager and import them into your project.
7. Move the Unity assets you downloaded to the `Audio` folder to keep everything organized and accessible.

In the next section, we will add background audio to our scene.

Adding background music with Global 2D audio sources

We can apply background music to our scene using a 2D audio source, similar to how we were able to apply global post-processing effects with a global volume. 2D audio sources play sound that appears to come from a fixed position in the game world, similar to the directional light but without any sense of direction or distance. They are typically used for background music, voice-overs, or sound effects that are not spatially relevant.

A key component of the Unity audio system is the `Audio Source` component. It allows developers to play audio in a Unity scene both globally and locally. It can be attached to any GO in the scene, such as a character or an object, and can be used to play sound effects, music, and other audio files.

The `Audio Source` component has several key features:

- **Audio clip**: This is the audio file that will be played by the `Audio Source` component. Developers can choose from a range of audio file formats, such as WAV, MP3, and Ogg Vorbis.
- **Volume**: This controls the volume of the audio that is played by the `Audio Source` component. It can be adjusted to create a range of audio levels, from soft background music to loud sound effects.
- **Pitch**: This controls the pitch of the audio that is played by the `Audio Source` component. It can be used to create a range of effects, such as slow-motion audio and high-pitched sound effects.

- **Looping**: This allows the audio clip to be played in a continuous loop so that it repeats indefinitely. This can be useful for background music or ambient sound effects.
- **Spatial blend**: This controls the balance between 2D and 3D audio for the `Audio Source` component. It can be used to create audio that is either fixed in position (2D) or appears to come from a specific location in the game world (3D).
- **Spatialize:** This feature enables spatial audio for the `Audio Source` component when the **Spatial Blend** is set to **3D**. It is used to simulate the way sound travels in real life by taking into account the direction and distance of the source and the position of the listener in the game world.

The `Audio Source` component is a powerful tool for adding audio to a Unity game. With its range of features and controls, developers can create a wide variety of audio experiences, from simple sound effects to complex musical compositions. To learn more about the `Audio Source` component, visit `https://docs.unity3d.com/Manual/class-AudioSource.html`.

In this lesson, we will learn how to add background music using a 2D audio source. Background music can enhance the user experience in your VR project, and adding it is a simple process.

To add background music to the scene, take the following steps:

1. Create an empty GO and name it `Audio`.
2. Create another empty GO as a child and name it `BackgroundAudio`.
3. Add an audio source to `BackgroundAudio`.
4. Make sure **Spatial Blend** is set to **2D** rather than **3D**. By default, it should be set to **2D**.
5. Enable **Loop**.
6. Add a sound to the **AudioClip** reference slot. I chose `14Door Of The Last Time` from the Lo-fi Music pack.

When you enter play mode, you will hear the background music play regardless of where you are in the scene.

In the next section, we will apply sound effects to our VR rig controllers.

Adding audio events to our VR rig

VR hand controller audio events are important because they help to create a more immersive and interactive experience in VR games and applications. By using audio events that are triggered by the movement of the user's hands and fingers, developers can enhance the sense of presence and realism in the virtual environment.

For example, in a VR game where the user is holding a virtual gun, the sound of the gun firing can be triggered by the user pulling the trigger on the hand controller. This creates a more realistic and engaging experience for the user and helps to reinforce the sense of control and agency they have within the game.

In addition to enhancing immersion, hand controller audio events can also be used to provide feedback to the user. For example, in a VR sculpting application, the sound of a brush stroke can be triggered when the user makes a gesture with the hand controller. This tells the user that they have successfully performed the intended action, and it can help to make the experience more intuitive and satisfying.

In this lesson, we will learn how to add sound effects to our VR rig to enhance the user experience and increase immersion. We will also create a prefab variant with sound to make the process more efficient.

To add an audio event to our VR rig (*Figure 7.1*), you will be working on the following interface:

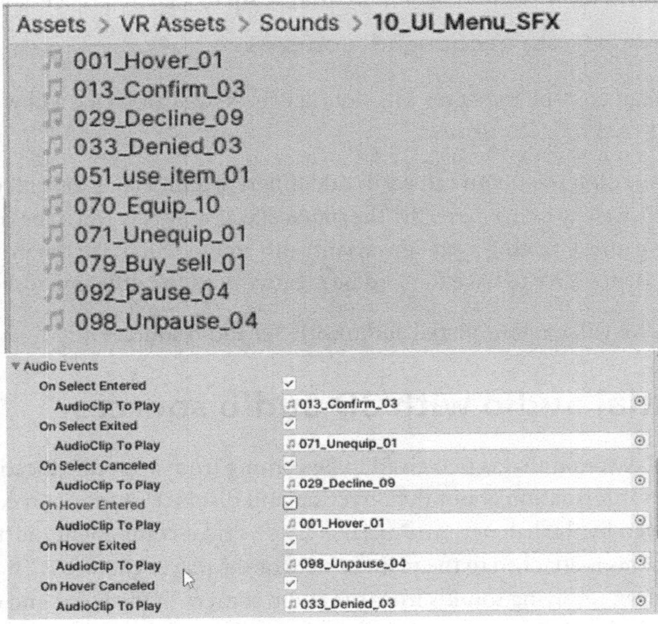

Figure 7.1 – Sound effects in the Project tab (top) and the hand controller Audio Events setup (bottom)

To add audio, go through the following steps:

1. Navigate to the `10_UI_Menu_SFX` folder where your audio files are in the **Project** tab.
2. Go to the VR rig and go to the **Audio Events** section on the `LeftHand Controller` GO.
3. Enable `On Select Entered`.
4. Add the `013_Confirm_03` audio file to the **AudioClip to Play** reference slot.
5. Enable `On Select Exited`.

6. Add the 071_Unequip_01 audio file to the **AudioClip to Play** reference slot.
7. Enable On Select Canceled.
8. Add the 029_Decline_09 audio file to the **AudioClip to Play** reference slot.
9. Enable On Hover Entered.
10. Add the 001_Hover_01 audio file to the **AudioClip to Play** reference slot.
11. Enable On Hover Exited.
12. Add the 098_Unpause_04 audio file to the **AudioClip to Play** reference slot.
13. Enable On Hover Canceled.
14. Add 033_Denied_03 audio file to the **AudioClip to Play** reference slot.
15. Repeat *steps 1–14* for the RightHand Controller GO.

With both of our hand controllers set up with sound effects, we can create a new VR rig variant and name it VR Rig Physics & Sound.

By following the preceding steps, you can easily add different audio clips for different events and test them out to ensure they are working correctly. The sound effects only play when the corresponding events are triggered in the game. Creating a prefab variant with sound will make the process more efficient for future projects. Remember to have fun and be creative with the different audio clips you choose!

In the next section, we will explore spatial audio with 3D audio sources.

Adding spatial audio with 3D audio sources

3D audio sources play sound that is perceived to be coming from a specific location in the 3D game world. This includes information about the direction and distance of the source, which affects how the sound is perceived by the listener. An Audio Listener component must also be present in the scene. Typically, this is attached to the main camera or the player character. The audio listener acts as the *ears* of the player, receiving sounds from the audio sources in the scene and outputting them to the player's speakers or headphones. For example, a sound that is further away from the audio listener will be quieter, and one that is to the left of the listener will be heard more prominently in the left ear. For 2D audio, it doesn't matter where the audio listener is in the scene because 2D audio does not compute distance and therefore will have a consistent volume level across the scene for the audio source.

By using 3D audio sources, developers can create a more immersive audio experience for players, with sounds that appear to come from specific locations in the game world. This can be useful for games that require players to locate sound sources, such as footsteps or enemies, as well as for creating a more realistic and engaging environment.

To create a radio, take the following steps:

1. Find the 3D Radio asset that we downloaded from the Asset Store at `https://assetstore.unity.com/packages/3d/props/radio-230712`.
2. Set the `Radio` prefab as a child of the `Audio` GO in our **Hierarchy**.
3. Increase the `Radio` prefab's **XYZ** scale to `6.5`.
4. Move the `Radio` to a location in the room. I chose the **XYZ** position `-13, 0, -2`.
5. Add an `Audio Source` component to the `Radio` prefab.
6. Add a sound to the `Audioclip`. I chose the `melody` audio clip.

With our radio placed in our scene, we can convert it from a 2D (global) audio source to a 3D (spatial) audio source. We will do that using the 3D sound settings. The **3D Sound Settings** (*Figure 7.2*) interface looks as follows:

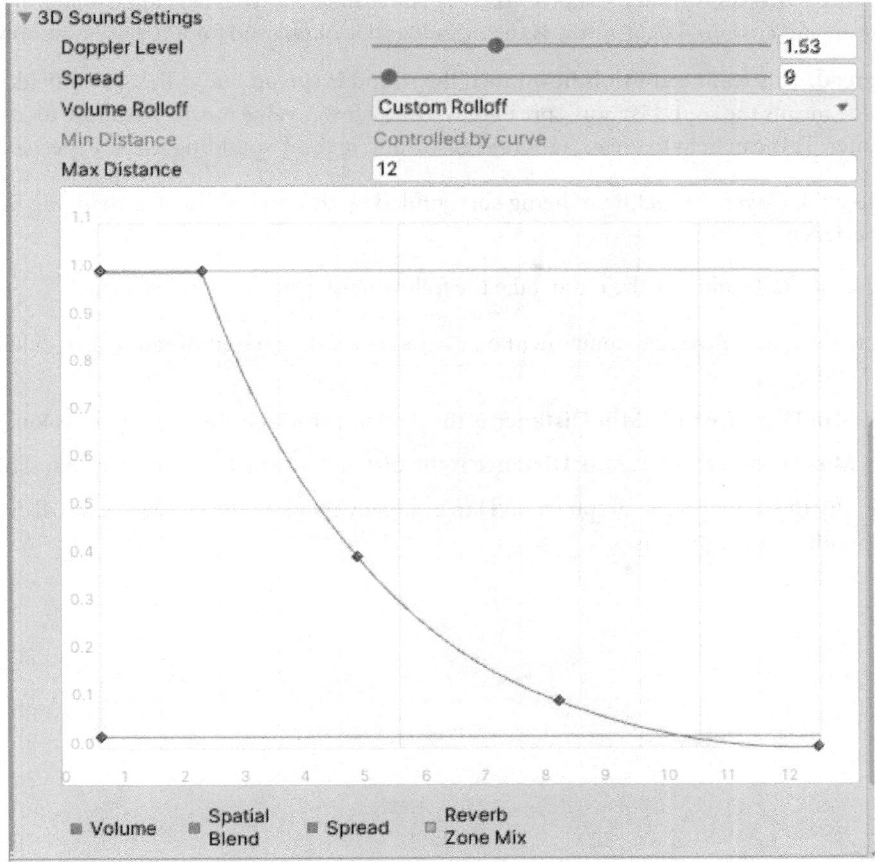

Figure 7.2 – 3D Sound Settings for spatial audio

In the preceding figure, we can see the following features:

- **Spatial Blend**: This feature determines how much of the sound is 2D or 3D. A value of 0 means the sound is completely 2D, while a value of 1 means the sound is completely 3D. By default, the value is set to 1, which means the sound is fully spatialized.
- **Doppler Level**: This feature simulates the change in frequency of a sound as it moves towards or away from the listener. A higher value means the Doppler effect is more pronounced, and a lower value means it is less noticeable. This can help to create a more realistic and immersive audio experience.
- **Min/Max Distance**: These features determine the minimum and maximum distances at which the sound can be heard. If the listener is outside the maximum distance, the sound will not be audible. If the listener is inside the minimum distance, the sound will be at its maximum volume.
- **Volume Rolloff**: This feature determines how quickly the sound decreases in volume as the listener moves away from the source. There are three different types of volume rolloff: logarithmic, linear, and custom. Logarithmic is the default and is often used for a natural-sounding rolloff.
- **Spread**: This feature controls how much the sound is spread out in the stereo field. A higher value means the sound is more spread out, while a lower value means it is more focused in the center. This can help to create a more realistic and natural-sounding audio experience.

We can give the player the feeling of being surrounded by the environment, enhancing the overall game experience.

To configure spatial audio for the radio, take the following steps:

1. In the `Audio Source` component on the radio, set the **Spatial Blend** to `1` to enable spatial 3D audio.
2. Set **Min Distance** to `3`. **Min Distance** is the distance at which the audio is at its loudest.
3. Set **Max Distance** to `13`. **Max Distance** is the distance at which the audio is inaudible.
4. Modify the spatial audio graph (rolloff) to gradually increase the volume as the distance from the audio source decreases.

You should end up with something like *Figure 7.3*:

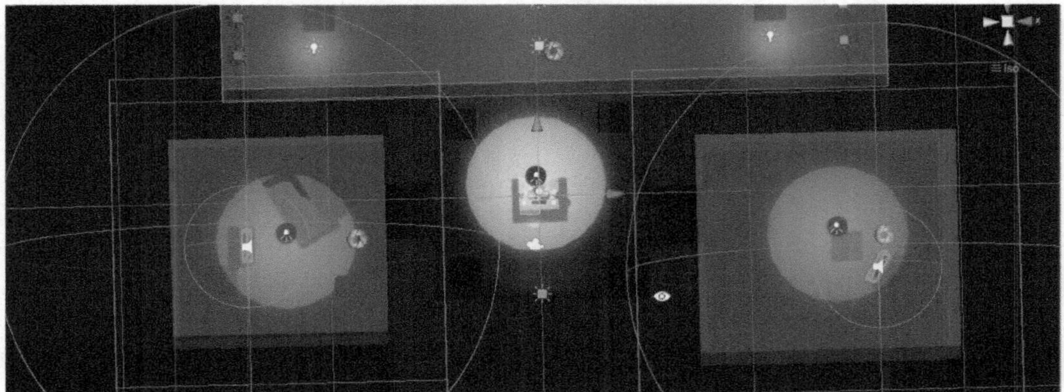

Figure 7.3 – Minimum and maximum sound distance indicators

When you get closer to the radio audio source, you will hear the sound louder. The further away, the less sound from the radio you can hear. When you have your first audio source set, you can place another one in another room to get more variations in sounds. I chose to have a different sound in each room I entered, similar to having the different post-processing effects in the different rooms in *Chapter 6*. You can combine both post-processing and spatial audio to create some interesting experiences in your projects.

Summary

Sound plays a vital role in creating an immersive and believable VR experience. With Unity's audio system, developers have a wide range of tools and features to create rich and immersive audio experiences in their VR games and applications. In this chapter, we have covered the basics of using Unity's audio system to create background audio, sound effects, and spatial audio effects. We have also explored how to download sound assets from the Unity Asset Store and use them to enhance the audio experience in VR. In the next chapter, we will delve into C# code and input assets to show how to create more advanced experiences in VR based on the various systems Unity provides. With the right approach, sound can truly enhance the VR experience and create a more engaging and convincing virtual environment.

8
Working with C#, Unity Events, and Input Actions

This chapter will explore the basics of C# and many of the XR-specific namespaces that are associated with VR SDKs and toolkits. Scripting for VR has a few quirks that make it different from scripting for games and apps. We will take a deep dive into all the features we can unlock with C# that can improve our VR development workflow.

This is probably the most important chapter of the book because it focuses on one of the core components of development, unlocking the potential of the Unity Editor to create the most immersive experiences possible. To be clear, this chapter is not meant to teach you how to code. The sole purpose of this chapter is to teach you how to navigate one of the most technical aspects of VR development, which is software development. You will learn how code can be used to enhance the capabilities of your VR scenes and how input actions and Unity Events can be used to complement that workflow.

By the end of this chapter, it may feel like we covered a lot in a small amount of time. In many ways, we will. As a developer, I have learned that mastery comes with time and experimentation. If, by the end of this chapter, you are able to apply what we cover here and rapidly iterate on the ideas you have, you will become more familiar with the applications of the skills and knowledge and you will find avenues to go beyond the topics introduced.

Ultimately, you will find that scripting is not as daunting as it seems. You will find joy in unlocking features of the editor you did know were there and, more importantly, you will be able to develop in a way that provides opportunities for scalability as your projects get more robust.

In this chapter, we will cover the following topics:

- How does C# work in Unity?
- Creating custom input actions
- Getting to know Unity Events

- Creating portals with colliders and events
- Switching between scenes with portals

Technical requirements

The complete source code for this chapter can be found at `https://github.com/PacktPublishing/Enhancing-Virtual-Reality-Experiences-with-Unity-2022/tree/main/EnhancingVRExperiencesFullProject/Assets/_VRProjectAssets/Scenes/Chapter_8`.

How does C# work in Unity?

C# (pronounced "C-sharp") is a programming language that is commonly used in Unity, a popular game engine used to create 2D and 3D games and interactive experiences. Unity supports C# as a scripting language, allowing developers to write scripts to control the behavior and functionality of their games. In Unity, C# scripts can be used to create character controllers, enemy AI, physics simulations, and other features that make a game interactive.

C# is used in Unity for scripting game logic and behavior that can be used to create a wide range of interactive and immersive experiences in VR, and Unity provides many built-in classes and functions to help with VR development, including the following:

- **Interaction**: C# can be used to create scripts that handle input from VR controllers, such as button presses and trigger pulls, and use this input to perform specific actions in the game or application, such as opening doors, picking up objects, or firing weapons.
- **Movement and teleportation**: C# can be used to create scripts that handle movement and teleportation in VR. For example, a script could be created that allows the player to move around the virtual environment using the joystick on a VR controller, or to teleport to specific locations using the trigger button.
- **Physics and collision detection**: C# can be used to create scripts that handle physics and collision detection in VR. For example, a script could be created that allows the player to grab and move objects in the virtual environment, or that allows objects to trigger events when they collide and interact with each other in realistic ways.
- **AI and NPC behavior**: C# can be used to create scripts that handle the behavior of **non-player characters (NPCs)** in VR. For example, a script could be created that allows NPCs to follow the player, or to react to the player's actions in the virtual environment.
- **User interface**: C# can be used to create scripts that handle the user interface in VR. For example, a script could be created that displays the player's health or score in the virtual environment, or that allows the player to access a menu or inventory.

- **Animation and sound**: C# can be used to create scripts that handle the animation and sound in VR. For example, a script could be created that triggers specific animations based on the player's actions or interactions, or that plays sound effects or music based on the player's location or actions.

To learn more about C# scripting in Unity, visit `https://docs.unity3d.com/Manual/ScriptingSection.html`.

We will now cover how to create a C# script in Unity.

To create a C# script, go through the following steps:

1. In the **Project** tab, create a new folder and name it `Scripts`. This is where we will place all our scripts to stay organized.
2. In the `Scripts` folder, create a C# script (*right-click* | **Create** | **C# Script**) and name it `TestScript_1`.
3. Once you have the script created, you can open it in a code editor such as Visual Studio to write the syntax.

We chose an arbitrary name right now to get started, but this is an important step because you must find a unique and functional way to name your scripts in larger projects. This will help you know what they are used for in a project as well as avoid any compile errors. As a best practice, give it a unique name based on its function, and be sure not to name it after an existing class or script. This can help you avoid any unwanted errors. For example, if you have a script that is supposed to manage all of your background 2D audio in your scene during runtime, it is best to name it `BackgroundAudioManager`. In the name, we use operational definitions, which give a brief description of what the function of the script actually is. A poor naming convention would be using something arbitrary such as `SoundsScript`. Compared to the first name, `SoundScript` doesn't give us much information to infer its function and would require us to open the script to see the code it contains.

Once you have created the script, you must apply it to a GO in our scene in order to utilize it. To use a C# script in your scene, follow these steps:

1. In a current scene, create an empty GO and name it anything relevant to the script created.
2. Select the GO, and drag the script onto the GO.

If you have any public variables or serializable fields, you will now be able to access them and input values. You can then add your own custom logic, functions, and variables to the script to define its behavior. Once you have written your code, you can save the script and return to Unity to see the changes in your game.

In the next sections, we will cover C# syntax and structure.

C# syntax

C# syntax is important for VR development in Unity because it is the primary programming language used in Unity, and provides the tools and syntax necessary to create complex VR applications. C# syntax has a few basic elements that are used to write C# code:

- **Variables**: Variables are used to store data in C# and are declared with a specific data type and a name. For example, to declare an integer variable called `x`, you would use the syntax `int x`.
- **Data types**: C# has a wide range of built-in data types, including numbers, characters, strings, and Booleans. The most commonly used data types are `int`, `float`, `double`, `char`, and `string`.
- **Operators**: C# has a variety of operators that can be used to perform calculations and compare values. The most commonly used operators are `+`, `-`, `*`, `/`, and `%` for arithmetic operations, and `==`, `!=`, `>`, `<`, `>=`, and `<=` for comparison operations.
- **Control structures**: C# has several control structures that are used to control the flow of a program, including `if-else` statements, `for` loops, `while` loops, and `switch` statements.
- **Classes**: A class is a blueprint for creating objects. It defines the properties and methods of the objects. In C#, classes are defined using the `class` keyword followed by the name of the class, and the properties and methods are defined inside the class.
- **Methods**: Methods are blocks of code that can be invoked by other code. They perform a specific task or calculation and may or may not return a value. Methods are defined using the keyword `void` or the type of the returned value, the name of the method, and parameters, if any.
- **Functions**: A function is a type of method that returns a value. Functions are defined using the type of the returned value, the name of the function, and parameters, if any.
- **Comments**: Comments are used to add notes to the code that are ignored by the compiler. They are used to explain the code and make it easier to understand. In C#, comments are denoted using `//` for single-line comments or `/* */` for multi-line comments.

These are the basics of C# syntax. Understanding these concepts is essential to writing and understanding C# code.

In the next section, we will explore how a C# script is organized.

C# structure

Understanding the structure of a C# script is essential for writing correct, readable, and maintainable code that follows best practices and has a logical flow. The basic structure of a C# script in Unity includes the following elements:

- **Library**: A library, also known as an assembly, is a compiled code that can be used by other applications. In C#, a library is typically packaged as a `.dll` file named `Assembly-CSharp.dll`.

DLL stands for **dynamic-link library**. These libraries can be added to a project in Unity by importing them through the Package Manager or as custom Unity packages.

- **Namespace**: A namespace declaration defines the namespace that the predefined script logic belongs to. In Unity, the namespace is typically set to `UnityEngine` or `UnityEngine.UI` for scripts that interact with Unity's built-in engine or UI components. Namespaces are often tied to whatever libraries you have imported into your project.
- **A class declaration**: This defines the main class for the script. The class name should be descriptive and meaningful, and it should typically inherit from `MonoBehaviour`.
- **Variables**: These are fields that store data for the script. They can be of various types, such as `int`, `float`, `string`, or `GameObject`.
- **Methods**: These are functions that perform specific tasks or actions. Unity has several built-in methods, such as `Start()` and `Update()`, which are called automatically at specific times during the game.
- **Statements**: A statement is a single instruction that tells the program to perform a specific action. In C#, statements are used to control the flow of a program, handle data, and perform calculations. Examples of statements include variable declarations, assignments, conditional statements, loops, and method calls.
- **Comments**: These are notes that you can add to your code to explain what it does or how it works. Comments are ignored by the compiler but they are very useful to understand the code. Comments are indicated by `//` before the statement.

Here's an example of a basic C# script in Unity that demonstrates the structure of a C# script:

```
//Example Comment
using ExampleNamespace;
public class ExampleScript : MonoBehaviour
{
    // Variables
    public int exampleInt = 0;
    public float exampleFloat = 0.0f;

    // Start is called before the first frame update
    void Start()
    {
        // Code that runs when the script starts
    }

    // Update is called once per frame
    void Update()
    {
```

```
        // Code that runs every frame
    }

    // Custom method
    public void ExampleMethod()
    {
        // Code that runs when the method is called
    }
}
```

In the next section, we will cover the importance of `public` and `private` access modifiers.

Public and private

In C#, `private` and `public` are access modifiers that determine the level of accessibility of a class, method, or variable.

A class, method, or variable that is declared as `private` can be accessed within the class in which it is defined or by nested classes within the same class they are defined in. It is not visible or accessible to any other classes, even if they are in the same namespace or assembly. This is known as **encapsulation**, which is a fundamental principle of object-oriented programming.

A class, method, or variable that is declared as `public` can be accessed from anywhere within the application, regardless of the class or namespace in which it is defined.

Here is an example of a class with a `private` and a `public` variable:

```
public class Example
{
    private int privateInt;
    public int publicInt;
}
```

In the preceding example, the `privateInt` variable can only be accessed within the `Example` class, while the `publicInt` variable can be accessed from any other class in the application.

If you want to have a `private` variable visible in **Inspector**, you can add `[SerializeField]` above it. `SerializeField` is an attribute that allows `private` variables to be serialized and displayed in the **Inspector** window. Using `SerializeField` with a `private` variable in Unity allows you to keep variables `private` while still being able to set their values in **Inspector**. This can be useful for data persistence, custom editor scripts, code organization, and debugging. It's a powerful tool that can help make your Unity projects more organized and efficient. Here is an example:

```
public class Example
{
```

```
    [SerializeField]
    private int privateInt;
    public int publicInt;
}
```

The main use of `private` variables and methods is to hide the implementation details of a class and expose only the necessary information to the outside. It allows for more control over the internal state of an object and prevents external code from accidentally modifying it. On the other hand, `public` variables and methods allow for easy access to the functionality of an object, making it more flexible and easier to use.

In the next section, we will learn about common methods, functions, and statements that are good to know when developing VR experiences in Unity.

Common functions and methods

In Unity, the `MonoBehaviour` class is a base class that provides a lot of common functionality for scripts that are attached to a GO. The `MonoBehaviour` class is inherited by any script that you create in Unity, and it provides several built-in methods and functions that you can use in your scripts. Some of the most commonly used methods and functions include the following:

- `Start()`: This method is called when the script component is first added to a GO. It is called before the first frame update and it is a good place to initialize variables or set up references.
- `Update()`: This method is called once per frame. It is the main function for updating the logic of a script. You can use it to check for inputs, perform calculations, or make changes to the GO.
- `Awake()`: This method is called when the script component is loaded and called before the `Start` method. It's useful for setting up references that are needed before the initialization of the script.
- `LateUpdate()`: This method is similar to `Update`, but it's called after all other `Update` calls have been processed. It's useful for cameras or other scripts that need to be updated after all other logic is processed.
- `OnEnable()`: This method is called when the script component is enabled. It's useful for resetting variables or starting coroutines when the script is enabled again.
- `OnDisable()`: This method is called when the script component is disabled. It's useful for stopping coroutines or cleaning up resources when the script is disabled.
- `OnDestroy()`: This method is called when the script component is destroyed. It's useful for cleaning up resources or stopping coroutines when the script is destroyed.
- `OnCollisionEnter()`: This method is called when the GO collides with another GO. It's useful for detecting collisions and performing actions based on the collision.

- `OnCollisionExit()`: This method is called when the GO exits a collision. It's useful for detecting when the GO stops colliding with another GO.
- `OnCollisionStay()`: This method is called every frame while the GO is in a collision. It's useful for performing actions while the GO is colliding with another GO.
- `OnTriggerEnter()`: This method is similar to `OnCollisionEnter`, but it's called when the GO enters a trigger collider. It's useful for detecting when the GO enters a specific area or volume.
- `OnTriggerExit()`: This method is called when the GO exits a trigger. It's useful for detecting when the GO stops being inside a specific area or volume.
- `OnTriggerStay()`: This method is called every frame while the GO is inside a trigger. It's useful for performing actions while the GO is inside a specific area or volume.
- `FindObjectOfType()`: This is a static method that allows you to find a specific component attached to a GO in the scene.
- `GetComponent()`: This method allows you to access a specific component attached to the GO. It's useful for getting references to other scripts or components attached to the same GO.
- `GetComponentInChildren()`: This method allows you to access a specific component that is attached to a child GO of the current GO.
- `GetComponentInParent()`: This method allows you to access a specific component that is attached to the parent GO of the current GO.
- `Invoke()`: This method allows you to call a specific method after a certain amount of time. It's useful for delaying the execution of a method.
- `OnApplicationQuit()`: This method is called when the application is about to quit. It's useful for saving data or cleaning up resources before the application closes.
- `OnBecameInvisible()`: This method is called when the GO becomes invisible to any camera. It's useful for disabling or pausing the script when it's not visible.
- `OnBecameVisible()`: This method is called when the GO becomes visible to any camera. It's useful for enabling or resuming the script when it becomes visible again.

We will be using a variety of these in this chapter and subsequent chapters.

In the next section, we will explore common statements to use.

Common statements

C# statements are important in VR development because they provide essential tools for controlling code execution, manipulating data, debugging, accessing scripting APIs, and improving code efficiency. Some of the most commonly used statements include the following:

- `for` loops: A `for` loop is a control structure that allows you to repeat a block of code a specific number of times. The syntax of a `for` loop includes an initialization statement, a condition that is evaluated before each iteration, and an increment statement that is executed after each iteration, as in this example:

```
for (int i = 0; i < 5; i++)
{
    // Code to execute
}
```

- `foreach` loops: A `foreach` loop is a control structure that allows you to iterate over a collection of items, such as an array or a list. The syntax of a `foreach` loop includes a variable that will hold the current item, the keyword `foreach`, and the collection of items to iterate over, as in this example:

```
foreach (int item in array)
{
    // Code to execute
}
```

- `if` statements: An `if` statement is a control structure that allows you to check a condition and perform different actions based on the result. The syntax of an `if` statement includes the keyword `if`, followed by a condition in parentheses, and a block of code to execute if the condition is true, as in this example:

```
if (x > 5)
{
    // Code to execute
}
```

- **Arrays**: An array is a collection of variables of the same type. Elements in an array are accessed by their index, which is an integer value. You can declare an array by specifying its data type, followed by the name of the array, and square brackets to indicate that it's an array, as in this example:

```
int[] array = new int[5];
```

- `switch` statements: A `switch` statement allows you to test a variable against a list of values and execute different code based on the value of the variable. The syntax of a `switch` statement includes the `switch` keyword followed by the variable to test, and a block of code with one or more `case` statements. Each `case` statement includes a value to test against and a block of code to execute if the variable matches the value. The `switch` statement also includes an optional default case, which is executed if none of the other cases match, as in this example:

```
switch (x)
{
case 1:
// Code to execute if x is 1
break;
case 2:
// Code to execute if x is 2
break;
default:
// Code to execute if x is not 1 or 2
break;
}
```

- `while` loops: A `while` loop is a control structure that allows you to repeat a block of code while a certain condition is true. The syntax of a `while` loop includes the keyword `while` followed by a condition in parentheses, and a block of code to execute while the condition is true, as in this example:

```
while (x < 10)
{
// Code to execute
x++;
}
```

- `do-while` loops: A `do-while` loop is similar to a `while` loop, but the block of code inside the loop is executed at least once before the condition is checked. The syntax of a `do-while` loop includes the keyword `do` followed by a block of code to execute, the keyword `while`, and a condition in parentheses, as in this example:

```
do
{
// Code to execute
x++;
} while (x < 10);
```

- **Coroutines**: A coroutine is a method that can be paused and resumed, allowing you to perform actions over a period of time rather than all at once. Coroutines are useful for creating animations, delays, and other time-based actions. To create a coroutine, you need to use the `yield` keyword and return an `IEnumerator` interface from the method, as in this example:

```
    void Start()
    {
        StartCoroutine(ExampleMethod(
            DelegationExampleValue)));
    }
    IEnumerator ExampleMethod(DelegationExample)
    {
        // Code to execute
        while (CoditionsEnxample) // While the
                                     duration hasn't
                                     elapsed
        {
            // Code to execute
            yield return null; // Wait for the next
                                  frame
        }
        // Code to execute
    }
}
```

These are some of the most commonly used control structures and data types in C#, and they provide different ways to control the flow of a program, handle data, and perform actions.

In the next section, we will create another basic demo scene and apply our C# knowledge to a few scripting actions.

Object rotation script

In this subsection, we will explore C# coding by diving deep into the code, specifically focusing on setting up a basic scene with some primitives, adding scripts for automatic and controlled rotation, and creating an XR interactable for the cube.

To create a primitive scene (*Figure 8.1*), go through the following steps:

1. Create a new scene.
2. Add a plane.
3. Add a cube.
4. Add a cylinder.

5. Add a sphere.
6. Line them up on top of the plane.
7. Add the `VR Rig Physics & Sound` prefab.

Figure 8.1 – Demo scene made of primitive shapes

Next, we will create a C# script for rotating the cube.

To create a script that will rotate an object, go through the following steps:

1. In the `Scripts` folder in the **Project** tab, create a new script.
2. Name it `RotateObject`.
3. Open the script file in Visual Studio code editor by double-clicking on the script file.
4. Apply the following code:

```
using UnityEngine;
public class RotateObject : MonoBehaviour
{
    public float rotationSpeed;

    // Update is called once per frame
    void Update()
    {
        transform.Rotate(Vector3.up * rotationSpeed *
            Time.deltaTime);

    }
}
```

5. Save the script and wait for it to compile.
6. Add the `RotateObject` script file to the cube.

7. Set the rotation speed to `35`.
8. Enter play mode and watch the cube rotate automatically.

In many ways, this is an alternative to creating animation in Unity, albeit with less flexibility. If we wanted to trigger the cube to rotate rather than it rotating automatically, we can do that with C# as well. We will modify the script to rotate only when the ray from our VR controller is pointed at the cube. It will not rotate if the ray is not hitting the cube.

To modify the rotation script to trigger a rotation (*Figure 8.2*), go through the following steps:

1. Open the `RotateObject` script.
2. Modify the script using the following code:

```
using UnityEngine;

public class RotateObject : MonoBehaviour
{
    public float rotationSpeed;
    bool isRotating;


    // Update is called once per frame
    void Update()
    {
        if (isRotating)
        {
            transform.Rotate(Vector3.up *
                rotationSpeed * Time.deltaTime);
        }
    }
    public void ToggleRotate()
    {
        isRotating = !isRotating;
    }
    public void Rotate()
    {
        isRotating = true;
    }
    public void NotRotate()
    {
        isRotating = false;
    }
}
```

3. Save it and compile.
4. Go to the cube in **Hierarchy**.
5. Add an `XRSimpleInteractable` component to the cube.
6. Set **Interaction Layer Mask** to **grabbable**.
7. For **Interactable Events**, go to **Hover**.
8. Click + for `Hover Entered`.
9. Add the `Cube` to the reference slot.
10. Set the function to **RotateObject | Rotate()**.
11. Click + for `Hover Exited`.
12. Add the `Cube` to the reference slot.
13. Set the function to **RotateObject | NotRotate()**.

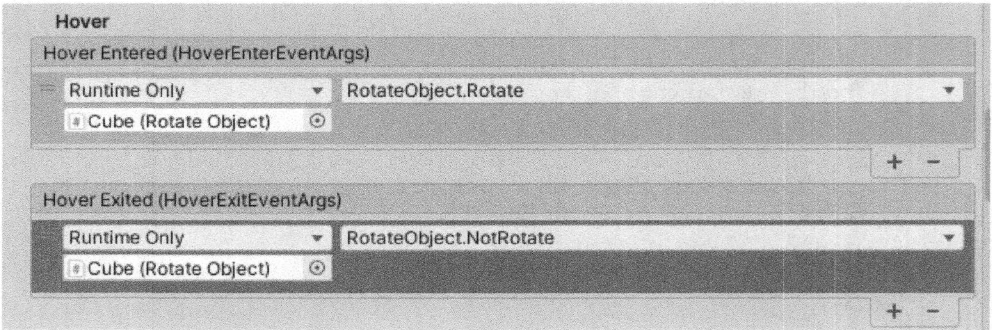

Figure 8.2 – Rotation script on the Cube applied to the Hover interaction

When we enter play mode after following these steps, we will be able to grab and release the cube, triggering a rotation based on our actions. The cube will rotate smoothly and responsively, creating an engaging VR experience. By modifying the rotation script and creating an XR interactable, we can add interactivity to our VR scenes and improve the user experience. With this knowledge, we can create more complex VR projects with even greater interactivity and user engagement.

In this section, we learned how to set up a basic scene, add automatic and controlled rotation scripts, and create an XR interactable. By using C# coding, we were able to create a smooth and responsive VR experience. By following the step-by-step guide in this section, you should now have a better understanding of C# coding in Unity and be able to create similar scripts for your own VR development projects.

In the next section, we will revisit input actions. This was a topic introduced in *Chapter 3*, when we covered the new Input System. We will dive deeper into how that can be used to create custom button interactions that can then be triggered by code to perform a wide array of functions.

Creating custom input actions

As a reminder, input actions are specific user inputs or gestures that are mapped to a particular action or behavior in the VR experience. Custom input actions are an essential tool for VR development, providing better control, interactivity, and flexibility in creating immersive VR experiences.

We will create custom input actions that allow us to use all the buttons on our VR hand controllers. Once we have these, we can use code to trigger events using specific button presses.

To create a custom input action (*Figure 8.3*), go through the following steps:

1. Go to the `XR Interaction Manager` GO in our **Hierarchy**.
2. In **Inspector**, double-click on the `XRI Default Input Actions` asset.
3. The **Input Actions** menu will open.
4. Click the + button in the **Action Maps** section to create a new action map.
5. Name it `Custom Inputs`.
6. Select **Save Asset.**

With our `Custom Inputs` action map created, we can create custom actions we can pair to buttons (*Figure 8.3*). To create custom input actions, go through the following steps:

1. In the **Actions** column, click +.
2. Name the new action string `MenuButton`.
3. Set the **Action Type** to **Button**.
4. Under **Binding**, enable **Generic XR Controller**.
5. Set **Path** to `menu` (**XR Controller | Optional Controls | menu**).
6. Select **Save Asset**.

We just paired the **Menu** button with an input action. We can now do the primary button (*Figure 8.3*):

1. In the **Actions** column, click +.
2. Name the new action string `PrimaryButton`.
3. Set the **Action Type** to **Button**.
4. Under **Binding**, enable **Generic XR Controller**.
5. Set **Path** to `PrimaryButton` (**XR Controller | Optional Controls | primaryButton**).
6. Select **Save Asset**.

We just paired the primary button with an input action. We can now do the secondary button (*Figure 8.3*):

1. In the **Actions** column, click +.
2. Name the new action string to `SecondaryButton`.
3. Set the **Action Type** to **Button**.
4. Under **Binding**, enable **Generic XR Controller**.
5. Set **Path** to `SecondaryButton` (**XR Controller | Optional Controls | secondaryButton**).
6. Proceed with mapping the rest of the buttons on the controller.
7. Select **Save Asset**.

We can perform another input action when the user presses and holds the button (*Figure 8.3*):

1. Duplicate the `PrimaryButton` input action.
2. Rename the action string `PrimaryButton_Hold`.
3. Under **Binding Properties**, press + for **Interactions** to add an interaction condition.
4. Select **Hold**.
5. Complete the previous steps for `SecondaryButton_Hold`.
6. Select **Save Asset**.

We can also do input actions based on pressing button combinations (*Figure 8.3*):

1. Add a new **Actions** slot.
2. Name the new action string `PrimaryButton_Trigger`.
3. Press + and select **Add Binding With One Modifier**.
4. Set the **Composite Type** reference to **Button With One Modifier**.
5. For the **Button** reference, set **Path** in **Binding Properties** to `primaryButton`.
6. For **Modifier Binding Properties**, set **Path** to `triggerPressed`.
7. Repeat these steps for `SecondaryButton_Trigger`.
8. Select **Save Asset**.

We have input actions for the trigger, but we can also have them work with the grip (*Figure 8.3*):

1. Duplicate `PrimaryButton_Trigger`.
2. Rename the action string to `PrimaryBuitton_Grip`.
3. Change the **Modifier Path** to `gripPressed`.
4. Repeat this for `SecondaryButton_Grip`.
5. Select **Save Asset**.

We can create an action for the grip and trigger press at the same time (*Figure 8.3*):

1. Add a new **Actions** slot.
2. Name the new action string to `PrimaryButton_TwoMods`.
3. Press + and select add **Binding With Two Modifiers**.
4. Set the **Composite Type** reference to **Button With Two Modifiers**.
5. For the **Button** reference, set **Path** in **Binding Properties** to `primaryButton`.
6. In **Binding Properties** for **Modifier 1**, set **Path** to `gripPressed`.
7. In **Binding Properties** for **Modifier 2**, set **Path** to `triggerPressed`.
8. Repeat these steps for `SecondaryButton_TwoMods`.
9. Select **Save Asset**.

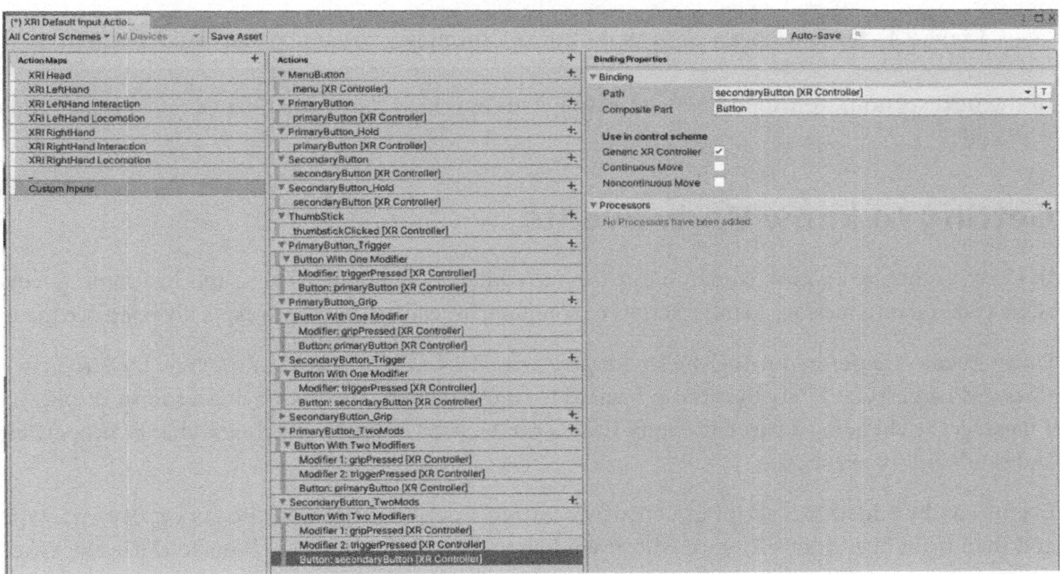

Figure 8.3 – List of custom input actions created

By following the step-by-step guide, we were able to bind different controller buttons to various actions and create combination buttons (*Figure 8.4*). With these custom input actions, we can now utilize all the buttons on our controllers and create more engaging VR experiences.

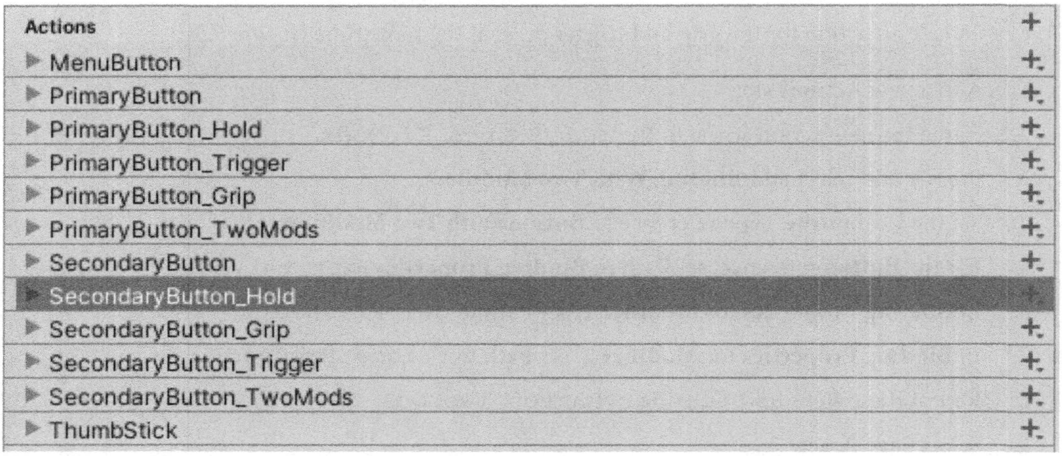

Figure 8.4 – Custom input actions for the primary, secondary, menu, and thumbstick buttons

In the next section, we will introduce Unity Events and how they can enhance our input actions with code.

Getting to know Unity Events

In Unity, events are a way to communicate between different components or scripts in a game. Events allow you to send a message to other scripts or components, without having to explicitly reference them.

Unity Events are defined using the `UnityEvent` class, which is part of the `UnityEngine.Events` namespace. Unity Events can be used to trigger actions, such as playing a sound, displaying a message, or changing a variable. Unity Events can be used to invoke methods, change properties, and send custom events.

Events can be added to a script in Unity by creating a public variable of the `UnityEvent` type and then using the `UnityEvent` editor window to add methods or functions to the event. Once the event is set up, other scripts or components can subscribe to the event using the + button in the `UnityEvent` editor window.

Unity Events are useful for creating a flexible and modular system in your project, where different parts of your game can communicate with each other without knowing about each other's existence. This makes it easy to add new functionality to a game without having to change existing scripts or components.

In the next section, we will use the Unity Event System to trigger events with input actions.

Triggering events with input actions

When it comes to VR development, the use of the Unity Event System can be particularly important because it allows you to map input actions to specific events. This means that you can use the input from your VR controllers to trigger events, which can be used to manipulate objects in the scene, play sounds, or even transition to a different scene.

For example, you might create an input action that triggers an event when the player presses a button on their VR controller. This event could be used to simulate a button press in the game world, such as opening a door or starting a vehicle. By using the Unity Event System, you can create a flexible and responsive control system that can be customized to suit the needs of your VR game or experience.

In this section, we will learn how to utilize input actions that we previously made by creating a new C# script. We will call it `BasicInputActionManager` and add an empty GO within it to reference the input action asset that we have. We will use the Unity Event System along with the Unity Engine Input System. By mastering the inputs and the events, you will be well on your way.

To create a C# `InputActionManager` script, go through the following steps:

1. Create a new C# script.
2. Name it `BasicInputActionManager`.
3. Create a new empty GO and name it `Managers`.
4. Create a new empty GO as a child of `Managers` and name it `BasicInputActionManager`.
5. Add the script to this GO.
6. Open the `BasicInputActionManager` script in Visual Studio.
7. Modify the script using the following code:

```
using UnityEngine;
using UnityEngine.InputSystem;
using UnityEngine.Events;

public class BasicInputActionManager : MonoBehaviour
{
    public InputActionAsset actionAsset;
    public InputActionReference actionReference;
    public UnityEvent actionEvent;


    private void Awake()
    {
        actionReference.action.performed +=
            OnButtonPressed;
    }
```

```
    private void OnDestroy()
    {
        actionReference.action.performed -=
            OnButtonPressed;
    }

    private void OnButtonPressed(
    InputAction.CallbackContext context)
    {
        actionEvent.Invoke();
    }
}
```

8. Save the script and recompile it.

We can now trigger an event using a function of code and an input action referencing one of the buttons we made. The script we created is simply a way to pair input actions with functions using the Unity Event System (*Figure 8.5*). Simple but effective. What we can do now is use a button to toggle the rotation of the cube on or off instead of hovering over it.

To do that, go through the following steps:

1. Open the `RotateObject` script.
2. Add the following code as a new method:

```
    public void ToggleRotate()
    {
        isRotating = !isRotating;
    }
```

3. Save it and recompile.
4. In the `BasicInputActionManager` GO, click + under **Action Event()**.
5. Add the cube to the reference slot.
6. Use the `ToggleRotate` function (*Figure 8.5*) to trigger the Cube to rotate using the script.
7. Set **Action Asset** to `XRI Default Input Actions`.
8. Set **Action Reference** to `Custom Inputs/PrimaryButton`.

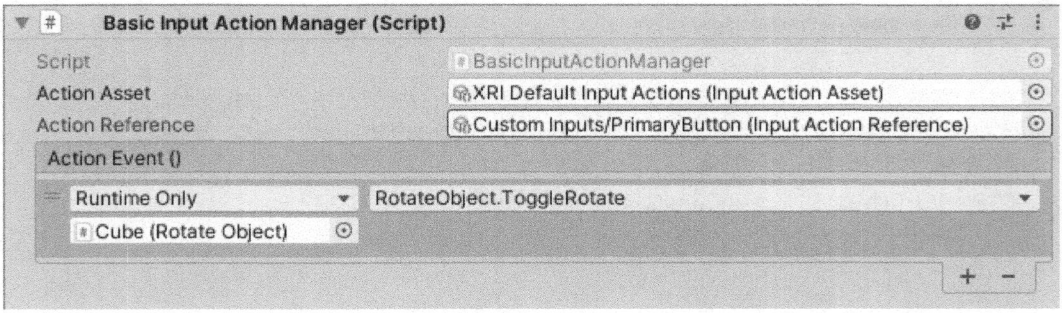

Figure 8.5 – Basic Input Action Manager C# component using toggle rotation

Now, we can make the cube rotate on and off with our primary button press.

The next one we will create is a script to toggle the visibility of a GO (*Figure 8.6*).

To do that, go through the following steps:

1. Create a new C# script.
2. Name it `ToggleVisibility`.
3. Open it, and modify the script using the following code:

```
using UnityEngine;

public class ToggleVisibility : MonoBehaviour
{
    public void ToggleVisibilty()
    {
        bool isActive = !gameObject.activeSelf;
        gameObject.SetActive(isActive);
    }
}
```

4. Save it and recompile.
5. Place the `ToggleVissibility` script on the `Sphere` GO.
6. Duplicate the `BasicInputActionManager` GO.
7. In the `BasicInputActionManager` script, set **Action Reference** to **Custom Inputs/SecondaryButton**.
8. Add the sphere to the **Action Event** reference slot.
9. Select the `ToggleVisibility` function.

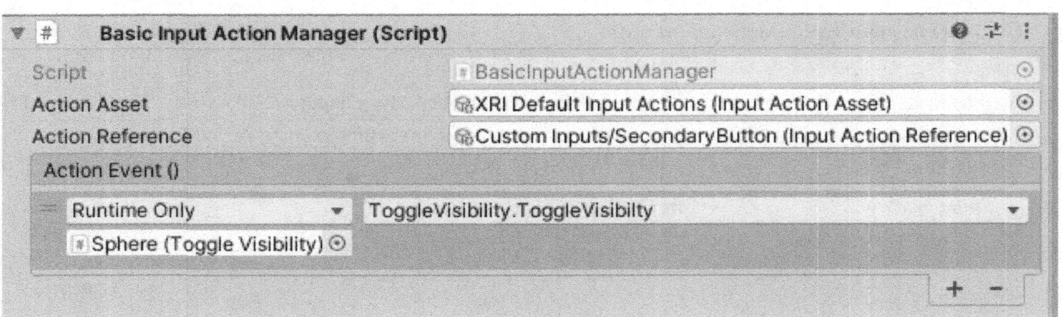

Figure 8.6 – Basic Input Action Manager C# component using Toggle Visibility

When you press the secondary button, the sphere will be enabled and disabled.

We just created a new C# script and used the Unity Engine Input System and the Unity Event System. We learned how to create an input action toggle and a script called `ToggleVisibility` that toggles off and on. We also learned how to create an input action manager and add custom actions to it.

We will create an input manager that allows us to create multiple buttons.

To create an input manager C# script (*Figure 8.7*), go through the following steps:

1. Create a new C# script.
2. Name it `InputActionManager`.
3. Create an empty GO, and name it `InputActionManager`.
4. Place the `InputActionManager` script on the `InputActionManager` GO.
5. Open the script and modify the script with the following code:

```
using UnityEngine;
using UnityEngine.InputSystem;
using UnityEngine.Events;

public class InputActionManager : MonoBehaviour
{

    [System.Serializable]
    public class CustomActions
    {
        public string actionName;
        public InputActionReference actionReference;
        public UnityEvent actionEvent;
    }
```

```
    public InputActionAsset actionAsset;
    public CustomActions[] actions;

    private void Awake()
    {
        for(int i=0; i < actions.Length; i++)
        {
            if(actions[i].actionReference != null)
            {
                actions[i].actionReference.action
                    .performed += OnButtonPressed;
            }
        }
    }

    private void OnDestroy()
    {
        for (int i = 0; i < actions.Length; i++)
        {
                actions[i].actionReference.action
                    .performed -= OnButtonPressed;
        }
    }

    private void OnButtonPressed(
    InputAction.CallbackContext context)
    {
        for (int i = 0; i < actions.Length; i++)
        {
            if (actions[i].actionReference != null &&
                actions[i].actionReference.action==
                context.action)
                actions[i].actionEvent.Invoke();
        }
    }
}
```

6. Save it and recompile.
7. In **Inspector**, set **Action Asset** to `XRI Default Input Action`.
8. Click + for **Actions** and open the dropdown menu.
9. Set **Action Name** to `ThumbStickPress`.
10. Set **Action Reference** to `CustomInputs/ThumbStick`.

11. Press + under **Action Event**.
12. Set the reference slot to the `Cylinder` GO.
13. Set the function to **MeshRenderer | Material material**.
14. Set the material to `Blue_Metallic`.
15. Repeat *steps 7 -14* for `PrimaryButton` and choose something to trigger. I chose the cube rotation from earlier.
16. Repeat *steps 7–14* for `SecondaryButton` and choose something to trigger. I chose the sphere toggle visibility from earlier.

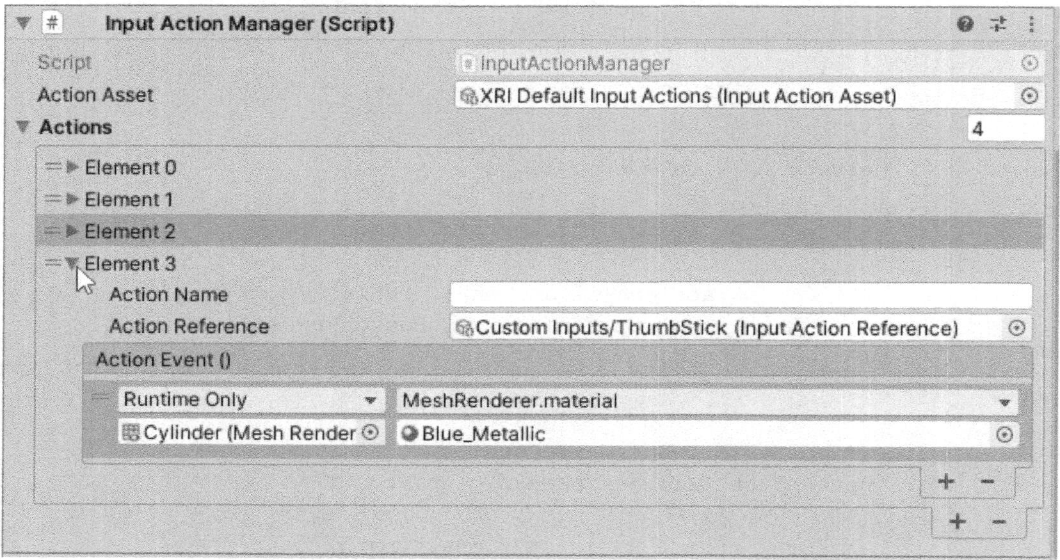

Figure 8.7 – Input Action Manager script component

We now have an input manager controller that lets us pair any button actions on our controller with any function within the Unity Editor. This is a powerful piece of code that can be used in a variety of situations.

We will next pair a `PrimaryButton_Hold` input action with a scale-up function and `SecondaryButton_Hold` with a scale-down function to increase and decrease the size of a GO depending on how long the button is held.

To create a `ToggleScale` C# script (*Figure 8.8*), go through the following steps:

1. Create a new C# script.
2. Name it `ToggleScale`.

3. Open it with Visual Studio.
4. Modify the script with the following code:

```
using UnityEngine;
using UnityEngine.InputSystem;

public class ToggleScale : MonoBehaviour
{
    public InputActionAsset inputActionAsset;
    public InputActionReference scaleUp;
    public InputActionReference scaleDown;
    private Vector3 intialscale;
    private bool isScalingUp;
    private bool isScalingDown;

    // Start is called before the first frame update
    void Start()
    {
        intialscale = transform.localScale;
        inputActionAsset.Enable();
        scaleUp.action.performed += ctx =>
            isScalingUp = true;
        scaleUp.action.performed += ctx =>
            isScalingUp = false;
        scaleDown.action.performed += ctx =>
            isScalingDown = true;
        scaleDown.action.performed += ctx =>
            isScalingDown = false;
    }
    private void OnDestroy()
    {
        inputActionAsset.Disable();
    }
    // Update is called once per frame
    private void Update()
    {
        if (isScalingUp)
        {
            transform.localScale += new Vector3(.01f,
                .01f, .01f);
        }
        else if (isScalingDown)
        {
```

```
                transform.localScale -= new Vector3(.01f,
                    .01f, .01f);
            }
        }
        public void ScaleUp()
        {
            isScalingUp = true;
            isScalingDown = false;
        }
        public void ScaleDown()
        {
            isScalingUp = false;
            isScalingDown = true;
        }
        public void ScaleNull()
        {
            isScalingUp = false;
            isScalingDown = false;
        }
    }
```

5. Save it and compile.
6. Add the script to the `Sphere` GO.
7. In `InputActionManager`, click + to add another action.
8. Set **Action Name** to `ScalingUp`.
9. Set **Action Reference** to `PrimaryButton_Hold`.
10. Click + for **Action Event**.
11. Set the reference to the `Sphere` GO.
12. Set the function to **ToggleScale | ScaleUp**.
13. Click + to add another action
14. Set **Action Name** to `ScalingDown`.
15. Set **Action Reference** to `SecondaryButton_Hold`.
16. Click + for **Action Event**.
17. Set the reference to the `Sphere` GO.
18. Set the function to **ToggleScale | ScaleDown**.

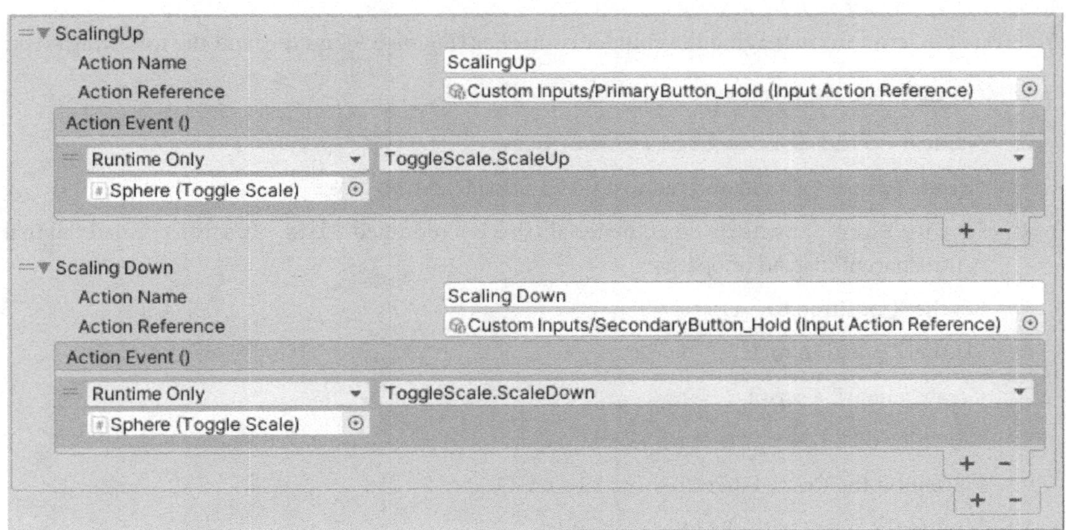

Figure 8.8 – Applying the Toggle Scale functions to our input actions

In this section, we have successfully created a script that allows for the scaling up and down of an object in Unity using input actions. We went through the process of declaring variables, defining methods, and assigning input actions to those methods. By following these steps, we can now add this functionality to our VR development projects in Unity.

In the next section, we will learn how to use colliders and triggers to perform Unity Events.

Triggering events with colliders

Using colliders and triggers to perform Unity Events is important for VR development because it allows the user to interact with objects and control the environment in a more intuitive and immersive way. By using colliders, the user can use their hand or a controller to touch or grab objects in the virtual environment, which triggers a Unity Event. These events can then be used to perform actions such as opening doors, activating buttons, or changing the state of objects in the environment.

It is crucial to create a seamless and intuitive experience for the user, and using colliders and triggers to perform Unity Events is an effective way to achieve this. By allowing the user to interact with the environment in a natural and intuitive way, the VR experience becomes more immersive and engaging. Additionally, the use of colliders and triggers allows for a wide range of interactions and actions to be performed in the virtual environment, which adds depth and complexity to the overall experience.

In this section, we will be creating an empty object and organizing our collider controllers. We will also be using the `OnTrigger` Event System to check whether something is triggered and then modify it. It will also change the color of the cube mesh based on specific conditions.

To create C# script for managing the collider controller (*Figure 8.9*), go through the following steps:

1. Create a new empty GO.
2. Name it `ColliderControllerManager`.
3. Create a cube as a child and name it `ColliderController`.
4. Give it a `Blue_Transparent` material. This is a modified `Blue_Standard` material that is transparent instead of opaque.
5. Set the **X** position to `-1`.
6. Set the **Z** position to `1`.
7. Create a new C# script.
8. Name it `Collider Controller`.
9. Place it on the `ColliderController` GO.
10. Modify the script with the following code:

```
using UnityEngine;
using UnityEngine.Events;

public class ColliderController : MonoBehaviour
{
    public string colliderTag;
    public UnityEvent enterEvent;
    public UnityEvent stayEvent;
    public UnityEvent exitEvent;

    private void OnTriggerEnter(Collider other)
    {
        if (other.tag == colliderTag)
        {
            enterEvent.Invoke();
        }
    }

    private void OnTriggerStay(Collider other)
    {
        if (other.tag == colliderTag)
        {
            stayEvent.Invoke();
        }
    }
```

```
    private void OnTriggerExit(Collider other)
    {
        if (other.tag == colliderTag)
        {
            exitEvent.Invoke();
        }
    }
}
```

11. Save it and recompile.
12. In **Inspector**, go to the `ColliderController` GO.
13. Enable **Is Trigger** on the `Box Collider` component.
14. Set **Collider Tag** to `LeftHand`. This predefined tag should correspond to the GO `Layer Tag` of the same name we set in the layer settings for the GO in **Inspector**. In this case, we will be using `LeftHand` as the tag, but you can choose any tag as long as **Collider Tag** and **Layer Tag** match exactly.
15. Click + for `Enter Event`, `Stay Event`, and `Exit Event`.
16. Add the `ColliderController` GO to all three event reference slots.
17. Set the functions for all three event reference slots to **MeshRenderer | Material material**.
18. Set the `Enter Event` material to `Red_Emission`.
19. Set the `Stay Event` material to `Green_Unlit`. This event will actually overwrite `Enter Event` if enabled.
20. Set the `Exit Event` material to `Blue_Transparent`.
21. Go to the `LeftHand Controller` GO.
22. Disable **Is Trigger** on the collider. Compared to the boxes that have **Is Trigger** enabled, we disable **Is Trigger** on our `LeftHand` collider because we only need one collider in an interaction to have **Is Trigger** enabled.
23. Set the layer to `LeftHand`. This is case-sensitive and should match the **Collider Tag** string exactly. If it does not exist, select the **Layer** dropdown, and add a new layer called `LeftHand` in an empty **Layer** slot.

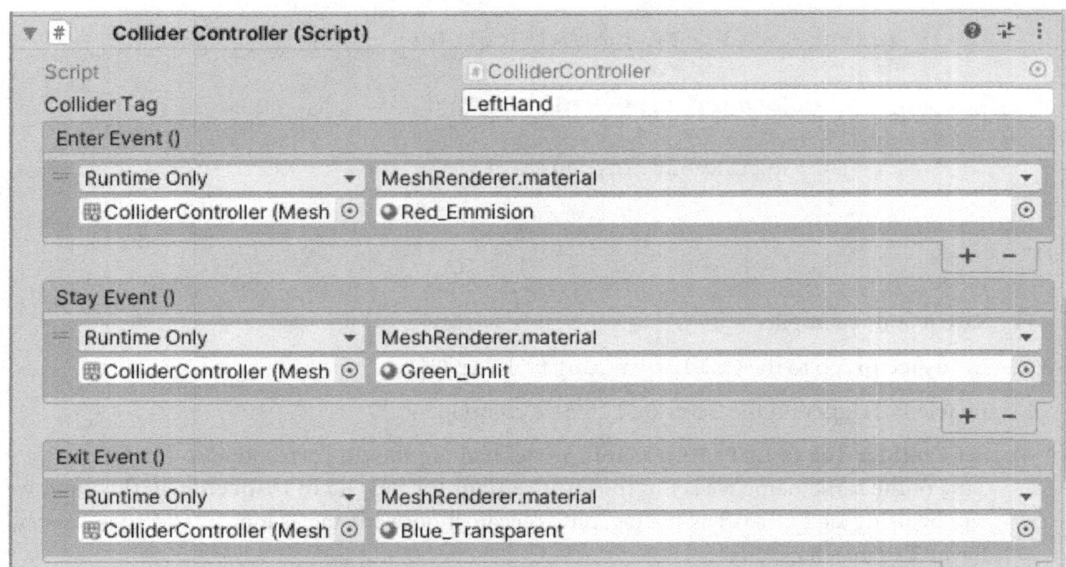

Figure 8.9 – Collider Controller C# component

When you place your hand in the cube, you will see that it changes colliders depending on whether your hand is in the cube or not. We can make this a prefab and reuse it in the scene now.

To create additional collider controllers (*Figure 8.10*), go through the following steps:

1. Duplicate `Collider Controller`.
2. Change the cube's material to `Orange_Transparent`.
3. Set `Exit Event` for this `ColliderController` to `Orange_Transparent`.
4. Set `Stay Event` to **Off**.
5. Add another `Enter Event` and `Exit Event` with +.
6. Set the reference slot for both to the `Sphere` GO in our scene (*Figure 8.10*).
7. Set the `Exit Event Sphere` function to **Toggle | ScaleNull**.
8. Set the `Enter Event Sphere` function to **Toggle | ScaleDown.**
9. Repeat *steps 4–7* for the blue `ColliderController`.
10. Set the `Enter Event Sphere` function to **Toggle | ScaleUp**.

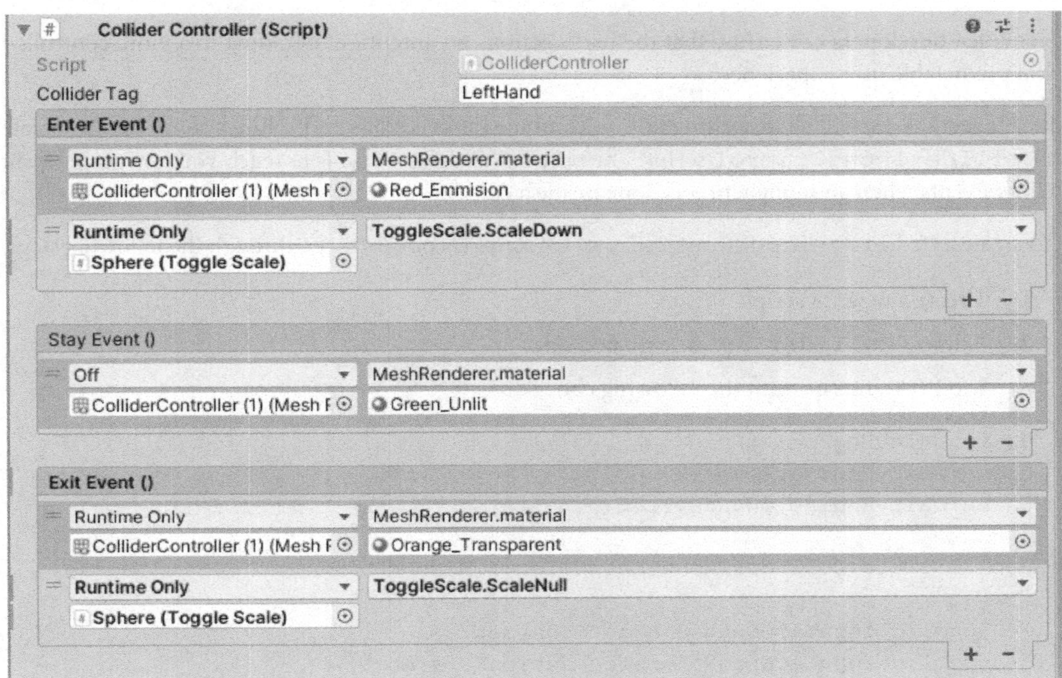

Figure 8.10 – Collider Controller C# component that triggers events affecting other GOs

We now have two colliders we can use to scale the sphere up and down when we place our hands in there.

In the next section, we will combine our knowledge of colliders, triggers, and input actions to trigger Unity Events only when an input action is performed inside a collider.

Combining collider triggers with input actions

Using colliders, triggers, and input actions to trigger Unity Events only when an input action is performed inside a collider is important for VR development because it allows for a more intuitive and immersive user experience. In VR, the user's hands and fingers are tracked, and by using colliders and triggers, developers can create virtual objects that react realistically to the user's actions.

For example, if a user's hand enters a collider trigger and performs a specific input action such as a button press or trigger pull, it can activate an event that performs a corresponding action in the virtual world, such as opening a door or firing a gun. This type of interaction allows the user to feel like they are truly interacting with the virtual world and can lead to a more immersive and engaging VR experience.

In addition, using colliders and triggers in this way can also help to prevent accidental input actions from triggering events. By restricting events to only occur when the input action is performed inside a collider, developers can ensure that the user's actions are intentional, leading to a more controlled and predictable user experience.

In this section, we will be discussing how to combine input actions and collider controllers to create a `ColliderInputControl` script. The purpose of this section is to teach you how to perform Unity Events when an input action is done inside a collider.

To create a `ColliderInputController` C# script (*Figure 8.11*), go through the following steps:

1. Create a new C# script.
2. Name it `ColliderInputController`.
3. Modify the script with the following code:

```
using UnityEngine;
using UnityEngine.Events;
using UnityEngine.InputSystem;

public class ColliderInputController : MonoBehaviour
{
    public InputActionAsset actionAsset;
    public InputActionReference actionReference;
    public string colliderTag;
    public UnityEvent enterEvent;
    public UnityEvent stayEvent;
    public UnityEvent exitEvent;
    public UnityEvent actionEvent;


    private void OnEnable()
    {
        actionAsset.Enable();
    }
    private void OnDisable()
    {
        actionAsset.Disable();
    }

    private void OnTriggerEnter(Collider other)
    {
        if (other.tag == colliderTag)
        {
            enterEvent.Invoke();
            actionReference.action.performed += ctx =>
```

```
                PerformedAction(ctx);
        }
    }

    private void OnTriggerStay(Collider other)
    {
        if (other.tag == colliderTag)
        {
            stayEvent.Invoke();
        }
    }

    private void OnTriggerExit(Collider other)
    {
        if (other.tag == colliderTag)
        {
            actionReference.action.performed -= ctx =>
                PerformedAction(ctx);
            exitEvent.Invoke();
        }
    }

    private void PerformedAction(
    InputAction.CallbackContext ctx)
    {
        actionEvent.Invoke();
    }
}
```

4. Save it and recompile.
5. Duplicate the `ColliderController` prefab.
6. Rename it `ColliderInputController`.
7. Add the `ColliderInputController` script to it.
8. Remove the `ColliderController` script from this prefab.

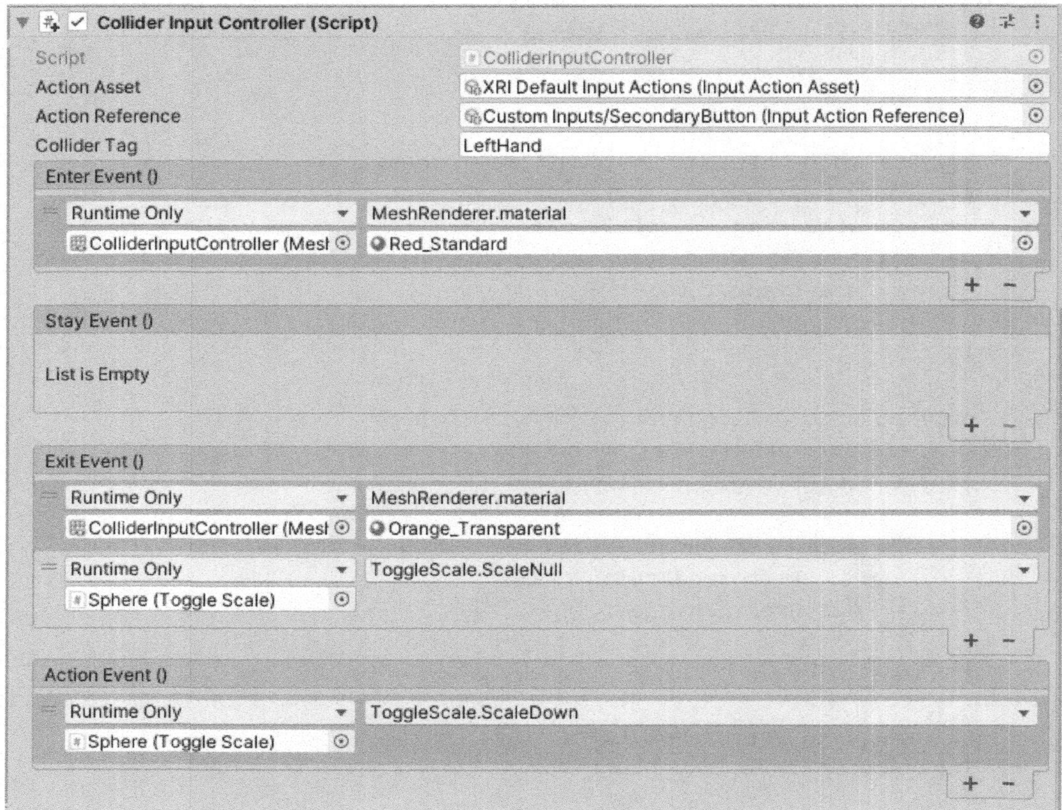

Figure 8.11 – Collider Input Controller C# component

By following the step-by-step guide, you now have the ability to create your own Collider Input Controller and apply it to your VR development projects.

In the next section, we will use colliders and Unity Events to create portals that teleport our player to other locations on the map.

Creating portals with colliders and events

Using colliders and Unity Events to create portals that teleport the player to other locations on the map is important for VR development because it enables seamless and immersive navigation within the virtual environment. By using colliders to trigger Unity Events when the player enters a specific area, we can create a mechanism for teleporting the player to another part of the map instantly. This can help to eliminate motion sickness and other discomforts associated with traditional movement in VR, such as joystick-based locomotion or teleporting through menus.

Portals can also be used to create interesting and engaging puzzles, challenges, and experiences in VR. For example, a puzzle game could require the player to find and activate several portals to unlock the final challenge. Or an adventure game could use portals to transport the player to different worlds, environments, or dimensions. Additionally, portals can help to save time and energy in game development by providing a faster and more efficient means of travel between different areas of the map.

In this section, we will cover how to create a portal in Unity using colliders and prefabs. We will also discuss the creation of a portal manager, a script to control all the portals that we have.

To create a portal with ProBuilder and C# (*Figure 8.12*), go through the following steps:

1. Create an empty GO.
2. Name it `Portal Manager`.
3. Create an empty GO as a child and name it `Portal`.
4. Set the **X** position to `4`.
5. Add a ProBuilder door (*right-click* | **ProBuilder** | **Door**) as a child of the `Portal` GO. If you have not installed ProBuilder, follow the steps found in the *Converting the floor plan to a 3D room with ProBuilder* section of *Chapter 4*.
6. Name it `PortalFrame`.
7. Set the material to `Yellow_Specular`.
8. Open the door in ProBuilder.
9. Set the **Y** rotation to `90`.
10. Set the **Z** position to `1.5`.
11. Add a `cube` GO as a child of the door.
12. Name it `PortalDoor`.
13. Enable **Is Trigger** on the `Box Collider` component.
14. Set the **X** scale to `3`.
15. Set the **Y** scale to `2.4`.
16. Set the **Z** scale to `.5`.
17. Set the **Y** position to `1.3`.
18. Set the **X** position to `.5`.
19. Set the material to `Blue_Metallic`.
20. Create a new GO as a child of the `Portal` GO.
21. Name it `PortalAnchor`.
22. Set the **X** position to `.5`.
23. Create a new C# script.

24. Name it `PortalManager`.
25. Open it with Visual Studio.
26. Modify the script with the following code:

```
using UnityEngine;

public class PortalManager : MonoBehaviour
{
    public string playerTag;
    public GameObject destination;
    public GameObject player;
    public float portalCooldown;
    private float cooldownTime;
    private bool onCooldown;

    private void Start()
    {
        cooldownTime = 0.0f;
        onCooldown = false;
    }
    private void Update()
    {
        if (onCooldown)
        {
            cooldownTime -= Time.deltaTime;
            if (cooldownTime <= 0.0f)
            {
                onCooldown = false;
            }
        }
    }
    public void StartCoolDown()
    {
        if (!onCooldown)
        {
            cooldownTime = portalCooldown;
            onCooldown = true;
        }
    }
    private void OnTriggerEnter(Collider other)
    {
        if (other.gameObject.tag ==
        playerTag&&!onCooldown)
```

```
            {
                StartCoolDown();
                player.transform.position =
                    destination.transform.position;
            }
        }
    }
```

27. Save it and recompile.
28. Add the `PortalManager` script to the `Portal` GO.
29. Set **Player Tag** to `Player`.
30. Set **Player** to the `XR Origin` GO.
31. Set **Portal Cooldown** to `3`.
32. Turn the `Portal` GO into a prefab.
33. Duplicate it.
34. Create another plane in your scene (*right-click* on **Hierarchy** | **Create** | **3D Object** | **Plane**) and place the second portal on it as a child of the new `Plane` GO using the `Transform` component to align the bottom `Portal` GO with the surface of the plane, as shown in *Figure 8.12*.

Figure 8.12 – Portal made with ProBuilder, a cube, and various materials

35. In the **Destination** reference slot in the `PortalManager` script component for each portal, place the opposing `PortalAnchor` GO in the slot. This is the location you will be teleported to when you enter the other portal. You may need to create a non-prefab `PortalAnchor` by duplicating the current `PortalAnchor` GO in the `Portal` prefab because the script may confuse one instance of the `PortalAnchor` prefab with another instance already in the scene.

To avoid this, duplicate the `PortalAnchor` GO you intend on using and use the duplicate `PortalAnchor` GO instead of the original `PortalAnchor` GO within the `Portal` prefab.

By following these step-by-step instructions, you should now have a better understanding of how to create a portal in Unity.

Figure 8.13 – Portal demo scene with two portals on planes

In the next section, we will create a portal that can take us to another scene.

Switching between scenes with portals

Portals can be used to create immersive experiences by allowing players to move between different environments. Unity Events and scene management are important for VR development because they allow you to create interactive objects and environments that can be controlled by player input. With these tools, you can create portals, teleportation systems, and other immersive features that enhance the VR experience. By using Unity Events, you can make your VR application more interactive and engaging, which can improve user engagement and immersion.

In this section, we will learn how to create a portal in Unity that can take us to another scene. We will use Unity Events and scene management to achieve this. This section is essential for VR development as it allows for seamless transitions between different areas of the virtual environment.

To create a portal that teleports to another scene (*Figure 8.14*), go through the following steps:

1. Create a new scene.
2. Name it `DemoRoomScene` and open it.
3. Delete the main camera. The main camera we will be using will come from our `VR Rig` prefab.
4. Add the `DemoRoom` prefab.
5. Add the `VR Rig Physics & Sounds` prefab. If you do not have this prefab, follow the instructions from the *Adding audio events to our VR rig* section of *Chapter 7*.
6. Save the scene and go back to the previous scene.

7. Duplicate the `Portal` GO and rename it `Portal_Scene`.
8. Place it in an open location on the plane.
9. Remove the `PortalManager` script.
10. Create a new C# script and name it `PortalSceneManager`.
11. Place it on the `Portal_Scene` GO.
12. Open it in Visual Studio.
13. Modify the script with the following code:

```
using UnityEngine;
using UnityEngine.SceneManagement;

public class PortalSceneManager : MonoBehaviour
{
    public string nextScene;
    public string playerTag;

    private void OnTriggerEnter(Collider other)
    {
        if (other.CompareTag(playerTag))
        {
            SceneManager.LoadScene(nextSceneName);
        }
    }
}
```

14. Save it and recompile.
15. In **Inspector**, set **Player Tag** to `Player`.
16. Turn `Portal_Scene` into a prefab variant. To create a prefab variant, follow the instructions in the *Creating Prefabs with our GOs* section in *Chapter 4*.
17. Set the **Next Scene** string name to `DemoRoomScene`. Remember that the string you use must match the name and case of the scene exactly.
18. Open **Build Settings (File | Build Settings)**.
19. Add `DemoRoomScene` to the **Scenes in Build** menu. This is a must or the scene-switching will not work. To effectively change scenes, you must have all potential scenes you intend to switch to in the **Scenes in Build** menu.
20. Save the scene and test the portal by entering Play mode and navigating your VR rig into the portal area you set to trigger the portal effect. The portal should take you to the new `DemoRoom` scene.

Figure 8.14 – Three portals in the demo scene; the two outer ones teleport between each other and the middle one teleports to another scene

You have successfully created a portal that takes you to another scene in Unity using Unity Events and scene management. This is an important technique to learn for VR development as it allows for seamless transitions between different areas in a virtual environment. In this section, we covered how to create a new scene, a portal, and a new script, load the scene, add the scene to the **Build** settings, and test the portal.

Summary

We have covered various aspects of VR development in Unity in this chapter. We started by discussing the importance of structuring C# code and understanding its syntax to make it clear, concise, and easily understandable for others. We also learned about the Unity Event System and how it can be used to trigger events with input actions, which is essential for VR development.

Next, we learned how to create portals that can transport us to another scene in Unity. We achieved this by using triggers and colliders to detect when the player enters a certain area, allowing us to load a new scene and move the player to that location. We also created a prefab variant for our portal scenes to make it easier to add them to our game.

We then explored the C# code required to make the portals work. We created a new C# script called `PortalSceneManager` that handles the transition between scenes. This script includes a public scene asset, which allows us to select the scene we want to load. We also added a player tag that ensures only the player triggers the portal, preventing other objects from accidentally triggering it. By understanding and implementing these concepts, we can create immersive and engaging VR experiences in Unity.

This concludes the basics of Unity development for VR. Next, we will briefly cover render pipelines before we move on to more robust Unity projects that incorporate all the skills we have developed over the past eight chapters.

9

Unlocking the Power of Render Pipelines

In VR, creating a believable and immersive world is essential for the user experience. To achieve this, it's necessary to render high-quality graphics at a high frame rate to maintain immersion, and that's where render pipelines come in!

A render pipeline is a set of instructions that dictate how the graphics in a Unity scene are processed and displayed to the user. There are several types of render pipelines, including the **built-in render pipeline**, as well as **High Definition Render Pipeline** (**HDRP**) and **Universal Render Pipeline** (**URP**).

Choosing the right render pipeline is crucial because it determines the quality and performance of your VR project. If your pipeline is inefficient or slow, it can lead to lower frame rates and decreased immersion, which can negatively impact the user experience.

Different render pipelines come with unique features and limitations, so it's crucial to choose the pipeline that best suits your project's needs. Some pipelines support advanced features such as real-time shadows and post-processing effects, while others focus on performance and compatibility with specific VR devices.

In this chapter, we will cover the following topics:

- What are render pipelines?
- Understanding which render pipeline is best for your project
- Exporting a project from the built-in render pipeline to another render pipeline
- Exploring and configuring URP
- Exploring and configuring HDRP
- Enabling post-processing in URP and HDRP
- Converting render pipelines within the same project

Render pipelines are crucial for VR development because they determine how the graphics in your scene are processed and displayed, affecting the performance and quality of your project. It's essential to choose the right pipeline for your project, depending on its requirements and limitations, to achieve optimal performance and immersion.

Getting to know Unity's Scriptable Render Pipeline

Unity's **Scriptable Render Pipeline** (**SRP**) is a powerful tool that allows developers to create custom render pipelines tailored to their specific VR projects. It provides full control over the rendering process and can significantly improve performance and visual quality. We mentioned URP and HDRP previously. They are both built on top of SRP. Creating a custom render pipeline requires a deep understanding of graphics programming and is not a beginner-friendly task.

Here are the key features of Unity's SRP:

- **Customizability**: Unity's SRP allows developers to customize the rendering pipeline as they can create shaders and rendering algorithms. This level of customization allows for better optimization and performance.
- **Improved performance**: SRP is designed to help developers improve performance by allowing them to create customized and more efficient rendering solutions for their experiences. It can be optimized for specific hardware and VR devices, leading to better frame rates and overall performance.
- **Enhanced visual quality**: SRP also allows developers to create high-quality graphics and visual effects. It supports advanced features such as volumetric lighting, real-time shadows, and global illumination, which can significantly enhance the immersive experience in VR.
- **Better workflows**: SRP is designed to improve workflows and reduce development time. With its flexible architecture and intuitive interface, developers can easily create and modify their render pipelines, saving time and resources.

The importance of Unity's SRP in VR development lies in its ability to create custom rendering solutions that are optimized for specific hardware and VR devices. This level of customization can improve performance and visual quality, leading to a more immersive VR experience.

Additionally, SRP's flexibility and ease of use make it an ideal tool for VR development. With the ability to create and modify custom pipelines quickly and efficiently, developers can save time and resources while ensuring the highest level of quality and performance for their VR projects.

To learn more about SRP, visit `https://docs.unity3d.com/Manual/ScriptableRenderPipeline.html`.

What are the different render pipelines?

Unity also allows you to use custom render pipelines, which is a way of creating your own render pipeline by using the SRP API. This allows you to create highly optimized and custom render pipelines that are tailored to your specific needs.

In Unity, a render pipeline is a set of instructions that dictate how 3D models, materials, and lights are rendered to the screen. Unity provides several built-in render pipelines, including the **built-in render pipeline**, URP, and HDRP. Render pipelines are responsible for tasks such as culling, lighting, shadows, reflections, and post-processing effects.

The built-in render pipeline is the default render pipeline in Unity. It's a simple and lightweight pipeline that provides basic support for 3D graphics and is suitable for most 2D and 3D games.

URP is a more advanced render pipeline that provides increased performance and improved visual quality over a wide range of devices. The performance and quality out of the box are better than using the built-in render pipeline. It's designed to be flexible, customizable, and easy to use. It uses the SRP API, which allows you to create custom render pipeline assets.

HDRP is a highly advanced and powerful render pipeline that provides photorealistic graphics and cinematic-quality visual effects. It's designed for use in high-end PC and console games, as well as architectural visualization, film, and animation. Although most VR standalone headsets such as the Oculus Quest 2 would not be suitable for HDRP, PC-based headsets such as the HTC Vive can support VR experiences created with HDRP.

Which one is best for your project?

Out of the box, the built-in render pipeline can be good to start with, but when you are trying to launch a project with the most optimal visuals and performance, you should consider using URP or HDRP. There are some great benefits in upgrading, but you must pay attention to the device you will be deploying to for the final render pipeline decision.

HDRP is the most advanced render pipeline provided by Unity and provides photorealistic graphics and cinematic-quality visual effects. It's designed for use in high-end PC and console games, as well as architectural visualization, film, and animation. It supports **physically based rendering** (**PBR**), advanced lighting and reflections, volumetric lighting and fog, advanced post-processing effects, and ray tracing. HDRP is considered to be the best option for visually stunning VR experiences if you intend to make experiences with the most realistic visuals, but it will require additional optimization and tweaking. This option is best for PC-based headsets or PlayStation VR experiences, where the headset is attached to a high-end computer and has a dedicated graphics card.

For lower-end headsets such as the Oculus Quest, URP is a good choice because it's designed to be lightweight and performant, and it provides improved visual quality compared to the built-in render pipeline. URP uses the SRP API, which allows you to create custom render pipelines; this can help you optimize the graphics and performance for the Oculus Quest 2. Additionally, URP supports GPU instancing, which allows you to render multiple instances of the same object with minimal CPU overhead. This can help improve performance.

Exporting our built-in render pipeline project

The built-in render pipeline is the default render pipeline in Unity. It is a simple and lightweight pipeline that provides basic support for 3D graphics and is suitable for most 2D and 3D games. It supports standard materials, forward and deferred rendering, and a limited set of post-processing effects. It also supports basic lighting and shadows, and a limited set of reflection and transparency features. We have done all of our projects in this render pipeline thus far, and that will continue in the remaining chapters, but here, we will cover how to take a project we created in the built-in render pipeline and export it to a project that is using either URP or HDRP. When we export the package, we will need to further configure the project to make it functional in the render pipeline of your choice, but this is the best option rather than converting the current project from a built-in pipeline into one that uses URP or HDRP. At the end of this chapter, we will explore the conversion process, but again, it is not a best practice for working on Unity projects that you expect to launch or get on app stores.

Since we know the most about the built-in render pipeline, let's export our project as a Unity package that can be imported into a project using another render pipeline.

To export a Unity project as a Unity package (*Figure 9.1*), go through the following steps:

1. Navigate to the `Scenes` folder in the **Project** tab.
2. Select all the folders containing scenes that you want to export.
3. Export it as a Unity package (*right-click* | **Export Package**).
4. Select the folder to save the package in.
5. Name the package `BuiltInDemo` and save it.

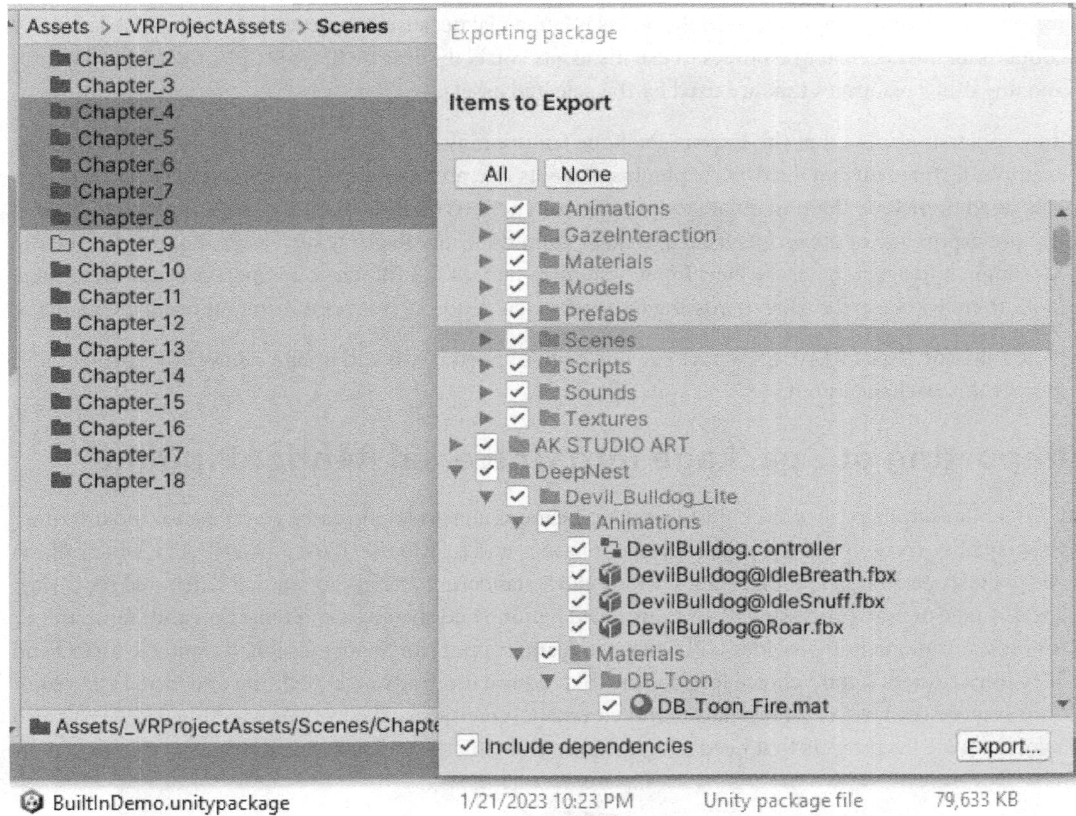

Figure 9.1 – Exporting the projects for Chapters 4 to 8 to a custom Unity package

When you export a package using the **Export Package** feature, you have the option to include all dependencies or exclude them. By default, Unity will export all the necessary dependencies, along with the assets you have selected to export. However, you can also choose to exclude certain dependencies if you do not want them to be included in the package.

> **Note**
>
> There may be some instances where the **Export Package** feature will not export all the dependencies. This is usually the case when the assets are in the `Editor` or `Packages` folder. Be sure to double-check which files were exported successfully before sharing the package with others.

Exporting dependencies along with the assets is beneficial because it ensures that the exported package contains all the necessary resources to use the assets correctly. This includes scripts, materials, textures, and any other resources that are used by the selected assets.

It's important to note that the **Export Package** feature may not always include all dependencies. For example, if you are using third-party plugins or assets that are not part of Unity's standard package, you may need to include them manually or provide instructions on how to obtain them separately. Also, it will not export any of the scripts from a package from the Unity Registry such as ProBuilder, Polybrush, XR Plugin Management, or the New Input System, to name a few. When you import projects using these tools, there will be errors due to missing dependencies. A quick fix is reimporting those dependencies.

Now that our `BuiltInDemo` package has been exported, we will create a new URP project and import this package into it.

Importing our package into Universal Render Pipeline

URP is more advanced than the built-in render pipeline as it provides increased performance and improved visual quality. It's designed to be flexible, customizable, and easy to use. It uses the SRP API, which allows you to create custom render pipelines. URP supports standard materials, forward and deferred rendering, a wide range of post-processing effects, advanced lighting and shadows, and reflection and transparency features. Additionally, it provides GPU instancing and support for Shader Graph. It's suitable for 2D and 3D games, and it's a good choice for projects that require more advanced lighting and visual effects but don't require the level of photorealism and cinematic-quality visual effects provided by HDRP. It's also a good choice for projects that need a high degree of flexibility and customizability.

Figure 9.2 – Universal Render Pipeline 3D sample scene

In this section, we will create a new URP project based on the premade Unity project template that Unity provides and import our `BuiltInDemo` package into the project.

To create a new URP project (*Figure 9.3*), go through the following steps:

1. Open Unity Hub.
2. Select **New Project** in the top-left corner.
3. Select **3D (URP)** from the project template menu.
4. If you have not downloaded the template yet, select **Download Template**.
5. Once you've downloaded the template, select a project name. I named mine `URP_VRProject`.
6. Select a location to save the project.
7. Select the **Editor Version** for the new project at the top of the menu.
8. Select **Create project** to open the project:

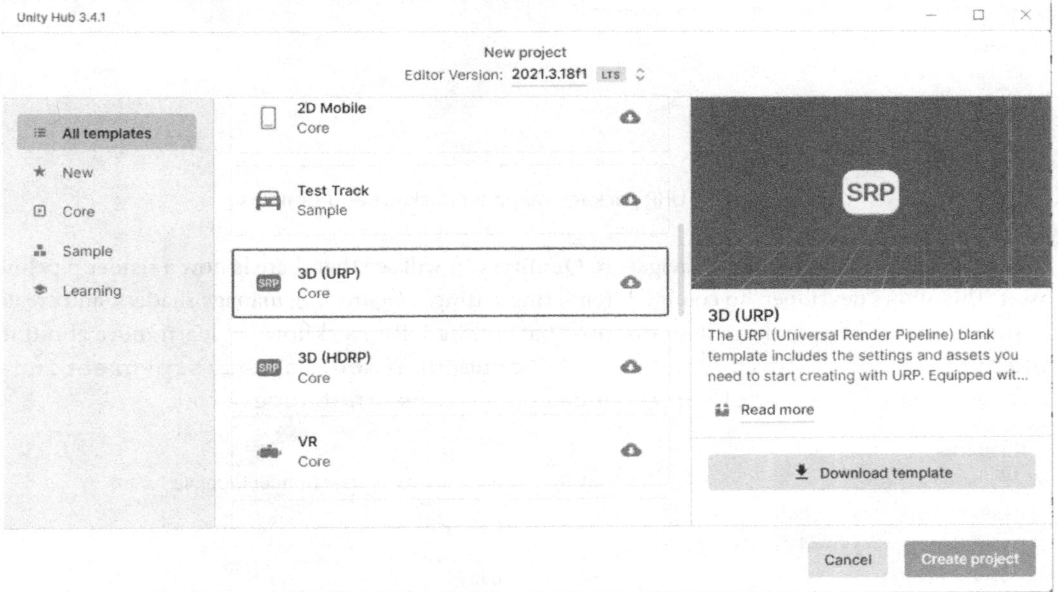

Figure 9.3 – URP project template in Unity Hub

To configure the URP project Registry packages (*Figure 9.4*), go through the following steps:

1. Go to **Package manager**.
2. Go to **Unity Registry**.
3. Install **XR Plugin Management**, as well as the included samples.
4. Install **XR Interaction Toolkit**. You will be asked to restart the project. Click **Confirm**. Your project will be restarted. Don't skip this step as it may cause problems. After the project reopens, install the samples provided.

5. You will notice that URP is enabled. Install the samples provided.
6. Install the **Polybrush** package.
7. Import `Shader Examples (URP)`.
8. Install the **ProBuilder** package.
9. Import **Universal Render Pipeline Support**:

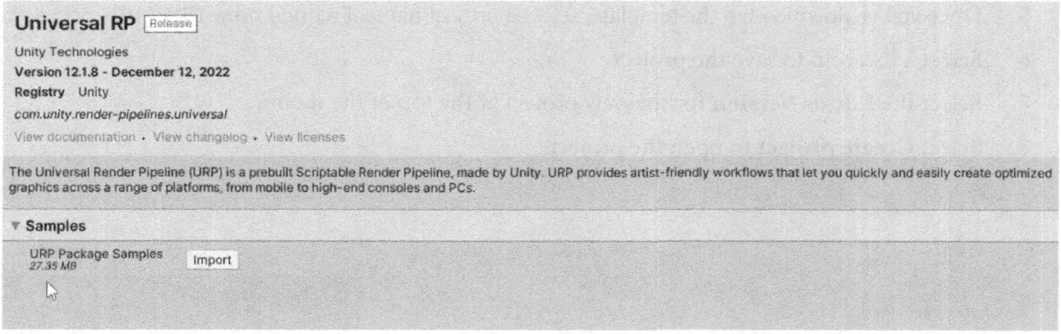

Figure 9.4 – URP package manager package and samples

In the **Project Settings** window, navigate to **Quality**; you will see that there is now a render pipeline asset. This allows developers to configure rendering settings (*Figure 9.5*), manage shaders, and create custom visual effects, making it an essential part of the URP workflow. To learn more about it, visit `https://docs.unity.cn/2019.3/Documentation/Manual/srp-creating-render-pipeline-asset-and-render-pipeline-instance.html`.

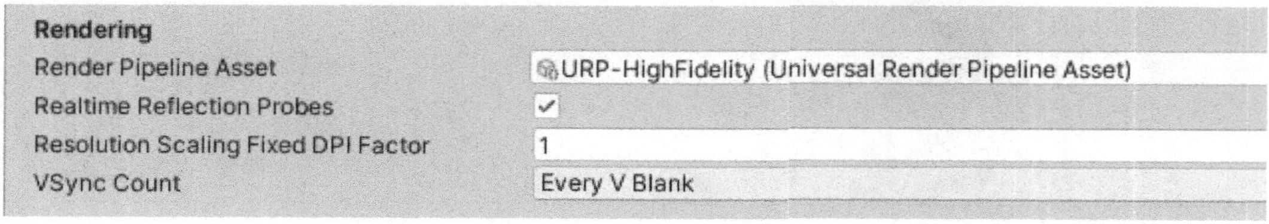

Figure 9.5 – URP quality setting in the Project Settings window

To configure the new URP project with the right settings, go through the following steps:

1. Navigate to **Project Settings**.
2. Under **Quality**, set the quality to **Medium** if you are on a low-end device. Set it to **High/Ultra** if you are on a high-end device.
3. In **XR Plugin Management**, enable **OpenXR**.
4. In **OpenXR**, enable **Oculus Quest Support** under the **Android** tab.

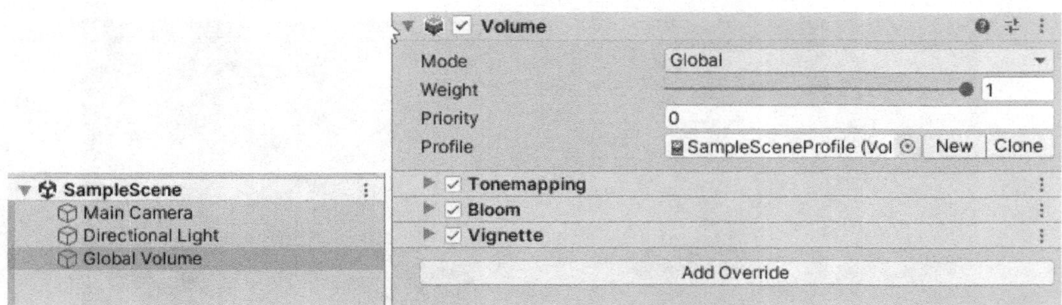

Figure 9.6 – URP Global Volume for applying post-processing effects

In the sample project that comes preinstalled with Unity, you will notice there is a `Global Volume` GO. This takes the place of the post-processing stack we would have downloaded for the original project using the built-in render pipeline. It is used to apply post-processing effects globally to the entire scene. It allows developers to control the look and feel of the scene by adjusting post-processing settings such as color grading, depth of field, motion blur, and ambient occlusion. It affects all the objects in the scene, including cameras, lights, and any other GOs.

To Import our demo package, go through the following steps:

1. Go to **Import Custom Package**.
2. Navigate to the location of the `BuiltInDemo` Unity package.
3. Select **Open**.
4. Select **Import** when the dialog box opens.

With our project imported, we can navigate to the last scene we made in the previous chapter called `DemoRoomScene`. When you open it, you will see that everything is pink (*Figure 9.7*). In URP, materials are created using shaders that are specifically designed for the pipeline. If a material from the original project is not compatible with URP, Unity will use the default "pink" material to replace it. This is done to indicate a shader error and make it easy to identify which materials are not compatible with the current render pipeline.

Figure 9.7 – Pink material error for incompatible render pipeline materials

The fix is pretty easy – you just need to replace the pink materials with materials that are compatible with URP. To do that, go through the following steps:

1. Go to the **Project** tab, select the asset search bar, and isolate all the materials in your project by selecting **Material** from the asset isolation menu, which is the second icon to the right of the search bar (*Figure 9.8*). Alternatively, search for all materials in your project by typing `t:Material` in the search bar.
2. Select all the materials that appear.
3. Open the **Edit** menu. Then, go to **Rendering | Materials | Convert Selected Materials**.

Figure 9.8 – Isolating all materials in the project from the search menu

This will convert most, if not all, materials so that they can work with URP. If you find that some did not convert, you may need to change the shader to the accurate one for that asset. Polybrush and ProBuilder provide URP-compatible shaders that we downloaded earlier in this section. You will have to change the shaders for these individually.

In the next section, we will cover using HDRP.

Importing our package into High Definition Render Pipeline

HDRP is the most advanced render pipeline provided by Unity as it provides photorealistic graphics and cinematic-quality visual effects. It's designed for use in high-end PC and console games, as well as architectural visualization, film, and animation. HDRP supports PBR, advanced lighting and reflections, volumetric lighting and fog, advanced post-processing effects, and ray tracing.

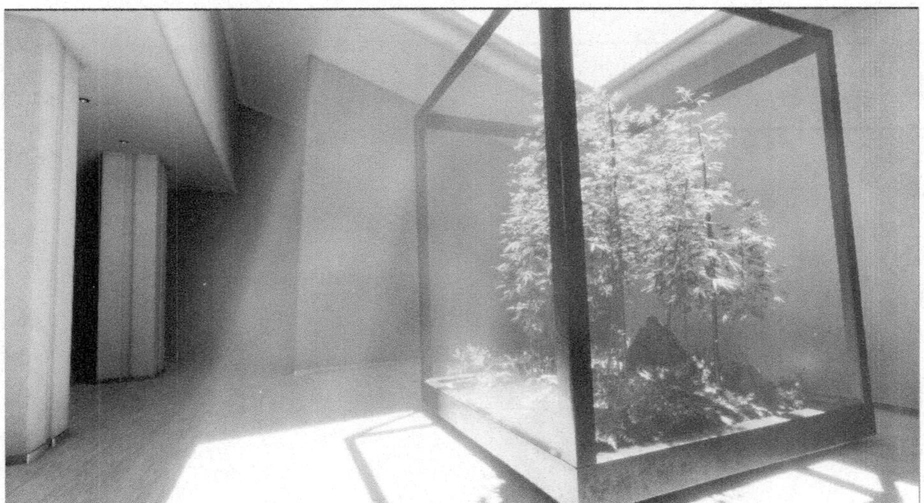

Figure 9.9 – High Definition Render Pipeline 3D sample scene

In this section, we will create a new HDRP project based on the premade Unity project template that Unity provides and then import our `BuiltInDemo` package into the project. As mentioned earlier in this chapter, HDRP is meant for higher-end PC and console VR experiences. That doesn't mean that developers cannot use lower-end devices for developing with HDRP, though. Also, most standalone headsets can be connected to PCs for playing more intensive experiences by utilizing the PC for its processing power. Connecting your headset also works for creating and testing experiences in the Unity Editor. This means that so long as you have a PC that meets the minimum requirements for HDRP development, you can use lower-end headsets such as the Oculus Quest 2 to develop PlayStation VR experiences with HDRP.

To create a new HDRP project (*Figure 9.10*), go through the following steps:

1. Open **Unity Hub**.
2. Select **New Project** in the top-left corner.
3. Select **3D (HDRP)** from the project template menu.
4. If you have not downloaded the template yet, select **Download Template**.

5. Once you've downloaded the template, select a project name. I named mine `HDRP_VRProject`.
6. Select a location to save the project.
7. Select the **Editor Version** for the new project at the top of the menu.
8. Select **Create project** to open the project:

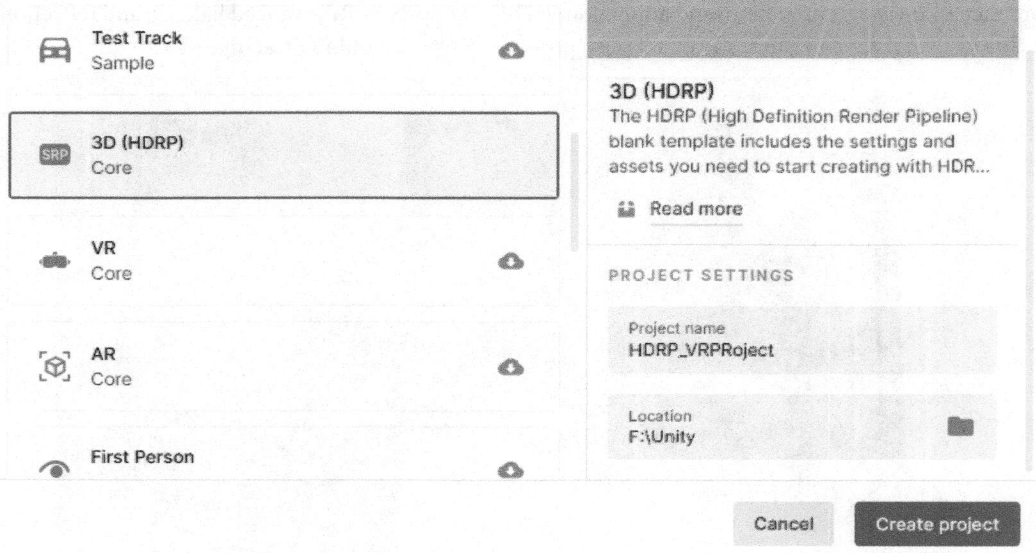

Figure 9.10 – HDRP project template in Unity Hub

When you open the project, you will be presented with the **HDRP Wizard**. This will further help you configure the project so that it works correctly.

To configure the HDRP project for VR, go through the following steps:

1. Go to the **HDRP + VR** tab in the **HDRP Wizard** window (*Figure 9.11*).
2. Select **Fix All**. Unity will try to install all the required packages for you automatically.
3. When it is complete, all the red icons will be removed.

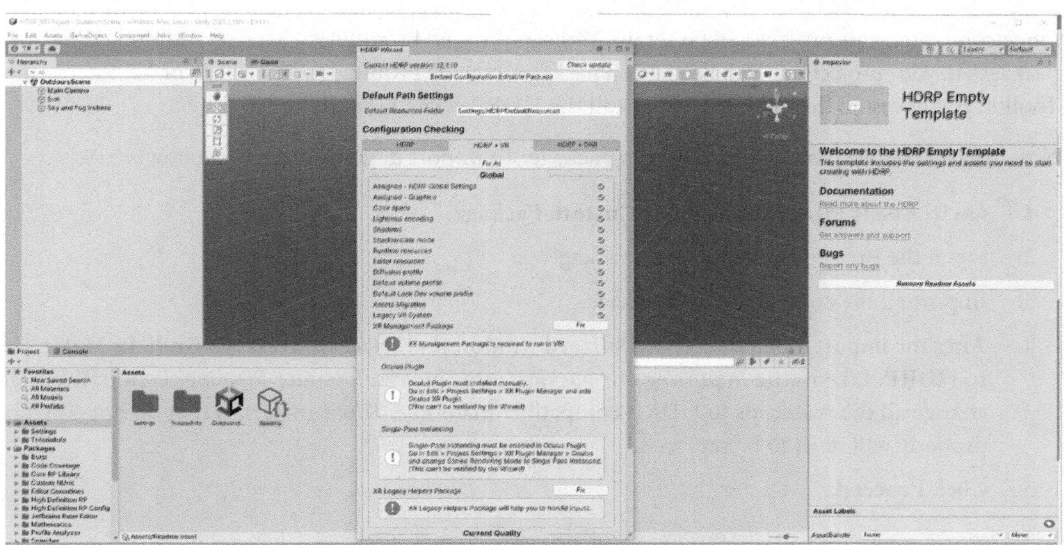

Figure 9.11 – HDRP Wizard window

There's some additional work you need to do for the Oculus Quest (*Figure 9.12*):

1. Go to **Project Settings**, then **XR Plug-in Management**.
2. Enable **OpenXR**. Wait for it to install. It will ask you to restart. Select **Yes**. Wait for it to reboot.
3. When it reboots, go to **Project Settings** under **OpenXR**.
4. Set **Interaction Profiles** to your desired device.
5. Under the **Android** tab, select **Meta Quest Support**.
6. A red icon will appear. Select it; the **OpenXR Project Validation** window will appear.
7. Select **Fix All**.

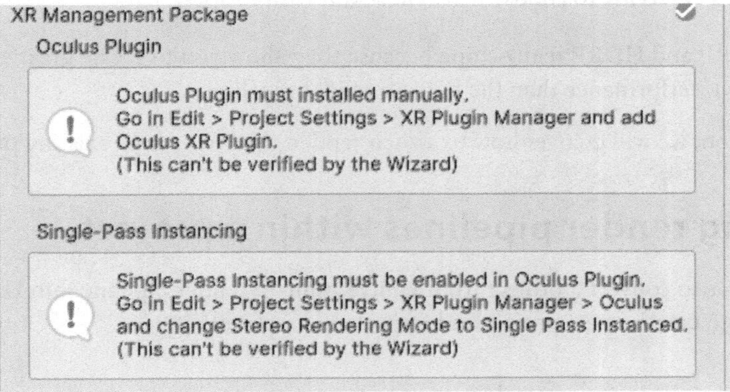

Figure 9.12 – HDRP Wizard configuration settings for low-end VR devices

Once complete, your project will be set up. You can proceed by adding whatever additional Registry packages to your project that you need. Such packages include ProBuilder, Polybrush, or XR Interaction Toolkit. If you install those, be sure to install the HDRP-related samples.

Now, we can import our `BuiltInDemo` package. To import it, go through the following steps:

1. Go to **Assets | Import Package | Custom Package**.
2. Open the `BuiltInDemo` Unity package.
3. Import all the contents of the package.
4. After the import, open the **HDRP Wizard** window and select **Convert All Built-In Materials to HDRP**. Like in the *Importing our package into Universal Render Pipeline* section, this will change all the materials to HDRP-compatible materials. Those materials that do not convert properly will need to be replaced.
5. Click **Proceed**.

In the next section, we will briefly cover how post-processing works in URP and HDRP.

Enabling post-processing in URP and HDRP

Compared to the built-in render pipeline, where you need to install a post-processing package and attach various components and layers, enabling post-processing in URP and HDRP is fairly straightforward. There is nothing you need to download. However, there may be a difference in what post-processing effects will be available for URP and HDRP.

To enable post-processing in both URP and HDRP, go through the following steps:

1. In your scene, create a new `Global Volume` GO (*right-click* | **Volume** | **Global Volume**).
2. In the `Global Volume` component, create a new profile.
3. Select **Add Override** to choose what effect you wish to apply.

This is where URP and HDRP really shine because they allow you to create great effects with more fidelity and better performance than the built-in render pipeline.

In the next section, we will go over how to switch render pipelines for an existing project.

Converting render pipelines within a project

While it's possible to convert a project from Unity's built-in render pipeline into URP or HDRP, it's generally better to create a new project and import the assets into it.

There are several reasons why this is the case:

- **Compatibility issues**: Converting a project from the built-in render pipeline into URP or HDRP can lead to compatibility issues as some assets may not be fully compatible with the new pipeline. This can lead to broken materials, lighting, or other issues that can be difficult to resolve.
- **Inefficient assets**: Assets created for the built-in pipeline may not be optimized for use with URP or HDRP, and may not take full advantage of the new pipeline's features. Starting a new project and importing assets allows you to rework or replace assets to make them more efficient and optimized for the new pipeline.
- **Workflow efficiency**: Starting a new project and importing assets allows you to set up your project's structure, settings, and configurations to better fit the new pipeline, leading to a more streamlined workflow.
- **Asset organization**: Importing assets into a new project allows you to better organize them according to the new pipeline's standards, which can lead to a cleaner and more efficient project.
- **Time-saving**: While starting a new project and importing assets may take more time initially, it can ultimately save time in the long run by avoiding compatibility issues and workflow inefficiencies that can arise from converting a project.

To convert a built-in project into URP, go through the following steps:

1. Go to **Package Manager**.
2. Find `Universal RP` in **Registry** and click **Install**.
3. Import `URP Package Samples`.
4. In the **Project** tab, create a new folder called `Pipeline Assets`.
5. Create a new **URP Asset**.
6. Create a new **URP Global Settings Asset**.
7. Go to **Project Settings**, under the **Quality** section.
8. Add **Render Pipeline Asset** to the reference slot.
9. Under **Graphics**, add **Render Pipeline Asset** to the **Scriptable Render Pipeline Settings** slot.
10. You can then convert all materials into **URP materials**.
11. If you want to convert into HDRP, install **High-definition RP** instead of **Universal RP**, and follow the HDRP Wizard.

> **Note**
>
> It will be difficult to revert everything to using the built-in render pipelines. Some assets and scripts may not work with URP, and converting a project pipeline within the project can break things unintentionally.

It's generally better to start a new project and import assets into URP or HDRP rather than converting a project from the built-in pipeline. Converting a project can lead to compatibility issues, inefficient assets, and workflow inefficiencies, while starting a new project allows you to better organize assets and set up a streamlined workflow that is optimized for the new pipeline.

Summary

Render pipelines are the backbone of creating stunning, high-performance VR experiences. Choosing the right pipeline is essential to achieve optimal performance and immersion in your project. In this chapter, we covered everything you need to know about render pipelines, from understanding their role in VR development to exploring and configuring both URP and HDRP. We also showed you how to enable post-processing and export your project to different pipelines. By mastering these topics, you can ensure your VR project is optimized for the best possible performance and quality, resulting in an immersive and engaging experience for your users.

But don't stop here – in the next section of this book, we'll be diving even deeper into creating immersive experiences with the skills we have developed thus far. We'll be combining many of the concepts that were introduced in past chapters and applying them to more complex projects. You'll learn how to design and create a variety of VR experiences, including games, simulations, and more. So, get ready to continue your VR development journey and take your skills to the next level.

Part 3: Projects: Putting Skills Together

In this dynamic, project-centric part, theory meets practice in a symphony of applied knowledge. By diving head-first into practical projects, you will cement the skills you've learned and see them in action, ultimately guiding you to becoming not just a spectator but also a creator within the VR world. The journey from concept to completion will not only instill a sense of accomplishment but will also provide you with a portfolio showcasing your newly acquired capabilities.

This part includes the following chapters:

10
Design Thinking for Virtual Reality Experiences

Now that we have acquired various tools and skills, it is time to learn about **design thinking** for VR experiences. Design thinking is a powerful concept that enables you to create immersive worlds and projects centered around humans. It emphasizes problem-solving and innovation through a systematic approach that enables us to create what we want and what people need. Through the tenets of design thinking, developers can empathize with users to understand their needs and design VR experiences that are more relevant to the user's interests and more engaging. This process requires a balance of technical and creative skills, thinking outside the box, and applying those nuances to develop a project that people can ultimately utilize.

Design thinking is an interdisciplinary approach that enables you to draw from different areas, industries, and experiences to incorporate the best results into your project. As a medical student with a vast amount of experience in visual storytelling and animation, I can create VR experiences centered around immersive medical education. With the goal of the experiences being both entertaining and educational, the innovation comes from the application of standard conventions interwoven into a novel experience, with VR being the access point for users to enjoy, instead of a book they would read or a video they would watch. This isn't gamifying learning; instead, it's making the learning experience an environment users can explore.

Applying design thinking to your VR experiences distinguishes you from other developers, as it allows you to incorporate your unique style and design aesthetic into your work. It is a continuous process that builds over time and enhances your design career and life's work. You can pull from many areas of expertise to create a solid foundation to build your project. This foundation can be translated into many projects or just be specific to the one project you are working on currently. For my immersive medical education and animation VR project, although I may only be working on it currently for medical school, I can extrapolate the approach I develop and apply it to any educational topic, such as physics, chemistry, or math. The content and subject matter can be different, but the core framework can be the same, like a template.

Once you finish this chapter, we will have a deeper understanding of design thinking and how to apply it to any project, regardless of its size. Furthermore, we will use the knowledge gained in this chapter, as well as insights from other chapters and projects, to create a comprehensive world that reflects our idea of immersive VR experiences and innovates on this concept to produce something unique.

In this chapter, we will cover the following topics:

- The basics of design thinking
- The main principles and processes that consist of design thinking
- How can design thinking be applied to VR development?
- Some things to consider while applying design thinking to VR development
- How to incorporate design thinking into a VR development workflow
- Developing a design document based on our design thinking approach
- Using the design document to build our roadmap for developing our immersive world
- Designing our level map and grayboxing the areas within the editor

Technical requirements

The complete source code for this chapter can be found at `https://github.com/PacktPublishing/Enhancing-Virtual-Reality-Experiences-with-Unity-2022/tree/main/EnhancingVRExperiencesFullProject/Assets/_VRProjectAssets/Scenes/Chapter_10`.

An introduction to design thinking

Design thinking is a human-centered approach to problem-solving that emphasizes empathy, creativity, and iterative prototyping. It aims to understand users' needs and desires, fostering a unifying language for multidisciplinary collaboration and leading to more innovative solutions more quickly.

The design thinking process consists of six main steps: *empathize*, *define*, *ideate*, *prototype*, *test*, and *implement* (*Figure 10.1*). It begins with empathizing with the customer and understanding their needs, gains, and pains. Next, the problem is defined based on gathered insights. During the ideate step, potential solutions are generated, followed by rapid prototyping and testing with real users for feedback. At the end of these five steps, we can implement the elements into the final production of our VR project. By prioritizing customers' needs, design thinking generates novel ideas that delight users, ensuring continuous improvement and refinement:

Figure 10.1 – Core elements of design thinking

In the following sections, we will explore how design thinking can be applied to VR development.

How can design thinking be applied to VR development?

Design thinking is crucial for VR development as it encourages user-centered and engaging experiences. By understanding users' needs and desires, developers can create immersive VR experiences tailored to their audience.

In VR development, it's essential to consider factors such as user comfort, motion sickness, and current VR technology limitations. Having a frame rate above 90 frames per second will reduce motion sickness; lower-end devices often have lower frame rates, depending on the amount of 3D objects rendered in a scene and the amount of code concurrently running in the background during runtime. Finding a happy medium among all the impacting variables to create a functional experience is at the core of why design thinking is important. Developers must design within hardware and software constraints while pushing innovation boundaries. Designing for a 3D environment requires attention to interaction design, spatial awareness, and the significance of sound and spatial audio.

Transitioning into the AR and VR field can be daunting due to high entry barriers, limited prototyping tools, and the need for a common communication language. However, drawing parallels with designing for flat surfaces such as smartphones and computers can ease the transition from 2D to 3D design. Familiarity with game engines, such as Unity, is also necessary for creating interactive high-fidelity prototypes.

Designing interfaces for AR and VR demands a departure from traditional 2D thinking because you have to design with three dimensions in mind. The benefit of XR is that you have a Z axis in space that users can access and utilize, as opposed to screen-based experiences where everything is built while considering an XY plane. Developers should prioritize information on all sides of objects (top, bottom, left, right, front, and back), ensuring users can access information from various viewpoints, leading to more immersive experiences.

To incorporate design thinking into VR development, developers must understand users' needs, experiment with new ideas and concepts, refine experiences based on feedback, and collaborate with others. This iterative process can be repeated until a VR experience meets users' needs and provides an engaging environment.

Although design thinking is a flexible philosophy without specific exercises or rules, understanding the philosophy and using structured frameworks such as design sprints can guide the design process, facilitating the creation of innovative, user-focused VR experiences. Think of design sprints as rapid prototyping. A developer quickly develops a design based on a core component or feature, moving to the prototyping and testing phase quickly so that they can validate whether that design choice is useful or not. This is helpful when implementing design choices modularly within a framework, such as using colliders instead of UI buttons to trigger events.

In the next section, we will talk about design documents and how they can be used to improve the workflow of our VR project experiences.

Developing a design document for a VR project

A design document is a comprehensive document that outlines the design, goals, and requirements for a project. It typically includes detailed information about the project's scope, target audience, user requirements, design guidelines, technical specifications, and timelines. The purpose of a design document is to provide a shared understanding of the project among team members, stakeholders, and clients. It serves as a roadmap for the design and development of the project and helps ensure that all team members are aligned on the project's goals, objectives, and deliverables. Developing a design document for a VR project based on the principles of design thinking can help ensure that the project meets user needs and provides a positive experience. Here are the steps to follow:

1. **Empathize**: Start by understanding the needs, desires, and challenges of the users for whom you're designing the VR experience. Conduct interviews or surveys, and observe how users interact with similar products.
2. **Define**: Use the insights you gathered from the *empathize* phase to define the problem you're trying to solve. For example, if you're creating a VR experience for a museum, the problem could be to provide an interactive and engaging way for visitors to learn about the exhibits.
3. **Ideate**: Brainstorm ideas on how to solve the problem you defined. Use techniques such as mind-mapping, sketching, or storyboarding to come up with a range of ideas. Encourage everyone on the team to contribute their ideas, and build on each other's suggestions.
4. **Prototype**: Create a low-fidelity prototype of your VR experience. Use simple materials such as cardboard, paper, or digital tools to create a rough version of the experience. Test it with users to see how they respond, and use their feedback to refine your design.
5. **Test**: Test your prototype with users and get feedback on how well it solves the problem you defined. Use this feedback to make improvements to the design.

6. **Implement**: Develop the final version of the VR experience based on the feedback you received from testing. Make sure it's user-friendly, engaging, and meets the needs of your target audience.
7. **Iterate**: Continue to iterate and improve the VR experience based on user feedback and new insights you gain. Design thinking is an iterative process, so it's important to continue to refine and improve the design over time. In your design document, include information on each of these steps, including the insights you gained from empathy, the problem you defined, the ideas you brainstormed, the prototype you created, the feedback you received from testing, and the final implementation of the VR experience. Make sure you also include information on how you plan to iterate and improve the experience over time.

In the next section, we will look at the various components of our design document and what is required to complete a fully functional design document.

Components of a design document

A design document details a project's goals, design, and requirements, covering its scope, audience, guidelines, technical specs, and timelines. It offers a shared understanding for team members and stakeholders, ensuring alignment on the project's objectives and deliverables. When creating a design document for a VR project, here are some key components to include:

- **Project overview**: This section should provide a brief summary of the project, its goals, and its target audience. It should also describe any existing products or services that the project is building upon or improving.
- **Design principles and guidelines**: This section should outline the principles and guidelines that will guide the design of the project. It should describe the project's visual style, typography, color palette, and other design elements.
- **User personas**: This section should describe the various user personas for the project. It should provide information on their age, gender, interests, and behaviors. It should also describe their goals, motivations, and pain points.
- **User scenarios**: This section should describe the various scenarios in which users will interact with the project. It should provide detailed descriptions of each scenario, including the user's goals, actions, and expected outcomes.
- **Wireframes and mockups**: This section should include wireframes and mockups of the project's key screens and interactions. It should provide a detailed description of each screen, including its purpose, content, and layout.
- **Technical specifications**: This section should provide technical specifications for the project, including the platforms and devices that the project will run on, the programming languages and frameworks that will be used, and any other technical requirements.

- **Project timeline**: This section should provide a timeline for the project, including key milestones and deliverables. It should also include any dependencies or constraints that may affect the project's timeline.

By including all of these components in a design document, you can ensure that all team members are aligned on the project's goals, objectives, and deliverables. A complete document can also help minimize misunderstandings and ensure that the project is completed on time and within budget.

In the following sections, we'll create a design document to guide our VR project development over the next few chapters. It's a comprehensive written outline that describes the project's goals, user requirements, technical specifications, and implementation details, serving as a reference for everyone involved. Design thinking principles can help us create a user-centric and scalable design that we can refine and improve with relevant questions at each stage of the process. The design document is a shared understanding of the project, guiding its development from start to finish.

Creating our design document

In the previous section, we discussed the importance of design thinking when creating immersive VR experiences. Now, we can use this foundation to design our own VR project by developing a comprehensive design document that clearly defines the project's goals, audience, and features. This document will also guide us through an iterative creative process so that we can refine our ideas.

To begin, we need to identify what our target audience can expect to gain from the VR experience and define the scope of the project. We will then start the iterative creative process, expanding on a list of key features and refining our ideas as we go. Throughout this process, we will explore relevant research, references, and resources to help us make informed design decisions.

Using the insights gained from our design thinking process, we will create a robust roadmap for the project that guides us from start to finish. This roadmap will detail the implementation of both simple and complex elements and features. With this plan in place, we can move forward confidently and efficiently, using our design document as a reference to ensure we stay on track and meet our project's goals.

By following this approach, we can create an immersive VR experience that not only meets the needs of our target audience but also delivers a positive and engaging experience. A well-crafted design document and a clear roadmap will allow us to tackle each aspect of the project with confidence and produce a final product that we can be proud of.

Empathy statement

Create an empathy statement for the VR experience you want to create. Consider addressing these questions when creating the empathy statement:

- Who are the users that we are creating this immersive world for?

- What are their needs, desires, and pain points?
- How can we make their experience in this world more engaging and meaningful?

The following statement is the one that I have created:

> *We are creating an immersive world for people who are tired of using regular controllers and want to experience VR. They want to perform moves like their favorite players and explore places beyond the 2D screen that provide depth and change as they navigate. They're tired of being disconnected from the immersion and want to be in the middle of it. Our target audience is someone who is seeking the same kind of immersive experience depicted in movies such as Ready Player One and Tron. Their pain point is that they want to play games and explore without leaving their house. We can create an immersive experience that includes interactions that mimic the real world with a fantastical twist. Users can walk in a park, climb mountains, swim in a lake, watch movies, and go on rides, all in VR.*

We can now move on to defining the project goal of our VR experience.

Defining the project goal

The goal in the next few chapters is to create an interactive virtual world that is interconnected based on the skills we have learned thus far, while also adding some extra skills to our repertoire.

Create a project definition for the VR experience you want to create. Consider addressing these questions when creating the project definition:

- What are the key features and functionalities that we want to include in this immersive world?
- What are the core design principles that will guide us in creating a cohesive and immersive experience?

The following statement is the one that I have created:

> *First, we will start by creating a park composed of different meshes that represent different elements of a familiar world. We will go through the full creative process from start to finish. Based on the overall picture, we will continue to add to our project until it is fully completed. By Chapter 15, we will have a fully immersive world complete, and we will be in a good position to test and optimize it to our liking.*

In the next section, we will look at how to create an ideation statement and a key features list for our VR experience.

Creating an ideation statement

Consider addressing these questions when creating the ideation statement:

- How can we come up with creative and innovative ideas for this immersive world?

- What are the different design concepts and themes that we can explore to make this world stand out?

The following statement is the one that I've created:

> *This fully immersive VR world will provide the user with the ability to navigate through different locations such as a park, city, mountain, art gallery, theatre, and lake. The VR rig allows for easy navigation with turn and walk capabilities and the use of raycasting, direct interactions, and gaze interactions. Additionally, the animated hands for controllers allow for a more realistic experience while jumping, running, and swimming in the virtual world. The dynamic lighting system changes with the time of day, adding an extra layer of immersion. The user can also travel to multiple locations, including hiking trails, to explore the highest mountain tops. The art gallery allows users to unleash their creativity by drawing on canvases, and the movie theatre provides a big screen to play animation videos. Finally, the park provides a relaxing atmosphere with walking trails, trees, and characters, giving the user a quiet place to chill out.*

Once you've done this, you need to create a key features list for the VR experience you want to create. The following is the one that I've created.

These are the key features of the experience:

- Navigate a virtual world with a VR rig using methods such as turning with the right joystick, walking with the left joystick, and using raycasting, direct interactions, and gaze interactions. Additionally, there are animated hands for controllers, and players can jump, run, and swim.
- Experience a fully immersive world with multiple locations on a map, including a park, city, mountain, art gallery, theatre, and lake, all with dynamic lighting that changes with the time of day.
- Embark on an adventure exploring the highest mountain top by traveling to multiple locations using various modes of transportation, such as hiking trails.
- Get creative and paint like Picasso in the art gallery with art canvases you can draw on.
- Enjoy a cinematic experience and watch movies on a big screen in the movie theatre.
- Relax and chill in the park with a walking trail, lake, trees, characters, and quiet places for meditation.

In the next section, I will briefly cover the process of researching, finding references, and allocating resources to prepare for developing robust VR experiences.

Researching, finding references, and allocating resources

To design immersive VR experiences with Unity that meet the needs of the target audience and deliver a seamless user experience, developers must take a thoughtful and strategic approach. This involves conducting research to gather information, understanding the target audience, and identifying best practices. Research can inform decisions about the project's scope, features, and aesthetics. Establishing a consistent visual language is also important, and this is where mood boards come in handy. A mood board is a visual tool that helps communicate the desired look and feel of a project, ensuring that the project's aesthetic matches the intended mood. Finally, developers must use available resources effectively, such as Unity's official documentation to know what development tools and features Unity offers for development, asset marketplaces such as the Unity Asset Store to add premade 3D objects and C# code, and tools such as Trello and Asana to streamline project management. In this section, we will explore the importance of research, mood boards, and resources in designing immersive VR experiences with Unity, and provide tips and best practices for utilizing them effectively.

To ensure a successful VR project, it is important to have a clear plan and roadmap from the beginning. This will help establish a solid foundation and guide the project through each stage of development. In the next section, we will explore the process of roadmapping and how it can be used to create a comprehensive plan for our VR experience. By following this process, we can ensure that our project stays on track, meets its goals, and delivers a positive and engaging experience for our target audience.

Roadmapping

A project development roadmap is a detailed plan that outlines the stages and activities necessary to complete a project from start to finish. It provides a strategic view of the entire project, including its goals, milestones, timelines, budget, and resources needed. The roadmap serves as a guide for project managers, team members, and stakeholders to stay focused and aligned throughout the project's life cycle.

In this section, we will create a roadmap based on our checklist and everything we've done so far with our design document. This roadmap will guide us through the next few chapters, helping us complete our VR experience and build upon the design elements we wish to prototype, iterate, test, implement, and expand. The roadmap will outline the key milestones for the project, the tasks that need to be completed to reach each milestone, and the timeline for completing each task.

We'll follow the format of splitting all the different sections we intend to implement into phases. Within those phases, we'll break down the necessary things to complete them and move on to the next phase. Some phases may not be fully completed when we move on, but the design document and roadmap are fluid and ever-expanding as we go through the development process.

As we develop, we may want to add things to the roadmap that were not initially there, thanks to the fluid nature of the design document. This will help us stay organized and on-task, ensuring that we go through a rigorous process of checks and balances, complete the project in a necessary amount of time, and explore only those ideas that lead to the most valuable aspects of our VR experience.

The roadmap will keep us accountable while allowing for flexibility and creativity in a technical space with guardrails that guide us down the path of least resistance.

To create the roadmap, we'll first define the phases and then figure out the necessary things we want to implement in each phase based on the feature list we just made. Finally, we'll incorporate minute details that we can check off as we implement them.

For example, in phase one, we'll design a map for all our areas, including the park, city, trail, and art areas. We'll want to include trees, trails, rocks, lakes, and paths, as well as designate buildings for sidewalks, theaters, demo rooms, art galleries, and more. We can convert this into a checklist, and once complete, that phase of our roadmap will be finished. We'll apply this process to every other phase we have.

Now that we understand what a roadmap is and how to implement one, let's move on to creating our roadmap for this project.

Create a project roadmap for the VR experience you want to create. The following statement is the one that I've created:

- **Phase 1 – map design**
    - *Design a full-level map, including a park, city, hiking trail, and roads*
    - *Design a park map with a walking trail, grass, trees, rocks, lake, and mountain hike path*
    - *Design an art gallery map with a hallway entry, separate room partitions, and different gallery rooms*
    - *Export the maps as .jpg images so that they can be imported as textures into Unity*
- **Phase 2 – prototype design**
    - *Create a new scene in Unity and place maps with accurate sizing*
    - *Use materials and shapes as placeholders for different areas of the map*
    - *Use primitives to create prefabs for people, animals, buildings, trees, and cars*
    - *Add tags to each primitive prefab placeholder*
- **Phase 3 – park experience design**
    - *Use kitbashing techniques to add various assets*
    - *Add a trail mesh, a grass mesh, tree prefabs, and a lake mesh*
    - *Add outdoor lighting*
- **Phase 4 – city experience design**
    - *Use kitbashing techniques to add various assets*
    - *Populate city blocks with streets, intersections, roads, sidewalks, buildings, and more*
    - *Add buildings for the theater, demo room, and art gallery*

- **Phase 5 – sound experience design**
    - *Add city environment sounds, forest sounds, and water sounds to the lake*
    - *Add bird sounds to the tree area*
    - *Add city sounds to the edges of the park*
    - *Add wind sounds to the top of the mountain*
- **Phase 6 – art gallery design**
    - *Create the art gallery as an indoor space that uses light components instead of environment lighting*
    - *Create local post-processing volumes for each room*
    - *Populate the art gallery with sculptures and art*
    - *Add art canvas with different colors*
    - *Design the markers, the canvas, and the eraser*
    - *Add sockets for colors and art to hang on the wall*
    - *Add indoor lighting*
- **Phase 7 – animation experience design**
    - *Write a script*
    - *Create storyboards*
    - *Create an animatic sequence*
    - *Create a previsualization sequence*
    - *Add 3D models to characters*
    - *Add animation clips to motions*
    - *Add sound effects*
    - *Add visual effects*
- **Phase 8 – theater experience design**
    - *Add a theater room and indoor lighting*
    - *Add a video to the screen that loops*
    - *Create a surround sound speaker system that uses the same audio source*
    - *Create speaker prefabs and modular code with an array manager*
    - *Record a city tour with a timeline recorder and play the sequence on the theater's big screen*
    - *Convert the sequence into a 360° video*

- **Phase 9 – trigger experiences design**
    - *Create a robust VR rig for user interactions*
    - *Add tags to each mesh*
    - *Create VR rig interactions for running, jumping, crouching, climbing walls and mountains, swimming in the lake, and turning with the right joystick and walking with the left joystick*
    - *Use raycasting, direct interactions, and gaze interactions with animated/dynamic hands instead of static hands*
    - *Add post-processing for water when the user goes underwater in the lake*
    - *Create a time of day feature with a sun and moon model and street lights that turn on at night and off in the morning*
    - *Add a demo room*
- **Phase 10 – optimization**
    - *Clean up the code*
    - *Bake all lightmaps*
    - *Use static GOs*
    - *Use occlusion culling*
    - *Adjust the quality settings*
    - *Improve the frame rate*

A project development roadmap is a strategic plan that outlines the stages, milestones, timelines, budget, and resources necessary to complete a project successfully. By following a roadmap, teams can stay on track, anticipate and address potential roadblocks, and ensure that the project is delivered on time and within budget.

To create our roadmap for the VR experience, we'll define the phases, identify necessary implementation details based on our feature list, and create checklists to track progress. The design document and roadmap are fluid and ever-expanding, allowing us to add ideas as we develop. It is important to recognize that changes should be made carefully to avoid scope creep. Scope creep can lead to delays and increased costs, so it's important to carefully consider any changes to the design document and roadmap.

Using a roadmap will keep us accountable while providing flexibility and creativity in a technical space with guardrails that guide us down a path of least resistance. Let's move on to creating our roadmap for this project and continue building an immersive and engaging VR experience.

Regardless of the scope of your project, developing something creative and technical can be daunting. As we get deeper and deeper into the development process, we can ask the following rhetorical questions based on design thinking to help generate ideas and further populate our design document as we move on to prototyping, testing, implementing, and iterating on our VR experiences. Here are the questions I have framed:

- **For prototyping**:
    - *How can we quickly iterate on our design ideas and test them in a virtual environment?*
    - *What tools and techniques can we use to create rapid prototypes that accurately simulate the immersive world?*
- **For testing**:
    - *How can we gather feedback from users and use it to refine and improve the immersive world?*
    - *What metrics and analytics can we use to measure the effectiveness of the experience and make data-driven design decisions?*
- **For implementing**:
    - *How can we ensure that the final VR experience is optimized for performance and delivers a high-quality user experience?*
    - *How can we effectively integrate feedback from user testing and iterate on the design to create the best possible VR experience?*
    - *How can we ensure that the VR experience is compatible with different hardware and software configurations, and across different platforms?*
- **For iterating**:
    - *How can we prioritize the most important improvements and iterate on the VR experience in a timely and efficient manner?*
    - *How can we use user feedback and data to identify opportunities for improvement and innovate on the VR experience? How can we ensure that each iteration builds on the success of the previous iteration and moves the VR experience closer to achieving its goals?*

Now that the design document is complete, it's time to start bringing our VR world to life. The first step in this process is designing our maps, and in the next section, we will explore the experience design process. Using Google Drawings, we will design 2D maps that can be used for grayboxing, kitbashing, and prototyping in Unity. This process will allow us to create a rough outline of our virtual world, experiment with different layouts and features, and ensure that everything is aligned with our design document's goals and objectives. By starting with 2D maps, we can create a solid foundation for our project and begin building upon it systematically and efficiently.

Experienced design

After completing the design document, the next step is to bring the VR experience to life in the Unity Editor. This involves a range of activities, including creating maps, custom assets, prototypes, and code, as well as downloading assets from the Unity Asset Store or other sources. In this chapter, we will focus on designing the map, which includes **grayboxing** and **kitbashing** techniques. By the end of this part of this chapter, we will have a fully populated space with assets, allowing us to navigate through it using our VR rig. This is a critical stage in the development process as it provides the foundation for the entire VR experience. Through careful design and iteration, we can create a space that is engaging, immersive, and intuitive for users to explore.

Designing the maps

To prepare building our virtual world maps, we'll create a 2D image map in Google Drawings to organize our layout and assets. This will save us time and provide us with a solid plan for our development process. There are more advanced tools such as GIMP or Photoshop, but simple tools such as Google Drawings or MS Paint are sufficient for this task. Our map will include a city, park, buildings, lake, grass, trees, walking path, and designations for specific buildings. We'll label streets and roads, color code them, and designate where the trees and grass will be. This map will be a guideline, not a detailed representation of the final product. Additionally, we'll create a floor plan for the art gallery, which will have specific details, while using premade assets for the theater and demo room. By the end of this section, we'll have an overall map (*Figure 10.2*) and an art gallery design for our project:

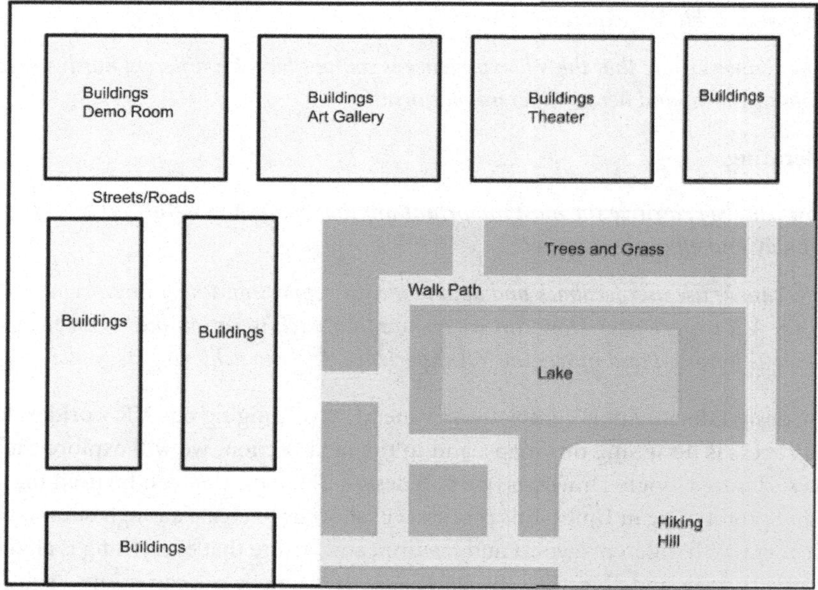

Figure 10.2 – Virtual world 2D map design

To design the VR experience map (*Figure 10.2*), go through the following steps:

1. Open an image editing app such as Google Drawings, Photoshop, Krita, or Procreate.
2. Create a new document and use the rectangle tool to make a large rectangle that covers the overall space and bounds of the map design.
3. Use smaller squares to partition out where the buildings will be located.
4. Label each square to designate the building type, such as the demo room, the art gallery, the theater, or regular buildings.
5. Use a larger square of a different color to indicate the park section.
6. Use different colors to differentiate the grass, trees, walking path, and hiking trail.
7. Add a lake or other water feature if desired.
8. Export the map as a `park.jpg` file.

To design the floor plan for our art gallery (*Figure 10.3*), go through the following steps:

1. Create a new document in an image editor or Google Drawings.
2. Draw a large rectangle to define the bounds of the space.
3. Use solid black rectangles to partition out the different wall areas of the space. This will help you know the thickness of the walls and how much area they will cover.
4. Leave an open space without doors to make it easier for users to navigate through the different spaces. Make sure there's enough room within the spaces to place statues and decorations to make the gallery feel like an actual gallery.
5. Look at how the space is organized and complete the floor plan of the art gallery.
6. Save the floor plan as `artgallery.jpg`.

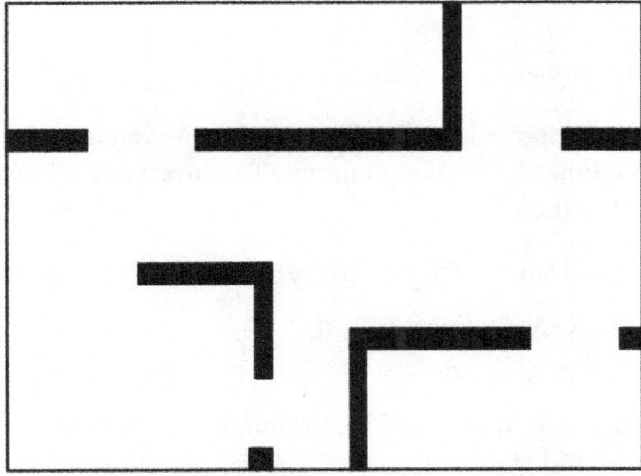

Figure 10.3 – Art gallery floor plan

We have created a 2D image map in Google Drawings to organize our layout and assets for our virtual world. Our map includes a city, a park, buildings, a lake, grass, trees, walking path, and designations for specific buildings. We also created a floor plan for the art gallery while using premade assets for the theater and demo room. These steps have provided us with a solid plan for our development process, allowing us to move on to grayboxing and kitbashing our maps in Unity.

In the next section, we will cover how to convert our 2D maps into 3D prototypes using primitive GOs in the Unity game engine.

Grayboxing the maps

Now that our VR maps have been designed, it's time to bring them into Unity and begin the grayboxing process. Grayboxing is a commonly used technique in video game development, VR, and other design fields to create a simplified, basic version of a level or environment. This process involves building simple, low-detail models or placeholders that represent various elements of the level, such as walls, floors, and objects. These models are usually created using basic shapes or geometry and textures and are often rendered in a single color or texture such as gray or white. The primary goal of grayboxing is to quickly and efficiently create a rough prototype or layout of a level or environment without spending excessive time or resources on detailed assets. Grayboxing can assist designers in testing and refining gameplay mechanics, exploring different design concepts, and gathering feedback from team members or stakeholders before committing significant resources to create more detailed assets.

To import the floor plan `.jpg` images into Unity, follow these steps:

1. Create a new folder called `Textures`.
2. Drag the `park.jpg` image from its saved location into the `Textures` folder in the **Project** window.
3. Select the image and change the image type to 2D (sprite and UI).
4. Select **Apply**.
5. Repeat *steps 2–4* for `artgallery.jpg`.

With our images created and imported into our Unity project, we can translate the 2D image into a 3D visualization that we can ultimately use as a prototype. To convert our 2D image into a 3D prototype with primitive shapes, follow these steps:

1. Create a new scene and label it `10_01_graybox map`.
2. Create a new empty GO and name it `VRMap`.
3. Set the **X**, **Y**, and **Z** positions to `0`.
4. Take the `park.jpg` image that you added to your floor plan `Textures` folder in the **Project** tab and place it as a child of the `VRMap` GO.
5. Set the **X** rotation to `90` and the **X** and **Y** scale to `30`. Set the **X** and **Y** position to `0`.

To define the road and grass sections of our map in the 3D prototype, follow these steps:

1. Create a new empty GO and name it `Roads`.
2. Set the position to `000`.
3. As a child of the `Roads` GO, create a new plane and set the **X** scale to `28`, **Y** scale to `20`, and **Z** scale to `20`.
4. Name the plane `Road_Plane`.
5. Give the `Road_Plane` GO a `dark gray` material.
6. Create a new empty GO and name it `Park`.
7. Set the position of the `Park` GO to `000`.
8. Create a new plane in the `Park` GO as a child and name it `Grass_Plane`.
9. Set the position of `Grass_Plane` to **X**: `50`, **Z**: `-34`.
10. Set the **X** scale to `17`, **Y** scale to `6`, and **Z** scale to `13`.
11. Give the `Grass_Plane` GO a green material.

To define the areas for our buildings, follow these steps:

1. Create a new empty GO and name it `buildings`.
2. As a child of the `buildings` GO, create a 3D cube and name it `Buildings_Cube`.
3. Set the position of `Buildings_Cube` to X: `-99`, Y: `28`, Z: `71`.
4. Set the **X** scale to `60`, **Y** scale to `16`, and **Z** scale to `50`.
5. Duplicate the `Buildings_Cube` GO.
6. Set the **X** position to `-25`.
7. Duplicate the `Buildings_Cube` GO again.
8. Set the **X** position to `48`.
9. Duplicate the `Buildings_Cube` GO once more.
10. Set the **X** position to `107` and **X** scale to `30`.
11. Duplicate the `Buildings_Cube` GO and set the **X** position to `-112`, **Z** position to `-13`, **X** scale to `30`, and **Z** scale to `88`.
12. Duplicate the `Buildings_Cube` GO again.
13. Set the **X** scale to `-65`.
14. Duplicate the `Buildings_Cube` GO.
15. Set **X Position** to `-90`, **Y Position** to `8`, and **Z Position** to `-85`.
16. Set the **X** scale to `78` and **Y** scale to `24`.
17. Set the material of the buildings GO to `Purple_Standard Material`.

To define the areas for our sidewalks on the roads under our buildings, follow these steps:

1. Create a new empty GO and name it `Sidewalks`.
2. Duplicate the `Buildings_Cube` GO.
3. Rename it `Sidewalk_Cube`.
4. Set the **Y** position to `0.05` and **Y** scale to `0.1`.
5. Set the `Sidewalk_Cube` material to `Gray_Standard`.
6. Place `Sidewalk_Cube` as a child of the `Sidewalks` GO.
7. Repeat *steps 2–6* for the remaining `Buildings_Cube` GOs.

To define the walking path in our park, follow these steps:

1. Create a new empty GO and name it `walking paths`, and then make it a child of the `Park` GO.
2. Set position to `0`, `0.02`, and `0`.
3. Create a new plane and name it `Walking Path_1`.
4. Set the **X** position to `8`, **Y** position to `0`, and **Z** position to `-85`. Set the **X** scale to `8.5`.
5. Duplicate `Walking Path_1`.
6. Set the **X** position to `51`, **Y** position to `0`, and **Z** position to `6`. Set the **X** scale to `13`.
7. Duplicate `Walking Path_1`.
8. Set **X** position to `9.5` and **Z** position to `-50`. Set the **X** scale to `5`.
9. Duplicate `Walking Path_1`. Set the **X** position to `-19.5` and **Z** position to `-27`. Set the **X** scale to `3`.
10. Duplicate `Walking Path_1`.
11. Set the **X** position to `-9` and **Z** position to `-39`. Set the **X** scale to `1` and **Z** scale to `9`.
12. Duplicate `Walking Path_1`.
13. Set the **X** position to `117.5` and **Z** position to `-85`. Set the **X** scale to `1` and **Z** scale to `8`.
14. Duplicate `Walking Path_1`.
15. Set the **X** position to `16` and **Z** position to `21`. Set the **X** scale to `1` and **Z** scale to `2`.
16. Duplicate `Walking Path_1`.
17. Set the **X** position to `29` and **Z** position to `-67.5`. Set the **X** scale to `1` and **Z** scale to `2.5`.
18. Apply `Orange_Standard Material` to all the `Walking Path_X` GOs.

To define the area for the lake in our park, follow these steps:

1. Create a new empty GO as a child of the `Park` GO.
2. Set the **Y** position to `0.02`.
3. Create a new plane and name it `Water_Plane`.
4. Set the **X** position to `48.5`, **Z** position to `-22.5`, and **Y** position to `0`. Set the **X** scale to `8`, **Y** scale to `1`, and **Z** scale to `3`.
5. Apply `Blue_Standard Material` to the `Water_Plane` GO.

To define the area for our hiking path up the mountain, follow these steps:

1. Create a new empty GO, name it `Mountains`, and make it a child of the `Park` GO.
2. Set the **X** position to `0`, **Y** position to `0`, **Z** position to `0`.
3. Create a cube GO and name it `Mountain_Cube`.
4. Set the position of `Mountain_Cube` to X `93`, Y `8`, Z `-73`. Set the **X** scale to `87`, **Y** scale to `16`, and **Z** scale to `47`.
5. Apply `Yellow_Standard material` to `Mountain_Cube`.

After going through all the steps in this section, you should end up with something that looks like this:

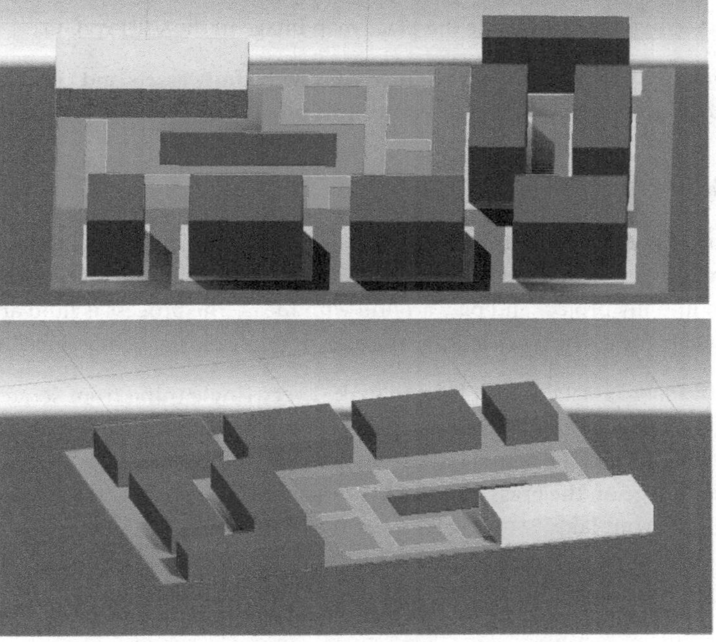

Figure 10.4 – Graybox of the map design

To design a placeholder for `NPC people`, follow these steps:

1. Create an empty GO and name it `People`.
2. Create another empty GO as a child of `People` and name it `People_Prototype`.
3. As a child of the `People_Prototype` GO, add a 3D capsule and name it `People_Body`.
4. Set the **Y** position of `People_Body` to `1`.
5. Drag `People_Prototype` to the `Prefabs` folder to turn it into a prefab.

To design a placeholder for our NPC cars, follow these steps:

1. Create a new GO and name it `Cars`.
2. Create a new GO as a child of `Cars` and name it `Car_Prototype`.
3. Set the **Y** position of `Car_Prototype` to `0.5`.
4. Add a quad as a child of the `Car_Prototype` GO and name it `Car_Bottom`.
5. Set the **X** rotation to `90` and **X** scale to `3`.
6. As a child of `Car_Bottom`, add a cube and name it `Car_Body`.
7. Set the **X** position to `0.09`, **Z** position to `-1.3`, **X** scale to `1.2`, **Y** scale to *2*, and **Z** scale to `1.7`.
8. Turn `Car_Prototype` into a prefab by dragging it to the `Prefabs` folder.

To see the final prototype, you can hide the place map image in the `VRMap` GO.

In the next section, we will replace our primitive GOs with Unity assets and custom 3D models that represent buildings, grass, mountains, and more. This process is known as kitbashing.

Kitbashing the maps

Kitbashing is one of my favorite things because it allows me to bring visuals to life in unique ways. Whether I'm creating my own assets or downloading them from the Unity Asset Store, it lets me implement them into my project and play around with ideas. The process is fluid and organic, and I can easily manipulate the assets. I can stick to the plan or pursue insights or gut feelings that come up.

By utilizing the available assets, I don't have to make every single thing from scratch. We will apply our kitbashing methodology to our grayboxed map to bring it to life beyond just having cubes and colors. First, we will download a nature pack from the Unity Asset Store. Next, we will use Polybrush to place trees and foliage on the grass textures in our park. Then, we will create our mountain range, city blocks, and finally our lake.

To download the **Free LowPoly Nature Forest** assets, follow these steps:

1. Open the Unity Asset Store.
2. Download the **Free Low Poly Nature Forest** assets from this link: `https://assetstore.unity.com/packages/3d/environments/landscapes/free-low-poly-nature-forest-205742`.
3. Import and download the assets from **Package Manager** into your project.
4. Create a new empty GO named `Nature`.

To place trees onto our `Grass_Plane` using Polybrush, follow these steps:

1. Open the **PolyBrush** window (**Tools | Polybrush**). To learn more about setting up **Polybrush**, visit the *Decorating the VR demo room with Polybrush and vertex painting* section in *Chapter 4*.
2. Go to **Scatter Prefabs** on the **Meshes** tab.
3. Set the brush outer radius to `3.68`, the inner radius to `.6`, and the strength to `1`.
4. In the **Project** tab, navigate to the `Free Low Poly Nature Forest Assets` folder, which is where all the nature assets are.
5. Drag the tree prefabs into the **Current Color Palette** section in the **Polybrush** window. This will prime Polybrush to use these prefabs when you paint on a texture.
6. Click the checkbox in the bottom left of each of the prefab indicators in the **Current Palette** section to make them available for painting on a mesh. They will then appear in the brush loadout section.
7. With your prefab selected, hover over `Grass_Plane` with your mouse in the **Scene** view, and hold the mouse button to place the selected prefabs onto the mesh.
8. Fill in the empty areas with the trees that you would like.
9. After you're done with the trees, you can replace the tree models in **Current Palette** with other GOs, such as flowers, grass, or rocks, and scatter them across `Grass_Plane` as well.
10. Once you're done, you will notice that `Grass_Plane` will have all the scattered prefabs as children of it. You can select all those child prefabs and move them to the `nature` folder that we created in the previous section.

To create our mountain range for the hike with prefabs imported from the Asset Store, follow these steps:

1. Create a new empty GO under the `Mountains` GO and name it `Mountain prefabs`.
2. In the `Prefabs` folder, find the `PC Forest Mountain Moss02` prefab and place it in our scene. This will be the main mountain top that we will use for our hike.
3. Set **X** position to `147`, **Y** position to `20`, and **Z** position to `-84`. Set the **X** scale to `2.5`, **Y** scale to `1.5`, and **Z** scale to `2`.

4. Duplicate the `Moss02` prefab.
5. Set the **X** position to `82.8`, **Y** position to `0`, and **Z** position to `-71.89`.
6. Set the **XYZ** scale to `0.6`.
7. Duplicate the `Moss02` prefab again.
8. Set the **X** position to `66` and **Z** position to `-103.3`.
9. Set the **XYZ Scale** to `0.51`.
10. Find the `PC Forest Mountain Moss01` prefab and add it to our scene.
11. Set the **X** position to `106.6`, **Y** position to `0.57`, and **Z** position to `-102`.
12. Duplicate the `Moss01` prefab.
13. Set the **X** position to `82.8`, **Y** position to `-0.2`, and **Z** position to `-103`.
14. Set the **XYZ** scale to `0.76`.
15. Duplicate the `Moss01` prefab again.
16. Set the **X** position to `105.7`, **Y** position to `1.6`, and **Z** position to `-69.3`.
17. Set the **XYZ** scale to `1`.
18. Duplicate the `Moss01` prefab again.
19. Set the **X** position to `64.8`, **Y** position to `0`, and **Z** position to `-71.9`.
20. Set the **XYZ** scale to `0.43`.
21. Hide the `Mountain_Cube` GO in **Inspector**.

To create a pathway leading up the mountain range, go through the following steps:

1. Create a new empty GO under the `Mountain prefabs` GO and name it `Mountain Pathway`.
2. Find the `PPMeadow Path 05` prefab in our project assets and add it to our scene as a child of the `Mountain Pathway` GO.
3. Set the **X** position to `61.5`, **Y** position to `-0.3`, and **Z** position to `-85`.
4. Set the **Z** rotation to `8`.
5. Duplicate the `PPMeadow Path 05` prefab.
6. Set the **X** position to `82.4`, **Y** position to `3.58`, and **Z** position to `-85`.
7. Set the rotation to `11.19`.
8. Duplicate the `PPMeadow Path 05` prefab.
9. Set the **X** position to `102.9`, **Y** position to `8.88`, and **Z** position to `-85`. Set the **Z** rotation to `16.89`.
10. Duplicate the `PPMeadow Path 05` prefab.

11. Set the **X** position to `122.32`, **Y** position to `16.58`, and **Z** position to `-85`. Set the **Z** rotation to `24.02`.

After going through all the steps provided in this section up to this point, you should end up with something similar to what's shown in *Figure 10.5*:

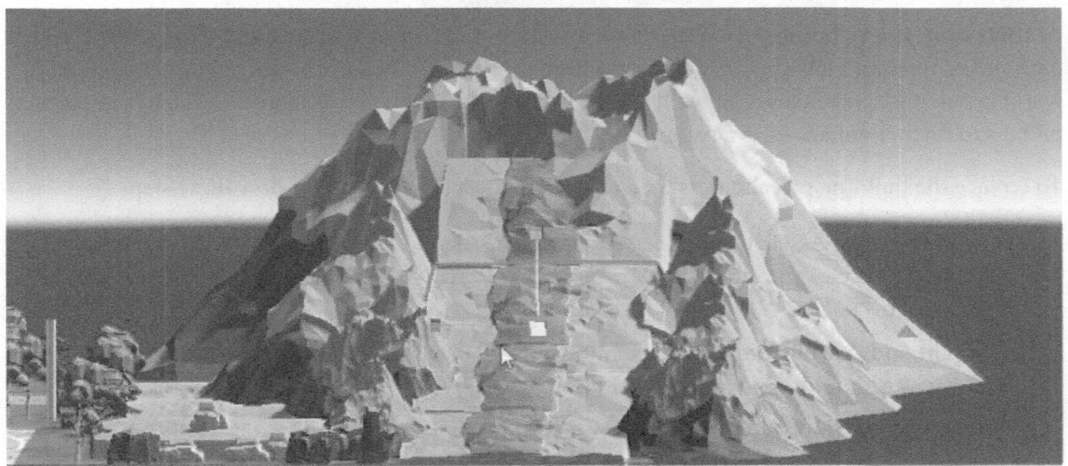

Figure 10.5 – Mountain range made of GOs

To give our lake area a water shader (*Figure 10.6*), follow these steps:

1. Open the Unity Asset Store and search for `Unlit Stylized Water Pack`: `https://assetstore.unity.com/packages/2d/textures-materials/water/unlit-stylized-water-pack-142285`.
2. Download and import **Unlit Stylized Water Pack** into your project via **Package Manager**.

3. In the **Project** tab, navigate to the downloaded assets and open the `Stylized Ocean Materials` folder.
4. Choose one of the materials provided and assign it to the `water_plane` object. For example, you can select `Ocean Material 04` and drag it onto the `water_plane` object in the **Scene** view.

Having added the water shader to the lake area, your VR world is becoming even more visually appealing:

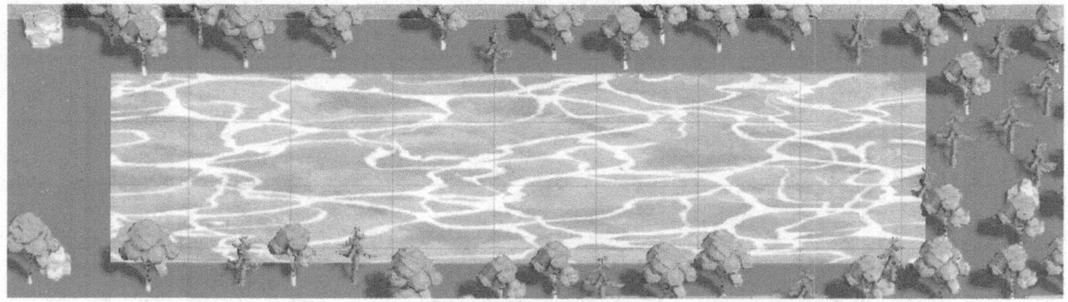

Figure 10.6 – Lake area with the water shader

At this point, you've brought your grayboxed map to life using kitbashing techniques. With a lush park full of trees and foliage, a realistic mountain range, and a beautiful lake (*Figure 10.6*), your VR world is starting to take shape. We will now dive into replacing the building placeholders with custom prefabs to further enhance the cityscape.

To replace the building placeholders with custom prefabs (*Figure 10.7*), follow these steps:

1. Go to the Unity Asset Store and search for a city package, such as `City Package`: `https://assetstore.unity.com/packages/3d/environments/urban/city-package-107224`.
2. Import and download the package into your project. The assets will appear in the `Polygon City Pack` folder in your **Project** tab.
3. Create a new empty GO in your **Hierarchy** and name it `Building Prefabs`. Set it as a child of the `Buildings` GO and set the **X**, **Y**, and **Z** positions to `0`.
4. In the **Scene** view, choose a sidewalk that has a building placeholder on it and hide that placeholder.
5. Drag a `Building` prefab from the prefab `Buildings` folder in the `Polygon City Pack` folder into your **Scene** view.
6. Make that building prefab a child of the `Building Prefabs` GO and place it within the area on the sidewalk. Ensure you don't have the building go past the sidewalk and also leave enough sidewalk space for people to walk on without the buildings obstructing their path.

7. Repeat *steps 4–6* with different building prefabs from the folder, filling up the sidewalk space with a variety of buildings.
8. Once you have completed this for one sidewalk, repeat *steps 4–7* for the remaining sidewalk placeholders.

With all of the primitive GOs now replaced, we have finally achieved a more comprehensive and impressive prototype of our VR world. The world is quite vast and enables us to navigate multiple areas within it. By following a systematic approach, we were able to identify the sections where we wanted buildings and separate the different areas. After separating those areas, we focused on one section at a time and put together a plan to guide us to where we are now:

Figure 10.7 – Placing building GOs in place of primitives

As we move toward the conclusion of this chapter, let's take a moment to appreciate the outcome of our VR world, as shown in *Figure 10.8*:

Figure 10.8 – Completed VR map with kitbashing assets

Congratulations! You have successfully transformed your initial grayboxed map into an immersive and visually engaging VR world using kitbashing techniques. As we move forward, we'll continue refining and enhancing our VR project, building on the strong foundation we've established here.

Summary

By following a systematic approach, we were able to create a prototype of our virtual world with various tools and skills. We focused on design thinking for VR experiences, which is a powerful concept that enables us to create immersive worlds and projects centered around humans. Design thinking is an interdisciplinary approach that emphasizes problem-solving and innovation through a systematic approach. We covered the basics of design thinking, its main principles and processes, how to apply it to VR development, and how to incorporate it into a VR development workflow. We should now have a deeper understanding of design thinking and how to apply it to any project, regardless of its size, and use it to create a comprehensive and innovative VR experience. In the next chapter, we will move on to phase five of our roadmap, where we will start to add audio to it.

11
Adding Audio to a Virtual Reality World

In this chapter, we will integrate many of the skills we learned in the previous sections to build our first project. Using the virtual world we created in the *Experienced design* section of *Chapter 10*, we will add spatial audio to populate our environment with interesting sounds, creating a fully immersive experience.

We will have environment sounds as well as 3D sounds in specific areas that accentuate what those areas represent. We'll also set up ambient sounds and use this as a foundation to build on as we add more visuals and interactions in the next couple of chapters. By the end of this chapter, you will be able to walk around a virtual park, go for a hike, and change your audio experience according to your unique specifications.

We will cover three main sections in this chapter. These include adding park audio, adding audio sources and sounds to our car, and adding audio sources and sounds to our non-playable characters or people. By the end of this, we should have a good idea of how to utilize code and creative approaches to implement sound in our VR experiences. In the next section, we will explore adding audio to the park section of our VR map.

This chapter covers the following topics:

- Revisiting the concept of spatial audio
- Creating local audio volumes and global audio volumes
- Utilizing code to enhance the features of the spatial audio and manage them

Technical requirements

The complete source code for this chapter can be found at `https://github.com/PacktPublishing/Enhancing-Virtual-Reality-Experiences-with-Unity-2022/tree/main/EnhancingVRExperiencesFullProject/Assets/_VRProjectAssets/Scenes/Chapter_11`.

Adding park audio

Since we spent so much time perfecting the visuals of our virtual world, it's time to pay attention to the audio. Audio can make or break any experience because it is a significant component of how we experience entertainment and other things. Therefore, we have to pay close attention to creating an immersive experience, particularly within a park setting. There are many sounds reminiscent of the tranquil nature of a park, and having birds chirping and water running is something people are all too familiar with. Recreating these sounds in VR will help us achieve our desired immersive experience.

If you recall from the *Roadmapping* section of *Chapter 10* where we talked about *Phase 5* of our roadmap, we specifically planned in our sound design experience to add city environmental sounds, forest sounds, and water sounds to the lake. To follow this, we'll add bird sounds to the tree areas and city sounds to the edge of the park. Finally, we'll add wind sounds to the top of the mountains. Understand that using the roadmap is just a guideline, and it's not something we have to stick to. Therefore, we can deviate from it a little bit, which is just part of the development process. Putting things into practice is different than planning things out, even though they're interconnected.

To download nature sounds for our park, follow these steps:

1. Go to the Unity Asset Store and search for `Nature Essentials`: `https://assetstore.unity.com/packages/audio/ambient/nature/nature-essentials-208227`.
2. Download and import the **Nature - Essentials** audio files using the Package Manager.
3. The downloaded audio files can be found in the `Nature Essentials` folder in the `Assets` folder of your project.

With our nature sounds downloaded, we can now proceed to add a local audio source, known as a *park audio source*, to our park.

To add local audio sources for the park audio, follow these steps:

1. Create an empty GO, and name it `Park Audio`.
2. Set the **X**, **Y**, and **Z** positions to `(0,0,0)`.
3. Create an `Audio Source` GO as a child of the `Park Audio` GO.
4. Name it `Park Audio Source`.
5. Set **Spatial Blend** in `Audio Source` to `1` to enable 3D sound. This means it will be affected by the position of the audio listener (usually attached to the main camera or player character in the scene).
6. Set **Max Distance** to `35`.
7. Adjust the **Max Distance** rolloff to the desired amount. You can refer back to *Chapter 7*, where we set up the first audio source for spatial audio in the last section.
8. Enable **Play On Awake** and **Loop**.
9. Save the `Park Audio Source` GO as a prefab.

We have just created a `Park Audio Source` prefab that we can use across our whole scene. We can duplicate it and distribute it across the multiple areas within our scene, which will have different audio sounds specific to the respective locations.

> **Note**
> The exact values of the position of each audio source are based on the specific layout of our park design, so the position may vary if your park layout differs from the example.

To distribute the local audio sources across the park area for wind sounds, follow these steps:

1. Go to the `Park Audio Source` prefab, which is a child of the `Park Audio` GO.
2. Set the **X** position to `119`, the **Y** position to `0`, and the **Z** position to `-6.9`.
3. Duplicate the `Park Audio Source` prefab.
4. Set the **X** position to `-7.8`, the **Y** position to `0`, and the **Z** position to `-40`.
5. Duplicate the `Park Audio Source` prefab again.
6. Set the **X** position to `0.3`, the **Y** position to `0`, and the **Z** position to `-80`.
7. Duplicate the `Park Audio Source` prefab again.
8. Set the **X** position to `73.8`, the **Y** position to `0`, and the **Z** position to `-73.7`.
9. Create an empty GO under `Park Audio` and name it `Wind Sounds`.
10. Place the `Park Audio Source` prefabs as children of the `Wind Sounds` GO.

Now that we have the different audio sound sources put in place, we can designate specific sounds for specific areas based on what we have planned in our roadmap. First, we will work on our bird sounds.

To create local audio sources for bird sounds, follow these steps:

1. Duplicate the `Park Audio Source` prefab.
2. Set the **X** position to `39.5`, the **Y** position to `0`, and the **Z** position to `1.5`.
3. Duplicate the `Park Audio Source` prefab.
4. Set the **X** position to `113.3`, the **Y** position to `0`, and the **Z** position to `-58.3`.
5. Duplicate the `Park Audio Source` prefab.
6. Set the **X** position to `7.4`, the **Y** position to `0`, and the **Z** position to `-58.8`.
7. Create an empty GO under `Park Audio` and name it `Bird Sounds`.
8. Place these `Park Audio Source` prefabs as children of the `Bird Sounds` GO.

With the bird sounds done, we can now add sounds to the water for the lake.

To create local audio sources for water sounds, follow these steps:

1. Duplicate the `Park Audio Source` prefab, and name the new file `Park Audio Source Water 1`.
2. Set the **X** position to `34.2`, the **Y** position to `0`, and the **Z** position to `27.2`.
3. Duplicate the prefab again, and name the new file `Park Audio Source Water 2`.
4. Set the **X** position to `74.8`, the **Y** position to `0`, and the **Z** position to `-27.2`.
5. Create an empty GO under `Park Audio` called `Water Sounds`.
6. Place the `Park Audio Source Water 1` and `Park Audio Source 2` prefabs as children of the `Water Sounds` GO.

The water sounds are complete and work for the lake, so now we can move on to the wind sounds for the mountains.

To create a local audio source for mountain wind, follow these steps:

1. Duplicate the `Park Audio Source Water 2` prefab, and name it `Park Audio Source Mountain Wind`.
2. Set the **X** position to `154.7`, the **Y** position to `29.5`, and the **Z** position to `-92`.
3. Set **Max Distance** in the `Audio Source` component to `60` so that the wind sounds can be heard further away, due to the height of the mountains.
4. Create an empty GO under `Park Audio` called `Mountain Sounds`.
5. Place the `Park Audio Source Mountain Wind` GO as a child of the `Mountain Sounds` GO.

With the mountain sounds in place, one thing we can explore is how to utilize a single GO or script to access all the local audio sources for that specific sound. We can add that specific sound to the local audio sources individually and have them play as local sounds.

To play an audio file on multiple local audio sources, follow these steps:

1. Create a new C# script in the `Scripts` folder under the **Project** tab, and name it `Multi Audio Source`.
2. Use the following namespaces:

```
using System.Collections;
using System.Collections.Generic;
using UnityEngine;
```

3. Under `public class MultiAudioSourceManager : MonoBehaviour`, add the following variables:

```
    public AudioClip audioClip
    public List<AudioSource> audioSources;
```

Within the `MultiAudioSourceManager` class, we define the `audioClip` and `audioSources` public variables to reference the audio clip to be played and a list of audio sources, respectively.

4. In the `void Start()` method, add the following code:

```
        foreach (AudioSource source in audioSources)
        {
            source.clip = audioClip;
            source.spatialBlend = 1f;
        }
    Play();
```

5. In the `Start()` method, the script iterates through each `AudioSource` in the `audioSources` list, assigns `audioClip`, and sets the `spatialBlend` property to `1`, ensuring that `AudioSource` is 3D and affected by the spatial properties of the scene. Create a new method called `public void Play()` and apply the following code:

```
        foreach (AudioSource source in audioSources)
        {
            source.Play();
        }
```

6. Create a new method called `public void Stop()` and apply the following code:

```
        foreach (AudioSource source in audioSources)
        {
            source.Stop();
        }
```

   The script includes the `Play()` and `Stop()` methods to control audio playback on all specified audio sources. Both methods iterate through each `AudioSource` in the `audioSources` list, calling the respective `Play()` or `Stop()` method on each `AudioSource` to start or stop audio playback, respectively.

7. Add the script to the `Wind Sounds` GO.
8. Add all the `Park Audio Source` children into the `Audio Sources` reference slot.
9. In the `Audio Clip` section, choose the `Ambiance_Wind_Forest_Loop_Stereo` audio file.
10. Make sure each of the `Audio Source` children does not have any audio clips in their reference slots. The only audio clip should be in the `Multi Audio Source Manager` component.
11. Repeat *steps 7–9* for `Mountain Audio Manager`, and use the `Ambiance_Wind_Forest_Loop_Stereo` audio clip.

12. Repeat *steps 7–9* for `Water Audio Manager`, and use the `Ambiance_Sea_Loop_Stereo` audio clip.
13. Repeat *steps 7–9* for `Birds Audio Manager`, and use the `Ambiance_Forest_Birds_Loop_Stereo` audio clip.

With these steps, we can now play an audio file on multiple local audio sources, creating a more immersive experience.

These nature sounds were just the tip of the iceberg. The next sound we will add to this virtual world is car audio, which we can customize to make it unique. This will allow us to involve the characteristics of car-like honking and engine sounds.

Adding car audio

In *Phase 5* of our roadmap, which we worked on in *Chapter 10*, we discussed adding environment sounds to our city. One of the ways we can do that is by adding sounds to cars because, primarily, environment sounds in a city are car sounds and people sounds. Since we have people sounds covered, we will focus on car sounds and how that environment can be built based on what we have already.

In this section, we will first focus on downloading our car audio sounds, and then we'll move on to adding spatial audio to the car prototypes that we created. Finally, we'll create a game manager script that allows us to control and vary car engine and honking sounds.

To add spatial audio to cars, follow these steps:

1. Go to the Unity Asset Store and search for `Engines`: `https://assetstore.unity.com/packages/audio/sound-fx/engines-123836`.
2. Download and import the **ENGINES** package, which contains audio files such as car engine and honking sounds.
3. You will find the imported files in the `Engines` folder under the `Assets` folder in the **Project** tab.

Now that we have our car audio sounds downloaded, we can add them to our car prototype using spatial audio.

To add spatial audio to our car prototype, follow these steps:

1. In the `Car_Prototype` prefab, add an `Audio Source` component.
2. Set **Spatial Blend** to `1`.
3. Set **Min Distance** to `1` and **Max Distance** to `10`.
4. Add an `Audio Source` GO as a child of the `Car_Prototype` GO.
5. Name it `HonkSource`.

6. Set **Spatial Blend** to `1`.
7. Set **Min Distance** to `5` and **Max Distance** to `20`.
8. Set the **X** position of the `HonkSource` GO to `2` and the **Y** position to `1`.

With the spatial audio set up for each one of our car prefabs (in my scene, I have 10, but you can choose however many you want in your scene), we can create a manager that is able to control and vary the honking and engine sounds. This is an important goal because we want to be able to continuously play the engine sounds when the scene starts, and then we want to add a randomizer to play the honking sound so that it's not always playing honking sounds or engine sounds; it's playing both at the same time.

To create a manager for all the car audio, perform the following steps:

1. Add a new script entitled `CarAudioManager`.
2. Add the following namespace to the script:

```
using UnityEngine;
```

3. Under the following `public class CarAudioManager : MonoBehaviour`, add the following variables:

```
    public AudioSource engineAudioSource
    public AudioSource honkAudioSource
    public AudioClip engineSound
    public AudioClip honkSound
    public float minHonkInterval = 10f;
    public float maxHonkInterval = 120f;
    public float honkCooldown = 120f;
    public float honkTimer = 0f;
    private float cooldownTimer = 0f;
    public bool playHonk;
```

The `CarAudioManager` script is designed to manage the car's audio sources, including the engine and honk sounds. In the script, the `UnityEngine` namespace is utilized to access Unity-specific functionalities. Within the `CarAudioManager` class, a list of public and private variables is defined to store references to the **audio sources**, **audio clips**, and **timer variables** and control the honking behavior.

4. In the `void Start()` method, add the following code:

```
        engineAudioSource.clip = engineSound;
        engineAudioSource.loop = true;
        engineAudioSource.Play();
        honkAudioSource.clip = honkSound;
```

In the `Start()` method, the audio clips are assigned to their respective audio sources. The engine audio source is set to loop, and the engine sound starts playing. The honk audio source is assigned its clip but not played immediately.

5. In the `void Update()` method, add the following code:

```
if (honkTimer <= 0f)
{
    honkTimer = Random.Range(minHonkInterval,
        maxHonkInterval);
    var honkplayer = maxHonkInterval / 2;
    if (honkTimer > honkplayer)
    {
        playHonk = true;
    }
    if (!honkAudioSource.isPlaying &&playHonk)
    {
        honkAudioSource.Play();
        playHonk = false;
    }
}
else
{
    honkTimer -= Time.deltaTime;
}
if (honkAudioSource.isPlaying)
{
    cooldownTimer -= Time.deltaTime;
    if (cooldownTimer <= 0f)
    {
        honkTimer =
            Random.Range(minHonkInterval,
                maxHonkInterval);
        cooldownTimer = honkCooldown;
    }
}
```

The honking behavior is managed in the `Update()` method. The method first checks whether `honkTimer` is less than or equal to `0`. If it is, the timer is reset with a random value between `minHonkInterval` and `maxHonkInterval`. Then, the script decides whether to play the honk sound based on the randomly generated value. If the honk sound should be played and isn't already playing, it is played, and the `playHonk` flag is reset. If the honk sound is playing, `cooldownTimer` is decremented by the time passed since the last frame. If the cooldown timer is less than or equal to `0`, the `honkTimer` and `cooldownTimer` values are reset for the next honk event.

6. In **Inspector** for the `Car Prototype` GO, set the `engineAudio` source to the car prototype audio source, by dragging the `Audio Source` component from the car prototype into the `engineAudioSource` field in the `CarAudioManager` script in **Inspector**.
7. Set `Honk Audio Source` to the `HonkSource` GO.
8. Set `Engine Sound` to `Engine 01`.
9. Set `Honk Sound` to `Car Horn 2`.
10. Apply all edits to the prefab and save it.

With this monster of a script, we're able to do a lot of complex things in a simple manner. All it does is allow you to use one audio source for the engine, another for the honking, and then have the Unity scripting time randomizer utilize different random numbers and an algorithm to play and vary the honking. This provides a lot of variability, and every time you open up the scene, you'll have a different experience with the honking and engine sounds. So, when you add 100 cars to your scene, each one will act differently, based on the unique characteristics created by your algorithm.

Now that our environment sounds from the cars are done, we can move on to adding audio to our `People_Prototype` prefabs. This way, we'll not only have a nice variability for the park sounds where people will be in the parks, but we can also add those sounds to the city. We'll have people walking around the city, saying different things, having conversations, and really adding to the environmental ambiance.

In the next section, we will add audio to our `NPC character`, which we created in the *Grayboxing the maps* section of *Chapter 10*.

Adding NPC audio

As mentioned in the previous section, adding audio to our `People_Prototype` prefabs really allows us to have a wholesome experience because we can populate our scenes with people, and then when you walk close to them, you'll be able to hear them talk about different things. We can utilize this within our VR experience so that it doesn't sound dull and boring. We can download an asset that allows us to have a variety of different dialogues and voices in different tones. Then, we can randomize that and apply it to the different prefabs. Using an algorithm similar to the car audio, we can have an algorithm that generates audio randomly, based on the tone and voice that we choose, creating variability in the audio that comes from different people.

In this section, we will create an audio source for our `People_Prototype` prefab and use the downloaded voices to create a dialogue system that allows us to choose whether a person is angry, sad, happy, or glad. Then, we can create a randomizer to populate our worlds with these people throughout, so we don't have to manually place them into our scenes. This saves time and energy because we can have a lot of variability, with the algorithms and C# working in our favor.

Before we move on to all of that, let's download our audio sounds and add them to our People_Prototype prefabs.

To add a local audio source to a People_Prototype prefab, follow these steps:

1. Go to the Unity Asset Store and search for Gibberish Dialogue and Voices, Volume One: https://assetstore.unity.com/packages/audio/sound-fx/voices/gibberish-dialogue-voice-pack-volume-1-32787.
2. Download and import the audio assets from the Package Manager.
3. The downloaded assets are located in the Assets folder under the Gibberish Dialog and Voice Pack Volume One folder.
4. Go to the People_Prototype prefab.
5. Add an Audio Source GO as a child of the prefab.
6. Set the **Y** position to 1.6 to position the Audio Source GO at the height of the People_Prototype prefab's mouth.
7. Set **Spatial Blend** to 1.
8. Set **Min Distance** to 0.2 because we want the dialogue to be heard at maximum volume when the audio listener is 0.2 meters away from the audio source.
9. Set **Max Distance** to 8. This indicates that the audio listener will not be able to hear any sound from the audio source beyond 8 meters.

With the audio sounds downloaded and the People_Prototype prefabs having the audio sources attached to them, it's time to create a dialogue manager that allows us to choose different categories of dialogue and then utilize those with our prefabs.

To add a Dialogue Audio Manager to the People_Prototype prefab, follow these steps:

1. Create a new script, and add it to the People_Prototype prefab.
2. Name it DialogueAudioManager.
3. Add the following namespaces to the script:

```
using System.Collections.Generic;
using UnityEngine;
```

4. In public class DialogueAudioManager : MonoBehaviour, add the following variables:

```
    public AudioSource audioSource;
    public List<AudioClip> angryClips;
    public List<AudioClip> answerClips;
    public List<AudioClip> braveClips;
    public List<AudioClip> carefulClips;
```

```
public List<AudioClip> excitedClips;
public List<AudioClip> happyClips;
public List<AudioClip> questionClips;
public List<AudioClip> sadClips;
public List<AudioClip> scaredClips;
public bool playAngryClips = true;
public bool playAnswerClips = false;
public bool playBraveClips = false;
public bool playCarefulClips = false;
public bool playExcitedClips = false;
public bool playHappyClips = false;
public bool playQuestionClips = false;
public bool playSadClips = false;
public bool playScaredClips = false;
private List<AudioClip>[] clipLists;
private List<AudioClip> currentList;
private int currentIndex;
```

In the `DialogueAudioManager` script, a variety of audio clips are defined as lists, each representing different emotions or dialogue types (e.g., angry, answer, brave, etc.). A public `AudioSource` component is also defined, which will be used to play the audio clips. There are also Boolean variables to control which type of clips should be played initially.

5. In the `void Start()` method, add the following code:

```
    clipLists = new List<AudioClip>[] {
        angryClips, answerClips, braveClips,
        carefulClips, excitedClips, happyClips,
        questionClips, sadClips, scaredClips };
    if (playAngryClips)
    {
        currentList = angryClips;
    }
    else if (playAnswerClips)
    {
        currentList = answerClips;
    }
    else if (playBraveClips)
    {
        currentList = braveClips;
    }
    else if (playCarefulClips)
    {
        currentList = carefulClips;
    }
```

```
        else if (playExcitedClips)
        {
            currentList = excitedClips;
        }
        else if (playHappyClips)
        {
            currentList = happyClips;
        }
        else if (playQuestionClips)
        {
            currentList = questionClips;
        }
        else if (playSadClips)
        {
            currentList = sadClips;
        }
        else if (playScaredClips)
        {
            currentList = scaredClips;
        }
        currentIndex =
            Random.Range(0, currentList.Count);
        audioSource.clip = currentList[currentIndex];
        audioSource.Play();
    }
```

In the `Start()` method, the script initializes an array of lists containing all the clip categories. It then checks which type of clips should be played first by looking at the Boolean variables (e.g., `playAngryClips`, `playAnswerClips`, etc.). The appropriate list is assigned to the `currentList` variable, and a random clip from that list is selected and played using the `AudioSource` component.

6. In the `void Update()` method, add the following code:

```
        if (!audioSource.isPlaying)
        {
            currentIndex =
                Random.Range(0, currentList.Count);
            audioSource.clip =
                currentList[currentIndex];
            audioSource.Play();
        }
```

In the `Update()` method, the script checks whether the `AudioSource` component is playing an audio clip. If it's not, the script selects a new random clip from the `currentList` variable and plays it using the `AudioSource` component.

7. Create a new method called `public void SetClipList(string category)` and add the following code:

```
        switch (category)
        {
            case "angry":
                currentList = angryClips;
                break;
            case "answer":
                currentList = answerClips;
                break;
            case "brave":
                currentList = braveClips;
                break;
            case "careful":
                currentList = carefulClips;
                break;
            case "excited":
                currentList = excitedClips;
                break;
            case "happy":
                currentList = happyClips;
                break;
            case "question":
                currentList = questionClips;
                break;
            case "sad":
                currentList = sadClips;
                break;
            case "scared":
                currentList = scaredClips;
                break;
            default:
                Debug.LogError("Invalid clip category:
                    " + category);
                break;
        }
    }
```

The `SetClipList(string category)` method is a public function that allows you to change the `currentList` variable, based on the input `category` string. It uses a `switch` statement to update the `currentList` variable according to the input category. If an invalid category is provided, an error message is logged.

> **Note**
>
> Each of the strings for the categories is case-sensitive. Make sure to correctly spell the category strings to avoid issues.

8. In **Inspector** for the `People_Prototype` prefab, you will find clip lists for the different clip categories that correspond to the categories of audio clips in the `Gibberish Dialogue and Voice Pack` asset.
9. Place all the audio clips with the title `Angry` in the `Angry Clips` reference slot.
10. Repeat *step 5* for the `Answer Clips`, `Brave Clips`, `Careful Clips`, `Excited Clips`, `Happy Clips`, `Question Clips`, `Sad Clips`, and `Scared Clips`.
11. Add the audio source from the `Audio Source` GO child of the `People_Prototype` prefab to the audio source in the `Dialogue Audio Manager` reference slot.
12. By clicking the box for the specific clip type or category, you can automatically loop between all the different audio files for a specific clip type automatically.
13. You can save the prefab by applying overrides.

This dialogue manager is very robust, and because we have so many clip options, from angry, brave, careful, and happy to questioning, sad, and scary, we can utilize all of them within the same script and manager to give us a lot of variability. More importantly, you can build on this script and add new sounds to it very easily by just clicking the + icon to add a new sound reference slot. You're literally rinsing and repeating. Now that you have the basic idea of how this script works, you can expand on it and apply it to a variety of different things. Even if you want to have animal sounds or any type of character, it's a great resource. And so, literally, you just place the `DialogueAudioManager` script on one GO, and because it's a prefab, it'll instantiate across all the different prefabs. Crafting something like this is very strategic because it saves you a lot of time, and you get a lot of bang for your buck.

Building on this, we can move on to creating a script that will randomize the generation of prefabs across different areas of our map. We could do that by creating a generator that will instantiate the same prefab across a variety of areas. And because there's already variability in the prefab, you'll get even more variability when you populate your world. So, by using these two different scripts (the `DialogueAudioManager` one and the `PersonSpawner` script we'll be working on shortly), we can populate a world that is very complex but simple under the hood.

To create a C# script that will randomly disperse our `People_Prototype` prefabs across our walking path area, you can follow these steps:

1. Create a new GO, and name it `Person Spawner Manager`.
2. Create a new C# script, and name it `PersonSpawner`.
3. Add the `PersonSpawner` script to the `Person Spawner Manager` GO.
4. Open the script in Visual Studio.
5. Add the following namespaces to the script:

```
using UnityEngine;
using UnityEditor;
using System.Linq;
using System.Collections.Generic;
```

6. Under `public class PersonSpawner : MonoBehaviour`, add the following variables:

```
    public GameObject[] personPrefabs;
    public int numberOfPeople = 10;
    [TagSelector]
    public string tagOptions = "";

    private Mesh mesh;
    private Vector3[] spawnPoints;
```

   The script defines several public and private variables. `personPrefabs` is an array of prefabs that will be spawned. `numberOfPeople` determines the number of people to spawn. `tagOptions` allows a user to specify a tag for the walking path area. `mesh` and `spawnPoints` are private variables used to store the mesh data and spawn positions, respectively.

7. In the `void Start()` method, add the following code:

```
    mesh = GetMeshWithTag(tagOptions);
    spawnPoints = GenerateSpawnPoints(numberOfPeople);
        for (int i = 0; i < numberOfPeople; i++)
        {
            Vector3 spawnPosition = spawnPoints[i];
            Quaternion spawnRotation =
                Quaternion.identity;
            Instantiate(personPrefabs[Random.Range(0,
                personPrefabs.Length)], spawnPosition,
                    spawnRotation);
        }
```

In the Start method, the script first calls GetMeshWithTag to find the combined mesh of all GOs with the specified tag. Then, it calls GenerateSpawnPoints to generate an array of spawn positions. For each spawn position, it randomly selects a prefab from personPrefabs and instantiates it in the scene.

8. Create a new method called Mesh GetMeshWithTag(string tag) and add the following code:

```
GameObject[] gameObjects =
    GameObject.FindGameObjectsWithTag(tag);
MeshFilter[] meshFilters = gameObjects
    .SelectMany(go =>
        go.GetComponentsInChildren<MeshFilter>())
    .Where(mf => mf != null && mf.sharedMesh !=
        null)
    .ToArray();
CombineInstance[] combineInstances = meshFilters
    .Select(mf => new CombineInstance()
    {
        mesh = mf.sharedMesh,
        transform =
            mf.transform.localToWorldMatrix
    })
    .ToArray();
Mesh mesh = new Mesh();
mesh.CombineMeshes(combineInstances, true, true);
return mesh;
```

This method finds all GOs with the specified tag and collects their MeshFilter. It creates a new array of CombineInstance, which stores the sharedMesh and localToWorldMatrix instances of each MeshFilter. The method then combines these meshes into a single mesh and returns it. By using the Where method, any null MeshFilter or those that don't have sharedMesh will be filtered out, ensuring that we only work with valid meshes when we combine the meshes with CombineInstance.

9. Create a new method called Vector3[] GenerateSpawnPoints(int count) and add the following code:

```
Vector3[] vertices = mesh.vertices;
Vector3[] spawnPoints = new Vector3[count];
for (int i = 0; i < count; i++)
{
    int randomIndex = Random.Range(0,
        vertices.Length);
    Vector3 vertex = vertices[randomIndex];
```

```
            spawnPoints[i] = vertex;
        }
        return spawnPoints;
```

This method takes a `count` integer as an argument and generates an array of `count` spawn points on the mesh's vertices. It iterates "count" times, selects a random vertex from the mesh's vertices, and adds it to the `spawnPoints` array. Finally, the method returns the `spawnPoints` array.

We can then set up a custom attribute in our **Inspector** that allows us to set the designated tag for the mesh we want to use to spawn our GOs. This `Tag` menu will be a dropdown menu that syncs with the `Tag` menu list that we normally see at the top of our **Inspector**.

To add the `Tag` menu dropdown that syncs with our `Tag` menu list, follow the following steps:

1. Add the following code to the bottom of our `PersonSpawner` script:

   ```
   [CustomPropertyDrawer(typeof(TagPickerAttribute))]
   ```

   This code defines a custom Unity Editor property drawer for a tag picker. The tag picker allows you to select a tag for an object in the Unity Editor more easily. The code is divided into two parts – the `TagPickerPropertyDrawer` class and the `TagPickerAttribute` class.

2. Create a new class named `public class TagPickerPropertyDrawer : PropertyDrawer`.

   The `TagPickerPropertyDrawer` class inherits from the `PropertyDrawer` class, which provides the functionality to customize how a specific type of property is displayed in the Unity Editor. The `OnGUI` method is overridden to implement the custom tag picker GUI.

3. In the new class, create a public override `void OnGUI(Rect position, SerializedProperty property, GUIContent label)` method and apply the following code:

   ```
           if (property.propertyType ==
               SerializedPropertyType.String)
               {
                   EditorGUI.BeginProperty(position, label,
                       property);
                   var attribute = this.attribute as
                       TagPickerAttribute;

                   if (attribute.UseStandardTagField)
                   {
                       property.stringValue =
                           EditorGUI.TagField(position,
                               label, property.stringValue);
                   }
   ```

```
        else
        {
            List<string> tags =
                new List<string>();
            tags.Add("<NoTag>");
            tags.AddRange(UnityEditorInternal
                .InternalEditorUtility.tags);
            string propValue =
                property.stringValue;
            int selectedIndex = -1;

            if (string.IsNullOrEmpty(propValue))
            {
                selectedIndex = 0;
            }
            else
            {
                for (int i = 1; i < tags.Count;
                     i++)
                {
                    if (tags[i] == propValue)
                    {
                        selectedIndex = i;
                        break;
                    }
                }
            }
```

The OnGUI method first checks whether the property type is a string. If so, it starts a new EditorGUI property block. It then retrieves TagPickerAttribute to check whether to use the standard Unity tag field. If UseStandardTagField is true, the standard Unity tag field is displayed. Otherwise, the custom tag picker is created.

The code continues as follows:

```
            selectedIndex =
                EditorGUI.Popup(position,
                    label.text, selectedIndex,
                        tags.ToArray());

            if (selectedIndex == 0)
            {
                property.stringValue = "";
            }
            else if (selectedIndex >= 1)
```

```
                {
                    property.stringValue =
                        tags[selectedIndex];
                }
                else
                {
                    property.stringValue = "";
                }
            }

            EditorGUI.EndProperty();
        }
        else
        {
            EditorGUI.PropertyField(position,
                property, label);
        }
    }
}
```

In the preceding snippet, the custom tag picker first initializes a list of tags, including the `<NoTag>` option. It then retrieves all the available tags in the Unity project using the `UnityEditorInternal.InternalEditorUtility.tags` property. The method then finds the index of the currently selected tag in the list of tags. If the property value is empty, `selectedIndex` is set to `0` (i.e., the `<NoTag>` option).

As a result of the preceding code, a pop-up menu is created using the `EditorGUI.Popup` method. `selectedIndex` is updated based on the user's selection. If `selectedIndex` is `0`, the property value is set to an empty string, indicating no tag. If `selectedIndex` is greater than or equal to `1`, the property value is set to the selected tag. If `selectedIndex` is `-1`, the property value is also set to an empty string, indicating no tag.

The `EditorGUI` property block is ended with the `EditorGUI.EndProperty` method.

4. Create a new class called `public class TagPickerAttribute : PropertyAttribute` and apply the following code:

```
    public bool UseStandardTagField = false;
```

The `TagPickerAttribute` class inherits from `PropertyAttribute` and contains a single Boolean field named `UseStandardTagField`. This field indicates whether the standard Unity `tag` field should be used instead of the custom tag picker. Setting this field to `true` will use the standard Unity `tag` field, while setting it to `false` will use the custom tag picker.

To configure the `PersonSpawner` script to disperse prefabs of our `People_Prototype` prefab along the area of our walking path, follow these steps:

1. In `Person Spawner Manager`, add our `People_Prototype` prefab to the `Person Prefabs` slot.
2. Set the number of people that you would like to spawn. I chose `15`, but you can choose any number. Just understand that the more people you spawn, the larger the impact on performance will be.
3. Go to the `Tags` menu and create a new tag called `WalkingPath`.
4. In our `WalkingPath` GO, set the tag to `WalkingPath`.
5. In `Person Spawner Manager`, set the tag options to `WalkingPath`.

When you press play, you will see multiple instances of the `People_Prototype` prefab spawned along the area of the walking path in random locations. To take it one step further, we can actually randomize which person will have which dialogue category enabled. We can do that with a simple randomized value that automatically triggers the category. This allows us to add some randomization and variability to the spawned persons. To do that, go to the `Start` function in our `DialogueAudioManager` script and add the following code:

```
int picker = Random.Range(1, 9);
if (picker == 1)
{
    playAngryClips = true;
}
else if (picker == 2)
{
    playAnswerClips = true;
}
else if (picker == 3)
{
    playBraveClips = true;
}
else if (picker == 4)
{
    playCarefulClips = true;
}
else if (picker == 5)
{
    playExcitedClips = true;
}
else if (picker == 6)
{
    playHappyClips = true;
```

```
    }
    else if (picker == 7)
    {
        playQuestionClips = true;
    }
    else if (picker == 8)
    {
        playSadClips = true;
    }
    else if (picker == 9)
    {
        playScaredClips = true;
    }
```

In the preceding code snippet, we create a dynamic and engaging emotional response system for VR characters by randomly selecting an emotional state and playing corresponding audio clips. To ensure consistency in the character's emotions, it's best to select only one category of audio clips at a time. The code implementation allows us to choose the type of audio for each player prefab, and it will randomly generate and play a sound from the selected category. Once a sound finishes playing, another sound within that category can be played, adding variety to the character's expressions.

While it's possible to play multiple sounds from different categories simultaneously, it's recommended to keep it limited to one category per prefab for a coherent emotional experience. By incorporating a randomizer for sound category selection, we add a layer of diversity and variability, which enhances the overall VR experience for both creators and users. This modular and customizable approach reflects the diversity we see in the real world, and utilizing code in this manner greatly benefits the development process.

Keeping these principles in mind during development allows for easy integration of diverse and variable elements into VR experiences. This strategic implementation results in a vast array of VR experiences that can be offered to the world, ensuring that your project stands out and caters to a wide audience.

Summary

This chapter covered a lot of material, focusing on *Phase 5* of our roadmap document, where we built out the sound design for our VR world. We created some `Park Audio` and `Audio Sources`, and made different audio managers for each category, such as the park, car, or NPC, and added new elements to give each area unique sounds. This was an easy task because we had the option to use audio sources from the Unity Asset Store, and more importantly, we were able to take a systematic approach to build C# code that allows us to add variability to the sounds, timing, content, categories, and implementation.

Playing with C# code, the Unity Editor, and our creativity allowed us to create immersive experiences with VR that we could literally walk around and experience in real time. This concept of creativity and the freedom to implement different ideas speaks to the power of VR development. As a developer myself, I really enjoy it because it allows me to unlock my potential as a creator, bouncing between code, designing, planning, sound design, and animation. These are the key skills that I mentioned in the first chapter and are now being implemented.

If you are not used to this sort of workflow as a VR developer, it is necessary to have this in your toolset, even if you do not use it every day. Having the capability to bounce from one area of expertise to another and build on those skills so that you can develop the best experience possible is essential. That is why this book exists and why VR experiences will be one of the biggest things in the next 5–10 years.

Now that we have completed our sound design, which ticks off *Phase 5* of our roadmap, we can move on to *Phase 6* – building our art gallery experience.

12
Building an Art Gallery

In the last chapter, we focused on a lot of passive interactions where you walk into different spaces, and you were able to have different experiences based on the locations you visited. You didn't have to input anything, but you were able to alter the experience and have a varied experience based on code and indirect interactions.

In this chapter, we'll revisit direct interactions by creating something that is interactive at its core – drawing. You don't need to be a true artist to draw in VR, but there are certain core elements that make for very interesting experiences. One of those is being able to interact with GOs and actually have alterations exist after those interactions. Something as simple as drawing on a wall can be very fun because you can explore all the variations of creativity within the virtual world and build the framework for it to be expanded across a whole environment. By the end of this chapter, you will understand that this feat is within arm's reach.

We will build off skills we developed in other chapters to build a virtual gallery space that takes on a life of its own. Going back to our roadmap in *Chapter 10*, we can look at *Phase 6* and see that our art gallery design experience is going to comprise creating an indoor art gallery from our floor plan. Then, we can have dynamic lighting indoors and create an art canvas that we can draw on using markers of different colors and sizes. We can then utilize the sockets that we created in a previous chapter to do things such as hanging art on a wall if it's not already there.

In this chapter, we will cover the following topics:

- Creating an art gallery 3D object from a floor plan image
- Creating a dynamic indoor lighting system
- Creating socket interactions to hang stuff on walls
- Creating a drawing system where you can use markers to draw on any canvas
- Creating a menu that can access and modify marker properties

Technical requirements

The complete source code for this chapter can be found at `https://github.com/PacktPublishing/Enhancing-Virtual-Reality-Experiences-with-Unity-2022/tree/main/EnhancingVRExperiencesFullProject/Assets/_VRProjectAssets/Scenes/Chapter_12`.

Creating a gallery mesh

This section should feel pretty familiar at this point because we've taken these steps many times before. We're going to revisit the idea of using a 2D image as a floor plan and then use ProBuilder to convert that floor plan into a 3D model. After doing that, we will utilize the available materials and assign the materials to our 3D model, and then we can add our lighting system. This is a straightforward implementation, and the approach is easy to follow. Once we have our art gallery 3D model, that's when the fun begins because we can start creating a system where we can draw in every nook and cranny of it.

To convert our gallery floor plan (*Figure 12.1*) into a 3D mesh (*Figure 12.2*) with ProBuilder, follow these steps:

1. Create a new, empty scene and name it `ArtGallery`.
2. In **Hierarchy**, create an empty GO and name it `ArtGallery`.
3. Set the **XYZ** position to `0,0,0` and the rotation to `0,0,0`.
4. Drag our `Art Gallery Map` floor plan into the scene from our `Textures` folder.
5. Set the **X** rotation to `90`.
6. Set the **XYZ** scale to `4`.
7. Make `Art Gallery Map` a child of the `ArtGallery` GO.
8. Open the **ProBuilder** window.
9. Choose the **New Poly Shape** option.
10. From an overhead view, use the **New Poly Shape** option to trace the internal walls of the floor plan.
11. After tracing all the walls, set the extrusion to `5` and enable **Flip Normals**.
12. Click the **Quit Editing** button to save your mesh.
13. If you have any internal walls, follow *steps 9–12* for those walls to create a new poly shape.
14. Choose all the poly-shaped GOs in **Hierarchy**, and in the **ProBuilder** window, click **Merge Objects** to merge them into one object.
15. We can now replace the mesh material with a white material.

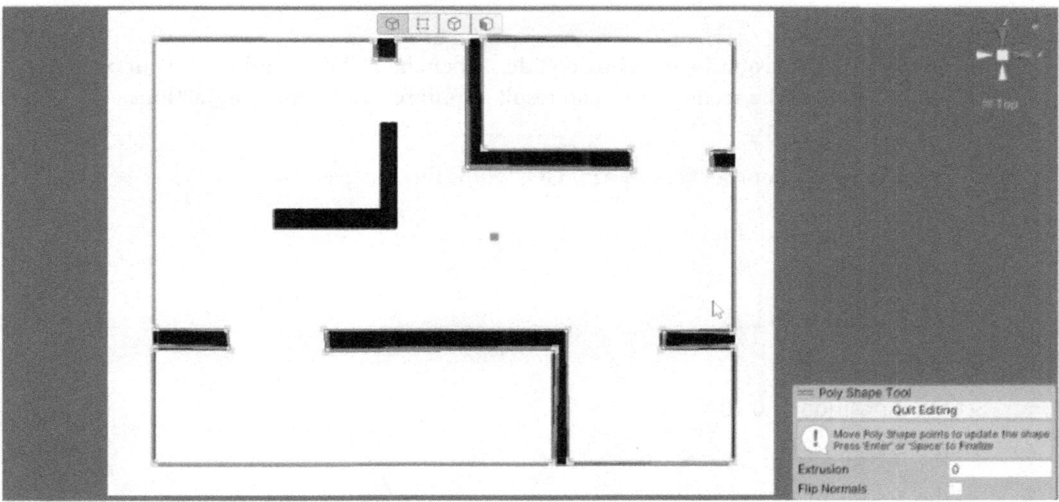

Figure 12.1 – 2D art gallery floor plan

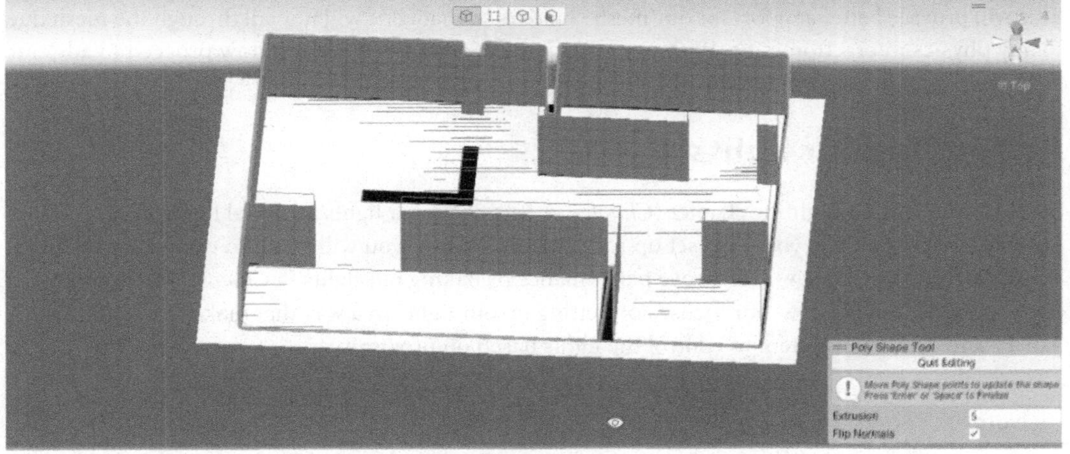

Figure 12.2 – 3D model based on the art gallery floor plan using ProBuilder

Now that the floor plan is completed and converted into a 3D model, we can move on to the next section, which focuses on implementing the art gallery part. But before we do, a best practice when you have a mesh that is made with a ProBuilder object and also has a mesh collider on it is to reinforce the ground with a box collider. This will prevent any bugs during the rendering of the physics and collisions, and ensure that objects and your VR rig won't go through the floor. The last thing you want is to apply complex art techniques to the canvas and ultimately fall through the floor because of a physics bug in Unity, causing you to free-fall into the abyss. This can have negative consequences for someone who is afraid of heights, so let's avoid that in the future by reinforcing our ground.

> **Note**
>
> While reinforcing the ground with a box collider is beneficial, be careful to prevent overlap with other colliders in the scene, as this can result in unforeseen physics interactions.

To reinforce the ground of our `ArtGallery` GO, follow these steps:

1. Create a 3D cube as a child of `ArtGallery`.
2. Name it `GalleryGround`.
3. Set the **X** position to `0.2`.
4. Set the **Y** position to `-2`.
5. Set the **Z** position to `0.03`.
6. Set the **X** scale to `35`.
7. Set the **Y** scale to `1`.
8. Set the **Z** scale to `27`.

This will provide better support for our mesh colliders so that GOs will not fall through the mesh due to any physics interaction bugs. With our gallery mesh completed, we can now proceed to add our lighting system in the next section.

Adding indoor lights

As I mentioned in the lighting chapter (*Chapter 6*), setting up our lights is crucial to increase visibility; but more importantly, if you don't set up your lights correctly, you will run into performance issues. We will cover more on how to improve performance by baking our lights in *Chapter 18*, which covers optimizations. But for now, our focus is on setting up our lights in a way that makes sense for the art gallery and creating a system to control the lights based on proximity.

> **Note**
>
> Overuse of dynamic lights can hinder performance, particularly in VR. Implementing baked lighting for static items is advisable to enhance performance.

To set up indoor lighting with spotlight prefabs (*Figure 12.3*), follow these steps:

1. Create a new, empty GO as a child of `ArtGallery`.
2. Name it `CeilingLights`.
3. From our `prefabs` folder, add a `CeilingLight` prefab as a child of the `CeilingLights` GO.
4. Set the **X** position to `0.09`.

5. Set the **Y** position to `5.53`.
6. Set the **Z** position to `1.64`.

Once the first light is positioned correctly, proceed to duplicate the lights and disperse them across the art gallery. I chose eight different lights and distributed them in the various rooms and hallways to have a good distribution of light. Remember our lighting chapter (*Chapter 6*), where in the *Modifying quality settings for lighting* section, we were able to control the amount of pixel light counts in our player settings based on the quality settings we had? So, if you want to have more lights, you will need to increase the pixel light count setting. But if you don't want to have too many lights, which is the case for our scene, you can limit the number of lights and the pixel light count setting. In the *Modifying quality settings for lighting* section of *Chapter 6*), we set the pixel light count to `10`, meaning we have a maximum of 10 lights before the lighting is impacted.

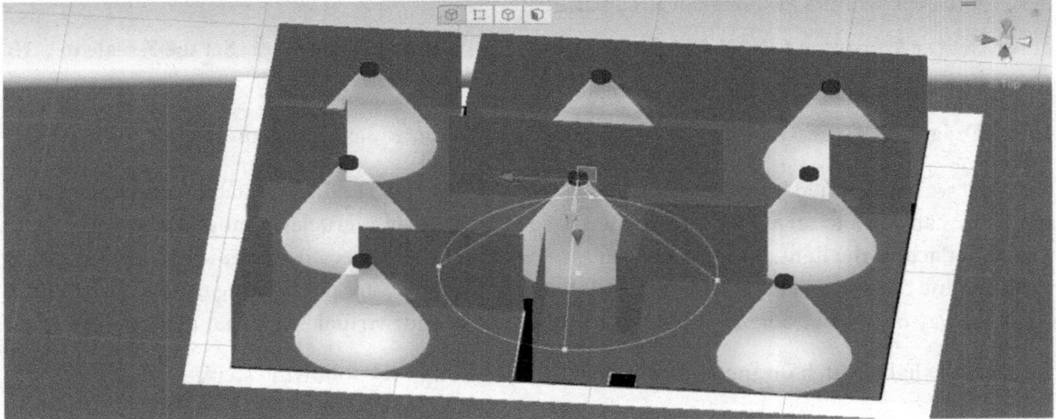

Figure 12.3 – Lights distributed in the art gallery

In the next section, we will learn how to create a light switch that can control lights within a certain proximity.

Adding light switches

We can provide a workaround to have high-quality lights and great performance while also limiting the number of lights that are turned on within a certain proximity. We can do that by creating a system where we press a light switch, and in doing so, turn off the lights that are within a specified distance of that light switch. Therefore, we're able to simulate a somewhat realistic experience of only having lights on that are turned on by us and turning off the lights that are not.

To create a light switch to place on the walls, go through the following steps:

1. Create an empty GO as a child of `ArtGallery`.
2. Name it `LightSwitches`.
3. Create another empty GO in `LightSwitches`.
4. Name it `LightSwitch`.
5. Create a cube as a child of the `LightSwitch` GO.
6. Name it `SwitchBody`.
7. Set the **Y** position to `.05`. Set the **X** scale to `.5`. Set the **Y** scale to `.1`. Set the **Z** scale to `.5`.
8. Give the cube a `DarkGray_Standard` material.
9. Create a cylinder and name it `SwitchButton`.
10. Set the **Y** position to `.15`. Set the **X** scale to `.35`. Set the **Y** scale to `.1`. Set the **Z** scale to `.35`.
11. Give the cylinder a `red unlit` material.
12. Drag the `LightSwitch` GO to the `prefabs` folder to save it as a prefab.

Now that we have created a prefab of our `LightSwitch`, we need to find a suitable location to place it so that we can use it to turn on the light when needed. Placement is crucial because if it is inaccessible, we cannot access the light, and without light, we won't be able to see anything. If you are struggling to determine the placement, consider the lights in the room you are in. They are usually placed in an open hallway or near a door. Try to find a location within your virtual space that makes sense.

To place the light switch on the wall (*Figure 12.4*), go through the following steps:

1. Set the **X** position to `-2.5`.
2. Set the **Y** position to `2.5`.
3. Set the **Z** position to `4`.
4. Set the **X** rotation to `-90`.
5. Set the **Z** rotation to `-90`.

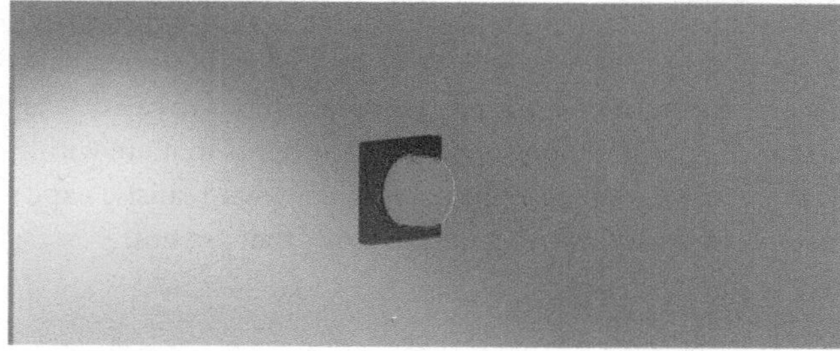

Figure 12.4 – Light switch placed on a wall in the art gallery

With the light switch placed on the wall, we can now proceed to add code that can be used to turn the lights on and off. Without this code, the light switch will theoretically be useless. Let's continue working toward building out this lighting system so we can have the best light possible for our gallery. This will contribute to us making wonderful art in the space.

To create a C# script that can turn on lights in the area, follow these steps:

1. Create a C# script and name it `LightSwitchController`.
2. Add it to the `LightSwitch` prefab.
3. Add the following namespaces to the C script:

```
using System.Collections.Generic;
using UnityEngine;
```

4. Within the `public class LightSwitchController : MonoBehaviour` class, add the following variables:

```
    public bool lightsOn = true;
    public Renderer buttonMesh;
    public Material onMaterial;
    public Material offMaterial;
    public float toggleRadius = 5.0f;
    public LayerMask toggleLayer;
```

5. Within the `void Start()` method, include the following code:

```
        SetLights(lightsOn);
        SetButtonMaterial(lightsOn);
```

   When the script starts, the `Start()` method initializes the lights' state and button appearance based on the `lightsOn` variable by calling the `SetLights()` and `SetButtonMaterial()` functions.

6. Create a method called `public void ToggleLights()`, and in the method, include the following code:

```
        lightsOn = !lightsOn;
        SetLights(lightsOn);
        SetButtonMaterial(lightsOn);
```

   The `ToggleLights()` method is responsible for toggling the `lightsOn` variable and updating the lights' state and button appearance accordingly. It calls the `SetLights()` and `SetButtonMaterial()` functions to achieve this.

7. Create a method called `void SetLights(bool state)` and add the following code:

```
Collider[] colliders =
    Physics.OverlapSphere(transform.position,
        toggleRadius, toggleLayer);
foreach (Collider collider in colliders)
{
    Light light =
        collider.GetComponent<Light>();
    if (light != null)
    {
        light.enabled = state;
    }
}
```

The `SetLights(bool state)` method finds all colliders within the `toggleRadius` distance from the script's position and within the specified `toggleLayer` using the `Physics.OverlapSphere()` function. It then iterates through these colliders, checks whether they have a `Light` component, and enables or disables the light based on the `state` parameter.

8. Create a method called `void SetButtonMaterial(bool state)` and add the following code:

```
if (state)
{
    buttonMesh.material = onMaterial;
}
else
{
    buttonMesh.material = offMaterial;
}
```

The `SetButtonMaterial(bool state)` method sets the button's material based on the `state` parameter. If `state` is `true`, the button material is set to `onMaterial`; otherwise, it's set to `offMaterial`.

9. Create a new method called `private void OnDrawGizmosSelected()` and apply the following code:

```
Gizmos.color = Color.yellow;
Gizmos.DrawWireSphere(transform.position, toggleRadius);
```

The `OnDrawGizmosSelected()` method visualizes the area of effect for toggling the lights in the editor. When the script's object is selected, it draws a yellow wireframe sphere in the **Scene** view, centered at the script's position with a radius equal to `toggleRadius`. This helps developers understand the coverage area for the light switch functionality (*Figure 12.5*):

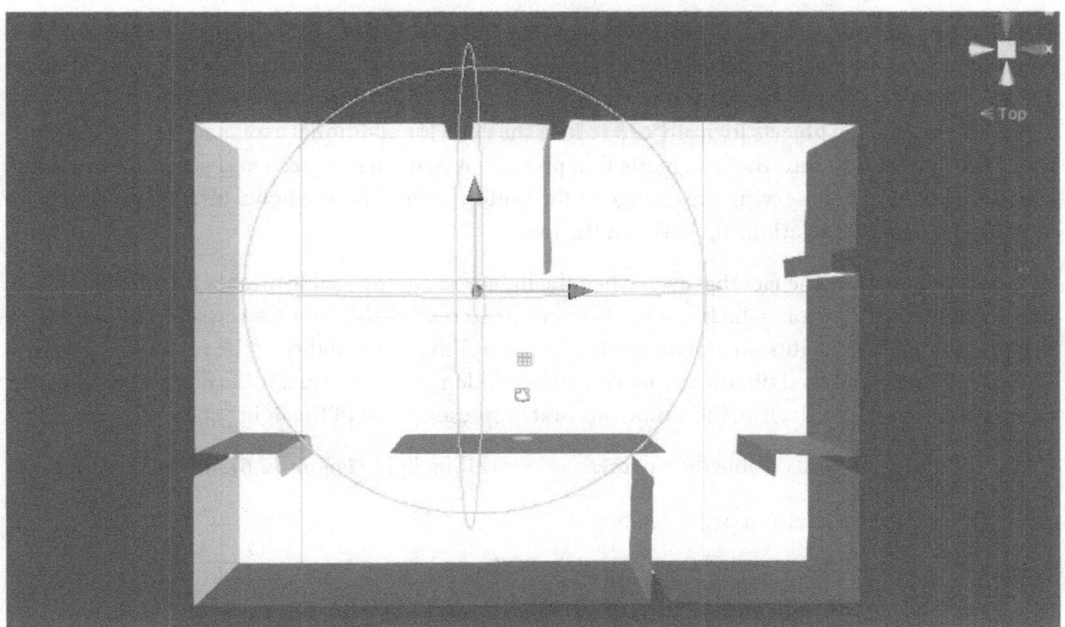

Figure 12.5 – Light switch radius visualized in the Scene view

10. Save the script and go back to the `LightSwitch` GO.
11. In **Inspector**, add `SwitchButton` to the `buttonMesh` reference.
12. Add the `green_emission` material to the `onMaterials` reference.
13. Add the `red_emission` material to the `offMaterial` reference.
14. Set **Toggle radius** to `12.5`.
15. In the **Layers** menu, create a new layer named `CeilingLights`.
16. In the `Toggle layers` reference in the `LightSwitch` prefab, set the **toggle layer** to `CeilingLights`.
17. On the `SwitchButton` GO, add an `XR Simple Interactable` component.
18. Set **Interaction Layer Mask** to **Everything**.
19. Set the `Select Entered Interactable` event to the `LightSwitch` GO.
20. Use the **Toggle lights** function from the `LightSwitch` GO script.

With the implemented code, we can now toggle the light on and off, and the button will provide a visual indicator of the light's current state by changing its material. This attention to detail enhances the user experience and effectively communicates the necessary information. Incorporating colors creatively and placing objects logically can reduce the need for additional explanations. For example, a red button on a wall intuitively suggests that pressing it may turn it green and activate something, such as the lights. By observing the change in the button's color and the lights turning on, users can easily understand the relationship between the two.

It's essential to address the fact that even when the lights are off, the visible meshes might still indicate that the light should be on, which can be distracting. To resolve this, our C# script should include a function to toggle the lights on and off while also controlling the visibility of the ray mesh. This way, when the lights are turned off, the ray mesh will be hidden, and the visual indicator provided by the mesh will be deactivated, ensuring a more accurate representation of the light's state.

To turn off the lights and disable the ray mesh in our ceiling light (*Figure 12.6*), follow these steps:

1. Go to the `CeilingLight` prefab.
2. Add a new C# script called `CeilingLightToggle`.
3. Add the `CeilingLightToggle` script to the `CeilingLight` prefab.
4. Add the following namespaces to the C# script:

```
using System.Collections;
using System.Collections.Generic;
using UnityEngine;
```

5. In the `public class CeilingLightToggle : MonoBehaviour` class, add the following variables:

```
    public Light spotlight;
    public MeshRenderer rayMesh;
    public Material onMaterial;
    public Material offMaterial;
    public MeshRenderer bulbMesh;
```

Within the `CeilingLightToggle` class, several variables are declared to manage different aspects of the light, including the `spotlight`, `rayMesh`, `onMaterial`, `offMaterial`, and `bulbMesh`.

6. In the `private void Start()` method, add the following code:

```
rayMesh.enabled = spotlight.enabled;
bulbMesh.material = spotlight.enabled ?
    onMaterial : offMaterial;
```

   In the `Start()` method, which runs at the beginning of the script execution, the initial state of the light rays and light bulb is set based on the spotlight's enabled state. If the light is on, `rayMesh` will be visible and `bulbMesh` will use `onMaterial`; if the light is off, `rayMesh` will be hidden and `bulbMesh` will use `offMaterial`.

7. In the `private void Update()` method, add the following code:

```
if (spotlight.enabled != rayMesh.enabled)
{
    rayMesh.enabled = spotlight.enabled;
    bulbMesh.material = spotlight.enabled ?
        onMaterial : offMaterial;
}
```

   In the `Update()` method, which runs once per frame, the code checks whether the spotlight's enabled state has changed and updates `rayMesh` and `bulbMesh` accordingly. If the spotlight's enabled state is different from `rayMesh`'s enabled state, `rayMesh`'s visibility is set based on the spotlight's enabled state, and `bulbMesh`'s material is set using either `onMaterial` if the light is on or `offMaterial` if it's off. This ensures that the appearance of the light and its rays stay consistent with the light's enabled state throughout the application's runtime.

8. Save the script and go back to the `CeilingLight` prefab in **Hierarchy**.
9. In the `Spotlight` reference, add a spotlight that's a child of `CeilingLight`.
10. Add the light ray to the `rayMesh` reference.
11. Add a `yellow emission` material to the `onMaterial` reference.
12. Add a `dark gray standard` material to the `offMaterial` reference.
13. Add the `bulb` GO to the `bulbMesh` reference.
14. Apply all the overrides to the `CeilingLight` prefab.

When you test this out, you will notice that any of the ceiling lights that are within the toggle radius of this light switch will turn off. When they turn off, the light bulb will change to dark gray, and the ray mesh will turn off or deactivate. When you turn on the lights, those within the range of the toggle ray will turn on by turning yellow, and they will have a ray mesh showing.

Figure 12.6 – Ceiling light turned on (left) and turned off (right)

Now that you have working light switches, you can distribute them around the art gallery to turn off specific lights or collections of lights in particular areas. A good use case for this is to place a light switch in every room that will automatically turn off all the lights within that room or area when pressed. This allows you to avoid designating specific lights to turn on/off, as the light switch will recognize, by default, all the lights available within its radius. In the next section, we can move on to creating our drawing canvas and ultimately building out our art experience.

Creating a drawing system

In this section, we'll be focusing on creating a drawing system that incorporates two core components: a canvas that can be drawn on and a marker that can be used for drawing. These two objects work together to create the drawing experience. Individually, they are just objects that you can interact with. You can expand on this system by modifying the canvas to cover a larger area, allowing you to draw on a larger surface instead of the predefined size we initially create.

To create a drawing canvas (*Figure 12.7*), go through the following steps:

1. Create a new plane.
2. Name it `Whiteboard`.
3. Set the **X** position to `3.6`, the **Y** position to `2.4`, and the **Z** position to `-0.4`.
4. Set the **X** rotation to `90`, the **Y** rotation to `90`, and the **Z** rotation to `90`.

5. Set the **X** scale to `0.3`, leave the **Y** scale at `1`, and set the **Z** scale to `0.3`.
6. Create a new C# script, name it `WhiteboardController`, and add it to the `Whiteboard` GO.
7. Add the following namespace to the C# script:

```
using UnityEngine;
```

The `UnityEngine` namespace is imported to provide access to Unity's classes and functions.

8. In the `public class WhiteboardController : MonoBehaviour` class, add the following variables:

```
    public Texture2D texture;
    public Vector2 textureSize = new Vector2(2048,
        2048);
```

Within the `WhiteboardController` class, two public variables are declared: a `Texture2D` named `texture` for the drawing canvas and a `Vector2` named `textureSize` for specifying its dimensions (2,048 x 2,048 in this case).

9. In the `void Start()` method, add the following code:

```
        var r = GetComponent<Renderer>();
        texture = new Texture2D((int)textureSize.x,
            (int)textureSize.y);
        r.material.mainTexture = texture;
```

In the `Start()` method, a reference to the `Renderer` component attached to the GO is obtained, which is responsible for rendering the visuals of the object. Then, a new `Texture2D` object is created using the dimensions from `textureSize` and assigned to the Renderer's material's main texture. This ensures that the texture is visible on the `Whiteboard` GO and can be drawn upon. The code sets up a drawing canvas by creating a new texture, setting its size, and assigning it to the `Whiteboard` GO, while also adding a script to the GO to handle the drawing functionality.

10. Save the code.
11. Save the `Whiteboard` GO as a prefab in the `prefabs` folder.

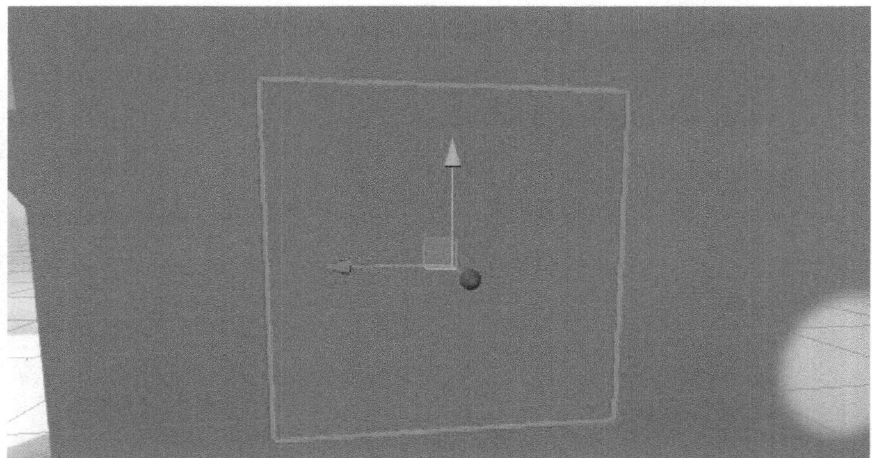

Figure 12.7 – Drawing canvas (Whiteboard GO) indicated by outline on the gallery wall

With the drawing canvas created, we can now create our markers. This process will involve a couple of steps, unlike the drawing board, where we're just using a simple plane. With the markers, we'll have to create the marker 3D objects and have them strategically separated from the body of the marker and the tip of the marker. We also need to set an anchor point so that we can hold the marker. After we have the model set up, we can proceed to the next section to add the code so that we can actually draw on the board.

To create a marker for drawing on the drawing board (*Figure 12.8*), follow these steps:

1. Create an empty GO and name it `WhiteboardMarker`.
2. Create another empty GO as a child of the `WhiteboardMarker` and name it `Anchor`.
3. On `Anchor`, set the **Y** position to `-0.2`.
4. Set the **X** rotation to `-90`.
5. Set the **X** scale to `0.05`, the **Y** scale to `0.05`, and the **Z** scale to `0.4`.
6. Create a cube as a child of `WhiteboardMarker` and name it `Handle`.
7. Set the **Y** position to `-0.23`.
8. Set the **Z** rotation to `-90`.
9. Set the **X** scale to `0.44`, the **Y** scale to `0.054`, and the **Z** scale to `0.054`.
10. Create another `Cube` GO as a child of `WhiteboardMarker` and name it `Marker Tip`.
11. Set the **Y** position to `0.0015`.
12. Set the **Z** rotation to `-90`.
13. Set the **X** scale to `0.05`, the **Y** scale to `0.05`, and the **Z** scale to `0.05`.

14. Create a new material named `MarkerMaterial` and add it to the `Tip` GOs `MeshRenderer` materials slot.
15. Take the `WhiteboardMarker` GO and make it a prefab to save it.

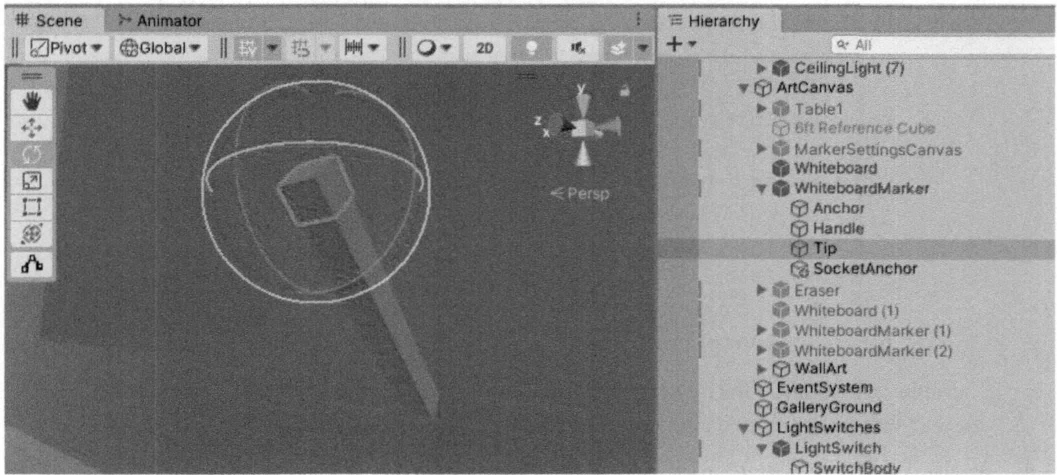

Figure 12.8 – WhiteboardMarker GO with the Tip GO indicated in the Scene view

Now that we have our 3D model of the marker made of primitive objects, we can move on to adding the functionality so that when the marker tip touches the drawing board, it will leave a mark that we can use to draw with. Since in VR there's no ink and everything is pixels, we have to simulate the canvas being drawn on. It's a simulation, but in VR, everything is a simulation. Using code and our creative problem-solving approach, we can create an interesting effect that I'm pleased with, and I hope you will be pleased with it as well.

To enable the marker to draw on the canvas, go through the following steps:

1. Create a new C# script called `WhiteboardMarker` and add it to the prefab.
2. Add the following namespaces to the C# script:

```
using System.Collections;
using System.Collections.Generic;
using System.Linq;
using UnityEngine;
```

3. In the `public class WhiteboardMarker : MonoBehaviour` class, add the following variables:

```
    public Transform markerTip;
    public int _penSize = 5;
```

```
    private MeshRenderer markerTipMesh;

    private Renderer _renderer;
    public string whiteboardTag;
    public Color markerColor;
    private Color previousColor;

    private Color[] _colors;
    private float _tipHeight;
    private RaycastHit _touch;
    private WhiteboardController _whiteboard;

    private Vector2 _touchPos,_lastTouchPos;
    private bool _touchedLastFrame;
    private Quaternion _lastTouchRot;
```

Variables are declared in the `WhiteboardMarker` class, which store information about the marker tip's position, pen size, color, and other related properties.

4. In the `void Start()` method, add the following code:

```
        previousColor = markerColor;
        _renderer =
            markerTip.GetComponent<Renderer>();
        _tipHeight = markerTip.localScale.y;

        markerTipMesh =
            markerTip.GetComponent<MeshRenderer>();
        PickColor();
```

In the `Start()` method, initial values for the marker tip's position, color, and size are set. The `PickColor()` method is called to set the initial color of the marker tip.

5. In the `void Update()` method, add the following code:

```
        if (markerColor != previousColor)
        {
            PickColor();
            previousColor = markerColor;
        }
        Draw();
    }
```

The `Update()` method is called every frame and checks whether the marker color has changed. If it has, the color is updated, and the `Draw()` method is called.

6. Create a new method called `private void PickColor()` and add the following code:

```
Material markerMaterial = new
    Material(Shader.Find("Standard"));
markerMaterial.color = markerColor;
markerTipMesh.material = markerMaterial;
SetColors();
```

The `PickColor()` method creates a new material with the current marker color and applies it to the marker tip's `Mesh Renderer`.

7. Create a new method called `private void SetColors()` and add the following code:

```
_colors =
    Enumerable.Repeat(_renderer.material.color
        , _penSize * _penSize).ToArray();
```

The `SetColors()` method generates an array of colors for the drawing, filling it with the current marker color.

8. Create a new method called `private void Draw()` and add the following code:

```
if(Physics.Raycast(markerTip.position,transform.up,
    out _touch, _tipHeight))
        {
            if (
            _touch.transform.CompareTag(whiteboardTag)
            )
            {
                if(_whiteboard == null)
                {
                    _whiteboard =
                        _touch.transform.GetComponent
                            <WhiteboardController>();
                }
                _touchPos = new
                    Vector2(_touch.textureCoord.x,
                        _touch.textureCoord.y);
                var x = (int)(_touchPos.x *
                    _whiteboard.textureSize.x -
                        (_penSize / 2));
                var y = (int)(_touchPos.y *
                    _whiteboard.textureSize.y -
                        (_penSize / 2));
                if (y < 0 || y >
                _whiteboard.textureSize.y || x < 0 ||
                x > _whiteboard.textureSize.x) return;
```

```
                    if (_touchedLastFrame)
                    {
                        _whiteboard.texture.SetPixels(
                            x, y, _penSize, _penSize,
                                _colors);
                        for(float f = 0.01f;
                            f < 1.00f; f += 0.01f)
                        {
                            var lerpX =
                                (int)Mathf.Lerp(
                                    _lastTouchPos.x,
                                        x, f);
                            var lerpY =
                                (int)Mathf.Lerp(
                                    _lastTouchPos.y,
                                        y, f);
                            _whiteboard.texture
                                .SetPixels(lerpX,
                                    lerpY, _penSize,
                                        _penSize,
                                            _colors);
                        }
                        transform.rotation =
                            _lastTouchRot;
                        _whiteboard.texture.Apply();
                    }
                    _lastTouchPos = new Vector2(x, y);
                    _lastTouchRot =
                        transform.rotation;
                        _touchedLastFrame = true;
                    return;
                }
            }
            _whiteboard = null;
            _touchedLastFrame = false;
        }
```

The `Draw()` method handles the actual drawing process by detecting whether the marker tip is touching a whiteboard surface using Raycast. If the marker is touching a whiteboard, it calculates the position on the texture and sets the appropriate pixels to the marker color. When drawing continuously, the method interpolates between the last touch position and the current one, creating a smooth line. If the marker is not touching the whiteboard, it resets the necessary variables.

9. Save the code and go back to the prefab. This script allows for a VR marker to draw on a whiteboard surface in Unity by continuously updating the marker tip's position and color and applying the drawing to the whiteboard's texture.
10. Add the `Tip` GO as a child of the `MarkerTip` object and set the reference.
11. Set the pen size to `60`.
12. Set the `whiteboard` tag to `Whiteboard`.
13. Set the marker color to any color you want.
14. Add a `Rigidbody` component to the `WhiteboardMarker` prefab.
15. Freeze rotation in the **X**, **Y**, and **Z** axes.
16. Add an `XR Grab Interactable` component.
17. Set **Interaction Layer Mask** to **grabbable**.
18. Set the attached transform to the `Anchor` GO.
19. Enable **Add Default Grab Transforms** in the **Grab Transformers Configuration** section.
20. Apply overrides to save the prefab.

With this, you can create a marker that you can use to draw on the whiteboard. You can adjust the pen size to change the thickness of the stroke on the canvas, and you can change the color of the marker. Additionally, you can change the style of the pen tip by changing the `Mesh Filter` from the default cube to a sphere, capsule, or any other mesh you want. This provides a lot of versatility in the drawing and writing tools you can use.

Having a complete marker with the code we've just created opens up many possibilities for control. We can adjust the size and color of the brushstroke when the marker hits the canvas. We can also create a settings menu that references the **Inspector** components and change everything on the fly. This allows us to work within the scene to control different settings and provide a better experience for users.

To create the menu, we'll start by creating a canvas and adding it to the world space. Then, we'll add sliders to reference the options we want to control in the menu. Finally, we'll pair that with the code we have to control all the different settings in real time.

To create a menu controller for the marker settings, follow these steps:

1. Add a `Canvas` GO and name it `MarkerSettingsCanvas`.
2. Set **Render Mode** in the `Canvas` component to **World Space**.
3. Set the **X** position to `0.76`.
4. Set the **Y** position to `2.4`.
5. Set the **Z** position to `-0.14`.
6. Set **Width** to `1290`.

7. Set **Height** to `1844`.
8. Set the **X** pivot to `0.5`.
9. Set the **Y** pivot to `0.5`.
10. Set the **Y** rotation to `-165.65`.
11. Set the **X** scale to `0.0015`.
12. Set the **Y** scale to `0.0015`.
13. Set the **Z** scale to `0.0015`.
14. Disable the `Graphic Ray Caster` component.
15. Add a `Tracked Device Graphic Raycaster` component.
16. Set **Blocking Mask** to **Everything**.
17. Set **Raycast Trigger Interaction** to **Ignore**.

The `Canvas` component is often underutilized in VR experiences because it's usually used for on-screen menus for mobile devices and traditional 2D screens. In VR, we don't have the opportunity to use touch screens, so instead of having stuff on the touch screen, we can add it to the space in front of us. To create a menu, we will take what would have been on a touch screen and apply it in the space that we occupy, utilizing UI components such as buttons and sliders and allowing the right interactor components to interact with them.

To add UI components to our **Marker** canvas to control our **Marker Settings** (*Figure 12.9*), follow these steps:

1. Create a `Panel` as a child of `MarkerSettingsCanvas`.
2. In the `Rect Transform` component of the panel, choose the option to stretch the panel to the edges of the canvas.
3. Set the panel color to black.
4. Set **Alpha** to `100`.
5. As a child of the panel, add a slider UI GO and name it `SaturationSlider`.
6. Set the **Y** position to `-298`.
7. Set the **X** position to `0`.
8. Set the **Z** position to `0`.
9. Set **Width** to `160`.
10. Set **Height** to `20`.
11. Set all the anchors and pivots to `0.5`.
12. Set the **X**, **Y**, and **Z** scale to `4.58`.
13. Enable the `Interactable` and the `Slider` component.

14. Set the **Direction** to **Left to Right**.
15. Set the minimum value to `0`.
16. Set the maximum value to `1`.
17. Set the value to `1`.
18. Duplicate `Saturation Slider` and name it `Size Slider`.
19. Set the **Y** Position to `-453`.
20. Set the minimum value in the slider component to `5`.
21. Set the maximum value to `30`.
22. Enable whole numbers.
23. Set the volume to `15`.
24. Duplicate `Size Slider` and name it `Hue Slider`.
25. Set the **X** position to `453`.
26. Set the **Y** position to `50`.
27. Set **Width** to `20`.
28. Set **Height** to `160`.
29. Set the direction in the slider component to **Bottom to Top**.
30. Set the minimum value to `0`.
31. Set the maximum value to `1`.
32. Disable whole numbers.
33. Set the value to `0.5`.
34. Add an image as a child of the panel and name it `Color Wheel Visual`.
35. Set the **X** position to `-10`.
36. Set the **Y** position to `18`.
37. Set **Width** and **Height** to `100`.
38. Set the **XYZ** scale to `5`.

With our sliders organized on our canvas, we have a functional menu that we can utilize. If you try to use it now, nothing will happen because it's not yet in the code, but you can see the possibilities of adding different settings to it. Having a menu like this isn't just limited to using settings – you could control an animation or trigger things on and off. Literally anything that you would have on a UI menu screen for a mobile device or any other experience in Unity, you can incorporate within your VR experience. The only difference is that you aren't touching the screen; you're just using your hand controller interactors and ray interactor to change the values.

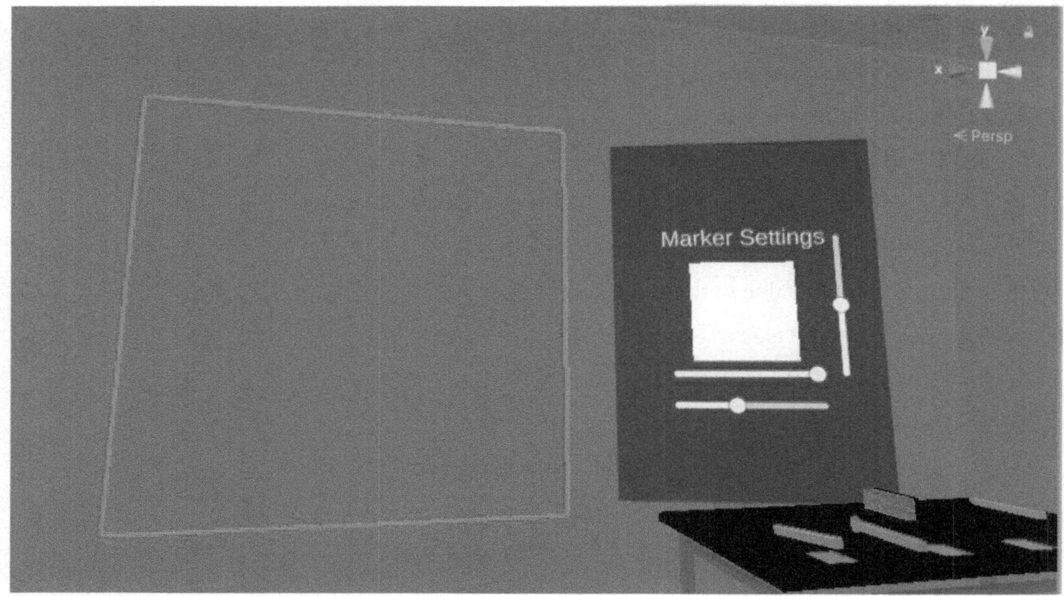

Figure 12.9 – MarkerSettingsCanvas with UI visualized next to the Whiteboard GO

With the UI menu complete, we can move on to setting up our code so that it references the UI components and we're able to control the marker settings in the UI.

To create a C# script to use sliders to control our marker settings, follow these steps:

1. Create a new C# script named `MarkerSettings` and add it to our `MarkerSettings-Canvas` GO.
2. Add the following namespaces to the C# script:

```
using UnityEngine;
using UnityEngine.UI;
```

3. In the `public class MarkerSettings : MonoBehaviour` class, add the following variables:

```
    public WhiteboardMarker[] markers;
    public Slider sizeSlider;
    private Image colorImage;
    public GameObject colorWheelUI;
    public Image colorWheel;
    private Image colorSelector;
    public Slider hueSlider;
```

```
public Slider saturationSlider;
private float previousSaturationValue;

private float previousHueValue;

private Color _selectedColor;
```

The `MarkerSettings` class inherits from `MonoBehaviour` and contains several public and private variables. These include an array of `WhiteboardMarker` objects, sliders for size, hue, and saturation, UI elements such as the color wheel and color selector, and color-related values.

4. In the `void Start()` method, add the following code:

```
_selectedColor = new Color(0.5f, 0.5f, 0.5f);

foreach(WhiteboardMarker marker in markers)
{
    marker.markerColor = colorImage.color;
    marker._penSize = (int)sizeSlider.value;
}
```

The `Start()` method initializes the `_selectedColor` variable and iterates through the `markers` array to set their initial color and pen size based on the `colorImage` color and `sizeSlider` value.

5. In the `void Update()` method, add the following code:

```
float hue = hueSlider.value;
float saturation = saturationSlider.value;

_selectedColor = Color.HSVToRGB(hue,
    saturation, 1f);
colorWheel.color = _selectedColor;
foreach (WhiteboardMarker marker in markers)
{
    if (marker.markerColor != _selectedColor)
    {
        marker.markerColor = _selectedColor;
        colorImage.color = _selectedColor;
    }
    if (marker._penSize !=
        (int)sizeSlider.value)
    {
        marker._penSize =
            (int)sizeSlider.value;
```

```
        }
        if (hueSlider.value != previousHueValue ||
        saturationSlider.value !=
        previousSaturationValue)
        {
            GetSelectedColor();
        }
    }
```

The `Update()` method is called every frame and updates the marker color and pen size based on the current slider values. It also calls the `GetSelectedColor()` method if hue or saturation values have changed.

6. Create a new method called `public void ToggleSettingsPanel(bool show)` and add the following code:

```
gameObject.SetActive(show);
```

The `ToggleSettingsPanel()` method takes a Boolean parameter to show or hide the settings panel.

7. Create a new method called `public void SelectColor()` and add the following code:

```
_selectedColor = GetSelectedColor();
colorWheelUI.SetActive(false);
```

The `SelectColor()` method sets the selected color and hides the color wheel UI.

8. Create a new method called `public void CancelColor()` and add the following code:

```
colorWheelUI.SetActive(false);
```

The `CancelColor()` method simply hides the color wheel UI.

9. Create a new method called `public void ShowColorWheel()` and add the following code:

```
colorWheelUI.SetActive(true);
```

The `ShowColorWheel()` method displays the color wheel UI.

10. Create a new method called `private Color GetSelectedColor()` and add the following code:

```
float hue = hueSlider.value * 360f;
float saturation = saturationSlider.value;
float chroma = saturation;
float huePrime = hue / 60f;
float x = chroma * (1f - Mathf.Abs(
    huePrime % 2f - 1f));
float r1 = 0, g1 = 0, b1 = 0;
if (huePrime < 1f)
{
    r1 = chroma;
    g1 = x;
}
else if (huePrime < 2f)
{
    r1 = x;
    g1 = chroma;
}
else if (huePrime < 3f)
{
    g1 = chroma;
    b1 = x;
}
else if (huePrime < 4f)
{
    g1 = x;
    b1 = chroma;
}
else if (huePrime < 5f)
{
    r1 = x;
    b1 = chroma;
}
else
{
    r1 = chroma;
    b1 = x;
}
float brightness = 1f;
float m = brightness - chroma;
float r = r1 + m;
```

```
        float g = g1 + m;
        float b = b1 + m;
        return new Color(r, g, b);
```

The `GetSelectedColor()` method converts hue and saturation values into an RGB color using a custom algorithm based on the HSL color model.

11. Create a new method called `public void UpdateColorSelector()` and add the following code:

```
        Vector2 localPos;
        RectTransformUtility
            .ScreenPointToLocalPointInRectangle(
                colorWheel.rectTransform,
                    Input.mousePosition, null,
                        out localPos);
        float hue = Mathf.Atan2(localPos.y,
            localPos.x) * Mathf.Rad2Deg;
        float saturation =
            Mathf.Clamp01(
                localPos.magnitude /
                    (colorWheel.rectTransform.rect
                        .width / 2f));
        colorSelector.rectTransform.anchoredPosition =
            localPos;
        _selectedColor = GetSelectedColor();
        colorImage.color = _selectedColor;
```

The `UpdateColorSelector()` method updates the color selector's position based on the mouse input, calculates the hue and saturation values, and sets the selected color accordingly.

12. Save the code. The script creates an interactive UI for adjusting marker settings, such as color and size, in a VR environment. The user can select the color using the color wheel and adjust the marker size using sliders, with the script updating the markers' properties in real time.
13. Return to the `MarkerSettingsCanvas` GO.
14. Add the markers to the markers reference array.
15. Add the `SizeSlider` GO to the size slider reference slot.
16. Add the `MarkerCanvas` GO to the color wheel UI reference slot.
17. Add the `ColorWheelVisual` image to the color wheel reference slot.
18. Add the `HueSlider` GO to the hue slider reference slot.
19. Add the `SaturationSlider` GO to the saturation slider reference slot.
20. Save `MarkerSettingsCanvas` as a prefab.

With the menu settings completed, we are able to control our drawing system by using the sliders to pick our colors, saturation, hue, and size. We can then save it as a setting within our marker controller at runtime. When we walk up to the canvas and place the marker on it, we can utilize all our artistic capabilities to create interesting pictures. Even if we just wanted to write our name, we can do that in VR by picking up a marker and drawing on the board. It sounds simple, but to be able to do that in VR when we're not actually picking up a physical marker is a remarkable experience. The possibilities are limitless. We can go a step further by making the drawing canvas larger, duplicating it, and placing it as a complete wall to have a full-wall canvas to apply our artistic talents to.

This is just the tip of the iceberg when it comes to combining the art and technology aspects of VR. We can be creative in the development process and encourage people to be creative in the experience that we develop. To top off the whole experience, we want to allow people to hang their artwork in the art gallery.

Hanging a picture frame

When you think about art galleries in general, you might wonder whether there's any point in having one if you can't hang things on the walls. Say you spent all this time working on a piece of art and you don't know what to do with it. You could take your art to the hypothetical art gallery and hang it on the art gallery wall so that people who visit the virtual gallery can see it. In many ways, you can have a virtual space that you have full control over to display your art. Even if you haven't set up the locations on the wall where you are going to place the art, you can set up sockets and places for you to place your art.

In this section, we'll proceed to make a picture frame that can hold art in it. We will be able to place it on our wall so that we can display the art in the frame. To do this, we will be utilizing sockets, which you should be familiar with from the introduction to all of the XR interactable components in *Chapter 3* (see the *Adding socket interactors to our demo scene* section). This is a very easy use case that we could apply to our gallery scene to really make the experience come full circle.

To make a picture frame you can hang on a wall, go through the following steps:

1. Create an empty GO and name it `Picture Frame`.
2. Create a ProBuilder cube as a child of `Picture Frame` and name it `Frame`.
3. Set the **Z** scale to `0.2`.
4. Open the **ProBuilder** window and select the **Face Selection** tool.
5. Hold the *Shift* button with the **Scale** tool active to scale the face down as an inset.
6. Use the **Move** tool while holding *Shift* to push the inseted face in about half the distance of the thickness of the cube.
7. Set the `Frame` material to `Yellow Metallic`.
8. Add a `Quad` as a child of `Picture Frame` and name it `Picture Canvas`.

9. Set the **X** position to `0.5`, the **Y** position to `0.5`, and the **Z** position to `0.16`.
10. Set the **Y** rotation to `180` and **XYZ** scale to `0.9`.
11. Set the material to `Violet Emission`.
12. In the `Picture Frame` GO, add an `XR Grab Interactable` component.
13. For **Interaction Layer Mask**, add a new layer called `Wall Art`.
14. Set **Interaction Layer Mask** to **grabbable** and `Wall Art`.
15. Add a `Box Collider` component to the `Picture Frame` GO.
16. In the `Box Collider` component, set the **X** center and **Y** center to `0.5` and **Z Center** to `0.1234`.
17. Set the **Z** scale to `0.2868`.
18. Create a new empty GO as a child of `Picture Frame` and name it `Picture Frame Anchor`.
19. Set the position to `0.5` for the X and Y axes and `-0.02` for the Z axis.
20. Add `Picture Frame Anchor` to the attached transform in `XR Grab Interactable`.

The picture frame is a quintessential element for hanging something on the wall because you can't just hang a picture on the wall without a frame. So, what better way to build on this experience than to add a socket capability so that only the picture frame can hang on the wall? We can do this very easily by adding an `XR Socket Interactor`, very much like the one that we created in *Chapter 3*.

To create a wall socket to hang the pictures on, go through the following steps:

1. Create an empty GO as a child of `ArtGallery` and name it `WallSockets`.
2. Add an `XR Socket Interactor` prefab from the one we made in the previous chapter.
3. In `XR Socket Interactor`, set the **Interaction Layer Mask** to `Wall Art`.
4. Set the attach point **Width** position to `0.025`. Set the **X** rotation to `-90`.
5. Change the socket indicator material to `Blue_Emission` so you can see it better on the walls.
6. Rename the prefab `Wall XR Socket` and add it to the `Prefabs` folder as a prefab variant.

Just like the light switch that we made earlier, you can scatter the wall XR sockets around on the different walls in the art gallery so you can hang up different pictures.

Figure 12.10 – Picture frame next to the light switch on the gallery wall

With the remainder of the space that you have in your gallery, decorate it with anything and everything that you could think of to make it eclectic and reflective of your artistic acumen.

Summary

In this chapter, we had a good mix of applying creativity and technical skills. Our goal, as outlined in *Chapter 10*, in *Phase 6* of our roadmap, was to create an art gallery experience. We began by designing a floor map and then creating a 3D model of it. We added lights and created a system to control them procedurally and automatically. After that, we built a drawing system that included a canvas and markers with customizable settings. Finally, we created a hanging system that allowed us to place picture frames on walls with socket indicators. These implementations utilized familiar concepts and were intuitive, allowing us to create various types of experiences.

In a later chapter, we will explore how to create a theater experience where users can watch a movie on the big screen. By tapping into familiar concepts, we can create memorable experiences that are novel in their presentation. The key is to add our own twist and set ourselves apart by applying these concepts in unique ways. VR provides ample opportunities for innovation, and we are still in the early stages of development.

In the next chapter, we will take a somewhat traditional approach by exploring the animation process and creating an animated show. This content will be original and can be repurposed in future chapters and shared on the internet if desired.

13
Animating a Virtual Reality Experience

If you're anything like me, animation has a special place in your heart. It's not just cartoons on a screen; it's also a way to bring ideas and stories to life. It's a fantastic skill to have, particularly if you're interested in the **extended reality** (**XR**) space.

We'll start from the basics—writing a synopsis and a script for your animated sequence. We'll then help you visualize your script by teaching you how to convert it into a storyboard. Once we've laid the groundwork, we'll move on to some hands-on practice with Unity Timeline.

But remember—these are more than just skills. They're tools that you can wield to give your animated sequences a unique style and flair. The processes we'll cover are just guidelines—feel free to play around and make them your own. After all, creativity is at the heart of all great animation.

If we look back at the roadmap that we have from *Chapter 10*, in *Phase 7*, it's all focused on our animation experience. We really want to focus on something that comes to life and compels people not only to play the animation but also experience it in a variety of different ways.

In *Chapter 5*, we introduced the Unity animation system. We covered important elements of Unity Timeline, created animation files, and showed how animation works in the Unity Editor. We will build on that knowledge so that we can create a fully animated sequence.

In this chapter, we will cover the following topics:

- Understanding the animation pipeline
- Writing a synopsis and a script for an animated sequence
- Converting that animated sequence script to a storyboard of visuals
- Creating an animatic using Unity Timeline and our storyboard visuals
- Adding audio to our animation timeline

- Creating a previsualization sequence
- Setting up camera angles with Cinemachine
- Downloading 3D characters and animation from Mixamo
- Applying animation clips to characters and Unity Timeline
- Adding visual effects so that the sequence pops
- Adding background characters

Technical requirements

The complete source code for this chapter can be found at `https://github.com/PacktPublishing/Enhancing-Virtual-Reality-Experiences-with-Unity-2022/tree/main/EnhancingVRExperiencesFullProject/Assets/_VRProjectAssets/Scenes/Chapter_13`.

Understanding the animation pipeline

Animation pipeline is a term used to describe the process that animation studios and professional animators follow to create animated sequences. This process typically involves several stages that work in tandem, starting from an idea to a rough outline, then a basic design, and finally, a finished product. Almost every animated sequence that you have seen across a variety of mediums has been created using this process in one way, shape, or form, making it a fundamental part of the animation industry.

If you are familiar with video production or game design, you will find that many of the same concepts are used in the animation pipeline. As an animator, I use a variation of this process and many of the workflows I have developed in making my VR experiences. The idea of going from an idea to written words on paper to creating simple visuals, and then building out the experience, all stems from core principles I learned in my training as an animator.

While this process is not specific to animation or unique to it, being able to streamline your process by using a stable and proven methodology can allow you to push the envelope of innovation and creativity without conflicting with other processes. Therefore, relying on a core concept that has been tried and tested can be valuable to any creative process.

The main stages in the animation pipeline are set out here:

1. **Concept development**: This is the initial stage where the story, characters, and world are conceived. Writers and concept artists collaborate to develop an overall vision of the project. This is what we normally do to start off any project—contemplate the idea and then put it on paper to have a rough idea of what we intend to embark on for a creative journey. When we designed our roadmap, it encompassed the empathy statement, defining factors, key features, and the ideation part of our development process.

2. **Scriptwriting**: Writers develop a detailed script based on storyboards, including dialogue and action descriptions for characters. You should be familiar with this because this is exactly what we did for our roadmap. This guide helps us know exactly what we want to do and intend to have in our animation sequence. If it's not in the script, then it's unlikely to be in the sequence. Therefore, putting a lot of time into this is crucial.

3. **Storyboarding**: In this stage, artists create storyboards to visualize the narrative and plan out scenes. Storyboards are a series of images that represent a sequence of events, allowing the team to refine the story and plan the animation. In a nutshell, this is a visual representation of the script that we have. If you're familiar with the process that we went through for designing our virtual world, all we did was take the roadmap that we had and create a gray box for it so that we could have a prototype. You do not need artistic skills to create a storyboard. If your artistic skills lack polish, you can utilize storyboard software to simplify the process.

4. **Character design**: Artists create detailed designs for characters, including expressions, poses, and outfits. These designs will be used as references for the animators. Animation is character-driven, and this animated sequence won't be too different. Even though it's simple, you will see that certain characters have certain qualities within our script that inform the character models that we will be using. No—we won't be designing characters per se, but we will be choosing characters that embody the qualities we want to have in our animated sequence.

5. **Previsualization/layout**: This step involves creating a rough 3D layout of scenes using basic models, called animatics. This helps the team plan camera angles, timing, and composition. It involves a lot of the core components of our animation process because it allows us to combine everything into an early render that we can be proud of. Once we have this done, all we have to do is kitbash assets and polish the sequence.

6. **Animation**: Animators create the final animation by bringing the characters and environments to life. They use voice tracks, storyboards, and animatics as references. There are several animation techniques, including traditional 2D animation, 3D computer animation, stop motion, and more. In this chapter, we'll be using a combination of kitbashing with premade `Animation Clips` and will also create original animations that can guide the `Animation Clips` from one area to the next. I personally think that this is the most powerful aspect of the animation system in the Unity game engine.

7. **Sound design**: Sound designers create and edit sound effects, music, and the final mix to enhance animated sequences. In this chapter, we will add animation to our timeline that captures the feel of our animated sequence. It may be a simple application of sound design, but any effort in this area is worth a try because, in our experience, involving as many senses as you can allows for the most immersive experience possible, as you may recall from *Chapter 1*.

8. **Post-production and color grading**: This stage involves final touches such as color correction, VFX, and any other adjustments to achieve the desired look and feel. In Unity, you can utilize the post-processing stack to improve visuals and the overall aesthetics of your animation. We won't be covering post-processing for this animated sequence in this chapter, but if you refer back to the *Global Post-Processing Volume* section of *Chapter 6*, you will have a good foundation of what post-processing can do for your animated sequence.
9. **Rendering**: The final animation is rendered as a series of images or video files. Since we are using a real-time rendering engine, we will actually be able to render stuff as it plays in the animation pipeline. This is great because we don't have to wait hours or days to see the animation as they used to do in the old days. We can look at it immediately. When we get to *Chapter 14*, we will explore some ways to render our animation as videos in close to real time as well.
10. **Distribution**: Once the animated project is complete, it is prepared for distribution through various channels such as theaters, television, or online platforms. In *Chapter 14*, we'll explore some of the ways we can distribute our animated sequence once it's created.

In this chapter, we will take a systematic approach to making an animated scene in our VR experience. Compared to traditional animation workflows, animation for VR incorporates 360-degree environments and requires consideration when developing a concept to completion. We'll start off by coming up with a premise for what our animated scene will be. We will write a script of the beat points that will happen in our animated scene. We will proceed to storyboard the scene and download resources such as characters, animations, and VFX. Then, we will move on to animating our scene in our timeline by blocking out the timing, adding sounds, cameras and camera angles, animation, and VFX. To finish it off, at the end, we will record it as a video that we can utilize in *Chapter 14*. Since this book is focused on VR, you will also be able to navigate this animated scene in VR to get the best camera angles and the best view overall.

Planning and organizing your animation process beforehand can save you a lot of time and effort in the long run. Here are a few tips that can help you along the way:

1. **Develop a clear synopsis**: Before you start writing the script, it's essential to have a clear idea of what you want to convey through your animation. Develop a brief synopsis or summary of the scene, outlining the main characters, setting, and story.
2. **Write a script**: Once you have a clear synopsis, start writing the script. Write down the dialogue, actions, and camera angles you want to use in each shot.
3. **Storyboard the script**: After you've written the script, create a storyboard that outlines each shot in the animation. A storyboard will help you visualize the scenes and determine the pacing of the animation.

4. **Create an animatic**: Using the storyboard, block out the timing of each shot in the timeline. This will help you ensure that the animation flows smoothly and that the timing of the dialogue and action is synchronized. This can be a time-consuming process but is crucial for making sure the timing and pacing of the animated scene are correct.
5. **Add sound and camera angles**: Once you've blocked out the timing, add sound effects and camera angles to the animation. This will help bring the scene to life and make it more immersive. Although Unity has a variety of tools to help with the sound design process, other audio-focused tools may be needed to finalize the project and give it the required polish it needs for the final render.
6. **Finalize the animation**: After you've added all the necessary elements to the animation, finalize it by fine-tuning the timing, camera angles, and sound effects. This is also the stage where you can add any special effects or visual enhancements to the animation.

By following these steps, you can create a well-planned and organized animation that is engaging and immersive for the viewer.

Writing a synopsis

A synopsis for an animation sequence is a brief summary or outline that provides an overview of key elements and story beats in the sequence. It highlights the main characters, setting, conflict, and resolution to give a clear understanding of the narrative without going into too much detail. A well-written synopsis can help guide the development of the animation and keep the creative team focused on core ideas.

When creating a synopsis for an animation sequence, some questions to ask yourself might include the following:

- Who are the main characters, and what are their roles in the story?
- What is the primary conflict or challenge faced by the characters?
- How do the characters overcome this conflict or challenge?
- What is the setting or environment in which the sequence takes place?
- What is the emotional tone or mood of the sequence?

To create a synopsis for an animation sequence, follow these steps:

1. **Identify the main characters**: Clearly define who the protagonist(s) and antagonist(s) are, as well as any supporting characters. Briefly describe their personalities, goals, and motivations.
2. **Establish the setting**: Describe the environment and time period in which the animation sequence takes place. This helps provide context and a sense of place for the story.

3. **Outline the conflict or challenge**: Clearly state the primary conflict or challenge faced by the characters in the sequence. This conflict can be internal (emotional or psychological) or external (physical or situational).
4. **Describe the resolution**: Explain how the characters overcome the conflict or challenge and how this resolution affects their relationships or circumstances.
5. **Summarize the emotional tone**: Briefly describe the overall mood or tone of the sequence, such as lighthearted, dramatic, or suspenseful. This helps set the stage for the visual and auditory elements of the animation.

My synopsis follows:

- **Title**: Dance Battle Chaos
- **Setting**: A bustling urban city with a lively park.
- **Main characters**:
    - **Man**: John, a curious and adventurous man who stumbles upon the dance battle
    - **Dancing duo**: A group of talented dancers competing against each other
    - **A crowd of spectators**: A group that is watching the dancers and cheering them on
    - **The big red monster**: A fearsome creature that suddenly appears and wreaks havoc in the city
- **Conflict**: A peaceful dance battle in the park is interrupted by the sudden appearance of a destructive monster, causing panic and chaos among the city's residents.
- **Emotional tone**: The sequence begins with a lighthearted and energetic atmosphere as John and the city's residents enjoy the dance battle. The tone shifts to suspense and tension when the monster appears.
- **Synopsis**: In a bustling urban city, a curious and adventurous man named John walks down the street and stumbles upon a group of talented dancers engaged in a dance battle at a lively park. As the energetic competition unfolds, a monstrous creature suddenly appears, attacking the city and causing panic among the residents. Explosions and chaos ensue as people flee for their lives.

This animated sequence is left pretty open-ended because I want to leave it up to you as the creator to determine how it finishes. And because it's a long process, we don't want something to drag on too long because it will take forever to complete. So, for practical purposes, we have consolidated the process in a way that is simple to achieve and yet teaches you what is necessary. We also want to give you a big enough challenge to build skills from in practice. With the idea conceptualized, let's make a script.

Writing a script

A script for an animation sequence is a written document that provides a detailed blueprint of the story, including character dialogue, actions, and scene descriptions. The script serves as a guideline for animators, directors, and other creative team members involved in the production process.

When creating a script for an animation sequence, some questions to ask yourself might include the following:

- Does the script effectively convey the story and its themes?
- Are the characters well developed and engaging?
- Does the dialogue sound natural and authentic for each character?
- Are the pacing and timing appropriate for the intended audience and medium?
- Is the script visually engaging, with clear descriptions of actions and scene settings?

To create an animation script, follow these steps:

1. **Develop your story idea**: Begin by brainstorming and outlining the central premise, themes, and plot points of your story. This will serve as a foundation for your script.
2. **Create and develop characters**: Design and flesh out the characters that will populate your story, including their appearances, personalities, backgrounds, and motivations.
3. **Write a treatment or synopsis**: Summarize the main events of your story in a brief narrative form, highlighting key plot points and character arcs.
4. **Break down the story into scenes or sequences**: Divide your story into smaller segments that can be more easily managed in the script format. This will help you organize the flow and pacing of your story.
5. **Write the script**: Using your treatment, character profiles, and scene breakdowns as a guide, write the full script. Include character dialogue, actions, and scene descriptions, ensuring that each element is clear and concise.

My script follows:

- **Opening shot**: A bustling cityscape at dusk, skyscrapers and buildings illuminated against the darkening sky.
- A man in his late 20s walks down the sidewalk, lost in his thoughts. He wears casual clothes and earphones, bobbing his head to the music.
- The man hears the cheers and claps of a crowd, which pique his curiosity. He removes his earphones, follows the sound, and discovers a group of people encircling two talented dancers engaged in a dance battle.

- As the man approaches, he is mesmerized by the skill and energy of the dancers. The crowd's excitement is palpable as they watch the performance, and the man can't help but be swept up in the atmosphere.
- Suddenly, a swirling portal opens above the water near the city square. The man and the crowd notice the strange phenomenon, their attention torn away from the dancers.
- A massive, terrifying monster emerges from the portal with a deafening roar. The crowd panics, screams filling the air as people scatter in every direction.
- The man watches in horror as the monster rampages through the city, destroying everything in its path. Buildings crumble, and explosions echo through the streets, the sounds of chaos and destruction all around.
- **Closing shot**: Flames consume the city skyline and the once-bustling metropolis is now reduced to ashes and ruins.

This script lays out a pretty detailed idea of what I was going for and allows me to use it as a roadmap or a guideline for my storyboarding. I probably won't include everything that is in here into the storyboard because there are limitations to visualizing, and there are constraints to the resources I have for creating the animation. But in general, having a fleshed-out idea and then pulling back from it is always the best approach, as opposed to having to add stuff later on because your script was not as robust as it could have been. With the script now complete, we can move on to our storyboarding.

Drafting storyboards

A storyboard is a visual representation of an animation sequence, film, or TV show, presented in the form of a series of illustrations or images. It acts as a blueprint for the production, depicting the flow of the story, camera angles, character movements, and transitions between scenes. A storyboard helps the production team to plan and communicate their ideas effectively.

When creating a storyboard, some questions to ask yourself might include the following:

- Does the storyboard effectively convey the story and emotion of the scene?
- Are character expressions and movements clear and consistent?
- Are camera angles and shots varied and engaging?
- Does the pacing of the storyboard match the intended tone of the scene?
- Have all important story beats and visual elements been considered?

Here are some simple steps to follow when creating a storyboard:

1. **Read and analyze the script**: Familiarize yourself with the story, characters, and key moments in the script. Identify scenes that need to be storyboarded and note any specific requirements.
2. **Plan the shots**: Determine the best camera angles, shots, and compositions to tell the story effectively. Consider using a mix of close-ups, medium shots, and wide shots to maintain visual interest.
3. **Sketch the scenes**: Draw rough sketches of each scene, focusing on the characters, their actions, and the environment. Include arrows or notes to indicate movement or camera motion.
4. **Add dialogue and action notes**: Include any important dialogue or action notes beneath the corresponding sketches to provide context and help guide the animators.
5. **Review and revise**: Evaluate your storyboard for clarity, continuity, and pacing. Make any necessary revisions to improve the visual storytelling.

To create storyboards (*Figure 13.1*) based on the script that we wrote, go through the following steps:

1. Open an image editor such as Photoshop or Google Drawings.
2. Create a storyboard template utilizing rectangles as containers for each storyboard.
3. Using the script as a reference, incorporate key details as visuals within your storyboard rectangles.
4. Review and revise as needed so that your storyboards capture the visuals that are described in the script.
5. Export each storyboard as individual JPGs.
6. Import the storyboard into your `textures` folder.
7. Select each image file in **Inspector** and set the texture type to `Sprite (2D and UI)`.
8. Click **Apply**.

Figure 13.1 – Storyboards read from left to right, then top to bottom

My approach to storyboarding is very loose and subjective. For me, storyboards serve as a guide throughout the process. They don't have to be robust or visually pleasing like fully rendered art pieces because they're just a guideline for the animated process. The power of storyboarding for me is that it allows me to get the idea on paper and take a step back to see whether it aligns with my overall vision for the animated scene. During this process, I can explore different camera angles or use place markers for actions I want to include in my sequence.

Storyboarding is important because it helps you recognize that each action and word in your script takes up time in your animation timeline. If you have too many actions or require more than the allotted time, you'll need to make tough decisions about what to include and what to cut. This internal conversation helps you focus on what's essential and complete your project within your time frame.

Once you're pleased with your storyboards, we can move on to blocking out the animatic sequence in Unity Timeline.

Creating a sequence animatic

A sequence animatic is a rough previsualization of an animation sequence, typically created using a series of storyboard images edited together with timing and basic movement and sometimes accompanied by voiceover, sound effects, or music. The purpose of an animatic is to visualize the narrative and pacing, plan out camera angles and movements, and make necessary adjustments before moving on to the final animation stage.

When creating a sequence animatic, some questions to ask yourself might include the following:

- Does the animatic effectively communicate the story and emotions of the scene?
- Are the pacing and timing of the sequence appropriate and engaging?
- Do camera angles and movements enhance the narrative and visual impact of the scene?
- Are there any elements of the scene that could be improved or changed for better clarity or storytelling?
- Does the animatic highlight key moments, expressions, or actions that are essential to the scene's overall impact?

To create a sequence animatic, follow these steps:

1. Go to **Package Manager**.
2. Go to the **Timeline** package in **Unity Registry** and install all the samples.
3. Install the **Sequences** sample.
4. Install the **Scene management** sample.
5. Add an empty GO and name it `AnimatedShow`.
6. Add an empty child GO and name it `AnimatedShowTimeline`.
7. Open the timeline and create a new **Timeline Track**.
8. Save it to the `Animations` folder.
9. In the timeline, add a `Storyboard Track`.
10. Add the storyboard images to the `Storyboard Track`.
11. Set the storyboards in a sequence that is about 30 seconds long.
12. Apply the following settings to the storyboards on the timeline:
    - *Storyboard image #1*—Start Time: `0:00`/Duration: 2 seconds
    - *Storyboard image #2*—Start Time: `0:02`/Duration: 2 seconds
    - *Storyboard image #3*—Start Time: `0:04`/Duration: 2 seconds
    - *Storyboard image #4*—Start Time: `0:06`/Duration: 2 seconds

- *Storyboard image #5*—Start Time: `0:08`/Duration: `4.7` seconds
- *Storyboard image #6*—Start Time: `0:12.7`/Duration: `2.233333` seconds
- *Storyboard image #7*—Start Time: `0:14.93333`/Duration: `2.533333` seconds
- *Storyboard image #8*—Start Time: `0:17.51667`/Duration: `2.25` seconds
- *Storyboard image #9*—Start Time: `0:19.76667`/Duration: `2.416667` seconds
- *Storyboard image #10*—Start Time: `0:22.18333`/Duration: `2.7` seconds
- *Storyboard image #11*—Start Time: `0:24.88333`/Duration: `2.533333` seconds
- *Storyboard image #12*—Start Time: `0:27.41667`/Duration: `2.583333` seconds

Creating an animatic is primarily focused on refining the visual elements and timing until you achieve a satisfying result. This often involves repeatedly playing the animatic on the timeline to assess the pacing and effectiveness of the visuals. The best approach is to experiment with different timing and pacing until you find what works best for your project. Start by adding all the frames to the timeline with equal time, then adjust the timing of individual frames based on how long they should be displayed. Remember that this is a fluid process, and it may take several iterations to achieve the desired outcome.

The following screenshot shows a sample storyboard layout on Unity Timeline:

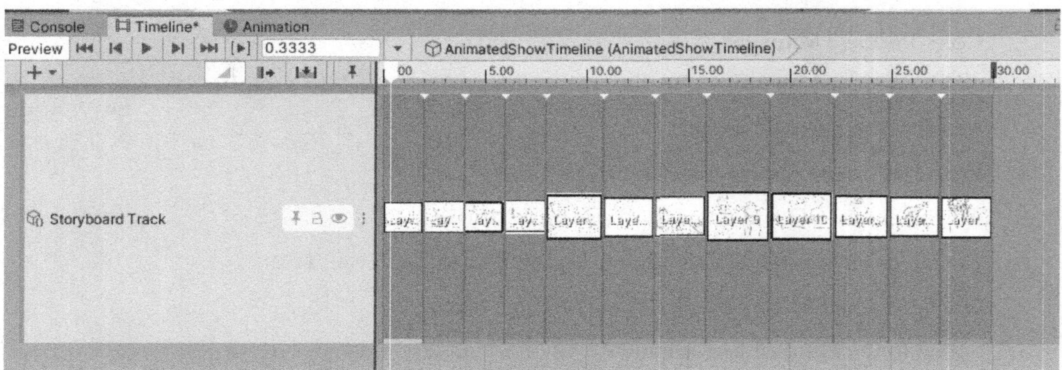

Figure 13.2 – Storyboard layout on Unity Timeline

With the first draft of our animatic done, we can move on to adding audio to our timeline in the next section.

Adding audio

This is my favorite part of the animation process because adding audio to the scene early on allows me to create a better visual sequence. Often, our animated experiences are driven by sounds that immerse our ears in each event on the screen. Using audio, you can set the tone and communicate shifts and actions without having to use words or extensive visuals. For this animated sequence, I wanted to stay simple, sweet, and efficient. Therefore, I decided to set the audio track based on the tones and shifts that take place on the screen. This ultimately required me to choose three different soundtracks/audio files that could highlight those tone shifts.

To create an audio track (*Figure 13.3*) for our animated sequence, follow these steps:

1. In our animation timeline, create a new `Audio Track`.
2. Find the `Dreams Of Her Best Friend` audio file and place it in the `Audio Track`.
3. Set the start time to `0`.
4. Set the duration to `17.46667`.
5. Find the `exploration_2B` audio file and place it in the `Audio Track`.
6. Set the start time to `14.93333`.
7. Set the duration to `9.95`.
8. Set the **Clip In** to `0.7666667`.
9. Find the `battle_final` audio file and place it in the `Audio Track`.
10. Set the start time to `22.18333`.
11. Set the duration to `7.941667`.

When choosing audio files, you'll notice that some of them overlap with others, and that's great to do because you don't want to have stark shifts from one sound to the next. That could be jarring for some users, depending on what sounds you have. Having seamless transitions is easy to do in Unity Timeline by setting the locations of different audio files. In **Inspector**, you'll notice that there will be a blend distance that indicates the blend in and the blend out for certain audio files. This isn't something you can control in **Inspector**, but as you move the easing in and easing out overlap indicators on Unity Timeline, those values will change:

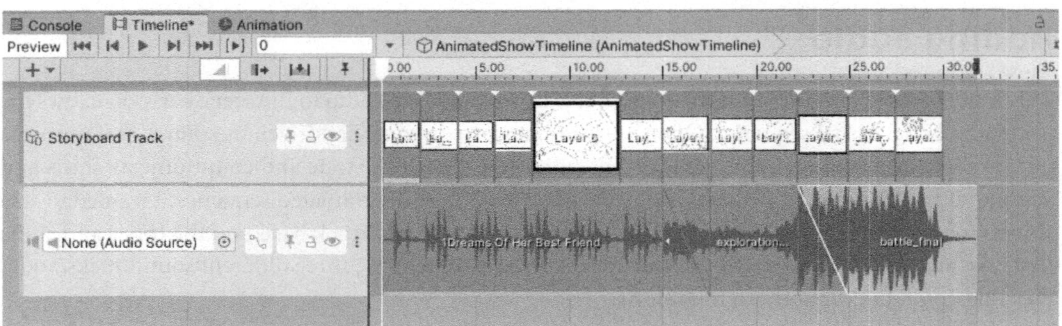

Figure 13.3 – Sound design layout in Unity Timeline

Sometimes, I'll go back and forth between working on the storyboard timing on my Timeline and matching it with the audio on the `Audio Track`. This is why I make it a point to select my audio tracks ahead of time. By aligning the storyboard's visual elements with the rhythm and musical beats within the track, I can create striking effects. This approach truly underscores the combined power of audio and visual elements. We all know our favorite movies and sequences in shows, and those are often tied to an audio track that sets the tone. It may be subtle or the highlight of why you like that sequence on the screen, because it just hits. It all starts out very meticulously on the part of the creator because they are going after a certain effect that the visuals and audio combined could achieve that no other combination could. I urge you to think about this as you continue making your animated scenes because this can be a defining element of that animated experience when people have it. Once you have your `Audio Track` done, we can move on to the previsualization process.

Previsualizing a sequence

Previsualization is an important step in this animation production process because this is where we convert our animatic from a collection of 2D images into a rough draft rendered in 3D. This is what I like to call the gray-box phase of development because we get to visualize what is intended to be seen in 3D. This process can take a considerable amount of time because we are carving out all the movement, but once it's done, applying unique animation clips becomes much easier and takes less time. To save ourselves the hassle, we can create primitives for our character GOs to use as placeholders. When we actually have our character models and animation clips, we can just place those in the locations as easily as we did when we converted our gray box to a kitbash scene.

To create placeholders for our animated characters, follow these steps:

1. Create a GO and name it `Main Character`.
2. Set the **Y** position to `1`.
3. Set the **X** position to `-5.5` and the **Z** position to `-30.24`.
4. Duplicate it and name it `Dancer_1`.

5. Set the **X** position to `15.85` and the **Z** position to `-2.16`.
6. Duplicate it and name it `Dancer_2`.
7. Set the **X** position to `18.14` and the **Z** position to `-2.78`.
8. Duplicate it and name it `NPC_1`.
9. Set the **X** position to `15.85` and the **Z** position to `-0.63`.
10. Duplicate it and name it `NPC_2`.
11. Set the **X** position to `19.45` and the **Z** position to `-1.37`.
12. Duplicate it and name it `NPC_3`.
13. Set the **X** position to `17.52` and the **Z** position to `0.39`.
14. Create a sphere GO and name it `Monster`.
15. Set the **X** position to `53.4` and the **Z** position to `-28.7`.
16. Set the **X** scale to `23`, the **Y** scale to `40`, and the **Z** scale to `23`.

After creating placeholders for all our characters and placing them where we expect them to be for our animation, we can now individualize the animation sequences for each one of our characters based on what we have in our animatic on our timeline already. This will essentially be the core animation that we will be creating for our characters. For the most part, it's nothing more than translational and rotational animation that we will create on our timeline. But that's all we need because we just need to make sure that the characters are in specific locations on specific timestamps so that they are in camera when all the action happens in the scene.

If you recall, in the *Creating an animation clip for GOs* section of *Chapter 5*, we placed keyframes to create a custom animation in Unity Timeline. That simply involved going to a particular timestamp, pressing the record button, placing the GO at that timestamp, and then going into **Inspector** and saving that keyframe. In order to give off the effect of animation, you just need two keyframes—one at a particular location and rotation, and then another at a different location and rotation. When you save the asset and press play, you will see that the objects will move from one location to the next, and that process of moving is animation.

You will become very familiar with this process because it will be the core focus of all the character animation for our previsualization. We will start with our main character and then move on to our other characters until all the animation for our characters is completed (*Figure 13.4*).

To create a custom animation for our `Main Character` GO, follow these steps:

1. Go to the `Main Character` GO in our **Hierarchy** and drag the GO to Unity Timeline.
2. Create a new `Animation Track` based on this GO.

3. Apply the following keyframes to the animation timeline for this character:

   - *Frame 0*—Position: `(-5.5, 0, -30.24)`/Rotation: `(0, 90, 0)`
   - *Frame 95*—Position: `(-28, -1, -0.829)`/Rotation: `(0, 90, 0)`
   - *Frame 108*—Position: `(-3, 1, -0.006)`/Rotation: `(0, 90, 0)`
   - *Frame 179*—Position: `(14.52, 1, 1.8)`/Rotation: `(0, 107.9, 0)`
   - *Frame 192*—Position: `(15.38, 1, 18)`/Rotation: `(0, 176, 0)`
   - *Frame 421*—Position: `(15.38, 1, 1.82)`/Rotation: `(0, 175.9, 0)`
   - *Frame 440*—Position: `(15.61, 2.09, 1.87)`/Rotation: `(.857, 163.5, 12.2)`
   - *Frame 478*—Position: `(15.38, 1, 1.8)`/Rotation: `(0, 175.9, 0)`
   - *Frame 658*—Position: `(-56, 1, -22.8)`/Rotation: `(0, -109, 0)`

To create a custom animation for our `dancer_1` GO, go through the following steps:

1. Go to the `dancer_1` GO in our **Hierarchy** and drag the GO to Unity Timeline.
2. Create a new `Animation Track` based on this GO.
3. Apply the following keyframes to the animation timeline for this character:

   - *Frame 503*—Position: `(15.85, .88, -2.16)`/Rotation: `(0, 0, 0)`
   - *Frame 516*—Position: `(10.98, .8, -1.81)`/Rotation: `(0, 0, 0)`
   - *Frame 540*—Position: `(-8, .8, -3.83)`/Rotation: `(0, 0, 0)`
   - *Frame 557*—Position: `(-29.8, .8, 3.8)`/Rotation: `(0, 0, 0)`
   - *Frame 690*—Position: `(-58.6, .8, 76.4)`/Rotation: `(0, 0, 0)`

To create a custom animation for our `dancer_2` GO, go through the following steps:

1. Go to the `dancer_2` GO in our **Hierarchy** and drag the GO to Unity Timeline.
2. Create a new `Animation Track` based on this GO.
3. Apply the following keyframes to the animation timeline for this character:

   - *Frame 503*—Position: `(18.14, .8, -2.78)`/Rotation: `(0, 0, 0)`
   - *Frame 516*—Position: `(13.38, .8, .03)`/Rotation: `(0, 0, 0)`
   - *Frame 540*—Position: `(-8.2, .8, -14.11)`/Rotation: `(0, 0, 0)`
   - *Frame 557*—Position: `(-27.5, .8, -14.4)`/Rotation: `(0, 0, 0)`
   - *Frame 690*—Position: `(-66.8, .8, -10.6)`/Rotation: `(0, 0, 0)`

To create a custom animation for our `NPC_1` GO, go through the following steps:

1. Go to the `NPC_1` GO in our **Hierarchy** and drag the GO to Unity Timeline.
2. Create a new `Animation Track` based on this GO.
3. Apply the following keyframes to the animation timeline for this character:
   - *Frame 503*—Position: `(15.85,0.8,-.63)`/Rotation: `(0,0,0)`
   - *Frame 516*—Position: `(11.54,0.8,1.05)`/Rotation: `(0,0,0)`
   - *Frame 540*—Position: `(-5.8,0.8,.07)`/Rotation: `(0,0,0)`
   - *Frame 557*—Position: `(-29.4,0.8,-5.1)`/Rotation: `(0,0,0)`
   - *Frame 690*—Position: `(-71.8,0.8,21.6)`/Rotation: `(0,0,0)`

To create a custom animation for our `NPC_2` GO, go through the following steps:

1. Go to the `NPC_2` GO in our **Hierarchy** and drag the GO to Unity Timeline.
2. Create a new `Animation Track` based on this GO.
3. Apply the following keyframes to the animation timeline for this character:
   - *Frame 503*—Position: `(19.45, 0.8, -1.37)`/Rotation: `(0,0,0)`
   - *Frame 516*—Position: `(12.81, 0.8, -1.94)`/Rotation: `(0,0,0)`
   - *Frame 540*—Position: `(-14.9, 0.8, -29.67)`/Rotation: `(0,0,0)`
   - *Frame 557*—Position: `(-24.8, 0.8, -23.4)`/Rotation: `(0,0,0)`
   - *Frame 690*—Position: `(-90.3, 0.8, -33.3)`/Rotation: `(0,0,0)`

To create a custom animation for our `NPC_3` GO, go through the following steps:

1. Go to the `NPC_3` GO in our **Hierarchy** and drag the GO to Unity Timeline.
2. Create a new `Animation Track` based on this GO.
3. Apply the following keyframes to the animation timeline for this character:
   - *Frame 503*—Position: `(17.52, 0.8, .39)`/Rotation: `(0,0,0)`
   - *Frame 516*—Position: `(13.95, 0.8, -0.99)`/Rotation: `(0,0,0)`
   - *Frame 540*—Position: `(-7.9, 0.8, -29.87)`/Rotation: `(0,0,0)`
   - *Frame 557*—Position: `(-33.6, 0.8, -27.8)`/Rotation: `(0,0,0)`
   - *Frame 690*—Position: `(-77.2, 0.8, -67.5)`/Rotation: `(0,0,0)`

To create a custom animation for our `Monster` GO, go through the following steps:

1. Go to the `Monster` GO in our **Hierarchy** and drag the GO to Unity Timeline.
2. Create a new `Animation Track` based on this GO.
3. Apply the following keyframes to the animation timeline for this character:

    - *Frame 360*—Position: `(53.4,-20.8,-28.7)`/Rotation: `(0,0,0)`
    - *Frame 442*—Position: `(53.4,-14.1,-28.7)`/Rotation: `(0,0,0)`
    - *Frame 482*—Position: `(53.4,5.4,-28.7)`/Rotation: `(0,0,0)`
    - *Frame 535*—Position: `(9,21.1,-28.7)`/Rotation: `(0,0,0)`
    - *Frame 599*—Position: `(-37.8,21.1,25.6)`/Rotation: `(0,0,0)`
    - *Frame 662*—Position: `(-73.1,21.1,34.6)`/Rotation: `(0,0,0)`
    - *Frame 716*—Position: `(-84.8,21.1,16.4)`/Rotation: `(0,0,0)`

After what may have seemed like a grueling and tedious process, we have completed the animation for all of our characters. My focus was on following the animatic as closely as possible, knowing where each character should be at specific parts of the animated sequence. By doing this, I was able to place them in the correct locations and constantly test the timing to ensure it was exactly what I wanted. Once I finished one character, I moved on to the next and repeated the same steps for placing keyframes.

Figure 13.4 – Custom keyframe animation for our characters on individual animation tracks

As you may have seen in this section, the previsualization process is very technical and meticulous because there are so many keyframes and details that need to be right for the animation effects to work as desired. Knowing this, you may be tempted in the future to simplify the script for your animation to avoid going through this long process. However, it is a necessary evil for animators because this is how animation is done.

Now that the bulk of our animation is completed, we can move on to setting up our cameras using the **Cinemachine** package.

Setting up cameras with Cinemachine

Cinemachine is a suite of camera tools for Unity, designed to help developers and creators build dynamic and complex camera systems for their games, animations, and interactive experiences without the need for extensive custom scripting. Cinemachine provides an intuitive and flexible system to control camera behavior, making it easier to create cinematic sequences, implement camera transitions, and manage multiple cameras within a scene. Cinemachine has two main components, as follows:

- **Virtual Cameras**: Cinemachine uses virtual cameras that can be placed throughout your scene to control the view and framing. These virtual cameras can have different priorities, allowing you to switch between them based on specific conditions or events.
- **Cinemachine Brain**: The Cinemachine Brain component is responsible for managing and blending the virtual cameras in your scene. It is attached to the main camera in your Unity project and acts as the central controller for all camera operations.

Cinemachine can be a powerful tool for creating dynamic and cinematic camera systems in Unity, simplifying the process of managing cameras and enabling developers to focus on building immersive and engaging experiences.

Now that we have a good idea of what Cinemachine is, we can add the package to our scene and utilize the virtual cameras to set up our camera angles on our timeline.

To set up our virtual cameras with Cinemachine, follow these steps:

1. Open **Package Manager** and go to **Unity Registry**.
2. Search for `Cinemachine`.
3. Download and import it. Also, import the Cinemachine example scenes.
4. Create a new empty GO in our **Hierarchy** named `Virtual Cameras`.
5. Right-click on the `Virtual Cameras` GO, go to **Cinemachine**, and select **Virtual Cameras**. This will create a virtual camera as a child called `CM VCam 1`, which will reference our main camera in our animated scene.
6. We will duplicate our virtual camera based on how many shots we will have. Since we have 12 storyboards representing 12 different shots, we will need a total of 12 virtual cameras. We will be using the virtual cameras to set up our camera angles in our scene instead of moving the main camera.
7. In our animated show timeline, create a new track called `Cinemachine Track`.
8. Add all the virtual cameras we created to the `Cinemachine Track` timeline (*Figure 13.5*).

9. Set the start frame, duration, transform position, and rotation to the following values in the Timeline Track **Inspector**:

   - *CM VCam 1*—Start: 0, Duration: 2, Position: (50.7,17.5,-38), Rotation: (6.9,-57,-2.7)
   - *CM VCam 2*—Start: 2, Duration: 2, Position: (2.2,3.5,-8.7), Rotation: (23.5,-94.9,0)
   - *CM VCam 3*—Start: 4, Duration: 2, Position: (-1.6,1.6,-1.26), Rotation: (5,79,.8)
   - *CM VCam 4*—Start: 6, Duration: 2, Position: (23,5.68,-6.79), Rotation: (24,-50.9,.25)
   - *CM VCam 5*—Start: 8, Duration: 47, Position: (18.74,1.57,2.42), Rotation: (18.4,193.4,0)
   - *CM VCam 6*—Start: 12.7, Duration: 2.233333, Position: (15.42,1.66,.41), Rotation: (9.97,-1.5,3.1)
   - *CM VCam 7*—Start: 14.93333, Duration: 2.583333, Position: (51.2,16,-40.72), Rotation: (8.25,-39.79,-.681)
   - *CM VCam 8*—Start: 17.51667, Duration: 2.25, Position: (15,1.9,4.6), Rotation: (-15.465,148.545,0)
   - *CM VCam 9*—Start: 19.7667, Duration: 2.416667, Position: (-2,1.4,7.4), Rotation: (9.1,123.96,0)
   - *CM VCam 10*—Start: 22.8333, Duration: 2.7, Position: (-46.3,.7,-8.9), Rotation: (-21.761,96.683,-.796)
   - *CM VCam 11*—Start: 24.88333, Duration: 2.533333, Position: (-114.6,18.6,32.5), Rotation: (-3.321,81.428,8.2)
   - *CM VCam 12*—Start: 27.41667, Duration: 2.708333, Position: (-132.82,24.1,13.86), Rotation: (8.222,420.084,6.79)

With the Cinemachine cameras in our timeline, we can use the storyboards and the scene we have to orient the camera angles in the proper locations. Try your best to match the locations and angles of the cameras to the storyboard that you've set up. Since the sequence of events is already done in our scene, it's just a matter of making sure that the camera angles accurately represent the plan we put in place with our previous phases of the animation pipeline workflow.

Figure 13.5 – Virtual cameras on the Cinemachine Track in Unity Timeline

We can now proceed to the next section where we will be adding 3D models that we downloaded from a service called Mixamo to our project.

Downloading 3D characters

Before we start downloading a whole bunch of different 3D assets to replace all our primitive models, the first thing we need to do is break down the actual assets and needs we require. This is a systematic approach to streamline our process so that we can be efficient and save on space and time within our development process. Going back to what our actual script requires, we have a main character, two dancers, some standard background characters that we'll call **non-playable characters** or **NPCs**, and our monster.

Instead of creating all these characters individually from scratch, we could use an asset library called **Mixamo**, which has characters and animations that we can utilize within our project. Looking at our project requirements, we'll need a variety of animations, but we'll also need specific characters that have unique elements. For our main character, we'll use the character named `James` from the Mixamo character library. For our dancers, we'll use the character models `Michelle` and `Sporty Granny`. For our NPCs, we'll use some standard mesh characters called `X Bot` and `Y Bot`. For the monster character, we will download a Unity asset for that later.

To download 3D characters from Mixamo, go through the following steps:

1. Create a new folder in the `3D Models` folder in the **Project** tab.
2. Name it `3D characters`.
3. Go to Mixamo and select the **Characters** tab:

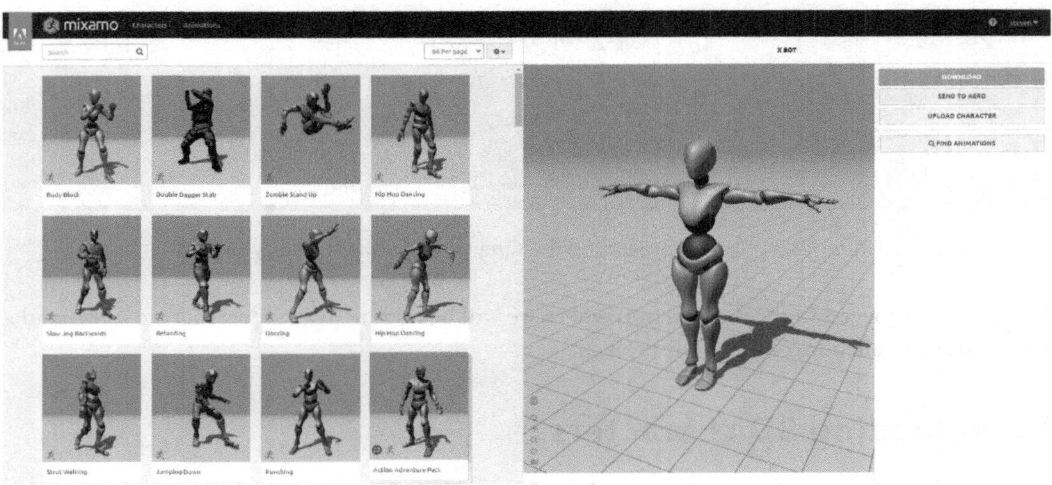

Figure 13.6 – Mixamo character and animation selection menu

4. Search for `James` and select **DOWNLOAD** on the top right.
5. For the format, select **FBX For Unity** (*Figure 13.7*):

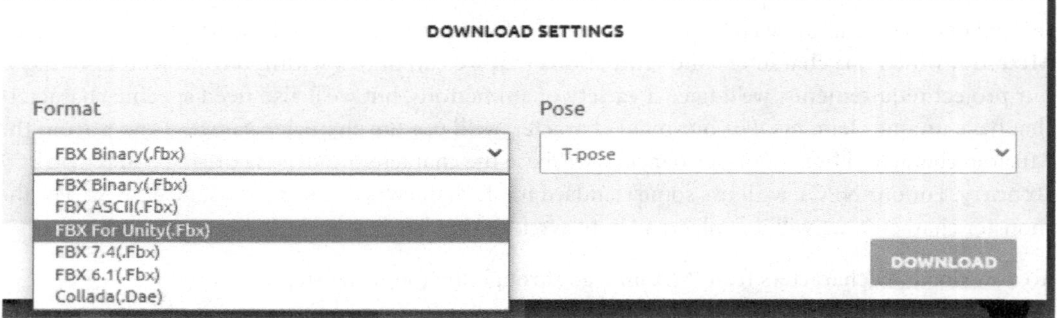

Figure 13.7 – Mixamo export settings

6. Select **DOWNLOAD**.
7. Save the `.fbx` file with the name `James.fbx` in a folder.
8. Import the 3D model file into our `3D Characters` folder in the **Project** tab.
9. Repeat *steps 3–6* for `Michelle`.
10. Repeat *steps 3–6* for `Sporty Granny`.
11. Repeat *steps 3–6* for `X Bot`.
12. Repeat *steps 3–6* for `Y Bot`

After all the models are downloaded, we can download our animation files. But before we start downloading a whole bunch of different animations that we probably won't be using, let's look at our roadmap and animation script and think about which animation files are needed to have the best animated experience. We don't want the animation to be bloated with unnecessary animation files and assets. We want it to be as efficient as possible.

For our main character, which is used by the `James` model, we need a walking animation, a jump animation, a running animation, and an idle animation. For our two dancing characters, we'll need two different dance animations, and we can reuse a running animation for both of those, so we'll only need one running animation for them. Our NPCs are pretty much standard characters, even though we're using two different meshes. To provide a little bit of variation, we could have four different cheering animations to mix it up within that crowd, and then we could have three different running-away animations that allow us to have some variation. To add a little bit of extra variation, we could also have some talking animations. We'll choose two of those, and then we'll have some idle animations, which we'll choose two of as well so that even though we're using the same assets, they have different characteristics that come across on the screen as different characters.

Resultantly, with very little effort, we're able to populate a scene that feels very lively without having too much bloat. For a VR experience, runtime is of the utmost essence. So, to have the biggest bang for your buck, having a larger-than-life scene that runs efficiently is the best approach.

With the 3D models of our characters downloaded from Mixamo, we can now download the necessary animation files to add to our 3D models in our timeline and scene.

Downloading animations from Mixamo

Even though we were able to download 3D models of characters from Mixamo, the true power of Mixamo is its extensive library of professionally curated animated sequences. Mixamo has been around for over a decade, and many creators and developers utilize this library to streamline their process of adding animation to their games and experiences. Just like the Unity Asset Store, Mixamo is a great resource for finding a variety of different animated clips that we could add to our characters in our scenes to enhance the animated experiences that we are creating. More importantly, this will save us a lot of time and allow us to have laser-focused searches for animations that have already been created. This is great because we don't have to imagine what it's going to look like; we could just utilize the Mixamo platform to test and prototype the animated sequences before we add them to our scene. While Mixamo is a great resource for 3D characters and animations, the assets downloaded from it may not always perfectly fit the needs of your project. They may require additional editing or adjustments in Unity or 3D modeling software.

We'll first download a walking animation for our main character since that's the first animation that plays in our animated sequence, and then we can proceed to search and download the rest of the animations that we need for our sequence.

To download an animated walk sequence for our main character, follow these steps:

1. In the **Project** tab, create a new folder called `Character Animations` in the `Animations` folder.
2. In the **Animations** tab, search for `walking with a swagger`.
3. Set **Overdrive** to `48`.
4. Set **Character Arm Space** to `78`.
5. Enable **In Place**.
6. Select **Download**.
7. Set **Format** to `FBX for Unity`.
8. Set **Frames per Second** to `24`.
9. Set **Skin** to `Without Skin`.
10. Select **Download**.
11. Name the downloaded animation file `Walking with Swagger.fbx`.
12. Import it into the `Character Animations` folder.

We will use this as the main walk sequence for our main character. Now that we have an idea of how to download animation files from Mixamo, we can proceed to download all the necessary files we need for our animated sequence for our main character.

To download the rest of the animation files from Mixamo, follow these steps:

1. For the main character's jump animation, search for `jump up` in the **Animations** search bar and download the animation.
2. For the running sequence for our main character, search for `run leaning back or forth`, enable **In Place**, and download the animation sequence.
3. For our `Michelle` character's dance sequence, search for `hip hop dance moonwalk`, and download the animation file.
4. For the `Sporty Granny` character's dance sequence, search for `Northern Soul flow combo`, and download the animation file.
5. For the run sequence, search for `running looking back`, enable **In Place**, and download the animation file.
6. For our NPCs, download four different cheering animations: `Cheering with Two Fist Pumps`, `Listening to Music`, `Standing Happily`, and `Rallying the Crowd`. Search for each of these and download them.
7. For the additional running animations, download three of them: `Turning to Silly Run`, `Looking Behind Run`, and `Run Forward, Facing Sideways`.

8. For the talking animations, search for and download two: `Asking a Question with Two Hands` and `General Conversation`.
9. For our idle animations, search for and download two: `Happy Idle Variation 2` and `Breathing Idle`.

With all of these files downloaded, import them into your `Character 3D Animation` folder in the **Project** tab so that we can apply them to our animation timeline. But before we do that, we must set up our animated characters so that they can work with the Unity animation system seamlessly.

Setting up animated characters

Now that we have our 3D character FBX models in our Unity project, as well as the `.fbx` animation files from Mixamo, we can set them up using a humanoid character rig that is predefined in Unity and apply the animation files to the models in our scenes.

To set up the 3D characters to be used in our scenes, follow these steps:

1. Go to our `3D characters` folder in the **Project** tab.
2. Choose the `James` 3D model.
3. In **Inspector**, go to the **Rig** tab (*Figure 13.8*).
4. Set the **Animation Type** dropdown menu to `Humanoid`.
5. Set the **Avatar Definition** dropdown menu to **Create From This Model**.
6. Click **Apply** to set up the rig 3D model with the humanoid animation system that Unity has.
7. Repeat *steps 2–6* for the `Michelle` model, the `Sporty Granny` model, the `X Bot` model, and the `Y Bot` model.

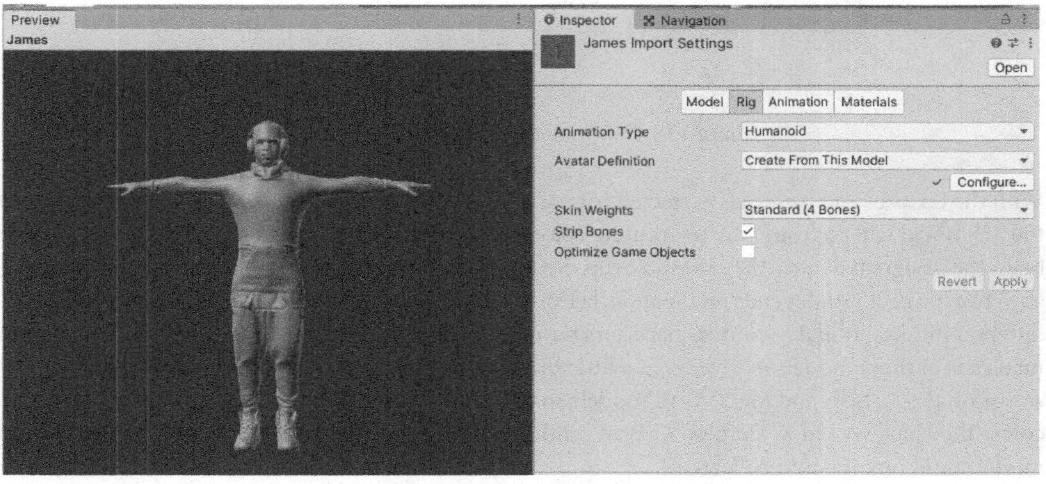

Figure 13.8 – 3D model character rigging setup

Now that we have all of our models completed, you may notice that the models don't actually have the textures and colors on their mesh. They're just gray meshes. That means the texture information within the `.fbx` file was not extracted when we imported the Unity model. To fix that, we have to extract the textures and materials from the FBX model in order to have them applied to our model and our Unity Editor.

To extract the textures and materials from the `.fbx` file, follow these steps:

1. Go to the `James` model in **Inspector**.
2. Choose the **Materials** tab.
3. Choose **Extract Textures**.
4. Save the textures in a new folder called `James Textures` in your textures folder in the **Project** tab. This will extract the textures from the `.fbx` file and apply them to the model.
5. If a popup appears to fix the normal maps, click **Fix now** (*Figure 13.9*).
6. Back in **Inspector** for the `James` 3D model, select **Extract Materials…** (*Figure 13.10*).
7. Save the materials in a new folder called `James Materials` in the `Materials` folder of the **Project** tab.
8. Repeat *steps 1–7* for the rest of the 3D models to extract their materials and textures.

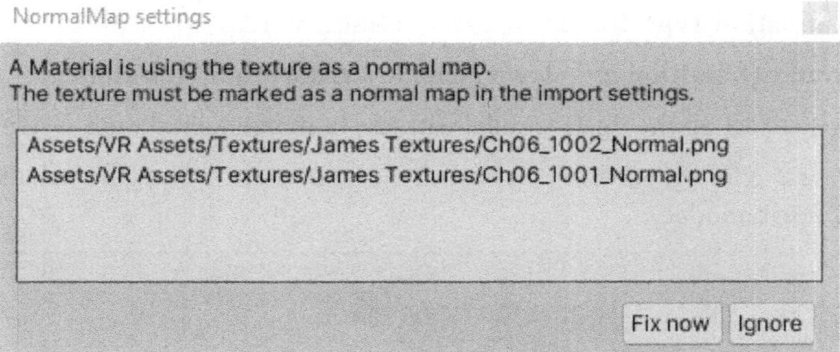

Figure 13.9 – NormalMap settings pop-up screen

With the textures and materials extracted from the `.fbx` file, you will see that the necessary colors for the 3D model will go from gray to accurate colors, and you'll see that all the remapped materials will be in the designated areas they should be in. Some models may have one material, while others may have five to six. It just depends on the model. This is also helpful because instead of having to download different meshes to make various characters have different qualities, you can modify the textures and materials of these models to give them a little bit of variation. A perfect example is swapping out the colors on the `X Bot` and the `Y Bot` models so that they have different characteristics related to the colors they have. A red `X Bot` or `Y Bot` model could be angry, whereas a blue `X Bot` or `Y Bot` model could be calm and collected:

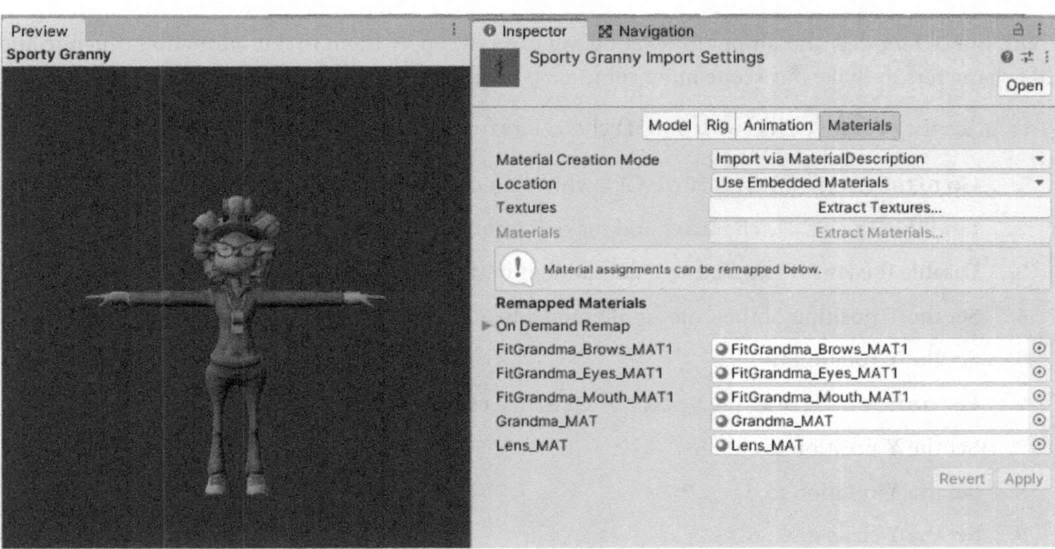

Figure 13.10 – 3D model material settings

With our characters set up with the humanoid rig and their materials extracted, we can set up our `Animation Clips` so that they can be applied to our characters in Unity Timeline.

Adding animation clips to our timeline

Now that we have imported our 3D models, we need to add the animated files we downloaded from Mixamo. This process is slightly different from importing 3D model characters into Unity, as we need to focus on the animations rather than the materials included in the `.fbx` files we import. We will follow the same process we did for the 3D models by creating custom humanoid rigs for the animations we intend to use on our characters in Unity. Then, we will move to the **Animation** tab to make them work efficiently.

To set up our animation files for the animated scene, follow these steps:

1. In the `Character Animation` folder, select the `breathing idle` animation.
2. Set the **Animation Type** dropdown menu to `Humanoid`.
3. Set the **Avatar Definition** dropdown menu to `Create from this Model`.
4. Click **Apply** to save the changes.
5. Go to the **Animation** tab.
6. Set **Animation compression** to **Optimal**.
7. Enable **Loop time**.
8. Click **Apply** to save the changes.
9. Repeat *steps 2–8* for the remaining animation files in the `Character Animation` folder.

With our 3D models and animations set up, we can now apply them to our animation timeline and 3D characters to make our scene more robust.

To replace the primitive GOs with our 3D characters from Mixamo (*Figure 13.11*), follow these steps:

1. Go to the `Main Character` GO, which is a child of the `Previz` GO.
2. Find the `James` 3D character and make it a child of the `Main Character` GO.
3. Disable the `Mesh Renderer` component in the `Main Character` GO.
4. Set the **Y** position of the `James` 3D model to `-1`.
5. Set the **Y** rotation to `-90`.
6. For `dancer_1`, drag the `Sporty Granny` character as a child of `dancer_1`.
7. Set the **Y** position to `-0.5`.
8. Set the **Y** rotation to `61`.
9. Set the **Y** scale to `0.625`.
10. Disable the `Mesh Renderer` in the `dancer_1` GO.
11. For `dancer_2`, add the `Michelle` model as a child of it.
12. Set the **Y** position to `-0.5`.
13. Set the **Y** rotation to `-45`.
14. Set the **Y** scale to `0.65`.
15. Disable the `Mesh Renderer` in the `dancer_2` GO.
16. For `NPC_1`, add the `X Bot` model as a child of it.
17. Set the **Y** position to `-0.5`.
18. Set the **Y** rotation to `-205`.
19. Set the **Y** scale to `0.65`.
20. Disable the `Mesh Renderer` in the `NPC_1` GO.
21. For `NPC_2`, add the `X Bot` model as a child of it.
22. Set the **Y** position to `-0.5`.
23. Set the **Y** rotation to `-112`.
24. Set the **Y** scale to `0.65`.
25. Disable the `Mesh Renderer` in the `NPC_2` GO.
26. Look for the `Beta_Joints` GO, which is a child of the `X Bot` 3D model.
27. Set the material to `Red Standard`.
28. In the `Beta_Surface` GO, set the material to `Violet Standard`.

29. For `NPC_3`, add the `Y Bot` model as a child of it.
30. Set the **Y** position to `-0.5`.
31. Set the **Y** rotation to `-190`.
32. Set the **Y** scale to `0.65`.
33. Disable the `Mesh Renderer` in the `NPC_3` GO.

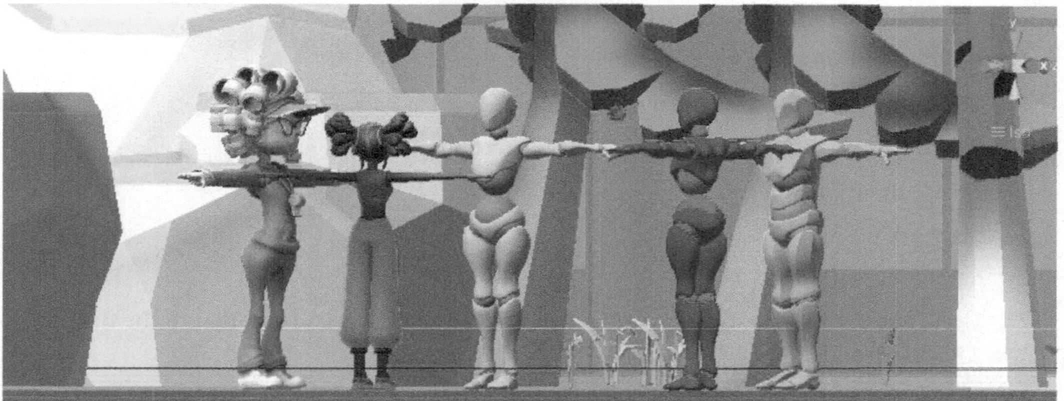

Figure 13.11 – 3D primitives replaced with 3D models from Mixamo

To add animation to the 3D characters, follow these steps:

1. Go to the `James` 3D model in **Hierarchy** and drag it under the `Main Character Animation Track` in the timeline.
2. Create a new `Animation Track` for the `James` 3D model.
3. Go to the `Character Animation` folder in the **Project** tab.
4. Choose the `Walking with Swagger Animation Clip`. You won't be able to drag the `.fbx` file onto the timeline for animation, but you can drag the animation file within the `.fbx` file.
5. Click on the triangle icon next to the `Walking with Swagger` FBX file. You will see a GO for Mixamo rig hips, a `Mixamo.com` file, and a `Walking with Swagger` avatar. The `Mixamo.com` file with a triangle and three lines is the `Animation Clip` we will drag to our timeline.
6. After you drag the `Animation Clip` to the animation timeline for `James`, place it at frame `0`.
7. Click on the `Animation Clip` in the timeline and go to **Inspector**.
8. In the **Clip Timing** section, set the duration to `4`.
9. In the **Animation extrapolation** section, set **Post-extrapolate** to **Loop**.
10. In the **Clip Transform Offsets** section, set the **Y** position to `-0.9`.

11. Set the **Y** rotation to `-90`.
12. Duplicate this `Animation Clip` on the timeline.
13. Set **Post-extrapolate** to **Hold**.
14. Set the **Y** rotation to `0`.
15. Go to the `Listening to Music` `Animation Clip` and add that to the timeline as the next animation. You will place it on the timeline at `8.05` seconds.
16. Set the duration of the clip to `9.47`.
17. Set the **Y** position to `-0.9`.
18. Add the `Jump Up` animation at `17.5167` seconds.
19. Set the duration to `2.375`.
20. Set the **Y** position to `-0.9`.
21. Set the **Y** rotation to `-14`.
22. Go to the `Turn to Silly Run` `Animation Clip` and add that to the timeline at `19.85` seconds.
23. Set the **Y** position to `-0.9`.
24. Add the `Run Leaning Back and Forth` `Animation Clip` to the timeline at `21.47` seconds.
25. Right-click on the `Animation Clip` in the timeline and select **Match Offsets to Previous Clip**. This will align the clip to the previous clip we had (the `Turn to Silly Run` animation) so that we can line up the motions more easily.
26. Set the **Y** rotation to `58`.
27. Set the duration to `10.4`.

With that, we have created our first animated sequence for our `Main Character` GO. We can go back and modify the camera angles so that they match up better with the character, such as close-ups or modifying the angle to get a better look at the composition. This is a brief overview of what can be done with animation timelines and creating animated sequences.

As a challenge for this chapter, try to utilize the animation clips that we used from Mixamo and apply them to the `dancer_1`, `NPC_one`, `dancer_2`, `NPC_2`, and `NPC_3` characters in our scene. Try to make it as fluid and cohesive as possible by creating an animation Timeline Track for each of the character 3D models and applying the animation clips to those timelines at specific time codes that correspond to the sequence of events you have storyboarded out.

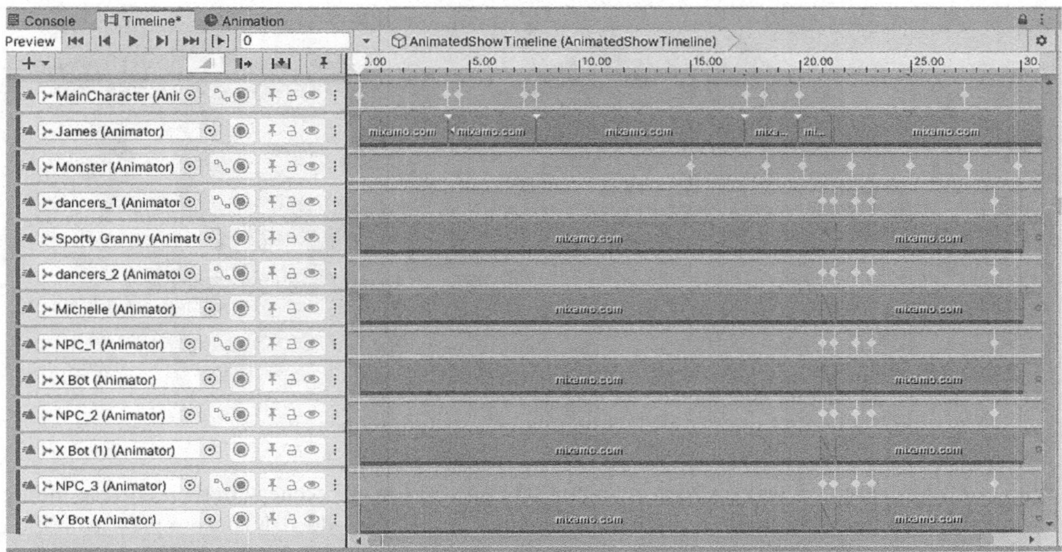

Figure 13.12 – Animation clips for each character's animation track

Now that we have all of our characters set up, we can proceed to add our monster into the scene to finish all the character animations. To add our monster character that pops out of the water, follow these steps:

1. Go to the Unity Asset Store and search for `Stylized Devil Bulldog Light Version`.
2. Download and import the asset from the Package Manager.
3. The imported assets will be in a folder called `Deepnest` in the **Project** tab.
4. Go to the `Deepnest` folder and open up the `devil_Bulldog_lite` folder.
5. Open the `Materials` folder.
6. Change the shader to a standard shader to correct the pink error caused by using a built-in render pipeline material in a URP project.
7. In the `Prefabs` folder, add the `DB_toon_fire` prefab as a child of our `Monster` GO.
8. In the `Monster` GO, disable the `Mesh Renderer`.
9. Drag the `DB_toon_fire` prefab that's a child of the `Monster` GO into the timeline and create an animation track.
10. In the `devil_Bulldog_lite` folder, go to the `Animation` folder.
11. Look for the `devil_bulldog_at_roar` animation file and add it to the animation track.
12. Click on the `roar` animation and look in **Inspector**.
13. Under **Animation Playable Asset**, set **Loop** to `On`.

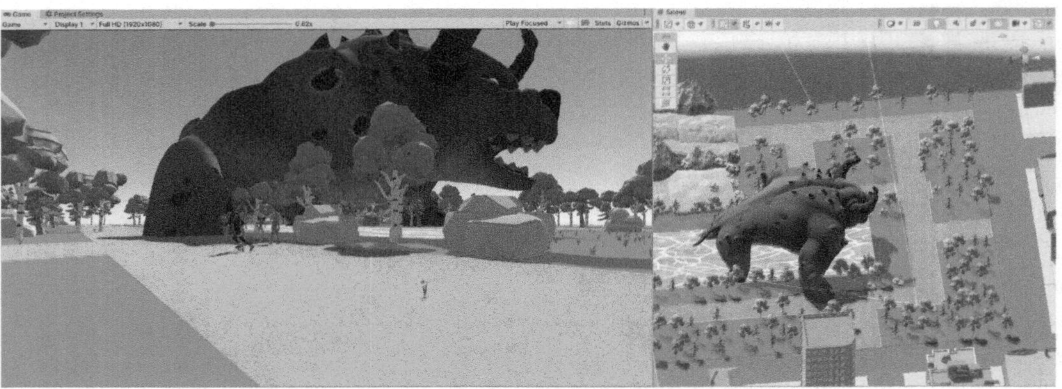

Figure 13.13 – The monster emerging from the water

With our monster added, we now have all of our 3D characters in our scene with their corresponding animated components. We also have our background music, which we added during our previsualization sequence to line everything up with the storyboards. The last thing we can do is add VFX to create explosions and make the experience uniquely come to life. When we experience this in VR, we'll see the characters running around, the larger-than-life monster, and all the explosions from the buildings. This can make the immersive experience of watching animation truly unbelievable. In the next section, we'll be adding VFX using prefabs to add accents to our animated sequence.

Adding VFX

So, we have everything we need to make our animated experience come to life in VR. The last thing we're going to do is really make it pop with explosions and VFX. These are the things that make the difference between having something that's enjoyable and having something that's memorable. If things such as explosions and particle beams are happening in front of you in VR, you know you're taking that immersive experience to the next level. We can make our own VFX or utilize the Unity Asset Store to drag and drop prefabs that have pre-made VFX into our scenes. We'll start by adding a particle beam to our monster so that it ups the ante of its destruction capabilities. Then, we can add a portal effect to show that the monster is coming out of some ethereal, crazy sci-fi origin place. Lastly, we'll add some explosions and fires to show the destructive damage to the actual city from the monster's rampage.

To add fire breath to the monster's mouth, follow these steps:

1. Go to the Unity Asset Store and search for `Cartoon FX Remaster Free` (`https://assetstore.unity.com/packages/vfx/particles/cartoon-fx-remaster-free-109565`).
2. Download and import it from the Unity Package Manager.
3. The contents will be in the `JMO Assets` folder in your **Project** tab.

4. In the `DB_Toon_Fire` prefab, go to the `tongue_root` GO and add an empty GO.
5. Name it `Monster Effects`.
6. Set the **X** position to `-.23`, the **Y** position to `-.07`, and the **Z** position to `.06`.
7. Set the **X** rotation to `20` and the **Y** rotation to `-90`.
8. From the `JMO Assets` folder, find the `CFXR fire breath` prefab and add it as a child to the monster effects.
9. In the timeline, create a `Control Track`.
10. Drag the `CFXR fire breath` prefab into the `Control Track` and set it to start at `21.3` seconds and end at `30` seconds.

To add portal effects to the monster's entry sequence, follow these steps:

1. Go to the Unity Asset Store and search for `Red Hollow Skill VFX` (`https://assetstore.unity.com/packages/vfx/red-hollow-skill-vfx-212627`).
2. Download and import it from the Unity Package Manager.
3. The contents will be in the `Hovl Studio` folder in your **Project** tab.
4. Create a new empty GO and title it `VFX`.
5. Set the **X** position, **Y** position, and **Z** position to `0`.
6. Create a new empty GO as a child of the `VFX` GO and call that `monster portal`.
7. Set the **X** position to `40.79` and the **Z** position to `-28.25`.
8. Set the **X** scale, **Y** scale, and **Z** scale to `3.5`.
9. From the `Hovl Studio` prefabs, add **Magic Circle** and **Magic Circle 2**.
10. For the magic circle, set the scale to `3`.
11. Create another `Control Track`.
12. Add **Magic Circle 1** to the `Control Track` we just created and place it at `14.93` seconds.
13. Set the duration to `6.7`.
14. Place **Magic Circle 2** on the top `Control Track` with the fire breath on it.
15. Set the start time to `15.76`.
16. Set the duration to `5.53`.

To add explosions and fire to the buildings and environment, follow these steps:

1. Create a new empty GO as a child of the `VFX` GO and name it `City Damage`.
2. Create an empty child GO and name it `Explosions`.
3. Create another empty child GO and name it `Fire_1`.

4. Create another empty child GO and name it `Fire_2`.
5. Create another empty child GO and name it `Fire_3`.
6. Add the `JMO Assets` to the `Fire Prefabs` folder.
7. Add the `CFX R Fire` prefab and the `CFX R2 Firewall` prefab to the `Fire_1` GO.
8. Duplicate the prefabs and scatter them across the areas that will be damaged by the monster's rampage. Use two firewalls and a fire prefab for the first set of damage and one fire and two firewalls for the second and third waves of damage to the city.
9. Drag `Fire_1` to the timeline to create an `Activation Track`.
10. Set the `Activation Track` to start at `21` seconds.
11. Set the duration to `8` seconds.
12. Create an `Activation Track` from `Fire_2`. Set the start time to `25` and set the duration to `5`.
13. Create an `Activation Track` from `Fire_3`. Set the start time to `26` and set the duration to `4`.
14. Create a new `Control Track`.
15. Go to the `Explosions` folder in the `JMO Assets` folder and select a variety of different explosion prefabs.
16. Place those as children of the `Explosions` child GO in the `City Damage` GO.
17. Set the explosion GOs along the damaged path in the city.
18. Add them to the `Control Track` so that they trigger at the right times on the timeline.

Figure 13.14 – The monster rampaging in the city with fire everywhere

With the VFX placed in the right areas, we have finally achieved our goal of creating an animated sequence that looks and feels worthy of being experienced in VR. You can go back and look at your storyboard and see how close you got to the idea that you came up with. Some of the defining things that I look at are the opening and closing shots because those are the first and last things that people will see when they watch your video. Making sure those two scenes and shots line up with what you imagine is a good way to gauge how successful you were in converting an idea into a finished product.

Adding background characters

An easy addition that we could quickly make is background characters. Even though we already have our animated sequence done, having background characters can liven up the environment even more. It's great to have a main cast, but just having people in the background who are talking and taking up space can make the environment feel a lot more immersive and fuller as opposed to having a big open space that feels lifeless. We can revisit the `People_Prototype` prefab that we made and add audio sequences and animations, as well as replace the 3D model with the `X Bot` and `Y Bot` models that we downloaded. The best part about these models is that we can switch up the materials on them, giving them a variety of different looks.

To replace our `People_Prototype` prefab with a 3D model, follow these steps:

1. In the `Prefabs` folder, double-click the `People_Prototype` prefab to open it.
2. Find the `X Bot` 3D model and add it as a child of the `People_Prototype` GO.
3. Hide the `Capsule` GO.
4. Copy the `animator` component from the `X Bot` model and add it to the `People_Prototype` prefab's parent.
5. Deactivate or delete the animator controller that is on the `X Bot` GO.
6. Click **Overrides** to apply overrides.

To add some variability, we can create a script that allows us to randomly generate different colors for our `X Bot` and `Y Bot` models when we instantiate them into the scene. To create a C# script that can randomly generate materials for our model, follow these steps:

1. Create a new C# script called `random color changer`.
2. Add it to our `People_Prototype`'s GO.
3. Open the script and apply the following namespaces to the C# code:

   ```
   using System.Collections;
   using System.Collections.Generic;
   using UnityEngine;
   ```

   These are the default namespaces required to access the main Unity Engine C# libraries.

4. Create a new method called `private void Awake()`, and add the following code to it:

   ```
           Renderer[] renderers =
               GetComponentsInChildren<Renderer>();
   ```

```
        foreach (Renderer renderer in renderers)
        {
            Material[] materials = renderer.materials;
            for (int i = 0; i < materials.Length; i++)
            {
                materials[i].color = new
                    Color(Random.value, Random.value,
                        Random.value, 1f);
            }
            renderer.materials = materials;
        }
    }
```

The `Awake()` method, a built-in Unity function that gets called when the script is loaded, is defined as private. Within this method, the script finds and loops through all `Renderer` components in the GO and its children. **Renderer components** are responsible for rendering the model's mesh with materials. The script then iterates through each `Renderer` component, obtains the `materials` array, and loops through each material in the array. A random color is assigned to each material using `Random.value`, which generates a random float value between `0` and `1`. The `Color` constructor creates a new color with the given red, green, blue, and alpha values, and sets the alpha value to `1f` for full opacity. After modifying the `materials` array, the updated materials are assigned back to the `Renderer` component to apply the changes to the GO and its children.

5. Save the code. This script assigns random colors to the materials of a 3D model in Unity. It is designed to be attached to the GO representing the 3D model.

When you press play, you will see that there will be randomized color variations for each of the prefabs that are instantiated. And every time you press play, there will be a different color combination. Now that we have variation in our characters' colors, we can add variation to their animations.

In this scenario, we're adopting a unique strategy because ordinarily, we would simply employ a standard C# script for such tasks. However, the animation system doesn't allow changes in animations during runtime as smoothly as it would for other assets, such as audio to add variation. As a result, we will create a state machine within an animator controller.

This controller is programmed to initiate a scripted behavior upon entering the state machine. The entry into the state machine prompts the selection of a random value, which corresponds to a distinct `Animation Clip` set within the state machine. Upon the completion of the `Animation Clip`, the `animator` component exits the state machine, subsequently entering another cycle.

In this new loop, it re-enters the state machine, selects a different random value, and plays the corresponding animation. Once the animation concludes, it departs from the state machine and the animated sequence we designed is once again repeated.

As different prefabs will have different animation instances, this will result in considerable variety. Each prefab will independently operate the same animation controller, negating the need for multiple controllers to run various animations. All we need is a single controller to be placed on our prefab.

To create a system that plays random animations on our background character, follow these steps:

1. In the `Animations` folder in the **Project** tab, create a new animator controller and name it `random animations`.
2. Add the `random animations` animator controller to the `animator` component on the `People_Prototype` prefab.
3. Double-click the animator controller to open up the **Animator** window.
4. Go to the `Character Animation` folder, which has all our animations downloaded from Mixamo.
5. Go to the `asking a question with two hands` animation file.
6. Select the `Mixamo.com` animation clip`Animation Clip` that's a child of this animation file.
7. Add it to the **Animator** window and set it as the layer default state.
8. Select the **Parameters** tab and add a new integer called `AnimID`.
9. Create a new substate machine and name it `random`.
10. In **Inspector**, go to **Add Behavior** and create a new behavior called `random animation behavior`.
11. In the `random animation behavior` script, remove the // comments from the `OnStateMachineEnter` method.
12. In the `override public void OnStateMachineEnter(Animator animator, int stateMachinePathHash)` method, add the following code:

    ```
    animator.SetInteger("AnimID", Random.Range(0, 5));
    ```

    This code will randomly pick a number from 0 to 5 and play the animation clip in the array according to its corresponding number.

13. Go back to the `Animation` folder and drag the `Breathing Idle` animation, the `Cheering with Two Fist Bumps` animation, the `General Conversation` animation, the `Listening to Music` animation, and the `Standing Happily` animation into the **Animator** window.
14. Right-click on **Entry state** and select **Make Transition.**
15. Drag the *transition* arrow to the `Breathing Idle` animation state that you chose to drag it into the **Animator** window.
16. Click on the triangle arrow line on the transition that you made.
17. In **Inspector**, go to **Conditions**.

18. In the dropdown menu for **Conditions**, choose `AnimID`.
19. Set the **Greater Than** dropdown menu to **Equals**.
20. Set the **Slot** field to `1`.
21. From the `Breathing Idle` animation state, right-click and select **Make Transition**.
22. Drag that transition to **Exit**.
23. Repeat *steps 14–22* for the remainder of the animation states.

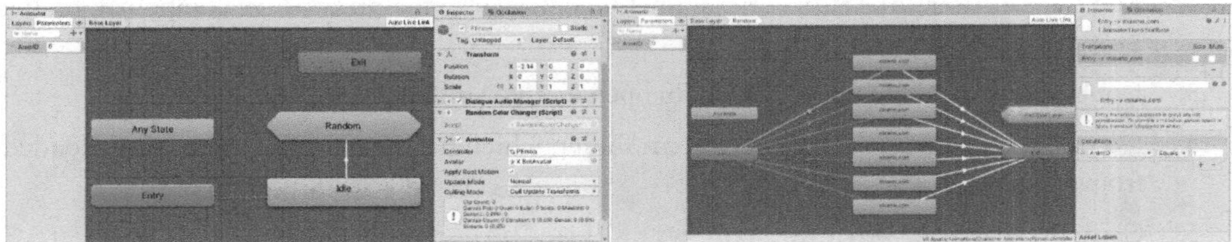

Figure 13.15 – Random animation animator controller (top) and state machine (bottom)

Since there are a total of 6 animations and 1 of them already has a default animation assigned, each condition for the animal ID should be assigned a different number from `0` to `5`. `0` will be assigned to the default animation, and we have already assigned number 1 to the animation we just discussed. The remaining animation states should be assigned either number `2`, `3`, `4`, or `5`.

To fix the `PersonSpawnerManager` so that it can place a `People_Prototype` prefab with a random rotation, go through the following steps:

1. In the `PersonSpawnerManager` script, find the following code:

   ```
   Quaternion spawnRotation = Quaternion.identity;
   ```

   Replace it with this:

   ```
   Quaternion spawnRotation = Quaternion.Euler(0, Random.Range(0,
   360), 0);
   ```

   Changing the code in this manner, from a standard rotation where every instance will have the same rotation value, will randomly apply a value from 0 to 360 for each of the spawned `People_Prototype` prefabs that are instantiated in the scene.

2. Save the script.

We can now revisit the `PersonSpawnerManager` that we created in *Chapter 11*. We can set the number of people to 50 and the tag options to `walking path`. Then, we can press play.

When you play the scene, there will be 50 `People_Prototype` prefabs scattered throughout the walking path, each with a different look due to the variation in materials and colors. They will also be randomly playing audio clips with different phrases. The script will randomly select an animation clip from the list and play it on the rigged character. After that animation clip finishes playing, the script will play another random animation when it enters the state machine state.

Summary

In this chapter, we went through the full animation pipeline workflow from start to finish. Hopefully, by the end of this, you have a better understanding of how animation works and how it can be created. If you are interested in pursuing more animation in Unity, it is the perfect tool to get started and integrate into more projects. This is just the tip of the iceberg because the animation system in Unity is so robust, as we have seen thus far. The power of real-time rendering is that you can utilize animation in many different ways that you otherwise wouldn't be able to in other programs such as Blender or Cinema 4D.

Just as our VR experiences are human-centered, the animation system and the way you create animation are interaction-centered, which in turn is human-centered as well. This is something to keep in mind as we craft interesting animated experiences, especially for VR because the utilization of these animations can be used across a variety of different mediums.

In the next chapter, we will be covering what some of those applications can be by way of recording the animations as videos, triggering them in the VR space, and converting them to 360 videos that can be played on YouTube.

14

Recording Virtual Reality Videos

In this chapter, we're going to be building on what we've already done with our animated show by utilizing the animation in a variety of different ways. The best part about animation is that it allows you to create experiences in VR, but then also record those as videos that you could play on a variety of different platforms. These platforms could be a local storage device, such as a mobile phone or a computer playing a video through a media player, or you could upload the video to a service such as YouTube or Vimeo and play it as a strip on a streaming platform. Since Unity is a real-time rendering engine, you can play that animation in real time, as we saw in the previous chapter. But you're not limited to that, and that's the best part about working in Unity and working on VR experiences. The same content that we create for VR can be rendered and saved as a video to play as a video file, or ported to a console to be played on a non-VR screen. The render can even be saved as a sequence of images that can be utilized as posters or in flipbooks.

If you recall our roadmap back in *Chapter 10*, we put in *Phase 8* that we were going to design a theater experience. Using that experience, we were going to add a theater room with some indoor lighting. Now, we're going to create a video that can play on the screen as a loop and have some surround sound. If possible, we could add some prefabs and a variety of different things that we've utilized in making array managers and everything such as that. We were also going to convert the animated sequence into a 360° video that can be played on any 3D-supported platform such as YouTube or even your local Windows Media Player. Again, you don't have to stick to this, but this is a good guideline for us to work on. Using the **Unity Recorder** and a variety of different tools that we will look at in this chapter, we will carve out an interesting array of experiences with the premade asset that we have with our animated show scene.

In this chapter, we will cover the following topics:

- Working with the Unity Recorder
- Recording our animation in a variety of different video formats
- Building a VR theater experience
- Creating a 360° video and understanding how to use that asset in a variety of different streaming platforms

Technical requirements

The complete source code for this chapter can be found at `https://github.com/PacktPublishing/Enhancing-Virtual-Reality-Experiences-with-Unity-2022/tree/main/EnhancingVRExperiencesFullProject/Assets/_VRProjectAssets/Scenes/Chapter_14`.

Working with the Unity Recorder

In order to utilize the animated clip that we made, we have to turn that into a video file so that we can play it in a variety of different settings. The best way to do that is using the Unity Recorder.

The Unity Recorder is a built-in tool in Unity that allows you to record gameplay footage and save it as video files or image sequences. It can capture a variety of output types, including screen captures, cameras, and audio sources. You can set up different recording sessions with various settings, such as **Resolution**, **Frame Rate**, and **File Format**. The Unity Recorder is useful for creating gameplay trailers, tutorials, and other promotional videos, as well as for debugging and analyzing game behavior.

In this section, we will first download the Unity Recorder from the Unity Package Manager, and then we will add it to our scene. After we've done that, we will create a new Unity Recorder track to Unity Timeline we have for our animation, use it to record a clip of our animation, and save it to a video file asset that we can utilize.

To record a video with the Unity Recorder, follow these steps:

1. Open **Package Manager** and navigate to Unity Registry.
2. Install the Unity Recorder.
3. Import all sample packages.
4. In the animated show timeline, create a new recorder track.
5. Right-click in the recorder track to add a recorder clip.
6. Set the start of the recorder clip to `0` and the duration to `30`.
7. Open the **Options** menu in the **Timeline** window by clicking the gear icon in the top right.

8. Set **Frame Rate** to `24` frames per second.
9. Set **Capture Source** to **Game View** and **Output Resolution** to `1080P`.
10. Enable **Include Audio**.
11. Set the format to `MP4` and **Quality** to `High`.
12. Give the output file a name.
13. If desired, set the `Recorder` folder (default is set to **Recordings**).
14. Enter play mode to begin recording.
15. Once the timeline reaches the end of the recording clip, it will automatically save when you exit play mode.
16. You will then have a recorded animation clip.

Now that we have our animation clip, the next step is to create a movie theater experience where we can watch the clip we just made on a big screen. To do this, we will download a theater asset and create a new scene centered around it. Then, we will place the video on the screen and press play to start the experience.

Building a VR theater experience

So, you may be wondering why we're going to create a theater experience in VR when you could just go to the theater. I think one of the values and beauties of VR, especially given the COVID pandemic, is that it is able to give people experiences that mimic the real-world places they want to go to but can't, right at home or wherever they may be limited to for a while. During the pandemic, people wanted that theater experience with surround sound and the ability to look around and see a huge screen. But they weren't able to do that because everything was shut down. VR can mitigate that. And because we have our animated scene created in the previous chapter, we can utilize that and put it on a big screen for a movie theater experience in the comfort of your living room. All you have to do is put on a headset and enjoy everything that comes with the theater experience. More importantly, you don't have to deal with noisy people talking and eating popcorn in your ear. That is a significant benefit.

To do this, we will download a theater asset from the Unity Asset Store and apply the animated video file that we created in the previous section to our big screen using a material projection.

To play the animation clip in a theater environment, follow these steps:

1. Go to the Unity Asset Store and search for **VR Cinema for Mobile**: `https://assetstore.unity.com/packages/3d/props/interior/vr-cinema-for-mobile-150120`.
2. Download and import the asset from the Unity Package Manager.
3. The files will be located in the `VRcinemaformobile` folder.
4. Create a new scene.

5. Add the demo scene from **VR Cinema for Mobile** to the **Hierarchy** window in the new scene.
6. Drag and drop the theater game object and theater light game object from the demo to the new scene.
7. Remove the demo scene without saving it.
8. Create a new empty game object named `movie timeline`.
9. Add a timeline asset to the movie timeline game object and save it in the `animations` folder.
10. Set the movie timeline to `24` frames per second.
11. Create a new `videos` folder in the assets called and add the recorded video to that folder.
12. In **Hierarchy**, create a new video player as a child of the movie timeline.
13. Set the video clip to the movie clip that was imported, set the **Render Mode** to **Material Override**, and set the renderer to the `Cinema Screen` GO.
14. Create a new material named `White_standard`.
15. Change the material of the cinema screen game object to `White_standard`.
16. Add a `Mesh Collider` component to the `theater_floor` GO.
17. In the `theater room` prefab, add a box collider around the entire theater:

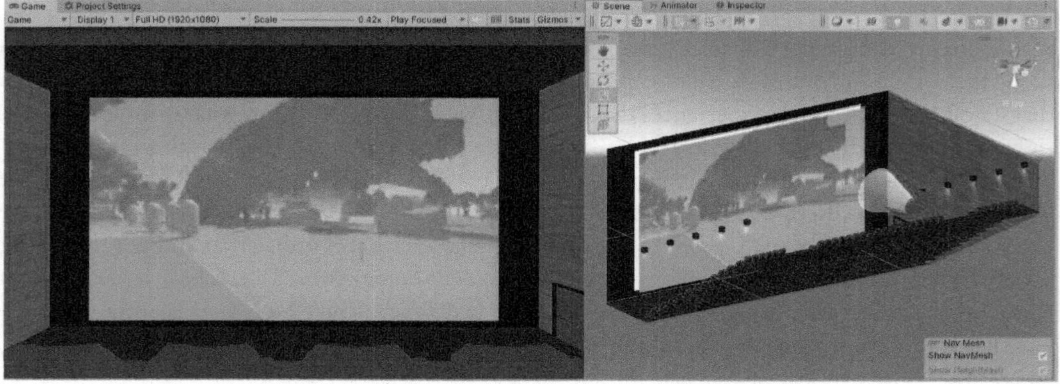

Figure 14.1 – VR theater experience with the animated show video playing on the big screen

In a few simple steps, we were able to create a theater experience very much like the ones that we're familiar with, without the limitations of physical theater space. We can make it large or small, change the size of the screen from big to small, or even make it bigger. There's a lot of stuff we can do with it, and it's great because, in a real-time rendering engine, we can rapidly iterate and then apply those principles to other things.

Now that we have a 2D experience done with our video, let's move on to creating a 3D experience using 360° video.

Creating a 360° video

Having 360° video in VR is quite interesting. You get to see that a lot in virtual tours, and you also see it in VR roller coasters. One of the best parts about having 360° video is that it makes videos much more accessible because you don't need a headset to have 360° video experiences. You can actually have those experiences on a web browser using tools from YouTube and a variety of other sources.

In this section, we will use the Unity Recorder to create a 360° video file from our animated show, much as we did with the animated show MP4 file. Then, we will add metadata to it so that the platforms we play the 360° video on understand that it's a 360° video. After that, we can upload it to a video source such as YouTube to stream and share.

To record a 360° video of the animated scene, follow these steps:

1. Duplicate the recorder track and disable the original recorder track.
2. Click on the recorder clip and change the source to 360° view.
3. Set the camera's **Main Camera** option.
4. Set the **Output Dimensions** option to `4096` width and `2048` height.
5. Set the **Cube Map Size** option to `2048`.
6. Disable **Record in Stereo** and enable **Include Audio**.
7. Give the video a name in the filename field.
8. Enter play mode to record the 360° video.
9. When finished, exit play mode to save the video.
10. It will be saved in the `recordings` folder.

You may be eager to see the magic of your 360° video at work and play it in Unity, but you will notice that everything appears distorted. This is a known bug that comes with recording 360° videos in Unity. Although you can export the actual file, it is missing valuable metadata information that programs need to properly interpret the video as a 360° video, including details about the projection type, field of view, and orientation. Without this metadata, the final video can appear distorted.

To overcome this, we need to use a third-party tool called **Spatial Media Metadata Injector**. This tool, hosted on a GitHub server, adds the necessary metadata to the video file. This metadata instructs 360° video players how to display the video correctly. By adding the metadata to our video, we can ensure that it will be recognized as a 360° video and displayed in the correct orientation when uploaded to YouTube or Vimeo or played on a 360° video player. So, let's add the necessary metadata to our video using the Spatial Media Metadata Injector.

To add the metadata to our 360° video to play correctly, go through the following steps:

1. Download **Spatial Media Metadata Injector v2.1** from `https://github.com/google/spatial-media/releases/tag/v2.1`.
2. Choose the appropriate download option for your operating system (Windows or Mac).
3. Open the Spatial Media Metadata Injector program.
4. Click **Open** and select the VR 360° video file that you exported from Unity.
5. Click **Inject Metadata** and choose where to save the newly created file.
6. Wait for the injection process to finish. The new file will have `_injected` added to its name.
7. You can now play the 360° video on a video player that supports this format.

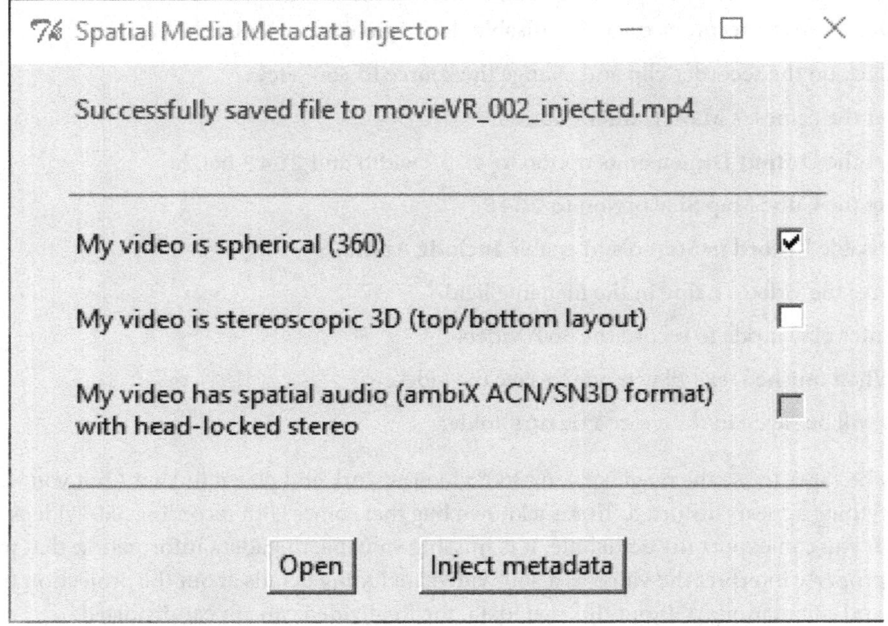

Figure 14.2 – Spatial Media Metadata Injector export settings

You can also upload this video to Vimeo or YouTube, and because we modified the metadata, it will automatically recognize the video you upload as a 360° video. That means that when the video has been uploaded, you will have the option to rotate your camera around 360° degrees as the video plays.

You can view my VR animated show 360° video here: `https://youtu.be/Om8LvVJh1iI`.

Here's a screenshot taken from this:

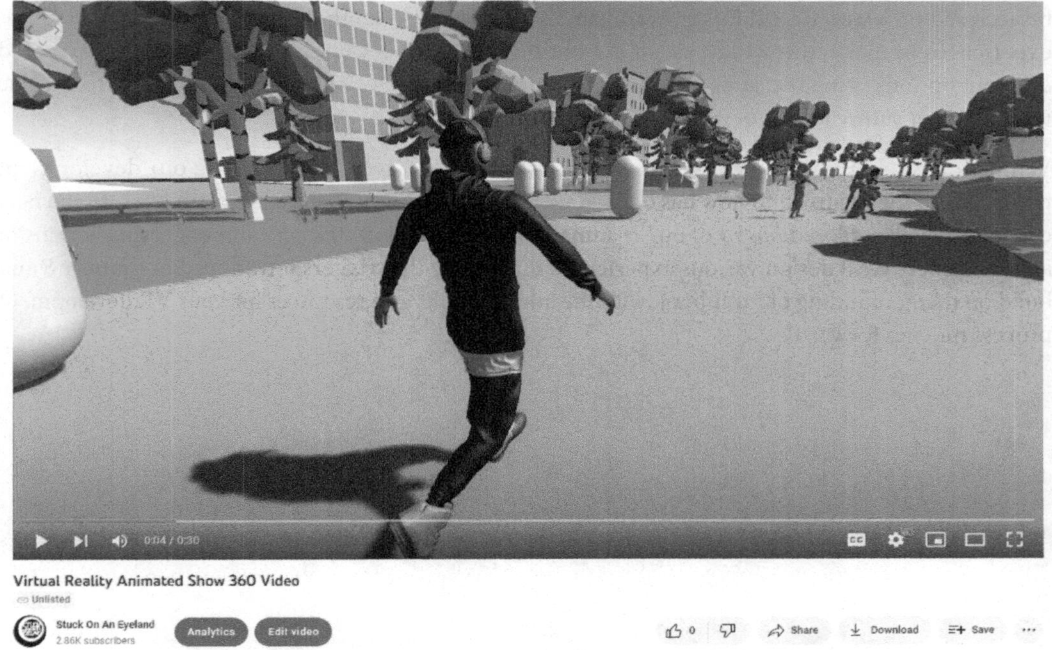

Figure 14.3 – Animated show 360° video playing on the YouTube streaming platform

Creating a VR movie theater experience and a 360° video from an animated sequence in Unity is a multi-step process, but it can lead to a truly immersive and interactive experience. The Unity Recorder and VR Cinema for Mobile assets allow for easy video and scene creation, while the Spatial Media Metadata Injector ensures that the 360° video is recognized as such by video players. With these tools, anyone can create their own virtual movie theater experience or 360° video and share it with others on platforms such as YouTube or Vimeo.

Summary

Using *Phase 8* of our roadmap as a guideline, we were able to explore how we can utilize our animated show assets in a variety of different ways. We first learned how to use the Unity Recorder to record our animated real-time rendered shell assets as a video file. Once we had that video file, we could place it on a big screen in a VR theater that we created. Then, we were able to convert that animated show into a 360° video file that we could use on 360° video players or upload to YouTube to stream 360° videos across the world and share them with friends.

At this point, you should understand that developing VR experiences is not limited to just headsets or mobile devices. You can create experiences through 360° video and streaming services that can be accessed on a variety of different platforms and devices. When thinking about what kinds of VR experiences to make, think hard about the options available because, in this chapter, we explored different options using the same core assets we built in previous chapters, applying them to specific use cases that showcase the power of VR.

While not as technical as the other chapters, utilizing VR assets and applying our development process from the roadmap to now has opened up our toolset to new skills and possibilities. In the next chapter, we will explore *Phase 9* of our roadmap, which focuses on triggers and triggering actions in an experience. We'll design various experiences that utilize the triggers introduced in *Chapter 8* and build on them, rounding out this book with meaningful skills and resources for your VR development process moving forward.

15

Enhancing Virtual Reality Rigs

The focus of this chapter is to start bringing everything we've covered so far in this entire book together. We've already created our virtual environment and learned a variety of skills, from animation to C# coding to the Unity Input System. Now, we'll use all of these skills to create experiences that allow us to explore a variety of VR interactions.

In this chapter, we will be building on all the knowledge you've gathered throughout this book. We will be adding new layers of interactivity to our VR rig, refining our VR development skills, and discovering new possibilities within the VR universe. Key enhancements will include introducing animated hands to our VR rig for a more realistic and immersive user experience. We'll also be incorporating the ability to switch between our indirect interactor and direct interactor components, offering a versatile and dynamic interactive experience. We're going to add more movement capabilities to our VR rig, including running, jumping, and crouching functions. These additions will bring a new level of immersion and interaction, allowing users to explore and navigate our VR environment in more engaging ways.

In this chapter, we will cover the following topics:

- Adding animated hands to our VR rig
- Implementing the ability to toggle between ray interactors and direct interactors
- Adding a running function to our VR rig
- Adding a jumping function to our VR rig
- Adding a crouching function to our VR rig

Technical requirements

The complete source code for this chapter can be found at `https://github.com/PacktPublishing/Enhancing-Virtual-Reality-Experiences-with-Unity-2022/tree/main/EnhancingVRExperiencesFullProject/Assets/_VRProjectAssets/Scenes/Chapter_15`.

Adding animated hands to the VR rig

Animated hands are a key component of VR experiences. They provide a layer of immersion, allowing users to interact with the virtual world in a more natural and intuitive way. They also provide feedback, expression, and personality to the experience, enhancing the overall engagement and enjoyment of the user. As VR technology continues to evolve, animated hands will continue to play an important role in creating more immersive and interactive experiences.

To set up rigged animated hands, follow these steps:

1. Go to this link to download the `Hands` asset: `https://drive.google.com/file/d/10b39IekUdpBHlcTslZ-BlNRyH5uqPUel`.
2. Import the hands into your project (*Figure 15.1*).

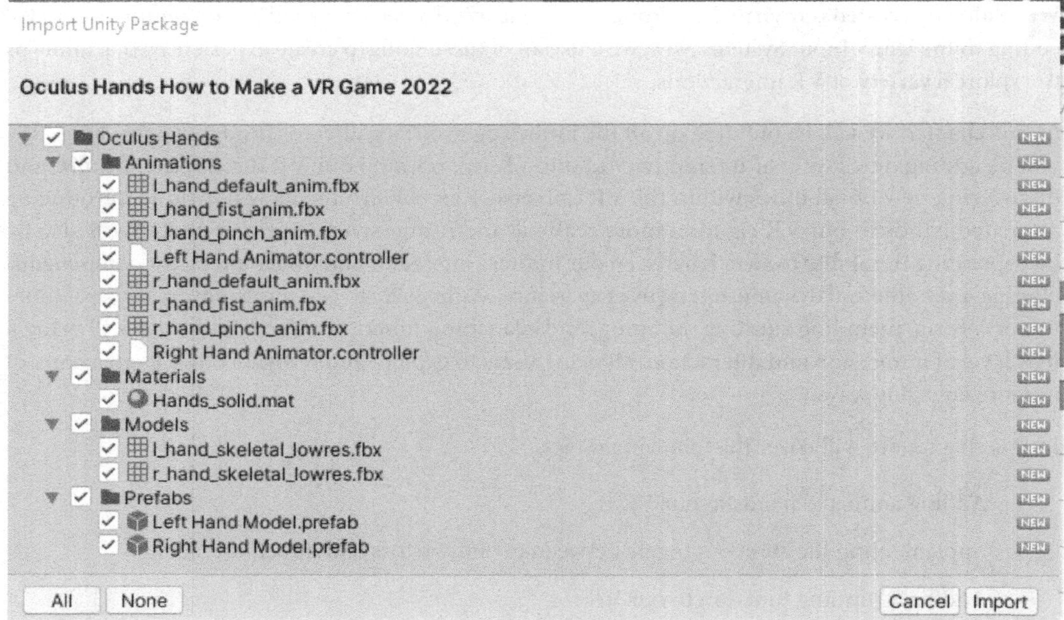

Figure 15.1 – Import Assets list for the Oculus Hands Unity package

   You will find the assets in the subfolder called `Oculus Hands`.

3. Open a new scene.
4. Drag your `VRPhysicsAndHandSound` variant prefab VR rig into the scene.
5. Find the `LeftHand Controller` and `RightHand Controller` GOs in your VR rig.
6. Go to the `Oculus Hands Prefabs` folder and drag `Left Hand Model` as a child of `LeftHand Controller`.

7. Set the **X** position to `-0.001`, the **Y** position to `2.001`, and the **Z** position to `-0.035`.
8. Set the **Z** rotation to `90`.
9. Set the **X**, **Y**, and **Z** scale to `1.5038`.
10. Drag `Right Hand Model` as a child of `RightHand Controller`.
11. Set the position and scale values to the same as `Left Hand Model`.
12. Set the Z rotation to `-90`.
13. You can hide or remove the `BlackHandLT` and `BlackHandRT` GOs that were added previously because we will be using the **Oculus Hands** package we imported instead.
14. Create new empty GOs as children of the `LeftHand` and `RightHand Controller`, and name them `left hand attach point` and `right hand attach point`, respectively.

By setting up rigged animated hands within Unity and using the provided `Oculus Hands` package, users can achieve a more immersive and realistic hand experience in VR. Additionally, the installed `Oculus Hands` package enables the incorporation of animations, allowing for simulated gripping actions when squeezing the VR hand controllers. These enhancements contribute to a heightened sense of presence and interaction within the VR environment. In the next section, we will add the grip animation.

Adding grip animations

Attention to detail in user interaction is paramount to achieving this goal. Having already established realistic hand representations through rigged animated hands, we now embark on an exhilarating adventure into grip animations. These animations enable users to simulate gripping the VR hand controllers, taking interactivity to new heights. Get ready to infuse our virtual worlds with lifelike hand movements, immersing users in dynamic and natural interactions.

To add grip animation to the hand controller simulation, follow these steps:

1. Create a C# script called `HandPinch`.
2. Open the script and apply the following namespaces to the code:

```
using UnityEngine;
using UnityEngine.InputSystem;
```

3. In the `public` class, `HandPinch`, add the following variables:

```
    public InputActionProperty grip;
    public Animator handAnimator;
```

   In the `HandPinch` class, we declare two variables: `grip` is a reference to the input action for gripping, which we will use to detect the gripping input from the user, and `handAnimator` is a reference to the `Animator` component attached to the hand model, which we will use to control the grip animation.

4. In the `void Update()` method, add the following code:

```
        float gripValue =
            grip.action.ReadValue<float>();
        handAnimator.SetFloat("Grip", gripValue);
```

   In the `Update()` method, we retrieve the current value of the `grip` input action using `grip.action.ReadValue<float>()` and store it in the `gripValue` variable. We then set the `Grip` parameter of the hand animator to this `gripValue`, which will control the intensity or strength of the grip animation.

5. Save the code.
6. Add the `HandPinch` script to both the left and right hand models.
7. For `Left Hand Model`, enable **Use Reference** and set the reference to `XRI Left Hand Interaction Select Value Input Action Reference`.
8. In the `Hand Animator` reference slot, add `Left Hand Model`.
9. Repeat *steps 6–8* for `Right Hand Model`, using `Right Hand Model` for the `Hand Animator` reference slot and the `XRI Right Hand Interaction Select Value Input Action Reference` asset for the grip reference.

With grip animations, we have elevated the level of interactivity in our VR experiences by allowing users to simulate holding the grip buttons on their VR hand controllers. This has brought a new level of realism and immersion to our virtual worlds. However, our exploration of lifelike hand interactions does not stop there. In addition to grip animations, we will now venture into the realm of pinch animations in the next section.

Adding pinch animations

Building upon our existing setup of rigged animated hands and the captivating grip animations we have incorporated, we now venture into the exciting domain of pinch animations. Pinch animations enable users to simulate the delicate act of pinching their fingers together, introducing a new layer of precision and realism to their virtual hand interactions. In this section, we will explore the process of integrating pinch animations into our Unity project, unlocking the ability to perform intricate gestures and interact with virtual objects in more nuanced ways.

To add pinch animation to hand controller activation simulation, follow these steps:

1. Open the `HandPinch` C# script.
2. Add the following variable code above the `Update` function:

```
public InputActionProperty pinch;
```

3. Add the following code inside the `Update` method:

```
float triggerValue = pinch.action.ReadValue<float>();
        handAnimator.SetFloat("Trigger", triggerValue);
```

   This code will read the current value of the `pinch` action and store it in the `triggerValue` variable. Then, set the `"Trigger"` parameter of `handAnimator` (an animator component) to the value of `triggerValue`. This will control the pinch animation based on the input.

4. Save the code.
5. For `Left Hand Model`, enable **Use Reference** under **Pinch**.
6. Set the reference to `XRI Left Hand Interaction Activate Value`.
7. Repeat *steps 5 and 6* for `Right Hand Model`.

Now, we have working animations for our hands that involve pressing the **Select** or **Trigger** buttons and the **Grip** buttons. Depending on how hard we press the **Trigger** or **Grip** buttons, we control how much of an animation is played when we have our hands. If we don't completely press the **Grip** or **Trigger**, the animation won't play completely.

In the next section, we will reduce the conflicting overlap in meshes when holding objects, by hiding the `hand` GOs when we hold virtual objects.

Hiding hands when holding objects

An important aspect of achieving this realism lies in addressing the visual representation of hands while holding these objects. When users grasp and manipulate virtual objects, it is crucial to hide or minimize the visibility of their hands. This serves two vital purposes: maintaining the illusion of direct interaction with the virtual world and preventing any visual inconsistencies that may disrupt the immersive experience. We will delve into the concept of hiding hands while holding virtual objects, exploring techniques to seamlessly conceal the user's hands and ensuring a more believable and engaging VR experience.

To hide hands when holding objects, follow these steps:

1. Go to the `RightHand Controller` GO.
2. In the `XR Controller` component, find the model reference.
3. Add the `Right Hand Model` GO to the model reference slot (do not use the model prefab or model parent as it will unintentionally create a duplicate instance of the hand model in the rig).
4. If you haven't done so already, go to the `XR Direct Interactor` and enable **Hide Controller on Select**.
5. Repeat *steps 2–4* for the `LeftHand Controller` GO, adding the `Left Hand Model` GO to the model reference slot instead of the `Right Hand Model` GO.

With the final step complete, we have successfully rigged animated hands, integrated grip animations, and explored the significance of hiding hands while holding virtual objects. With these elements in place, we have made remarkable strides in enhancing the realism and interactivity of our VR experiences. However, our journey does not end here. As we continue to deepen our understanding of VR development, the next stage brings us to the realm of interactors. These powerful components play a pivotal role in enabling seamless interactions between users and the virtual environment. In the upcoming section, we will unravel the magic of interactors, exploring how they facilitate object grabbing, interaction events, and more. We will achieve that by adding the ability to toggle between the ray and direct interactors on both hands of our VR rig.

Adding and toggling between the ray interactor and the direct interactor

A ray interactor allows the user to interact with objects in the virtual environment using a laser-like pointer, which is useful for selecting or pointing at objects from a distance. On the other hand, a direct interactor allows the user to interact with objects in the virtual environment using their hand or a controller, which is useful for grabbing, pushing, or manipulating objects up close.

Adding interactors

By having both a ray interactor and a direct interactor on the same hand controller, the user has more options and flexibility in how they interact with the virtual environment. They can use the ray interactor to select objects from a distance and the direct interactor to manipulate or grab objects up close, providing a more intuitive and immersive experience.

To add ray interactors to both hands, follow these steps:

1. Create a new empty GO and name it `Right Hand Ray`.
2. Go to the `RightHand Controller` GO and select the three dots at the top right of the `XR Controller` component.
3. Click **Copy Component** to copy the component and its values.
4. Go to the `Right Hand Ray` GO.
5. Press the three dots in the top right of the `Transform` component.
6. Click **Paste Component as New**. This will copy the component and paste it into the `Right Hand Ray` GO.
7. Repeat *steps 2-6* to add the `XR Ray Interactor`, the `Line Renderer`, and the `XR Interactor Line Visual` components.
8. In the `XR Controller` component, set the model to `Right Hand Model`.
9. In the `XR Ray Interactor` component, set **Interaction Layer Mask** to **Everything**, and the attached transform to `Right Hand Attach Point`.

10. Under **Selection Configuration**, enable **Hide Controller on Select**. This will hide the hand model when you select something with Ray Interactor.
11. Duplicate the `Right Hand Ray` GO and name it `Left Hand Ray`.
12. In the `XR Controller` component of `Left Hand Ray`, replace all the `XRI Right Hand` references with `XRI Left Hand`.
13. Set the model to `Left Hand Model`.
14. In the `XR Ray Interactor` component, set the attach point to `Left Hand Attach Point`.

To add direct interactors to both hands, follow these steps:

1. Go to the `RightHand Controller` and remove the `XR Ray Interactor`, the `Line Renderer`, and the `XR Interactor Line Visual` components.
2. Add an `XR Direct Interactor` component to the `RightHand Controller` GO.
3. Set the interaction manager to **XR Interaction Manager**.
4. Set **Interaction Layer Mask** to **grabbable** and **Object**.
5. Enable **Hide Controller on Select**.
6. Go to the `LeftHand Controller` GO.
7. In the `XR Direct Interactor` component, enable **Hide Controller on Select**.
8. Copy the `Sphere Collider` component.
9. Go back to the `RightHand Controller` GO and paste the `Sphere Collider` component as a new component.
10. Lastly, you can change the material on the `Left Hand Model` and the `Right Hand Model` by looking for the `Hands: L Hand` or `Hands: R Hand` GOs and swapping out the material. I chose the example hand gradient material that I had on my previous hands.
11. Rename the `VR Rig` prefab as `VR Rig Physics Sound Animated Hands Variant`.
12. Drag it into our `Prefabs` folder to make a prefab variant.

Now that we have added our `Interactor` components to our hands, we will create a script to toggle the interactors on and off.

Creating a flexible toggle for independent direct and ray interactors

We constantly strive to refine and enhance the level of interactivity and realism in our VR experiences. In our quest to achieve this, we embark on a new frontier of flexibility by creating a script that allows independent toggling of the direct and ray interactors for each hand. This powerful scripting capability grants us the freedom to customize how we interact with virtual objects, providing a new level of versatility and control. To toggle ray interactors on both hands with C# script and input actions, follow these steps:

1. Create a new C# script and name it `ToggleRay`.
2. Open the script and apply the following namespaces to the code:

   ```
   using System.Collections.Generic;
   using UnityEngine;
   using UnityEngine.XR.Interaction.Toolkit;
   [RequireComponent(typeof(XRRayInteractor))]
   ```

   We import the necessary namespaces and indicate that the script requires an `XRRayInteractor` component.

3. In the `public` class, `ToggleRay`, add the following code to the script:

   ```
       [Tooltip("Switch even if an object is selected")]
       public bool forceToggle = false;
       [Tooltip("The direct interactor that's switched
           to")]
       public XRDirectInteractor directInteractor = null;
       private XRRayInteractor rayInteractor = null;
       private bool isSwitched = false;
   ```

   We declare some `public` variables for toggling the ray and specifying the direct interactor. We also create `private` variables for the ray interactor and a Boolean to track the current state.

4. In the `private void Awake()` method, add the following code to the script:

   ```
           rayInteractor =
               GetComponent<XRRayInteractor>();
           SwitchInteractors(false);
   ```

   In the `Awake` method, we assign the `Ray Interactor` component to the variable and initially disable both interactors.

5. Create a method called `public void ActivateRay()`, and add the following code to the script:

   ```
           if (!TouchingObject() || forceToggle)
               SwitchInteractors(true);
   ```

   Here, we create a `public` method called `ActivateRay` that checks that there are no objects being touched and whether `forceToggle` is `true`, and then it enables the ray by calling `SwitchInteractors` with a value of `true`.

6. Create a method called `public void DeactivateRay()`, and add the following code to the script:

```
if (isSwitched)
    SwitchInteractors(false);
```

Here, we create a `public` method called `DeactivateRay` that checks whether the ray is currently switched on, and then it disables the ray by calling `SwitchInteractors` with a value of `false`.

7. Create a method called `TouchingOIbject()` (private Boolean) and add the following code to the script:

```
List<XRBaseInteractable> targets = new
    List<XRBaseInteractable>();
directInteractor.GetValidTargets(targets);
return (targets.Count > 0);
```

Here, we define a `private` method called `TouchingObject` that retrieves a list of valid targets using the direct interactor and returns `true` if there is at least one target being touched.

8. Create a private void method called `SwitchInteractors` (Boolean value), and add the following code to the script:

```
isSwitched = value;
rayInteractor.enabled = value;
directInteractor.enabled = !value;
```

Here, we create a `private` method called `SwitchInteractors` that takes a Boolean value. It updates the `isSwitched` variable, enables or disables the ray interactor based on the value, and enables or disables the direct interactor accordingly.

9. Save the preceding code.
10. Add the `ToggleRay` script to both the `left-hand Ray` GO and the `right-hand Ray` GO.
11. For the `ToggleRay` script on the left-hand ray, add the `LeftHand Controller` GO to the `Direct Interactor` reference slot.
12. For the right-hand ray, add the `RightHand Controller` GO to the `Direct Interactor` reference slot.

With our script complete, we will now create input actions to connect our toggle script to the VR hand controller trigger action.

Adding triggers for individual toggling

We will now need to create a trigger specifically for the left hand and the right hand so that we can toggle them individually. We can do this by creating new input actions, as we did in the previous chapter. To create input actions specifically for the toggle rays on the left and right hand, go through the following steps:

1. Go to the `XR Interaction Manager` GO and double-click `XRI Default Input Actions` in the `Input Action Manager` reference slot. This will open the `XRI Default Input Actions` asset.
2. In the **Action Maps** section, choose `XRI Left Hand Interaction`.
3. Create a new action and call it `X Button`.
4. Set the action type to **Button**.
5. Click + and choose **Add Binding**.
6. For the binding, set the path to `Primary Button` for the left-hand XR controller. Be sure to choose the left-hand XR controller specifically and not the general XR controller as we did with our custom inputs in the *Creating custom input actions* section of *Chapter 8*.
7. Create another action and name it `Y Button`.
8. Click + and choose **Add Binding**.
9. For the binding, set the path to `Secondary Button` for the left-hand XR controller.
10. Select the `XRI Right Hand Interaction` action map.
11. Repeat *steps 2–9* to create the input actions for the right VR controller. Instead of using `X` for the primary button and `Y` for the secondary button as on the left VR controller, the equivalent on the right VR controller is `A button` for the primary button and `B button` for the secondary button. Make sure you also choose the XR controller for the right hand instead of the left hand.

Adding an input manager

Now that we have specific input actions for left- and right-hand interactions on our controller, it's time to add an input manager to our VR rig. This input manager will handle all of our input actions and trigger events from scripts, which will be particularly useful when incorporating actions such as jumping, running, crouching, and other VR-specific interactions. By creating a prefab from this setup, we eliminate the need to repeat the setup process.

In *Chapter 8*, in the *Triggering events with input actions* section, we learned how to reference input actions from the new Input System and pair them with the Unity Event System. This allowed us to easily add desired methods to the input actions using **Inspector**. This dynamic and scalable approach simplifies the development of actions, enabling us to expand our Input System efficiently. In this case, we will focus on the toggle action, but we can also utilize this script to scale other input actions with additional methods in the future. By leveraging the power of the Input Manager and the Unity Event System, we achieve a flexible and streamlined development process for our VR interactions.

To add an input manager to our VR rig and set up the toggles with the hands and the new interactions, follow these steps:

1. Create a new empty GO as a child of our VR rig and name it `VRHandInteractionsManager`.
2. Create a new script called `ToggleInputActionManager` and add it to the `VRHandInteractionsManager` GO.
3. Apply the following namespaces to the code:

```
using UnityEngine;
using UnityEngine.InputSystem;
using UnityEngine.Events;
```

These namespaces grant access to the necessary Unity classes and functionalities.

4. In the `ToggleInputActionManager` class, add a nested class called `ButtonPressedActions` and include the following variables:

```
    [System.Serializable]
    public class ButtonPressedActions
    {
        public string actionName;
        public InputActionReference actionReference;

        public UnityEvent actionEvent = new
            UnityEvent();
        public bool showPressedAndReleasedEvents;
        public UnityEvent pressedEvent = new
            UnityEvent();
        public UnityEvent releasedEvent = new
            UnityEvent();
```

5. The `ButtonPressedActions` class holds information about each button's name, input action reference, associated events, and an optional Boolean to determine whether pressed and released events should be shown. This class provides a structured way to store and manage specific button actions, including their input actions and events, without the need for separate variables for each button. Also, add the following variables below the nested `ButtonPressedActions` class:

```
    public InputActionAsset actionAsset;
    public ButtonPressedActions[] actions;
```

The script includes two important variables: the `inputActionAsset` and an array of `ButtonPressedActions`. `InputActionAsset` represents all the defined input actions for the game, while the array of `ButtonPressedActions` holds the specific button actions and their associated events. These public variables provide the necessary references and data structures to manage and handle input actions effectively in the game.

6. Create an `Awake()` method and add the following code.

```
for (int i = 0; i < actions.Length; i++)
{
    if (actions[i].actionReference != null)
    {
        actions[i].actionReference.action
            .performed += OnButtonPerformed;
        actions[i].actionReference.action
            .started += OnButtonPressed;
        actions[i].actionReference.action
            .canceled += OnButtonReleased;
    }
}
```

In the `Awake()` method, a `for` loop iterates through the `actions` array and assigns event handlers for the performed, started, and canceled events of each input action. This enables us to listen and respond to button interactions effectively within the `ButtonPressedActions` array.

7. Create an `OnDestroy()` method and add the following code:

```
for (int i = 0; i < actions.Length; i++)
{
    actions[i].actionReference.action
        .started -= OnButtonPressed;
    actions[i].actionReference.action
        .canceled -= OnButtonReleased;
}
```

In the `OnDestroy()` method, we take the necessary step of removing the event handlers to prevent memory leaks when the script is destroyed. By unsubscribing from the started and canceled events of each input action, we ensure that no references are retained, allowing the script to be cleaned up properly. This practice is crucial for maintaining memory efficiency and avoiding potential issues that can arise from lingering event subscriptions.

8. In the `OnEnable` method, enable the input actions for all the defined actions:

```
for (int i = 0; i < actions.Length; i++)
{
    actions[i].actionReference.action.Enable();
}
```

9. In the `OnDisable` method, disable the input actions for all the defined actions:

```
for (int i = 0; i < actions.Length; i++)
{
    actions[i].actionReference.action
```

```
                .Disable();
        }
```

The `OnEnable()` and `OnDisable()` methods play a crucial role in enabling and disabling the input actions. Enabling the input actions ensures that the button actions respond to user input, enabling interaction and triggering associated events. On the other hand, disabling the input actions prevents any response, effectively pausing the button actions and halting event triggering. These methods provide control over the responsiveness of button interactions, allowing you to enable or disable them as needed.

10. Create three new methods, called `OnButtonPerformed`, `OnButtonPressed`, and `OnButtonReleased`, and apply the following code to the respective methods:

```
    private void OnButtonPerformed(
        InputAction.CallbackContext context)
    {
        for (int i = 0; i < actions.Length; i++)
        {
            if (actions[i].actionReference != null &&
                actions[i].actionReference.action ==
                context.action)
            {
                actions[i].actionEvent.Invoke();
            }
        }
    }
    private void OnButtonPressed(
        InputAction.CallbackContext context)
    {
        for (int i = 0; i < actions.Length; i++)
        {
            if (actions[i].actionReference != null &&
                actions[i].actionReference.action ==
                context.action)
            {
                if (actions[i]
                    .showPressedAndReleasedEvents)
                {
                    actions[i].pressedEvent.Invoke();
                }
            }
        }
    }

    private void OnButtonReleased(
```

```
            InputAction.CallbackContext context)
        {
            for (int i = 0; i < actions.Length; i++)
            {
                if (actions[i].actionReference != null &&
                    actions[i].actionReference.action ==
                    context.action)
                {
                    if (actions[i]
                        .showPressedAndReleasedEvents)
                    {
                        actions[i].releasedEvent.Invoke();
                    }
                }
            }
        }
    }
```

This script provides three essential methods for handling button events: `OnButtonPerformed()` triggers the general action event associated with the performed input action, `OnButtonPressed()` invokes the button press event when the `showPressedAndReleasedEvents` option is enabled, and `OnButtonReleased()` triggers the button release event under the same condition. By iterating through the `actions` array and appropriately invoking the associated events based on the input action that triggered the callback, this script enables efficient management of button interactions you create with the Input System.

The `ToggleInputActionManager` script simplifies the management of button actions in your game or application, enabling interactive and responsive experiences. With this script, you can easily handle various input actions and trigger associated events, resulting in engaging user interactions.

11. Save the script and go to the `ToggleInputActionManager` script component in **Inspector**.
12. Under **Actions**, click +.
13. In the action reference slot, add the `XRI Left Hand Interaction Y Button` asset.
14. Click + for **Action Event**.
15. In the reference slot, add the `left-hand Ray` GO.
16. Choose the **Activate Ray** function from the `ToggleRay` script in the **Function** menu.
17. For **Released Event**, click +.
18. Add the `left-hand Ray` GO to the reference slot.
19. Choose the **Deactivate Ray** function from the `ToggleRay` script in the **Function** menu.

20. Repeat *steps 2–10* using the `XRI Right Hand Interaction` for the **B** button. In the action reference slot, use the `right-hand Ray` GO for **Action Event** and **Released Event**.

We now have our ray interactors set up so that we can toggle them on and off while also being able to use the direct interactor for both of our hands. We can toggle them on or off by pressing down the **Y** button for the left hand and the **B** button for the right hand to activate the ray and interact with objects as normal. When we release our fingers from the **Y** or **B** button, then the ray will deactivate.

In the next section, we will add the ability to increase the speed of our VR rig with a button press.

Making the VR rig run

Being able to make your VR rig run or increase speed to sprint is crucial in Unity VR experiences because it provides a more immersive and engaging experience for the user. In VR, movement is a critical component of the experience, and the ability to move quickly and fluidly can greatly enhance the sense of presence and realism.

By increasing the speed of the VR rig, you can simulate running or sprinting, which can be especially useful in games that involve exploration or fast-paced action. For example, in a VR game where the player is running away from enemies or racing against other players, being able to sprint can add a new level of excitement and challenge to the game.

Moreover, the ability to adjust the speed of the VR rig can also help to reduce motion sickness and enhance comfort for the user. If the VR rig is moving too slowly or too quickly, it can cause discomfort or disorientation for the user. Therefore, having control over the speed of the VR rig can help to create a more comfortable and enjoyable experience.

To increase the speed of our VR rig and simulate running, follow these steps:

1. Create a new C# script and name it `SpeedAction`.
2. Open the script and apply the following namespaces to the code:

```
using UnityEngine;
using UnityEngine.XR.Interaction.Toolkit;
```

   The preceding code imports necessary namespaces for Unity and XR Interaction Toolkit.

3. In the `public class SpeedAction` class, add the following variables to the script:

```
    public ContinuousMoveProviderBase moveProvider;
    public float speedBoost;
    public bool superSpeed;
    private float currentSpeed;
```

   Here, we are declaring variables for the script, including a move provider, speed boost, a flag for super speed, and a variable to store the current speed.

4. In the `void Start()` method, add the following code to the script:

   ```
   moveProvider =
   FindObjectOfType<ContinuousMoveProviderBase>();
   currentSpeed = moveProvider.moveSpeed;
   ```

   In the `Start()` method, we find and assign the `ContinuousMoveProviderBase` component in the scene to the `moveProvider` variable, and store its initial move speed in the `currentSpeed` variable.

5. In the `void Update()` method, add the following code to the script:

   ```
   if (superSpeed)
   {
       moveProvider.moveSpeed =
           currentSpeed* speedBoost;
   }
   else
   {
       moveProvider.moveSpeed = currentSpeed;
   }
   ```

   In the `Update()` method, we check whether the `superSpeed` flag is `true`. If it is, we set the move speed of `moveProvider` to `currentSpeed`, effectively increasing the speed. If the flag is `false`, we set the move speed to a default value of `1f`, representing normal speed.

6. Create a method called `public void SpeedOn()` and add the following code to the script:

   ```
   superSpeed = true;
   ```

   The `SpeedOn()` method sets the `superSpeed` flag to `true`, enabling the super speed effect.

7. Create a method called `public void SpeedOff()` and add the following code to the script:

   ```
   superSpeed = false;
   ```

   The `SpeedOff()` method sets the `superSpeed` flag to `false`, disabling the super speed effect.

8. Save the code.
9. Add the `SpeedAction` script to our `XR Origin` GO.
10. Set the speed boost value to `3`.
11. Open the `XRI Default Input Actions` asset menu.
12. For `XRI Left Hand Interactions`, create a new action and name it `Left Thumbstick Press`.
13. Set the action type to **Button**.
14. For the path, use `Thumbstick Clicked` for the left XR controller.

15. Go to `VRHandInteractionsManager` component.
16. Under **Actions**, press + to create a new action.
17. Set **Action Name** to `Sprinting`.
18. In the action reference, add the `XRI Left Hand Interaction Thumbstick Clicked` input asset reference we just made.
19. Click + for the pressed event.
20. Add the `XR Origin` GO.
21. Set the function for the `SpeedAction` script to **SpeedOn**.
22. Click + for the released event.
23. Add the `XR Origin` GO.
24. Set the function for the `SpeedAction` script to **SpeedOff**.

Now, we have the ability to hold the left thumbstick button down to increase our speed and simulate running, and when we release the thumbstick, we will go back to walking at a normal speed.

In the next section, we will add the ability to make our VR rig jump with a button press.

Making our VR rig jump

Being able to make your VR rig jump in Unity VR experiences can greatly enhance the level of immersion and interactivity for the user.

Jumping is a basic and instinctive human movement that we use in our daily lives, and incorporating it into VR experiences can make the user feel more connected to the virtual environment.

By allowing the VR rig to jump, users can explore and navigate the virtual environment in a more natural and intuitive way, as they would in the real world. This can make the VR experience feel more realistic and engaging and can help to reduce motion sickness, which some users may experience in VR.

In addition, incorporating jumping into VR experiences can provide opportunities for gameplay mechanics and puzzles that are unique to VR. For example, users may need to jump over obstacles or onto platforms to progress through the game or solve puzzles.

To make our VR rig jump with a button press, follow these steps:

1. Create a new C# script and name it `JumpingAction`.
2. Open the script and apply the following namespaces to the code:

```
using UnityEngine;
using UnityEngine.InputSystem;
using UnityEngine.XR.Interaction.Toolkit;
[RequireComponent(typeof(Rigidbody))]
```

The `using` statements at the beginning of the code allow us to access specific Unity libraries and components that we'll be using in our script.

3. In the `JumpingAction` public class, add the following variables to the script:

```
public float jumpForce;
     [SerializeField] private float groundCheckRadius =
        0.5f;
     [SerializeField] private LayerMask groundLayer;
     [SerializeField] private Transform
        groundCheckPoint;
     private Rigidbody _rigidbody;
     public bool jumping;
```

These variables will hold various properties and references that we'll use in our script. The `jumpForce` variable determines the force applied when jumping, `groundCheckRadius` defines the radius for checking whether the character is on the ground, `groundLayer` specifies the layer used to detect ground objects, and `groundCheckPoint` is the transform position from where the ground check is performed. The `_rigidbody` variable will hold a reference to the `Rigidbody` component attached to our VR rig, and `jumping` is a Boolean variable to track whether the character is currently jumping.

4. In the `private void Awake()` method, add the following code to the script:

```
_rigidbody = GetComponent<Rigidbody>();
```

In the `Awake()` method, we retrieve the `Rigidbody` component attached to our VR rig and assign it to the `_rigidbody` variable for later use.

5. Create a method called `private bool IsGrounded()` and add the following code to the script:

```
return Physics.OverlapSphere(
     groundCheckPoint.position,
          groundCheckRadius, groundLayer)
               .Length > 0;
```

The `IsGrounded()` method checks whether the character is touching the ground. It performs an overlap sphere check using `Physics.OverlapSphere()` at the position of `groundCheckPoint` with a radius of `groundCheckRadius`, and returns `true` if any objects in the specified `groundLayer` are detected.

6. Create a method called `public void Jump()` and add the following code to the script:

```
if (IsGrounded())
{
     _rigidbody.AddForce(Vector3.up *
          jumpForce, ForceMode.Impulse);
```

```
            Debug.Log("Jumped!");
        }
```

The `Jump()` method is responsible for making the VR rig jump. It first checks whether the character is on the ground by calling `IsGrounded()`. If the character is on the ground, it applies an upward force to `_rigidbody` using `AddForce()` and logs a debug message.

7. Create a method called `private void OnDrawGizmos()` and add the following code to the script:

```
        if (groundCheckPoint != null)
        {
            Gizmos.color = Color.green;
            Gizmos.DrawWireSphere(
                groundCheckPoint.position,
                    groundCheckRadius);
        }
```

   The `OnDrawGizmos()` method is used to visualize the ground check sphere in the Unity Editor. It draws a wire sphere with a green color at the position of `groundCheckPoint` with a radius of `groundCheckRadius`. This helps us visually inspect the ground detection area while editing the scene in the Unity Editor.

8. Save the code.
9. Add the `JumpingAction` script to our `XR Origin` GO.
10. Set the jump force to `500`, the ground check radius to `0.5`, and the ground layer to `Ground`.
11. Create a new GO as a child of `XR Origin`, and name it `GroundChecker`.
12. Set the **Y** position of `GroundChecker` to `-1`.
13. Add the `GroundChecker` GO to the **Ground Checkpoint** reference slot.
14. Go to the `VRHandInteractionsManager` GO. Press the + button to add a new action to the **Actions** list.
15. Set the action reference to the `A button` for the `XRI Right Hand Interaction` asset.
16. Press the + button for the action event.
17. Add the `XR Origin` to the reference slot.
18. Set the function to the `Jump` function of the `JumpingAction` script.

Now, when we press the **A** button on our right-hand controller, the physics system will apply a force of 500 newtons in the outward direction, propelling our VR rig rigid body attached to our `XR Origin` GO into the air, simulating a jumping action. After a small amount of time, gravity will take over and bring the XR origin back to the ground. The script also includes a checker to determine whether the VR rig is touching the ground or not. If it is, jumping is possible. If it is not, jumping is deactivated.

To activate jumping, we set the ground layer in our `JumpingAction` script to `Ground`. This means that you must choose all the GOs that you intend to use as ground layers for it to work. If you don't have any ground layers chosen as GOs with the layer of `Ground`, you won't be able to activate jumping. This is done to ensure that there are no double or triple jumps. You only get one jump. In order to have that, you have to designate a ground layer, so you're only able to jump when you're touching the ground. If you're not touching the ground, you can't activate the jump.

In the next section, we will add the ability to crouch to decrease the height of our VR rig with a button press.

Making the VR rig crouch

Being able to make your VR rig crouch is great in Unity VR experiences because it adds a new level of immersion and interactivity for the user.

Crouching is a natural movement for humans, and when a user can physically crouch down in a VR experience, it creates a more realistic and engaging experience. For example, if you're playing a first-person shooter game in VR and need to hide behind a wall or object to avoid enemy fire, crouching down in real life to do so will make the experience feel more authentic and immersive.

In addition to adding realism to the experience, crouching in VR also allows for more dynamic gameplay mechanics. For example, in a puzzle game, crouching down may be necessary to see a hidden object or solve a puzzle.

To add a crouching action to our VR rig, follow these steps:

1. Create a new C# script called `CrouchingAction`.
2. Open the script and apply the following namespaces to the code:

```
using System.Collections;
using System.Collections.Generic;
using UnityEngine;
using UnityEngine.XR.Interaction.Toolkit;
[RequireComponent(typeof(SpeedAction))]
[RequireComponent(typeof(Rigidbody))]
```

   Include the necessary namespaces: `System.Collections`, `System.Collections.Generic`, `UnityEngine`, and `UnityEngine.XR.Interaction.Toolkit`. These provide the required classes and functionality for VR development.

3. In the public `CrouchingAction` class, add the following variables to the script:

```
    [Header("Crouching")]
    private float crouchSpeed;
    private float crouchSpeedBoost;
    [Range(0f, 1f)]
```

```
public float crouchSpeedModifier;
public float crouchYScale;
public float startYScale;
public bool isCrouching;
[Header("References")]
public Transform orientation;
public Rigidbody rb;
public ContinuousMoveProviderBase moveProvider;
public SpeedAction speedAction;
private float currentSpeed;
private float currentSpeedBoost;
```

4. In the `private void Awake()` method, add the following code to the script:

```
    rb = GetComponent<Rigidbody>();
    moveProvider = FindObjectOfType
        <ContinuousMoveProviderBase>();
    speedAction = FindObjectOfType<SpeedAction>();
```

In the `private void Awake()` method, assign references to the `rb`, `moveProvider`, and `speedAction` variables using the `GetComponent` and `FindObjectOfType` functions. This ensures the script can access the required components.

5. In the `void Start()` method, add the following code to the script:

```
    currentSpeed = moveProvider.moveSpeed;
    startYScale = transform.localScale.y;
```

In the `void Start()` method, set the `currentSpeed` variable to the initial movement speed of the player obtained from `moveProvider.moveSpeed`. Also, store the initial vertical scale of the player's transform in `startYScale`.

6. In the `void Update()` method, add the following code to the script:

```
    crouchSpeed = moveProvider.moveSpeed *
        crouchSpeedModifier;
    crouchSpeedBoost = speedAction.speedBoost *
        crouchSpeedModifier;
    if (isCrouching)
    {
        Crouched();
    }
    else
    {
        Standing();
    }
```

In the `void Update()` method, update `crouchSpeed` and `crouchSpeedBoost` based on the current movement speed and speed boost, respectively, modified by `crouchSpeedModifier`. Then, check whether the player is crouching and call the appropriate method: `Crouched()` or `Standing()`.

7. Create a method called `public void CrouchDown()` and add the following code to the script:

```
isCrouching = true;
```

Inside the method, set the `isCrouching` flag to `true`, indicating that the player is crouching.

8. Create a method called `public void StandUp()` and add the following code to the script:

```
isCrouching = false;
```

Inside the method, set the `isCrouching` flag to `false`, indicating that the player is standing up.

9. Create a method called `private void Crouched()` and add the following code to the script:

```
transform.localScale = new
    Vector3(transform.localScale.x,
        crouchYScale, transform.localScale.z);
rb.AddForce(Vector3.down * 5f,
    ForceMode.Impulse);
moveProvider.moveSpeed = crouchSpeed;
speedAction.speedBoost = crouchSpeedBoost;
```

This method handles the behavior when the player is crouching. Inside the method, adjust the player's transform's vertical scale to `crouchYScale`, apply a downward force to the `Rigidbody` component, and set the movement speed and speed boost to their crouching values (`crouchSpeed` and `crouchSpeedBoost`).

10. Create a method called `private void Standing()`, and add the following code to the script:

```
transform.localScale = new
    Vector3(transform.localScale.x,
        startYScale, transform.localScale.z);
moveProvider.moveSpeed = currentSpeed;
speedAction.speedBoost = currentSpeedBoost;
```

This method handles the behavior when the player is standing up. Inside the method, restore the player's transform's vertical scale to `startYScale`, and set the movement speed and speed boost to their original values (`currentSpeed` and `currentSpeedBoost`).

11. Save the code.

12. Add the C# script to the `XR Origin` GO.

13. In the `CrouchingAction` script, set the crouch speed modifier to `0.6`. Since we move slower in a crouched position, I arbitrarily chose 60% of our original speed, but you can choose any speed less than the value of the current speed for the crouch speed modifier.
14. Go to the `XRI Default Input Actions` input action asset.
15. For the `XRI LeftHand and RightHand Interaction` action maps, add a new action and name it `thumbstick Pressed`.
16. Set the action type to **Button**.
17. Press the + button to add a binding.
18. For the binding path, go to the `Thumbstick Clicked` action asset for the right-hand XR controller.
19. In our `VRHandInteractionsManager` GO, add a new action in the `Toggle Input Actions Manager` component.
20. In the action reference, add the `thumbstick Pressed` action asset for the `XRI Right Hand Interaction`.
21. Show pressed and released events.
22. For the pressed event, click the + button and add the `XR Origin` GO to it.
23. In the function reference, choose the `Crouched down` function in the `CrouchingAction` script.
24. Add a released event and add the `XR Origin` GO to it.
25. In the function reference, choose the `Stand up` function in the `CrouchingAction` script.

Now that we have this code added to our VR rig and object, we are able to press the right thumbstick down; when we hold it down, our character will crouch down. When we release it, the character will stand up. You will notice that when you move around while you're crouching, you will be able to move about 40% slower or 60% of the speed when you walk or try to run with the speed action. If you want to adjust the speed relative to the crouch, you can use the slider that we added to modify it. We have it set so that when you're crouching, you will move slower than when you're standing up, but you could make modifications as you see fit.

Summary

In this chapter, we enriched the user experience by adding animated hands and unique functionalities such as running, jumping, and crouching. This is just the start of the possibilities for interaction and movement within your virtual worlds. We've also developed an interactive environment by adding functions to toggle between the ray interactors and direct interactors. This opens up a world of actions and reactions within our VR universe. These additions set the groundwork for you to explore and implement even more complex interactions at your own pace. In the next chapter, we'll explore various ways to interact with elements within our virtual world, from triggering animations to play to teleporting from one area of the VR world to another.

16
Triggering Actions in Virtual Reality

We've ventured far and wide in the VR realm, from creating immersive environments to animating lifelike movements, and from mastering C# coding to understanding the Unity input system. Now, we're ready to apply all these skills to design dynamic, interactive experiences in the VR world. In this chapter, we'll focus on constructing a VR rig menu system to control various settings, using triggers to command animations, employing portals for seamless travel between the diverse scenes we've crafted, and harnessing the power of the physics system to create lively bouncing balls such as basketballs.

We will start by creating a VR settings menu that can control the different values we added for our VR rig abilities, including running, jumping, and crouching from *Chapter 15*. We will then move on to triggering our animations from the *Adding animation clips to our timeline* section of *Chapter 13*, enabling the animated experience to play while we're literally in the scene, taking the idea of a 360° video to the next level.

After we learn how to trigger our animations, we will apply that same concept to portals so that we can connect all the virtual projects and scenes we've created thus far into one experience, where we can jump from one scene to the next seamlessly by just walking through a door.

In this chapter, we will cover the following topics:

- Creating a VR rig menu system to control the different settings of our VR rig
- Using triggers to play and pause animation in our VR world
- Utilizing portals to travel between the various scenes we've created in this book
- Utilizing the physics system to create bouncing basketballs

Technical requirements

The complete source code for this chapter can be found at `https://github.com/PacktPublishing/Enhancing-Virtual-Reality-Experiences-with-Unity-2022/tree/main/EnhancingVRExperiencesFullProject/Assets/_VRProjectAssets/Scenes/Chapter_16`.

Creating and configuring a VR settings menu

Settings menus are crucial for VR experiences and any experience made in Unity because if you're not able to control the settings at runtime, you're often stuck in developer mode instead of exploration mode. Quite often, you want to be able to modify different abilities within the VR world that don't require you to take off the headset, and creating a VR settings menu allows you to do that. More importantly, you can add fun little elements that allow you to improve or obscure the VR experience, because modifying the way we navigate in the world is a whole experience in and of itself.

By the end of this section, you will have a VR settings menu that accesses the run, jump, and crouch abilities, and you can control those different abilities using sliders on a mini screen. We will attach this menu screen to a menu button on our left VR controller that we can toggle on and off easily with the press of a button. This whole experience combines the use of UI element code, custom input actions, and the previous assets we created.

To create a VR rig menu that controls the jump, crouch, and speed actions, follow these steps:

1. Create a new GO as a child of the `XR Origin` GO.
2. Name it `VRRigMenuManager`.
3. Create a new canvas as a child of `VRRigMenuManager` and name it `VRMenuCanvas`.
4. For the `VRMenuCanvas` GO, set the **X** position to `0`, the **Y** position to `2.391`, and the **Z** position to `0`.
5. Set **Width** to `1290` and **Height** to `1845`.
6. Set the **XYZ** scale to `0.0015`.
7. Set **Render Mode** in the `Canvas` component to **World Space**.
8. Disable **Graphic Raycaster**.
9. Add a `Track Device Graphic Raycaster` component (**Add Component** | search for - `Track Device Graphic Raycaster`).
10. Add a panel as a child of `VRMenuCanvas` and name it `VRMenuPanel`.
11. Set **Rect Transform** to **stretch**.
12. Set the **RGBA** values to `0`, `0`, `0`, and `215`.

Now that we have our `VRRigMenu` set up, it's time to add some sliders so that we can eventually use them to control the values of our actions in our `XR Origin` GO.

Creating sliders for our VR settings menu

To create sliders for our `VRRigMenu`, follow these steps:

1. Create a slider as a child of `VRMenuPanel` and name it `Speed Slider`.
2. Set the **XYZ** scale to `4.5`.
3. Set the **X** position to `0`.
4. Set the **Y** position to `-160`.
5. Set **Width** to `160` and **Height** to `20`.
6. Set **Direction** to **Left to Right**.
7. Set the minimum value to `1` and the maximum value to `3`.
8. Disable **Whole Numbers**.
9. Create another slider and call it `CrouchSpeedSlider`.
10. Set the **XYZ** scale to `4.5`.
11. Set the **X** position to `0`.
12. Set the **Y** position to `-498`.
13. Set **Width** to `160` and **Height** to `20`.
14. Set **Direction** to **Left to Right**.
15. Set the minimum value to `0` and the maximum value to `1`.
16. Create another slider and name it `JumpForceSlider`.
17. Set the **XYZ** scale to `4.5`.
18. Set the **X** position to `-25`.
19. Set the **Y** position to `190`.
20. Set **Width** to `160` and **Height** to `20`.
21. Set **Direction** to **Left to Right**.
22. Set the minimum value to `250` and the maximum value to `1000`.
23. Enable **Whole Numbers**.

After adding the sliders, we will add some text so that when you open up the VR rig, you will know which slider is associated with which values you will be changing.

Adding text indicators for the settings menu sliders

To add text indicators for our `VRRigMenu` sliders, follow these steps:

1. Create a TextMeshPro text in the `VRMenuCanvas` GO as a child of `VRMenuPanel` (**VRRigMenuManager | VRMenuCanvas | VRMenuPanel**), and name it `VRMenuTitle` (see *Figure 16.1*).
2. Set the **Y** position to `689`.
3. Set **Width** to `1000` and **Height** to `225`.
4. Set **Text Input** to `VRMenuSettings`.
5. Enable **Auto-Size**.
6. Create another TextMeshPro text, and name it `JumpText`.
7. Set the **Y** position to `345`.
8. Set **Width** to `803` and **Height** to `150`.
9. Set **Text Input** to `Jump Force`.
10. Enable **Auto-Size**.
11. Create another TextMeshPro text, and name it `Speed Text`.
12. Set the **Y** position to `-11`.
13. Set **Width** to `803` and **Height** to `150`.
14. Set **Text Input** to `Sprint Speed`.
15. Enable **Auto-Size**.
16. Create another TextMeshPro text, and name it `Crouch Text`.
17. Set the **Y** position to `-376`.
18. Set **Width** to `803` and **Height** to `150`.
19. Set **Text Input** to `Crouch Speed`.
20. Enable **Auto-Size**.

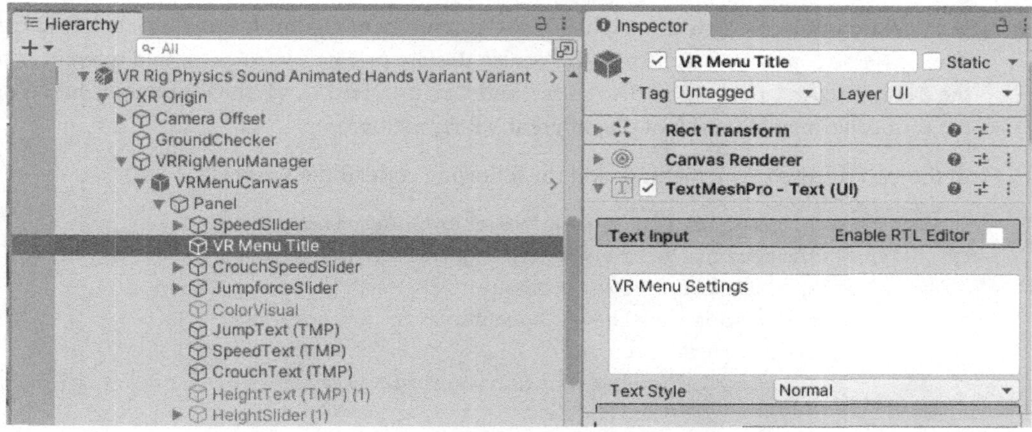

Figure 16.1 – A textbox in the VRRigMenu Hierarchy pane

Now that we have our menu set up and our sliders ready to go, it's time to create a C# script that allows us to use the sliders to modify the values of our jump, crouch, and speed values on our VR rig. We will do that in the next section.

Controlling the jump, crouch, and speed values with sliders

To create a C# script that controls the jump, crouch, and speed values with sliders, follow these steps:

1. Create a C# script called `VRRigMenuSettings`.
2. Add it to our `XR Origin` GO.
3. Open the C# script and add the following namespaces:

```
using UnityEngine;
using UnityEngine.UI;
```

   We include the necessary namespaces for Unity and Unity UI to access the required classes and components.

4. In the `public class VRRigMenuSettings` class, add the following code to the script:

```
    public Slider jumpForce;
    public Slider speedBoost;
    public Slider crouchSpeed;
    private JumpingAction jumpingAction;
    private SpeedAction speedAction;
    private CrouchingAction crouchingAction;
```

We declare public `Slider` variables to hold references to the sliders for `jumpForce`, `speedBoost`, and `crouchSpeed`. We also declare private variables to hold references to the `JumpingAction`, `SpeedAction`, and `CrouchingAction` components based on the scripts we made for each of the different VR rig actions.

5. In the `void Start()` method, add the following code to the script:

```
jumpingAction = GetComponent<JumpingAction>();
jumpForce.value = jumpingAction.jumpForce;
speedAction = GetComponent<SpeedAction>();
speedBoost.value = speedAction.speedBoost;
crouchingAction =
    GetComponent<CrouchingAction>();
crouchSpeed.value =
    crouchingAction.crouchSpeedModifier;
```

In the `Start()` method, we assign the appropriate component references to the private variables. These variables are from the `Jump`, `Speed`, and `Crouch` action classes that we created for our VR rig in *Chapter 15*. We also set the initial values of the sliders to match the current values of the corresponding actions.

6. In the `void Update()` method, add the following code to the script:

```
jumpingAction.jumpForce = jumpForce.value;
speedAction.speedBoost = speedBoost.value;
crouchingAction.crouchSpeedModifier =
    crouchSpeed.value;
```

In the `Update()` method, we continuously update the values of the `jumpForce`, `speedBoost`, and `crouchSpeedModifier` properties of the corresponding actions with the current values from the sliders.

7. Save the code.
8. Go to the `VRRigMenuSettings` script component and select `XR Origin` GO.
9. Add the jump force slider to the `Jump Force` reference slot.
10. Add the speed slider to the `Speed Boost` reference slot.
11. Add the crouch speed slider to the `Crouch Speed` reference slot.

With these steps completed, we can pair our sliders with the references for jump, speed, and crouch. If we test it out, we can look at the menu and use the ray interactor on the hand controller to move the slider, increasing or decreasing the values. Once you modify these values and perform different actions, you'll notice that the values for *Jump Force*, *Speed Boost*, and *Crouch Speed* have changed, based on the values you selected.

Adding an on/off toggle to the VR settings menu

Now that we have completed the VR settings menu, let's learn how to toggle it on and off so that we can use it when needed and hide it when not required. Follow these steps to create a C# script that we can use to toggle the `VR Menu` on and off:

1. Create a C# script called `VRRigMenuManager`.
2. Open the script and add the following code:

```
using UnityEngine;
```

3. In the `public class VRRigMenuManager` class, add the following code to the script:

```
    public GameObject menu;
    public Transform head;
    public float spawnDistance = 2;
```

   We declare public variables to hold references to the `VRMenu` GO, the head transform, and the spawn distance.

4. Create a new method called `public void ToggleMenu()` and add the following code to the script:

```
        menu.SetActive(!menu.activeInHierarchy);
        menu.transform.position = head.position +
            new Vector3(head.forward.x, 0,
                head.forward.z).normalized *
                    spawnDistance;
        menu.transform.LookAt(new Vector3(
            head.position.x,
                menu.transform.position.y,
                    head.position.z));
        menu.transform.forward *= -1;
```

   This method is responsible for toggling the `VRMenu` on and off. When called, it will activate or deactivate the menu GO based on its current state. It also sets the position and rotation of the menu relative to the head position, creating a spawn distance in front of the user.

5. Save the code.
6. Create a new empty GO, name it `VRRigMenu`, and add the `VR Rig Physics Sound Animated Hands` prefab to it.
7. Add the `VRRigMenuManager` code to the `VRRigMenu` GO.
8. Add the main camera GO (that is, a child of the camera offset and the `XR Origin` GO) to the head transform slot.
9. Add the `VRRigMenuCanvas` GO to the **Menu** slot for the menu.

10. Go to the `VRHandInteractionsManager` GO.
11. Create a new action reference in the **Actions** menu of `VRHandInteractionManager`.
12. Set the action reference to **Custom Inputs | Menu Button**.
13. Create a new **Action Event**.
14. Drag the `VRRigMenuManager` GO into the reference slot.
15. Set the function to **Toggle Menu** from the `VRRigMenuManager` script.

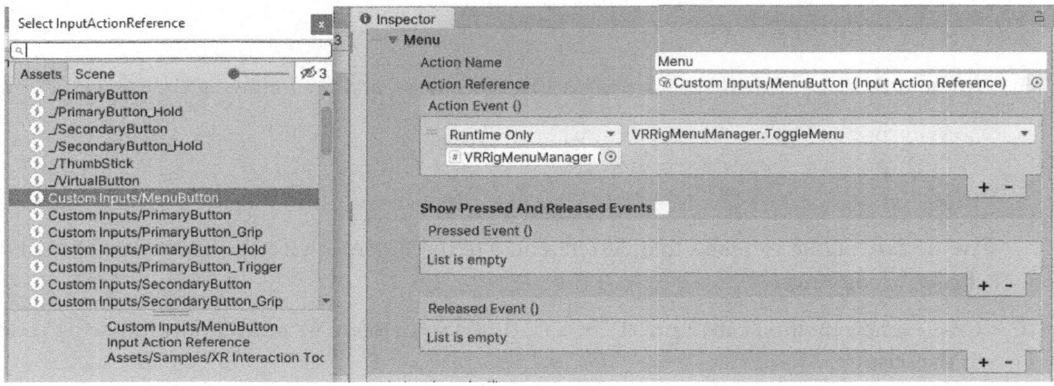

Figure 16.2 – Setting up the menu button in the VRRigMenuManager script component

With this setup, we can now open up a menu that appears 2 meters away from our head, regardless of its location. This menu allows us to change the force of our jump, the speed of our crouch while walking and running, and the speed of our running when we're standing. This gives us more flexibility when we're in the experience to modify it, based on what we want to do in the virtual world. In a nutshell, we can control how high we jump and how fast we move by opening up the menu and modifying the values of the slider.

In the next section, we will learn how to trigger our animated show within the virtual world that we will navigate again. This should be familiar to you because we did something similar in the *Recording with the Recorder* section of *Chapter 14*, where we triggered the animation to play while we recorded the animation to a video file.

Triggering animations in the scene

One of the best things about creating animations is that you can reuse the content you create over and over again. However, animations are often created just for videos and don't exist anywhere else. This will change with VR, as we can now utilize the same animated assets we created for videos and experience them in VR. This is possible because VR uses real-time rendering, which allows us to walk around animated scenes and view them from any angle we desire. Triggering animated scenes is especially fun for animators and those interested in visual storytelling because it changes the way stories can be told and experienced.

In this section, we will cover how to reuse our collider controller script with a new collider that we can use as a portal. We will step into the portal and trigger the animation to play. When we step out of the portal, the animation will pause. This is a simple implementation, but it can be expanded on with multiple animated scenes and other content.

To create a portal to trigger our animated scene, follow these steps:

1. Go to the `AnimatedShow` GO, and select the `AnimatedShowTimeline` GO.
2. Disable play on the timeline in **Playable Director**.
3. In the timeline, create a new `Activation Track`.
4. Set the previous GO as the reference to `Activation Track`.
5. Place the `VFX` GO into the previous GO as a child.
6. Deactivate the previous GO.
7. Go to the `AnimatedShowTimeline` GO.
8. Create a new empty GO and name it `Animation Trigger`.
9. In the `Animation Trigger` GO, add a capsule collider.
10. Set the center **Y** position to `1`.
11. Set the radius to `.5`.
12. Set the height to `2`.
13. Set **Is Trigger** to **true**.

Now, let's learn how to trigger the animated show while in the VR scene by following these steps:

1. Add a `Collider Controller` script from our script library.
2. Add an `Enter Event` and choose the `AnimatedShowTimeline` GO.
3. Set the function to the **Playable Director Play** function.
4. Add an `Exit Event`.
5. Add the `AnimatedShowTimeline` GO.
6. Set **Playable Director** to the **Play the Pause** function.
7. Add a cylinder as a child of `Animation Trigger`.
8. Give it an `orange-transparent` material.
9. Set the **Y** position to `1`.

When we walk into the capsule collider of `Animation Trigger`, it will start playing our animated show. We have it set to play only when we enter the collider, and it will continue to play as long as we stay on the collider. If we leave the collider, it will trigger the exit function, which will pause the animated show. In the *Triggering events with colliders* section in *Chapter 8*, we used colliders in place of button presses to trigger Unity events. This is exactly what we did here. Not only can you trigger simple functions but you can also trigger entire animated sequences by standing in a space and watching what happens. In many ways, you get a front-row seat to the animated experiences that you created earlier in this book.

In the next section, we will revisit our portals, and we will use them to go from the art gallery to the other scenes we have created.

Adding portals for navigation

As we saw in the *Creating portals with colliders and events* section in *Chapter 8*, where we created our portals to move between different scenes and areas of our map, they are very powerful tools for navigation. If you want to go to the other side of an area or to a completely different location, such as walking into a building or walking out of a building, you can do that by walking into a portal and being placed exactly where you need to be.

We will use the portals we created in the *Creating portals with colliders and events* section in *Chapter 8* and expand on them so that they can be used within our VR world, allowing us to bounce from one aspect of the VR experience to another. We will start by adding a portal to go to our art gallery. After we finish the art gallery, we will move on to the VR theater and then to the demo room scene that we worked on in the first half of this book. Essentially, we will put all of the scenes we've worked on in this book into one VR experience that can be navigated seamlessly.

The first portal that we will make will lead to our art gallery. Think of this part of the experience as simply going to an art gallery with your friends, something that you would normally do in the US on the first Fridays or last Thursdays of the month. Maybe you want to draw something on the wall or hang up a picture. This is a perfect way to create an experience that is subtle and mundane but very effective when it comes to VR development, as the technical aspects of it meet the implementation and applications of the technology. With the power of VR in your living room, you can do something that would otherwise cost you gas, money, and time to do in the real world.

Creating a portal between the art gallery and the virtual world

To create a portal to go back and forth between the art gallery and the virtual world, follow these steps:

1. In **Build Settings**, add the art gallery scene to the **Scenes in Build** section.
2. Open the `Virtual World` scene.
3. Add another `portal_scene` variant prefab to the `Portals` GO.
4. Set the **X** position to `-16.9`, the **Y** position to `0`, and the **Z** position to `42.3`.
5. Set the **Y** rotation to `-90`.

6. In the `Portal Scene Manager` component, set the next scene to the art gallery string, matching the name and case exactly as it is in the **Scenes in Build** menu. In my case, the `ArtGallery` scene is named `12_01_Art Gallery`.
7. Open the art gallery scene.
8. Create a new empty GO as a child of the art gallery GO called `Portals`.
9. Add the `portal_scene` variant prefab to the `Portals` GO.
10. Set the **X** position to `-0.5`, the **Y** position to `0`, and the **Z** position to `12`.
11. Set the **Y** rotation to `90`.
12. Add the `VirtualWorld` string that matches the name of the desired scene in the **Scenes in Build** menu to the `Next Scene` reference slot in the `Portal Scene Manager` component. My virtual world scene is labeled `15_VirtualWorld`.

With this setup, we are able to go back and forth between the virtual world scene and the art gallery by walking through the portal in each scene, respectively, to go to the next scene.

We can now do the same thing again but apply it to the VR theater scene that we worked on in the *Building a VR theater experience* section of *Chapter 14*. This simulates going to a movie theater in VR, where instead of having to go to a physical movie theater, you can go to a theater in VR and still see a big screen, and then when you're done, you can just leave the theater and go to another area of the VR world.

Creating a portal between the theatre scene and the virtual world

To trigger a portal to go to our VR theater scene, follow these steps:

1. Find the animated show scene that we created in *Chapter 14*, and rename it `Virtual World`.
2. Open **Build Settings**, and add the `Virtual World` scene we just renamed to the **Scenes in Build** section.
3. Go to the VR theater room scene that we created in *Chapter 14*, and add that to the **Scenes in Build** section.
4. In the `Virtual World` scene, disable the animated show timeline by turning off **Play on Awake** and **Playable Director** because we currently do not need the animated show animation playing in our VR scene, since we will be playing the animation on a theater screen instead.
5. Create a new empty GO named `Portals`.
6. Add a `portal_scene` variant prefab from the `Prefabs` folder as a child of the `Portals` GO.
7. Set the **X** position to `-92`, the **Y** position to `0`, and the **Z** position to `43`.
8. Set the **Y** rotation to `-90`.
9. In the `Portal Scene Manager` component, set the player tag to **Player**.

10. Set the next scene to the VR theater room string. Mine is labeled `VRTheaterRoom`.
11. Open the `VRTheaterRoom` scene.
12. Set the `Theater` GO in the `VRTheaterRoom` scene to `1.66` in the **X**, **Y**, and **Z** scales.
13. Create a new empty GO and name it `Portals`.
14. Add a `portal_scene` variant prefab.
15. Set the **X** position to `13.56`, the **Y** position to `2.78`, and the **Z** position to `-5.06`.
16. In the `Portal Scene Manager` component, set the next scene to the string for the `Virtual World` scene.
17. Set the player tag to **Player**.

Now, we are able to go to the theater room by walking through the portal in the `Virtual World` scene, and then if we want to go back to the `Virtual World` scene, we can walk through the portal in the theater room to go back to the virtual world.

The last portal that we will make is going to be our demo room. This takes us back to *Chapters 2–9* in the first half of the book, where we worked on our demo room so that we could test out different functions and features. Now, we can revisit this by connecting the functions and features with the implementations of the virtual world. Say you have another implementation that you want to try out. You could go to the demo room to try it out, and then you could go back to the VR scenes and worlds that you created, such as the art gallery or the theater, which are already baked in and completed, to have a nice balance of experimentation and implementation.

Creating a portal between the demo room and the virtual world

To create a portal to go back and forth between the `DemoRoom` scene and the virtual world, follow these steps:

1. Take the `DemoRoom` scene that we had in *Chapter 8*, and add it to the **Scenes in Build** menu if you haven't already.
2. In the `DemoRoom` scene, create a new empty GO named `Portals`.
3. Add a `portal_scene` variant prefab as a child of the `Portals` GO.
4. Set the **X** position to `0`, the **Y** position to `0`, and the **Z** position to `-4`.
5. Set the **Y** rotation to `90`.
6. In the `Next Scene` reference slot, add the string for the `Virtual World` scene.
7. Open the `Virtual World` scene.
8. Add another `portal_scene` variant to the `Portals` GO.
9. Set the **X** position to `50`, the **Y** position to `0`, and the **Z** position to `42.3`.

10. Set the **Y** rotation to `-90`.
11. In the `Next Scene` reference slot, add the string for the `DemoRoom` scene. Mine is labeled `DemoRoomScene`.

With this setup, we are now able to go from the `Virtual World` scene to the `DemoRoom` scene and back to the `Virtual World` scene, just like we did with the art gallery and the theater room.

In the next section, we will learn how to use triggers and code with colliders to make a bouncing ball. This may be a simple implementation, but to make it feel as realistic and natural as possible is actually a feat in and of itself.

Creating and controlling a bouncing basketball

Creating a bouncing ball requires a variety of different systems in Unity. Whether it's the physics system, the C system, the scripting render pipeline, the animation system, or even the XR interaction toolkit, all of these things have to work together with your coordination in order to have a successfully bouncing ball that you can dribble down the sidewalk. This is a very simple implementation, but it's very effective because through this, you can add different object-to-object interactions, and you can make them continuously and directly interact with objects using your hand controllers. Bouncing a ball may appear deceptively simple, yet in the realm of VR, it proves to be a challenging endeavor. As we strive to simulate real-world physics within the virtual realm, we come to appreciate the intricate coordination required to achieve realistic ball bouncing. Often taken for granted in reality, the interaction between objects with different materials and the resulting ball bounce demand heightened attention and skill in VR.

For this project, we will cover making an actual 3D object of a ball instead of having to download one. We will first make a simple ball object, and then we'll create C# code that we can use for the ball that utilizes the physics system and the XR interaction toolkit, as well as a variety of other elements of the Unity game engine. After that, we can go out and test it and try to improve our coordination so that we can become skilled VR basketball dribblers.

Creating a basketball object

To create a basketball in our scene, follow these steps:

1. Create an empty GO and name it `basketball`.
2. Add a `Sphere Collider` component.
3. Set **Radius** to `0.2`.
4. Add a `Rigidbody` component.
5. Set **Interpolate** to **Interpolate** to have a smooth simulation of motion when the basketball GO moves during a physics simulation.

6. Set **Collision Detection** to **Continuous Dynamic**. This will provide a more realistic bouncing and hand interaction when interacting with the hand controller and the surfaces it collides with.
7. Set the mass to `1.5`.
8. Add a sphere as a child of the `basketball` GO.
9. Set the **X**, **Y**, and **Z** scale of the sphere to `0.4`.
10. Remove the sphere collider.
11. Add an `orange_standard` material.
12. Create a new empty GO as a child of the basketball and name it `attach point`.
13. Set the **Y** position to `0.2`.
14. Set the **XYZ** scale of the sphere to `0.4`.

Figure 16.3 – A basketball with the orange_standard material applied to the MeshRenderer

With the basketball created, we can now create C# code that can handle the functions of the bouncing ball so that we can utilize it in our dribbling experience.

Controlling the bounce of our basketball object

To create a C# script that controls the bouncing of the ball, follow these steps:

1. Create a C# script called `Basketball`.
2. Attach it to the `basketball` GO.
3. Open the script and apply the following namespaces:

```
using UnityEngine;
using UnityEngine.XR.Interaction.Toolkit;
```

We include the necessary namespaces for Unity and the XR Interaction Toolkit to access the required classes and components.

4. In `public class Basketball class`, add the following code to the script:

```
public float forceMultiplier = 10f;
public float maxVelocity = 10f;
public float dribbleThreshold = 0.1f;
public float bounceThreshold = 0.2f;
public float bounceMultiplier = 0.8f;
public AudioClip bounceSound;
private XRGrabInteractable grabInteractable;
private Rigidbody rb;
private AudioSource audioSource;
```

We declare public variables to control the behavior of the ball, such as the force applied to dribbling, the maximum velocity, and the thresholds for dribbling and bouncing. We also declare private variables to hold references to the `XRGrabInteractable` component, the `Rigidbody` component, and the `AudioSource` component.

5. In the `private void Start()` method, add the following code to the script:

```
    grabInteractable =
        GetComponent<XRGrabInteractable>();
    rb = GetComponent<Rigidbody>();
    audioSource = GetComponent<AudioSource>();
```

In the `Start()` method, we assign the appropriate component references to the private variables.

6. In the `private void Update()` method, add the following code to the script:

```
    if (grabInteractable.isSelected)
    {
        // Dribble the basketball
        Vector3 velocity = rb.velocity;
        float verticalVelocity = velocity.y;
        float horizontalVelocity =
            Mathf.Sqrt(velocity.x * velocity.x +
                velocity.z * velocity.z);
        float speed =
            Mathf.Sqrt(horizontalVelocity *
                horizontalVelocity +
                    verticalVelocity *
                        verticalVelocity);
        if (speed < dribbleThreshold)
        {
            rb.AddForce(transform.up *
                forceMultiplier,
                    ForceMode.Impulse);
```

```
        }
    }
```

In the `Update()` method, we check whether the ball is currently grabbed. If it is, we calculate the speed of the ball and check whether it is below the dribble threshold. If it is, we add an upward force to the ball to simulate dribbling.

7. Create a new method called `private void OnCollisionEnter(Collision collision)` and add the following code to the script:

```
        float force =
            collision.relativeVelocity.magnitude *
                bounceMultiplier;
        if (force > bounceThreshold)
        {
            rb.AddForce(collision.contacts[0].normal *
                force, ForceMode.Impulse);
            audioSource.PlayOneShot(bounceSound);
        }
```

This method is called when the ball collides with another object. We calculate the force based on the relative velocity of the collision and apply a bounce force to the ball if it exceeds the bounce threshold. We also play a bounce sound using the `AudioSource` component.

8. In the `private void FixedUpdate()` method, add the following code to the script:

```
        if (rb.velocity.magnitude > maxVelocity)
        {
            rb.velocity = rb.velocity.normalized *
                maxVelocity;
        }
```

In the `FixedUpdate()` method, we check whether the magnitude of the ball's velocity exceeds the maximum velocity. If it does, we normalize the velocity vector and scale it to the maximum velocity to limit the ball's speed.

9. Save the code and go back to the `basketball` GO.
10. Add an audio source to the `basketball` GO.
11. Set the spatial blend to `1`.
12. Set the minimum distance to `0.4`.
13. Set the maximum distance to `2`.
14. For the bounce sound, add the `45_landing_01` audio clip.

So, when you open up the scene and add the bouncing ball, all you have to do is grab the ball with the grip button. Then, when you swing your arm down, you can release the grip button and the ball will bounce, hit the ground, and then come back up. All you have to do is press the grip button again and you will be able to hold the ball.

We covered a lot in this chapter, including creating a VR menu, triggering animation, adding portals and going from scene to scene, and bouncing a basketball. These are the many different interactions that you can trigger with simple grip and trigger presses, as well as by using code that utilizes colliders. In many ways, we use the same approach and implementation for each interaction, but we apply it in different ways and get different results. As a VR developer, utilizing these strengths and focusing on the creative aspects will take you very far.

Summary

The magic of VR truly comes alive as we bring in trigger interactions to animate our VR world. With a simple trigger, you can summon a VR menu, set off animated sequences, or even whisk yourself away through portals to different corners of your virtual universe. One of our more whimsical achievements was creating a bouncing basketball. As simple as a bouncing basketball sounds, this opens up numerous fun and interactive experiences for the user, enhancing their coordination and engagement with the VR world around them. At this point, your project may seem hefty, but think of it as a treasure trove of assets, ready for you to use and create experiences that would have otherwise taken much longer.

In the next chapter, we will conclude our projects by implementing a system to destroy virtual objects with projectiles, adding impact with various particle effects.

17
Destroying Objects in Virtual Reality

Even though we are not solely focused on making video games in VR, we're concentrating on creating experiences in general. Having the ability to manipulate destruction and destroy buildings is a valuable asset because, just as much as people enjoy building things, they also like tearing them apart and recreating them into something else. Even if you want to create something that allows you to make destruction less destructive through VR, implementing a destruction system into those experiences can take you very far.

Mastering the nuances of dismantling virtual GOs, particularly in Unity, is an intricate art. Efficiently creating and erasing objects, while ensuring their seamless integration into the experience, paves the way for captivating virtual realities. While the act of destroying objects may seem straightforward—employing a basic method to eliminate the object—it's the strategic application of this method within diverse coding contexts that brings the magic to life. Users should experience fluid transitions without waiting for object removals; it should feel intuitive, occurring before they even contemplate it. Immersing someone in a VR setting, where objects actively respond to their applied force, exemplifies the zenith of destruction capabilities.

In this chapter, we'll focus on creating weapons and projectiles that can apply force in a variety of different ways. After we apply those forces, we'll be able to interact with GOs and provide different visual effects that can give the illusion of objects hitting and interacting with things, such as impact effects and sound effects. We will create projectiles that have a variety of different properties that interact with a variety of different objects that we can define. Then, we'll move on to destroying those GOs. We can implement a "one code fits all" destruction system where a projectile automatically destroys something, or we could give our virtual objects hit points so that it takes a certain amount of hits from certain projectiles and weapons and interactions to destroy them. Having this variability is great because you don't want everything to be a one-size-fits-all. You need some variability and some variation in that. We can accomplish this by approaching it modularly, similar to the `BasicInputActionManager` script in the *Triggering events with input actions* section of *Chapter 8* and the `ToggleInputActionManager` script in the *Adding an input manager* section in *Chapter 15*, where you only need one or two scripts that can do so many different things depending on how you utilize them.

In this chapter, we will cover the following topics:

- Creating objects with ProBuilder and Polybrush
- Adding particle effects and projectiles that can be used to destroy virtual objects.
- Making a virtual world that is completely destructible

We will start by creating a grenade that can provide destructive capabilities in our virtual scene. When the grenade is initiated, it will apply force in all directions to create a realistic explosion effect.

Technical requirements

The complete source code for this chapter can be found at `https://github.com/PacktPublishing/Enhancing-Virtual-Reality-Experiences-with-Unity-2022/tree/main/EnhancingVRExperiencesFullProject/Assets/_VRProjectAssets/Scenes/Chapter_17`.

Creating a grenade

Our first project is creating a grenade, and we will use it as a way of applying force in a variety of different directions so that there is a broad impact in our VR scene. Creating a grenade requires a strategic approach, specifically because it requires you to grab the grenade, arm it, and then throw it. Once the grenade is thrown and armed, it will detonate after a certain amount of time. If you don't arm the grenade and throw it, it won't detonate. And if you don't throw it soon enough, it can detonate in your hand. Being able to create this experience is unique and can be fun because it allows you to implement something very simple and get a nice result.

For this project, we'll start by creating a grenade mesh with simple objects. Then, we'll create a C# script that can be used to arm our grenade and apply different settings and properties, such as impact force and other things. We will then create a spawn portal that will automatically replace the grenade we picked up so that we have a continuous supply of grenades in our VR scene. This is a great implementation because if you have a spawner, you can set up different stations around your VR scene, pick stuff up, throw it, and have fun. With that said, let's go ahead and start creating our mesh for the grenade.

To create a grenade mesh (*Figure 17.1*), follow these steps:

1. Create an empty GO and name it `Grenade`.
2. Create a `capsule` GO as a child of `Grenade` and name it `GrenadeBody`.
3. Set all **Position** and **Rotation** values to `0`.
4. Set the **XYZ** scale to `0.1`.

5. Remove the `Capsule Collider` component.
6. Set the material to `dark gray_standard` (**Create** | **Material** | **Color: dark gray**).
7. Create a ProBuilder arch as a child of the `Grenade` GO and name it `GrenadeArch`.
8. Set the **X** position to `0.043`, the **Y** position to `0.059`, and the **Z** position to `-0.011`.
9. Set **Rotation** to `-90`.
10. Set the **XYZ** scale to `0.026`.
11. Set the material to `orange_standard` (refer to the *Creating custom materials* section of *Chapter 4*).
12. Remove the `Mesh Collider` component.
13. Create a ProBuilder `Torus` as a child of the `Grenade` GO and name it `ArmIndicator`.
14. Set the **X** position to `-0.09`, the **Y** position to `0.042`, and the **Z** Position to `-0.085`.
15. Set the material to `red_emission` (refer to the *Creating custom materials* section of *Chapter 4*).
16. Remove the `Mesh Collider` component.
17. Go to the `Grenade` parent GO in **Hierarchy**.
18. In the **Layer** dropdown menu, create a new layer called `Grenade` and assign it to the `Grenade` parent GO.
19. Add a `Box Collider` component.
20. Set the **X** size to `0.13`, the **Y** size to `0.24`, and the **Z** size to `0.13`.
21. Add an `XR Grab Interactable` component.
22. Set **Interaction Layer Mask** to **grabbable** and **Object**.
23. Add an `Audio Source` component.
24. Set **Spatial Blend** to `1`.
25. Set **Min Distance** to `2`.
26. Set **Max Distance** to `10`.

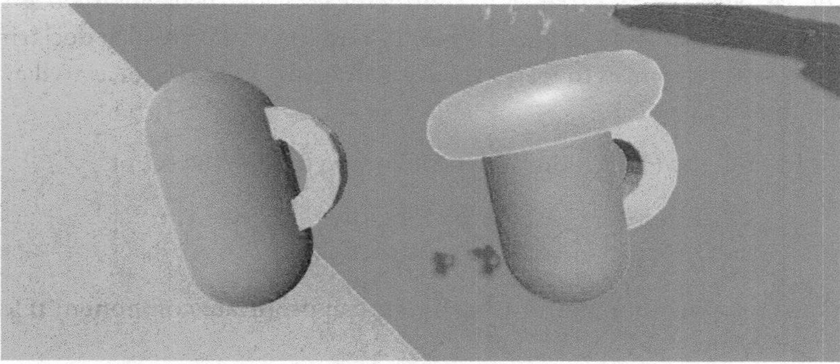

Figure 17.1 – The Grenade mesh (left) and the Grenade mesh with ArmIndicator active (right)

We now have a 3D model of a grenade that we can use to create an explosion in a virtual world. To make the explosion possible, we need to create a script that will play a prefab and a sound.

Creating an explosion

To create a script that will arm the grenade, follow these steps:

1. Create a new C# script called `VRGrenade`.
2. Open the script and add the following namespace:

```
using UnityEngine;
[RequireComponent(typeof(Rigidbody))]
[RequireComponent(typeof(AudioSource))]
```

   We are including the necessary namespace for Unity and applying the `[RequireComponent]` attribute to ensure the script requires certain components.

3. In the `public class VRGrenade` class, add the following variables to the script:

```
    public AudioClip explosionSound;
    public GameObject explosionParticles;
    public float armTime = 4f;
    public float explosionRadius = 5f;
    public float explosionForce = 500f;
    public GameObject proximityIndicator;
    public AudioClip proximitySound;
    public float proximitySoundStartDistance = 2f;
    public float proximitySoundMaxDistance = 5f;
    private Rigidbody rigidbody;
    private bool isArmed = false;
    private float armTimer = 0f;
    private AudioSource audioSource;
    private bool isPlayingProximitySound = false;
```

   We are declaring `public` variables to control the grenade's behavior, such as the explosion's sound, particles, arm time, explosion radius, and force. We are also declaring `private` variables to hold references to `Rigidbody` and `Audio Source`, as well as track various states and timers.

4. In the `void Start()` method, add the following code to the script:

```
        rigidbody = GetComponent<Rigidbody>();
        audioSource = GetComponent<AudioSource>();
```

   In the `Start()` method, we must assign the appropriate component references to the `private` variables.

5. In the `void Update()` method, add the following code to the script:

```
if (isArmed)
{
    armTimer += Time.deltaTime;
    if (armTimer >= armTime)
    {
        Explode();
    }
    UpdateProximityIndicator();
    UpdateProximitySound();
}
```

   In the `Update()` method, if the grenade is armed, we increment `armTimer` and check whether it has reached `armTime`. If it has, we call the `Explode()` method. We also update the proximity indicator and proximity sound.

6. Create a new method called `public void Arm()`, and add the following code to the script:

```
isArmed = true;
```

   The `Arm()` method sets the `isArmed` flag to `true`, indicating that the grenade is armed.

7. Create a new method called `public void Throw(Vector3 throwVelocity)`, and add the following code to the script:

```
rigidbody.isKinematic = false;
rigidbody.velocity = throwVelocity;
transform.parent = null;
Arm();
```

   The `Throw()` method is called to throw the grenade. We enable `Rigidbody`, set its velocity to the provided `throwVelocity`, unparent the grenade from any object it might be attached to, and arm the grenade.

8. Create a new method called `void Explode()`, and add the following code to the script:

```
AudioSource.PlayClipAtPoint(explosionSound,
    transform.position);
Instantiate(explosionParticles,
    transform.position, Quaternion.identity);
Collider[] colliders =
    Physics.OverlapSphere(transform.position,
        explosionRadius);
foreach (Collider collider in colliders)
{
    Rigidbody otherRigidbody =
        collider.GetComponent<Rigidbody>();
```

```
            if (otherRigidbody != null)
            {
                otherRigidbody.AddExplosionForce(
                    explosionForce,
                        transform.position,
                            explosionRadius);
            }
        }
        Destroy(gameObject);
```

The `Explode()` method is called when the grenade is fully armed. It plays the explosion sound, instantiates the explosion particles, applies explosion forces to nearby `Rigidbody` components within the explosion radius, and destroys the grenade object.

9. Create a new method called `void UpdateProximityIndicator()`, and add the following code to the script:

```
        float progress =
            Mathf.Clamp01(armTimer / armTime);
        float blinkInterval = Mathf.Lerp(1f, 0.1f,
            progress);
        blinkInterval *= Mathf.Lerp(1f, 2f, progress);
        if (proximityIndicator.activeSelf)
        {
            proximityIndicator.SetActive(false);
            Invoke("ToggleProximityIndicator",
                blinkInterval);
        }
        else
        {
            proximityIndicator.SetActive(true);
            Invoke("ToggleProximityIndicator",
                blinkInterval);
        }
```

In the `UpdateProximityIndicator()` method, we calculate the progress of `armTimer` relative to `armTime`. Based on the progress, we determine `blinkInterval` to control the blinking rate of the proximity indicator. We toggle the visibility of the proximity indicator using `SetActive()` and schedule the next toggle using `Invoke()`.

10. Create a new method called `void ToggleProximityIndicator()`, and add the following code to the script:

```
proximityIndicator.SetActive
    (!proximityIndicator.activeSelf);
```

The `ToggleProximityIndicator()` method toggles the visibility of the proximity indicator by inverting its active state.

11. Create a new method called `void UpdateProximitySound()`, and add the following code to the script:

```
float distance =
    Vector3.Distance(transform.position,
        Camera.main.transform.position);
if (distance < proximitySoundMaxDistance)
{
    float pitch = Mathf.Lerp(1f, 2f,
        1f - (distance -
        proximitySoundStartDistance) /
        (proximitySoundMaxDistance -
        proximitySoundStartDistance));
    audioSource.pitch = pitch;
    if (!isPlayingProximitySound)
    {
        audioSource.clip = proximitySound;
        audioSource.loop = true;
        audioSource.Play();
        isPlayingProximitySound = true;
    }
}
else
{
    if (isPlayingProximitySound)
    {
        audioSource.Stop();
        isPlayingProximitySound = false;
    }
}
```

In the `UpdateProximitySound()` method, we calculate the distance between the grenade and the main camera. If the distance is within `proximitySoundMaxDistance`, we calculate the pitch based on the distance. We then update the pitch of `audioSource` accordingly and play the proximity sound if it's not already playing. If the distance exceeds `proximitySoundMaxDistance`, we stop the proximity sound if it's currently playing.

12. In the `void UpdateProximitySound()` method, add the following code to the script:

```
if (isArmed)
{
    float progress = Mathf.Clamp01(armTimer /
        armTime);
    float pitchMultiplier = Mathf.Lerp(1f, 2f,
        progress);
    audioSource.pitch = pitchMultiplier;
    int numPlays = 0;
    if (progress >= 0.1f)
    {
        numPlays = 1;
    }
    if (progress >= 0.3f)
    {
        numPlays = 2;
    }
    if (progress >= 0.6f)
    {
        numPlays = 3;
    }
    if (progress >= 0.75f)
    {
        numPlays = 4;
    }
    for (int i = 0; i < numPlays; i++)
    {
        AudioSource.PlayClipAtPoint(
            proximitySound,
                transform.position);
    }
}
```

If the grenade is armed, we calculate the progress of `armTimer` and adjust the pitch and number of plays of the proximity sound accordingly. We play the proximity sound multiple times based on the progress to create an audio effect.

13. Save the code and add it to the `Grenade` GO.
14. Add the proximity indicator and the `ArmIndicator` GO.
15. For these, select `Enter Interactable Event` and add a function.
16. Place the `Grenade` GO as the reference.
17. Choose the `VRGrenade` script and select the arm function.

With this, we can grab our grenade, hold it, and when we press the trigger button, it will arm the grenade. From there, we will have a default arming time of 4 seconds to throw the GO before it explodes.

Now that we have our explosion function working, we can add visuals to it by including explosion sounds and visual effects.

Adding detonation visuals

To add visuals, we can add prefabs of particles so that when an object detonates, we get the full effect of the explosion. This is something that would typically only be applied to the physics system and invisible GOs, but we can have actual visuals to create a fully immersive experience as well.

To add the explosion sound and prefab, follow these steps:

1. Go to the Unity Asset Store and search for the particle pack: `https://assetstore.unity.com/packages/vfx/particles/particle-pack-127325`.
2. Download and import it from the Package Manager.
3. You will find the imported assets in the Unity `Technologies` folder.
4. For the proximity sound, I chose `092_pause_04` as the audio clip.
5. For the explosion sound, choose `04_fire_explosion_04_medium` as the audio clip.
6. For the explosion particle, I will choose the `SmallExplosion` particle, which can be found in the fire and explosion effects folder of our particle pack.
7. We can drag the `SmallExplosion` prefab into our scene and open **Hierarchy**. You will see that each one of the GOs in `SmallExplosion` has a particle system on it. By default, it is set to looping.
8. To deactivate the looping functionality, we need to click the `SmallExplosion` GO, the `embers` GO, the additional `SmokeEffect` GO, and the `shockwave` GO.
9. In the `particle system` component, disable **Looping**.
10. Click the **Add component** button in **Inspector**.
11. Click **New script** and name it `ExplosionDestroyer`.
12. Open the script and apply the following namespace:

    ```
    using UnityEngine;
    ```

13. Create a method called `private void OnEnable()`, and add the following code to the script:

    ```
            Destroy(gameObject, 3f);
    ```

    The `OnEnable()` method is called when the GO this script is attached to becomes enabled. In this case, it destroys the GO after a delay of 3 seconds using the `Destroy()` method.

14. In the SmallExplosion GO, override the prefab.
15. Remove the SmallExplosion GO from the scene.
16. Hide the ArmIndicator GO.
17. Finally, save the Grenade as a prefab.

With this code, you will be able to automatically destroy the SmallExplosion GO that is instantiated after it finishes the explosion animation. This prevents it from causing the scene to loop or stand any longer than necessary. By default, we have it set at 3 seconds. You can make it longer if you would like, but this is based on how long the animated sequence for the explosion will be, so 3 seconds should suffice before the GO is destroyed.

We can now create a spawning portal that allows the Grenade to be instantiated in that spot so that you can grab it and throw it, and then after the Grenade is removed, another one will be instantiated after 5 seconds for you to grab and throw again.

Creating a grenade-spawning portal

To create a spawner to instantiate Grenades (*Figure 17.12*), follow these steps:

1. Create an empty GO and name it GrenadeSpawner.
2. Add a Box Collider component.
3. Set the center **Y** position of Box Collider to 1 and the **Y** size to 2.
4. Create a cylinder as a child of the empty GO and name it Spawn Portal.
5. Remove the Capsule Collider component.
6. Change the material to blue transparent.
7. Set the **Y** position to 1.
8. Create a new empty GO as a child of GrenadeSpawner and name it SpawnPoint.
9. Set the **Y** position to 1.75.
10. Create a new C# script called GrenadeSpawner.
11. Add it to the GrenadeSpawner GO.
12. Open the script and apply the following namespaces:

```
using System.Collections;
using UnityEngine;
```

13. In the `public class GrenadeSpawner` class, add the following variables to the script:

```
public GameObject grenadePrefab;
public Transform spawnPoint;
public float respawnDelay = 5f;
private bool isSpawned = false;
private GameObject currentGrenade;
private Rigidbody rb;
```

We are declaring `public` variables to control the `GrenadeSpawner`'s behavior, such as the `grenadePrefab`, `spawnPoint`, and `respawnDelay`. We are also declaring `private` variables to track the state of the spawner and hold references to the current grenade and `Rigidbody`.

14. In the `private void Start()` method, add the following code to the script:

```
        SpawnGrenade();
```

In the `Start()` method, we call the `SpawnGrenade()` method to initially spawn a grenade.

15. Create a new method called `private void SpawnGrenade()`, and add the following code to the script:

```
        currentGrenade = Instantiate(grenadePrefab,
            spawnPoint.position, spawnPoint.rotation);
        isSpawned = true;
```

The `SpawnGrenade()` method instantiates a new grenade at the `SpawnPoint` and sets the `isSpawned` flag to `true`.

16. Create a new coroutine called `private IEnumerator RespawnGrenade()`, and add the following code to the script:

```
        yield return new WaitForSeconds(respawnDelay);
        if (!isSpawned)
        {
            SpawnGrenade();
        }
```

The `RespawnGrenade()` coroutine waits for the specified respawn delay and then checks if a grenade is already spawned. If not, it calls the `SpawnGrenade()` method to spawn a new grenade.

17. Create a new method called `private void OnTriggerStay(Collider other)`, and add the following code to the script:

    ```
    if (other.GetComponent<Rigidbody>()  != null)
    {
    other.GetComponent<Rigidbody>().useGravity = false;
    }
    ```

    The `OnTriggerStay()` method is called when another collider stays within the trigger collider attached to the spawner. In this case, we disabled the gravity for the other object's `Rigidbody` to prevent it from falling.

18. Create a new method called `private void OnTriggerExit(Collider other)`, and add the following code to the script:

    ```
            if (other.gameObject.CompareTag("grenade"))
            {
                isSpawned = false;
                StartCoroutine(RespawnGrenade());
            }
    ```

    The `OnTriggerExit()` method is called when another collider exits the trigger collider attached to the spawner. If the other object has the `grenade` tag, we set the `isSpawned` flag to `false` and start the `RespawnGrenade()` coroutine to respawn a new grenade. If you haven't done so already, set the `Grenade` prefab to the `grenade` tag in the **Inspector** area.

19. Save the code and go back to the **Inspector** area.
20. In the `GrenadeSpawner` component, add the `Grenade` prefab from our `prefabs` folder to the reference slot.
21. Add the `SpawnPoint` GO to the `SpawnPoint` reference point.
22. Go to the `Grenade` prefab in the **Inspector** area.
23. In the `Rigidbody` component, set **Interpolate** to **Interpolate**.
24. Set **Collision Detection** to **Continuous Dynamic**.
25. In the `XR Grab Interactable` component, set **Force Gravity On Detach** to **Enable**.
26. Add another activated event and set the `grenade` GO's `Rigidbody` component to **Use Gravity**. Then, set the function to `true`.
27. You can save this by making the `GrenadeSpawner` a prefab.

With this complete, we now have a grenade spawner (*Figure 17.2*) that will spawn a grenade every 5 seconds after the original grenade was removed from the portal indicator. This means that you will have unlimited grenades that you have access to, regardless of how much time you spend in the world.

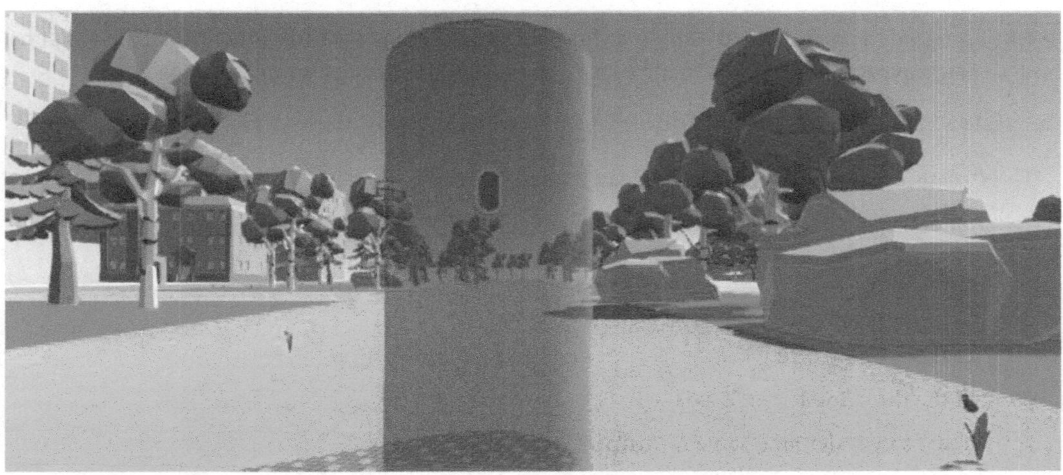

Figure 17.2 – Grenade Spawner containing a Grenade prefab within it

As you can see, making a grenade fully functional takes quite a bit of work in a VR scene. But this gives you a good idea and a good foundation of the core elements of what it's like to build experiences out piece by piece. There's never a one-size-fits-all approach, but if you take it step by step and break things down into bite-sized pieces, something that seems daunting can be really simple and easy to create and follow.

In the next section, we will proceed to create a `HandCannon` GO that can be used to fire projectiles.

Making a simple hand cannon

When I was considering what approach to take with projectiles, I reflected on what I enjoyed about my personal experiences with them, which mainly involved video games. One of my favorite games was *Mega Man*, and what I liked about it was that he utilized the resources in his hands to do a lot of interesting things. It just so happened that one of his hands was a hand cannon.

To be respectful of the idea of guns and their use, which is infrequent in reality, I wanted to approach weapons in a way that felt approachable for everyone. This is something to keep in mind when working on VR experiences since there isn't a one-size-fits-all solution, but there is a solution for every problem. Projectiles are here to stay, but when creating experiences, some people may not want to use guns all the time, and that's perfectly fine. Understanding this in the development process is essential because it allows you to find ways to address sensitive topics while also implementing standard practices and adding elements that are common across the most popular experiences.

Therefore, a good approach is to think outside the box and try to relate to people on a personal level while also not alienating anyone. The idea of navigating guns in VR can be touchy, but if you can find a fun twist on the approach, you can go far with it.

We will proceed to create a hand cannon to fire projectiles. It functions like other projectile weapons, and we can explore some utilities that make it very versatile for such a simple form factor.

To create a 3D model of a `HandCannon` GO (*Figure 17.3*), follow these steps:

1. Create a new empty GO and name it `HandCannon`.
2. Add a `Capsule Collider` component.
3. Set **Radius** to `0.17`.
4. Set the **Z** center to `0.06`.
5. Set **Height** to `0.52`.
6. Set the direction to the **Z** axis.
7. Create a cylinder and name it `CannonBase`.
8. Set the **X** rotation to `90`.
9. Set the **X** scale to `0.2`, the **Y** scale to `0.1`, and the **Z** scale to `0.2`.
10. Remove the `Collider` component.
11. Add a `Red_Metallic` material.
12. Create a ProBuilder `Torus` and name it `CannonNozzle`.
13. Open the **ProBuilder** window and select **Center pivot**.
14. Set the **Z** position to `0.2`.
15. Set the **X** rotation to `90`.
16. Set the **X** scale to `0.07`, the **Y** scale to `0.1`, and the **Z** scale to `0.076`.
17. Remove the `Mesh Collider` component.
18. Add a `Red_Unlit` material.
19. Create a capsule and name it `CannonShaft`.
20. Set the **Z** position to `0.06`.
21. Set the **X** rotation to `90`.
22. Set the **X** scale to `0.3`, the **Y** scale to `0.14`, and the **Z** scale to `0.3`.
23. Remove the `Collider` component.
24. Add a `Blue_Standard` material.
25. Create an empty GO and name it `CannonAnchor`.
26. Set the **Z** position to `-0.067`.
27. Create another empty GO and name it `CannonSource`.

28. Set the **Z** position to `0.237`:

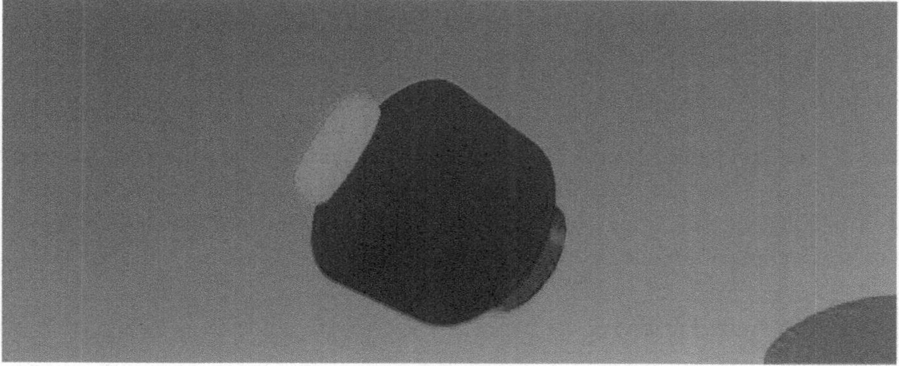

Figure 17.3 – The HandCannon GO

To wield the cannon effectively, we must now focus on attaching it to our hands. By doing so, we can seamlessly hold and manipulate the cannon while launching projectiles into the virtual world. In the next section, we will explore the process of attaching the 3D cannon to our hand, enabling a natural and immersive experience as we interact with the VR environment.

Attaching the cannon to a hand

To fully harness the potential of this powerful projectile launcher, it is crucial to establish a means of securely holding it in our hands. This allows us to precisely aim the cannon in the desired direction for projectile firing. Alternatively, we can choose to maintain the cannon's fixed position while aligning its firing direction to match its orientation. However, to provide a more immersive and flexible experience, we will explore adding components to the cannon's GO. By holding the grip button, we can affix the cannon to our hand and seamlessly move it around, aligning it with our hand's position. Join us as we embark on the journey of enhancing control and immersion by attaching `HandCannon`, enabling dynamic manipulation and precise aiming within our VR environment. To make it attachable, follow these steps:

1. Go to the `HandCannon` GO.
2. Add an `Audio Source` component.
3. Set **Spatial Blend** to `1`.
4. Set **Min Distance** to `0.03` and the **Max Distance** to `3`.
5. Add a `Rigidbody` component.
6. Enable **Use Gravity**.
7. Set **Interpolate** to **Interpolate**.

8. Set **Collision Detection** to **ContinuousDynamic**.
9. Add an `XR Grab Interactable` component.
10. Set the **Interaction Layer Mask** to **Everything**.
11. Set the attached transform to the `CannonAnchor` GO.

By successfully attaching `HandCannon`, we now have the foundation for a dynamic and engaging VR experience. In the next section, we will explore the ability to fire projectiles from the `HandCannon` GO. This capability not only adds excitement and gameplay depth but also provides an essential element of interaction within our virtual environment.

Enabling cannon firing

The ability to launch projectiles from `HandCannon` not only adds a thrilling aspect to our VR environment but also offers an essential means of interaction and gameplay depth. We will explore the mechanics of firing `HandCannon` in VR, enabling you to aim, shoot, and engage with virtual targets or environments with precision and excitement.

To fire a projectile from `HandCannon`, follow these steps:

1. Create a new C# script and name it `CannonBlaster`.
2. Add the script to the `HandCannon` GO.
3. Open the script and add the following namespace:

```
using UnityEngine;
```

4. In the `public class CannonBlaster` class, add the following variables to the script:

```
    public GameObject projectilePrefab;
    public float projectileSpeed = 10f;
    public float impactForce = 10f;
    public GameObject cannonNozzle;
    public AudioClip blastSound;
    private AudioSource cannonAudio;
```

We are declaring `public` variables to control the `CannonBlaster`'s behavior, such as the `projectilePrefab`, `Speed`, `impactForce`, `cannonNozzle` reference, and `blastSound`. We are also declaring a `private` variable to hold a reference to the `AudioSource` component.

5. In the `private void Awake()` method, add the following code to the script:

```
        cannonAudio = GetComponent<AudioSource>();
```

In the `Awake()` method, we are assigning the appropriate component reference to the `private` variable.

6. Create a new method called `public void FireProjectile()`, and add the following code to the script:

```
GameObject projectile =
    Instantiate(projectilePrefab,
        cannonNozzle.transform.position,
            cannonNozzle.transform.rotation);
Rigidbody rb =
    projectile.GetComponent<Rigidbody>();
rb.velocity = transform.forward *
    projectileSpeed;
cannonAudio.PlayOneShot(blastSound);
```

   The `FireProjectile()` method is called to fire a projectile from the cannon. We instantiate a new projectile at the cannon nozzle's position and rotation. We then get the `Rigidbody` component of the projectile and set its velocity to be in the forward direction of the cannon, multiplied by the projectile speed. Finally, we play `blastSound` using the `AudioSource` component.

7. Save the code and go back to the `HandCannon` GO.
8. Add the `CannonSource` GO to the `CannonNozzle` reference slot.
9. Add an audio clip to the `blastSound` reference slot (I chose `08_Bite_04`).
10. In the `XR Grab Interactable` component, add a new `Activated Interaction Event`.
11. Drag the `CannonBlaster` script into the reference slot.
12. In the **Function** menu, choose the `CannonBlasterFireProjectile` function.
13. Rename `HandCannon` to `Hand Cannon_Simple` and turn it into a prefab.

Now, when you fire `CannonBlaster`, it will send out a projectile from `HandCannon`, which will go toward wherever `HandCannon` is facing and pointing. It's as easy as just pressing the trigger button. Just note that you have to keep holding the grip button while you press the trigger button; otherwise, `HandCannon` will fall to the ground, float away, or do whatever it does, and you won't be able to utilize it.

Making a hand cannon is pretty simple. Just like with the grenade, it's pretty much the same process: make a mesh, add a script to it, add some functionality, and test it out. It's a pretty standard development process. Now that we have that under our belt, we can iterate even more by adding more advanced features and creating different types of projectiles that can be shot through the hand cannon.

In the next section, we will build on our simple hand cannon, and we'll make a more complex hand cannon that we can utilize to create some very interesting destruction effects.

Making a complex hand cannon

This section is going to be somewhat beefy, partly because we will be implementing a lot of different features into this hand cannon. Although it would probably be good to split this up into multiple chapters and focus on the different implementations of `HandCannon`, we'll cover all the hand cannon stuff first before revisiting the concepts of projectiles. More importantly, this builds on the foundation we already have, so it's not necessary to walk through the basics of developing something like this at this point in this book. By the end of this section, you'll have a solid understanding of how to create projectile sources, which will lay the foundation for when we add our projectiles since it'll give you a lot of ideas of what projectiles can be used for this cannon.

As mentioned previously, we're going to cover a lot of different things. We'll start by making a C# script that allows us to put everything we need for the complex cannon into one solid piece of code. We'll start by adding a class for particle properties that can have a variety of different properties that work for all the different projectiles. Then, we'll go to the main class and set up a trigger function for when you press the trigger button. This function will replace `FireProjectile` and use it to do what it did in the simple implementation of the cannon. However, we'll also have an implementation for non-projectiles, such as flamethrowers, which don't shoot out but remain static and work interestingly.

Next, we'll add an implementation for our release trigger so that when the trigger is pressed, it'll fire a function, and when it's released, it'll fire another function. We should be familiar with this from the input action managers that we've created. Finally, we'll have a feature where we can press a button to switch from one projectile set to another projectile set. This way, instead of having multiple hand cannons and projectile sources, we can have one projectile source that can use multiple projectiles, and all you have to do is press a button to switch to the next projectile.

There's a lot to cover in this section, and it can be daunting to implement, but once you get through it, you'll have a solid foundation for making something complex that someone can use in a VR experience.

To create a complex hand cannon with advanced features, follow these steps:

1. Create a new C# script and name it `CannonBlasterComplex`.
2. Add it to the `HandCannon` GO.
3. Open the C# script and apply the following namespaces:

```
using System.Collections;
using System.Collections.Generic;
using UnityEngine;
using UnityEngine.XR.Interaction.Toolkit;
[System.Serializable]
```

   We are including the necessary namespaces for Unity, XR Interaction Toolkit, and `System.Collections` to access the required classes and components.

4. Create a new class called `public class ProjectileProperties`, and add the following code to the class:

```
public string projectileName;
public GameObject projectilePrefab;
public GameObject impactPrefabs;
public bool isProjectile;
public bool rapidFireEnabled;
public int rapidFireRate;
public float rapidFireDelay = 0.1f;
```

We have created a `ProjectileProperties` class as a subclass to define properties for each projectile type. It includes fields such as the projectile name, projectile prefab, impact prefabs, whether it is a projectile or not, and options for rapid fire.

With our `ProjectileProperties` class done, we can proceed with the rest of the C# script.

5. In the `public class CannonBlasterComplex` class, add the following code to the script:

```
public List<ProjectileProperties>
    projectileProperties;
public int currentProjectileIndex = 0;
public GameObject cannonNozzle;
private GameObject currentNonProjectile;
public float speed = 10f;
public AudioClip blastSound;
private AudioSource cannonAudio;
public bool cannonHeld;
```

We have declared `public` variables to hold the `ProjectileProperties` list, `currentProjectileIndex`, `CannonNozzle` reference, `currentNonProjectile` object, `speed`, `blastSound`, and `cannonHeld` status.

6. In the `private void Awake()` method, add the following code to the script:

```
    cannonAudio = GetComponent<AudioSource>();
```

In the `Awake()` method, we assign the `AudioSource` component to the `cannonAudio` variable.

7. Create a new method called `public void PressTrigger()`, and add the following code to the script:

```
    ProjectileProperties properties =
        projectileProperties
            [currentProjectileIndex];

    if (properties.isProjectile)
    {
```

```
        if (properties.rapidFireEnabled)
        {

            StartCoroutine(RapidFireProjectile(
                properties,
                    properties.rapidFireRate));

        }
        FireProjectile(properties);
    }
    else
    {
        NonProjectile(properties);
    }
```

The `PressTrigger()` method is called when the trigger is pressed. It checks if the current projectile is a projectile or not and calls the appropriate methods accordingly.

8. Create a new method called `private void FireProjectile(ProjectileProperties properties)`, and add the following code to the script:

```
    GameObject projectile =
        Instantiate(properties.projectilePrefab,
            cannonNozzle.transform.position,
                transform.rotation);
    cannonAudio.PlayOneShot(blastSound);
    Rigidbody rb =
        projectile.GetComponent<Rigidbody>();
    rb.velocity = transform.forward * speed;
```

The `FireProjectile()` method instantiates a new projectile at the cannon nozzle's position and rotation. It plays `blastSound` and sets the velocity of the projectile to move forward based on the specified speed.

9. Create a new coroutine called `private IEnumerator RapidFireProjectile(ProjectileProperties properties, int numberOfTimes)` and add the following code to the script:

```
    for (int i = 0; i < numberOfTimes; i++)
    {
        FireProjectile(properties);
        yield return new WaitForSeconds(
            properties.rapidFireDelay);
    }
```

The RapidFireProjectile() coroutine is used for rapid-fire functionality. It fires the projectile multiple times with a delay specified by the rapid-fire delay.

10. Create a new method called private void NonProjectile(ProjectileProperties properties), and add the following code to the script:

```
GameObject projectile =
    Instantiate(properties.projectilePrefab,
        cannonNozzle.transform.position,
            transform.rotation,
                cannonNozzle.transform);
currentNonProjectile = projectile;
projectile.SetActive(true);
```

The NonProjectile() method is called when the current projectile is not a projectile. It instantiates the non-projectile object at the cannon nozzle's position and rotation. The current non-projectile object is stored for later use, and it is set to active.

11. Create a new method called public void ReleaseTrigger(), and add the following code to the script:

```
If
(!projectileProperties[currentProjectileIndex]
.isProjectile)
{
    Destroy(currentNonProjectile);
}
```

The ReleaseTrigger() method is called when the trigger is released. If the current projectile is not a projectile (that is, a non-projectile), the current non-projectile object is destroyed.

12. Create a new method called public void NextProjectile(), and add the following code to the script:

```
if (cannonHeld == true)
{
    currentProjectileIndex =
        (currentProjectileIndex + 1) %
            projectileProperties.Count;
}
```

The NextProjectile() method is called to switch to the next projectile. If the cannon is held (cannonHeld is true), the current projectile index is incremented to the next index in a circular manner.

13. Create a new method called `public void PreviousProjectile()`, and add the following code to the script:

```
if (cannonHeld == true)
{
    currentProjectileIndex--;
    if (currentProjectileIndex < 0)
    {
        currentProjectileIndex =
            projectileProperties.Count - 1;
    }
}
```

The `PreviousProjectile()` method is called to switch to the previous projectile. If the cannon is held (`cannonHeld` is `true`), the current projectile index is decremented to the previous index in a circular manner. If the index goes below `0`, it wraps around to the last index.

14. Create a new method called `public void HoldCannon()`, and add the following code to the script:

```
cannonHeld = true;
```

The `HoldCannon()` method is called when the cannon is being held. It sets the `cannonHeld` variable to `true`.

15. Create a new method called `public void ReleaseCannon()`, and add the following code to the script:

```
cannonHeld = false;
```

The `ReleaseCannon()` method is called when the cannon is released. It sets the `cannonHeld` variable to `false`.

16. Save the code and go back to the scene.
17. Look for the `HandCannon_Simple` prefab.
18. Duplicate it and name it `HandCannon_complex`.
19. Remove the `CannonBlaster` script and replace it with the `CannonBlastercomplex` script.
20. Set `CannonNozzle` to the `CannonSource` GO.
21. Set its speed to `15`.
22. Set `blastsound` to `08_bite_04`.
23. In the `XR Grab Interactable`, set the `Select Entered` event to `HandCannon` and set the function to `hold cannon`.
24. In the `Select Exited` event, set the function to `release cannon`.

25. In the `Activated` event, set the function to `press trigger`.
26. In the `Deactivated` event, set the function to `release trigger`.

You can now save this as a prefab variant and move on to adding it to our VR hand interactions manager GO.

As you may recall, `ToggleInputActionManager` from the *Adding an input manager* section in *Chapter 15* is where we put all of our toggle input interactions from our manager script. We can use this for all the toggle rays – that is, for jumping, sprinting, crouching, and the menu. Adding the ability to toggle our projectiles as well is a perfect thing to add to this list. To set up `ToggleInputActionManager` with our `HandCannon` so that we can toggle the projectiles, follow these steps:

1. Add a new slot in the **Actions** reference slot and name it `Toggleprojectiles`.
2. Set the action reference to `XRI left hand interaction X button`.
3. Add a new action event.
4. Set the reference slot to `HandCannon`.
5. Set the function to `next projectile` in the `CannonBlastercomplex` script.

Now this this is set up, whenever you hold `CannonBlaster`, you can press the *X* button on the left XR controller to toggle from one projectile to the next in a list. If you want, you can set up another button to go to the previous item in the list, but this one only goes to the next item. If you have a lot of items, it may take you a while to get back around, but having a lot of variability would be nice as well.

In the next section, we will work on a project to create projectiles for our cannon blasters to fire. This will involve designing the visual and physical properties of the projectile, as well as programming its behavior when fired. By the end of this next section, you will have a fully functional cannon system that can shoot realistic projectiles in your Unity VR project.

Making projectiles

Making projectiles is not as complicated as creating the actual projectile sources. However, they can be customized if you give them different properties that react differently in the virtual world. The best part about projectiles is their variability and versatility. In this section, we will explore a variety of ways to customize the experience of using our hand cannon.

Projectiles are what make hand cannon fun to use. By creating immersive experiences with sound, impacts, force, and physics, we can make some exciting experiences using a simple projectile. In this section, we will cover how to create a simple projectile, add an impact prefab to indicate that it hit an object, and make complex prefabs to utilize a variety of different properties that we created the framework for in our complex hand cannon. We will start with the basics and then build up to more complex features, leaving it to you to create the variance and variability as you see fit.

To create a prefab to use as a projectile, follow these steps:

1. Create a new empty object and name it `projectile`.
2. Add a `Capsule Collider`.
3. Set **Radius** to `0.03`.
4. Set **Height** to `0.25`.
5. Set **Direction** to **X axis**.
6. Add a `Rigidbody` component.
7. Set **Use Gravity** to **False**.
8. Set **Interpolate** to **Interpolate**.
9. Set **Collision Detection** to **Continuous Dynamic**.
10. Create a sphere as a child of the `projectile` GO.
11. Set the **X** scale to `0.05`, **Y** scale to `0.05`, and **Z** scale to `0.2`.
12. Remove the `Sphere Collider`.
13. Set the material to `red_emission`.
14. Save the `projectile` as a prefab.
15. In the `CannonBlaster` script, add the `projectile` to the `projectilePrefab` reference slot.

For the most part, our projectile prefab is just a red pill that we are firing. It's simple but sufficient for what we need. If you want to change the visuals, you can do so easily once you have the foundation of the projectile made. It's as simple as swapping out the mesh or adding a mesh as a child of this projectile prefab. To make it more interesting, focus on implementing a way for the projectile to test whether it impacted something or not.

Creating a simple projectile

To make a simple projectile that can detect whether it hit a mesh after it was fired from `HandCannon`, follow these steps:

1. Create a new C# script and call it `CannonProjectile`.
2. Open it and apply the following namespaces:

```
using UnityEngine;
```

3. In the `public class CannonProjectile` class, add the following code to the script:

```
public float impactForce = 10f;
public float destroyDelay=2f;
private CannonBlaster cannonBlaster;
```

We have declared `public` variables to hold the impact force and destroy delay for the projectile. We also have a reference to the `CannonBlaster` script.

4. In the `private void Awake()` method, add the following code to the script:

```
cannonBlaster = GetComponent<CannonBlaster>();
impactForce = cannonBlaster.impactForce;
```

In the `Awake()` method, we are getting the `CannonBlaster` component from the same GO and assigning its impact force to the `impactForce` variable of this projectile.

5. Create a new method called `private void OnCollisionEnter(Collision collision)` and add the following code to the script:

```
    Rigidbody rb =
        collision.gameObject.GetComponent
            <Rigidbody>();
    if (rb != null)
    {
        rb.AddForce(transform.forward *
            impactForce, ForceMode.Impulse);
    }
    Destroy(this.gameObject, destroyDelay-.1f);
}
```

The `OnCollisionEnter()` method is called when the projectile collides with another object. We retrieve the `Rigidbody` component from the collided object and add a force in the forward direction of the projectile with the specified impact force using `ForceMode.Impulse`. We then destroy the `projectile` GO after a delay, which allows time for any impact effects to play before cleanup.

6. Save the code.
7. Apply the script to the projectile that you have.
8. Create a prefab of this and save it.

With this code, we can have the projectile check whether it hits something after it leaves `HandCannon`. Once it leaves `HandCannon`, `HandCannon` cannot check anything, so it's up to the projectile to do all the calculations and collisions. By putting in this code and having it stay on while the projectile is moving, it can provide a lot of information in terms of what hits where and how it triggers other stuff once there's a hit.

Speaking of triggering things, we can implement an impact visual to go with the impact force that the projectile has when it connects with a collision.

To add a projectile impact, follow these steps:

1. Open the `CannonProjectile` C# script and apply the following code as `public` variables:

   ```
   public GameObject impactPrefab;
   ```

   Here, we have declared a `public` variable to hold the impact prefab for the projectile.

2. Apply the following code to the `Awake()` method:

   ```
   impactPrefab = cannonBlaster.impactPrefab;
   ```

   In the `Awake()` method, we are assigning the impact prefab from the `CannonBlaster` script to the `impactPrefab` variable of this projectile.

3. Apply the following code to the `OnCollisionEnter()` method:

   ```
   GameObject impact = Instantiate(impactPrefab,
       collision.contacts[0].point,
           Quaternion.identity);
   Destroy(impact, 2.0f);
   ```

   The `OnCollisionEnter()` method is called when the projectile collides with another object. We instantiate the impact prefab at the contact point of the collision with the collided object. `Quaternion.identity` means no rotation is applied to the impact prefab. We destroy the `impact` GO after a delay of 2.0 seconds to allow time for any impact effects to play before cleanup.

4. Save the code and go back to the prefab.

With this additional code, we can add a prefab for whatever visual impact we want to have on our projectile. This can be projectile-specific, which is the best part about it. You can choose whatever prefab you want, and it will place the impact exactly where the projectile hits a mesh. So, if it hits the side of a building, the impact will be placed on the side of the building. More importantly, it will be automatically destroyed once the visual is done playing, so you don't have to worry about it hogging up too much memory.

Creating a complex projectile

Now that we have impact features for our projectiles, we can further individualize the properties of our projectiles with something more complex, just like we did with the complex `HandCannon` from the simple `HandCannon`.

To create a complex projectile that can be fired from `HandCannon` in Unity, follow these steps:

1. Create a new C# script and name it `CannonProjectileComplex`.
2. Open the script and add the following namespaces:

```
using UnityEngine;
```

3. In the `public class CannonProjectileComplex` class, add the following variables to the script:

```
    public GameObject impactPrefab;
    public float impactForce = 10f;
    public float destroyDelay = 2f;
```

   We have declared `public` variables to hold the impact prefab, impact force, and destroy delay for the projectile.

4. Create a new method called `private void OnCollisionEnter(Collision collision)` and add the following code to the script:

```
            Rigidbody rb =
                collision.gameObject.GetComponent
                    <Rigidbody>();
            if (rb != null)
            {
                rb.AddForce(transform.forward *
                    impactForce, ForceMode.Impulse);
            }
            GameObject impact =
                Instantiate(impactPrefab,
                    collision.contacts[0].point,
                        Quaternion.identity);
            ContactPoint contact =
                collision.contacts[0];
            Quaternion rotation =
                Quaternion.FromToRotation(Vector3.up,
                    contact.normal);
            Instantiate(impactPrefab, contact.point,
                rotation);
            Destroy(collision.gameObject);
        Destroy(impact, destroyDelay);
        Destroy(this.gameObject, destroyDelay-2f);
```

   The `OnCollisionEnter()` method is called when the projectile collides with another object. We retrieve the `Rigidbody` component from the collided object and add a force in the forward direction of the projectile with the specified impact force using

ForceMode.Impulse. We instantiate the impact prefab at the contact point of the collision and also rotate it based on the surface normal. We destroy the collided object, impact prefab, and the projectile itself with appropriate delays.

5. Save the code.
6. Go to the Projectile prefab that you already have.
7. Duplicate it and give it a new name, such as Projectile_complex.
8. Add the code you created earlier to the new Projectile prefab.
9. Save it as a prefab variant.

By creating this prefab variant, we can now use more complex features such as specifying the impact prefab and applying a specific impact force. These elements are crucial when thinking about how projectiles affect virtual objects in the game world. These characteristics are separate from the visual appearance of the projectile, allowing for distinct functionality for each prefab.

In the next section, we will cover how to create different variants of projectiles and implement them into our complex HandCannon to create unique experiences with each new projectile that we use.

Making projectile variants

As mentioned in the previous section, projectile variants are crucial when we're trying to add variability to the HandCannon experience. This allows us to add features that are unique to that projectile and remove features that are probably unnecessary. In the context of not having a one-size-fits-all solution, you could create a variety of different projectiles that have gravity effects, force effects, and visual effects that are interesting and appealing. By providing this variability, you allow your users to choose what they enjoy and avoid what they don't. In many ways, this is all about customization and creating variants that have the same concept but are implemented differently within the virtual world. That's the way to go.

Making a rapid-fire projectile

We will start by making a projectile variant that utilizes the default projectile that we had but has slightly different properties such as rapid fire. To make a rapid-fire projectile variant, go through the following steps:

1. Go to the HandCannon_complex GO.
2. In the CannonBlaster_complex script, add a new projectile property.
3. Set **Projectile Name** to RapidFire.
4. Set **Projectile Prefab** to projectile_simple.
5. Set **Impact Prefab** to TinyExplosion (*Figure 17.4*).
6. Enable **isProjectile**.

7. Enable **Rapid Fire Enabled**.
8. Set **Rapid Fire Rate** to `3`.
9. Set **Rapid Fire Delay** to `0.15`.

Figure 17.4 – The TinyExplosion impact prefab has been activated

This variant will use the regular projectile prefab that we made and the simple prefabs, but will have an impact prefab that's a tiny explosion. And since we have it set to a projectile with rapid fire, it will be able to fire multiple projectiles in succession. So, all you have to do is press the trigger once, and it'll fire three projectiles. This is a simple implementation. All we did was tweak the fire rate, but now, it feels like a different projectile that we could utilize within our scene.

Making an energy shot projectile

The next projectile we can create is an energy shot. It will shoot an energy beam that will have a force and a plasma explosion attached to it. It's not going to be a rapid fire, and it'll look significantly different and feel different than our original projectile. To create an energy shot projectile variant, go through the following steps:

1. Duplicate the `projectile_simple` prefab and name it `Projectile_EnergyShot`.
2. In the `Rigidbody` component, set **Mass** to `1`.
3. Set **Drag** to `0`.
4. Set **Angular Drag** to `0.05`.
5. Enable **Use Gravity**.
6. Set **Interpolate** to **Interpolate**.

7. Set **Collision Detection** to **Continuous Dynamic**.
8. In the `CannonProjectile_complex` script, set the impact prefab to `PlasmaExplosionEffect`.
9. Set **Impact Force** to `10`.
10. In the `CannonBlaster_complex` script, add a new `projectile` property.
11. Set **Projectile Name** to `energyshot`.
12. Set **Projectile Prefab** to `Projectile_EnergyShot`.
13. Set **Impact Prefab** to `PlasmaExplosionEffect` (*Figure 17.5*).
14. Enable **isProjectile**.

Figure 17.5 – The PlasmaExplosionEffect impact prefab has been activated

Since this isn't rapid fire, you don't have to enable rapid fire, change the rapid fire rate, or change the rapid fire delay. But that concludes making our projectile variant. We didn't cover the visuals of the actual projectile partly because that is creative liberty that you can have. Creating engaging visuals for projectiles from scratch requires an understanding of many additional systems within Unity that we have not covered. Those include the Particle System, the VFX Graph, and the Shader Graph. You can learn more about these systems at the following links:

- **Particle System**: `https://docs.unity3d.com/Manual/class-ParticleSystem.html`
- **VFX Graph**: `https://unity.com/visual-effect-graph`
- **Shader Graph**: `https://unity.com/features/shader-graph`

The core components of the projectile outside of the visuals are vastly different, though. When it impacts an object, it looks completely different and reacts differently than the rapid fire or simple projectile. In many ways, creating original particle effects is not required to add diversity to the cannon projectiles because we can control many other characteristics of the projectiles from the script we created. In the next section, we will create a projectile variant with fireball characteristics.

Making a fireball projectile

To make a `FireBall` projectile variant, go through the following steps:

1. Duplicate the `projectile_simple` prefab and name it `Projectile_FireBall`.
2. In the prefab, add a `FlameStream` prefab as a child of the parent GO.
3. Set the **XYZ** position to `0,0,0`.
4. In the `Rigidbody` component, set **Mass** to `6`.
5. Set **Drag** to `0`.
6. Set **Angular Drag** to `0.05`.
7. Enable **Use Gravity**.
8. Set **Interpolate** to **Interpolate**.
9. Set **Collision Detection** to **Continuous Dynamic**.
10. Create a new **Physics Material**.
11. Name it `Fireball`.
12. Set **Dynamic Friction** to `0.19`.
13. Set **Static Friction** to `0.09`.
14. Set **Bounciness** to `0.75`.
15. Set **Friction Combine** to **Average**.
16. Set **Bounce Combine** to **Average**.
17. Add it to the **Material** slot in the `Capsule Collider` component.
18. In the `CannonProjectile_complex` script, set **Impact Prefab** to `LargeFlames`.
19. Set **Impact Force** to `10`.
20. In the `CannonBlaster_complex` script, add a new `projectile` property.
21. Set **Projectile Name** to `fire ball`.
22. Set **Projectile Prefab** to `Projectile_FireBall`.
23. Set **Impact Prefab** to `LargeFlames` (*Figure 17.6*).
24. Enable **isProjectile**.

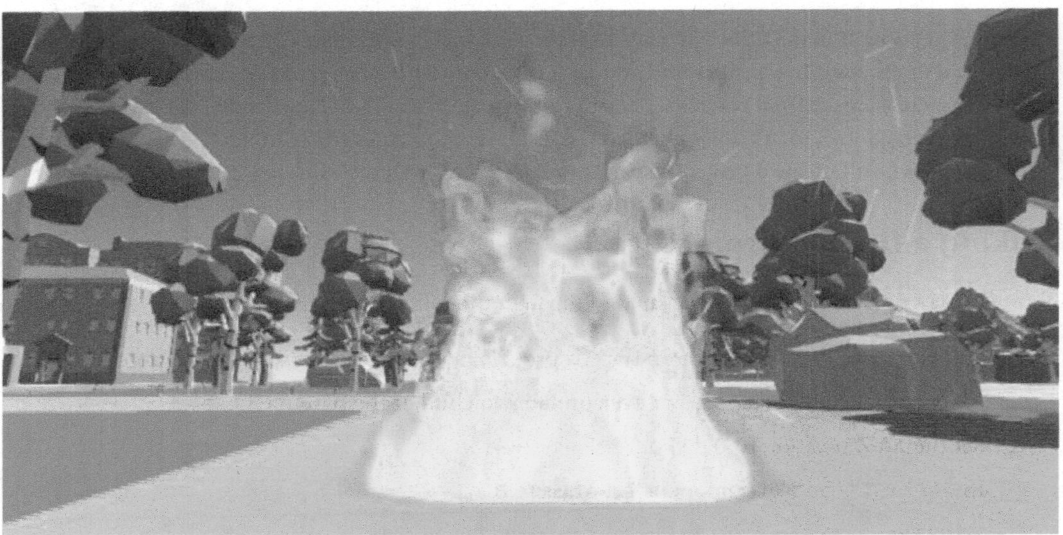

Figure 17.6 – The LargeFlames impact prefab has been activated

While rapid fire offers a continuous stream of ammunition, the addition of fireball projectiles introduces a new dimension of impact and damage characteristics. Intuitively, we recognize that these fireballs will interact with the virtual world in distinct ways compared to rapid-fire projectiles. By displaying these differences within the Unity Editor, we provide users with a range of immersive projectile experiences.

Building upon our progress, the next section focuses on further enriching our projectile library by introducing yet another exciting addition: the grenade projectile. With the inclusion of grenades, we extend our arsenal, opening up a whole new realm of tactical possibilities and explosive encounters.

Making a grenade projectile

To make a grenade projectile variant, go through the following steps:

1. Duplicate the `Projectile_Simple` prefab and name it `Projectile_Grenade`.
2. Add the `VRGrenade` script to this prefab.
3. Disable the `Cannon Projectile` script component.
4. Set **Explosion Sound** to `04_Fire_explosion_04_medium audio file`.
5. Set **Explosion Particles** to the `BigExplosion` prefab.
6. Set **Arm Time** to `3`.
7. Set **Explosion Radius** to `5`.
8. Set **Explosion Force** to `500`.
9. Set **Proximity Indicator** to this prefab.

10. Set **Proximity Sound** to `092__Pause_04`.
11. Set **Proximity Sound Start Distance** to `2`.
12. Set **Proximity Sound Max Distance** to `5`.
13. Enable **Is Armed**.
14. Set **Impact Force** to `20`.
15. In the `CannonBlasterCannonBlaster_Complex` script, add a new `projectile` property.
16. Set **Projectile Name** to `Grenade`.
17. Set **Projectile Prefab** to `Projectile_Grenade`.
18. Set **Impact Prefab** to the `BigExplosion` prefab (*Figure 17.7*).
19. Enable **isProjectile**.

Figure 17.7 – The BigExplosion impact prefab has been activated

We have now created a grenade projectile variant, expanding our projectile library with an explosive and tactically engaging option. Our VR experience is enriched with the ability to launch powerful grenades. We will continue our journey by introducing a water drop projectile variant. This variant will bring a refreshing twist to our VR experience, offering unique properties and interactions. In the next section, we will add an elemental projectile based on water.

Making a water drop projectile

To make a water drop projectile variant, go through the following steps:

1. Duplicate the `Projectile_Simple` prefab and name it `projectile_WaterDrop`.
2. In the `Rigidbody` component, set **Mass** to `4`.

3. Set **Drag** to `0`.
4. Set **Angular Drag** to `0.05`.
5. Enable **Use Gravity**.
6. Set **Interpolate** to **Interpolate**.
7. Set **Collision Detection** to **Continuous Dynamic**.
8. In the `CannonProjectileComplex` script, set **Impact Prefab** to `BigSplash`.
9. Set **Impact Force** to `10`.
10. In the `CannonBlasterCannonBlaster_Complex` script, add a new `projectile` property.
11. Set **Projectile Name** to `Water Drop`.
12. Set **Projectile Prefab** to `Projectile_WaterDrop`.
13. Set **Impact Prefab** to the `BigSplash` prefab (*Figure 17.8*).
14. Enable **isProjectile**.

Figure 17.8 – The BigSplash impact prefab has been activated

Offering a refreshing and fluid experience, the water drop projectile variant is launched in the air with reduced gravity, and upon impact, it triggers a captivating water splash effect, immersing the surroundings in liquid splendor. In the next section, we will add an earth-themed projectile.

Making a rock slide projectile

To make a rock slide projectile variant, go through the following steps:

1. Duplicate the `Projectile_Simple` prefab and name it `Projectile_RockSlide`.
2. In the `Rigidbody` component, set **Mass** to `15`.
3. Set **Drag** to `1.26`.
4. Set **Angular Drag** to `0.4`.
5. Enable **Use Gravity**.
6. Set **Interpolate** to **Interpolate**.
7. Set **Collision Detection** to **Continuous Dynamic**.
8. In the `CannonProjectile_complex` script, set the **Impact Prefab** to the `EarthShatter` prefab.
9. Set **Impact Force** to `100`.
10. In the `CannonBlaster _Complex` script, add a new `projectile` property.
11. Set **Projectile Name** to `Rock Slide`.
12. Set **Projectile Prefab** to `Projectile_RockSlide`.
13. Set **Impact Prefab** to the `EarthShatter` prefab (*Figure 17.10*).
14. Enable **isProjectile**.

Figure 17.9 – The EarthShatter impact prefab has been activated

The rock slide projectile variant embodies the strength and solidity of the earth. With its increased mass and substantial drag, the rock slide projectile carries significant weight and momentum. When it collides with objects or surfaces, it creates a powerful impact that raises the ground from beneath, causing earth-shaking tremors. In the next section, we will create an ice-themed projectile variant.

Making an ice shard projectile

To make an ice shard projectile variant, go through the following steps:

1. In the `CannonBlaster _Complex` script, add a new `projectile` property.
2. Set **Projectile Name** to `ice shard`.
3. Set **Projectile Prefab** to the `IceLance` prefab *(Figure 17.10)*.
4. Set **Impact Prefab** to `null`.
5. Disable **isProjectile**.

Figure 17.10 – The IceLance projectile prefab has been activated from the HandCannon GO

Using the chilling power of ice and frost, the ice shards create a stunning visual spectacle. As they are propelled through the air, they leave behind a trail of frost and frigid particles. In the next section, we will create a flamethrower variant. Although a flamethrower technically does not shoot traditional projectiles, we can still incorporate non-projectile options into the cannon experience, adding diversity and unique elemental qualities. In the next section, we will create a non-projectile variant based on fire.

Making a flamethrower projectile

To make a flamethrower projectile variant, go through the following steps:

1. In the `CannonBlaster _Complex` script, add a new `projectile` property.
2. Set **Projectile Name** to `Flamethrower`.
3. Set **Projectile Prefab** to the `FlameThrower_Projectile` variant prefab (*Figure 17.11*).
4. Set **Impact Prefab** to `null`.
5. Disable **isProjectile**.

For each of these projectile variants, you can customize the visual effects and adjust other properties to create unique experiences for the users. By having multiple projectile variants available, you can provide a more diverse and engaging gameplay experience, allowing the user to choose what they enjoy and avoid what they don't. Remember to test each variant thoroughly to ensure it works as intended and provides a satisfying experience for the user.

Figure 17.11 – The Flamethrower projectile prefab has been activated

With all the projectiles we've just created, we've covered a lot of ground. It's amazing because, with `HandCannon` and all the different projectiles, you could have fun for days. You have the foundations for so much destruction within a world that it's almost unimaginable. It's worth noting that platformers have taken this simple implementation, expanded on it, and created a whole series of games, movies, and everything based on that. *Samus* and *Metroid Prime* are perfect examples, and let's not forget about *Mega Man*. I urge you not to stop here when it comes to thinking about projectile variants because there are so many different things you can uncover and so many experiences you could have with these variations that allow you to impact the worlds you're creating in unimaginable ways.

Now that we have all of our projectiles and projectile sources under our belt, it's time to let them destructively impact the virtual world. In the next section, we'll be covering how to destroy all GOs with projectiles.

Destroying GameObjects with projectiles

The core focus of this section is on destroying GOs, not just using the destroy function within a C# script, but creating a destructive experience and putting that in the hands of the user who navigates the virtual world. It's not fun if everything is pristine and perfect without any damage or water damage on anything. Nobody wants curated experiences that don't have a chink in their armor. By allowing users to interact with the virtual world and have consequences for those interactions, whether good or bad, we can tap into the risk-reward feature and element of VR. If there's something to lose, that means there's a risk and a reward, and people will risk what they have to lose to go for that reward. It creates an innate challenge that is interesting to see play out when you release your projects and share them with the world.

To destroy GOs when they are hit by projectiles, follow these steps:

1. Open the `CannonProjectileComplex` C# script, and add the following code to the `variables` area:

```
public bool destroy;
[TagSelector]
public string destructionTag;
public GameObject destructionPrefab;
```

   We have added new variables to the script. The `destroy` variable determines whether the projectile can destroy objects. `destructionTag` is used to specify the tag of the objects that can be destroyed by the projectile. `destructionPrefab` is the prefab to be instantiated upon destruction.

2. Implement the following code for the `OnCollisionEnter` function:

```
        GameObject impact =
            Instantiate(impactPrefab,
                collision.contacts[0].point,
                    Quaternion.identity);
    if (collision.gameObject.CompareTag(
    destructionTag))
    {
        ContactPoint contact =
            collision.contacts[0];
        Quaternion rotation =
            Quaternion.FromToRotation(Vector3.up,
                contact.normal);
        Instantiate(impactPrefab, contact.point,
            rotation);
```

```
                Destroy(collision.gameObject);
                Destroy(destructionPrefab);
            }
            else
            {
                Rigidbody rb =
                    collision.gameObject.GetComponent
                        <Rigidbody>();
                if (rb != null)
                {
                    rb.AddForce(transform.forward *
                        impactForce, ForceMode.Impulse);
                }
            }
```

Within the `OnCollisionEnter()` method, we instantiate the impact prefab at the contact point of the collision as before. If the collided object has a tag that matches the `destructionTag` method specified in the script, we instantiate another impact prefab at the contact point and destroy both the collided object and `destructionPrefab`. If the collided object doesn't have the specified tag, we proceed to add the impact force to the object using its `Rigidbody` component.

3. Save the code.
4. Choose a projectile with the script attached to it and set the tag to `destructible`.
5. Enable **Destroy** if you want this to be able to destroy a GO in the virtual world.
6. Go to the virtual world scene and set a GO to the `destructible` tag as well.

When you test it out, you can fire projectiles anywhere and add them to anything, but when you fire the projectile that has the `destructible` tag on it using the `destructible` tag projectile, that object will be destroyed. So, the way this works now is that if you want to set an object to be destroyed by a particular projectile, all you have to do is set the tag for that in the projectile using the dropdown menu made within the script. Then, you can set the object you want it to destroy with the same tag. If you don't have a tag, you can create one in the tag menu and then set the projectile and the specific object so that they interact the way you want them to. This is a modular approach to using code and applying it in a variety of different ways for many different use cases.

In this section, we laid down the foundation for how to destroy GOs when they're hit by projectiles. In the next section, we will expand on this concept so that we can designate how many hits it's going to take for an object to be destroyed. It's no fun if it only takes one hit to destroy an object. Adding some variability would be nice, and more importantly, something that is small and soft should not take as many hits as something that is big and large such as a building. Additionally, this allows us to have different damage indicators for our different projectiles.

In the next section, we will cover how to implement a health system for our virtual objects using Unity.

Adding health to an object

A health system, or hit points as it's known in the gaming world, is a way to determine how many projectile impacts a virtual object can withstand before it's destroyed. This is the perfect way to implement our destruction system because we want to be able to set a building's destruction to something high and a rock's destruction to something low. Having this variability while also keeping it simple is ideal for a health system within a virtual world, especially since you don't want to waste too much time on this implementation when you have other things you want to do with the experience.

In this section, we will cover how to add health points to an object and then add damage points to our projectiles. The interplay of these two elements gives us a robust damage and health system that allows us to lay the foundation for how our objects are destroyed in our VR scene.

Adding health points

To add health points to an object, follow these steps:

1. Create a new C# script called `ObjectHealth`.
2. Open the script and apply the following namespace:

   ```
   using UnityEngine;
   ```

3. In the `public class ObjectHealth` class, add the following variable to the script:

   ```
       public float health = 5f;
   ```

   This variable represents the initial health points of the object.

4. Create a new method called `public void TakeDamage(float amount)`, and add the following code to the script:

   ```
           health -= amount;
           if (health <= 0f)
           {
               Shatter();
           }
   ```

   This code subtracts the damage amount from the object's health and checks whether the health has reached zero or below. If so, it calls the `Shatter()` method to handle the object's destruction.

5. Create a new method called `void Shatter()` and add the following code to the script:

   ```
           DestroyGameObjectAndChildren(this.gameObject);
   ```

   This line of code invokes the `DestroyGameObjectAndChildren` method to destroy the object and its child objects upon reaching zero or negative health.

6. Create a new method called `void DestroyGameObjectAndChildren(GameObject gameObject)`, and add the following code to the script:

```
foreach (Transform child in
gameObject.transform)
{
    Destroy(child.gameObject);
}
Destroy(gameObject);
```

This iterates through each child object of the specified GO and destroys them. Finally, it destroys the GO itself.

7. Save this script and add it to any virtual objects you want to be part of the health and damage system in your virtual world.
8. For the GO that has this script on it, create a new tag called `Destruction` and give this GO a `Destruction` tag.
9. In the `ObjectHealth` script, set the health to `5`.

Adding damage points

To add damage points to a projectile, follow these steps:

1. Open the `CannonProjectileComplex` C# script and modify the following code by adding a new `public float` variable:

```
public float projectileDamagePoints;
```

We have added a new `public float` variable called `projectileDamagePoints` to hold the damage points that the projectile will apply to objects.

2. Reference the `Object Health` C# script we just made:

```
ObjectHealth health =
    collision.transform.GetComponent
        <ObjectHealth>();
if (health != null)
{
    health.TakeDamage(
        projectileDamagePoints);
}
else
{
    Destroy(collision.gameObject);
}
```

Within the `OnCollisionEnter()` method, we retrieve the `ObjectHealth` component from the collided object using `GetComponent`. If the object has an `ObjectHealth` component, we call the `TakeDamage()` method on that component, passing in `projectileDamagePoints`. If the object doesn't have an `ObjectHealth` component, we destroy the collided object.

Implementing a health system and damage system is essential for creating a realistic and dynamic VR experience. By following the steps outlined in this section, you can easily add health points to virtual objects and damage points to projectiles, providing a foundation for how objects are destroyed in your VR scene. With this foundation in place, you can focus on creating more engaging and interactive experiences without having to worry about the technical details of object destruction. By using a health and damage system, you can enhance the realism of your virtual world, making it more immersive and enjoyable for your users.

In the next section, we will create a prefab with a shatter effect that can be used with the script we just created.

Creating a shatter prefab

One of the challenges of creating VR applications is creating realistic effects, such as the destruction of GOs. In this section, we will explore how to create a `ShatterParticles` prefab in Unity to simulate the destruction of a GO. We will go through the steps involved in creating this effect, including creating a C# script, adding Rigidbodies and colliders, and distributing the particles in a variable area. We will also learn how to make variant `ShatterParticles` prefabs that can be used in different contexts. By the end of this book, you will have a solid understanding of how to create realistic destruction effects in your VR applications using Unity.

To create a prefab that simulates the shattered destruction of a GO, follow these steps:

1. Create an empty GO and name it `ShatteredParticles`.
2. Create a new C# script and name it `ObjectDestruction`.
3. Open the script and apply the following namespace:

```
using UnityEngine;
```

4. In the `public class ObjectDestruction` class, add the following variables to the script:

```
    public Collider[] particles;
    public float explosionRadius = 5f;
    public float explosionForce = 500f;
    public float delayTime;
    public Transform explosionCenter;
```

5. We have declared `public` variables to hold the shattered particles (colliders), explosion radius, explosion force, delay time before destroying the particles, and the transform of the explosion center.

6. Create a new method called `private void OnEnable()`, and add the following code to the script:

```
foreach (Collider collider in particles)
{
    Rigidbody otherRigidbody =
        collider.GetComponent<Rigidbody>();
    if (otherRigidbody != null)
    {
        otherRigidbody.AddExplosionForce(
            explosionForce,
            explosionCenter.transform.position
            , explosionRadius);
    }
    Destroy(collider.gameObject,delayTime);
}
Destroy(gameObject, delayTime);
```

   In the `OnEnable()` method, we iterate through each collider in the `particles` array. We retrieve the `Rigidbody` component from the collider and apply an explosion force to it using `AddExplosionForce()`. We also destroy the collider's GO after a specified delay. Finally, we destroy the GO of this script (`ShatteredParticles`) after the same delay.

7. Save the code and apply it to your `Shattered Particles` GO.
8. Set **Explosion Radius** to `5`.
9. Set **Explosion Force** to `300`.
10. Set **Delay Time** to `2`.
11. Set the explosion center to the `Shattered Particles` GO.
12. Create a cube as a child of the GO and name it `Destruction Particle`.
13. Scale it down in the **X**, **Y**, and **Z** axes to `0.05`.
14. Add a `Rigidbody` component to it.
15. Set **Mass** to `0.5`.
16. Enable **Use Gravity**.
17. Make `Destruction Particle` a prefab so that it can be duplicated and edited easily.
18. After saving the prefab, duplicate the `Destruction Particle` prefab 15 to 20 times as children of the `Shattered Particles` GO.

19. Add all the destruction particles to the `particles` array in the `ObjectDestruction` script.
20. Randomly distribute the particles around the center of the explosion point while keeping the variation of the particles to within -1 to 1 on each of the **X**, **Y**, and **Z** axes.
21. Add a dust particle by adding a `CFX3_Hit_SmokePuff` prefab from the downloaded VFX assets to the Shattered Particles prefab (*Figure 17.12*).
22. Save the `Shattered Particles` GO as a prefab.

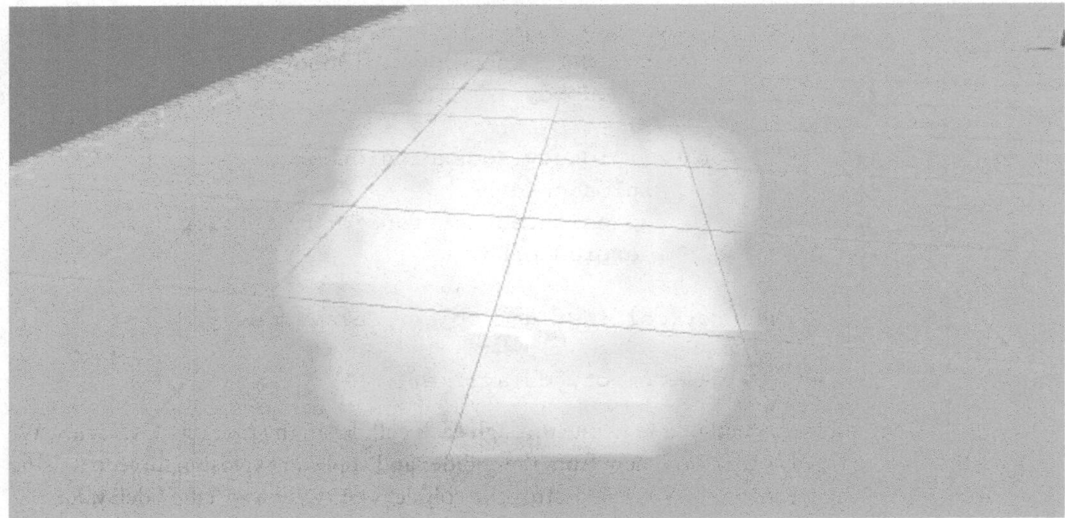

Figure 17.12 – The ShatterdParticles prefab has been activated with smoke effects

Now that we've created a prefab that shows a shatter effect, it is time to create a script that will place the prefab in the exact moment that we want it to be – when the explosion happens. This gives us the effect of having collateral damage within our scene based on the projectile that we fire and its interaction with the environment around it.

Instantiating a shatter prefab

To instantiate the shatter prefab on your object, follow these steps:

1. Open the `Object Health` script.
2. Add the following code to the `public` variable area:

```
public GameObject shatterPrefab;
public float shatterTime = 2f;
```

We have added a new `public GameObject` variable called `shatterPrefab` to hold the reference to the `ShatterParticles` prefab. The `shatterTime` variable determines how long `ShatterParticles` should exist before being destroyed.

3. Apply the following code to the `Shatter()` method:

```
Instantiate(shatterPrefab, transform.position,
    transform.rotation);
Destroy(shatterPrefab, shatterTime);
```

   Within the `Shatter()` method, we instantiate `shatterPrefab` at the position and rotation of the object. Then, we destroy `shatterPrefab` after the specified `shatterTime`.

4. Save the code.
5. In the `Object Health` component (*Figure 17.13*), set the `ShatterParticles` prefab to the **Shatter Prefab** reference section.
6. Set `shatterTime` to `2`.
7. Add this to your `ObjectHealth` script whenever you want to have an object become destructible.

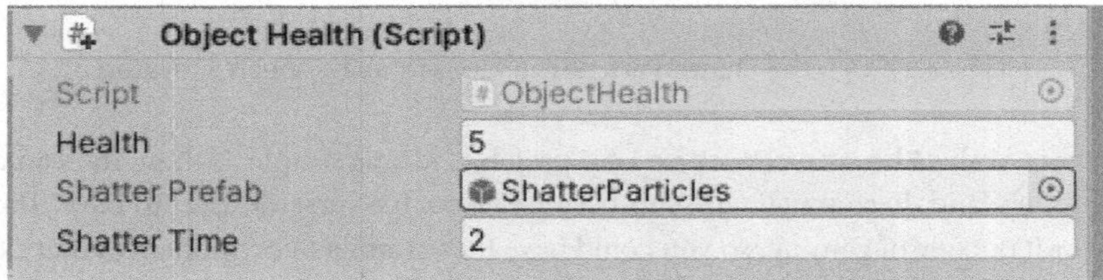

Figure 17.13 – Inspector component for the Object Health script

Now, when an object is destroyed after taking a lot of damage, it will spawn a shatter prefab that has an impulse that spreads particles all over the place to show that the object was destroyed. This is an easy and simple way to give off the effect of destruction within an environment without having to break down different meshes. The best part about it is that with this template, you can expand on it by adding different prefab elements. Maybe you want to have different GOs that burst out – the world is your oyster when it comes to creating the effect with this simple implementation.

Creating a shatter prefab variant

To create a shatter prefab variable, follow these steps:

1. Add the `ShatterParticles` prefab to a scene.
2. Rename it `ShatterParticles_BigBang`.
3. Find the `CFXR Explosion Smoke 2 Solo` prefab and add it as a child of the `ShatterParticles` prefab.

4. Set **Position** to `0,0,0` for `CFXR Explosion Smoke 2 Solo` (*Figure 17.14*).
5. Drag it to the `prefabs` folder and save it as a prefab variant. Make sure that the prefab is enabled before you make it a prefab; otherwise, you will have to enable it in the **Inspector** area from the `assets` folder.

Figure 17.14 – The ShatterParticles variant prefab has been activated

Making variants of the `ShatterParticles` prefab is just as simple as that. You can add things, change the models, and do so much with this because it's such a versatile asset to have. There are a lot of use cases for it outside of gaming, so you could have these immersive experiences that excite people about going through your experiences. The best part about the `ShatterParticles` prefab is that the only thing you need to do to activate it is to turn it on because it uses the `OnEnable()` method. The `OnEnable()` method triggers the code to play when it's activated. So, when you're thinking about interesting use cases to apply, think about using the `OnEnable()` method as well as using these types of activating experiences to beef up the things you have to offer within your VR worlds.

Summary

The real game-changer in this powerhouse of a chapter is the destruction and health system we've built for our VR objects. Imagine a world where every building or rock can be destroyed with hand cannons, grenades, or projectiles. This comes to life spectacularly through the use of visual effect prefabs from the Asset Store, adding that touch of pizzazz. At this point, you're equipped with a treasure trove of assets to craft immersive experiences, a process that would have taken years without our shared journey. Use these skills to develop unforgettable VR experiences.

In the next chapter, we'll focus on the crucial aspect of optimization. Without it, VR experiences can crash devices or run slowly, leading to poor user feedback. For independent developers and small studios, avoiding poor reviews is essential. Always remember that optimization isn't just a buzzword – it's a key to building trust with your users and ensuring a smooth, immersive VR experience.

Part 4: Final Touches

This final part elevates your VR creation journey to the next level, focusing on the art of optimization. Here, you will uncover the secrets to refining your VR experiences, ensuring that they run smoothly and are tailored to perform to the highest standards. By the time you turn the final page, you will have gained not just the knowledge of creating VR experiences but also the wisdom to optimize them for maximum impact and efficiency.

This part includes the following chapter:

- *Chapter 18, Optimizing Your Virtual Reality Experiences*

18

Optimizing Your Virtual Reality Experiences

In this chapter, we will cover a variety of ways to improve our VR experience during and after development, including tried-and-true optimization techniques that enhance usability and accessibility. Unity offers best practices and tools for optimization, and there is a wealth of information available online and in asset stores to improve your VR experiences.

In an ideal world, we wouldn't need to optimize because everything we create would run flawlessly on every device. However, this is not the case.

By the end of this chapter, you will understand the importance of optimization in making or breaking the experiences you hope to create. As a developer, you are aware of the effort and challenges that optimization requires, but this chapter will equip you with skills and approaches to improve the performance of your VR experiences, regardless of the intended device.

In *Phase 10* of our roadmap, we introduced optimizations, such as cleaning up code, baking lightmaps, making objects static, adding occlusion culling, adjusting quality settings, and improving the frame rate. Although this was a defined list, there is a lot of overlap between these techniques.

In this chapter, we will cover the following topics:

- What is optimization, and why is it important?
- How to use optimization tools such as the **Unity Profiler** and the **Stats** window
- Common techniques for optimizing Unity experiences while maintaining performance and quality
- How to approach improving the frame rate

Technical requirements

The complete source code for this chapter can be found at `https://github.com/PacktPublishing/Enhancing-Virtual-Reality-Experiences-with-Unity-2022/tree/main/EnhancingVRExperiencesFullProject/Assets/_VRProjectAssets/Scenes/Chapter_18`.

Optimization in Unity

Optimization is a critical aspect of developing interactive experiences such as games, animated videos, and VR applications. It focuses on improving performance and ensuring accessibility and playability, while minimizing issues such as lags, bugs, and other problems that could lead to user discomfort, such as nausea or vertigo.

Early optimization during development is essential as it allows for seamless performance across various devices without sacrificing visual quality. This practice also prevents potential challenges that may arise when trying to optimize a project after it has been fully developed.

Profiling plays a crucial role in the optimization process, as it helps developers identify specific areas that require improvement based on their individual projects. Since each project is unique, developers need to examine their Profilers to pinpoint performance bottlenecks and prioritize optimization efforts accordingly.

Achieving a high frame rate is a primary goal for optimization, especially in VR experiences where maintaining 90 fps is considered the standard. A consistent frame rate reduces performance-related issues such as lag, jittering, and overheating, ultimately providing users with a smoother, more enjoyable experience.

Biggest performance impacts

Preserving a 90 fps rate in VR is pivotal for minimizing motion sickness and guaranteeing pleasurable experiences. Not meeting this benchmark will detrimentally affect user interaction. Hence, we need to be cognizant of all factors that influence performance and, consequently, our frame rate.

The components in a Unity-based VR experience that most significantly affect performance can fluctuate based on the specific application and hardware setup. Nonetheless, here are some components that typically exert a considerable influence on performance:

- **Real-time rendering**: Real-time rendering, including lighting, shadows, and reflections, can have a significant impact on performance in VR applications. These elements require a lot of processing power and can cause frame rate drops if not optimized properly.
- **Physics**: Physics calculations, such as collisions, can also have a significant impact on performance in VR applications. This is because physics calculations can be complex and require a lot of processing power.

- **Triangles**: The number of triangles in your models can also have a significant impact on performance in VR applications. Models with a high number of triangles can require a lot of processing power to render and can cause frame rate drops if not optimized properly.
- **Animation**: Complex animations, especially those with a high number of bones or vertices, can have a significant impact on performance in VR applications.
- **Audio**: Audio processing can also have a significant impact on performance in VR applications, especially if the application uses a lot of positional audio or real-time audio effects.
- **Particles**: Particle effects, such as smoke, fire, and explosions, can have a significant impact on performance in VR applications. These effects require a lot of processing power to simulate and render.
- **Post-processing effects**: Post-processing effects, such as depth of field, bloom, and motion blur, can also have a significant impact on performance in VR applications. These effects require a lot of processing power to render, especially at high resolutions.
- **Dynamic objects**: Dynamic objects, such as objects that move or change shape frequently, can have a significant impact on performance in VR applications. This is because dynamic objects require more processing power to simulate and render than static objects.
- **Scripting**: Poorly optimized scripts, especially those that run frequently or perform complex calculations, can have a significant impact on performance in VR applications. It's important to write efficient and optimized scripts to minimize their impact on performance.
- **Reflections**: Real-time reflections, especially in complex environments, can have a significant impact on performance in VR applications. These reflections require a lot of processing power to render, especially at high resolutions.

What can you do to improve performance?

To improve performance, the following three-step approach can be used:

1. **Profile**: Analyze your game to identify resource-intensive areas.
2. **Plan**: Brainstorm at least three solutions to address the identified issues.
3. **Perform**: Implement the changes and evaluate their effectiveness.

Optimization of VR experiences is crucial to unlock their full capabilities and maintain user interest. It's also important to factor in the target devices, as this affects the level of optimization needed. Lower-end devices, such as the Oculus Quest or mobile phones, necessitate more optimization for ideal performance than high-end devices such as the Meta Quest Pro or PC-based VR headsets, which leverage more robust GPU and CPU resources. You can learn more about optimizing for performance here: `https://learn.unity.com/project/optimizing-for-performance-2019-3`.

In the next section, we will create a tool that can help us visualize and control the frame rate in our VR experience.

Frame rate manager

A simple optimization technique for VR experiences is setting the target frame rate. By doing this, we avoid using extra processing power to exceed the ideal frame rate, allocating more resources to other tasks. We'll set it to 90 fps, as that is the most suitable frame rate for VR experiences.

To set a target frame rate, go through the following steps:

1. Create a new C# script and call it `Frame Rate Manager`.
2. Open the script and apply the following namespaces to the code:

```
using System.Collections;
using System.Threading;
using UnityEngine;
```

3. In the `FrameRateManager : MonoBehaviour` public class, add the following variables:

```
[Header("Frame Settings")]
int MaxRate = 9999;
public float TargetFrameRate = 90.0f;
float currentFrameTime;
```

4. In the `Awake()` method, apply the following code:

```
QualitySettings.vSyncCount = 0;
Application.targetFrameRate = MaxRate;
currentFrameTime = Time.realtimeSinceStartup;
StartCoroutine("WaitForNextFrame");
```

5. This code disables **vertical synchronization (vSync)** to allow the frame rate to go as high as possible and sets the application's target frame rate to a specified maximum rate when the scene is first run on the first frame. Create a new method called `IEnumerator WaitForNextFrame()` and apply the following code:

```
while (true)
{
yield return new WaitForEndOfFrame();
currentFrameTime += 1.0f / TargetFrameRate;
var t = Time.realtimeSinceStartup;
var sleepTime = currentFrameTime - t - 0.01f;
if (sleepTime > 0)
Thread.Sleep((int)(sleepTime * 1000));
while (t < currentFrameTime)
t = Time.realtimeSinceStartup;
}
```

`IEnumerator WaitForNextFrame()` is a coroutine that manages the application's frame rate to align with the `TargetFrameRate` value we set in **Inspector**.

6. Save the code and go to **Hierarchy**.
7. Create a new GO and name it `frame rate manager`.
8. Apply the code to the `frame rate manager` GO.

A 90 fps setting ensures compatibility with lower-end devices. Once confirmed, build and run the file, then connect your device to test performance. The frame rate will not exceed the set value but may drop if performance issues arise. To display the frame rate on screen, use a UI canvas and a text element referencing the frame rate.

In the next section, we will make a UI text element and another script to show the frame rate at runtime.

Display frames per second

Having set the frame rate, it's essential to monitor it consistently to optimize performance. Check the frame rate during testing to identify any impacts on performance during specific scene elements. Displaying the frame rate in the corner allows for easy tracking, reducing the need to switch between the editor and play mode. This is particularly helpful when using a VR headset, as it enables focused optimization within specific contexts of the VR experience.

To display your current frame rate, go through the following steps:

1. Create a new canvas by right-clicking in the **Hierarchy** window and selecting **UI | Canvas**.
2. Add a text component to the canvas by selecting the canvas in the **Hierarchy** window, right-clicking on the canvas, and selecting **UI | Text**.
3. Select the text component in the **Hierarchy** window and rename it `FPSCounter`.
4. Set the font size, color, and other text properties for `FPSCounter` as desired.
5. Create a new script by right-clicking in the **Project** window and selecting **Create | C# Script**.
6. Name the script `FPSDisplay` and open it in your code editor.
7. Apply the following namespaces to the script:

```
using UnityEngine;
using UnityEngine.UI;
```

8. In the `FPSDisplay : MonoBehaviour` public class, apply the following variable:

```
    public Text fpsCounter;
```

9. In the `Update()` method, apply the following code:

```
    {
        float fps = 1f / Time.deltaTime;
```

```
            fpsCounter.text = "FPS: " + fps.ToString("F0");
        }
```

The preceding code calculates FPS based on the time taken to render each frame and updates the text component with the current FPS value. It is beneficial for testing optimizations within the experience being optimized.

10. Attach the `FPSDisplay` script to the canvas object by dragging the script from the **Project** window onto the canvas object in the **Hierarchy** window.
11. Drag the `FPSCounter` text component from the canvas object in the **Hierarchy** window into the `fpsCounter` field in the **Inspector** window for the `FPSDisplay` script.
12. Play the scene in Unity and you should see the `FPSCounter` text updating with the current FPS value in real time.

Monitoring the frame rate during every event is a valuable implementation during both early and late development stages. Even if not included in the final build, having this feature in prototypes is useful. It helps assess the impact of novel features on performance, allowing developers to make informed decisions on whether to proceed or find alternatives.

In the next section, we will look at the optimization tools that Unity provides for us to improve our performance.

Optimization tools

Unity provides various optimization tools to improve the performance of games and VR applications. These tools include the Profiler for real-time performance analysis, occlusion culling to hide non-visible objects, static and dynamic batching to reduce draw calls, **Level of Detail** (**LOD**) for distance-based object detail reduction, texture compression to optimize memory usage, and script optimization to optimize code for performance. By utilizing these tools, developers can ensure their games or VR applications run smoothly and provide a high-quality experience for users.

To access most of the Unity optimization tools, go through the following steps:

1. Go to the **Window** section of the toolbar.
2. Go to the **Analysis** tab. Here, you will find a variety of different things that will be useful for your optimization workflow.

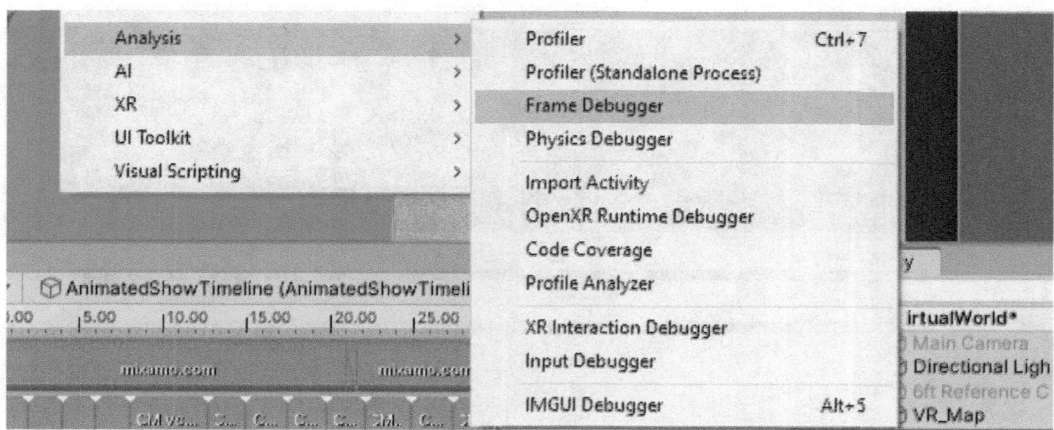

Figure 18.1 – Accessing Frame Debugger in the Unity Window dropdown menu

In the next section, we will introduce and explore the Unity **Profiler** and how it can be used to improve our performance.

Working with the Unity Profiler

One powerful tool to assist you in performance optimization is the **Profiler**. In this section, we will cover the basics of using the **Profiler** to analyze our VR application, identify areas for improvement, and optimize its performance to achieve a consistent 90 fps with good visuals on the target device.

To use the Profiler for optimizing your VR experience, follow these steps:

1. Open the Profiler by navigating to **Window** | **Analysis** | **Profiler** in your development environment.
2. Initiate play mode to activate the **Profiler** window, which will provide an overview of your application's performance in real time.
3. Observe the performance of various aspects of your application, such as CPU, GPU, memory, rendering, audio, and physics.
4. Look for spikes or high usage in any of the **Profiler** sections, which may indicate bottlenecks or areas that require optimization.
5. Pause the live view and switch to **Hierarchy** mode for a detailed breakdown of the time taken to complete a single frame and each call made during that frame.
6. Identify the specific scripts, assets, or resources causing performance issues by examining the detailed information provided in the **Profiler** window.
7. Optimize the problematic elements of your application to improve performance and maintain a consistent 90 fps.

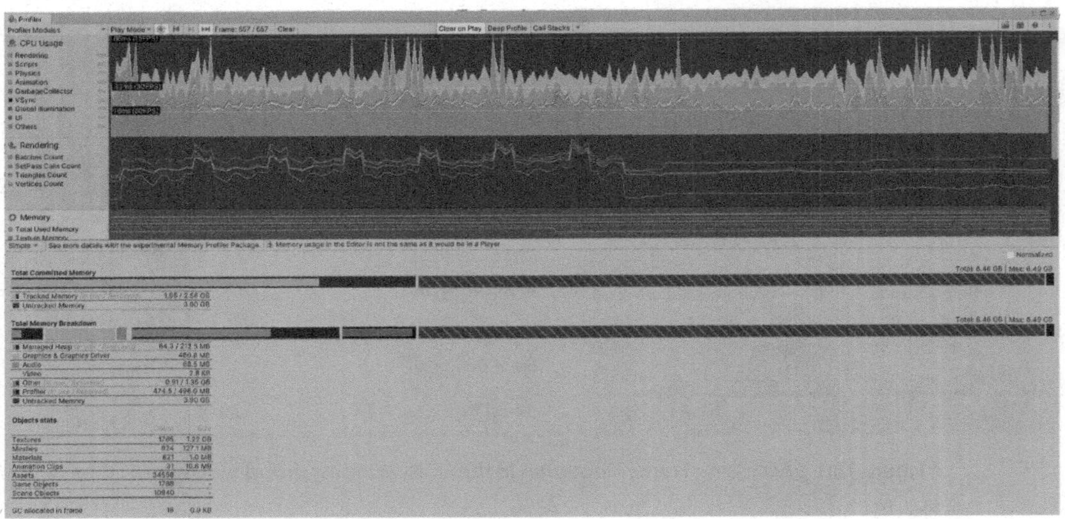

Figure 18.2 – Memory view of the Profiler analyzing the AnimatedShow scene performance

Here are some tips for optimizing specific aspects of your VR experience:

- For scripts taking a long time to complete, refactor the code to make it more efficient or offload computationally expensive tasks to background threads
- If animation is consuming a significant amount of time, consider using lower-polygon models, simplifying animations, or using LOD techniques to reduce the complexity of the scene as the distance from the viewer increases
- For memory optimization, consider using asset bundles or addressable assets to load resources on demand and unload them when they are no longer needed
- Optimize audio by using compressed audio formats, limiting the number of simultaneous audio sources, and using spatial audio techniques to prioritize important sounds in the environment
- To improve physics performance, you can simplify or approximate collision meshes, use layers and a collision matrix to limit the interactions between objects, and consider using physics engines optimized for VR

By following these tips and using the Profiler to identify bottlenecks, you can create a VR experience that maintains optimal performance and visual quality on the target device. Remember that optimization is an ongoing process, and regular testing and analysis are essential to ensure the best possible user experience.

In the next section, we will look at the **Stats** window, which allows us to look at different frame rates and other stats within our scene from the **Game** view.

Using the Stats window

Developers must be mindful of the target device's capabilities and limitations while creating immersive experiences. In this chapter, we will discuss various optimization tools and best practices, with a particular focus on using the **Stats** window in Unity for performance monitoring and improvement.

The Unity **Stats** window is a powerful tool for monitoring your VR project's real-time performance metrics, such as frame rate, draw calls, and memory usage. Regularly monitoring these metrics allows developers to identify areas requiring optimization and make necessary changes to achieve optimal performance and visuals. For an enjoyable VR experience, it is crucial to maintain a consistent frame rate of 90 fps on the target device.

To utilize the **Stats** window in Unity for optimization, follow these steps:

1. Open your Unity project and navigate to the **Game** view.
2. Enable the **Stats** window by clicking the **Stats** button located in the top-left corner of the **Game** view.
3. Run your game and observe the real-time performance metrics displayed in the **Stats** window, including frame rate, draw calls, and memory usage.
4. Customize the **Stats** window display settings by clicking the *gear* icon in the top-right corner of the window. Choose which metrics to display and adjust the refresh rate as needed.

Analyze the information provided by the **Stats** window to pinpoint areas requiring optimization. Make necessary changes to improve your game's performance. Here is an example:

- If the frame rate is below 90 fps, consider adjusting graphics settings, such as lowering texture resolution or reducing the render distance
- If draw calls are too high, try implementing techniques such as mesh batching, occlusion culling, or using LOD groups

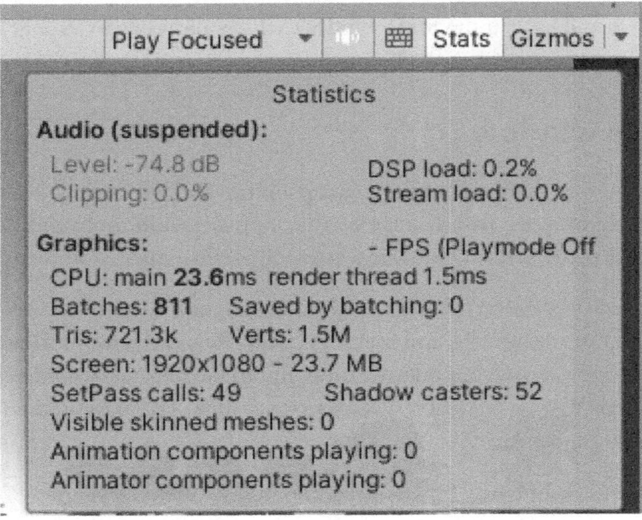

Figure 18.3 – The Stats window showing stats for the Animation scene

In the next section, we will look at **Frame Debugger** and how it could be used to identify bottlenecks.

Using Frame Debugger

One key aspect of optimization is maintaining a high frame rate, ideally around 90 fps, for the target device. In this section, we will discuss Frame Debugger to analyze the rendering process of each frame in your game or VR application, identifying performance bottlenecks and areas for improvement.

Frame Debugger is a valuable tool for identifying and addressing performance issues in your Unity projects, particularly for VR applications. To use Frame Debugger in Unity, go through the following steps:

1. Open your game or VR application in Unity and enter play mode.
2. Navigate to **Window** | **Analysis** | **Frame Debugger** to open the **Frame Debugger** window.
3. Click on the **Enable** button to activate **Frame Debugger**. Unity will pause the game and show you a snapshot of the rendering process for the current frame.
4. Use the controls in the **Frame Debugger** window to navigate through the rendering process and view information about each object in the scene, such as draw calls, materials, and textures.
5. Identify any performance issues, such as objects causing too many draw calls or materials that are too complex.
6. Make changes to your scene or assets to address the performance issues, and test your changes by exiting play mode and re-entering it.
7. Remember to adjust the debug level on your URP asset when needed. Increasing the debug level can provide more information but may reduce performance. Be sure to turn it off when not profiling.

8. Review any custom renderer features you may have active in your pipeline asset to understand their impact on the rendering loop and make adjustments as necessary.

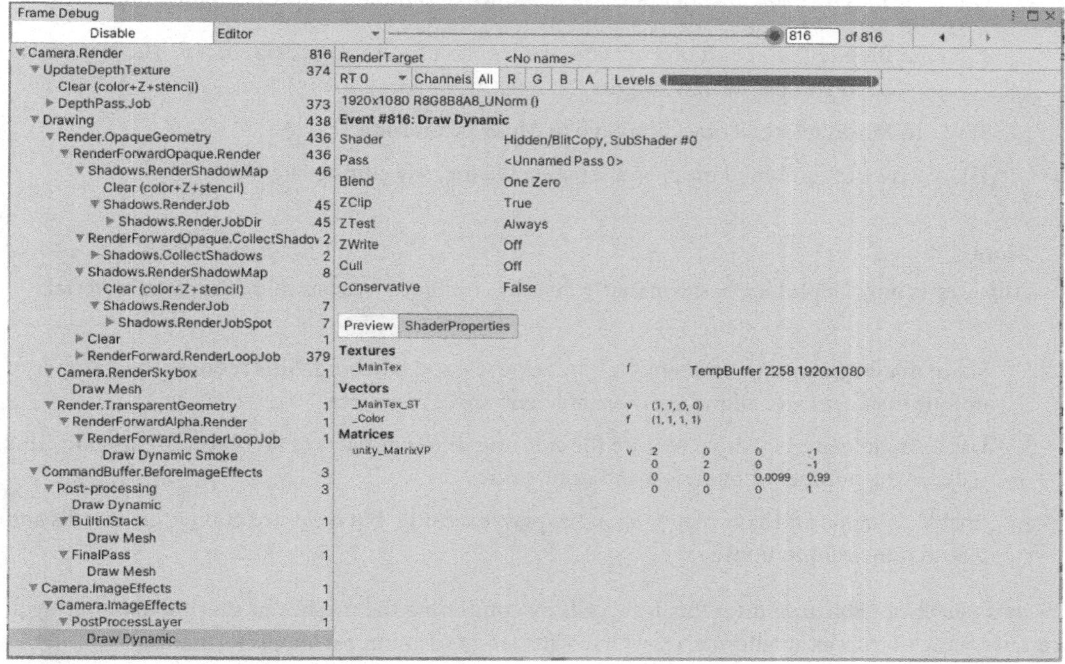

Figure 18.4 – Frame Debugger stats from the Animation scene

By using Frame Debugger, you can optimize your VR experience, ensuring that it runs smoothly and provides a high-quality experience for users on the target device.

In addition to Frame Debugger, don't forget to utilize the Unity Profiler to gain insights into the performance of your application. Combining the use of Frame Debugger and Profiler will enable you to identify and resolve performance bottlenecks and create an optimized VR experience that runs at 90 fps with good visuals and performance on the target device.

With an understanding of various optimization tools in Unity for enhancing VR experiences, we can now focus on optimizing specific aspects such as draw calls, assets, and other materials. This will further improve runtime, enabling us to achieve a smooth 90 fps. Let's begin by examining draw call optimization.

Optimizing draw calls

One critical aspect of optimizing VR applications is reducing draw calls, which are commands sent to the GPU to render a mesh. The number of draw calls can quickly add up and have a significant impact on performance.

To optimize draw calls in your VR experience, follow these steps:

1. Combine meshes using Blender or Maya to reduce the amount of faces to render for each asset:

   I. In Blender, select all objects you want to combine and press *Ctrl* + *J*. The last object selected will be the new origin.

   II. In Maya, select all objects and go to **Mesh | Combine**.

   III. Save the combined mesh as a separate file for easy editing later on.

> **Note**
>
> This step is only helpful for performance when the combined meshes share the same material.

2. Share materials among different GOs to achieve good batching. This reduces the number of unique instances and allows for more efficient use of resources.
3. Use a single material with a texture for coloring different parts of an object, if possible. This reduces the number of materials and draw calls.
4. Enable dynamic and static batching in the player settings, but be aware of their drawbacks and research their limitations.

Even if you're not able to reduce the draw calls by combining the meshes or sharing materials, you can use static objects as an alternative, which is just as good at improving performance.

Static objects

VR experiences require high-quality visuals and performance to ensure an immersive and enjoyable experience for users. To achieve this, developers must optimize their VR applications by using various tools and best practices. This section will provide an overview of optimization techniques that can help maintain a consistent frame rate of 90 fps while still providing good visuals and performance for VR devices. We will discuss various optimization tools, settings, and best practices to ensure that your VR experience is both visually stunning and performs optimally.

Set objects that are not supposed to move to **Static**. To set an object to **Static** in Unity, go through the following steps:

1. Select the object that you want to set to static in the **Hierarchy** window or **Scene** view.
2. In the **Inspector** window, locate the **Static** checkbox under the `Mesh Renderer` component or the `Collider` component.
3. Check the **Static** checkbox to set the object to **Static**.

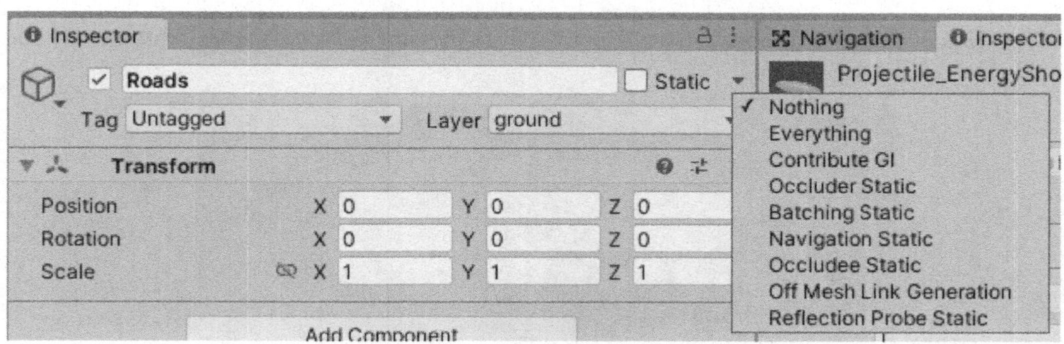

Figure 18.5 – Static GO options in the Inspector window

Note that setting an object to **Static** means that it will not move or change at runtime, and can be batched with other static objects to reduce draw calls and improve performance. However, this also means that the object cannot be moved, rotated, or scaled at runtime. If you need an object to be dynamic and changeable at runtime, you should not set it to **Static**.

Another hack to improve performance by reducing draw calls is using occlusion culling. We will explore that in the next section.

Occlusion culling

One effective method to optimize VR experiences is by using occlusion culling, which helps reduce the rendering workload by only drawing the visible geometry in a scene. By calculating occlusion data and ignoring geometry that is hidden behind other objects, you can significantly improve the performance and maintain a stable frame rate in your VR applications.

To use occlusion culling in Unity for VR optimization, follow these steps:

1. Open your project in Unity and select the scene you want to optimize.
2. In the **Scene** view, select the static objects that you want to calculate occlusion data for, such as objects behind walls or in closed rooms.
3. In the top menu, select **Window | Rendering | Occlusion Culling**.
4. In the **Occlusion Culling** window, click on the **Bake** button to calculate occlusion data for the selected objects.
5. Unity will display a progress bar as it calculates the occlusion data. This process may take some time depending on the complexity of the scene and the number of objects.
6. Once the occlusion data has been calculated, you can enable occlusion culling in the **Scene** view by clicking on the **Occlusion Culling** button in the top-left corner of the **Scene** view.

7. Unity will now hide objects that are not visible to the camera based on the occlusion data that was calculated in *step 4*.

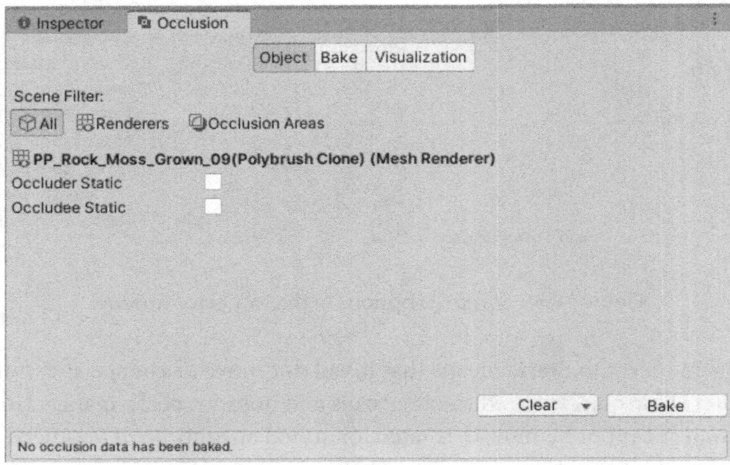

Figure 18.6 – Object occlusion options in the Occlusion window

Here are some exact values and settings to use for optimal VR experiences running at 90 fps with good visuals and performance:

- For the **Smallest Occluder** setting in the **Occlusion Culling** window, use a value of `5`
- For the **Smallest Hole** setting, use a value of `0.25`
- For the **Backface Threshold** setting, use a value of `100`

These settings should help you achieve better performance and visuals in your VR application on the target device. Remember that occlusion culling works best with static objects, and dynamic objects may require additional optimization techniques.

Now that we have a better understanding of how to optimize draw calls, we can optimize the materials on our meshes.

Optimizing material settings

Optimizing materials is essential for enhancing the performance and user experience of Unity games and VR applications. By streamlining material complexity, enabling GPU instancing, and using appropriate shaders, developers can significantly increase rendering speed, reduce memory usage, and achieve a stable 90 fps on target devices similar to *Oculus Quest 2*. This optimization ensures a visually appealing and responsive VR experience for users.

GPU instancing

By utilizing various techniques such as batching, GPU instancing, and choosing appropriate settings, we can ensure that our VR content runs smoothly at 90 fps while maintaining excellent visuals on the target device. To achieve this, we will delve into specific optimization tips and step-by-step instructions to maximize the performance and efficiency of your VR project.

To improve performance when rendering multiple instances of the same object with the same mesh and material, consider using GPU instancing. This technique allows you to render several instances of an object with a single draw call, reducing the number of draw calls required and, ultimately, improving performance.

To use GPU instancing in Unity, follow these steps:

1. Select the object you want to instance and create a new material for it by selecting **Create | Material** in the **Project** window.
2. Choose a shader that supports GPU instancing, such as the **Standard Shader**, in the **Inspector** window for the new material.
3. Enable GPU instancing for the material by checking the **Enable Instancing** checkbox in **Material Inspector**.
4. With the object selected in the **Hierarchy** window, access the `Mesh Renderer` component in the **Inspector** window.
5. In the `Mesh Renderer` component, navigate to the **Materials** section and add the material to the list of materials.

Remember, GPU instancing is most effective for objects sharing the same mesh and material, making it ideal for objects such as trees, rocks, and grass in outdoor environments. However, it might not be as effective for objects with unique meshes and materials. GPU instancing cannot be used simultaneously with static batching, so choose the technique that best suits your specific use case.

Out of the box, Unity provides a shader that is optimal for mobile rendering and that is the Mobile shader. We will explore that in the next section.

Using Mobile shaders

Mobile shaders are a powerful tool for optimizing VR experiences on devices with limited processing power and memory. Complex shaders are great for providing robust detail to objects in your scene, but often, performance is more of a priority during runtime. Shaders with multiple textures and complex shader features can be resource-heavy. By utilizing these specialized shaders, developers can create visually stunning and high-performance VR experiences that run optimally at 90 fps. This section will discuss optimization tools and best practices for leveraging Mobile shaders in Unity, ensuring that your VR application maintains excellent visuals and performance.

To use Mobile shaders in Unity and optimize your VR experience, go through the following steps:

1. Open your project in Unity and navigate to the **Materials** folder in the **Project** window.
2. Right-click in the **Materials** folder and select **Create | Material** to create a new material.
3. Select the newly created material in the **Project** window and look for the **Shader** dropdown in the **Inspector** window.
4. Expand the **Mobile** section of the **Shader** dropdown and choose an appropriate Mobile shader, such as **Mobile/Diffuse** for a basic diffuse material or **Mobile/Bumped Specular** for a material with specular highlights and normal maps.
5. Adjust the material properties, such as color and texture, in the **Inspector** window to align with your desired visual effects. For optimal performance, use texture resolutions of *1,024 x 1,024* or lower.
6. Apply the material to a GO by dragging and dropping it onto the object in the **Scene** view or **Hierarchy** window.

For advanced users, consider creating custom Mobile shaders using Unity's ShaderLab language. This requires knowledge of Shader programming and offers more control over the optimization process.

With our materials optimized, we can move on to our camera settings so that we can have the best camera settings for our VR rendering experiences.

Optimizing camera settings

Understanding Unity camera settings is essential for boosting your VR experience's performance. The camera renders everything in the scene, and knowing which options to adjust can lead to significant performance improvements. Two important settings are the camera **clipping planes** and camera **field of view** (**FOV**), which determine how much the Unity camera can view. However, be cautious not to set these values too low, as it may prevent the camera from rendering essential elements.

In the next section, we will optimize our camera settings by adjusting the FOV.

FOV

Adjusting the camera's FOV can significantly impact the overall performance, as it determines the number of objects being rendered on the screen at once. In this section, we will discuss how to optimize the FOV for an optimal VR experience while maintaining good visuals and performance on the target device.

To optimize the FOV for a VR experience, follow these steps:

1. Select the camera in the **Scene** or **Hierarchy** window.
2. In the **Inspector** window, look for the **Field of View** property under the `Camera` component.

3. Set **FOV** to around `90`.
4. Test the performance and visuals on the target device, and fine-tune the **FOV** value as needed to achieve the desired balance between performance and visual quality.

Remember that finding the right FOV value is a process of trial and error. Continuously test your VR experience on the target device to determine the optimal setting that offers the best combination of performance and visuals while maintaining a comfortable experience for the user.

With our FOV adjusted, we can move on to adjusting our clipping planes.

Clipping planes

One of the key aspects of optimization is managing the clipping planes, which determine the closest and farthest distances at which the camera can render objects. Balancing these settings can help improve performance while maintaining a high level of visual quality.

Based on the provided notes, here are the step-by-step instructions for optimizing clipping planes:

1. Select the camera in the **Scene** or **Hierarchy** window.
2. In the **Inspector** window, locate the **Clipping Planes** property under the `Camera` component.
3. Adjust the **Near** value to control the closest distance at which objects are rendered. A value of `0.3` is recommended to prevent visual artifacts.
4. Adjust the **Far** value to control the farthest distance at which objects are rendered. This value should be set based on your specific scene requirements. Start with a value of `1000` and adjust as needed for best performance and visual quality.
5. Test your VR experience with the adjusted clipping planes to ensure that the visuals and performance are optimal. Make any necessary adjustments before finalizing your build.

Remember that it's important to test and fine-tune these values based on the specific requirements of your VR experience to achieve the best balance between performance and visual quality.

With our clipping planes adjusted, we can move on to optimizing our render paths in the next section.

Render paths

In this subsection, we will discuss optimization tools and best practices for creating VR experiences with a focus on rendering techniques, camera settings, and performance considerations. We'll explore two rendering paths, **Forward Rendering** and **Deferred Rendering**, and their trade-offs in terms of performance and visual quality. Additionally, we will delve into camera components that can impact performance, such as culling masks, depth textures, and camera effects, and provide tips for optimizing these settings for a smooth VR experience targeting 90 fps on the desired device.

Forward Rendering is the default rendering path and works well for scenes with few lights and no dynamic objects. However, it lacks support for advanced features such as soft shadows and may struggle with scenes containing many lights.

Deferred Rendering, on the other hand, is designed for complex scenes with numerous lights, as it separates the rendering process into two passes: geometry and lighting. Although more efficient for rendering many lights, it may not be as performant with high-vertex-count objects and anti-aliasing.

To choose the right rendering path, consider your application's specific requirements, and the number of lights and dynamic objects present. Be aware that Deferred Rendering might not be supported on all devices and may not work optimally with some features such as anti-aliasing or semi-transparent objects.

Now that we have our camera settings optimized, we can move on to optimizing our images and textures in the next section.

Optimizing images and textures

Texture optimization involves configuring texture map settings such as resolution, format, compression, and mipmapping to balance performance and image quality. In this section, we will discuss best practices and step-by-step instructions for optimizing textures in Unity to achieve the desired results.

To optimize textures in Unity for VR experiences, follow these steps:

1. Select the texture in the Unity project.
2. In the **Inspector** window, enable the **Generate MipMaps** option.
3. Set **Max Size** to an appropriate value, such as `512`. For UI elements, you can use `128` or `256`.
4. Enable the **Crunch Compression** option.
5. Set the **Quality** value to balance between compression and image quality, such as `50`.
6. Click **Apply** to save the changes.

We can repeat these steps to apply to all of our textures and images in our VR scenes so that we save space and improve our rendering speed. In the next section, we will explore optimizations for our audio files.

Optimizing audio files

Efficient audio management helps maintain high frame rates, reduces memory usage, and minimizes latency, ensuring a smooth and enjoyable experience for the user. In this section, we will explore various tools and best practices for optimizing audio in Unity, targeting an optimal performance of 90 fps and high-quality visuals on standalone VR devices.

To optimize audio in Unity for VR experiences, follow these steps:

1. Select the audio file in the Unity project.
2. Enable the **Force to Mono** option for 3D audio sources to save memory, as 3D audio essentially plays in mono. This does not affect the sound quality but reduces the file size.
3. Enable the **Normalize** option to adjust the gain of the mono sound to the same volume as the original audio file.
4. Set these options based on your requirements to manage how and when audio files are loaded in your VR application.
5. Enable the **Ambisonic** option if the audio file has ambisonic encoded audio.
6. Choose between **Decompress On Load**, **Compressed In Memory**, or **Streaming** based on the size and performance needs of your audio files. For most cases, use **Compressed In Memory**.
7. Select the appropriate compression format (**PCM**, **ADPCM**, or **Vorbis**) for your audio files. **ADPCM** is recommended for reducing CPU load while maintaining sound quality, and **Vorbis** is recommended for high compression ratios without compromising sound quality. For most cases, use **Vorbis**.
8. Adjust the **Quality** option to decrease the size of the compressed audio file in exchange for sound quality. Keep the value between `100` and `70` for optimal performance without significant quality loss. Start with `75` and adjust from there.
9. Choose between **Preserve Sample Rate**, **Optimize Sample Rate**, or **Override Sample Rate** based on your audio management expertise and the desired audio quality for your VR experience. For background sound, use `44 Hz`. For sound effects, use `8-22 Hz`.

Now that we have a better understanding of optimizing our audio files, we repeat this in a variety of different ways to save our frame rate from being impacted. In the next section, we will focus on optimizing our animation files.

Optimizing animation files

Animations play a vital role in creating immersive and engaging experiences in games and VR applications. However, they can also significantly impact performance if not optimized effectively. By utilizing proper optimization techniques, developers can enhance the performance of animations in Unity, ensuring smooth and responsive gameplay or VR experiences for users.

High-frame-rate animations can consume substantial resources, leading to decreased performance. It's essential to evaluate the current frame rate of your animations to identify potential areas for optimization. To improve performance, consider lowering the frame rate of animations in the Timeline. This will reduce resource consumption and lead to a more responsive experience. For optimal performance on the target device, aim for animations to run at 90 fps.

The best way to optimize our animation files is to reduce the keyframes. We will explore that in the next section.

Keyframe reduction

Optimizing VR experiences is crucial to maintaining high-quality visuals and performance while ensuring a smooth and immersive experience for users. One key aspect of optimization is reducing the memory and computational overhead associated with animations. In this section, we will explore optimization tools and best practices, with a focus on keyframe reduction and compression techniques, to help you achieve optimal performance in your VR applications.

To use keyframe reduction in Unity for optimizing your animations, follow these steps:

1. Select the animated object in the **Scene** or **Project** view window.
2. In the **Inspector** window, click on the **Animation** tab.
3. Select the animation clip that you want to optimize.
4. Click on the **Optimize Curve** button to open the **Curve Editor** window.
5. In the **Curve Editor** window, you will see a visual representation of the animation's curves.
6. Select the curves that you want to optimize.
7. Click on the **Key Reduction** dropdown and select one of the options: **All Keys**, **Selected Keys**, or **Curves with Overlapping Keys**.
8. Adjust the **Keyframe Reduction Threshold** slider to your desired value. For the target device, use a value of `0.2` for rotation, position, and scale error, which corresponds to approximately 20% keyframe reduction.
9. Preview the optimized animation by clicking on the **Preview** button in the **Curve Editor** window.
10. If you're satisfied with the optimized animation, click on the **Apply** button to apply the changes.

Keep in mind that keyframe reduction is a balance between performance and visual quality. Removing too many keyframes can result in a less smooth or accurate animation, so it's important to find the right balance between optimization and visual fidelity. Also, not all animations are suitable for keyframe reduction, such as those with subtle movements or complex movements that require precise timing. It's recommended to test the optimized animation thoroughly before using it in your VR application.

With our keyframes reduced, we are sure to gain extra rendering power with the space that we save. In the next section, we will revisit a concept we learned in *Chapter 6*: light baking to optimize our lighting system.

Optimizing the lighting system

VR experiences require optimization tools and best practices to achieve the best possible performance and visual fidelity. One crucial aspect of optimizing VR experiences is managing lighting, as it can greatly impact both visual quality and performance. By following these guidelines, developers can create VR experiences that run smoothly at 90 fps on target devices.

The best way to optimize our lighting system is to explore light baking, which we will do in the next section.

Light baking

Creating immersive and high-quality VR experiences requires a balance between visual quality and performance. To achieve optimal performance on target devices, it is essential to utilize optimization tools and best practices. One critical aspect of optimizing VR experiences is the efficient management of lighting within the scene, which can be achieved through a process known as baking. In this section, we will discuss the benefits of baking lights, how to perform the process in Unity, and tips for maintaining high-quality visuals while achieving the desired 90 fps performance on your target device.

To bake lights and optimize performance, follow these steps:

1. Set up your scene and objects in Unity, ensuring that all objects and light sources are placed as desired.
2. Mark your lights as baked by selecting them and choosing **Baked** from the **Mode** dropdown.
3. Mark **Geometry** in your scene as **Static** to include geometry objects in lightmapping calculations and contribute to bouncing light from global illumination.
4. Open the **Lighting** window (**Window | Rendering | Lighting**) and create a new `Lighting Settings` asset.
5. Set up your lightmapping settings using the **Progressive Lightmapper**, with the following settings:
    - **Direct samples**: `12`
    - **Indirect samples**: `12`
    - **Environment samples**: `12`
    - **Lightmap resolution**: `19.1`
    - **Lightmap size: 2048x2048 (2K) maximum**
6. Click on **Generate Lighting** to begin the baking process.

When you're satisfied with the scene, gradually increase the resolution, size, and sample settings for your final build. Strive to maintain between one and three lightmap sprite sheets for optimal performance, minimizing draw calls.

We just improved our light system and so now we have to focus on the shadows so that they don't bog us down. We will explore that in the next section.

Shadows

Shadows play an essential role in creating realistic and immersive visuals in VR applications. However, they can also be resource-intensive, affecting the overall performance of the experience. In this section, we'll cover how to optimize shadows in a VR application, ensuring good visuals while maintaining a consistent 90 fps for optimal performance on target devices.

To optimize shadow settings for VR applications, follow these steps:

1. To set hard shadows, in the **Directional Light** settings, change **Shadow Type** to **Hard Shadows**. Hard shadows are less resource-intensive and are recommended for VR applications.
2. In the **Directional Light** settings, adjust the **Shadow Strength** slider to `0.75`.
3. Go to **Edit | Project Settings | Quality**.
4. Select a **Medium** preset.
5. Disable **Anisotropic Textures**.
6. Set **Shadow Type** to **Hard Shadows Only**.
7. Set **Shadow Resolution** to **Medium**.
8. Set **Shadow Cascades** to **No Cascades**.
9. Disable **Soft Particles**, if not needed.

We now have a fully optimized lighting system that has lightmaps that are baked and shadows that are a good resolution for us to use across our scenes. In the last section, we will explore project setting optimizations so that we can improve the performance across all of our scenes in our whole project.

Optimizing project settings

Optimizing project settings in Unity is an important step to ensure that your project runs smoothly and efficiently. The settings that you can optimize include **Rendering**, **Physics**, **Audio**, and **Scripting**. For example, in the rendering settings, you can adjust the graphics quality and set up LOD to improve performance. In the physics settings, you can adjust the timestep and gravity to ensure that the physics simulation runs smoothly. In the audio settings, you can optimize the audio quality and set up audio occlusion to ensure that sounds are only heard in the appropriate areas. In the scripting settings, you can adjust the compilation settings and choose the appropriate scripting backend to optimize the performance of your code. By optimizing these settings, you can improve the performance of your Unity project and ensure that it runs smoothly on different devices and platforms.

We will go through some settings that all VR experiences must have so that they run the best that they possibly could on any device. We'll first start off with build settings and then we'll move on to other settings.

Build settings

One of the essential areas to optimize is the build settings, specifically for the Android platform. By following the steps outlined, you can enhance your VR experience by reducing game file size and improving texture compression.

To optimize build settings for Android and enable **Adaptive Scaler Texture Compression** (**ASTC**), go through the following steps:

1. Open your project in your preferred game engine or development environment.
2. Go to **File | Build Settings** to access the **Build Settings** panel.
3. If not already done, switch to the Android platform. This may take a moment to complete.
4. Once switched to the Android platform, locate the **Texture Compression** setting.
5. Change the **Texture Compression** option to **ASTC**.

By following these steps, you will have successfully optimized your build settings for the Android platform and enabled ASTC, a newer form of texture compression that reduces game file size and covers a wider range of textures.

In the next section, we will look at different player settings that we can implement that will further improve the performance of our VR projects.

Player settings

By carefully configuring these settings, developers can tailor their VR projects to the target platform, meeting the demanding requirements of high frame rates and visual fidelity. This section will guide you through the process of optimizing **Player Settings** in Unity and provide best practices to achieve optimal results for VR experiences.

To optimize **Player Settings** in Unity for VR experiences, go through the following steps:

1. Open the Unity project you are working on.
2. Click on **Edit** in the top menu and select **Project Settings** from the dropdown menu to access the **Project Settings** window.
3. In the **Project Settings** window, click on the **Player** tab to access **Player Settings**.
4. Under the **Resolution and Presentation** section, set **Default Orientation** to **Landscape Left** for optimal VR performance.

5. **Player Settings** has a variety of different subsections, such as **Rendering** settings, **Configuration** settings, and other settings that can be adjusted and modified so that we can have the best frame rate and rendering quality that devices can possibly reach.

In the next section, we will explore rendering settings that allow us to reach the most optimal frame rate with the best quality visuals.

Rendering settings

In this section, we will discuss optimization tools and best practices for VR experiences, focusing on rendering settings for optimal visuals and performance. Ensuring your VR application runs at 90 fps with high-quality visuals is crucial for an immersive and enjoyable experience on the target device.

To optimize the rendering settings in Unity, follow these steps:

1. Set **Color Space** to **Linear**:

   I. Go to **Edit | Project Settings | Player**.

   II. Under the **Other Settings** section, find the **Color Space** option.

   III. Change the **Color Space** setting from **Gamma** to **Linear**.

   Linear lighting provides a more realistic interaction of light with objects compared to gamma space.

2. Configure the **Graphics APIs** settings:

   I. In the same **Player** settings, locate the **Graphics API** section.

   II. Deselect **Auto Graphics API** to manually choose the API.

   III. Remove **Vulkan** from the list of APIs, as it is still in the experimental phase.

   IV. Ensure **OpenGLES3** is the selected API, as it is required for linear color spaces.

3. Enable **Multi-threaded Rendering**:

   I. In the **Player** settings, find the **Multi-threaded Rendering** option.

   II. Enable this setting to utilize CPUs with multiple cores, speeding up the rendering process.

4. Enable **Static Batching** and **Dynamic Batching**:

   I. Still in the **Player** settings, locate **Static Batching** and **Dynamic Batching**.

   II. Enable both options to reduce draw calls and lighten the load on the system.

5. Set **Texture Compression Format**:

   I. In the **Player** settings, find the **Texture Compression Format** option.

   II. Change the format to **ASTC** to use the optimal compression format for the target device.

6. Set **Minimum API Level** to **Android 10**:

   I. Navigate to the **Identification** section in the **Player** settings.

   II. Change **Minimum API Level** to **Android 10**.

   III. Ensure **Target API Level** is set to **Automatic (highest installed)**.

   This is a requirement by Meta and not directly related to performance improvement.

With our rendering settings optimized, we can move on to the next subsection of the **Player Settings** tab, which is **Configuration** settings.

Configuration settings

In this section, we will discuss important topics such as choosing the appropriate scripting backend, target architecture, and installation location.

IL2CPP (which stands for **Intermediate Language To C++**) is a Unity-developed scripting backend that provides better support for a wider range of platforms and improvements in performance when compared to Mono, an open source implementation of Microsoft's .NET Framework.

To choose IL2CPP as the scripting backend, follow these steps:

1. In Unity, go to **Edit | Project Settings | Player**.
2. Under the **Configuration** section, locate **Scripting Backend** and select **IL2CPP**.
3. Set the target architecture to **ARM64**. ARM64 is required for compatibility with certain application storefronts, which only allow 64-bit applications.

   To set the target architecture to **ARM64**, follow these steps:

   I. In the **Player** settings, go to **Edit | Project Settings | Player**, and navigate to the **Configuration** section.

   II. Locate **Target Architectures** and uncheck **ARMv7**.

   III. Make sure **ARM64** is checked.

4. Set **Install Location** to **Automatic**. Setting the **Install Location** to **Automatic** allows the operating system to choose the best location to install the application on the target device.

Now that we have our configuration settings done, we can move to the **Quality** settings tab so that we can improve the quality of our graphics while also saving ourselves some performance load by turning off different rendering options that we don't need.

Quality settings

We will focus on quality settings and discuss how to balance performance with visual fidelity. Additionally, we will provide tips on giving the player control over the game's performance by allowing them to adjust the quality settings at runtime.

To optimize the quality settings for VR experiences, go through the following steps:

1. In the **Quality Levels** section, click on **Medium**.

   You will notice in this section that there are some icons for the different device modules that we have in our project. Under **Android** and **iOS**, if you have those installed, you will see that, for **Medium**, there are green checkboxes. Those green checkboxes mean that the rendering setting is the most ideal for those devices. Since most VR devices are Android devices, I usually go with **Medium**. Alternatively, you can select **Add Quality Level** and rename it to a suitable name to serve as the custom settings for your target device.

2. Change the pixel light count to `1`, as suggested by Meta. This reduces the number of lights considered important for rendering, which improves performance.
3. Set the anti-aliasing to `4x`. This balances the smoothness of object edges while maintaining performance.
4. Turn on real-time reflection probes to improve the visuals in your VR experience.
5. Ensure **Texture Quality** is set to **Full Res** for better visuals.
6. Set **Anisotropic Textures** to **Per Texture** to save processing and GPU work.
7. Turn off soft particles to optimize performance.
8. Ensure **Billboards Face Camera Positions** is checked for proper rendering of billboards.
9. Consider disabling shadows, or use hard shadows only to improve performance. Experiment with these settings to find the best balance between visual quality and performance.

Adjusting our quality settings gives us a happy medium between improving our performance and having the best visuals we possibly can for our VR experiences. There are a lot of different individual settings that we could optimize here, but for the basics, we just covered those. Out of the box, Unity provides us with very good initial settings with very low, low, medium, high, very high, and ultra quality. If you decide to use the URP, then it provides you with other settings that you could do to improve the quality of your visuals while also maintaining a good level of performance.

The second to last section that we will move on to is stereo rendering, which is perfect for VR experiences because we need to render on both eyes.

Stereo rendering settings

Typically, VR requires rendering two separate images for each eye, which can be quite taxing on processing power. However, an alternative approach called **single-pass stereo rendering** can be used to improve performance. This method shares data and processes it for both eyes simultaneously, reducing the overall rendering workload. To enable single-pass stereo rendering, follow these steps:

1. Open your Unity project and go to **Edit** | **Project Settings**.
2. Navigate to **XR Plug-in Management** and click on the **Oculus** tab.
3. Select the **Android** tab to access the **Stereo Rendering Mode** settings.
4. Change **Stereo Rendering Mode** from **Multipass** to **Multiview**. This will enable single-pass stereo rendering for your VR experience.

By adjusting the stereo rendering settings, we're able to save some bandwidth by not completely rendering two scenes because we have two different eyes that will be rendered for. We can actually do a hybrid of single and stereoscopic rendering by using the multiview settings.

In the next section, we will explore changing our screen scale resolution so that we save on rendering a large amount of pixels by defining a smaller range to render.

Screen scale resolution

One optimization technique that can significantly improve the performance on mobile devices is adjusting the screen scale resolution. Screen scale resolution allows you to render your VR experience at a lower resolution, which reduces the strain on the GPU and enhances overall performance. This is particularly useful for mobile devices, which may have high-resolution displays but limited GPU and CPU capabilities. In many cases, reducing the resolution to 70% or 80% does not result in a noticeable visual difference, yet it can greatly improve performance, allowing the VR experience to run at a smooth 90 fps.

To set the screen scale resolution for optimal performance and visuals, follow these steps:

1. Open the Unity Editor and select the target platform for your project.
2. Go to **File** | **Build Settings**.
3. In the **Build Settings** window, select the platform you are building for, and click on the **Player Settings** button.
4. In the **Player Settings** window, go to the **Player** | **Android (icon)** tab and the **Resolution and Presentation** section.
5. Set **Resolution Scaling Mode** to **Fixed DPI** to control how the game content scales to fit the screen size.
6. Set **Target DPI** to `300` or under to reduce the number of pixels needed to be rendered on a screen and preserve processing power.

By reducing the screen scale resolution, we can decrease the rendering required to produce a visually appealing image in our VR experience through the headset. Lowering the resolution from 2K to a fraction of that saves rendering space, as we're already rendering at 90 fps. Cutting corners in these areas allows for more bandwidth to be devoted to the experience, ensuring the best possible outcome without glitches or holdups caused by wasted processing power.

In the next section, we will take all the information we have learned about optimizations and put them into practice to improve the VR project we worked on from *Chapters 10–17*.

Applying optimizations to our VR world

Throughout the first half of this book, we laid a strong foundation. In the second half, we dove deep into design thinking and the entire development process, bringing to life a dynamic virtual world. This world boasts a powerful VR rig, an expansive environment, and even an animated show that plays at its center. However, if you've tested it by pressing play, you might have noticed it doesn't perform as smoothly as desired.

In this section, we'll delve into optimizing our VR scene. Using the insights gathered in this chapter, our goal is to free up memory bandwidth and enhance frame rates during real-time playback. To achieve this, we need to first understand how our scene functions. Unity's profiling tools will be invaluable in this endeavor, allowing us to pinpoint what affects the runtime experience.

Assessing our scene

Let's begin by entering play mode to evaluate our VR scene's performance. We'll observe the scene in three phases:

- In play mode without any movement or interactions with our VR rig
- Moving within the scene to gauge any impact on performance
- Playing the animated show from *Chapter 14* to determine its effect on performance

Upon first running the VR scene in Unity's play mode, it consistently averaged 120 fps without any movement (*Figure 18.7*). However, as soon as there was movement, the fps dipped to around 100. The most significant drop, to a range of 5–10 fps, occurred when the animated Timeline played.

From our observation, static scenes maintain an ideal fps, but movement brings it closer to the bare minimum required for a comfortable VR experience—above 90 fps—to prevent motion sickness. Yet, the animated Timeline's performance is well below the acceptable threshold, which is a significant concern we need to address.

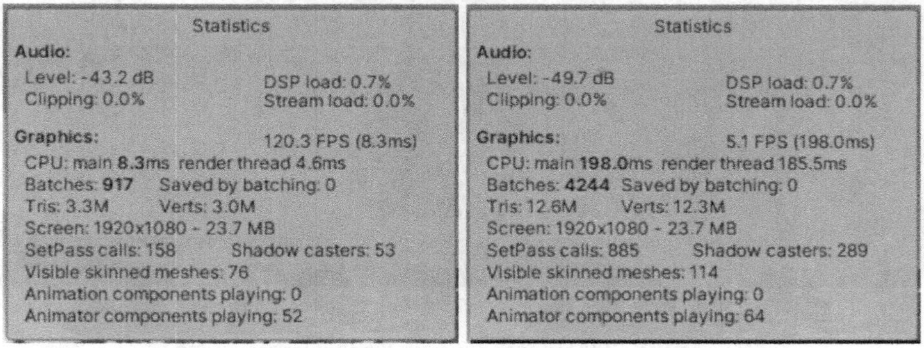

Statistics
Audio:
Level: -43.2 dB DSP load: 0.7%
Clipping: 0.0% Stream load: 0.0%
Graphics: 120.3 FPS (8.3ms)
CPU: main **8.3**ms render thread 4.6ms
Batches: **917** Saved by batching: 0
Tris: 3.3M Verts: 3.0M
Screen: 1920x1080 - 23.7 MB
SetPass calls: 158 Shadow casters: 53
Visible skinned meshes: 76
Animation components playing: 0
Animator components playing: 52

Statistics
Audio:
Level: -49.7 dB DSP load: 0.7%
Clipping: 0.0% Stream load: 0.0%
Graphics: 5.1 FPS (198.0ms)
CPU: main **198.0**ms render thread 185.5ms
Batches: **4244** Saved by batching: 0
Tris: 12.6M Verts: 12.3M
Screen: 1920x1080 - 23.7 MB
SetPass calls: 885 Shadow casters: 289
Visible skinned meshes: 114
Animation components playing: 0
Animator components playing: 64

Figure 18.7 – Frame rate before (left) and after (right) playing the animation Timeline

While in play mode, if I deactivate the animation Timeline, the frame rate promptly rebounds to between 100 and 120 fps. However, when I play the animation from its start to its conclusion, there's a consistent decline in frame rate. By the animation's peak, filled with its most intense action, we see frame rates plunge into the single digits. Such substantial resource demand at this peak can cause grave performance issues, potentially crashing or overheating the device if tested in real conditions.

A sound strategy to pinpoint these issues is by examining performance using Unity's Profiler tool.

Running the Profiler

As mentioned earlier in the chapter, the Profiler tool in Unity offers an array of functionalities to inspect what might be affecting our performance, especially on the CPU and memory fronts. However, since our goal is the optimization of an existing experience, there's no need to delve into every detail of profiling. Our primary areas of concern will be the CPU performance, which correlates with frame rate, and the memory profile, indicative of the assets present in our scene and their potential to constrain performance due to memory consumption.

It's essential to understand that this memory pertains to **Random Access Memory** (**RAM**). A larger footprint in the memory profile signals a heightened risk of crashing the device. Typically, devices can handle up to 3 to 4 GB of RAM before encountering issues.

Exploring the CPU

To begin, open the Profiler by navigating to **Window** | **Analysis** | **Profiler**, and then dock it adjacent to the **Game** view. This setup allows us to simultaneously observe both the **Stats** and **Profiler** windows. Upon entering play mode, the CPU usage remains minimal for the initial few seconds, with the graph illustrating rates well below the standard 60 fps commonly expected for video games. However, after those initial moments, especially when the animation from our Timeline plays, there's a noticeable spike, leveling off around 15 fps (*Figure 18.8*). A closer look reveals that the primary cause of this spike is the rendering process and its substantial demand on the CPU.

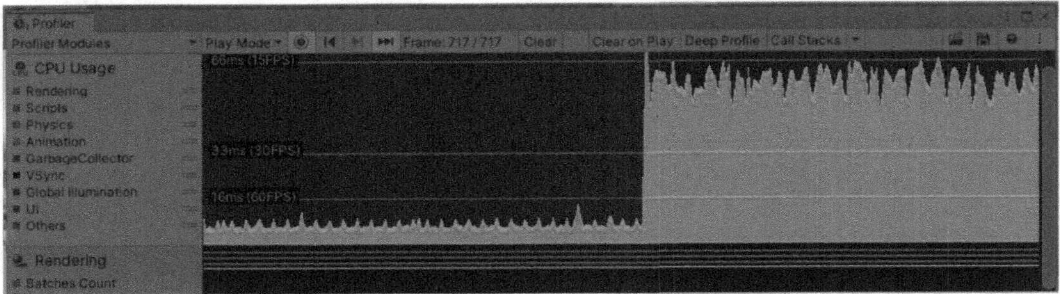

Figure 18.8 – CPU usage view from the Profiler at runtime

We've established that the CPU is impacted, which in turn affects our performance and frame rate. However, that's just one aspect of the narrative. To gain a full understanding, we must examine the memory profile. This will reveal the true extent of the load on our memory and any further constraints hampering our performance.

Exploring memory

Upon selecting the **Memory** tab in the Profiler, various categories emerge that impact our performance. Notably, out of our committed memory, 2.82 GB is allocated, with 2.0 GB already in use. This tight margin leaves minimal room for in-scene interactions, interactivity, and runtime processes, suggesting that our scene's assets consume significant memory.

Breaking down the memory allocation further (*Figure 18.9*), we have the following:

- Out of the total 2.99 GB, 0.61 GB is earmarked for graphics and their associated drivers
- An **Other** category occupies 0.81 GB out of a possible 1.5 GB
- The Profiler alone reserves half a GB
- Audio components use roughly 70 MB
- Some miscellaneous elements fall into untracked memory

The significant takeaways are the extensive memory usage in the **Other** category and the allocation for graphics and drivers.

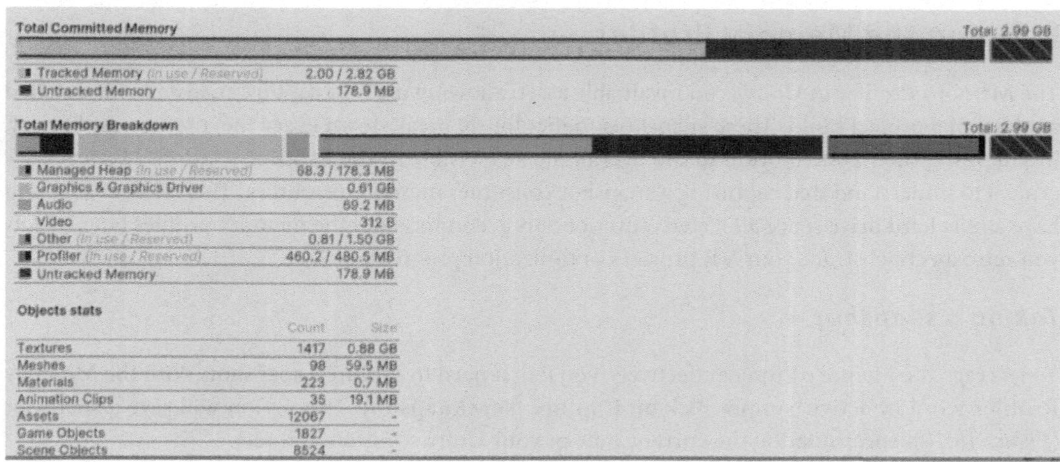

Figure 18.9 – Memory view from the Profiler window

A closer examination of the factors contributing to our memory footprint reveals that textures dominate, consuming 0.92 GB of memory. This is indicative of the sheer volume of assets and GOs populating our scene. To provide perspective, our scene contains 1,827 GOs, 8,524 scene objects, and an overwhelming 12,076 assets. Even the count of our meshes and materials surpasses 300. Such a densely populated scene inevitably impacts performance, a fact that becomes even more evident when confronted with these numerical values.

Installing the detailed Memory Profiler

The **Memory Profiler** is an extension of the standard Profiler in Unity. It offers a granular examination of elements impacting performance by breaking down individual files contributing to our memory footprint. Although this tool requires a separate installation, it's conveniently accessible directly from the **Profiler** window. To install it, follow these steps:

1. Navigate to the **Profiler** window.
2. Select the **Memory** tab.
3. Click on **Install Memory Profile Package**.

Once installed, the Memory Profiler provides a detailed breakdown of factors contributing to memory usage. This granularity enables pinpoint identification of memory concerns, facilitating targeted optimizations.

To access its insights, simply click **Open Memory Profiler** to launch the dedicated window.

Running the Memory Profiler

The Memory Profiler in Unity is an invaluable asset, allowing users to capture snapshots for detailed analysis of a project build. These snapshots meticulously break down every file, process, and script, highlighting their contribution to the overall file size visible in the **Profiler** window. However, it's crucial to understand that capturing a snapshot consumes memory resources. Therefore, ensure you have ample hard drive space allocated. This not only accommodates the memory profiles but also lets you retrospectively trace your VR project's optimization progress.

Taking a snapshot

To leverage the Memory Profiler effectively, you'll first need to capture a snapshot. With the **Memory Profiler** window active, simply click on **Capture New Snapshot**. This action will save a snapshot (*Figure 18.10*), encapsulating the current state of your Unity scene and project.

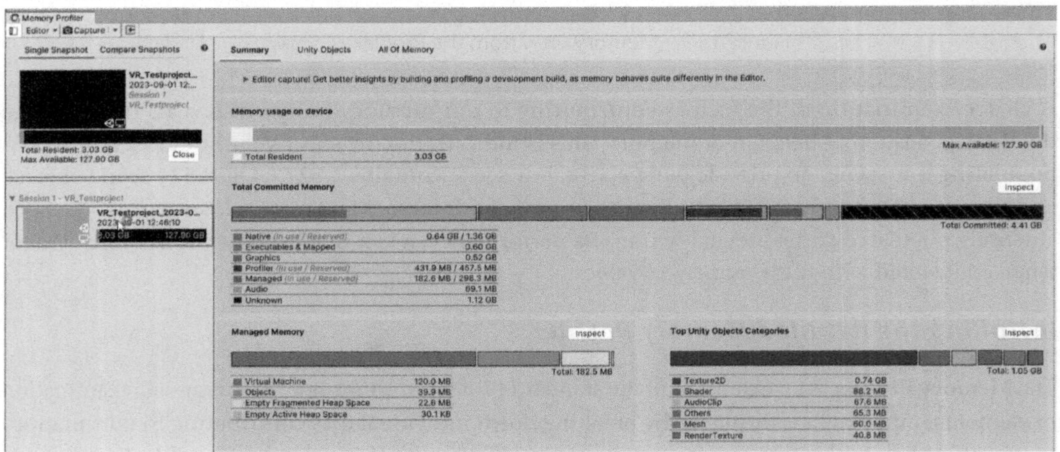

Figure 18.10 – Memory Profiler snapshot representing the baseline memory distribution

The snapshot taken in the Memory Profiler is organized into three sections:

- **Summary**: This offers an extended overview of the data seen in the **Memory** tab of the Profiler
- **Unity Objects**: This tab lists all objects in the build, sorted by their type
- **All Of Memory**: Generally, this section takes a while to load and might not be as relevant for smaller projects, but it can be insightful for larger-scale projects, even if we won't delve deep into it here

Adjacent to categories such as **Managed Memory**, **Total Committed Memory**, and **Top Unity Object**, you'll notice **Inspect** buttons. These are instrumental in diving deeper into the specific files and elements causing memory bottlenecks. The real strength of the Memory Profiler lies in its capability to pinpoint exact sources of performance issues.

Exploring the memory profile

With a clearer understanding of the Memory Profiler's functionalities, it's time for a comprehensive exploration of our memory profile to identify potential bottlenecks. My preferred approach begins with taking an initial snapshot, ensuring a baseline that captures the system's status when the play mode is inactive. However, to pinpoint precise bottlenecks and their root causes, I simulate the specific moments in the experience where these bottlenecks peak, capturing a dedicated snapshot. This approach provides an accurate representation of the memory and frame rate's strain at those crucial instances. By addressing these specific stress points, it's possible to enhance performance more broadly.

To facilitate this analysis, I keep the Memory Profiler, the general Profiler, and the **Game** view's **Stats** window open concurrently. Once in play mode, I initiate the animation Timeline, closely observing the performance until the frame rates drop to single digits. At this juncture, capturing a new snapshot is essential. Exiting play mode allows for a comparative study of these snapshots. For instance, while the initial snapshot indicated a memory usage of 3.03 GB, during the performance trough, this escalates dramatically to 4.48 GB. This near 2 GB jump, merely from the peak bottleneck, underscores the significance of these evaluations. As developers, understanding the disparity between optimal performance (when the system is inactive) and its lowest ebb (during intensive animations) is crucial for refining the experience.

While I took three distinct snapshots for a comprehensive perspective—including one at the onset of play mode—it's most pragmatic to base our optimizations on the snapshot reflecting the lowest frame rate (*Figure 18.11*):

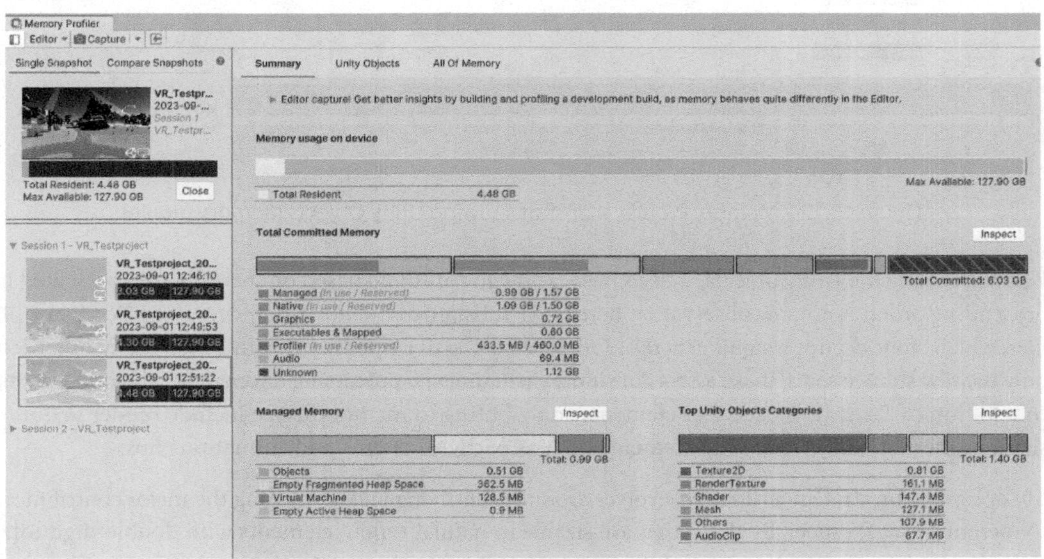

Figure 18.11 – Memory Profiler snapshot representing the lowest frame rate at runtime

Delving into the specifics, the disk's memory usage is at 4.48 GB, with the total committed memory hitting 6.03 GB. A significant chunk of this is consumed by graphics, executable maps, managed resources, and native resources. Notably, **Unity Objects** categories alone account for 1.4 GB. Given that devices such as the Oculus Quest typically offer between 3 and 4 GB of memory, this consumption poses a challenge. When Unity objects alone eat up nearly half of the available memory, it restricts the potential for creating rich, interactive experiences, thus elevating the risk of suboptimal or even malfunctioning outcomes.

To gain a more granular insight into the **Unity Objects** categories, we can either navigate via the **Unity Objects** tab (*Figure 18.12*) located next to the **Summary** tab or select the **Inspect** button within the **Unity Objects** categories section.

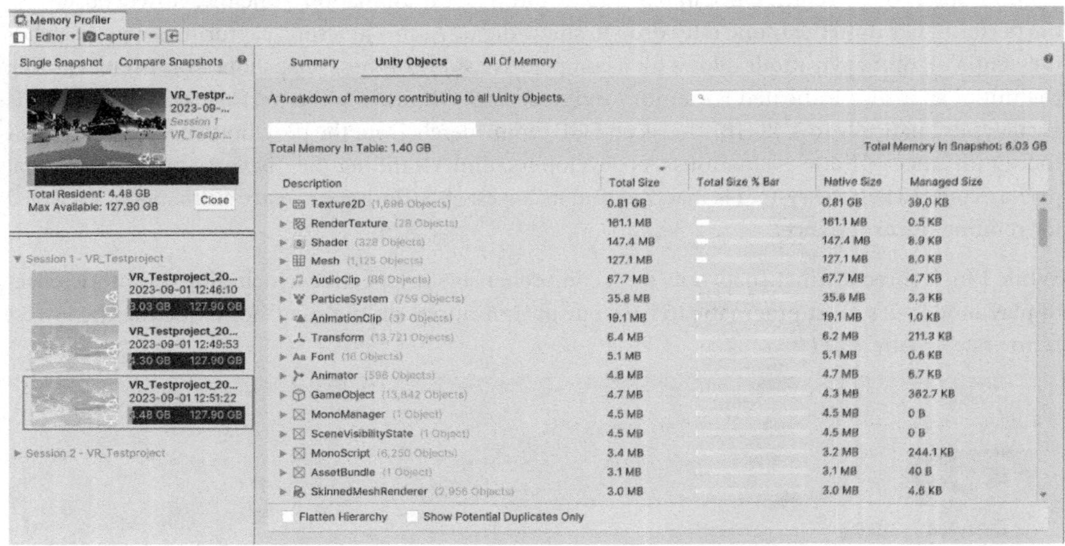

Figure 18.12 – Memory Profiler snapshot showing Unity Objects memory profiles

Upon accessing the Unity objects, it becomes feasible to sort them based on their file size, presented in descending order. A notable observation here is the substantial memory footprint of the `Texture2D` files, which alone occupy a significant 0.81 GB. It's essential to emphasize that this measurement reflects only the raw storage space these assets consume, excluding any processing or operational requirements. In addition to `Texture2D`, other elements contributing to memory usage include render textures, shaders, meshes, audio clips, and elements such as particle systems and animation clips.

My optimization strategy primarily revolves around identifying and addressing the major contributors to memory usage, especially those that are sizable in nature. Often, elements with double-digit total sizes demand immediate attention. Leveraging Unity's suite of optimization and compression tools, I aim to reduce these file sizes, ensuring that we recapture valuable memory that might otherwise be squandered due to unoptimized assets. Equipped with this knowledge, we can now embark on fine-tuning our memory profile by targeting and rectifying unoptimized asset issues.

Optimizing the memory profile

From our snapshot via the Memory Profiler, it's evident that the predominant performance bottleneck stems from uncompressed and unoptimized textures. Our primary focus should be to address these textures. Following that, we can move on to compressing the audio files, refining the meshes and animations, and subsequently, fine-tuning the entire scene. This systematic approach will ensure the most optimal frame rate for our scene exploration.

Compressing textures

Upon inspecting our `Texture2D` files, it's evident that the sheer volume, despite each having a minimal footprint, accumulates significantly. For a comprehensive view, instead of manually navigating through folders, simply select the icon (comprising a triangle, circle, and square) next to the search bar in the **Project** window. This will filter to the **Texture** category, displaying all textures from the `Assets` folder. To optimize, navigate to each texture's **Inspector** and adjust settings to strike the right balance between file size and performance. I've provided a chart (*Figure 18.13*) detailing settings based on targeted devices, ranging from mobile VR experiences to performance-focused PC headsets using the URP to high-end, quality-centric VR headsets. My chosen optimizations are tailored for standalone VR headsets, such as the Oculus Quest.

		Mobile VR for Android and iOS	**Standalone VR Headsets**	**PC-Based VR for Performance (URP)**	**PC-Based VR for Quality (HDRP)**
Image Optimizations	**Max Size**	256	512	1024	2048
	Compression	Low quality	Low quality or normal quality	Normal quality	High quality
	Use Crunch Compression	Enabled	Enabled	Enabled	Optional
	Compressor Quality	30	50	75	N/A

Figure 18.13 – Image optimization settings chart for lower- to higher-end VR devices

Compressing audio files

While the audio clips in our scene might seem negligible in size compared to textures, every bit of conserved space is essential, given the resource constraints of typical VR devices. To ensure efficient experiences, it's crucial to optimize these audio files, enhancing both performance and auditory quality. To do this, navigate to the **Project** window and filter by audio clips using the category selector next to the search bar. After selecting the desired clips, apply the most suitable settings for your target device. My recommendations (*Figure 18.14*) are geared toward standalone VR headsets but refer to the provided chart to tailor settings for your specific needs.

		Mobile VR for Android and iOS	**Standalone VR Headsets**	**PC-Based VR for Performance (URP)**	**PC-Based VR for Quality (HDRP)**
Audio Optimizations	**Force to Mono**	Enabled	Enabled	Optional	Optional
	Load type	Compressed in Memory	Compressed in Memory	Compressed in Memory	Decompressed on Load or Streaming
	Compression Format	Vorbis	Vorbis	Vorbis	Vorbis or PCM
	Quality	25–40	30–50	50–75	75–100

Figure 18.14 – Audio optimization settings chart for lower- to higher-end VR devices

Compressing meshes

Meshes consume double the memory of audio clips in our scene. Given the significant memory savings we achieved with audio optimizations, it's imperative to reduce the mesh footprint for more efficient memory use. Similar to our approach with audio and textures, we'll search using the **Model** category. Through Unity's **Model Import** settings in **Inspector**, we can access the platform's mesh compression tools. The primary adjustment is to switch **Mesh Compression** from **None** to the desired quality level. For guidance, refer to my chart (*Figure 18.15*) detailing various compression levels. This will help you find the right balance between performance and mesh quality.

		Mobile VR for Android and iOS	**Standalone VR Headsets**	**PC-Based VR for Performance (URP)**	**PC-Based VR for Quality (HDRP)**
Mesh Optimizations	**Mesh Compression**	High	Medium	Low	Off

Figure 18.15 – Mesh optimization settings chart for lower- to higher-end VR devices

Reducing keyframes

Although animation clips in our scene exert a lesser impact compared to textures, audio clips, and meshes, optimizing them is crucial. Given that these clips often run concurrently across multiple characters, their collective render load can strain the device. By minimizing keyframes, we can mitigate this effect.

Unlike textures or audio clips, animations often reside within FBX or model files. Hence, they're accessed through the import settings used for meshes. In our project, these animations—specifically for characters such as the devil and bulldog and those sourced from Mixamo—are housed in specific folders. To locate them, head to the `Animations` folder within `VRAssets and Characters`, and the `Devil Bulldog` subfolder from the Asset Store. Once inside, model assets will appear, allowing you to access their respective animation settings in **Inspector**. For the ideal keyframe reduction, consult the provided chart (*Figure 18.16*).

		Mobile VR for Android and iOS	Standalone VR Headsets	PC-Based VR for Performance (URP)	PC-Based VR for Quality (HDRP)
Animation Optimizations	**Animation Compression**	Keyframe Reduction	Keyframe Reduction	Optimal	Optimal or Off

Figure 18.16 – Animation optimization settings chart for lower- to higher-end VR devices

With the essential memory profile optimizations complete, our next step is to enhance the scene of our VR experience. This will ensure maximum rendering efficiency during play mode testing.

Optimizing our scene

Tackling the memory profile is just one aspect; equally crucial is ensuring optimal lighting and proper object categorization in our VR experience. This entails marking non-moving objects as static, transitioning real-time lights to mixed lights, toning down shadow quality, and, importantly, baking our lightmaps.

Making objects static

First, we'll designate the non-moving 3D objects in our scene as static (*Figure 18.17*). This includes the following GOs: `VRMap`, `Roads`, `Park`, `Buildings`, `Nature`, `Park audio`, `City audio`, `Person Spawner Manager`, and `Portals`. We'll avoid marking the `AnimatedShow` GO, `VirtualCameras`, `VRRig`, and other projectiles as static since they have movement components. To mark the indicated objects as static, select the necessary GOs, navigate to **Inspector** on the top right, and tick the **Static** checkbox. Upon doing this, a prompt will inquire about making all child objects static as well. Opt for **Yes, change children**.

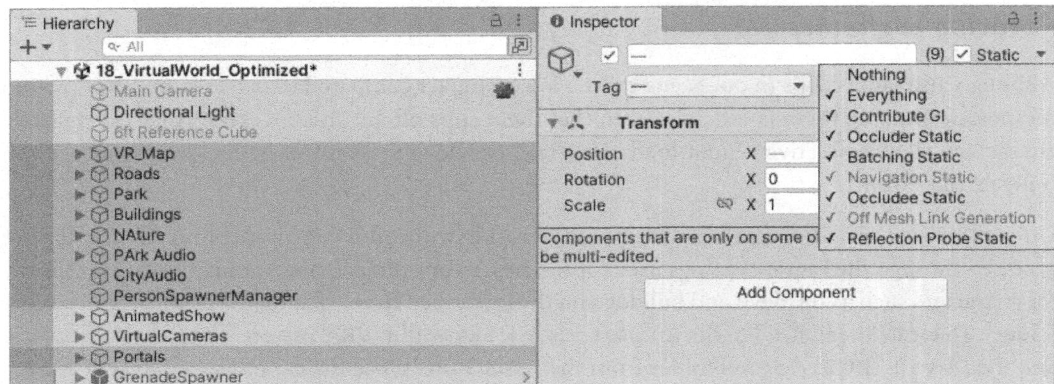

Figure 18.17 – Static GOs in the VR scene

Optimizing our directional light

Optimizing the directional light is straightforward, as it governs both real-time and baked light settings through a singular component. Plus, it provides the flexibility to adjust shadows for every object in the scene by merely fine-tuning this component. Perform the following steps:

1. Navigate to the `Directional Light` GO.
2. In the `Lighting` component, switch the mode from **Real-Time** to **Mixed**.
3. Alter **Shadow Type** to **Hard Shadows**.
4. For **Real-Time Shadows Resolution**, select **Medium Resolution**.

With these adjustments, the **Lighting Settings** are optimized. Next, you'll want to head over to the **Lighting** window to bake your lightmaps.

Baking lightmaps

Light baking has been a recurring topic across various chapters. Now, let's delve into the device-specific application of settings for optimal performance. As we've navigated through the options for compressing textures, audio files, and other assets in our memory profile, it's essential to apply the same targeted approach for our lightmap settings.

For the sake of this guide, I've optimized the VR experience for standalone VR headsets. Please refer to the provided chart (*Figure 18.18*) to adjust settings in alignment with your device's capabilities. Perform the following steps:

1. Open the **Lighting** window.
2. Head to the **Scene** tab.

3. Create a new `Lighting Settings` asset.
4. Refer to the provided chart to determine the ideal settings.

For devices on the lower end, avoid real-time lighting due to the added resource demands. Instead, emphasize mixed lighting and lightmapping for scene illumination. While those with higher-end devices might experiment with real-time lighting, standalone and mobile VR devices benefit most from mixed and baked lighting.

		Mobile VR for Android and iOS	**Standalone VR Headsets**	**PC-Based VR for Performance (URP)**	**PC-Based VR for Quality (HDRP)**
Realtime Lighting	**Realtime Global Illumination**	Disable	Disable	Enable	Enable
	Realtime Indirect Resolution	N/A	N/A	.5–1	1–2
Mixed Lighting	**Baked Global Illumination**	Enabled	Enabled	Enabled	Enabled
	Lighting Mode	Baked Indirect	Baked Indirect	Subtractive or Realtime GI	Realtime GI

Figure 18.18 – Real-time and mixed lighting settings chart for lower- to higher-end VR devices

Lightmap settings are pivotal for two main reasons: achieving optimal lighting while enhancing performance and reducing the baking process duration. My personal setup is powered by the NVIDIA 3090 RTX graphics card with a 24 GB memory capacity, positioning it among the top performers in light baking efficiency.

However, if you're utilizing a laptop or a less robust PC, your hardware might not afford the same luxury. In such cases, strategic settings choices can expedite your development cycle, preventing protracted lightmap baking times.

Direct and indirect samples play a significant role in this process. For developers targeting devices such as the Oculus Quest or other standalone VR headsets, it's advantageous to lean toward the lower end of the sample spectrum. This approach minimizes waiting time during the optimization phase, allowing for faster iteration of your projects.

Refer to the chart (*Figure 18.19*) provided to discern the ideal lightmap settings for your target headset. While my settings are tailored for the Oculus Quest, those developing for PC-based VR might want to explore both URP and HDRP settings. While this chart offers a solid foundation, you might discover a unique combination of settings that best complements your specific VR experience.

		Mobile VR for Android and iOS	Standalone VR Headsets	PC-Based VR for Performance (URP)	PC-Based VR for Quality (HDRP)
Lightmapping Settings	**Lightmapper**	Progressive CPU	Progressive CPU	Progressive CPU	Progressive CPU
	Direct Samples	16	32	64	128–256
	Indirect Samples	128	256	512	1024–2048
	Environment Samples	8–32	16–64	64–128	128–256
	Light Probe Sample Multiplier	Reduced	Default	Default	Default or Increased based on quality
	Max Bounces	1	1 or 2	2	3–5
	Filtering	Advanced	Advanced	Advanced	Advanced
	Direct, Indirect, and Ambient Occlusion Denoiser and Filter	Optix Gaussian	Optix Gaussian	Optix Gaussian or A-Trous	Optix A-Trous
	Direct Filter Radius	.7	.8	.5	.5
	Indirect Filter Radius	1.3	1.5	1	1–2
	Ambient Occlusion Filter Radius	1.3	1.5	1	1–2
	Lightmap Resolution	10–20	20–40	40–60	80–100
	Lightmap Padding	2	2	2	2+
	Max Lightmap Size	256–512	512–1024	1024–2048	2048–4096
	Lightmap Compression	Low Quality	Normal Quality	Medium Quality	Optional
	Ambient Occlusion	Disabled	Enabled	Enabled	Enabled
	Max Distance	N/A	.5–1	.5–1	1–2
	Indirect Contribution	N/A	1	1	1–2

	Direct Contribution	N/A	.8	1	1
	Directional Mode	Non-Directional	Non-Directional	Directional	Directional
	Albedo Boost	1	1	1	1–2
	Indirect Intensity	1	1	1	1–2
	Lightmap Parameters	Very Low or Low Resolution	Low or Medium Resolution	Medium Resolution	High Resolution

Figure 18.19 – Lightmap settings chart for lower-end to high-end VR devices

In the **Environment** tab within the **Lighting** window, do the following:

- Ensure your **Skybox** material is correctly configured, which it should be by default.
- Set your `Directional Light` GO as the sun source. This facilitates a precise light bake by providing scene context during the process.

For the optimal settings, refer to the provided chart (*Figure 18.20*). While I've optimized mine for standalone VR headsets, it's advisable to adjust based on your specific headset's specifications to achieve peak performance and visuals.

		Mobile VR for Android and iOS	**Standalone VR Headsets**	**PC-Based VR for Performance (URP)**	**PC-Based VR for Quality (HDRP)**
Environment Reflections	**Resolution**	16–64	64–128	128–256	128–256
	Compression	Compressed	Compressed	Auto	Uncompressed
	Intensity Multiplier	1	1	1	1
	Bounces	1	1–2	2	3–5

Figure 18.20 – Environment lighting settings chart for lower- to higher-end VR devices

Once you've configured all the settings in the **Lighting** window, initiating **Generate Lighting** will commence the baking process using both the GPU and CPU. The duration can vary significantly, sometimes due to factors that are hard to pinpoint.

In my experience, the estimated time isn't always accurate. For this project, even though the indicator projected 12 minutes, it took about 25 minutes to complete. Given that light baking is resource-intensive, it's advisable to avoid running other heavy tasks on the machine during the process. If the projected time is considerably long, you might consider baking overnight, especially if working on a lower-end machine or with a complex scene.

In my case, my GPU consumed nearly 5 GB (*Figure 18.21*) of memory solely for the baking process. Considering that this is a large chunk of the total memory available in many GPUs, we should be conscious of resource management during the bake.

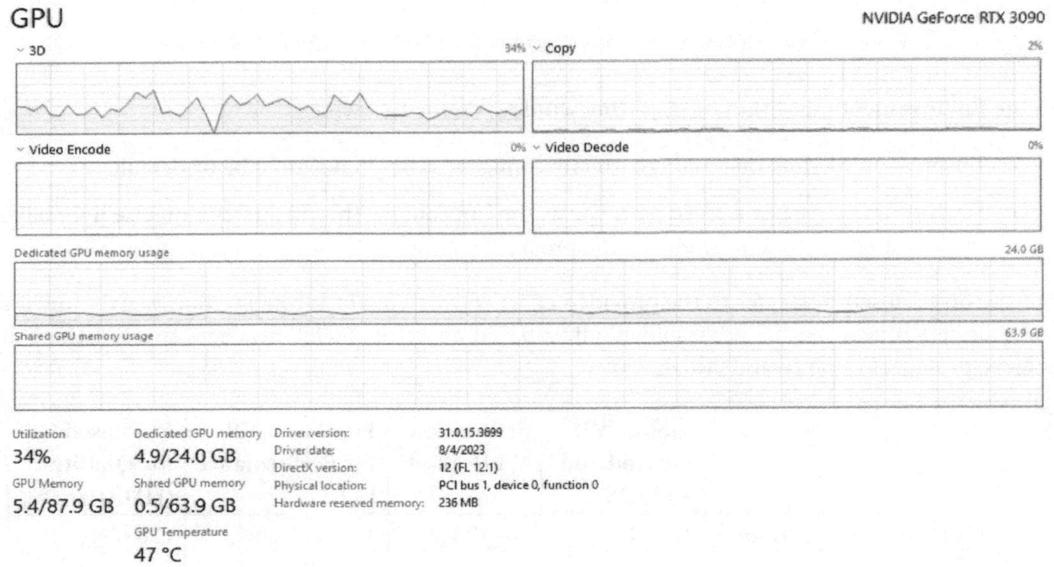

Figure 18.21 – GPU usage chart while baking lightmaps

Upon completion of the light baking, the **Baked Lightmaps** tab (*Figure 18.22*) within the **Lighting** window provides insights into the lightmaps produced.

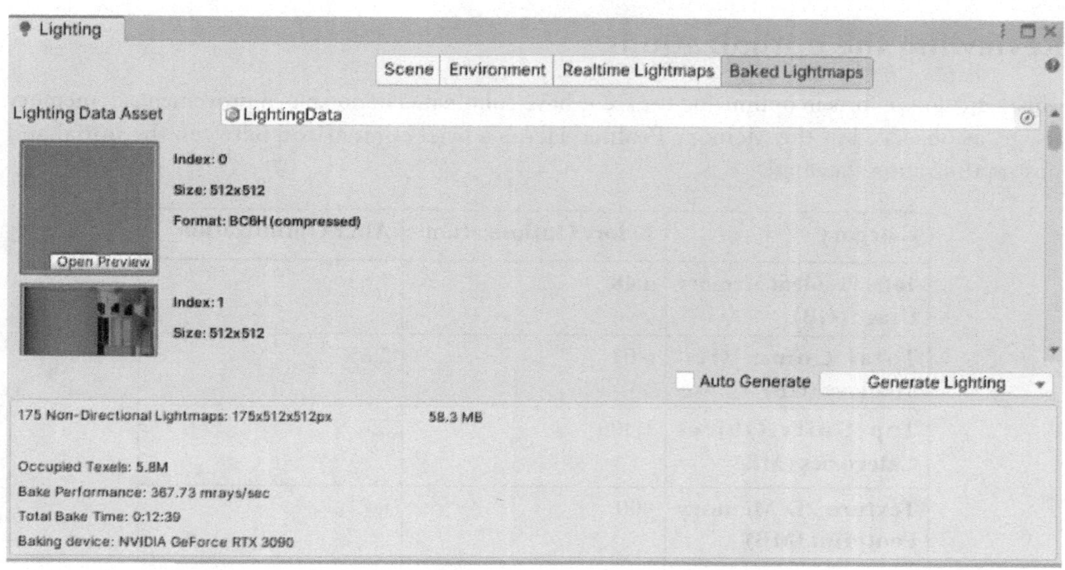

Figure 18.22 – Baked lightmap results

In this case, we see the following:

- 175 individual lightmaps were generated
- These maps occupied approximately 58 MB of memory

The optimizations made previously on animations, audio, and meshes essentially made room for these lightmaps in the memory, which means that our previous efforts to save space have now been efficiently used.

Moreover, since we're utilizing baked lightmaps and shadows, the scene will benefit from enhanced performance. This is because we've reduced the dependency on real-time shadows and lighting, which typically demand more computational resources.

Aesthetically, post-baking, the scene exhibits richer vibrancy (*Figure 18.23*). Shadows and lights are more evenly distributed, making the scene's darker regions more uniformly illuminated compared to their state before the baking process.

Figure 18.23 – Lighting on objects in the scene before light baking (left) and after light baking (right)

Reviewing the optimizations

The meticulous efforts in optimizing the scene have culminated in notable improvements in memory usage, as observed in the Memory Profiler. Here's a brief comparison between the initial and post-optimization statistics:

Category	Before Optimization	After Optimization
Total Resident Memory Usage (GB)	4.48	1.63
Total Committed Memory (GB)	6.03	2.55
Top Unity Object Categories (MB)	1,400	352.9
Texture 2D Memory Footprint (MB)	800	86.1
Mesh Memory (MB)	127	59

Figure 18.24 – Comparing Memory Profiler statistics before (left) and after (right) optimizations

The considerable decline in memory usage across the board signifies the effectiveness of the applied optimizations. As the next step, entering play mode will provide insights (*Figure 18.25*) into the performance enhancement achieved due to these memory optimizations.

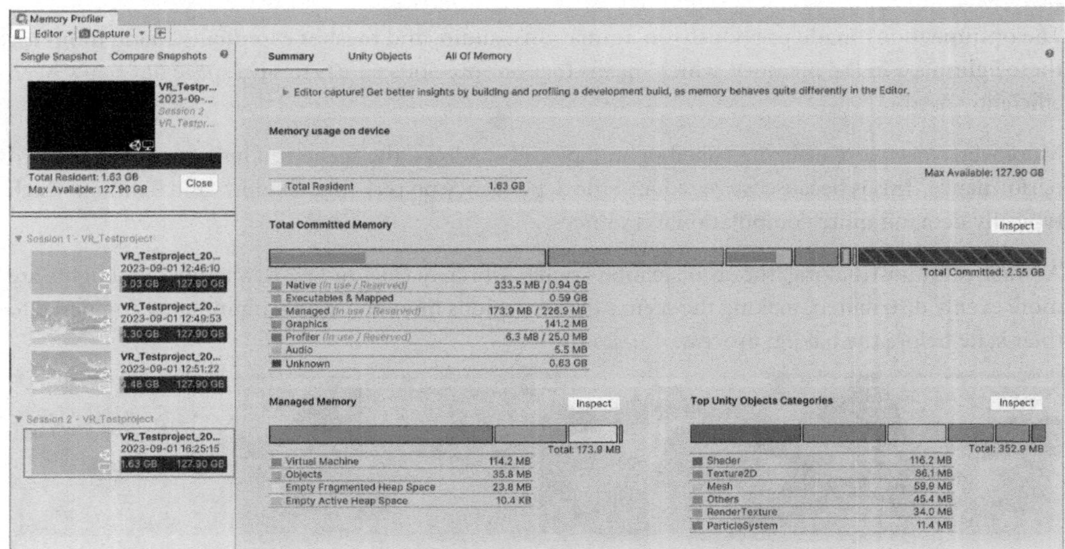

Figure 18.25 – Memory Profiler snapshot after implementing optimizations

As the scene loads, there's an immediate and palpable difference; the world unveils itself in a seamless motion. Gone are the days when entering this realm felt like trudging through a quagmire. Now, it's as swift as turning a page in one of our favorite manga epics.

Our protagonist doesn't just move—they dance. As the narrative's animation Timeline unfolds, our hero doesn't falter. No longer held back by the shackles of choppiness, their movements reflect their true potential. Their speed may vary, darting at 150 fps, sometimes slowing to a contemplative 80 or 90 (*Figure 18.25*), but never does it stumble down to a crawl.

This transformation wasn't achieved through some mystical power-up or ancient scroll; no, it was the result of meticulous craftsmanship. Each texture, shadow, and sound was optimized to perfection, ensuring that our story's flow remains uninterrupted. Even during the most intense moments, the animation never dips below 60 fps. It's like witnessing a martial arts master: every move deliberate, every action impactful.

The realm has now reached a new equilibrium, where artistry meets performance. But, as any storyteller knows, the journey doesn't end here. With each new chapter and each new element added, the balance will need to be reassessed, retuned, and reoptimized. And that is the never-ending saga of creation, one where we, the creators, are always eager for the next challenge.

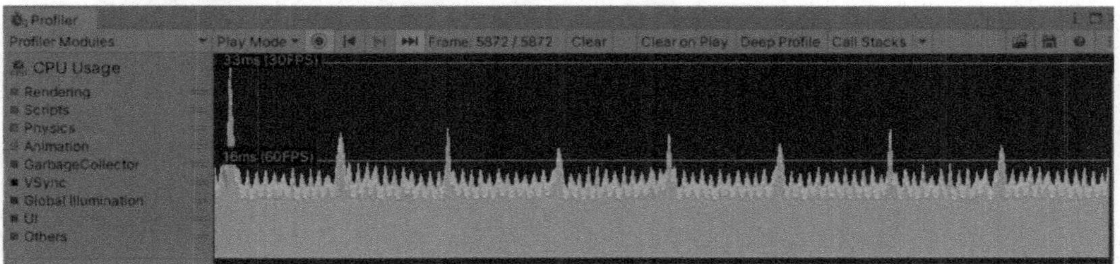

Figure 18.26 – Profiler window showing CPU and frame rate usage

Venturing back into our realm, the difference is palpable. Jarring spikes have smoothed out and been replaced by a consistent flow. Thanks to our meticulous work with Unity's tools, the stuttering past is gone, revealing a VR experience now running at its zenith. From chaos to a masterpiece, we've not just optimized; we've transformed.

Summary

In the final stretch of our VR journey, we've dug deep into the art of optimization. We've used all the Unity tools at our disposal, including compression and the Unity Profiler, to keep a keen eye on our frame rate and performance throughout the runtime.

We've fine-tuned our camera settings, squished our images to lighten their load, and even given the same treatment to our audio files. After all, while we love a rich soundscape, we can't afford to let it weigh us down.

We've even done some spring cleaning on our 3D models, trimming the fat on mesh and draw calls, and cutting out the excess frames on our animation files. We're even baking our lights so we can keep things bright without slowing things down.

We've also revisited our project settings to tweak the quality of our rendering and the backend player settings. It's all about making our algorithms work for us, not against us. This keeps things running smoothly, saves time on development, and above all, delivers an unforgettable VR experience to our users.

This book might be coming to an end, but the journey doesn't stop here. You've been equipped with the tools, principles, and know-how to design VR experiences that put the user front and center. Now, it's your turn to bring those ideas to life and make your mark on the world of VR.

Index

Symbols

A

B

D

E

H

I

J

K

L

M

N

O

P

T

U

W

X

Y

Z

Other Books You May Enjoy

If you enjoyed this book, you may be interested in these other books by Packt:

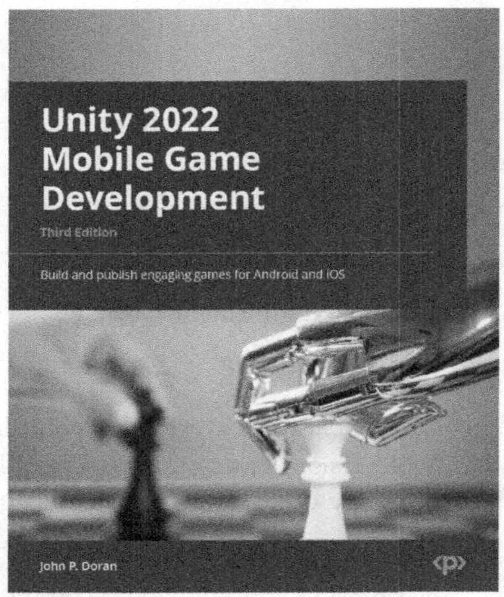

Unity 2022 Mobile Game Development

John P. Doran

ISBN: 978-1-80461-372-6

- Design responsive UIs for your mobile games
- Detect collisions, receive user input, and create player movements
- Create interesting gameplay elements using mobile device input
- Add custom icons and presentation options
- Keep players engaged by using Unity s mobile notification package
- Integrate social media into your projects
- Add augmented reality features to your game for real-world appeal
- Make your games juicy with post-processing and particle effects

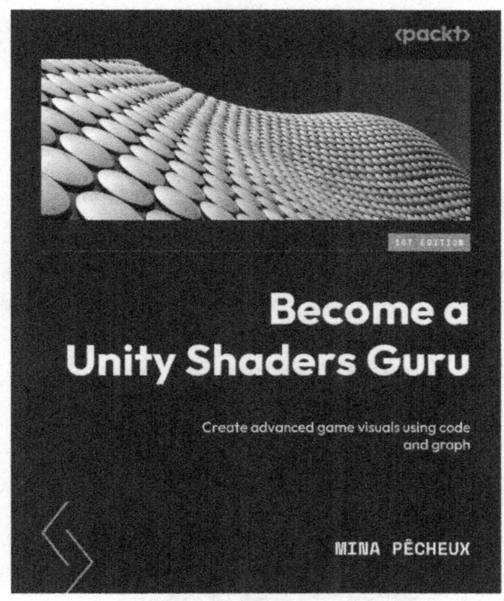

Become a Unity Shaders Guru

Mina Pêcheux

ISBN: 978-1-83763-674-7

- Understand the main differences between the legacy render pipeline and the SRP
- Create shaders in Unity with HLSL code and the Shader Graph 10 tool
- Implement common game shaders for VFX, animation, procedural generation, and more
- Experiment with offloading work from the CPU to the GPU
- Identify different optimization tools and their uses
- Discover useful URP shaders and re-adapt them in your projects

Packt is searching for authors like you

If you're interested in becoming an author for Packt, please visit `authors.packtpub.com` and apply today. We have worked with thousands of developers and tech professionals, just like you, to help them share their insight with the global tech community. You can make a general application, apply for a specific hot topic that we are recruiting an author for, or submit your own idea.

Share Your Thoughts

Now you've finished *Enhancing Virtual Reality Experiences with Unity 2022*, we'd love to hear your thoughts! Scan the QR code below to go straight to the Amazon review page for this book and share your feedback or leave a review on the site that you purchased it from.

`https://packt.link/r/1-804-61953-1`

Your review is important to us and the tech community and will help us make sure we're delivering excellent quality content.

Download a free PDF copy of this book

Thanks for purchasing this book!

Do you like to read on the go but are unable to carry your print books everywhere?

Is your eBook purchase not compatible with the device of your choice?

Don't worry, now with every Packt book you get a DRM-free PDF version of that book at no cost.

Read anywhere, any place, on any device. Search, copy, and paste code from your favorite technical books directly into your application.

The perks don't stop there, you can get exclusive access to discounts, newsletters, and great free content in your inbox daily

Follow these simple steps to get the benefits:

1. Scan the QR code or visit the link below

`https://packt.link/free-ebook/9781804619537`

2. Submit your proof of purchase
3. That's it! We'll send your free PDF and other benefits to your email directly

Made in the USA
Las Vegas, NV
14 May 2024